The Aims of Argument
A Text and Reader

SEVENTH EDITION

The Aims of Argument
A Text and Reader

Timothy W. Crusius
Southern Methodist University

Carolyn E. Channell
Southern Methodist University

Mc
Graw
Hill

Connect
Learn
Succeed™

Published by McGraw-Hill, a business unit of The McGraw-Hill Companies, Inc., 1221 Avenue of the Americas, New York, NY 10020. Copyright © 2011, 2009, 2006, 2003, 2000, 1998, 1995 by The McGraw-Hill Companies, Inc. All rights reserved. No part of this publication may be reproduced or distributed in any form or by any means, or stored in a database or retrieval system, without the prior written consent of The McGraw-Hill Companies, Inc., including, but not limited to, any network or other electronic storage or transmission, or broadcast for distance learning. Some ancillaries, including electronic and print components, may not be available to customers outside the United States.

This book is printed on acid-free paper.

2 3 4 5 6 7 8 9 0 DOC/DOC 1 5 4 3 2

ISBN: 978-0-07-734379-8
MHID: 0-07-734379-4

Vice President, Editorial: *Michael Ryan*
Director, Editorial: *Beth Mejia*
Publisher: *David S. Patterson*
Sponsoring Editor: *Christopher Bennem*
Development Editor: *Janice Wiggins-Clarke*
Managing Editor: *Marley Magaziner*
Marketing Director: *Allison Jones*
Marketing Manager: *Tierra Morgan*
Media Project Manager: *Bethuel Jabez*
Production Editor: *Ruth Sakata Corley*
Cover Designer: *Andrei Pasternak*
Photo Researcher: *LouAnn Wilson*
Senior Buyer: *Laura Fuller*
Production Service: *Matrix Productions, Inc.*
Composition: *10/12 Sabon by Laserwords Private Limited*
Printing: *45# New Era Matte by R.R. Donnelley & Sons*

Cover image: © *2009 Corey Holms/Flickr/Getty Images*

Credits: *The credits section for this book begins on page 630–632 and is considered an extension of the copyright page.*

Library of Congress Cataloging-in-Publication Data

Crusius, Timothy W., 1950-
   The aims of argument: a text and reader/Timothy W. Crusius,
Carolyn E. Channell.—7th ed.
      p. cm.
   ISBN 978-0-07-734379-8
   1. English language—Rhetoric—Problems, exercises, etc.   2. Persuasion (Rhetoric)—
Problems, exercises, etc.   3. Report writing—Problems, exercises, etc.   4. College
readers.   I. Channell, Carolyn E.   II. Title.

PE1431.C78 2010
808'.042—dc22   2010040271

The Internet addresses listed in the text were accurate at the time of publication. The inclusion of a website does not indicate an endorsement by the authors or McGraw-Hill, and McGraw-Hill does not guarantee the accuracy of the information presented at these sites.

www.mhhe.com

For W. Ross Winterowd

As its first six editions were, the seventh edition of *The Aims of Argument* is different from other argumentation texts because it remains the only one that focuses on the aims, or purposes, of argument. That this book's popularity increases from edition to edition tells us that our approach does in fact satisfy the previously unmet need that moved us to become textbook authors.

NOTES ON THIS TEXT'S ORIGINS

With more than sixty years of teaching experience between us, we had tried most argument books. Many of them were good, and we learned from them. However, we found ourselves adopting a text not so much out of genuine enthusiasm but because it had fewer liabilities. We wondered why we were so lukewarm about even the best argumentation textbooks. We boiled our dissatisfaction down to a few major criticisms:

- Most treatments were too formalistic and prescriptive.
- Most failed to integrate class discussion and individual inquiry with written argumentation.
- Apart from moving from simple concepts and assignments to more complicated ones, no book offered a learning sequence.
- Despite the fact that argument, like narrative, is clearly a mode or means of discourse, not a purpose for writing, no book offered a well-developed view of the aims or purposes of argument.

We thought that these shortcomings had undesirable consequences in the classroom, including the following:

- The overemphasis on form confused students with too much terminology, made them doubt their instincts, and drained away energy from inventing and discovering good arguments. Informal argumentation is not formal logic but open-ended and creative.

- The separation of class discussion from composing created a hiatus between oral and written argument. Students had difficulty seeing the relation between the two and using insights from each to improve the other.

- The lack of a learning sequence—of assignments that build on each other—meant that courses in argumentation were less coherent and meaningful than they could be. Students did not understand why they were doing what they were doing and could not envision what might come next.

- Finally, inattention to what people actually use argument to accomplish resulted in too narrow a view of argument and in unclear purposes for writing. Because instruction was mainly limited to what we call arguing to convince, students took argument only as monologues of advocacy. They ignored inquiry.

We set out to solve these problems. The result is a book different from any other argument text because it focuses on four aims of argument:

Arguing to inquire, questioning opinions

Arguing to convince, making cases

Arguing to persuade, appealing to the whole person

Arguing to mediate, finding common ground between conflicting positions

COMMON QUESTIONS ABOUT THE AIMS OF ARGUMENT

Instructors have certain questions about these aims, especially how they relate to one another. Here are some of the most frequently asked questions:

1. *What is the relative value of the four aims? Because mediation comes last, is it the best or most valued?* No aim is "better" than any other aim. Given needs for writing and certain audiences, one aim is more appropriate than another for the task at hand. Mediation comes last because it integrates inquiry, convincing, and persuading.

2. *Must inquiry be taught as a separate aim?* No. It *may* be taught as a separate aim, but we do not intend this "may" as a "must." Teaching inquiry as a distinct aim has certain advantages. Students need to learn how to engage in constructive dialogue, which is more disciplined and more focused than most class discussion. Once they see how it is done, students enjoy dialogue with one another and with texts. Dialogue helps students think through their arguments and imagine reader reaction to what they say, both of which are crucial to convincing and persuading. Finally, as with mediation, inquiry offers avenues for assignments other than the standard argumentative essay.

3. *Should inquiry come first?* For a number of reasons, inquiry has priority over the other aims. Most teachers are likely to approach inquiry as prewriting, preparatory to convincing or persuading. And commonly, we return to inquiry when we find something wrong with a case we are trying to construct, so the relationship between inquiry and the other aims is also recursive.

   Moreover, inquiry has psychological, moral, and practical claims to priority. When we are unfamiliar with an issue, inquiry comes first psychologically, as a felt need to explore existing opinion. Regardless of what happens in the "real world," convincing or persuading without an open, honest, and earnest search for the truth is, in our view, immoral. Finally, inquiry goes hand in hand with research, which requires questioning the opinions encountered.

4. *Isn't the difference between convincing and persuading more a matter of degree than kind?* Sharp distinctions can be drawn between inquiry and mediation and between both of these aims and the monologues of advocacy, convincing, and persuading. But convincing and persuading do shade into one another so that the difference is clearest at the extremes, with carefully chosen examples. Furthermore, the "purest" appeal to reason—a legal brief, a philosophical or scientific argument—appeals in ways beyond the sheer cogency of the case. Persuasive techniques are submerged but not absent in arguing to convince.

   Our motivation for separating convincing from persuading is not theoretical but pedagogical. Case-making is complex enough that attention to logical appeal by itself is justified. Making students conscious of the appeals to character, emotion, and style while they are learning to cope with case-making can overburden them to the point of paralysis.

   Regardless, then, of how sound the traditional distinction between convincing and persuading may be, we think it best to take up convincing first and then persuasion, especially because what students learn in the former can be carried over intact into the latter. And because one cannot make a case without unconscious appeal to character, emotional commitments (such as values), and style, teaching persuasion is a matter of exposing and developing what is already there in arguing to convince.

Here are the central tenets of an approach based on aims of argument:

- *Argumentation is a mode or means of discourse, not an aim or purpose for writing;* consequently, we need to teach the aims of argument.
- *The aims of argument are linked in a learning sequence so that convincing builds on inquiry, persuasion on convincing, and all three contribute to mediation;* consequently, we offer a learning sequence for conceiving a course or courses in argumentation.

We believe in the sequence as much as the aims. We think that many will come to prefer it over any other approach.

Of course, textbooks are used selectively, as teachers and programs need them in achieving their own goals. As with any other text, this one can be used selectively, ignoring some parts, playing up others, designing other sequences, and so on. If you want to work with our learning sequence, it's there for creative adaptation. If not, the text is flexible enough for almost any course structure or teaching method.

A NOTE ABOUT THE READINGS

Since the fourth edition, we have divided the readings into two sections: casebooks and readings chapters. The former may need some explanation. We introduced the casebook for two reasons: to allow deeper exploration of some topics and to provide enough readings to permit research assignments drawing on source material only from the textbook. Obviously, as teachers struggle more and more with plagiarism and with problems connected with skillful paraphrasing and summarizing of sources, the casebook offers significant advantages over less controlled outside research.

However, concerns regarding the book's length prompted us in this edition to reduce both the number and the length of the pieces chosen, while still retaining greater depth and the potential to evaluate more easily student use of sources.

We have avoided the "great authors, classic essays" approach. We tried instead to find bright, contemporary people arguing well from diverse viewpoints—articles and chapters similar to those that can be found in our better journals and trade books, the sort of publications students should read most in doing research. We have not presented any issue in simple pro-and-con fashion, as if there were only two sides.

Included in the range of perspectives are arguments made with both words and images. We include a full instructional chapter examining visual arguments such as editorial cartoons, advertisements, public sculpture, and photographs.

A FINAL WORD ABOUT THE APPROACH

Our approach is innovative. But is it better? Will students learn more? Will instructors find the book more satisfying and more helpful than what they currently use? Our experience—both in using the book ourselves and in listening to the responses of those who have read it or tested it in the classroom or used it for years—is that they will. Students complain less about having to read this book than about having to read others used in our program. They do seem to learn more. Teachers claim to find the text stimulating, something to work with rather than around. We hope your experience is as positive as ours has been. We invite your comments and will use them in the perpetual revision that constitutes the life of a text and our lives as writing teachers.

NEW TO THE SEVENTH EDITION

The writing assignments in the book have been thoroughly revised, and we did so through a lengthy process of writing, rewriting, and revision, aided by extensive input from reviewers and classroom testing. Here are the results:

1. **A new assignment chapter, Chapter 4, "Writing a Critique"** Following Chapter 2, "Reading an Argument," and Chapter 3, "Analyzing an Argument," this chapter offers a fully developed pedagogy for responding critically to arguments. It can be used to guide a distinct assignment or to help students assess arguments they encounter in research.

2. **A new version of "Arguing to Inquire," Chapter 8** Inquiry in argument amounts to "joining the conversation," comparing existing arguments on controversial issues. Our new chapter takes students through understanding and assessment of conflicting positions, with the goal of discovering the good reasons and evidence in each and reaching a position of their own. Cultivating rational inquiry has always been an important goal for this book, but we think this new chapter does it better than before.

3. **A new version of "Arguing to Convince," Chapter 9** The familiar emphasis on case-making remains central, but we think the process offered is easier for students to understand and more efficient to teach.

4. **A new version of "Arguing to Persuade," Chapter 10** "Motivating action" remains our focus, which means, as it always has for us, appealing to the whole person, integrating argument with ethical, emotional, and stylistic inducement. We believe, however, that the instruction offered makes the challenge of persuading more accessible to students, with advice and guidance they can more readily implement in their own writing.

5. **New readings and student examples in all four of the new assignment chapters** Nothing enlivens teaching composition quite like some fresh material. Besides new readings to work with, we offer more of them on topics we think your students will find especially engaging. The new student examples were gathered not only to provide better models but also for the following key innovation.

6. **Greater emphasis on revision** In most books, student examples are finished products, models only, which reveal little of what went on to make the examples successful. We now have excerpts from early drafts, motivations for revising them are addressed, followed by revised drafts so that students can see the concrete improvements only genuine revision can achieve. As all writing teachers know, better writing cannot result so long as students think of writing as "cleaning up" a first draft. They must learn to revise. We think our new way of presenting student examples will help.

7. **A new reading chapter, Chapter 17, "Declining Civility: Is Rudeness on the Rise?"** From the ubiquitous cell phone used inappropriately to the extreme polarization of national politics, civility is becoming a lost virtue. This chapter examines several of the many varieties of incivility and asks what can and should be done.

Besides these major additions and changes, those familiar with the Sixth Edition will detect many more: other new readings and visual examples, for instance, and an updating of "Writing Research-Based Arguments." We have enlarged the Glossary and developed the entries to help your students understand the terminology of argument better. We think the work that went into this new edition of *Aims* was well worth the effort and hope you will too.

Revised Online Learning Center

In addition to the many changes the seventh edition offers in the text itself, this edition of *Aims* is accompanied by a newly revised Online Learning Center, accessible at www.mhhe.com/crusius. The site features all the tools of Catalyst 2.0, McGraw-Hill's award-winning writing and research Web site. You will find integrated references throughout the text, pointing you to additional online coverage of the topic at hand.

The instructor's manual has been significantly revised by the authors and is available on the instructors' side of the Online Learning Center. Contact your McGraw-Hill sales representative for access.

Online Course Delivery and Distance Learning

In addition to the Web site, McGraw-Hill offers the following technology products for composition classes. The online content of *The Aims of Argument* is supported by WebCT, Blackboard, eCollege.com, and most other course systems.

ACKNOWLEDGMENTS

We have learned a great deal from the comments of both teachers and students who have used this book, so please continue to share your thoughts with us.

We wish to acknowledge the work of the following reviewers who guided our work on the seventh edition: Cora Agatucci, Central Oregon Community College; Allan Johnston, DePaul University & Columbia College; Ann Krooth, Diablo Valley College; Michael Lee, Columbia Basin College; Dorothy Leman, Central Oregon Community College; Judy M. Lloyd, Southside Virginia Community College; Jim McKeown, McLennan Community College; Anne M. Reid, Colorado State University, Ft. Collins; and Daniel Asher Wolkow, Eastern New Mexico University-Roswell.

Aaron Downey of Matrix Productions, our production editor, and Kay Mikel, our copyeditor, went far beyond the call of duty. Christopher Bennem and Janice Wiggins-Clarke, our editors, showed their usual brilliance and lent their unflagging energy throughout the process that led to this new edition of *Aims*.

A special thanks to Marcella Stark, research librarian at SMU, for all her help with updating the research chapter.

Timothy Crusius
Carolyn Channell
Dallas, Texas

Our goal in this book is not just to show you how to construct an argument but also to make you more aware of why people argue and what purposes argument serves. Consequently, Part Two of this book introduces four specific aims that people have in mind when they argue: to inquire, to convince, to persuade, and to mediate. Part One precedes the aims of argument and focuses on understanding argumentation in general, reading and analyzing arguments, writing a critique, doing research, and working with such forms of visual persuasion as advertising.

The selections in Parts One and Two offer something to emulate. All writers learn from studying the strategies of other writers. The object is not to imitate what a more experienced writer does but to understand the range of strategies you can use in your own way for your own purposes.

Included are arguments made with words and images. We have examples of editorial cartoons, advertisements, and photographs.

The additional readings in Parts Three and Four serve another function. To learn argument, we have to argue; to argue, we must have something to argue about. So we have grouped essays and images around central issues of current public discussion. Part Three's two casebooks offer expanded treatment of two subjects we think you'll find especially interesting: the consumer society, and sex and relationships. We selected the essays of Part Four rather than others for two main reasons. One is that the included essays have worked better than those we tried and rejected. The other is that most of the topics of these essays deal centrally with difference, which causes people to disagree with one another in the first place.

People argue with one another because they do not see the world the same way, and they do not see the world the same way because of different backgrounds. Therefore, in dealing with how people differ, a book about argument must deal with what makes people different, with the sources of disagreement itself—including gender, race/ethnicity, class, sexual orientation, and religion. Rather than ignoring or glossing over difference, the readings in Parts Three and Four will help you better understand it.

This book concludes with two appendixes. The first is on editing, the art of polishing and refining prose, and finding common errors. The second deals with fallacies and critical thinking. Consult these resources often as you work through the text's assignments.

Arguing well is difficult for anyone. We have tried to write a text no more complicated than it has to be. We welcome your comments to improve future editions. Write us at

The Rhetoric Program
Dallas Hall
Southern Methodist University
Dallas, Texas 75275

or e-mail your comments to

cchannel@mail.smu.edu
tcrusius@mail.smu.edu

Timothy W. Crusius is professor of English at Southern Methodist University, where he teaches beginning and advanced composition. He's the author of books on discourse theory, philosophical hermeneutics, and Kenneth Burke. He resides in Dallas with his wife, Elizabeth, and their children, Micah and Rachel.

Carolyn E. Channell taught high school and community college students before coming to Southern Methodist University, where she is now a senior lecturer and specialist in first-year writing courses. She resides in Richardson, Texas, with her husband, David, and "child," a boxer named Gretel.

BRIEF CONTENTS

CONTENTS

CHAPTER 7

Ethical Writing and Plagiarism   167

PART TWO

THE AIMS OF ARGUMENT   177

CHAPTER 8

Joining the Conversation: Arguing to Inquire   179

CHAPTER 9

Making Your Case: Arguing to Convince   207

CHAPTER 13

Romantic Relationships: Sex, Love, and Maybe Marriage   371

BOXES BY TYPE

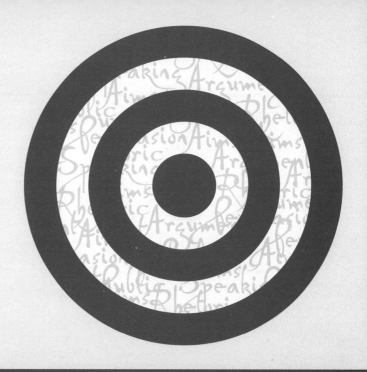

Resources for Reading and Writing Arguments

RESOURCES FOR READING AND WRITING ARGUMENTS

Understanding Argument

The Aims of Argument is based on two key concepts: argument and rhetoric. These days, unfortunately, the terms *argument* and *rhetoric* have acquired bad reputations. The popular meaning of *argument* is *disagreement;* we think of raised voices, hurt feelings, winners and losers. Most people think of *rhetoric,* too, in a negative sense—as language that sounds good but evades or hides the truth. In this sense, rhetoric is the language we hear from the politician who says anything to win votes, the public relations person who puts "positive spin" on dishonest business practices, the buck-passing bureaucrat who blames the foul-up on someone else, the clever lawyer who counterfeits passion to plead for the acquittal of a guilty client.

The words *argument* and *rhetoric,* then, are commonly applied to the darker side of human acts and motives. This darker side is real—arguments are often pointless and silly, ugly and destructive; all too often, rhetoric is empty words contrived to mislead or to disguise the desire to exert power. But this book is not about that kind of argument or that kind of rhetoric. Here we develop the meanings of *argument* and *rhetoric* in an older, fuller, and far more positive sense—as the language and art of mature reasoning.

WHAT IS ARGUMENT?

In this book, **argument** means *mature reasoning*. By *mature*, we mean an attitude and approach to argument, not an age group. Some older adults are incapable of mature reasoning, whereas some young people reason very well. And all of us, regardless of age, sometimes fall short of mature reasoning. What is "mature" about the kind of argument we have in mind? One meaning of *mature* is "worked out fully by the mind" or "considered" (*American Heritage Dictionary*). Mature decisions, for example, are thoughtful ones, reached slowly after full consideration of all the consequences. And this is true also of mature reasoning.

The second term in this definition of argument also needs comment: *reasoning*. If we study logic in depth, we find many definitions of reasoning, but *reasoning* here means *an opinion plus a reason (or reasons) for holding that opinion*. As we will see shortly, good arguments require more than this; to be convincing, reasons must be developed with evidence like specific facts and examples. However, understanding the basic form of "opinion-plus-a-reason" is the place to begin when considering your own and other people's arguments.

WHAT IS RHETORIC?

Over time, the meanings of most words in most languages change—sometimes only a little, sometimes a lot. The word *rhetoric* is a good example of a big change. As indicated already, the popular meaning of *rhetoric* is empty verbiage—the art of sounding impressive while saying little—or the art of verbal deception. This meaning of *rhetoric* confers a judgment, and not a positive one.

In contrast, in ancient Greece, where rhetoric was invented about 2,500 years ago, *rhetoric* referred to the art of public speaking. The Greeks recognized that rhetoric could be abused, but, for their culture in general, it was not a negative term. They had a goddess of persuasion (see Figure 1.1), and they respected the power of the spoken word to move people. It dominated their law courts, their governments, and their public ceremonies and events. As an art, the spoken word was an object of study. People enrolled in schools of rhetoric to become effective public speakers. Further, the ancient rhetoricians put a high value on good character. Not just sounding ethical but being ethical contributed to a speaker's persuasive power.

This old, highly valued meaning of rhetoric as oratory survived well into the nineteenth century. In Abraham Lincoln's day, Americans assembled by the thousands to hear speeches that went on for hours. For them, a good speech held the same level of interest as a big sporting event does for people today.

In this book, we are interested primarily in various ways of using *written* argument, but the rhetorical tradition informs our understanding of mature reasoning.

If argument is mature reasoning, then rhetoric is its *art*—that is, how we go about arguing with some degree of success. Just as there is an art of

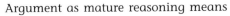
Defining Mature Reasoning

Argument as mature reasoning means

- Defending *not the first position* you might take on an issue *but the best position,* determined through open-minded inquiry
- Providing reasons for holding that position that can earn the respect of an audience

painting or sculpture, so is there an art of mature reasoning. Since the time of Aristotle, teachers of rhetoric have taught their students *self-conscious* ways of reasoning well and arguing successfully. The study of rhetoric, therefore, includes both what we have already defined as reasoning *and* ways of appealing to an audience. These include efforts to project oneself as a good and intelligent person as well as efforts to connect with the audience through humor, passion, and image.

Figure 1.1

Peitho, the goddess of persuasion, was often involved in seductions and love affairs. On this piece (a detail from a terra-cotta kylix, c. 410 BCE), Peitho, the figure on the left, gives advice to a dejected-looking woman, identified as Demonassa. To the right, Eros, the god of love, stands with his hand on Demonassa's shoulder, suggesting the nature of this advice.

Defining Rhetoric

Rhetoric is the art of argument as mature reasoning. The study of rhetoric develops self-conscious awareness of the principles and practices of mature reasoning and effective arguing.

AN EXAMPLE OF ARGUMENT

So far, we have been talking about argument in the abstract—definitions and explanations. We need a concrete example of mature reasoning. One thing mature reasoning does is challenge unexamined belief, the stances people take without much thought. The following argument by a syndicated columnist would have us reassess a word that often has negative associations.

The Other F Word

LEONARD PITTS

1   Women must stop recoiling from the very word that stands for their liberation. Brace yourself. I'm going to use a word that offends folks. I'm talking the "F" word. Feminist.

2   This woman sent me an e-mail Monday and it got me thinking. See, in describing herself, she assured me she was not a "women's libber"—the late 1960s equivalent of feminist. She also said she was retired from the U.S. Navy. There was, it seemed to me, a disconnect there: She doesn't believe in women's liberation, yet she is retired from a position that liberation made possible.

3   Intrigued, I asked my 17-year-old daughter if she considers herself a feminist. She responded with a mildly horrified no. This, by the way, is the daughter with the 3.75 GPA who is presently pondering possible college majors including political science, psychology and . . . women's studies. I asked her to define "feminist." There began a halting explanation that seemed to suggest shrillness wrapped around obnoxiousness. Abruptly, she stopped. "It's hard to explain," she said.

4   Actually, it's not. Jessica Valenti, author of *Full Frontal Feminism: A Young Woman's Guide to Why Feminism Matters,* calls it the I'm-Not-A-Feminist-But syndrome. As in the woman who says, "I'm not a feminist, but . . ." and then "goes on to espouse completely feminist values. I think most women believe in access to birth control, they want equal pay for equal work, they want to fight against rape and violence against women."

5   "Feminist," it seems, has ended up in the same syntactical purgatory as another once-useful, now-reviled term: liberal. Most people endorse what that word has historically stood for—integration, child labor laws, product safety—yet they treat the word itself like anthrax. Similarly, while it's hard to imagine that any young woman really wants to return to the days of barefoot, pregnant and making meatloaf, many

now disdain the banner under which their gender fought for freedom. They scorn feminism even as they feast at a table feminism prepared.

6   Says Ms. Valenti, "The word has been so effectively misused and so effectively mischaracterized by conservatives for so long that women are afraid to identify with it. They'll say everything under the sun that's feminist, but they won't identify with it because they've been taught feminists are anti-men, feminists are ugly."

7   Dr. Deborah Tannen agrees. She is a professor of linguistics at Georgetown University and author of a number of books on gender and communication, including: *You're Wearing That? Understanding Mothers and Daughters in Conversation.* "The reason, I believe, is that meanings of words come from how they're used. And since the word 'feminist' is used as a negative term rather than a positive one, people don't want to be associated with it."

8   With apologies to Malcolm X, they've been had, they've been hoodwinked, they've been bamboozled. And it's sad. I've lost track of how many times, visiting high schools or teaching college classes, I have met bright girls juggling options and freedoms that would've been unthinkable a generation ago, smart young women preparing for lives and careers their foremothers could not have dreamt, yet if you use the "F" word, they recoil.

9   We have, I think, lost collective memory of how things were before the F-word. Of the casual beatings. Of casual rape. Of words like "old maid" and "spinster." Of abortion by coat hanger. Of going to school to find a man. Of getting an allowance and needing a husband's permission. Of taking all your spirit, all your dreams, all your ambition, aspiration, creativity, and pounding them down until they fit a space no larger than a casserole dish.

10   "I'm not a feminist, but . . . ?" That's a fraud. It's intellectually dishonest. And it's a slap to the feminists who prepared the table at which today's young women sup.

11   So for the record, I am a feminist. My daughter is, too.

12   She doesn't know it yet.

Leonard Pitts, "The Other F Word," *Miami Herald*, February 14, 2008, p.19A. Reprinted by permission of McClatchey Interactive West.

Discussion of "The Other F Word"

Leonard Pitts's argument is an example of a type or *genre* of written persuasion, the opinion column. Let's examine his argument and what makes it mature.

The first question we should ask of any argument we are analyzing is, What is Pitts's *claim* or position? *All claims are answers to questions.* In this case, the question is, How should we assess the statement "I'm not a feminist, but . . ."? His answer: "That's a fraud. It's intellectually dishonest. And it's a slap to the feminists who prepared the table at which today's young women sup" (paragraph 10). His claim is that "women must stop recoiling from the very word that stands for their liberation" (paragraph 1).

What reasoning does he use to justify his claim? He points to a fundamental contradiction. Women reject the label "feminist" but support most or all of what feminism achieved for women. In essence, they are denying what they are. He goes on to support this reasoning with evidence drawn from expert opinion, from Jessica Valenti and Deborah Tannen.

What makes Pitts's argument mature, an example of the kind of reasoning worth learning how to do? His position is obviously more mature than his daughter's, who thinks that a feminist is always "shrillness wrapped around obnoxiousness." However, the difference here is not age but rather *awareness*. The retired Navy woman has the same problem as the much younger daughter: recoiling from the very word that stands for her liberation. Neither seem aware of what feminism has accomplished for women or the history of oppression that Pitts summarizes so well in paragraph 9. Pitts's greater awareness contributes greatly to the maturity of his reasoning.

However, another sign of maturity may be equally important. *Pitts's opinion is consistent with his actual beliefs.* Too often we are reluctant to claim what we actually think, usually because we are overly concerned about the reactions of other people. Of course, nothing is gained by offending others needlessly. Tact matters. But we need to be honest, and we need to be consistent—more than that, we must have the courage to say what we think. We also gain nothing by being evasive.

In recognizing the maturity of Pitts's argument, we should not be too respectful of it. Mature reasoning should be challenged by mature criticism. For instance, is it always the case that "I am not a feminist, but . . ." amounts to intellectual fraud? Perhaps the retired Navy woman did not know that her opportunities resulted from feminist agitation. You cannot commit fraud—tell a lie about what you know the truth is—if you do not know the truth. Nor is it necessarily fraudulent to know the truth but also wish to avoid a label that puts you at a disadvantage. Perhaps some women know they are feminists but wish to be called something else because the word has negative connotations. If so, being a good strategist is not the same thing as committing fraud.

◎◎ FOLLOWING THROUGH

Any good piece of writing can give you ideas for your own writing. The Pitts editorial calls labeling into question, and you can probably recall when someone applied a label with negative connotations to you or to some group to which you belong. Choose an instance and either accept the label and defend it as something positive or reject it and show why it should not be applied to you or your group.   •

FOUR CRITERIA OF MATURE REASONING

Students often ask, "What does my professor want?" Although you will be writing many different kinds of papers in response to the assignments in this textbook, your professor will most likely look for evidence of mature reasoning. When we evaluate student work, we use four criteria.

Mature Reasoners Are Well Informed

Your opinions must develop from knowledge and be supported by reliable and current evidence. If the reader feels that the writer "doesn't know his or her stuff," the argument loses all weight and force.

You may have noticed that people have opinions about all sorts of things, including subjects they know little or nothing about. The general human tendency is to have the strongest opinions on matters about which we know the least. Ignorance and inflexibility go together because it is easy to form an opinion when few or none of the facts get in the way and we can just assert our prejudices. Conversely, the more we know about most topics, the harder it is to be dogmatic. We find ourselves changing or at least refining our opinions more or less continuously as we gain more knowledge.

Mature Reasoners Are Self-Critical and Open to Constructive Criticism from Others

We have opinions about all sorts of things that do not matter much to us, casual opinions we have picked up somehow and may not even bother to defend if challenged. But we also have opinions in which we are heavily invested, sometimes to the point that our whole sense of reality, right and wrong, good and bad—our very sense of ourselves—is tied up in them. These opinions we defend passionately.

On this count, popular argumentation and mature reasoning are alike. Mature reasoners are often passionate about their convictions, as committed to them as the fanatic on the street corner is to his or her cause. A crucial difference, however, separates the fanatic from the mature reasoner. The fanatic is all passion; the mature reasoner is able and willing to step back and examine even deeply held convictions. "I may have believed this for as long as I can remember," the mature reasoner says, "but is this conviction really justified? Do the facts support it? When I think it through, does it really make sense? Can I make a coherent and consistent argument for it?" These are questions that do not concern the fanatic and are seldom posed in the popular argumentation we hear on talk radio or TV.

In practical terms, being self-critical and open to well-intended criticism boils down to this: Mature reasoners can and do change their minds when they have good reasons to do so. In popular argumentation, changing one's mind can be taken as a weakness, as "wishy-washy," and so people tend to go on advocating what they believe, regardless of what anyone else says. But there is nothing wishy-washy about, for example, confronting the facts, about realizing that what we thought is not supported by the available evidence. In such a case, changing one's mind is a sign of intelligence and the very maturity mature reason values.

Mature Reasoners Argue with Their Audiences or Readers in Mind

Nothing drains energy from argument more than the feeling that it will accomplish nothing. As one student put it, "Why bother? People just go on thinking what they want to." This attitude is understandable. Popular, undisciplined argument often does seem futile: minds are not changed; no progress is made; it is doubtful that anyone learned anything. Sometimes the opposing positions only harden, and the people involved are more at odds than before.

Why does this happen so often? One reason is that nobody is listening to anyone else. We tend to hear only our own voices and see only from our own points of view. But there is another reason: The people making the arguments have made no effort to reach their audience. This is the other side of the coin of not listening—when we do not take other points of view seriously, we cannot make our points of view appealing to those who do not already share them.

To have a chance of working, arguments must be *other-directed,* attuned to the people they want to reach. This may seem obvious, but it is also commonly ignored and not easy to do. We have to imagine the other guy. We have to care about other points of view, not just see them as obstacles to our own. We have to present and develop our arguments in ways that will not turn off the very people for whom we are writing. In many ways, *adapting to the audience* is the biggest challenge of argument.

Mature Reasoners Know Their Arguments' Contexts

All arguments are part of an ongoing conversation. We think of arguments as something individuals make. We think of our opinions as *ours,* almost like private property. But arguments and opinions have pasts: Other people argued about more or less the same issues and problems before—often long before—we came on the scene. They have a present: Who's arguing what now, the current state of the argument. And they have a future: What people will be arguing about tomorrow, in different circumstances, with knowledge we lack now.

So most arguments are not the isolated events they seem to be. Part of being well informed is knowing something about the history of an argument. By understanding an argument's past, we learn about patterns that will help us develop our own position. To some extent, we must know what is going on now and what other people are saying to make our own reasoning relevant. And although we cannot know the future, we can imagine the drift of the argument, where it might be heading. In other words, there is a larger context we need to join—a big conversation of many voices to which our few belong.

WHAT ARE THE AIMS OF ARGUMENT?

The heart of this book is Part Two, the section titled "The Aims of Argument." In conceiving this book, we worked from one basic premise: Mature reasoners do not argue just to argue; rather, they use argument to accomplish something: *to inquire* into a question, problem, or issue (commonly part of the research process); *to convince* their readers to assent to an opinion, or

Four Criteria of Mature Reasoning

MATURE REASONERS ARE WELL INFORMED

Their opinions develop out of knowledge and are supported by reliable and current evidence.

MATURE REASONERS ARE SELF-CRITICAL AND OPEN TO CONSTRUCTIVE CRITICISM FROM OTHERS

They balance their passionate attachment to their opinions with willingness to evaluate and test them against differing opinions, acknowledge when good points are made against their opinions, and even, when presented with good reasons for doing so, change their minds.

MATURE REASONERS ARGUE WITH THEIR AUDIENCES OR READERS IN MIND

They make a sincere effort to understand and connect with other people and other points of view because they do not see differences of opinion as obstacles to their own points of view.

MATURE REASONERS KNOW THEIR ARGUMENTS' CONTEXTS

They recognize that what we argue about now was argued about in the past and will be argued about in the future, that our contributions to these ongoing conversations are influenced by who we are, what made us who we are, where we are, what's going on around us.

---

claim; *to persuade* readers to take action, such as buying a product or voting for a candidate; and *to mediate* conflict, as in labor disputes, divorce proceedings, and so on.

Let's look at each of these aims in more detail.

Arguing to Inquire

Arguing to **inquire** is using reasoning to determine the best position on an issue. We open the "Aims" section with inquiry because mature reasoning is not a matter of defending what we already believe but of questioning it. Arguing to inquire helps us form opinions, question opinions we already have, and reason our way through conflicts or contradictions in other people's arguments on a topic. Inquiry is open-minded, and it requires that we make an effort to find out what people who disagree think and why.

The ancient Greeks called argument as inquiry *dialectic*; today we might think of it as **dialogue** or serious conversation. There is nothing confrontational about such conversations. We have them with friends, family, and colleagues, even with ourselves. We have these conversations in writing too, as we make notations in the margins of the arguments we read.

Inquiry centers on questions and involves some legwork to answer them—finding the facts, doing research. This is true whether you are inquiring into what car to buy, what major to choose in college, what candidate to vote for, or what policy our government should pursue on any given issue.

Arguing to Convince

The goal of inquiry is to reach some kind of conclusion on an issue. Let's call this conclusion a **conviction** and define it as "an earned opinion, achieved through careful thought, research, and discussion." Once we arrive at a conviction, we usually want others to share it. The aim of further argument is to secure the assent of people who do not share our conviction (or who do not share it fully).

Argument to **convince** centers on making a case, which means offering reasons and evidence in support of our opinion. Arguments to convince are all around us. In college, we find them in scholarly and professional writing. In everyday life, we find arguments to convince in editorials, courtrooms, and political speeches. Whenever we encounter an opinion supported by reasons and asking us to agree, we are dealing with arguing to convince.

Arguing to Persuade

Like convincing, persuasion attempts to earn agreement, but it wants more. **Persuasion** attempts to influence not just thinking but also behavior. An advertisement for Mercedes-Benz aims to convince us not only that the company makes a high-quality car but also that we should go out and buy one. A Sunday sermon asks for more than agreement with some interpretation of a biblical passage; the minister wants the congregation to live according to its message. Persuasion asks us to do something—spend money, give money, join a demonstration, recycle, vote, enlist, acquit. Because we do not always act on our convictions, persuasion cannot rely on reasoning alone. It must appeal in broader, deeper ways.

Persuasion appeals to readers' emotions. It tells stories about individual cases of hardship that move us to pity. It often uses photographs, as when charities confront us with pictures of poverty or suffering. Persuasion uses many of the devices of poetry, such as patterns of sound, repetitions, metaphors, and similes to arouse a desired emotion in the audience.

Persuasion also relies on the personality of the writer to an even greater degree than does convincing. The persuasive writer attempts to represent something higher or larger than him- or herself—some ideal with which the reader would like to be associated. For example, a war veteran and hero like Senator John McCain naturally brings patriotism to the table when he makes a speech.

Arguing to Mediate

By the time we find ourselves in a situation where our aim is to **mediate**, we will have already attempted to convince an opponent to settle a conflict or

Comparing the Aims of Argument

The aims of argument have much in common. For example, besides sharing argument, they all tend to draw on sources of knowledge (research) and to deal with controversial issues. But the aims also differ from one another, mainly in terms of purpose, audience, situation, and method, as summarized here and on the inside back cover.

	Purpose	Audience	Situation	Method
Inquiry	Seeks truth	Oneself, friends, and colleagues	Informal; a dialogue	Questions
Convincing	Seeks assent to a thesis	Less intimate; wants careful reasoning	More formal; a monologue	Case-making
Persuading	Seeks action	More broadly public, less academic	Pressing need for a decision	Appeals to reason and emotions
Mediating	Seeks consensus	Polarized by differences	Need to cooperate, preserve relations	"Give-and-take"

We offer this chart as a general guide to the aims of argument. Think of it as the big picture you can always return to as you work your way through Part Two, which deals with each of the aims in detail.

dispute our way. Our opponent will have done the same. Yet neither side has secured the assent of the other, and "agreeing to disagree" is not a practical solution because the participants must decide what to do.

In most instances of mediation, the parties involved try to work out the conflict themselves because they have some relationship they wish to preserve—as employer and employee, business partners, family members, neighbors, even coauthors of an argument textbook. Common differences requiring mediation include the amount of a raise or the terms of a contract. In private life, mediation helps roommates live together and families decide on everything from budgets to vacation destinations.

Just like other aims of argument, arguing to mediate requires sound logic and the clear presentation of positions and reasons. However, mediation challenges our interpersonal skills more than do the other aims. Each side must listen closely to understand not just the other's case but also the emotional commitments and underlying values. When mediation works, the opposing sides begin to converge. Exchanging viewpoints and information and building empathy enable all parties to make concessions, to loosen their hold on their original positions, and finally to reach consensus—or at least a resolution that all participants find satisfactory.

CHAPTER 2

Reading an Argument

In a course in argumentation, you will read many arguments. Our book contains a wide range of argumentative essays, some by students, some by established professionals. In addition, you may find arguments on your own in books, newspapers, and magazines, or on the Internet. You will read them to develop your understanding of argument. That means you will analyze and evaluate these texts—known as **critical reading.** Critical reading involves special skills and habits that are not essential when you read a book for information or entertainment. This chapter discusses those skills and habits.

By the time most students get to high school, reading is no longer taught. While there is plenty to read, any advice on *how to read* is usually about increasing vocabulary or reading speed, not reading critically. This is too bad because in college you are called on to read more critically than ever.

Have patience with yourself and with the texts you work with in this book. Reading will involve going through a text more than once, no matter how careful that single reading may be. You will go back to a text several times, asking new questions with each reading. That takes time, but it is time well spent. Just as when you see a film a second time, you notice new details, so each reading increases your knowledge of a text.

Before we start, a bit of advice: Attempt critical reading only when your mind is fresh. Find a place conducive to concentration—such as a table in the library. Critical reading requires an alert, active response.

THE FIRST ENCOUNTER: SEEING THE TEXT IN CONTEXT

Critical reading begins not with a line-by-line reading but with a fast overview of the whole text, followed by some thinking about how the text fits into a bigger picture, or *context,* which we describe shortly.

We first **sample** a text rather than read it through. Look at the headings and subdivisions. They will give a sense of how the text is organized. Note what parts look interesting and/or hard to understand. Note any information about the author provided before or after the text itself, as well as any publication information (where and when the piece was originally published). Look at the opening and closing paragraphs to discern the author's main point or view.

Reading comprehension depends less on a large vocabulary than on the ability to see how the text fits into contexts. Sampling will help you consider the text in two contexts that are particularly important:

1. *The general climate of opinion* surrounding the topic of the text. This includes debate on the topic both before and since the text's publication.

2. *The rhetorical context* of the text. This includes facts about the author, the intended audience, and the setting in which the argument took place.

Considering the Climate of Opinion

Familiarity with the climate of opinion will help you view any argument critically, recognize a writer's biases and assumptions, and spot gaps or errors in the information. Your own perspective, too, will affect your interpretation of the text. So think about what you know, how you know it, what your opinion is, and what might have led to its formation. You can then interact with a text, rather than just read it passively.

◎◎ FOLLOWING THROUGH

An argument on the topic of body decoration (tattoos and piercing) appears later in this chapter. "On Teenagers and Tattoos" is about motives for decorating the body. As practice in identifying the climate of opinion surrounding a topic, think about what people say about tattooing. Have you heard people argue that it is "low-class"? a rebellion against middle-class conformity? immoral? an artistic expression? a fad? an affront to school or parental authority? an expression of individuality? If you would not want a tattoo, why not? If you have a tattoo, why did you get it? In your writer's notebook, jot down some positions you have heard debated, and state your own viewpoint.   •

Considering the Rhetorical Context

Critical readers also are aware of the **rhetorical context** of an argument. They do not see the text merely as words on a page but as a contribution to some debate among interested people. Rhetorical context includes the author, the intended audience, and the date and place of publication. The reader who knows something about the author's politics or affiliations will have an advantage over the reader who does not. Also, knowing if a periodical is liberal, like *The Nation,* or conservative, like *National Review,* helps.

An understanding of rhetorical context comes from both external and internal clues—information outside the text and information you gather as you read and reread it. You can glean information about rhetorical context from external evidence such as publishers' notes about the author or about a magazine's editorial board or sponsoring foundation. You can find this information in any issue of a periodical or by following an information link on the home page of an online publication.

You also may have prior knowledge of rhetorical context—for example, you may have heard of the author. Or you can look in a database (see pages 111, 112–115) to see what else the author has written. Later, when you read the argument more thoroughly, you will enlarge your understanding of rhetorical context as you discover what the text itself reveals about the author's bias, character, and purpose for writing.

In sum, the first encounter with a text is preliminary to a careful, close reading. It prepares you to get the most out of the second encounter. If you are researching a topic and looking for good sources of information and viewpoints about it, the first encounter with any text will help you decide whether you want to read it at all. A first encounter can be a time-saving last encounter if the text does not seem appropriate or credible.

◎◎ FOLLOWING THROUGH

Note the following information about "On Teenagers and Tattoos."

When published: In 1997, reprinted fall 2000.

Where published: In the *Journal of the American Academy of Child & Adolescent Psychiatry,* published by the American Academy of Child and Adolescent Psychiatry, then reprinted in *Reclaiming Children and Youth.*

Written by *whom:* Andrés Martin, MD. Martin is an associate professor of child psychiatry at the Yale Child Study Center in New Haven, CT.

Then do a fast sampling of the text itself. In your writer's notebook, make some notes about what you expect to find in this argument. What do you think the author's perspective will be, and why? How might it differ from that of a teen, a parent, a teacher? Do the subheadings give you any idea of the main point? Do you notice at the opening or closing any repeated ideas that might give a clue to the author's claim? To whom do you imagine the author was writing, and what might be the purpose of an essay in a journal such as the one that published his argument?

•

Guidelines for Determining Rhetorical Context

To determine an argument's rhetorical context, answer the following questions:

Who wrote this argument, and what are his or her occupation, personal background, and political leanings?

To whom do you think the author is writing? Arguments are rarely aimed at "the general public" but rather at a definite target audience, such as "entertainment industry moguls," "drivers in Dallas," or "parents of teenagers."

Where does the article appear? If it is reprinted, where did it appear originally? What do you know about the publication?

When was the argument written? If not recently, what do you know about the time during which it appeared?

Why was the article written? What prompted its creation, and what purpose does the author have for writing?

AN ARGUMENT FOR CRITICAL READING

On Teenagers and Tattoos

ANDRÉS MARTIN

The skeleton dimensions I shall now proceed to set down are copied verbatim from my right arm, where I had them tattooed: as in my wild wanderings at that period, there was no other secure way of preserving such valuable statistics.

—Herman Melville, *Moby Dick*

1   Tattoos and piercing have become a part of our everyday landscape. They are ubiquitous, having entered the circles of glamour and the mainstream of fashion, and they have even become an increasingly common feature of our urban youth. Legislation in most states restricts professional tattooing to adults older than 18 years of age, so "high end" tattooing is rare in children and adolescents, but such tattoos are occasionally seen in older teenagers. Piercings, by comparison, as well as self-made or "jailhouse" type tattoos, are not at all rare among adolescents or even among school-age children. Like hairdo, makeup, or baggy jeans, tattoos and piercings can be subject to fad influence or peer pressure in an effort toward group affiliation. As with any other fashion statement, they can be construed as bodily aids in the inner struggle toward identity consolidation, serving as adjuncts to the defining and sculpting of the self by means of external manipulations. But unlike most other body decorations, tattoos and piercings are set apart by their irreversible and permanent nature, a quality at the core of their magnetic appeal to adolescents.

2   Adolescents and their parents are often at odds over the acquisition of bodily decorations. For the adolescent, piercing or tattoos may be seen as personal and beautifying statements, while parents may construe them as oppositional

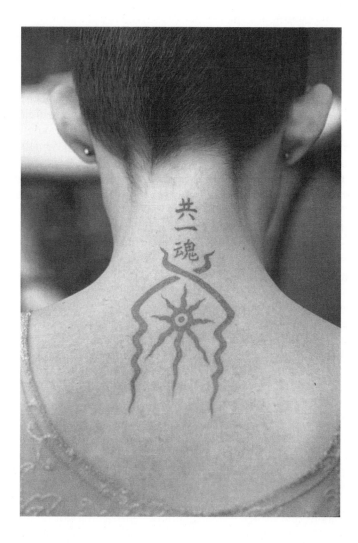

and enraging affronts to their authority. Distinguishing bodily adornment from self-mutilation may indeed prove challenging, particularly when a family is in disagreement over a teenager's motivations and a clinician is summoned as the final arbiter. At such times it may be most important to realize jointly that the skin can all too readily become but another battleground for the tensions of the age, arguments having less to do with tattoos and piercings than with core issues such as separation from the family matrix. Exploring the motivations and significance underlying tattoos (Grumet, 1983) and piercings can go a long way toward resolving such differences and can become a novel and additional way of getting to know teenagers. An interested and nonjudgmental appreciation of teenagers' surface presentations may become a way of making contact not only in their terms but on their turfs: quite literally on the territory of their skins.

3   The following three sections exemplify some of the complex psychological underpinnings of youth tattooing.

IDENTITY AND THE ADOLESCENT'S BODY

4   Tattoos and piercing can offer a concrete and readily available solution for many of the identity crises and conflicts normative to adolescent development. In using such decorations, and by marking out their bodily territories, adolescents can support their efforts at autonomy, privacy, and insulation. Seeking individuation, tattooed adolescents can become unambiguously demarcated from others and singled out as unique. The intense and often disturbing reactions that are mobilized in viewers can help to effectively keep them at bay, becoming tantamount to the proverbial "Keep Out" sign hanging from a teenager's door.

5   Alternatively, feeling prey to a rapidly evolving body over which they have no say, self-made and openly visible decorations may restore adolescents' sense of normalcy and control, a way of turning a passive experience into an active identity. By indelibly marking their bodies, adolescents can strive to reclaim their bearings within an environment experienced as alien, estranged, or suffocating or to lay claim over their evolving and increasingly unrecognizable bodies. In either case, the net outcome can be a resolution to unwelcome impositions: external, familial, or societal in one case; internal and hormonal in the other. In the words of a 16-year-old girl with several facial piercings, and who could have been referring to her body just as well as to the position within her family: "If I don't fit in, it is because I say so."

INCORPORATION AND OWNERSHIP

6   Imagery of a religious, deathly, or skeletal nature, the likenesses of fierce animals or imagined creatures, and the simple inscription of names are some of the time-tested favorite contents for tattoos. In all instances, marks become not only memorials or recipients for dearly held persons or concepts: they strive for incorporation, with images and abstract symbols gaining substance on becoming a permanent part of the individual's skin. Thickly embedded in personally meaningful representations and object relations, tattoos can become not only the ongoing memento of a relationship, but at times even the only evidence that there ever was such a bond. They can quite literally become the relationship itself. The turbulence and impulsivity of early attachments and infatuations may become grounded, effectively bridging oblivion through the visible reality to tattoos.

7   Case Vignette: "A," a 13-year-old boy, proudly showed me his tattooed deltoid. The coarsely depicted roll of the dice marked the day and month of his birth. Rather disappointed, he then uncovered an immaculate back, going on to draw for me the great "piece" he envisioned for it. A menacing figure held a hand of cards: two aces, two eights, and a card with two sets of dates. "A's" father had belonged to Dead Man's Hand, a motorcycle gang named after the set of cards (aces and eights) that the legendary Wild Bill Hickock had held in the 1890s when shot dead over a poker table in Deadwood, South Dakota. "A" had only the vaguest memory of and sketchiest information about his father, but he knew he had died in a motorcycle accident: The fifth card marked the dates of his birth and death.

8 The case vignette also serves to illustrate how tattoos are often the culmination of a long process of imagination, fantasy, and planning that can start at an early age. Limited markings, or relatively reversible ones such as piercings, can at a later time scaffold toward the more radical commitment of a permanent tattoo.

THE QUEST OF PERMANENCE

9 The popularity of the anchor as a tattoo motif may historically have had to do less with guild identification among sailors than with an intense longing for rootedness and stability. In a similar vein, the recent increase in the popularity and acceptance of tattoos may be understood as an antidote or counterpoint to our urban and nomadic lifestyles. Within an increasingly mobile society, in which relationships are so often transient—as attested by the frequencies of divorce, abandonment, foster placement, and repeated moves, for example—tattoos can be a readily available source of grounding. Tattoos, unlike many relationships, can promise permanence and stability. A sense of constancy can be derived from unchanging marks that can be carried along no matter what the physical, temporal, or geographical vicissitudes at hand. Tattoos stay, while all else may change.

10 Case Vignette: A proud father at 17, "B" had had the smiling face of his 4-month-old baby girl tattooed on his chest. As we talked at a tattoo convention, he proudly introduced her to me, explaining how he would "always know how beautiful she is today" when years from then he saw her semblance etched on himself.

11 The quest for permanence may at other times prove misleading and offer premature closure to unresolved conflicts. At a time of normative uncertainties, adolescents may maladaptively and all too readily commit to a tattoo and its indefinite presence. A wish to hold on to a current certainty may lead the adolescent to lay down in ink what is valued and cherished one day but may not necessarily be in the future. The frequency of self-made tattoos among hospitalized, incarcerated, or gang-affiliated youths suggests such motivations: A sense of stability may be a particularly dire need under temporary, turbulent, or volatile conditions. In addition, through their designs teenagers may assert a sense of bonding and allegiance to a group larger than themselves. Tattoos may attest to powerful experiences, such as adolescence itself, lived and even survived together. As with Moby Dick's protagonist, Ishmael, they may bear witness to the "valuable statistics" of one's "wild wandering(s)": those of adolescent exhilaration and excitement on the one hand; of growing pains, shared misfortune, or even incarceration on the other.

12 Adolescents' bodily decorations, at times radical and dramatic in their presentation, can be seen in terms of figuration rather than disfigurement, of the natural body being through them transformed into a personalized body (Brain, 1979). They can often be understood as self-constructive and adorning efforts, rather than prematurely subsumed as mutilatory and destructive acts. If we bear all of this in mind, we may not only arrive at a position to pass more reasoned clinical judgment, but become sensitized through our patients' skins to another level of their internal reality.

REFERENCES

Brain, R. (1979). *The decorated body.* New York: Harper & Row.
Grumet, G. W. (1983). Psychodynamic implications of tattoos. *American Journal of Orthopsychiatry, 53,* 482–92.

Andrés Martin, "On Teenagers and Tattoos," *Journal of the American Academy of Child & Adolescent Psychiatry,* vol. 36, no. 6 (June 1997), pp. 860–861. Reprinted by permission of Lippincott Williams & Wilkins.

THE SECOND ENCOUNTER: READING AND ANALYZING THE TEXT

We turn now to suggestions for reading and analyzing. These are our own "best practices," what we do when we prepare to discuss or write about a written text. Remember, when you read critically, your purpose goes beyond merely finding out what an argument says. The critical reader is different from the target audience. As a critical reader, you are more like the food critic who dines not merely to eat but to evaluate the chef's efforts.

To see the difference, consider the different perspectives that an ant and a bird would have when looking at the same suburban lawn. The ant is down among the blades of grass, climbing one and then the next. It's a close look, but the view is limited. The bird in the sky above looks down, noticing the size and shape of the yard, the brown patches, the difference between the grass in this yard and the grass in the surrounding yards. The bird has the big picture, the ant the close-up. Critical readers move back and forth between the perspective of the ant and the perspective of the bird, each perspective enriching the other. The big picture helps one notice the patterns, even as the details offer clues to the big picture.

Because critical reading means interacting with the text, be ready with pencil or pen to mark up the text. Highlighting or underlining is not enough. Write comments in the margin.

Wrestling with Difficult Passages

Because one goal of the second encounter is to understand the argument fully, you will need to determine the meanings of unfamiliar words and difficult passages. In college reading, you may encounter new words. You may find allusions or references to other books or authors that you have not read. You may encounter metaphors and irony. The author may speak ironically or for another person. The author may assume that readers have lived through all that he or she has or share the same political viewpoint. All of this can make reading harder. Following are common features that often make reading difficult.

Unfamiliar Contexts

If the author and his or her intended audience are removed from your own experience, you will find the text difficult. Texts from a distant culture or time will include concepts familiar to the writer and original readers but not to you. This is true also of contemporary writing intended for specialists. College increases your store of specialized knowledge and introduces you to new (and old) perspectives. Accepting the challenge of difficult texts is part of college. Look up concepts you don't know. Your instructors can also help you to bridge the gap between your world and the text's.

Contrasting Voices and Views

Authors may state viewpoints that contradict their own. They may concede that part of an opposing argument is true, or they may put in an opposing view to refute it. These voices and viewpoints may come as direct quotations or paraphrases. To avoid misreading these views as the author's, be alert to words that signal contrast. The most common are *but* and *however.*

Allusions

Allusions are brief references to things outside the text—to people, works of art, songs, events in the news—anything in the culture that the author assumes he or she shares knowledge of with readers. Allusions are one way for an author to form a bond with readers—provided the readers' and authors' opinions are the same about what is alluded to. Allusions influence readers. They are persuasive devices that can provide positive associations with the author's viewpoint.

In "On Teenagers and Tattoos," the epigraph (the quotation that appears under the title of the essay) is an allusion to the classic novel *Moby Dick.* Martin alludes to the novel again in paragraph 11. He assumes that his readers know the work—not just its title but also its characters, in particular, the narrator, Ishmael. And he assumes his readers would know that the "skeleton dimensions" of a great whale were important and that readers would therefore understand the value of preserving these statistics. The allusion predisposes readers to see that there are valid reasons for permanently marking the body.

Specialized Vocabulary

If an argument is aimed at an audience of specialists, it will undoubtedly contain vocabulary peculiar to that group or profession. Martin's essay contains social science terminology: "family matrix" and "surface presentations" (paragraph 2), "individuation" (paragraph 4), "grounded" (paragraph 6), "sense of constancy" (paragraph 9), and "normative uncertainties" (paragraph 11).

The text surrounding these terms provides enough help for most readers to get a fair understanding. For example, the text surrounding *individuation* suggests that the person would stand out as a separate physical presence; this is not quite the same as *individuality,* which refers more to one's character. Likewise, the text around *family matrix* points to something the single word *family* does not: it emphasizes the family as the surroundings in which one develops.

If you need to look up a term and a dictionary does not seem to offer an appropriate definition, go to one of the specialized dictionaries available on the library reference shelves. (See pages 102–112 for more on these.)

If you encounter an argument with more jargon than you can handle, you may have to accept that you are not an appropriate reader for it. Some readings are aimed at people with highly specialized graduate degrees or training. Without advanced courses, no one could read these articles with full comprehension, much less critique their arguments.

◎◎ FOLLOWING THROUGH

Find other words in Martin's essay that sound specific to the field of psychology. Use the surrounding text to come up with laypersons' terms for these concepts.   •

Missing Persons

A common difficulty with scientific writing is that it can sound disembodied and abstract. You won't find a lot of people doing things in it. Sentences are easiest to read when they take a "who-does-what" form. However, these can be rare in scientific writing. Many of Martin's sentences have abstract subjects and nonaction verbs like *be* and *become*:

> *An interested and nonjudgmental appreciation of teenagers' surface presentations* may become a way of making contact not only in their terms but on their turfs. . . .

In at least one other sentence, Martin goes so far in leaving people out that his sentence is grammatically incorrect. Note the dangling modifier:

> Alternatively, *feeling prey to a rapidly evolving body over which they have no say,* self-made and openly visible decorations may restore adolescents' sense of normalcy and control, a way of turning a passive experience into an active identity.

The italicized phrase describes adolescents, not decorations. If you have trouble reading passages like this, take comfort in the fact that the difficulty is not your fault. Recasting the idea into who-does-what can clear things up:

> Teens may feel like helpless victims of the changes taking place in their bodies. They may mark themselves with highly visible tattoos and piercings to regain a sense of control over their lives.

Passive Voice

Passive voice is another common form of the missing-person problem. In an active-voice sentence, we see our predictable who-does-what pattern:

> *Active voice:* The rat ate the cheese.

In passive-voice sentences, the subject of the verb is not an agent; it does not act.

Passive voice: The cheese was eaten by the rat.

At least in this sentence, we know who the agent is. But scientists often leave out any mention of agents. Thus, in Martin's essay we have sentences like this one:

Adolescents' bodily decorations . . . *can be seen* in terms of figuration rather than disfigurement. . . .

Who can see them? Martin means that *psychiatrists should see tattoos* as figuration rather than disfigurement. But that would sound too committed, not scientific. Passive-voice sentences are common in the sciences, part of an effort to sound objective.

If you learn to recognize passive voice, you can often mentally convert the troublesome passage into active voice, making it clearer. Passive voice takes this pattern:

A helping verb in some form of the verb *to be: Is, was, were, has been, will be, will have been, could have been,* and so forth.

Followed by a main verb, a past participle: Past participles end in *ed, en, g, k,* or *t.*

Some examples:

The car *was being driven* by my roommate when we had the wreck.

Infections *are spread* by bacteria.

The refrain *is sung* three times.

◎◎ FOLLOWING THROUGH

Convert the following sentences into active voice. We have put the passive-voice verbs in bold type, but you may need to look at the surrounding text to figure out who the agents are.

A sense of constancy **can be derived** from unchanging marks that **can be carried** along no matter what the physical, temporal, or geographical vicissitudes at hand. (paragraph 9)

To edit this one, ask *who* can derive what and *who* can carry what.

The intense and often disturbing reactions that **are mobilized** in viewers can help to effectively keep them at bay, becoming tantamount to the proverbial "Keep Out" sign hanging from a teenager's door. (paragraph 4)

To edit, ask *what* mobilizes the reactions in other people.   •

Using Paraphrase to Aid Comprehension

As we all know, explaining something to someone else is the best way to make it clear to ourselves. Putting an author's ideas into your own words, **paraphrasing** them, is like explaining the author to yourself. For more on paraphrasing, see Chapter 6, pages 127–129.

Paraphrase is often longer than the original because it loosens up what is dense. In paraphrasing, try to make both the language and the syntax (word order) simpler. Paraphrase may require two sentences where there was one. It looks for plainer, more everyday language, converts passive voice to active voice, and makes the subjects concrete.

Analyzing the Reasoning of an Argument

As part of your second encounter with the text, pick out its reasoning. The reasoning is the author's case, which consists of the *claim* (what the author wants the readers to believe or do) and the *reasons* and *evidence* offered in support of it. State the case in your own words and describe what else is going on in the argument, such as the inclusion of opposing views or background information.

If a text is an argument, we can state what the author wants the readers to believe or do, and just as important, *why*. We should look for evidence presented to make the reasons seem believable. Note claims, reasons, and evidence in the margins as you read.

Reading Martin's Essay

Complex arguments require critical reading. Two critical-reading skills will help you: subdividing the text and considering contexts.

Finding Parts

Critical readers break texts down into parts. By *parts*, we mean groups of paragraphs that work together to perform some role in the essay. Examples of such roles are to introduce, to provide background, to give an opposing view, to conclude, and so on.

Discovering the parts of a text can be simple. Authors often make them obvious with subheadings and blank space. Even without these, transitional expressions and clear statements of intention make subdividing a text almost as easy as breaking a Hershey bar into its already well-defined segments. However, some arguments are more loosely constructed, their subdivisions less readily discernible. Even so, close inspection will usually reveal subdivisions, and you should be able to see the roles played by the various chunks.

We have placed numbers next to each paragraph in the essays reprinted in our text. Numbering makes it easier to refer to specific passages and to discuss parts.

Martin helps us see the parts of his essay by announcing early on, in paragraph 3, that it will have three sections, each "exemplify[ing] some of the complex psychological underpinnings of youth tattooing." Martin's essay can thus be subdivided as follows:

1. Epigraph
2. Paragraphs 1, 2, and 3: the introduction

Guidelines for Paraphrasing

- Use your own words, but do not strain to find a different word for every single one in the original. Some of the author's plain words are fine.

- If you take a phrase from the original, enclose it in quotation marks.

- Use a simpler sentence pattern than the original, even if it means making several short sentences. Aim for clarity.

- Check the surrounding sentences to make sure you understand the passage in context. You may want to add an idea from the context.

- Try for who-does-what sentences.

3. Paragraphs 4 and 5: an example
4. Paragaphs 6, 7, and 8: another example
5. Paragraphs 9, 10, and 11: a third example
6. Paragraph 12: the conclusion

Using Context

Taking the larger view again, we can use context to help pick out the reasoning. Although a quick reading might suggest that Martin is arguing that teens have good reasons for decorating their bodies, we need to recall that the essay appeared in a journal for psychiatrists—doctors, not parents or teachers. Martin is writing to other psychiatrists and psychologists, clinicians who work with families. Reading carefully, we learn that his audience is an even smaller portion of this group: clinicians who have been "summoned as the final arbiter" in family disputes involving tattoos and other body decoration (paragraph 2). Because journals such as the *Journal of the American Academy of Child & Adolescent Psychiatry* are aimed at improving the practice of medicine, we want to note sentences that tell these readers what they ought to do and how it will make them better doctors.

Identifying the Claim and Reasons

The claim: Martin is very clear about his claim, repeating it three times, using just slightly different wording:

> His readers should "[explore] the motivations and significance [underlying] tattoos and piercings. . . ." (paragraph 2)

> His readers should have "[a]n interested and nonjudgmental appreciation of teenagers' surface presentations. . . ." (paragraph 2)

> His readers should see "[a]dolescents' bodily decorations . . . in terms of figuration rather than disfigurement. . . ." (paragraph 12)

Asked to identify Martin's claim, you could choose any one of these statements.

The reason: The reason is the "because" part of the argument. Why should the readers believe or do as Martin suggests? We can find the answer in paragraph 2, in the same sentences with his claim:

> Because doing so "can go a long way toward resolving . . . differences and can become a novel and additional way of getting to know teenagers."

> Because doing so "may become a way of making contact not only in their terms but on their turfs. . . ."

And the final sentence of Martin's essay offers a third version of the same reason:

> Because "we may not only arrive at a position to pass more reasoned clinical judgment, but become sensitized through our patients' skins to another level of their internal reality."

Again, we could choose any one of these sentences as the stated reason, or paraphrase his reason. Using paraphrase, we can begin to outline the case structure of Martin's argument:

> **Claim:** Rather than dismissing tattoos as disfigurement, mental health professionals should take a serious interest in the meaning of and motivation behind the tattoos.

> **Reason:** Exploring their patients' body decorations can help them gain insight and make contact with teenagers on teenagers' own terms.

Where is Martin's evidence? Martin tells us that the three subsections will "exemplify some of the complex psychological underpinnings of youth tattooing." In each, he offers a case, or vignette, as evidence.

> **Example and evidence** (paragraphs 4 and 5): Tattoos are a way of working out identity problems when teens need either to mark themselves off from others or to regain a sense of control of a changing body or an imposing environment. The sixteen-year-old-girl who chose not to fit in.

> **Example and evidence** (paragraphs 6, 7, and 8): Tattoos can be an attempt to make the intangible a tangible part of one's body. The thirteen-year-old boy remembering his father.

> **Example and evidence** (paragraphs 9, 10, and 11): Tattoos are an "antidote" to a society that is on the run. The seventeen-year-old father.

THE THIRD ENCOUNTER: RESPONDING CRITICALLY TO AN ARGUMENT

Once you feel confident that you have the argument figured out, you are ready to respond to it, which means evaluating and comparing it with other perspectives, including your own. Only by *writing words* can you respond critically. As the reading expert Mortimer Adler says in *How to Read a Book,*

> Reading, if it is active, is thinking, and thinking tends to express itself in words, spoken or written. The person who says he knows what he thinks but cannot express it in words usually does not know what he thinks. (49)

Ways to Annotate

- Paraphrase the claim and reasons next to where you find them stated.

- Consider: Does the author support his or her reasons with evidence? Is the evidence sufficient in terms of both quantity and quality?

- Circle the key terms. Note how the author defines or fails to define them.

- Ask: What does the author assume? Behind every argument, there are assumptions. For example, a baseball fan wrote to our local paper arguing that the policy of fouls after the second strike needs to be changed. His reason was that the fans would not be subjected to such a long game. The author assumed that a fast game of hits and outs is more interesting than a slow game of strategy between batters and pitchers. Not every baseball fan shares that assumption.

- Note any contradictions you see, either within the text itself or with anything else you've read or learned.

- Consider the implications of the argument. If we believe or do what the author argues, what is likely to happen?

- Think of someone who would disagree with this argument, and say what that person might object to.

- If you see any opposing views in the argument, question the author's fairness in presenting them. Consider whether the author has represented opposing views fairly or has set them up to be easily knocked down.

- Ask: What is the author overlooking or leaving out?

- Consider: Where does the argument connect with anything else you have read?

- Consider: Does the argument exemplify mature reasoning as explained in Chapter 1, "Understanding Argument"?

- Ask: What aim does the argument seem to pursue? One of the four in the box on page 13, or some combination of them?

- Ask: What kind of person does the author sound like? Mark places where you hear the author's voice. Describe the tone. How does the author establish credibility—or fail to?

- Note the author's values and biases, places where the author sounds liberal or conservative, religious or materialistic, and so on.

- Note places where you see clues about the intended audience of the argument, such as appeals to their interests, values, tastes, and so on.

Annotation Is Key

We suggest that you annotate heavily. **Annotation** simply means making a note. Use the margins, and/or writer's notebook, for these notes of critical response. Many writers keep reading journals to practice active interaction with what they read and to preserve the experience of reading a text they want to remember.

What should you write about? Think of questions you would ask the author if he or she were in the room with you. Think of your own experience with the subject. Note similarities and contrasts with other arguments you have read or experiences of your own that confirm or contradict what the author is saying. Write about anything you notice that seems interesting, unusual, brilliant, or wrong. *Comment, question*—the more you actually write on the page, the more the text becomes your own. And you will write more confidently about a text you own than one you are just borrowing.

The list in the Best Practices box on page 29 will give you more ideas for annotations.

A concluding comment about responses: Even if you agree with an argument, think about who might oppose it and what their objections might be. Challenge the views you find most sympathetic.

Following is an example of annotation for part of Martin's argument.

Sample Annotations

How is he defining "solution"? Do tattoos solve a problem or just indicate one?

It seems like there are more mature ways to do this.

Or would it cause parents to pay attention to them rather than leave them alone?

Is he implying that the indelible mark is one they will not outgrow? What if they do?

Tattoos and piercing can offer a concrete and readily available <u>solution</u> for many of the identity crises and conflicts normative to adolescent development. In using such decorations, and by marking out their bodily territories, adolescents can support their efforts at autonomy, privacy, and insulation. Seeking individuation, tattooed adolescents can become unambiguously demarcated from others and singled out as unique. The intense and often disturbing reactions that are mobilized in viewers can help to effectively <u>keep them at bay</u>, becoming tantamount to the proverbial "Keep Out" sign hanging from a teenager's door.

Alternatively, feeling prey to a rapidly evolving body over which they have no say, self-made and openly visible decorations may restore adolescents' sense of <u>normalcy</u> and control, a way of turning a passive experience into an active identity. By indelibly marking their bodies, adolescents can strive to reclaim their bearings within an environment experienced as alien, estranged, or suffocating or to lay claim over their evolving and increasingly unrecognizable bodies. In either case, the net outcome <u>can be a resolution to</u> <u>unwelcome impositions</u>: external, familial, or societal in one case, internal and hormonal in the other. In the words of a 16-year-old girl with several facial piercings, and who could have been referring to her body just as well as to the position within her family: "If I don't fit in, it is because I say so."

5

What is normal?

Would he say the same about anorexia?

Does he assume this family needs counseling—or will not need it? He says the problem is "resolved."

CHAPTER 3

Analyzing an Argument: The Toulmin Method

In Chapter 2, we discussed the importance of reading arguments critically: breaking them down into their parts to see how they are put together, noting in the margins key terms that are not defined, and raising questions about the writer's claims or evidence. Although these general techniques are sufficient for analyzing many arguments, sometimes—especially with intricate arguments and with arguments we sense are faulty but whose weaknesses we are unable to specify—we need a more systematic technique.

In this chapter, we explain and illustrate such a technique based on the work of Stephen Toulmin, a contemporary philosopher who has contributed a great deal to our understanding of argumentation. This method will allow you to analyze the logic of any argument; you will also find it useful in examining the logic of your own arguments as you draft and revise them.

A PRELIMINARY CRITICAL READING

Before we consider Toulmin, let's first explore the following argument carefully. Use the general process for critical reading we described in Chapter 2.

Rising to the Occasion of Our Death

WILLIAM F. MAY

> William F. May (b. 1927) is a distinguished professor of ethics at Southern Methodist University. The following essay appeared originally in *The Christian Century (1990).*

1   For many parents, a Volkswagen van is associated with putting children to sleep on a camping trip. Jack Kevorkian, a Detroit pathologist, has now linked the van with the veterinarian's meaning of "putting to sleep." Kevorkian conducted a dinner interview with Janet Elaine Adkins, a 54-year-old Alzheimer's patient, and her husband and then agreed to help her commit suicide in his VW van. Kevorkian pressed beyond the more generally accepted practice of passive euthanasia (allowing a patient to die by withholding or withdrawing treatment) to active euthanasia (killing for mercy).

2   Kevorkian, moreover, did not comply with the strict regulations that govern active euthanasia in, for example, the Netherlands. Holland requires that death be imminent (Adkins had beaten her son in tennis just a few days earlier); it demands a more professional review of the medical evidence and the patient's resolution than a dinner interview with a physician (who is a stranger and who does not treat patients) permits; and it calls for the final, endorsing signatures of two doctors.

3   So Kevorkian-bashing is easy. But the question remains: Should we develop a judicious, regulated social policy permitting voluntary euthanasia for the terminally ill? Some moralists argue that the distinction between allowing to die and killing for mercy is petty quibbling over technique. Since the patient in any event dies—whether by acts of omission or commission—the route to death doesn't really matter. The way modern procedures have made dying at the hands of the experts and their machines such a prolonged and painful business has further fueled the euthanasia movement, which asserts not simply the right to die but the right to be killed.

4   But other moralists believe that there is an important moral distinction between allowing to die and mercy killing. The euthanasia movement, these critics contend, wants to engineer death rather than face dying. Euthanasia would bypass dying to make one dead as quickly as possible. It aims to relieve suffering by knocking out the interval between life and death. It solves the problem of suffering by eliminating the sufferer.

5   The impulse behind the euthanasia movement is understandable in an age when dying has become such an inhumanly endless business. But the movement may fail to appreciate our human capacity to rise to the occasion of our death. The best death is not always the sudden death. Those forewarned of death and given time to prepare for it have time to engage in acts of reconciliation. Also, advanced grieving by those about to be bereaved may ease some of their pain. Psychiatrists

have observed that those who lose a loved one accidentally have a more difficult time recovering from the loss than those who have suffered through an extended period of illness before the death. Those who have lost a close relative by accident are more likely to experience what Geoffrey Gorer has called limitless grief. The community, moreover, may need its aged and dependent, its sick and its dying, and the virtues which they sometimes evince—the virtues of humility, courage, and patience—just as much as the community needs the virtues of justice and love manifest in the agents of care.

6   On the whole, our social policy should allow terminal patients to die, but it should not regularize killing for mercy. Such a policy would recognize and respect that moment in illness when it no longer makes sense to bend every effort to cure or to prolong life and when one must allow patients to do their own dying. This policy seems most consonant with the obligations of the community to care and of the patient to finish his or her course.

7   Advocates of active euthanasia appeal to the principle of patient autonomy— as the use of the phrase "voluntary euthanasia" indicates. But emphasis on the patient's right to determine his or her destiny often harbors an extremely naïve view of the uncoerced nature of the decision. Patients who plead to be put to death hardly make unforced decisions if the terms and conditions under which they receive care already nudge them in the direction of the exit. If the elderly have stumbled around in their apartments, alone and frightened for years, or if they have spent years warehoused in geriatrics barracks, then the decision to be killed for mercy hardly reflects an uncoerced decision. The alternative may be so wretched as to push patients toward this escape. It is a huge irony and, in some cases, hypocrisy to talk suddenly about a compassionate killing when the aging and dying may have been starved for compassion for many years. To put it bluntly, a country has not earned the moral right to kill for mercy unless it has already sustained and supported life mercifully. Otherwise we kill for compassion only to reduce the demands on our compassion. This statement does not charge a given doctor or family member with impure motives. I am concerned here not with the individual case but with the cumulative impact of a social policy.

8   I can, to be sure, imagine rare circumstances in which I hope I would have the courage to kill for mercy—when the patient is utterly beyond human care, termi- nal, and in excruciating pain. A neurosurgeon once showed a group of physicians and an ethicist the picture of a Vietnam casualty who had lost all four limbs in a landmine explosion. The catastrophe had reduced the soldier to a trunk with his face transfixed in horror. On the battlefield I would hope that I would have the courage to kill the sufferer with mercy.

9   But hard cases do not always make good laws or wise social policies. Regular- ized mercy killings would too quickly relieve the community of its obligation to provide good care. Further, we should not always expect the law to provide us with full protection and coverage for what, in rare circumstances, we may morally need to do. Sometimes the moral life calls us out into a no-man's-land where we cannot expect total security and protection under the law. But no one said that the moral life is easy.

A STEP-BY-STEP DEMONSTRATION OF THE TOULMIN METHOD

The Toulmin method requires an analysis of the claim, the reasons offered to support the claim, and the evidence offered to support the reasons, along with an analysis of any refutations offered.

Analyzing the Claim

Logical analysis begins with identifying the *claim,* the thesis or central contention, along with any specific qualifications or exceptions.

Identify the Claim

First, ask yourself, *What statement is the author defending?* In "Rising to the Occasion of Our Death," William F. May spells out his claim in paragraph 6:

> [O]ur social policy should allow terminal patients to die, but it should not regularize killing for mercy.

In his claim, May supports passive euthanasia (letting someone die by withholding or discontinuing treatment) but opposes "regularizing" (making legal or customary) active euthanasia (administering, say, an overdose of morphine to cause a patient's death).

Much popular argumentation is sometimes careless about what exactly is being claimed: Untrained arguers too often content themselves with merely taking sides ("Euthanasia is wrong"). Note that May, a student of ethics trained in philosophical argumentation, makes a claim that is specific. Whenever an argument does not include an explicit statement of its claim, you should begin your analysis by stating the writer's claim yourself.

Look for Qualifiers

Next, ask, *How is the claim qualified?* Is it absolute, or does it include words or phrases to indicate that it may not hold true in every situation or set of circumstances?

May qualifies his claim in paragraph 6 with the phrase "On the whole," indicating that he recognizes possible exceptions. Other qualifiers include "typically," "usually," and "most of the time." Careful arguers are wary of making absolute claims. Qualifying words or phrases are used to restrict a claim and improve its defensibility.

Find the Exceptions

Finally, ask, *In what cases or circumstances would the writer not press his or her claim?* Look for any explicit exceptions the writer offers.

May is quite clear in paragraph 8 about when he would not press his claim:

> I hope I would have the courage to kill for mercy—when the patient is utterly beyond human care, terminal, and in excruciating pain.

Once he has specified these abstract conditions, he offers a chilling example of a case in which mercy killing would be appropriate. Nevertheless, he insists that such exceptions are rare and thus do not justify making active euthanasia legal or allowing it to become common policy.

Summarize the Claim

At this point it is a good idea to write out the claim, its qualifiers, and its exceptions so that you can see all of them clearly:

(qualifier)   "On the whole"

(claim)   "our social policy should allow terminal patients to die,
              but it should not regularize killing for mercy"

(exception)   "when the patient is utterly beyond human care, terminal,
              and in excruciating pain"

Analyzing the Reasons

Once you have analyzed the claim, you should next identify and evaluate the reasons offered for the claim.

List the Reasons

Begin by asking yourself, *Why is the writer advancing this claim?* Look for any statement or statements that are used to justify the thesis. May groups all of his reasons in paragraph 5:

The dying should have time to prepare for death and to reconcile with
   relatives and friends.

Those close to the dying should have time to come to terms with the
   impending loss of a loved one.

The community needs examples of dependent but patient and courageous people who sometimes do die with dignity.

The community needs the virtues ("justice and love") of those who
   care for the sick and dying.

When you list reasons, you need not preserve the exact words of the arguer; often, doing so is impossible because reasons are not always spelled out. Be very careful, however, to adhere as closely as possible to the writer's language. Otherwise, your analysis can easily go astray, imposing a reason of your own that the writer did not have in mind.

Note that reasons, like claims, can be qualified. May does not say, for instance, that "the aged and dependent" *always* show "the virtues of humility, courage, and patience." He implicitly admits that they can be ornery and cowardly as well. But for May's purposes it is enough that they sometimes manifest the virtues he admires.

List the reasons following your summary of the claim, qualifiers, and exceptions. One possibility is to list them beneath the summary of the claim in the form of a tree diagram (see the model diagram in the Concept Close-up box on page 38).

Examine the Reasons

There are two questions to ask as you examine the reasons. First, *Are they really good reasons?* A reason is only as good as the values it invokes or implies. A value is something we think is good—that is, worth pursuing for its own sake or because it leads to attaining other goods. For each reason, specify the values involved and then determine whether you accept those values as generally binding.

Second, *Is the reason relevant to the thesis?* In other words, does the relationship between the claim and the reason hold up to examination? For example, the claim "You should buy a new car from Fred Freed" cannot be supported by the reason "Fred is a family man with three cute kids."

Be careful as you examine whether reasons are good and whether they are relevant. No other step is as important in assessing the logic of an argument.

To illustrate, consider May's first reason: Those who know they are about to die should have time to prepare for death and to seek reconciliation with people from whom they have become estranged. Is this a good reason? Yes, because we value the chance to prepare for death and to reconcile with estranged friends or family members.

But is the reason relevant? May seems to rule out the possibility that a dying person seeking active euthanasia would be able to prepare for death and reconcile with others. However, terminally ill people who decide to arrange for their own deaths may make any number of preparations beforehand, so the connection between this reason and May's claim is weak. To accept a connection, we would have to assume that active euthanasia necessarily amounts to a sudden death without adequate preparation. We are entitled to question the relevance of the reason, no matter how good it might be in itself.

◎◎ FOLLOWING THROUGH

Examine May's second, third, and fourth reasons on your own. Make notes about each reason, evaluating how good each is in itself and how relevant it is to the thesis. Create your own diagram based on the model on page 38. •

Analyzing the Evidence

Once you have finished your analysis of the reasons, the next step is to consider the evidence offered to support any of those reasons.

List the Evidence

Ask, *What kinds of evidence (data, anecdotes, case studies, citations from authority, and so forth) are offered as support for each reason?* Some arguments advance little in the way of evidence. May's is a good example of a moral argument about principles; such an argument does not require much evidence. Lack of evidence, then, is not always a fault. For one of his reasons, however, May does offer some evidence: After stating his second reason in paragraph 5—the chance to grieve before a loved one dies—he invokes authorities who agree with him about the value of advanced grieving.

Examine the Evidence

Two questions apply. First, *Is the evidence good?* That is, is it sufficient, accurate, and credible? Second, *Is it relevant to the reason it supports?* The evidence May offers in paragraph 5 is sufficient. We assume his citations are accurate and credible as well. We would also accept them as relevant because, apart from our own experience with grieving, we have to rely on expert opinion. (See Chapter 6 for a fuller discussion of estimating the adequacy and relevance of evidence.)

Noting Refutations

A final step is to assess an arguer's refutations. In a refutation, a writer anticipates potential objections to his or her position and tries to show why they do not undermine the basic argument. A skilled arguer uses them to deal with any obvious objections a reader is likely to have.

First, ask, *What refutations does the writer offer?* Summarize them. Then ask, *How does the writer approach each objection?* May's refutation occupies paragraph 7. He recognizes that the value of free choice lends weight to the proeuthanasia position, and so he relates this value to the question of "voluntary euthanasia." Because in our culture individual freedom is so strong a value, May does not question the value itself; rather, he leads us to question whether voluntary euthanasia is actually a matter of free choice. He suggests that unwanted people may be coerced into "choosing" death or may be so isolated and neglected that death becomes preferable. Thus, he responds to the objection that dying people should have freedom of choice where death is concerned.

Summarizing Your Analysis

Once you have completed your analysis, it is a good idea to summarize the results in a paragraph or two. Be sure to set aside your own position on the issue, confining your summary to the argument the writer makes.

Although May's logic is strong, it is not fully compelling. He qualifies his argument and uses exceptions effectively, and his single use of refutation is skillful. However, he fails to acknowledge that active euthanasia need not be a sudden decision leading to sudden death. Consequently, his reasons for supporting passive euthanasia can be used to support at least some cases of active euthanasia as well. It is here—in the linkage between reasons and claim—that May's argument falls short. Furthermore, we may question whether the circumstances under which May would permit active euthanasia are in fact as rare as he suggests. Many people are beyond human care, terminal, and in pain, and many others suffer acute anguish for which they might legitimately seek the relief of death.

Model Toulmin Diagram for Analyzing Arguments

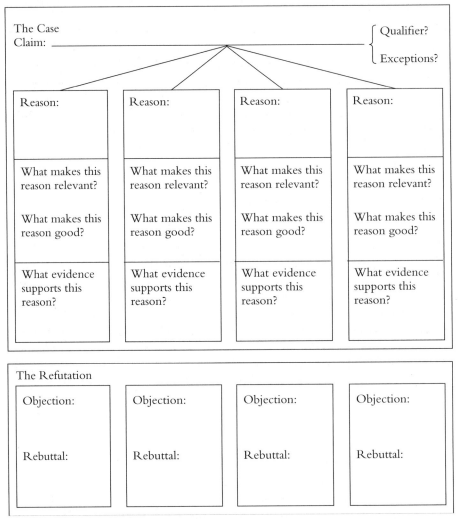

A FINAL NOTE ABOUT LOGICAL ANALYSIS

No method for analyzing arguments is perfect, and no method can guarantee that everyone using it will assess an argument the same way. Uniform results are not especially desirable anyway. What would be left to talk about? The point of argumentative analysis is to step back and examine an argument carefully, to detect how it is structured, to assess the cogency and power of its logic. The Toulmin method helps us move beyond a hit-or-miss approach to logical analysis, but it cannot yield a conclusion as compelling as mathematical proof.

Toulmin Analysis

A. ANALYZE THE CLAIM

1. **Find the claim.** In many arguments, the claim is never explicitly stated. When it isn't, try to make the implied claim explicit by stating it in your own words. (Note: If, after careful analysis, you aren't sure *exactly* what the writer is claiming, you've found a serious fault in the argument.)

2. **Look for qualifiers.** Is the claim absolute? Or is it qualified by some word or phrase like *usually* or *all things being equal?* If the claim is absolute, can you think of circumstances in which it might not apply? If the claim is qualified, why is it not absolute? That is, is there any real thought or content in the qualifier—good reasons for qualifying the claim?

3. **Look for explicit exceptions to the claim.** If the writer has pointed out conditions in which he or she would not assert the claim, note them carefully.

Summarize steps 1–3. See the diagram on page 38.

B. ANALYZE THE REASONS

1. **Find the reason or reasons advanced to justify the claim.** All statements of reason will answer the question "Why are you claiming what you've claimed?" They can be linked to the claim with *because.* As with claims, reasons may be implied. Dig them out and state them in your own words. (Note: If, after careful analysis, you discover that the reasons aren't clear or relevant to the claim, you should conclude that the argument is either defective and in need of revision or invalid and therefore unacceptable.)

2. **Ponder each reason advanced.** Is the reason good in itself? Is the reason relevant to the thesis? Note any problems.

List the reasons underneath the claim. See the diagram on page 38.

C. ANALYZE THE EVIDENCE

1. **For each reason, locate all evidence offered to back it up.** Evidence is not limited to hard data. Anecdotes, case studies, and citations from authorities also count as evidence. (Note: Not all reasons require extensive evidence. But we should be suspicious of reasons without evidence, especially when it seems that evidence ought to be available. Unsupported reasons are often a sign of bad reasoning.)

2. **Ponder each piece of evidence.** Is it good? That is, is it accurate and believable? Is it relevant to the reason it supports? Note any problems.

List the evidence underneath the claim. See the diagram on page 38.

D. EXAMINE THE REFUTATIONS

If there are refutations—efforts to refute objections to the case—examine them. If not, consider what objections you think the writer should have addressed.

Convincing and persuading always involve more than logic, and, therefore, logical analysis alone is never enough to assess the strength of an argument. For example, William May's argument attempts to discredit those like Dr. Jack Kevorkian who assist patients wishing to take their own lives. May depicts Kevorkian as offering assistance without sufficient consultation with the patient. Is his depiction accurate? Clearly, we can answer this question only by finding out more about how Kevorkian and others like him work. Because such questions are not a part of logical analysis, they have not been of concern to us in this chapter. But any adequate and thorough analysis of an argument must also address questions of fact and the interpretation of data.

Writing a Critique

In Chapter 2 you learned how to read an argument critically, in Chapter 3 how to analyze one. This chapter pulls those lessons together around the genre of critique, a written assessment of an argument.

WHAT IS A CRITIQUE?

When you evaluate someone else's argument, you offer a **critique,** "a written estimate of the merits of a performance" (*New Grolier's Webster International Dictionary*). We encounter them in "Letters to the Editor" in newspapers, in magazines that include reader responses to articles in previous issues, and in blogs devoted to some controversial issue or cause. The basic situation is always the same: Someone writes an argument urging readers to believe or do something; a reader responds by "estimat[ing] the merits" of the argument, agreeing or disagreeing (or some of both), and explaining why.

A critique, then, is part of a public conversation conducted in writing. It is not a put-down, an attack on someone's argument, but rather rational assessment, part of a search for truth.

Context and Critique

Most written arguments are "stand-alone" texts—an opinion column in a newspaper or online, an article in a magazine or on a Web site, and so on. However, they are not as isolated as they seem. Authors create **context**, a background against which they want you to see their argument—current events, an ongoing debate about the topic, and so on.

Context *always* matters for the following reasons:

- *Context is the key to understanding an argument.* For example, increasing the availability of loans for college students makes sense within the rapid increase of higher education costs.

- *Context is the key to understanding why people disagree.* Those who favor increasing loans often see the issue in the context of opportunity, making college possible for modest-income students. Those who oppose it often see loans in the context of too much personal debt.

- *Context is the key to understanding your response.* If you or your family cannot afford college and you have taken full advantage of other forms of aid, loans may be very appealing.

We'll return to context often in this chapter.

WHY CRITIQUE AN ARGUMENT?

See Chapter 9, "Making Your Case: Arguing to Convince" for convincing, concerned with influencing what people think. See Chapter 10, "Motivating Action: Arguing to Persuade" for persuasion, concerned with motivating people to act.

On occasion you will make arguments designed to change someone's mind or to move others to action. Every day, however, you will hear or read the arguments of other people, in conversation, in books and magazines, on television, radio, and the Net, in business meetings and community gatherings. Short of becoming a hermit, there is no way to avoid arguments designed to influence what you think and do. Professors assign critiques because they know how often you will need to assess arguments.

Good arguments must be distinguished from bad ones. That is the stake that you and all thoughtful people have in evaluating arguments.

HOW DOES CRITIQUING AN ARGUMENT WORK?

You may have noticed that most people only react to arguments. They just agree or disagree, sometimes with much heat and noise. A good example is talk radio: Listeners call in to voice all kinds of opinions about political issues or the performance of their local sports team. Many people avoid such exchanges because they feel nothing is accomplished. "It's just a shouting match," they say.

Why does public discussion often seem pointless? The problem is not in exchanging opinions. Saying what we think gets things off our chest. Hearing what other people think is stimulating. The problem is that public discussion tends to *stop* at exchanging opinions and reacting to them.

The crucial next step is critique, evaluating arguments, the move from stating opinions to questioning them. How does it work?

The Art of Questioning: Probing an Opinion

Opinions take the form of claims or statements. For example,

> The United States should promote the spread of democracy as part of its foreign policy in the Middle East.

Because democracy has a high value for us, this opinion can easily go unchallenged. To open it up for assessment, what questions could you ask?

- You could ask about *key terms*. What does "promote" mean? For the Bush administration after the 9/11 terrorist attack, it meant using our military to remove totalitarian governments in both Afghanistan and Iraq. Should we go that far in promoting democracy?

- You could ask about *context*. What is the potential for democracy in the Middle East? Muslim countries typically do not separate religion from government; without such a separation, can we promote democracy as we understand it?

- You could ask about what the *data* indicate. How many Middle Eastern countries were democratic ten years ago? How many are now? What's the trend? How stable are the democracies in the Middle East?

- You could ask about various ways to *interpret the data*. Is democracy an advantage for the United States in the Middle East? Have the outcomes of elections favored our interests? How many of the friendly governments in the region are not democracies?

FOLLOWING THROUGH

Bring the op-ed pages from two or three days of your local newspaper to class. Examine the opinions expressed by the editorial staff, letters to the editor, and opinion columnists. Select two or three of the most interesting ones and probe them in class using the four assessment questions.

Evaluating arguments includes more than assessing claims and many more questions than the four discussed so far. Nevertheless, *the basic move for evaluating arguments is posing questions*. Without it discussion stalls at merely reacting to opinions.

READING

The following reading will help you see in detail how critiques work and what to do in a situation that calls for evaluating an argument.

Responses to Arguments Against the Minimum Legal Drinking Age

DAVID J. HANSON

> David J. Hanson is Professor Emeritus of Sociology at SUNY, Potsdam, and an expert on issues related to alcohol use. This piece came from his Web site, funded by the Distilled Spirits Council of the United States.
>
> Hanson responds to arguments advanced by a government agency, the National Institute on Alcohol Abuse and Alcoholism (NIAAA), against lowering the drinking age to eighteen. As you read, consider how important *point of view* is in critiquing arguments. Being clear about what you think is one of the keys to a good critique.

Context: The first two sentences identify the source of the argument critiqued and what it's about.

The federal government is spending taxpayer money in a questionable political campaign to defend the minimum drinking age against attempts in some states to lower it. In "Responses to Arguments against the Minimum Drinking Age," the National Institute on Alcohol Abuse and Alcoholism (NIAAA) identifies arguments against the minimum legal drinking age and then suggests counter-arguments. But in doing so, it plays fast and loose with the facts, a common tactic in politics.

Preview: Summarizes major point.

Argument: "If I'm old enough to go to war, I should be old enough to drink."

The long list of what people can do legally at age eighteen makes prohibition of alcohol seem much more arbitrary than the usual point about fighting in a war.

Actually the argument is much stronger than the NIAAA acknowledges. The fact is that citizens are legally adults at the age of 18. They can marry, vote, adopt children, own and drive automobiles, have abortions, enter into legally binding contracts, operate businesses, purchase or even perform in pornography, give legal consent for sexual intercourse, fly airplanes, hold public office, serve on juries that convict others of murder, hunt wildlife with deadly weapons, be imprisoned, be executed, be an employer, sue and be sued in court, and otherwise conduct themselves as the adults they are. And, of course, they can serve in the United States armed services and give their lives defending their country. One of the very few things they can't legally do is consume an alcohol beverage. They can't even have a celebratory sip of champagne at their own weddings.

Counter-Argument: Federal agents suggest pointing out that people can obtain a hunting license at age 12 and a driver's license at age 16.

Part of what makes this critique so powerful is that Hanson responds not only to the NIAAA's arguments but also to their counter-arguments, what they say in response to challenges from the other side.

Ironically, this actually strengthens the argument against treating legal adults as children with regard to alcohol beverages. People can hunt wildlife with a deadly weapon at age 12 but can't be trusted with a beer at age 20?

The government also suggests pointing out that people must be 25 to serve in the U.S. House of Representatives, 30 to serve in the Senate, and 35 to serve as President. But these unusual restrictions were imposed well over two hundred years ago in a new country that was still largely reluctant to grant rights and in which neither women nor African Americans were trusted to vote. We're now in the 21st century enjoying widespread rights and also a time when young people are infinitely more sophisticated. Clearly, the agency's arguments are extremely weak and unconvincing.

6   **Argument:** "Europeans let their teens drink from an early age, yet they don't have the alcohol-related problems we do."

7 | **Counter-Argument:** The NIAAA responds that "the idea that Europeans do not have alcohol-related problems is a myth." But no one suggests that Europeans have no drinking-related problems. Here the agency is guilty of using the straw person tactic—create a very weak argument and then shoot it down.

8 | In reality, research for decades has demonstrated that those countries and groups in Europe and elsewhere in which most people regularly drink but have few drinking-related problems all share three common characteristics:

1. Alcohol is seen as a rather neutral substance in and of itself. It's neither a poison nor a magic elixir. It's how it's used that's important.

2. People have two equally acceptable choices:

    • Abstain or

    • Drink in moderation.

    What's never acceptable is the abuse of alcohol by anyone of any age. Period.

3. People learn about drinking alcohol in moderation from an early age in the safe and supportive environment of the home, and they do so by good parental example. All of these groups would agree that it's better to learn about drinking in the parents' house than in the fraternity house.

These three points show how research information can be used for critique and how to summarize what it says effectively.

9 | Age 21 is actually the highest minimum legal drinking age in the entire world and is a radical social experiment both internationally and in terms of our own national history. Those who call for all adults to be able to drink are traditionalists, whereas those who insist on age 21 are radicals.

10 | **Argument:** Lower rates of alcohol-related crashes among 19- to 20-year-olds aren't related to the age 21 policy, but rather they're related to increased drinking-driver educational efforts, tougher enforcement, and tougher drunk-driving penalties."

Good use of historical and current knowledge about the drinking age to show that the current law is out of step.

11 | **Counter-Argument:** The agency wants us to argue that "Careful research has shown the decline was not due to DUI enforcement and tougher penalties, but is a direct result of the legal drinking age" and that "Achieving long-term reductions in youth drinking problems requires an environmental change so that alcohol is less accessible to teens."

12 | However, there are a number of weaknesses in what the bureaucrats want us to say. It's true that lower rates of alcohol-related traffic accidents now occur among drivers under the age of 21. But they've also been declining among those age 21 and older, with one notable exception.

13 | Raising the minimum legal drinking age has resulted in an apparent displacement of large numbers of alcohol-related traffic fatalities from those under the age of 21 to those age 21 to 24. In short, raising the drinking age simply changed the ages of those killed.

Arguments often cite only those facts that support their position. Critique should cite evidence damaging to the argument that has been omitted.

14 | The argument that we need to make alcohol less accessible to adults under the age of 21 fails to recognize the fact, well established by governmental surveys, that it's easier for young people to obtain marijuana than alcohol.

When you can show a past policy has failed, one like the present one advocated or defended, you have a strong point for critique.

It's also foolish to think that effective prohibition can be imposed on young adults. The U.S. already tried that with the entire population during National Prohibition (1920–1933). The result was less frequent drinking but more heavy, episodic drinking. The effort to impose prohibition on young adults has driven drinking underground and promoted so-called binge drinking. This is a natural and totally predictable consequence of prohibition.

Argument: "We drank when we were young and we grew out of it. It's just a phase that all students go through."

Exposes what may be the hidden agenda: a desire to discourage alcohol use altogether. Shows that the NIAAA's argument is at odds with the 21 age position defended.

Counter-Argument: Interestingly, NIAAA wants us to argue that "Unfortunately, many teens will not 'grow out of it.'" Implicit is the belief that adults should not consume alcohol even when legally able to do so. The agency apparently envisions a society in which abstention from alcohol is the norm, a vision that it shares with temperance and prohibition advocates.

While not all students will try alcohol, virtually all normal young people will do so and they will do so without ill effects. But NIAAA wants us to promote the discredited and simplistic "stepping stone" hypothesis that suggests that drinking leads to smoking, which leads to marijuana, which leads to crack, which leads to cocaine, which leads to degradation and illness, which leads to death.

19   **Argument:** "Making it illegal to drink until 21 increases the desire for the 'forbidden fruit.' Then, when students turn 21, they'll drink even more."

20   **Counter-Argument:** NIAAA wants us to assert incorrectly that "Actually the opposite is true. Early legal access to alcohol is associated with higher rates of drinking as an adult."

Critique ends with the author's strongest point: that the 21 age has an effect opposite to its intention.

In reality, research has clearly demonstrated the "forbidden fruit" phenomenon among adults under the age of 21. On the other hand, there is no evidence that the increased desire to drink continues after students turn 21. In fact, upon turning age 21, many adults find that it's no longer so much fun to get into bars and drink precisely because it is legal for them to do so.

QUESTIONS FOR DISCUSSION

1. There is no question that alcohol abuse is connected with many problems: highway deaths and serious injuries, date rape, spousal abuse, and ruined careers. Are any of these problems connected to the current legal drinking age?

2. Critiques can be critiqued. For example, Hanson points to the ambiguous results of National Prohibition (paragraph 15). But if we set the legal drinking age at eighteen, we will still be prohibiting alcohol consumption below eighteen. The issue, then, is not prohibition, but where we draw the line. Isn't what happened between 1920 and 1933 irrelevant to the argument?

Strategies for Critiquing Arguments

It is one thing to know that you do not agree with an argument you hear or read, quite another to respond to it with more than just "I'm not convinced." Hanson shows us some of the many ways we can say something about arguments, both those we support and those we do not.

In paragraph 3, for instance, Hanson expands on the assertion that people old enough to fight in a war should be old enough to drink. As he points out, eighteen-year-olds have many freedoms and responsibilities. One way to respond to a point you agree with is to *offer more examples* that illustrate the validity of the point.

In paragraphs 7 and 8, Hanson responds to the NIAAA argument that Europeans do have alcohol-related problems. You can use his strategies:

1. *Resist allowing an argument to "shift ground."* The NIAAA claims something no one denies: there are problems with alcohol in Europe. The issue is whether the lower drinking age in Europe is relevant to the problems.

2. *Supply counter-evidence.* Hanson goes on to specify the social conditions in regions such as Europe where alcohol is consumed from an early age with few negative consequences.

3. *Put the issue in a wider context.* Hanson points out that twenty-one is the "highest legal drinking age in the entire world" and deviates from the usual practice in our own history.

◎◎ FOLLOWING THROUGH

In class discussion, characterize the strategies Hanson uses in paragraphs 10–21. Which seem most convincing to you? Why do they work so well?   •

CLAIMING VOICE IN EVALUATING AN ARGUMENT

The voice of critique or analysis shares much in common with the voice of case-making: the emphasis is on stating your position clearly, directly, and forcefully, favoring a middle style more formal than conversation, but less formal than a public speech. Also like making a case, critique's voice should be the calm voice of reason, of opinions stated precisely and defended well. (See Chapter 9, pages 214–215, for claiming voice in making a case.)

Here is a good example of the analytical voice in paragraph 1 of Hanson's critique:

> The federal government is spending taxpayer money in a questionable political campaign to defend the minimum drinking age against attempts in some states to lower it. In "Responses to Arguments against the Minimum Drinking Age," the National Institute on Alcohol Abuse and Alcoholism (NIAAA) identifies arguments against the minimum legal drinking age and then suggests counter-arguments. But in doing so, it plays fast and loose with the facts, a common tactic in politics.

Notice that you can say that an argument "plays fast and loose with the facts" or that it is illogical or inconsistent, providing you can back it up and make your accusations stick, as Hanson does in the rest of his article.

Your voice in critique, therefore, depends largely on *how you assess the quality of the argument you are critiquing.* Hanson clearly thinks the NIAAA's argument is politically motivated, not supported by available data, and poorly reasoned as well. He therefore does not give it the respect he might extend to an argument with only minor flaws, an argument that needs revision rather than rejection.

THE ASSIGNMENT

If your instructor does not assign one, locate any short (750–1,000 words) argument on a controversial topic and write a paper of about the same length critiquing it.

Topic and Focus

Obviously, you need to respond to what the article says. However, you can relate the argument's topic to matters the author does not mention. For example, an article advocating laws prohibiting handheld cell phone use by drivers may focus entirely on this particular device. You might respond by pointing to other driver distractions that also contribute to accidents, such as putting CDs in audio equipment. Perhaps the real problem is driver distraction in general, not cell phone use in particular?

Audience

Usually you will write to the same readership your argument addresses. However, when an argument you are responding to targets only one of several readerships with a stake in the topic, it is legitimate to respond by addressing your critique to one of the other audiences. For example, an argument addressed only to parents about a public school issue, such as classes that are too large, might well address the students affected by too large classes instead.

Voice and Ethos

Be sincere, project confidence, have command of the facts and what they mean, and show respect for the argument you are evaluating.

Writing Assignment Suggestions

This assignment could be written in many genres, the most common being a letter to the editor of a newspaper or magazine; as an op-ed piece; as a response to a blog; as a short article for a newspaper or magazine or newsletter; as an assessment of a classroom discussion, debate, chat room exchange; public speech; or some other oral argument.

We suggest that you pick an argument you disagree with or an argument you partly agree with and partly disagree with in almost equal measure. It makes little sense to critique an argument you find wholly convincing.

CHOOSING AN ARGUMENT

When you have a choice, opt for the provocative or extreme argument. They almost beg for critique, and evaluating them is more fruitful than the predictable position defended in predictable ways.

You can locate suitable arguments by recalling something you read in a newspaper, magazine, or on a Web site, by doing subject searches on LexisNexis (see page 111 for how to use this resource), and by Googling a topic in the news. Consider also the following possibilities.

- *Class readings.* Class readings can provide arguments for critique, especially if the readings themselves are arguments.
- *Local news or observation.* Read your local and campus newspapers for arguments relating to your community. Sometimes these can be more interesting than overworked topics like abortion or gun control.
- *Internet discussions.* Blogs are often good sources for arguments. Visit blogs on issues of public concern, such as National Public Radio's blog at www.npr.org/blogs/talk/.

EXPLORING YOUR TOPIC

So that you can see how to explore the argument you have selected or been assigned, we need to work with an example argument. Here's one on an issue of some concern on most college campuses. Read it once or twice, just to understand what it says and to form a first reaction to it.

Open Your Ears to Biased Professors

DAVID FRYMAN

> David Fryman was a senior at Brandeis University when he wrote this opinion column for the school's newspaper, *The Justice.* He's offering advice to younger college students who often encounter professors with political opinions different from those endorsed at home or in their local communities. Fryman's question is, How should they respond?

1   One of the most important lessons I've learned in three years of higher education is the value of creativity and critical thinking, particularly when confronted with a professor whose ideology, political leanings or religious viewpoint fly in the face of what I believe. In fact, with a good professor, this should happen often. It is part of a professor's job to challenge you, force you to reconsider, encourage you to entertain new ideas and the like.

2   My first year here, it bothered me. Some professors subtly endorsed certain ways of thinking over others without always justifying their biases. They offered opinions on issues beyond their academic expertise. Many showed partiality to the political left or right.

3   How should we react when a professor with a captive audience advances a perspective we find offensive, insulting or just ridiculous? Perhaps we would benefit from treating our professors, who often double as mentors and advisers, the same way that we're taught to approach great works of literature: With critical respect.

4   The truth is many faculty members are at the top of their fields. They read, write and teach for a living. We're generally talking about the most well-educated and well-read members of society. So when a professor has something to say about politics, religion, war or which movie should win the Academy Award, I think it's a good idea to take him seriously.

5   It certainly doesn't follow, though, that there's a direct relationship between what a professor says and what's true. In fact, there may be no relationship at all. While our professors generally are leading scholars, some are also biased and fallible. I don't mean this as an insult. Professors are human beings and, as such, carry with them a wide array of hang-ups and prejudices.

6   Interestingly enough—if not ironically—our professors often teach us how to deal with biased and opinionated scholars like themselves. When we read novels, journal articles, essays and textbooks for class, we're taught—or at least this has been my experience—to be critical. We're expected to sift through material and distinguish between what holds water and what doesn't, what is based on reasoned analysis and what is mere speculation.

7   If we treat our professors similarly it should no longer bother us when they use the classroom as their soapbox. They have important things to say and we're here to learn from them. I've come to appreciate professors' opinions on a variety of issues not directly related to the subject at hand, and I think it helps us build relationships with them. While it's unfair for a professor to assign high grades only to students who echo their view or to make others feel uncomfortable to disagree, I prefer that professors be honest about what they think.

8   While it's a disservice to our own education to be intimidated or too easily persuaded by academic clout, it's just as problematic, and frankly silly, to categorically reject what a professor has to say because we take issue with his ideology, political leanings, religious views or cultural biases.

9   It's become popular, particularly among conservatives responding to what they perceive as a liberal bias in academia, to criticize professors for espousing personal views in the classroom. The ideal, they argue, is to leave students ignorant to their instructors' beliefs.

10   First of all, I think there's a practical problem with this strategy. It's more difficult to be critical if we're unsure where our professors stand. For the same reason that it's often helpful to have background information about an author before analyzing his work, it's useful to see our professors' ideological cards on the table. For instance, if I know my professor loves hunting and believes everybody should have firearms in his basement then when I hear his interpretation of the Second Amendment, I'm better equipped to evaluate his thoughts.

11   Secondly, if we proscribe what views may or may not be expressed in the classroom, we limit our own access to potentially useful information. Even if most

of the extraneous digressions aren't worthy, every once in a while we might hear something that goes to the heart of an important issue. To limit this because we don't trust our own critical abilities is cowardly.

12   To return to the question I posed above: How should we respond to politically charged, opinionated, biased professors? I think we should listen.

Forming a First Impression

It is impossible to read an argument without having some kind of response to it. Let's not imagine that objectivity or neutrality is either possible or desirable. Start by being honest with yourself about what your first impression is.

◎◎ FOLLOWING THROUGH

After reading your argument, state your reaction simply and directly. Write it down in your notebook or a computer file reserved for this assignment. Read the selection again. Is your reaction changing? How? Why?

The first response of most of our students to Fryman was favorable. He offered practical advice, and more appealing yet, *safe* advice. You may have had an entirely different reaction. First reactions cannot be right or wrong, good or bad. They just are what they are. The important thing is that *you* know what your reaction is.   •

Stepping Back: Analyzing the Argument

Critiques require **critical distance** from first responses. "Critical distance" does not mean "forget your first response." On the contrary, first impressions often turn out to be sound. Critical distance does mean setting your first response aside for a while so that you can think the argument through carefully.

Use the questions in the Best Practices box to guide your analysis. It deals with parts of an argument that can be challenged. In contrast, there is nothing to be gained by challenging the following items:

- *Values everyone in our culture accepts.* For example, Fryman appeals to "creativity and critical thinking" (paragraph 1). Who can argue against these two values?

- *Statements of personal feelings.* For example, Fryman states that he was bothered at first by opinionated professors (paragraph 2). We can't say, "No you weren't."—or "You shouldn't have been." What would be the point?

- *Information only the author would know.* For example, if Fryman had mentioned something he read or heard that caused him to be more tolerant of bias in the classroom, we would just have to accept what he says.

- *Incidental facts whose accuracy is not important for the argument.* For example, if Fryman had referred to a particular class and professor, we

Concepts and Questions for Analyzing an Argument

1. *The claim or thesis.* Find the main point the writer wants you to believe and/or be persuaded to do. Sometimes the claim will be stated, sometimes implied. Ask, Is the claim clear and consistent? Is it absolute, no exceptions allowed? Assess the claim: Is it reasonable, desirable, practical?

2. *The reasons.* Find answers to the question, Why? That is, given the claim, what explains or justifies it? Like the claim, reasons will be stated or implied. Ask, Does each reason actually explain or justify the thesis? How convincing is the reason?

3. *The evidence.* Reasons will be supported or developed with something: more reasoning, examples, data, or expert opinion. Look at the evidence offered for each reason and ask, Does the evidence actually support the reason? How convincing is each piece of evidence, and how convincing is the evidence for each reason taken together?

4. *Key terms.* Often without defining them, writers use words that should be carefully pondered. When a claim is justified, for instance, as the right or moral thing to do, we need to ask what "right" or "moral" means in this case.

5. *Assumptions.* It is impossible to argue without assuming many things— and "assume" means "often not stated." Ask, What must I believe to accept that claim, or reason, or piece of evidence? Is the assumption "safe," something that any reasonable person would also assume?

6. *Implications.* Like assumptions, implications are usually not stated. To uncover them, ask, If I accept this statement, what follows from it? Are its implications acceptable or not?

7. *Analogies.* Many arguments use comparisons and some depend on them—on reasoning based on something being like something else. Look for analogies. Ask, Are the items compared close enough to permit reasoning by similarity? How important are the differences between the items compared?

---

would have to accept the information as factual. Even if his memory was faulty, it does not matter so far as assessing the argument is concerned.

Here are some illustrations of how the analytical concepts and questions apply to Fryman's argument:

1. *Thesis*

   Fryman: College students should listen to biased and opinionated professors with critical respect.

   Comment: Note that you have to piece together the thesis from several statements he makes. We can respond by saying, "What sort of opinions *merit* critical respect?"

2. *Reasons*

   Fryman: "Many faculty members are at the top of their fields."

   Comment: Clearly, this statement is a reason—it explains why the author thinks students should accord professors respect. We can respond by saying, "Yes, some professors are quite accomplished *in their fields*. But when they venture outside them, do their opinions count for more than any other relatively well-informed person's?"

3. *Evidence*

   Fryman: "Many [professors] showed partiality to the political left or right."

   Comment: In backing up one of his statements—that it bothered him at first when professors offered their opinions—he points to political bias as one of the irritating factors. We can respond by saying, "*Under what circumstances* would expression of political opinions be appropriate?"

4. *Key terms*

   Fryman: "hang-ups and prejudices"

   Comment: Fryman admits that professors have such things when he talks about the relationship between opinions and truth (paragraph 5). We can respond by saying, "What exactly is a 'hang-up,' and how do we distinguish it from a legitimate concern with something?" Or, "We *all* have 'prejudices.' When are they justified and therefore worth taking seriously?"

5. *Assumptions*

   Fryman: He assumes that there are no ethical constraints on what professors should talk about in class.

   Comment: We can respond by asking, "Shouldn't there be professional ethics at work here? What moral or ethical principles should govern what's discussed and under what conditions?"

6. *Implications*

   Fryman: He implies that students should tolerate whatever the professor dishes out.

   Comment: We can respond by saying, "How much student toleration is too much toleration? Suppose that a professor is openly sexist, for instance? Shouldn't we not only reject the opinions but also report the behavior to university authorities?"

7. *Analogies*

   Fryman: He compares the approach students should take to opinionated professors with the critical respect accorded great works of literature (paragraph 3).

   Comment: We can respond by saying, "Great works of literature have typically survived for years. We call them classics. Does it make sense to meet the casual opinions of professors the same way that we approach Shakespeare?"

⊙⊙ FOLLOWING THROUGH

If you are working alone on an argument, use the seven questions in the Best Practices box. Record the results in your notebook, your computer file for this assignment, or online as a blog that presents the argument and your analysis of it.

If your class is working on the same argument, divide into small groups of about three or four people and do an analysis. Share what your group found with the class as a whole in discussion.   •

Doing Research

Logical analysis focuses on *what an argument says*. The challenge of analysis is to discover what you can say back.

As important as analysis is, there is another way to explore an argument. Test what it says *against reality*, your experience with life and the world, what you know about the topic, and what you can find out from research.

The Art of Questioning: Inquiry into the Fit of Argument and Reality
The following questions should help you test the argument against reality:

1. What is my own experience with the topic or issue or problem the argument takes up?

    > In the case of Fryman's argument, when have the comments of "biased teachers" been illuminating or helpful to you? When have they been boring, irritating, or useless? What's the difference between the two?

2. What relevant information do I have from reading or from some other source?

    > Perhaps you have heard other students complain about professors pushing their political convictions on their students. What did they say? Did their complaints seem justified? Why or why not?

3. What could I find out from research that might be relevant to assessing the argument?

    > Most arguments suggest opportunities for at least checking up on information relevant to the argument. For instance, you might investigate the idea of academic freedom. How does it apply to professors? How does it apply to students? (For detailed guidance on ways to research any topic, see Chapter 6, pages 97–115.)

4. If the argument reasons from data, in what other ways might the data be interpreted?

    > Research will often lead you to other arguments that interpret the same or similar data differently or that supply additional data the argument you are critiquing did not know or ignored. For example, arguments for stronger border patrol enforcement sometimes

fail to mention that about 40% of illegal immigrants got here legally and simply stayed. Enhanced border control obviously will have no effect on that group.

5. In what other contexts might the argument be placed?

All arguments state or assume a context within which what they say is valid or true. What other contexts might be relevant? For instance, using the Constitution as context, the Supreme Court has ruled that public flag-burning qualifies as free speech. You could reason based on some other context, such as the wisdom of burning a flag as a gesture of protest. Does it make a point or just make people mad?

◎◎ FOLLOWING THROUGH

In your notebook or computer file, sum up the results of applying the above questions. Highlight the best insight you gained. It could be a major point in your critique, perhaps even the central point around which you structure it. •

Preparing to Write

Thoughtful exploration of an argument—responding to what it says and pondering its fit with reality—results in much you *could* say. However, a critique is not a collection of comments or a list of criticisms. Rather it's *a coherent evaluation from a particular point of view,* your view. Consequently, in preparing to write, formulating your stance matters most.

Formulating Your Stance

Stances toward an argument range from total acceptance to total rejection, with many possibilities in between. You can reject an argument in general, but see value in a part of it. You can accept an argument in general, but with major reservations. The key question is, *What do you really think?*

Here are a few of the stances our students took on "Opening Your Ears to Biased Professors."

1. He focuses entirely on what *students* should do. He's one-sided. The key question is, What should professors do to deserve the critical respect Fryman says students should have?

2. He says students should listen with critical respect. Fine, but shouldn't we do more than that? If professors are free to give their opinions on just about anything in class, shouldn't students have at least the freedom to question the opinions offered?

3. Professors should limit their opinions to the subject matter of the course and topics they have special knowledge about. They shouldn't offer opinions on "politics, religion, war, or which movie should win the Academy Award" if these topics do not arise from the course's subject matter.

FOLLOWING THROUGH

Using the examples above as models, write down your stance. If you are having difficulty, consider the following possibilities:

- *Return to your first impression.* Perhaps a revised version can be your stance.
- *Review the statements in the argument that you found open to question.* Is there a pattern in your criticisms? Or perhaps one statement stands out from the rest and seems central? Your stance may be implied in your most important criticism.
- *Do you detect one place where the reasoning breaks down?* Try fashioning your stance around the reasoning you think the author should have used to reach conclusions you favor.
- *Look for places where the author's view of reality or what is needed or desirable part company with yours.* Your stance may be implied in it.
- *Talk through possible stances with another student or your instructor.* Just talking helps, and sometimes a comment from someone else can help your stance emerge.

Sometimes you will discover your best stance only through writing a first draft. For now, try out the stance that appeals to you most. You can always revise and rewrite.

Consider Your Reader, Purpose, and Tone

As you approach the first draft, review the key variables discussed earlier (page 47). In sum,

> **Reader.** Most critiques address the same audience as the argument.
>
> **Purpose.** A critique contributes to a conversation seeking the truth about a controversial issue or question. Connect your criticisms with the truth as you see it.
>
> **Tone.** You want to sound engaged, fair, balanced, and respectful. Assert your criticisms firmly and forcefully.

FOLLOWING THROUGH

Add notes about the key variables to your stance statement. Answer these questions: Do you intend to address the same readers that the argument does? Why or why not? How *exactly* does your version of the truth differ from the author's and how great is the difference? How friendly to the author do you want to sound?

DRAFTING YOUR PAPER

As you write your paper, focus on organization and development. The following guidance should help.

Organization

Whether you write first drafts in chunks and then fit them together or write from a plan more or less in sequence, beginning to end, have the following organizational principles in mind:

Introduction

Begin by identifying the argument you are critiquing: who wrote it and for what group of readers, when and where it appeared, what it is about, and the position the author takes. Make your own stance clear and give it an emphatic position, near the end of your introduction.

Body

From everything you found questionable in the argument, select *only* what is relevant to your stance. No one expects a critique to deal with everything an argument says or everything that can be said about it.

Do not let the order of the argument determine the order of your critique. Order in relation to your stance and for maximum impact on your readers.

If you can say positive things, deal with these points first. Readers listen to the negative more willingly after hearing the positive.

Conclusion

Short critiques of short arguments do not need summarizing conclusions. Strive instead for a clincher, the memorable "parting shot" expressing the gist or main thrust of your response.

Development

For each part of your critique, you have many options for development. Here are some of them.

Introduction

Besides identifying the argument and taking your stance, you can also include material about context, background information, and a preview of your critique. A critique of Fryman, for instance, might deal with his argument in the context of efforts to restrict academic freedom; research about the author might reveal relevant background information, such as what was happening at Brandeis University when he wrote the article. Previews summarize the points you are going to make in the order in which you are going to discuss them.

Body

Take up one point at a time. Each point will challenge either the reasoning of the argument or its fit with reality. If the former, be sure to explain inconsistencies or contradictions fully, so that your reader understands exactly where and why the reasoning went wrong. See Hanson's critique (pages 44–46) for examples. If the latter, provide counter-evidence from personal experience, general knowledge, or research.

Conclusion

To clinch your critique, consider the following possibilities: a memorable quotation with a comment on it from you; a return to a key statement or piece of information in your introduction that you can now develop more fully; remind the reader of your strongest point with additional support or commentary.

REVISING YOUR DRAFT

Whenever time permits, it is best to get away from your draft for a day or two, come back to it fresh, assess it first yourself, and then seek input from others. The Best Practices checklist should help both you and the persons you consult in assessing the first draft.

Excerpts from a Sample Discovery Draft

The following excerpts come from student D. D. Solomon's draft in response to the Fryman argument.

Excerpt 1: Introduction

"Open Your Ears to Biased Professors," by David Fryman, deals with a common complaint among students: teachers who express their political or religious views in class. The article was published in *The Justice*, Brandeis University's student newspaper. In the article Fryman discusses how students should deal with a professor's opinion that differs from a student's own. By examining the situation from a student perspective, Fryman illuminates the implications and ramifications of professor bias. The author concludes that bias should be avoided, but if it isn't, students should deal with the situation by following several basic guidelines.

Excerpt 2: D. D.'s Critique

Although Fryman is right about how students should respond, he left out the obligations professors have. Fryman dealt with how teachers sometimes deviate from the topic at hand, and begin to speak of their own personal opinions on a topic. In my ethics class last year, my teacher told us she was a lesbian. In one of our discussions we spoke about gay rights, and whether or not marriage should be legal for homosexuals. She believed strongly in the right of homosexuals to marry. Some of the students, including myself, did not agree with her. Yet, when we tried to discuss our side of the issue, she cut us off. Fryman neglected to discuss such instances when a teacher's opinions infringe on the students' right to open debate.

Critique Revision Checklist

1. Look at all places where you have summarized or paraphrased the argument. Compare them against the text. Are they accurate? Do they capture the author's apparent intent as well as what she or he says?

2. Locate the argument's context—the existing view or views the author addressed. If the critique does not mention context, would it improve if it did? If so, where might a discussion of context work best?

3. Critiques are written either to the same readers the author attempted to reach or for readers with a stake in the argument the author left out. Where in the critique can you detect the writer appealing to readers? Compare the opening paragraphs with the ending ones. Is the reader conception consistent?

4. Critiques seek the truth about some controversial issue or question. What is the issue or question the argument addresses? Is it stated in the critique? Does the difference between the author's view of the truth and the view in the critique emerge clearly? If not, what could be done to make the difference sharper?

5. Underline the critique's stance. Is it stated explicitly and early in the essay? Examine each critical point. How does it develop, explain, or defend the stance? Consider cutting anything not related to the stance.

6. Check the flow of the critical points. Does each connect to the one before it and the one after? If not, consider rearranging the sequence. How might one point set up or lead to another better?

7. How does the critique sound? The tone should be thoughtfully engaged, fair, balanced, and respectful, but also confident and forceful. Look for places where the tone might make the wrong impression. Consider ways to improve it.

Fryman believed that professors should express their stands on controversial issues. When expressing his or her opinion, professors should not neglect to introduce all aspects of the issue at hand. Sometimes professors get caught up in their own view too much and fall into preaching, rather than sharing what they know with the class. Students should hear about other viewpoints so they can view many sides of the issue. The professor should offer his own position as an opinion, not as fact, and should encourage students to form their own opinions.

Fryman fails to deal with the negative impact when teachers stray from the subject matter of the course. His point that teachers should express their opinions is relevant only when related to the topic at hand. In my ethics class, the teacher was always returning to the issue of gay rights, even when the topic of discussion didn't relate to it. She wanted to convert students to her point of view more than teach us ethics.

Example Assessment: Sizing Up D. D.'s First Draft

D. D. felt that his first draft lacked punch and that the body of his critique did not unfold the way he wanted it to. Questions 4 and 5 in the revision checklist helped him see why he felt his paper lacked punch. Fryman sees biased professors as a fact that students must cope with as constructively as they can. For D. D. the professor–student relationship should be a two-way street. He did not bring out this fundamental difference well.

A student collaborator helped him see why his critical points did not flow as well as he wished. "What should come first," D. D.'s partner asked, "staying on topic or not ignoring student opinions?"

Finally, D. D.'s instructor helped him detect another problem, a place where he did not represent Fryman's position accurately. "The author concludes that bias should be avoided," D. D. claimed. "Does he?" his teacher asked, adding, "Where?" D. D. could not find it in the argument because Fryman does not say it.

D. D. had much to consider and a number of decisions to make. The revised draft appears below and on page 61.

Develop a Revision Strategy

Make a list of both your assessments of the draft and those of anyone who responded helpfully to it. Which criticisms seem valid or sound? Take these and plan your second draft. It can be a sentence or two, "I'll cut this, rearrange that, and add a point here," a full-blown outline, or something in between. *The important thing is to have a clear idea of what you plan to do and in what order.*

Before attempting your revision, read D. D.'s revised draft. It is a good example of what cutting, adding, and rearranging can do.

REVISED DRAFT: D. D. SOLOMON'S EVALUATION OF FRYMAN'S ARGUMENT

"How Professors Should Deal with Their Biases"

D. D. SOLOMON

1   "Open Your Ears to Biased Professors," by David Fryman, deals with a common complaint among students: teachers who express their political or religious views in class. Fryman believes that students should treat the personal opinions of professors with critical respect. I agree, but think that his view is one-sided and therefore not fully persuasive.

2   Because he is writing only to students, he has very little to say about how professors should conduct themselves. Fryman deals with the problem of bias as if only what students should do matters. Actually, professors have more responsibility.

They're older, more knowledgeable, and more experienced. I think if professors are going to express their political and religious views in class, they should do so in certain ways or not do it at all.

3   Fryman fails to consider professors who try to convert students to their own ideology. Because professors know so much, they can appear very appealing to students who have not encountered an issue before. By leaving out other interpretations, the professor assures that students hear only the teacher's side, which does not allow students to form their own conclusions. I saw this happen in a government class which discussed the 2008 Presidential election. Most of the class did not know much about politics, and therefore accepted the professor's view completely. They didn't have the critical capacity Fryman assumes all college students have. Certainly professors should challenge students, but what my government professor did was convert.

4   Sometimes professors get caught up in their own view too much and fall into preaching, rather than sharing all they know with the class. Students should hear about other viewpoints so they can view all sides of the issue. Furthermore, the professor should offer his own opinion as an opinion, not as a fact, and encourage students to form their own opinions.

5   Unfortunately, professors who want to convert students don't want students to form their own opinions but rather believe what the professor thinks. In my ethics class last year, my teacher told us she was a lesbian. In one of our discussions we spoke about gay rights, and whether or not marriage should be legal for homosexuals. She believed strongly in the right of homosexuals to marry. Some of the students, including me, did not agree with her. Yet, when we tried to discuss our side of the issue, she cut us off. Fryman neglects to discuss such instances when a teacher's opinions infringe on the students' right to open debate. I believe that if teachers can express their opinions openly in class, the students should be able to express theirs.

6   Finally, Fryman fails to deal with the negative impact when teachers stray from the subject matter of the course. In my ethics class, the teacher was always returning to the issue of gay rights, even when the topic of discussion didn't relate to it. She wanted to convert students to her point of view more than teach us ethics. Because she lacked restraint, the class spent too much class time on one issue.

7   I agree that professors should share their opinions with the class and students should listen and learn from them. But opinions must be distinguished from facts. Students should hear about other opinions besides the professor's. There should be open discussion, and students who have opinions different from the professor's should feel free to express them. Professors should stay on topic and not allow themselves to talk about just whatever happens to be on their mind. Most of all, education shouldn't be conversion. A professor is not a preacher and shouldn't take that role.

Responding to D. D.'s Revision Draft

It is remarkable how much a paper can improve if genuine effort goes into revising. Note especially in D. D.'s revised draft that

- He got his own view stated "up front," in the introduction, and sharply distinguished from Fryman's.

- He completely reorganized his key point, that education should not be a process of conversion.
- He pulled his whole view together well at the end.

Edit Your Paper

Edit your own draft to eliminate errors.

It is easy to overlook small-scale editing problems. Someone else's eyes and ears can be a big help. Exchange your edited paper with another student. Help each other find and correct any remaining errors.

Make a list of the editing problems. List words you misspelled. If you did not punctuate a sentence correctly, write the sentence down and circle or underline the correct mark of punctuation. Add to this list when you get the marked paper back from your instructor.

Always check your next paper for the problems listed first. In this way you can gradually reduce error. Continue this practice with everything you write. It will improve your grades and make you a better writer.

CHAPTER SUMMARY

For nearly everything people do, there is a natural way to go about it and an educated way. The natural way to approach disagreement is to "have at it" in a free-for-all kind of way. People want to be heard, but too often they do not want to listen; hardly anything receives careful thought or discussion. The natural way is open, democratic, often exciting, and even therapeutic. But too often the point of it all—finding the truth insofar as we can hope to discover it—gets lost.

The educated way of critique works by listening, taking in what other people say, and probing it through questions, testing it thoughtfully for both logical cogency and for its adequacy in coping with reality. It enables thought and discussion rather than merely an exchange of opinion.

CHAPTER 5

Reading and Writing about Visual Arguments

We live in a world awash in pictures. We turn on the TV and see not just performers, advertisers, and talking heads but also dramatic footage of events from around the world, commercials as visually creative as works of art, and video images to accompany popular music. We boot up our computers and surf the Net; many of the waves we ride are visual swells, enticing images created or enhanced by the very machines that take us out to sea. We drive our cars through a gallery of street art—on billboards and buildings and on the sides of buses and trucks. We go to malls and window-shop, entertained by the images of fantasy fulfillment each retailer offers. Print media are full of images; in our newspapers, for instance, photos, drawings, and computer graphics vie with print for space. Even college textbooks, once mostly blocks of uninterrupted prose with an occasional black-and-white drawing or photo, now often have colorful graphics and elaborate transparency overlays.

Like language, visual images are rhetorical. They persuade us in obvious and not-so-obvious ways. And so we need some perspective on visual rhetoric; we need to understand its power and how to use it effectively and responsibly.

UNDERSTANDING VISUAL ARGUMENTS

Visual rhetoric is *the use of images, sometimes coupled with sound or appeals to the other senses, to make an argument or persuade us to act as the image-maker would have us act.* Probably the clearest examples are advertisements and political cartoons, a few of which we will examine shortly. But visual rhetoric is everywhere. We do not ordinarily think, say, of a car's body style as "rhetoric," but clearly it is, because people are persuaded to pay tens of thousands of dollars for the sleekest new body style when they could spend a few thousand for an older car that would get them from home to work or school just as well.

"READING" IMAGES

Rhetorical analysis of visual rhetoric involves examining images to see how they attempt to convince or persuade an audience. Pictures are symbols that must be read, just as language is read. To read an argument made through images, a critic must be able to recognize allusions to popular culture. For example, Americans know that the white mustaches on the celebrities in the milk commercials refer to the way children drink milk; more recently, the milk mustache symbolizes the ad campaign itself, now part of our culture.

As with inquiry into any argument, we ought to begin with questions about rhetorical context: When was the visual argument created and by whom? To what audience was it originally aimed and with what purpose? Then we can ask what claim a visual argument makes and what reasons it offers in support of that claim. Finally, as with verbal texts that make a case, we can examine visual arguments for evidence, assumptions, and bias, and we can ask what values they favor and what the implications of accepting their argument are.

However, many visuals do not even attempt reasoning; they rely instead on emotional appeals. Such appeals are most obvious in advertising, where the aim is to move a target audience to buy a service or product. In many advertisements, especially for products like beer, cigarettes, and perfume, where the differences are subjective, emotional appeal is all there is. Most emotional appeals work by promising to reward our desires for love, status, peace of mind, or escape from everyday responsibilities.

Advertisements also use ethical appeals, associating their claim with values the audience approves of and wants to identify with—such as images that show nature being preserved, races living in harmony, families staying in touch, and people attaining the American dream of upward mobility.

In evaluating the ethics of visual rhetoric, we need to consider whether the argument is at least reasonable: Does the image demonstrate reasoning, or does it oversimplify and mislead? We will want to look at the emotional and ethical appeals to decide if they pander to audience weaknesses and prejudices or manipulate fantasies and fears.

Figure C-1

Figure C-2

SOUTHAMPTON ANTI-BIAS TASK FORCE • 516-287-5734

Figure C-3

Figure C-4

Figure C-5

Figure C-6

Figure C-7

Figure C-8

ANALYSIS: FIVE COMMON TYPES OF VISUAL ARGUMENT

In this section, we analyze some visual arguments in various genres: advertisements, editorial cartoons, public sculpture, news photographs, and graphics. We show how "reading" visual texts requires interpretive skills and how interpretive skills, in turn, depend on cultural knowledge.

Advertisements

We begin with a classic ad for Charlie perfume from 1988 that created quite a stir when it first appeared (see Figure C-1 in the color section). As James B. Twitchell noted in his *Twenty Ads That Shook the World,* the shot of a woman giving a man an encouraging fanny pat "subverted sexism, turned it on its head, [and] used it against itself." At first the editors at the *New York Times* "refused to run the ad, saying it was in 'poor taste.'" But the ad proved irresistibly appealing when it appeared in women's magazines. Why did it work so well?

Twitchell argues that "Charlie is not just in charge, she is clearly enjoying dominance."

> She is taller than her partner. . . . Not only does he have part of his anatomy removed from the picture so that the Charlie bottle can be foregrounded, and not only does she have the jaunty scarf and the cascading hair of a free spirit, but she is delivering that most masculine of signifiers, the booty pat. . . . In football especially, the pat signifies comradeship . . . and is applied dominant to submissive. . . . The coach delivers it to a hulking [player] returning to the field of battle. . . . When Charlie bestows it on her gentleman friend . . . , she is harvesting a rich crop of meaning. The tide has turned, and now men are getting their butts slapped, by of all people, women. (170)

It is possible, of course, to read the pat in other ways—for example, as the kind of thing a dominant man might do to a subordinate woman at the office, inappropriate behavior now widely understood as sexual harassment. But no matter how you read it, there is no doubt that the ad tapped into the woman's movement at a time when women routinely endured sexism at work. No wonder that the ad was hugely popular.

The other ads in our color section work in different ways. Try your hand at analyzing their persuasive power.

QUESTIONS FOR DISCUSSION

1. Figure C-2 may look like a poster but it is actually a "semi-postal" stamp, so called because a percentage of its cost goes to the cause it advocates. This stamp has raised over $22 million for breast cancer research since it was issued in 1998. What are the sources of its appeal?

2. Figure C-3, from the Southampton Anti-Bias Task Force, depends for full impact on remembering a crayon labeled *flesh* that was the color of the

center crayon in the photo. People in their forties and fifties or older remember that crayon. What, then, is the ad's appeal for them? What does it say about skin color to younger people who do not remember the crayon?

3. Figure C-4 is a striking example of the power of photography and probably digital and other ways of enhancing photographs. How might women respond to it? How might men?

4. If Figure C-4 features the art of photography in selling a product through making it glamorous, C-5 is deliberately unglamorous, depicting women more as they are. How does it work to promote Dove products?

5. Figure C-6, the Adidas ad, ingeniously exploits how the eye can be fooled by what it *expects* to see rather than what is actually there. Did you see the shadow at first simply as the runner's shadow? What made you reevaluate what you were seeing? What's the impact of playing with perception in this case?

6. As a class project, find ads for the same product in magazines that appeal to different market segments, as defined by age, income, sex, ethnicity, and so on. Compare and contrast the ads to see how they are designed to appeal to their target audiences.

Editorial Cartoons

Editorial cartoons comment on events and issues in the news. They are funny but offer concise arguments too. Most political cartoons rely on captions and dialogue to make their argument, combining the visual and verbal. Consider the one by Mike Keefe (Figure 5.1) that comments on the impact of computers.

Figure 5.1

Mike Keefe, dePIXion Studios. Reprinted with permission.

The cartoon illustrates well how "reading" a visual argument depends on shared cultural knowledge. The image of a thirsty man crawling on hands and knees through a desert stands for anything important that humans lack. The cartoon depicts our common metaphor for the Internet, the "information superhighway," literally. The man has too much information and not enough wisdom. To read the argument of the cartoon and appreciate its humor, the viewer has to know about the overwhelming glut of information on the Internet, suggested by the size of the letters on the road. The cartoon "argues" that relying on the Internet will deprive a civilization of the wisdom to sustain a good life.

QUESTIONS FOR DISCUSSION

1. Cartoons probably are most persuasive when they satirize a familiar problem, as in the information superhighway example in Figure 5.1. A similar cartoon is Stuart Carlson's in Figure 5.3 (page 69). However, although most Americans struggle with the Net's information glut, fewer, but still a large percentage, drive gas-guzzling vehicles. If you do not, how do you react to Carlson's cartoon? Why do you react the way you do? If you drive a gas guzzler or would like to, is the cartoon still amusing? Why or why not?

2. Some cartoons are "factional," created by one side in a controversy to ridicule the position of the other side. Contrasting examples appear in Figure 5.2. Clearly, neither cartoon will persuade anyone whose position is held up to ridicule. Yet, factional cartoons are common. They must serve some purpose. How do you think they work?

3. Find a recent editorial cartoon on an issue prominent in the news. Bring it to class and be prepared to explain its persuasive tactics. Consider also the fairness of the cartoon. Does the cartoon minimize the complexity of the issue it addresses?

Public Sculpture

Public sculptures, such as war memorials, aim to teach an audience about a nation's past and to honor its values. An example that can be read as an argument is the Marine Corps Memorial, erected in 1954 on the Mall in Washington, D.C. (see Figure 5.4). It honors all Marines who have given their lives by depicting one specific act of bravery, the planting of the American flag on Iwo Jima, a Pacific island captured from the Japanese in 1945. The claim the sculpture makes is clear: Honor your country. The image of the soldiers straining every muscle gives the reason: These men made extreme sacrifices to preserve the values symbolized by this flag. The sculpture also communicates through details like the wind-whipped flag.

The Iwo Jima sculpture is traditional, glorifying victory on enemy soil. Compare it with the Vietnam War Memorial, dedicated in Washington, D.C., in November 1982. Maya Lin designed what we now call "the Wall" while

Figure 5.2

Jim McCloskey, *The News Leader,* Staunton, Virginia. Reprinted by permission.

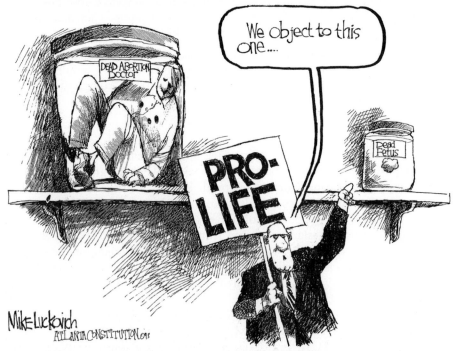

By permission of Mike Luckovich and Creators Syndicate, Inc.

Figure 5.3

Figure 5.4

Figure 5.5

Figure 5.6

an undergraduate student at Yale. Her design was controversial because it was so unconventional (see Figures 5.5 and 5.6, page 70) and antiwar. Its black granite slates are etched with the names of war dead; it honors individuals who died in a war that tore the nation apart.

QUESTIONS FOR DISCUSSION

1. Because it does not portray a realistic scene as the Iwo Jima Memorial does, the Wall invites interpretation and analysis. If you have visited it, try to recall your reaction. What details led to your interpretation? Could you characterize the Wall as having logical, ethical, and emotional appeals?

2. Find public sculpture or monuments to visit and analyze. Alone or with some classmates, take notes and photographs. Then develop your interpretation of the sculpture's argument, specifying how visual details contribute to the case, and present your analysis to the class. Compare your interpretation with those of your classmates.

News Photographs

While some news photographs may seem merely to record an event, the camera is not objective. The photographer makes many decisions—whether to snap a picture, when to snap it, what to include and exclude from the image—and decisions about light, depth of field, and so on. Figure 5.7 (page 72), a photograph that appeared in the *New York Times,* shows a scene photographer Bruce Young encountered while covering a snowstorm that hit Washington, D.C. in January 1994. The storm was severe enough to shut down the city and most government offices. Without the caption supplied by the *New York Times,* readers might not recognize the objects in the foreground as human beings, homeless people huddled on benches, covered by undisturbed snow.

The picture depicts homelessness in America as a national disgrace. The White House in the background is our nation's "home," a grand and lavishly decorated residence symbolic of national wealth. In the foreground, the homeless people look like bags of garbage, marring the picture of the snow-covered landscape. No blame attaches to the homeless for their condition; they are too pathetic under their blankets of snow. The picture shows the homeless as a fact of life in our cities, challenging the idealized image of our nation.

QUESTIONS FOR DISCUSSION

1. Figure C-7 in the color section depicts the family of Sgt. Jose M. Velez standing over his casket. Sgt. Velez was killed in Iraq. Any thoughtful response to such a photo has to be complex. How would you describe your response? To what extent is your view of the war in Iraq relevant?

Figure 5.7

2. Figure C-8 is a shot of the Tour de France, the annual bicycling race that Lance Armstrong made almost as big an event in the United States as it is in Europe. What impression does the photo convey? What details in the photo convey the impression?

3. The news photos in Figure 5.8 show events of humanitarian concern: U.S. Army personnel helping earthquake victims in Haiti, and refugees in Chad fleeing from Arab militias as a result of civil war in that African country. What details make the photographs effective in arousing viewers' interest and sympathy for the victims of such events? What do such photos add to news stories?

4. In a recent newspaper or news magazine, look for photos you think are effective when combined with a story about a controversial issue. What perspective or point of view do the pictures represent? How do you read their composition, including camera angle, light conditions, foreground and background, and so on?

www.mhhe.com/crusius To find more photographs to analyze, check out:
Writing > Visual Rhetoric Tutorial > Catalyst Image Bank

Figure 5.8

Graphics

Visual supplements to a longer text such as an essay, article, or manual are known as **graphics.** Most graphics fall into one of the following categories:

Tables and charts (typically an arrangement of data in columns and rows that summarizes the results of research)

www.mhhe.com/**crusius**

If you want information on using PowerPoint to create graphics, go to

Writing > PowerPoint Tutorial

Graphs (including bar, line, and pie graphs)

Photographs

Drawings (including maps and cartoons)

Although charts and tables are not images, they present data in visual form. Tables display information economically in one place so that readers can assess it as they read and find it easily afterward if they want to refer to it again. Consider Figure 5.9, which combines a table with bar graphs. It comes from a study of poverty in the United States. Note how much information is packed into this single visual and how easy it is to read, moving top to bottom and left to right through the categories. Consider how many long and boring paragraphs it would take to say the same thing in prose.

Graphs are usually no more than tables transformed into visuals we can interpret more easily. Bar graphs are best at showing comparisons at some single point in time. In contrast, line graphs reveal trends—for example, the performance of the stock market. Pie graphs highlight relative proportions well. When newspapers want to show us how the federal budget is spent, for example, they typically use pie graphs with the pieces labeled in some way to represent categories such as national defense, welfare, and entitlement programs. What gets the biggest pieces of the pie becomes *instantly clear* and *easy to remember*—the two major purposes of all graphs. Graphs do not make arguments, but they deliver evidence powerfully.

www.mhhe.com/**crusius**   For more help with visual design, go to:

Writing > Visual Rhetoric Tutorial > Visualizing Data

and

Writing > Visual Rhetoric Tutorial > Designing Documents

As graphics, photographs represent people, objects, and scenes realistically. For instance, owner's manuals for cars often have a shot of the engine compartment that shows where fluid reservoirs are located. Clearly, such photos serve highly practical purposes, such as helping us locate the dipstick. But they're also used, for example, in biographies; we get a better sense of, say, Abraham Lincoln's life and times when pictures of him, his family, his home, and so on are included. But photographs can do much more than inform. They can be highly dramatic and powerfully emotional in ways that only the best writers can manage with prose. Photos are often potent persuaders.

Photographs, however, are not analytical—by their nature, they give us the surface, only what the camera can "see." A different type of graphic, the drawing, is preferable when we want to depict how something is put together or structured. For instance, instructions for assembling and installing a ceiling

Figure 5.9

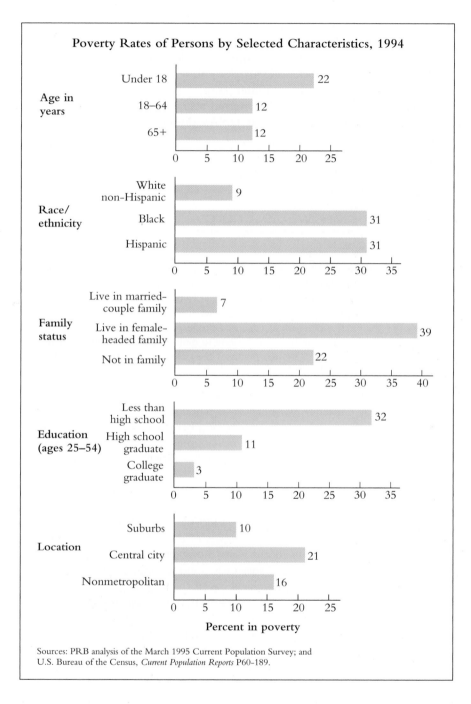

Poverty Rates of Persons by Selected Characteristics, 1994

Age in years
- Under 18: 22
- 18–64: 12
- 65+: 12

Race/ethnicity
- White non-Hispanic: 9
- Black: 31
- Hispanic: 31

Family status
- Live in married-couple family: 7
- Live in female-headed family: 39
- Not in family: 22

Education (ages 25–54)
- Less than high school: 32
- High school graduate: 11
- College graduate: 3

Location
- Suburbs: 10
- Central city: 21
- Nonmetropolitan: 16

Percent in poverty

Sources: PRB analysis of the March 1995 Current Population Survey; and
U.S. Bureau of the Census, *Current Population Reports* P60-189.

fan or a light fixture usually have many diagrams—a large one showing how all the parts fit together and smaller ones that depict steps in the process in more detail. Corporate publications often include diagrams of the company's organizational hierarchy. Scientific articles and textbooks are full of drawings or illustrations created with computer graphics; science writers want us to understand structures, particularly internal structures, impossible to capture on film. For example, our sense of DNA's double-helical structure comes entirely from diagrams.

The following article illustrates how a variety of graphics can contribute to the effectiveness of a written text.

The Rise of Renewable Energy

DANIEL M. KAMMEN

This article appeared in the September 2006 issue of *Scientific American*. Daniel Kammen is Distinguished Professor of Energy at the University of California, Berkeley, where he founded and directs the Renewable and Appropriate Energy Laboratory.

Renewable energy refers to any source of power that does not depend on the limited supply of fossil fuels, such as oil or coal, and produces relatively little or none of the greenhouse gases that contribute significantly to global warming. There are many renewable energy sources. Kammen discusses the potential of solar power, wind power, and biofuels such as ethanol.

1   No plan to substantially reduce greenhouse gas emissions can succeed through increases in energy efficiency alone. Because economic growth continues to boost the demand for energy—more coal for powering new factories, more oil for fueling new cars, more natural gas for heating new homes—carbon emissions will keep climbing despite the introduction of more energy-efficient vehicles, buildings and appliances. To counter the alarming trend of global warming, the U.S. and other countries must make a major commitment to developing renewable energy sources that generate little or no carbon.

2   Renewable energy technologies were suddenly and briefly fashionable three decades ago in response to the oil embargoes of the 1970s, but the interest and support were not sustained. In recent years, however, dramatic improvements in the performance and affordability of solar cells, wind turbines and biofuels—ethanol and other fuels derived from plants—have paved the way for mass commercialization. In addition to their environmental benefits, renewable sources promise to enhance America's energy security by reducing the country's reliance on fossil fuels from other nations. What is more, high and wildly fluctuating prices for oil and natural gas have made renewable alternatives more appealing.

3   We are now in an era where the opportunities for renewable energy are unprecedented, making this the ideal time to advance clean power for decades to come. But the endeavor will require a long-term investment of scientific, economic and political resources. Policymakers and ordinary citizens must demand action and challenge one another to hasten the transition.

LET THE SUN SHINE

4   Solar cells, also known as photovoltaics, use semiconductor materials to convert sunlight into electric current. They now provide just a tiny slice of the world's electricity: their global generating capacity of 5,000 megawatts (MW) is only 0.15 percent of the total generating capacity from all sources. Yet sunlight could potentially supply 5,000 times as much energy as the world currently consumes. And thanks to technology improvements, cost declines and favorable policies in many states and nations, the annual production of photovoltaics has increased by more than 25 percent a year for the past decade and by a remarkable 45 percent in 2005. The cells manufactured last year added 1,727 MW to worldwide generating capacity, with 833 MW made in Japan, 353 MW in Germany and 153 MW in the U.S.

5   Solar cells can now be made from a range of materials, from the traditional multicrystalline silicon wafers that still dominate the market to thin-film silicon cells and devices composed of plastic or organic semiconductors. Thin-film photovoltaics are cheaper to produce than crystalline silicon cells but are also less efficient at turning light into power. In laboratory tests, crystalline cells have achieved efficiencies of 30 percent or more; current commercial cells of this type range from 15 to 20 percent. Both laboratory and commercial efficiencies for all kinds of solar cells have risen steadily in recent years, indicating that an expansion of research efforts would further enhance the performance of solar cells on the market.

6   Solar photovoltaics are particularly easy to use because they can be installed in so many places—on the roofs or walls of homes and office buildings, in vast arrays in the desert, even sewn into clothing to power portable electronic devices. The state of California has joined Japan and Germany in leading a global push for solar installations; the "Million Solar Roof" commitment is intended to create 3,000 MW of new generating capacity in the state by 2018. Studies done by my research group, the Renewable and Appropriate Energy Laboratory at the University of California, Berkeley, show that annual production of solar photovoltaics in the U.S. alone could grow to 10,000 MW in just 20 years if current trends continue.

7   The biggest challenge will be lowering the price of the photovoltaics, which are now relatively expensive to manufacture. Electricity produced by crystalline cells has a total cost of 20 to 25 cents per kilowatt-hour, compared with four to six cents for coal-fired electricity, five to seven cents for power produced by burning natural gas, and six to nine cents for biomass power plants. (The cost of nuclear power is harder to pin down because experts disagree on which expenses to include in the analysis; the estimated range is two to 12 cents per kilowatt-hour.) Fortunately, the prices of solar cells have fallen consistently over the past decade, largely because of improvements in manufacturing processes. In Japan, where 290 MW of solar generating capacity were added in 2005 and an even larger amount was exported, the cost of photovoltaics has declined 8 percent a year; in California, where 50 MW of solar power were installed in 2005, costs have dropped 5 percent annually.

8   Surprisingly, Kenya is the global leader in the number of solar power systems installed per capita (but not the number of watts added). More than 30,000 very small solar panels, each producing only 12 to 30 watts, are sold in that country

A world of clean energy could rely on wind turbines and solar cells to generate its electricity and biofuels derived from switchgrass and other plants to power its vehicles.

KENN BROWN

annually. For an investment of as little as $100 for the panel and wiring, the system can be used to charge a car battery, which can then provide enough power to run a fluorescent lamp or a small black-and-white television for a few hours a day. More Kenyans adopt solar power every year than make connections to the country's electric grid. The panels typically use solar cells made of amorphous silicon; although these photovoltaics are only half as efficient as crystalline cells, their cost is so much lower (by a factor of at least four) that they are more affordable and useful for the two billion people worldwide who currently have no access to electricity. Sales of small solar power systems are booming in other African nations as well, and advances in low-cost photovoltaic manufacturing could accelerate this trend.

9   Furthermore, photovoltaics are not the only fast-growing form of solar power. Solar-thermal systems, which collect sunlight to generate heat, are also undergoing a resurgence. These systems have long been used to provide hot water for homes or factories, but they can also produce electricity without the need for expensive

solar cells. In one design, for example, mirrors focus light on a Stirling engine, a high-efficiency device containing a working fluid that circulates between hot and cold chambers. The fluid expands as the sunlight heats it, pushing a piston that, in turn, drives a turbine.

10   In the fall of 2005 a Phoenix company called Stirling Energy Systems announced that it was planning to build two large solar-thermal power plants in southern California. The company signed a 20-year power purchase agreement with Southern California Edison, which will buy the electricity from a 500-MW solar plant to be constructed in the Mojave Desert. Stretching across 4,500 acres, the facility will include 20,000 curved dish mirrors, each concentrating light on a Stirling engine about the size of an oil barrel. The plant is expected to begin operating in 2009 and could later be expanded to 850 MW. Stirling Energy Systems also signed a 20-year contract with San Diego Gas & Electric to build a 300-MW, 12,000-dish plant in the Imperial Valley. This facility could eventually be upgraded to 900 MW.

GROWING FAST, BUT STILL A SLIVER

Solar cells, wind power and biofuels are rapidly gaining traction in the energy markets, but they remain marginal providers compared with fossil-fuel sources such as coal, natural gas and oil.

THE RENEWABLE BOOM

Since 2000 the commercialization of renewable energy sources has accelerated dramatically. The annual global production of solar cells, also known as photovoltaics, jumped 45 percent in 2005. The construction of new wind farms, particularly in Europe, has boosted the worldwide generating capacity of wind power 10-fold over the past decade. And the production of ethanol, the most common biofuel, soared to 36.5 billion liters last year, with the lion's share distilled from American-grown corn.

Photovoltaic Production

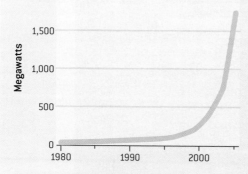

Wind Energy Generating Capacity

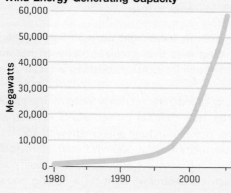

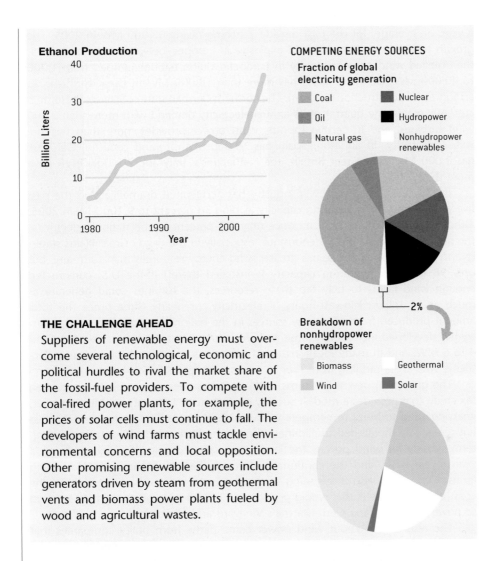

Ethanol Production

Billion Liters / Year

COMPETING ENERGY SOURCES

Fraction of global electricity generation

- Coal
- Oil
- Natural gas
- Nuclear
- Hydropower
- Nonhydropower renewables

— 2%

Breakdown of nonhydropower renewables

- Biomass
- Wind
- Geothermal
- Solar

THE CHALLENGE AHEAD

Suppliers of renewable energy must overcome several technological, economic and political hurdles to rival the market share of the fossil-fuel providers. To compete with coal-fired power plants, for example, the prices of solar cells must continue to fall. The developers of wind farms must tackle environmental concerns and local opposition. Other promising renewable sources include generators driven by steam from geothermal vents and biomass power plants fueled by wood and agricultural wastes.

11 The financial details of the two California projects have not been made public, but electricity produced by present solar-thermal technologies costs between five and 13 cents per kilowatt-hour, with dish-mirror systems at the upper end of that range. Because the projects involve highly reliable technologies and mass production, however, the generation expenses are expected to ultimately drop closer to four to six cents per kilowatt-hour—that is, competitive with the current price of coal-fired power.

BLOWING IN THE WIND

12 Wind power has been growing at a pace rivaling that of the solar industry. The worldwide generating capacity of wind turbines has increased more than 25 percent

a year, on average, for the past decade, reaching nearly 60,000 MW in 2005. The growth has been nothing short of explosive in Europe—between 1994 and 2005, the installed wind power capacity in European Union nations jumped from 1,700 to 40,000 MW. Germany alone has more than 18,000 MW of capacity thanks to an aggressive construction program. The northern German state of Schleswig-Holstein currently meets one quarter of its annual electricity demand with more than 2,400 wind turbines, and in certain months wind power provides more than half the state's electricity. In addition, Spain has 10,000 MW of wind capacity, Denmark has 3,000 MW, and Great Britain, the Netherlands, Italy and Portugal each have more than 1,000 MW.

13   In the U.S. the wind power industry has accelerated dramatically in the past five years, with total generating capacity leaping 36 percent to 9,100 MW in 2005. Although wind turbines now produce only 0.5 percent of the nation's electricity, the potential for expansion is enormous, especially in the windy Great Plains states. (North Dakota, for example, has greater wind energy resources than Germany, but only 98 MW of generating capacity is installed there.) If the U.S. constructed enough wind farms to fully tap these resources, the turbines could generate as much as 11 trillion kilowatt-hours of electricity, or nearly three times the total amount produced from all energy sources in the nation last year. The wind industry has developed increasingly large and efficient turbines, each capable of yielding 4 to 6 MW. And in many locations, wind power is the cheapest form of new electricity, with costs ranging from four to seven cents per kilowatt-hour.

14   The growth of new wind farms in the U.S. has been spurred by a production tax credit that provides a modest subsidy equivalent to 1.9 cents per kilowatt-hour, enabling wind turbines to compete with coal-fired plants. Unfortunately, Congress has repeatedly threatened to eliminate the tax credit. Instead of instituting a long-term subsidy for wind power, the lawmakers have extended the tax credit on a year-to-year basis, and the continual uncertainty has slowed investment in wind farms. Congress is also threatening to derail a proposed 130-turbine farm off the coast of Massachusetts that would provide 468 MW of generating capacity, enough to power most of Cape Cod, Martha's Vineyard and Nantucket.

15   The reservations about wind power come partly from utility companies that are reluctant to embrace the new technology and partly from so-called NIMBY-ism. ("NIMBY" is an acronym for Not in My Backyard.) Although local concerns over how wind turbines will affect landscape views may have some merit, they must be balanced against the social costs of the alternatives. Because society's energy needs are growing relentlessly, rejecting wind farms often means requiring the construction or expansion of fossil fuel–burning power plants that will have far more devastating environmental effects.

GREEN FUELS

16   Researchers are also pressing ahead with the development of biofuels that could replace at least a portion of the oil currently consumed by motor vehicles. The most common biofuel by far in the U.S. is ethanol, which is typically made from corn and blended with gasoline. The manufacturers of ethanol benefit from a

substantial tax credit: with the help of the $2-billion annual subsidy, they sold more than 16 billion liters of ethanol in 2005 (almost 3 percent of all automobile fuel by volume), and production is expected to rise 50 percent by 2007. Some policy-makers have questioned the wisdom of the subsidy, pointing to studies showing that it takes more energy to harvest the corn and refine the ethanol than the fuel can deliver to combustion engines. In a recent analysis, though, my colleagues and I discovered that some of these studies did not properly account for the energy content of the by-products manufactured along with the ethanol. When all the inputs and outputs were correctly factored in, we found that ethanol has a positive net energy of almost five megajoules per liter.

17   We also found, however, that ethanol's impact on greenhouse gas emissions is more ambiguous. Our best estimates indicate that substituting corn-based ethanol for gasoline reduces greenhouse gas emissions by 18 percent, but the analysis is hampered by large uncertainties regarding certain agricultural practices, particularly the environmental costs of fertilizers. If we use different assumptions about these practices, the results of switching to ethanol range from a 36 percent drop in emissions to a 29 percent increase. Although corn-based ethanol may help the U.S. reduce its reliance on foreign oil, it will probably not do much to slow global warming unless the production of the biofuel becomes cleaner.

18   But the calculations change substantially when the ethanol is made from cellulosic sources: woody plants such as switchgrass or poplar. Whereas most makers of corn-based ethanol burn fossil fuels to provide the heat for fermentation, the

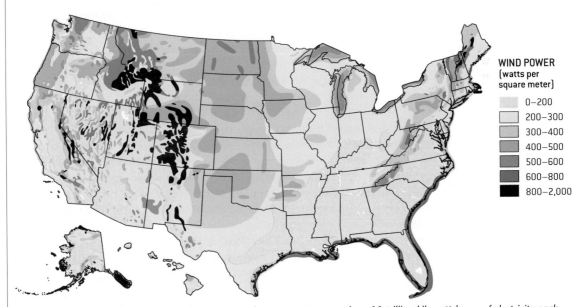

America has enormous wind energy resources, enough to generate as much as 11 trillion kilowatt-hours of electricity each year. Some of the best locations for wind turbines are the Great Plains states, the Great Lakes and the mountain ridges of the Rockies and the Appalachians.

producers of cellulosic ethanol burn lignin—an unfermentable part of the organic material—to heat the plant sugars. Burning lignin does not add any greenhouse gases to the atmosphere, because the emissions are offset by the carbon dioxide absorbed during the growth of the plants used to make the ethanol. As a result, substituting cellulosic ethanol for gasoline can slash greenhouse gas emissions by 90 percent or more.

19   Another promising biofuel is so-called green diesel. Researchers have produced this fuel by first gasifying biomass—heating organic materials enough that they release hydrogen and carbon monoxide—and then converting these compounds into long-chain hydrocarbons using the Fischer-Tropsch process. (During World War II, German engineers employed these chemical reactions to make synthetic motor fuels out of coal.) The result would be an economically competitive liquid fuel for motor vehicles that would add virtually no greenhouse gases to the atmosphere. Oil giant Royal Dutch/Shell is currently investigating the technology.

THE NEED FOR R&D

20   Each of these renewable sources is now at or near a tipping point, the crucial stage when investment and innovation, as well as market access, could enable these attractive but generally marginal providers to become major contributors to regional and global energy supplies. At the same time, aggressive policies designed to open markets for renewables are taking hold at city, state and federal levels around the world. Governments have adopted these policies for a wide variety of reasons: to promote market diversity or energy security, to bolster industries and jobs, and to protect the environment on both the local and global scales. In the U.S. more than 20 states have adopted standards setting a minimum for the fraction of electricity that must be supplied with renewable sources. Germany plans to generate 20 percent of its electricity from renewables by 2020, and Sweden intends to give up fossil fuels entirely.

21   Even President George W. Bush said, in his now famous State of the Union address this past January, that the U.S. is "addicted to oil." And although Bush did not make the link to global warming, nearly all scientists agree that humanity's addiction to fossil fuels is disrupting the earth's climate. The time for action is now, and at last the tools exist to alter energy production and consumption in ways that simultaneously benefit the economy and the environment. Over the past 25 years, however, the public and private funding of research and development in the energy sector has withered. Between 1980 and 2005 the fraction of all U.S. R&D spending devoted to energy declined from 10 to 2 percent. Annual public R&D funding for energy sank from $8 billion to $3 billion (in 2002 dollars); private R&D plummeted from $4 billion to $1 billion (see box, "R&D Is key").

22   To put these declines in perspective, consider that in the early 1980s energy companies were investing more in R&D than were drug companies, whereas today investment by energy firms is an order of magnitude lower. Total private R&D funding for the entire energy sector is less than that of a single large biotech company. (Amgen, for example, had R&D expenses of $2.3 billion in 2005.) And as R&D spending dwindles, so does innovation. For instance, as R&D funding for photovoltaics and wind

power has slipped over the past quarter of a century, the number of successful patent applications in these fields has fallen accordingly. The lack of attention to long-term research and planning has significantly weakened our nation's ability to respond to the challenges of climate change and disruptions in energy supplies.

23   Calls for major new commitments to energy R&D have become common. A 1997 study by the President's Committee of Advisors on Science and Technology and a 2004 report by the bipartisan National Commission on Energy Policy both recommended that the federal government double its R&D spending on energy. But would such an expansion be enough? Probably not. Based on assessments of the cost to stabilize the amount of carbon dioxide in the atmosphere and other studies that estimate the success of energy R&D programs and the resulting savings from the technologies that would emerge, my research group has calculated that public funding of $15 billion to $30 billion a year would be required—a fivefold to 10-fold increase over current levels.

24   Greg F. Nemet, a doctoral student in my laboratory, and I found that an increase of this magnitude would be roughly comparable to those that occurred during previous federal R&D initiatives such as the Manhattan Project and the Apollo program, each of which produced demonstrable economic benefits in addition to meeting its objectives. American energy companies could also boost their R&D spending by a factor of 10, and it would still be below the average for U.S. industry overall. Although government funding is essential to supporting early-stage technologies, private-sector R&D is the key to winnowing the best ideas and reducing the barriers to commercialization.

25   Raising R&D spending, though, is not the only way to make clean energy a national priority. Educators at all grade levels, from kindergarten to college, can stimulate public interest and activism by teaching how energy use and production affect the social and natural environment. Nonprofit organizations can establish a series of contests that would reward the first company or private group to achieve a challenging and worthwhile energy goal, such as constructing a building or appliance that can generate its own power or developing a commercial vehicle that can go 200 miles on a single gallon of fuel. The contests could be modeled after the Ashoka awards for pioneers in public policy and the Ansari X Prize for the developers of space vehicles. Scientists and entrepreneurs should also focus on finding clean, affordable ways to meet the energy needs of people in the developing world. My colleagues and I, for instance, recently detailed the environmental benefits of improving cooking stoves in Africa.

26   But perhaps the most important step toward creating a sustainable energy economy is to institute market-based schemes to make the prices of carbon fuels reflect their social cost. The use of coal, oil and natural gas imposes a huge collective toll on society, in the form of health care expenditures for ailments caused by air pollution, military spending to secure oil supplies, environmental damage from mining operations, and the potentially devastating economic impacts of global warming. A fee on carbon emissions would provide a simple, logical and transparent method to reward renewable, clean energy sources over those that harm the economy and the environment. The tax revenues could pay for some of the social

R&D IS KEY

Spending on research and development in the U.S. energy sector has fallen steadily since its peak in 1980. Studies of patent activity suggest that the drop in funding has slowed the development of renewable energy technologies. For example, the number of successful patent applications in photovoltaics and wind power has plummeted as R&D spending in these fields has declined.

U.S. R&D SPENDING IN THE ENERGY SECTOR

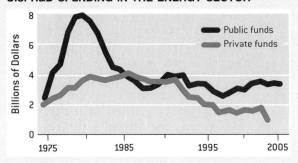

LAGGING INNOVATION IN PHOTOVOLTAICS . . .

. . . AND IN WIND POWER

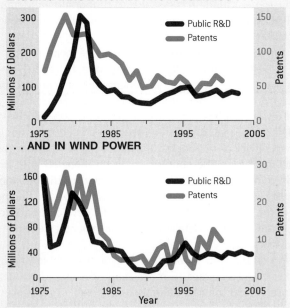

Spending amounts are expressed in 2002 dollars to adjust for inflation.

costs of carbon emissions, and a portion could be designated to compensate low-income families who spend a larger share of their income on energy. Furthermore, the carbon fee could be combined with a cap-and-trade program that would set limits on carbon emissions but also allow the cleanest energy suppliers to sell permits to their dirtier competitors. The federal government has used such programs with great success to curb other pollutants, and several northeastern states are already experimenting with greenhouse gas emissions trading.

27   Best of all, these steps would give energy companies an enormous financial incentive to advance the development and commercialization of renewable energy sources. In essence, the U.S. has the opportunity to foster an entirely new industry. The threat of climate change can be a rallying cry for a clean-technology revolution that would strengthen the country's manufacturing base, create thousands of jobs and alleviate our international trade deficits—instead of importing foreign oil, we can export high-efficiency vehicles, appliances, wind turbines and photovoltaics. This transformation can turn the nation's energy sector into something that was once deemed impossible: a vibrant, environmentally sustainable engine of growth.

Understanding Kammen's Graphics

The article certainly informs, and the graphics present information economically, clearly, and memorably. However, Kammen's central purpose is to convince us that renewable energy has enormous potential and needs significantly more public attention, research investment, and commercial development than it is currently getting. "Let's commit ourselves to renewable energy" is its central message, and so this apparently informative article is actually an argument. The graphics, therefore, function mainly as evidence to back up Kammen's main contentions. Let's examine the first two and reserve the others for your own analysis.

The opening drawing, an example of what's called an "artist's conception," depicts a green world, powered entirely by renewables, where agriculture and city exist side by side. The combine in the field runs on electricity generated by huge solar panels, perhaps using biofuels on days without sun, while wind (note the turbines in the background) and sun (note the solar panels on the roof of the houses in the right foreground) work together to provide all the power needed by the city. In the original color drawing, the sky is deep blue merging into purple, suggesting lack of pollution, and the fields are various shades of green and gold, with obvious implications.

"Why an artist's conception?" you might ask. The obvious answer, of course, is no such communities exist today to photograph. The article needs a way to stimulate our imagination, to help us envision a world that could be, where energy is cheap, abundant, inexhaustible, and, most of all, clean. Caught as we are in a world that burns oil, natural gas, and coal to supply nearly all energy, we have trouble conceiving a world powered by renewables. Anything we cannot conceive, we cannot aspire to—hence the importance of establishing this vision of the future.

The drawing, then, is persuasive: "Just imagine the possibilities" is the message. The box titled "Growing Fast . . ." (pages 80–81), in contrast, gives us the facts. Solar, wind, and ethanol production are all sharply up worldwide, as the three line graphs show, but the top pie graph puts the upswing in perspective—only a tiny sliver, 2%, of the world's power comes currently from renewables. The pie graph on the bottom depicts the relative proportions of green energy in use, showing us, among other things, that the enormous potential of wind and solar power has yet to be aggressively exploited. Finally, the prose combined with the visuals summarizes knowledge that the graphs and photos could not supply, making the box a fine example of combining visuals with words.

The "Growing Fast . . ." box packs a lot of information into an attractive space; it would take many pages to describe it in prose, boring pages of data that would not have half the impact of the graphics. That is part of why it is persuasive—we can see the big picture without trudging through many pages of text. But to appreciate its full persuasive power, the implications of the box and the opening drawing must be combined. The drawing seems almost futuristic, as if we will wait a long time to see anything like it, whereas the box shows us that it is all tantalizingly within reach. We just have to do more with what we have. And so, in sum, the message is simple and upbeat: "We can do it."

QUESTIONS FOR DISCUSSION

1. Graphics, we must always remember, *supplement* texts. Reread the section "Blowing in the Wind," an allusion to a famous song by Bob Dylan, and then examine the map of the United States (page 83), which depicts the 11 trillion kilowatt-hours of wind energy that could be generated in the United States each year. What do text and graphic working together "say"?

2. We see what could happen in the map—wind power harnessed to full potential. And so we ask, Why not? The box "R&D Is Key" (page 86) tells us what the main problem is—not nearly enough R&D. The problem is not putting enough money in research and scientific innovation. We are not going to get there if we don't. Work backwards from this box: How do all the graphics link to one another to answer closely related questions? How much of Kammen's case for renewables is made in the graphics? If we had only the text without the graphics, how much persuasive power would be lost?

3. To see the potential for adding graphics in your own writing, bring a recent paper you wrote to class. If you did not use graphics, consider whether the paper can be improved with graphic support. If so, given your audience and purposes, what graphic types would you use and why? If you did use graphics, be prepared to discuss them—what you did and why, and how you went about securing or creating the visuals. If you now see ways to improve them, discuss what you would do as well.

WRITING ASSIGNMENTS

Assignment 1: Analyzing an Advertisement or Editorial Cartoon

Choose an ad or cartoon from a current magazine or newspaper. First, inquire into its rhetorical context: What situation prompted its creation? What purpose does it aim to achieve? Where did it originally appear? Who is its intended audience? What would they know or believe about the product or issue? Then inquire into the argument being made. Consider the following points: What visual metaphors or allusions appear? What prior cultural knowledge and experiences would the audience need to "read" the image? Consider how the visual argument might limit the scope of the issue or how it might play to the audience's biases, stereotypes, or fears. After thorough inquiry, reach some conclusion about the effectiveness and ethics of your ad or cartoon. Write your conclusion as a thesis or claim. Use your analysis to convince, supporting it with evidence gathered during inquiry.

| STUDENT SAMPLE | Analysis Of Visual Rhetoric

The following student essay is an example of Assignment 1. Before you begin your own essay, read it and discuss the conclusions reached about an advertisement for Eagle Brand condensed milk. We were unable to obtain permission to reprint the advertisement under discussion, but the descriptions of it should make the analysis easy to follow.

A Mother's Treat
Kelly Williams

1 Advertisements are effective only if they connect with their audiences. Advertisers study the group of people they hope to reach and know what the group values and what images they have of themselves. Often these images come from social expectations that tell businessmen, mothers, fathers, teens that they should look or act a certain way. Most people adhere to the norms because they give social status. Advertisers tend to look to these norms as a way to sell their products. For example, an ad depicts a man in an

---

expensive suit driving a luxury car, and readers assume he is a lawyer, physician, or business executive. Such people will buy this car because they associate it with the status they want to project. Likewise, some advertisements manipulate women with children by associating a product with the ideal maternal image.

2   An advertisement for Eagle Brand condensed milk typifies this effort. The advertisement appeared in magazines aimed at homemakers and in *People* magazine's "Best and Worst Dressed" issue of September 1998. The readers are predominantly young women; those with children may be second-income producers or single mothers. They are struggling to raise a family and have many demands on their time. They feel enormous pressure to fulfill ideal work and domestic roles.

3   The advertisement creates a strong connection with a maternal audience. The black-and-white photograph depicts a young girl about kindergarten age. The little girl's facial expression connotes hesitation and sadness. In the background is a school yard. Other children are walking toward the school, their heads facing down, creating a feeling of gloom. All readers will recognize the situation. The little girl is about to attend her first day of school. One could easily guess that she is looking back at her mother with a sense of abandonment, pleading for support.

4   The wording of the text adds some comic relief. The ad is not intended to make the readers sad. The words seem to come from the mind of the child's mother. "For not insisting on bunny slippers for shoes, for leaving Blankie behind, for actually getting out of the car. . . ." These words show that the mother is a good mother, very empathetic. Even the print type is part of the marketing strategy. It mimics a "proper" mother's handwriting. There are no sharp edges, implying softness and gentleness.

5   The intent is to persuade mothers that if they buy Eagle Brand milk and make the chocolate bar treat, they will be good mothers like the speaker in the ad. It tells women that cooking such treats helps alleviate stressful situations in everyday family life. The little girl reminds mothers of their duty to comfort their kids. She evokes the "feminine" qualities of compassion, empathy, and protectiveness.

6   The ad also suggests that good mothers reward good behavior. As the ad says, "It's time for a treat." But good mothers would also know that "Welcome Home Chocolate Bars" are rich, so this mother has to say, "I'll risk spoiling your dinner." The invisible mother in the ad is ideal because she does care about her child's nutrition, but more about the emotional state of her child.

7   In many ways this ad is unethical. While the ad looks harmless and cute, it actually reinforces social pressures on women to be "perfect" mothers. If you don't bake a treat to welcome your child back home after school, you are failing as a mother. The recipe includes preparation time, showing that the treat can be made with minimal effort. It gives mothers no excuse for not making it. Moreover, the advertisement obviously exploits children to sell their product.

8   Desserts do not have much nutritional value. It would be hard to make a logical case for Welcome Home Bars, so Eagle Brand appeals to emotion. There's nothing wrong with a treat once in a while, but it is wrong to use guilt and social pressure to persuade mothers to buy a product.

Assignment 2: Analyzing and Creating Posters or Flyers

As a class project, collect copies of posters or flyers you find around your campus. It is true that information in our culture is plentiful and cheap, but attention is at a premium. Creators of posters and flyers must compete not only with each other but with all other visual sources of information to catch and keep our attention. How well do the posters and flyers your class found work? Why do some catch and hold attention better than others?

Create a poster or flyer to publicize an event, an organization, a student government election, or anything else relevant to your campus life. Use the best posters and flyers you found as a model, but do not be reluctant to use color, type sizes, images, and so on in your own way.

Assignment 3: Using Visual Rhetoric to Promote Your School

Colleges and universities compete fiercely for students and are therefore as concerned about their image as any corporation or politician. As a class project, collect images your school uses to promote itself, including brochures for prospective students, catalogs, class lists, and Web home pages. Choose three or four of the best ones, and in class discussions analyze them. Then, working in groups of three or four students or individually, do one or all of the following:

1. Find an aspect of your college or university overlooked in the publications that you believe is a strong selling point. Employing photographs, drawings, paintings, or some other visual medium, create an image

appropriate for one of the school publications. Compose an appealing text to go with it. Then, in a page or two, explain why you think your promotional image would work well.

2. If someone in the class has the computer knowledge, create an alternative to your school's home page, or make changes that would make it more appealing to prospective students and their parents.

3. Imagine that for purposes of parody or protest you wanted to call attention to aspects of your school that the official images deliberately omit. Proceed as in item 1. In a short statement, explain why you chose the image you did and what purpose(s) you want it to serve.

4. Select a school organization (a fraternity or sorority, a club, etc.) whose image you think could be improved. Create a promotional image for it either for the Web or for some other existing publication.

5. As in item 3, create a visual parody of the official image of a school organization, perhaps as an inside joke intended for other members of the organization.

Assignment 4: Analyzing Your Own Visual Rhetoric

Study all the images your class created as argument and/or persuasion in the previous assignment. Select an image to analyze in depth. Write an essay that addresses these questions:

What audience does the image intend to reach?

What goal did the creator of the image seek to accomplish?

If something is being argued, ask:

What thesis is advanced by the image or accompanying text?

Do aspects of the image or text function as reasons for holding the thesis?

If an image persuades more than it argues, attempt to discover and understand its major source of appeal. Persuasion appeals to the whole person in an effort to create **identification,** a strong linking of the reader's interests and values with the image that represents something desired. Hence, we can ask

How do the images your class created appeal to the audience's interests and values?

Do the images embody emotional appeals? If so, how?

Assignment 5: Using Graphics to Supplement Your Own Writing or Other Texts

Select an essay that could be improved either by adding graphics or by revising the graphics used. Working alone or collaboratively with a writing group, revise it. For help with using graphics effectively in your writing, see the

Guidelines for Using Visuals

Graphics come in a variety of useful forms: as tables to display numerical data economically, as graphs to depict data in a way that permits easy comparison of proportions or trends, as photographs to convey realism and drama, and as drawings to depict structures. Whatever graphics you use, be sure to do the following:

- Make sure every graphic has a definite function. Graphics are not decorative and should never be "thrown" into an essay.

- Choose the kind or form of visual best suited to convey the point you are trying to make.

- Design graphics so that they are easy to interpret. That is, keep them simple, make them large enough to be read without strain, and use clear labeling.

- Place graphics as close as possible to the text they explain or illustrate. Remember, graphics should be easier to understand than the text they supplement.

- Refer to all your graphics in the text. Readers usually need both the graphic and a text discussion for full understanding.

- Acknowledge the creator or source of each graphic next to the graphic itself. As long as you acknowledge the source or creator, you can borrow freely, just as you can with quotations from texts. Of course, if you wish to publish an essay that includes borrowed graphics, you must obtain written permission.

Best Practices box "Guidelines for Using Visuals." You have many revision options: Besides adding visuals, you can cut unneeded ones, redesign existing ones, change media (for example, from a photo to a drawing), change image types (for example, from a table to a graph), and so on. Revising graphics always means reworking the text as well. Expect changes in one to require changes in the other.

Assignment 6: Presenting Information Using PowerPoint

Revise and present the written text in Assignment 6 as an oral presentation using PowerPoint. If you do not know how to use PowerPoint, have another student who does show you how, or use the tutorial that comes with the program.

PowerPoint is a powerful tool for presenting visuals in a talk. *But it is more often used poorly, as a crutch for nervous speakers, than it is used well, to supplement a talk.* Inexperienced speakers want the audience's eyes on anything else but them, so they pack everything they have to say into the PowerPoint slides and have the audience looking at the projections all through

www.mhhe.com/**crusius**

For further help on using Power-Point, visit the online tutorial at:

Writing > PowerPoint Tutorial

the speech. Do not do this. Use PowerPoint to present your graphics to the audience and to summarize major points. Otherwise, keep the audience looking at and listening to you, not staring at a projection screen. Show them a graphic, for instance, and then discuss it, but do not leave it on screen to distract attention from you. Do not read from your text or memorize it, but talk from a few notes to remind yourself of what you need to say. Remember: PowerPoint complements a speech in much the same way graphics complement a written text. Do not let it take over or allow anxiety to cause you to lean on it too hard.

Writing Research-Based Arguments

Most arguments are researched writing. You need to read sources to inform yourself about your topic, and then you need to cite sources in order to convince your readers that you have a good case. An argument with no research behind it is generally weak. Many published arguments may not appear to have research behind them. In journalism, sources may not be documented, but the authors have had to dig to learn the facts, and when they use someone else's views, they introduce that person as an authority because naming authorities' credentials strengthens a case.

Nevertheless, a researched argument must be your own case, with your own angle on the topic, not a case borrowed from your sources. The trick to writing well with sources is to keep them from taking over. You must be in charge, using your sources as supporting characters in what must remain your own show. This chapter will cover finding sources, evaluating them, using them in your own writing, and citing them correctly. To help you stay in charge through this whole process, we will emphasize the role of writing "behind the scenes" *before* you begin drafting your paper. The more you use writing to interact with your sources, to know them well, and to see what supporting parts they might play, the more you will be ready to write as the

www.mhhe.com/**crusius**

For a wealth of research resources, go to:

Research

author—the authority—of an argument of your own: an argument with your own claim, your own voice, your own design.

Using your sources with this kind of confidence helps reduce the possibility of misusing a source. Misuse of a source includes

- Taking material out of context and misrepresenting the viewpoint of the author. Most texts include "multiple voices"—that is, writers may describe opposing views, or they may speak ironically, so a casual reader may misunderstand their viewpoint. Applying the critical reading skills described in Chapter 2 will keep you from misusing a source.

- Using material without giving credit to the source. If you use someone else's words, you must put quotation marks around them. If you use someone else's ideas, even in your own words, you must give that other person credit. Failure to do so is plagiarism. Because plagiarism is a growing problem, partly owing to the ease with which material can be cut and pasted from online sources, we have devoted Chapter 7 to ethical writing and plagiarism. Because some plagiarism is not intentional—students may not understand what constitutes fair use of a source or may not realize how to paraphrase adequately and accurately—we recommend that you read this brief chapter before you start working with the sources you find.

Research takes time and patience; it takes initiative; it takes genuine curiosity. You have to recognize what you do not know and be willing to accept good evidence even if it contradicts what you previously believed. The first step in research is finding an issue that is appropriate.

www.mhhe.com/**crusius**

For more information on plagiarism, go to:

Research > Plagiarism

FINDING AN ISSUE

Let's say you have been assigned to write an argument on an issue of current public concern. If you have no idea what to write about, what should you do?

Understand the Difference between a Topic and an Issue

People argue about issues, not about topics. For example, global warming is a topic. It is the warming of the earth's atmosphere, a scientific observation. However, people argue about many issues related to the topic of global warming, such as whether human activity has contributed to the temperature increase. This was the argument made by the film *An Inconvenient Truth*. The conversation on that issue is subsiding because even the oil companies have come to accept the evidence about the effects of manmade greenhouse gases. But other issues remain, such as what sources of energy are the best alternatives to the fuels that produce greenhouse gases and how individuals might change their lifestyles to make less of an impact on global climate. The point here: To write a good argument, you must explore genuine questions at issue, not just topics. Furthermore, you should explore a question that really interests you. You also must care about your issue.

Find Issues in the News

Pay attention to the news and to the opinions of newsmakers, leaders, and commentators. College students are busy, but there are some easy ways to keep abreast of issues in the news. Here are hints for various news sources.

The Internet

Set one of the major news organizations or newspapers as your home page so that when you turn on your computer, the news will be the first thing you see. Some options are

Cable News Network	<http://www.cnn.com>
Microsoft NBC News	<http://www.msnbc.com>
National Public Radio News	<http://www.npr.org/>
The *New York Times*	<http://www.nytimes.com>
The *Wall Street Journal*	<http://www.wsj.com>

If you moved away to go to college, choose the online version of your hometown paper as a way of keeping in touch with events back home as well as around the world.

Library Online Databases and Resources

Your college library likely subscribes to many online databases and resources that you can search to find issues of current interest. See pages 107–112 for more about online library resources. A good place to look for issues is CQ Researcher. See Figure 6.1 for a look at this Web site. This division of Congressional Quarterly (CQ Press) allows you to search for issues and browse reports and pro–con statements from professional researchers. Although the reports offer only a general overview, they are a good starting point for further research, as each report concludes with a bibliography listing books, articles, and Web sites about the issue.

Magazines and Newspapers

Browse your campus bookstore or library for magazines devoted to news and current affairs. In the library, ask for directions to the "recent periodicals" area. In addition to the obvious choices such as *Time* and *Newsweek,* look for the more opinionated magazines such as *Utne Reader, New Republic,* and *National Review.* For more coverage of issues, look for *Atlantic Monthly, Harper's, Science,* and *National Geographic.*

Lectures, Panel Discussions, Class Discussions, Conversations

Hearing in person what others have to say on an issue will help expose the important points and raise questions for research. Seek out discussion of issues you are considering for research.

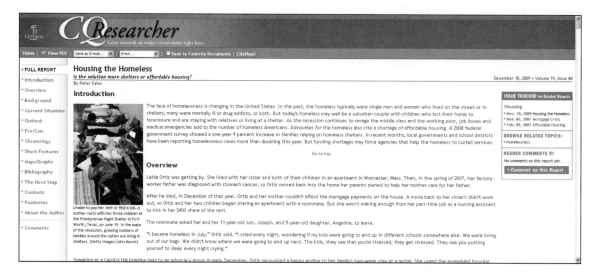

Figure 6.1

CQ Researcher home page. The menu on the left allows you to browse through a list of issues and find articles for researching them.

Personal Observations

The best way to find an engaging issue is to look around you. Your instructor may not give you total freedom to choose an issue, but many current events and social concerns touch our daily lives. For example, the student whose paper we use as an example of researched writing found her issue when she realized the connection between something close to home that had been bothering her and the general topic area her instructor had specified for the class: global warming.

Finding an Issue on the Topic of Global Warming: A Student Example

Student Julie Ross was in a class that had been assigned the topic of global warming. To find an issue, Julie attended an on-campus screening of *An Inconvenient Truth,* followed by a panel discussion featuring representatives of government agencies, environmentalists, and professors of earth science. Julie asked the panelists what individual citizens could do to reduce their contributions to greenhouse gases. One panelist suggested that consuming "less stuff" would make a difference because the production of consumer goods contributes to carbon dioxide and other greenhouse gases. Because Julie was already fuming about old houses on her street being torn down and replaced with supersized McMansions, she decided to research the question of how destructive this kind of development is, not just to the immediate neighborhood, but also to the planet. She began wondering about its contribution to global warming and how much more energy it demands, because the new houses use much more energy than the ones they replace. She decided to write her paper to an audience of home buyers. If she could discourage them from buying these huge new houses, the developers would have to stop building them. To make a convincing case, Julie needed to find good arguments for preserving the older homes and evidence about how much more energy the large new homes use than the older, smaller ones. Julie's paper appears on pages 157–166.

 **www.mhhe.com/crusius** You'll find more tools to help you find an issue at:
Learning > Links Across the Curriculum > Refdesk.com

FINDING SOURCES

The prospect of doing research can be overwhelming, given the many possible avenues to explore: the Internet, newspapers, magazines and journals, and all kinds of books. You need a strategy to guide you most efficiently to the best sources on your topic. The quality of your paper depends on its ingredients; you want to find not just *any* sources but the most credible, appropriate, and—if you are writing about current events—the most recent.

As you begin your research, two tips will make the journey much more efficient and orderly—and less stressful.

1. Keep a research log. Keep a record of your research by writing informally about what you do in each session of searching. Some things to record are:

    *   search terms you used, noting which ones were good and which were less productive

    *   ideas and questions that occur to you while browsing and reading

    *   notes about catalogs and indexes you searched on any particular day

    *   complete bibliographical information about each source you plan to use and notes about what the source contains and how you might use it

    *   personal responses to sources you read and notes about how different sources compare or contrast on the same topic or issue

    Your research log could be handwritten in a notebook or typed into a computer file or an electronic source management tool like Zotero or EndNote, available through many schools' library Web sites. You may have folders for different kinds of notes (such as search terms or responses to sources). You may organize all or part of your log like a diary with daily notes on the progress of your research. In whatever form or forms you choose, a research log helps you keep track of sources so you do not have to retrace steps, and it positions you to have your own views and voice when writing your argument.

2. Make and store complete copies of sources that you may use. Depending on the source, you may make photocopies or printouts or download documents (such as PDFs) of sources you think you will use. You will want to annotate all your sources and mark them up, and your instructor might require that you submit them with your paper. When copying, be sure to get all the information; avoid cutting off page numbers. With a book, capture the title page and the copyright page on the flip side; you will need this information when citing the source. With online sources, when given the option, choose to print out PDF files because these have page numbers, which makes citing much easier. Also copy any information about the author. Clip, clamp, and label these copies. Keep them in a file folder or binder.

Field Research

Consider beginning your research with what you can observe. That means going out into the "field," as researchers call it, and recording what you see, either in written notes or with photographs or drawings. Field research also can include recording what you hear, in audiotapes and in notes of interviews and conversations. An interview can take place online, through e-mails or a chat, if you can preserve it. Following are some suggestions for field research.

Observations

Do not discount the value of your own personal experiences as evidence in making a case. You will notice that many writers of arguments offer as evidence what they themselves have seen, heard, and done.

Alternatively, you may seek out a specific personal experience as you inquire into your topic. For example, one student writing about homelessness in Dallas decided to visit a shelter. She called ahead to get permission and schedule the visit. Her paper was memorable because she was able to include the stories and physical descriptions of several homeless women, with details of their conversations.

Julie Ross began her research by walking the streets of her neighborhood, photographing the stark contrasts of size and style between the older homes and the new ones built on the sites of torn-down houses. Her photographs provided evidence for her case against supersized homes in historic communities.

Questionnaires and Surveys

You may be able to get information on some topics, especially if they are campus related, by doing surveys or questionnaires. This can be done very efficiently in electronic versions (Web-based or e-mail). Be forewarned, however, that it is very difficult to conduct a reliable survey.

First, there is the problem of designing a clear and unbiased survey instrument. If you have ever filled out an evaluation form for an instructor or a course, you will know what we mean about the problem of clarity. For example, one evaluation might ask whether an instructor returns papers "in a reasonable length of time"; what is "reasonable" to some students may be too long for others. As for bias, consider the question "Have you ever had trouble getting assistance from the library's reference desk?" To get a fair response, this questionnaire had better also ask how many requests for help were handled promptly and well. If you do decide to draft a questionnaire, we suggest you do it as a class project so that students on all sides of the issue can contribute and troubleshoot for ambiguity.

Second, there is the problem of getting a representative response. For the same reasons we doubt the results of certain magazine-sponsored surveys of people's sex lives, we should be skeptical about the statistical accuracy of surveys targeting a group that may not be representative of the whole. For example, it would be impossible to generalize about all first-year college students in the United States based on a survey of only your English class—or even the entire first-year class at your college.

Surveys can be useful, but design, administer, and interpret them carefully.

Interviews

You can get a great deal of current information by talking to experts. As with any kind of research, the first step in conducting an interview is to decide exactly what you want to find out. Write down your questions.

The next step is to find the right person to interview. As you read about an issue, note the names (and possible biases) of any organizations mentioned; these may have local offices, the telephone numbers of which you could easily find. In addition, institutions such as hospitals, universities, and large corporations have public relations offices whose staffs provide information. Also, do not overlook the expertise available from faculty members at your own school.

Once you have determined possible sources for interviews, you must begin a patient and courteous round of telephone calls, continuing until you connect with the right person; this can take many calls. If you have a subject's e-mail address, you might write to introduce yourself and request an appointment for a telephone interview.

Whether your interview is face to face or over the telephone, begin by acknowledging that the interviewee's time is valuable. Tell the person something about the project you are working on, but withhold your own position on any controversial matters. Sound neutral and be specific about what you want to know. Take notes, and include the title and background of the person being interviewed and the date of the interview, which you will need to cite this source. If you want to tape the interview, ask permission first. Finally, if you have the individual's mailing address, send a thank-you note after the interview.

If everyone in your class is researching the same topic and more than one person wants to contact the same expert, avoid flooding that person with requests. One or two students could do the interview and report to the class, or the expert could visit the class.

Library and Internet Research

Since much of what is now published in print is also available online, the distinction between library and Internet research has blurred. You will be able to find many magazines, scholarly journals, and newspapers through the Internet, and many Internet sites through your library's online directories. Because so many documents are now electronic—even if they appeared first in print—librarians have coined the term "born digital" to distinguish purely cyberspace documents from documents that were born in print but have been made available online.

With the daily additions to information, articles, images, and even books available online, the resources for searching it are constantly being upgraded. The advice in this chapter should get you started, but it's always a good idea to consult your library's reference librarians for help with finding sources on your topic. They know what is in your school's library, what is online, and what the latest tools are for finding any kind of source. You will find these librarians at the reference desk; every library has one.

 **www.mhhe.com/crusius**   To find online guidance for using the library, check out:
Research > Using the Library

Kinds of Sources

The various kinds of sources available in print and online include books and periodicals as well as electronic media.

Books   Nonfiction books generally fall into three categories:

Monographs: Monographs are sustained arguments on a single topic. To use them responsibly, you should know the complete argument; that means reading the entire book, which time may not allow. Possibly, reading the introduction to a book will acquaint you with the author's argument well enough that you can selectively read sections of the book. Decide if you have time to use a book responsibly. Sometimes you can find a magazine or journal article by the author that covers some of the same ground as the book but in a condensed way.

Anthologies: These are collections of essays and articles, usually by many different writers, selected by an editor, who writes an introductory essay. Anthologies are good sources for short papers because they offer multiple voices, and each argument can be read in one sitting. Pay attention to whether a book is an anthology because you will cite these anthology selections differently from a regular book. Look near the back of the book for information about the author of any selection you choose to use.

Reference books: These are good for gathering background information and specific facts on your topic. You can find these online and on the library shelves; they cannot be checked out. Reference books include specialized encyclopedias on almost any subject, such as *The Encyclopedia of Politics and Religion* (CQ Press, 2007). We will tell you below how to search for encyclopedias and other reference books. Many reference books are now available electronically.

A note of caution about Wikipedia: *Wikipedia* is not a scholarly publication. In fact, it encourages a democratic notion of knowledge in which anyone can contribute, add to, alter, or delete material that has been posted on a topic. Although the editors scan it regularly for misinformation, errors, and deliberate lies, there is no guarantee that what you find there is credible. We suggest you use it for background information and for links to other, more authoritative sources whose authors' credentials you can confirm. Check any facts you plan to use in your papers against other, more scholarly sources.

A note of caution about general encyclopedias: Multivolume online and print encyclopedias such as *Britannica* and *Microsoft Encarta* are good for background knowledge as you begin research on a topic or for fact-checking while you are writing. However, college students should not use general encyclopedias as primary sources. The entries do not cover topics in depth and are not usually products of original research. It is better to use specialized encyclopedias and reference works or books and articles by specialists in your topic.

Periodicals Periodicals are published periodically—daily, weekly, monthly, quarterly. They include the following types:

Articles in scholarly journals: These journals are usually published by university presses and aimed at readers in a particular scholarly discipline: Both the authors and intended readers are professors and graduate students. Scholarly articles are contributions to ongoing debates within a discipline. Therefore, they are credible sources, but scan them for accessibility. If you are not familiar with the debate they are joining, you may not find them accessible enough to use responsibly. Seek your instructor's help if you find a source hard to comprehend. Scholarly journals are usually born in print and put online, but some are born digital.

Articles in magazines: Magazines—print, online, and the born digital "e-zines"—are good sources for short papers. Magazine articles vary greatly, depending on their intended readership. Some magazines, such as *Atlantic Monthly, Harper's, National Review, New Republic,* the *New Yorker,* and even *Rolling Stone,* offer articles by scholars and serious journalists. They give arguments on current public issues by the same people who write for scholarly journals, but the articles are aimed at an educated public readership, not other scholars. These are perfect for familiarizing yourself with viewpoints on an issue. You can find even more accessible articles and arguments in weekly newsmagazines, including columns by nationally syndicated writers. Trade magazines are good for business-related topics; Julie Ross found several online magazines published for the building industry. Many advocacy groups also publish magazines in print and online. Julie found ecological advocacy groups' magazines, such as *E: The Environmental Magazine,* helpful in her research.

Newspapers: Newspapers are ideal sources for arguments and information on current as well as historical issues. Feature articles, which are long and in-depth, usually present the reporter's angle on the topic; opinion columns are arguments and therefore good for getting perspectives on your topic. Major national newspapers such as the *Washington Post, Wall Street Journal,* and *New York Times* should be available online through your library's catalog, as will the local newspaper for your college's city or town. Below, we tell more about how to search for newspaper articles.

Audiovisual Materials   You should be aware of the many resources for finding visuals to use in your paper and also to view as sources of information. You can find images by searching the Internet. Also, your library's online resources page may have a link to digital resources, as does the Library of Congress's Digital Collections and Services, which is a free resource available online. See Figure 6.2, for a look at this Web site.

Web Sites   Web sites include nearly every kind of source described above and more. You have to evaluate everything you find in the wild and open world of cyberspace, but nearly all research institutes and centers associated with universities, advocacy groups, government bureaus, and political organizations are excellent sources for your arguments. Also, most writers these days have their own page on the Web, where you can go to find more about their lives, views, and other writing, so the Web is a great resource for learning more about your sources. The only problem is searching the Web efficiently, and we offer advice later in this chapter on how to zero in on the best sites for your topic.

Blogs, Listservs, Usenet Groups, Message Boards   The Web has become an exciting place for dialogue, where scholars within an area of interest can argue with each other and ask each other for help with their research. Although a first-year student may not feel ready to enter these discussions,

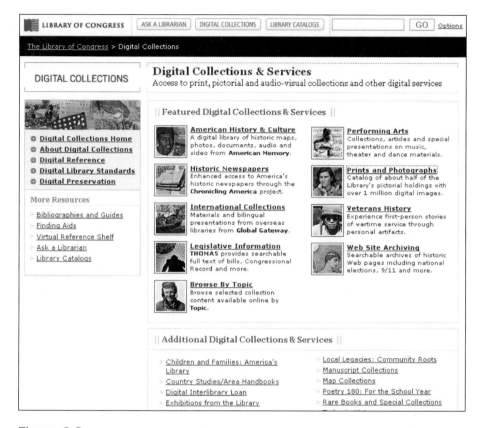

Figure 6.2

This page from the Library of Congress Web site gives you an idea of the range of audiovisual material available to you.

"lurking"—reading a discussion without contributing to it—is a great way to learn about the debates firsthand. And an intelligent question will find people ready to share their knowledge and opinions. We'll tell you later in this chapter about directories that will take you to the most relevant resources for your topic.

Choose the Best Search Terms

The success of your search depends on what terms you use. Before beginning, write down, in your notebook or research log, possible terms that you might use in searching for sources on your topic. Do this by examining your research question to find its key terms. As you begin doing your research, you will discover which of these terms are most productive and which you can cross out. Adapt your search terms as you discover which ones are most productive.

We'll use Julie's search to illustrate how to find the best search terms. Julie's research question was, What are the negative effects of tearing down older homes and replacing them with bigger new ones? Julie wanted to know more about the environmental effects of large homes, both on climate change globally and on the local neighborhoods.

Use Keyword Searching   Keyword searches use as search terms the words that most often are used to refer to your topic. Julie's topic, the construction of large new houses replacing old ones, is often referred to as the teardown trend, so she used "teardowns" in a keyword search.

Use Phrase Searching   You can combine words to create a search term. When you do this, your search engine may want you to put quotation marks or parentheses around the combined terms so it recognizes them as one idea. For example, Julie also used the phrase "neighborhood preservation" to find sources on her topic.

Use Boolean Searching   Boolean searching (named after nineteenth-century English logician George Boole) allows you to narrow or broaden your search by joining words with AND OR NOT

> **AND:** "home size" AND "energy consumption"

Using AND narrowed Julie's search. However, she found nothing by combining "home size" AND "global warming." She needed to think more specifically about the connection between home size and global warming: Energy consumption is the link. (Note: Google and most other search engines automatically put AND in when you type words in succession.)

> **OR:** "green houses" OR "sustainable homes"

Using OR broadened the search, yielding more hits. Using OR is helpful if you know your subject has many synonyms, such as *youth, teenagers, students.*

> **NOT:** "green house" NOT agriculture

Using NOT limited the search by eliminating references to hothouses in agriculture.

Use Subject Words   Keyword searches may not work well in some indexes and databases that have been compiled under strict subject headings. Different search engines and databases will have different official subject headings. For example, the Library of Congress uses "electric automobiles" as a subject heading, whereas the online library subscription database Academic OneFile uses the subject heading "electric cars."

Most university libraries use the Library of Congress subject words for books in their online catalogs. You can go to the Library of Congress Subject

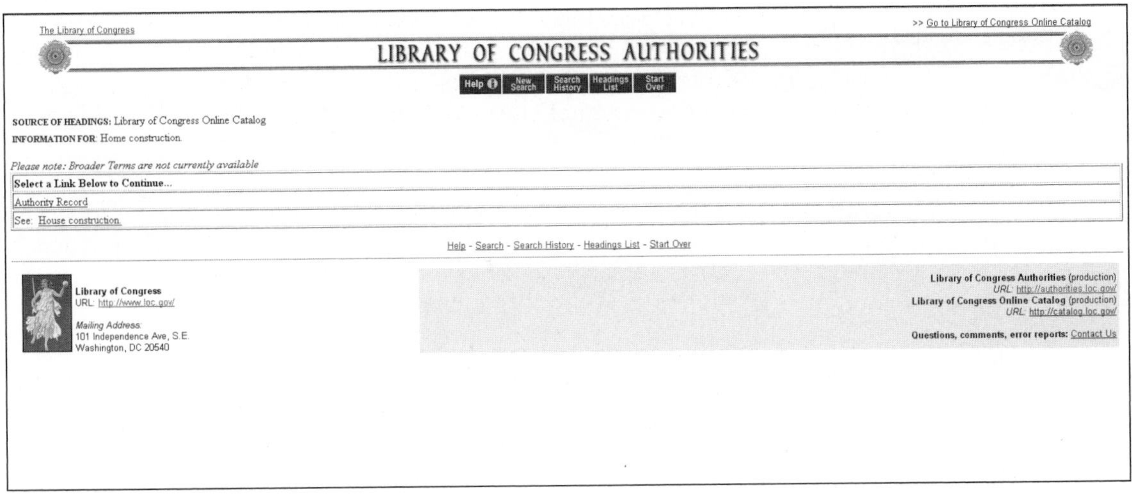

Figure 6.3

The Library of Congress Authorities Web site will tell you the correct search term for finding books on your topic.

Authorities site to find the correct subject headings. When Julie went to the Library of Congress Subject Authorities site, she found that "house construction" was the correct search term, not "home construction."

The Library of Congress helps you find correct subject headings at its Library of Congress Authorities Web site: <http://authorities.loc.gov/>. Figure 6.3 shows the results of a search for correct subject headings. Or you can go directly to your library's catalog and type what you think might a good search term. The catalog should then direct you to the correct subject heading for that topic. For example, if you type in "electric cars" in your library catalog, you will be told to "See 'electric automobiles'."

Searching Your Library

Because much of the research material on the Internet is available for free through your school's library, it makes sense to start with your library's resources. Why pay for something that you already have free access to through your college or university? Also, unlike much of what you find on the Internet, the materials available through your library have been selected by scholars, editors, and librarians, so you can be more confident about the credibility of what you find.

Don't assume that searching the library means using bound books and periodicals only, or even going there in person. Libraries are going electronic, giving you online access to more high quality, full-text sources than you will find on the Web. Libraries subscribe to online indexes and

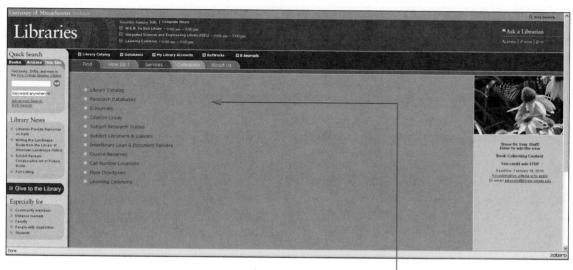

Figure 6.4
A library home page

Use the link to research databases (often called online resources) to find articles in magazines, newspapers, and scholarly journals.

journals that cannot be found through search engines like Google and Yahoo!. Your enrollment at school gives you access to these resources, which are described later in this chapter. Your library's online home page is the gateway to all the library's resources. Figure 6.4 is an example of a library home page. Many librarians create research guides to the resources their library offers in various subject areas, including first-year writing, as shown in Figure 6.5.

Your Library's Online Catalog

Your library's online catalog is the gateway to a wealth of sources: books, both printed and online in the form of e-books that you can "check out" and download; full-text online newspapers, including the complete archives of these papers; indexes to individual articles in magazines, newspapers, and scholarly journals, including links to the full text of most of them online; audiovisual materials; maps; and reference books of all kinds. Visit the home page of your library's online catalog and explore the places it will take you. In the library catalog, you can search for books by title, author, subject, and keyword, as well as their Library of Congress call numbers. Here are some tips:

> *In a title search:* If you know a title you are looking for, do a title search with as much of the title needed to distinguish it from other titles. Omit initial articles (*a, the, an*).

> *In a subject search:* You will need to know what "subject heading" the Library of Congress has given your topic. Julie, for example, found

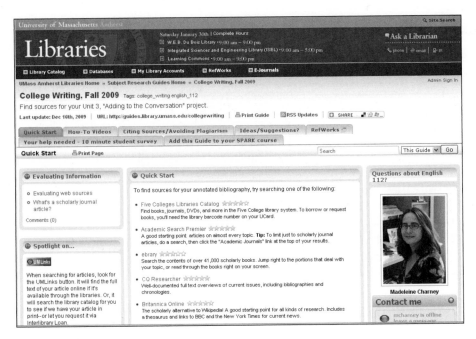

Figure 6.5

A research guide to college writing

no books in her library catalog when she typed in "home construction" but found twenty-five books when she typed in "house
construction." See pages 105–107 for more about subject headings.
Or just try a keyword search, described below.

In a keyword search: This kind of search is more forgiving than a
subject search and can be helpful if you don't know the exact right
word. Put quotation marks around phrases: "global warming." You
can use AND or OR to combine terms: "teardowns" AND "neighborhood preservation."

The library's online catalog will also tell you if your library subscribes to a
particular newspaper or magazine. The catalog will not tell you about individual articles or stories in these periodicals, but you can find them by searching the publication's own online index or the online databases in your library,
described on the next page. Most university libraries now subscribe to major
U.S. newspapers and have full-text archives online. Do a title search to find
out if your library has a particular newspaper.

To locate reference books, combine your keyword search with words like
encyclopedia, dictionary, or *almanac,* and you will find both online and

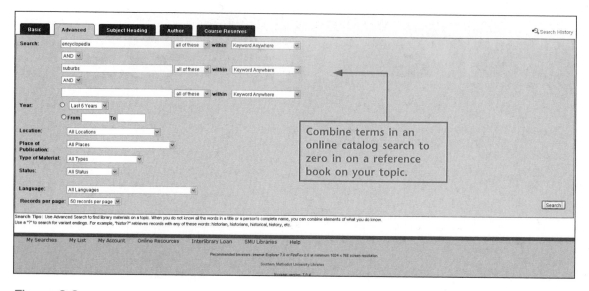

Figure 6.6

A search in an online catalog for specialized encyclopedias about suburbs

on-the-shelf reference books. For an example of such a search and an example of a result, see Figures 6.6 and 6.7.

Your Library's Online Resources

Your school library's purchased online resources are available only to students, faculty, and staff. Students can access them on campus or off campus by using a password. The main Web page of most university libraries offers a link to a page listing the online resources available to you. These usually include reference resources: dictionaries such as the Oxford English Dictionary; electronic encyclopedias, journals, and magazines; and most important, licensed databases to help you search for a wide variety of sources on any topic, both on and off the Web.

These databases are indexes to articles in periodicals: magazines, scholarly journals, and newspapers. You search them by typing in a subject, keyword, author, or title. In most cases the search will produce a list of articles, an abstract of the article, and often, a link to full text of the article, which you can then save or print out.

If the full text is not available online, the database will tell you if the periodical is in your library's holdings. You may be able to access it electronically through the online catalog. This is why it is good to know which magazines, journals, and newspapers are cataloged along with the books in your library's online catalog.

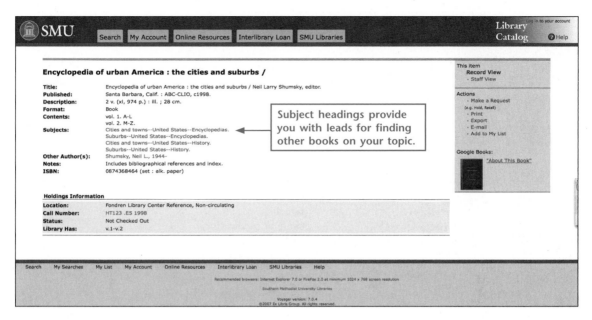

Figure 6.7

The result of an online search for encyclopedias about suburbs

Never use the abstract of an article as a source. Abstracts may not be written by the source's author; they may not be accurate. Most important, you cannot get the in-depth understanding of a source that would allow you to use it accurately.

The following are some common databases subscribed to by college libraries:

Academic Search Complete

Academic OneFile

LEXIS-NEXIS Academic

Business Source Complete

Communication and Mass Media Complete

Film and Television Literature Index

TOPICsearch (good for social, political, and other topics popular in classroom discussions)

Using the "advanced search" in databases like Academic OneFile and Academic Search Complete (illustrated in Figure 6.8) allows you to combine terms to narrow your search. Julie Ross eliminated all hits not related to housing by including "houses" as a second term in her search. Note that both

Figure 6.8
Results of an advanced search for newspaper articles in a database

databases allow you to select from academic journals, popular magazines, newspapers, or all three. The search in Figure 6.8 targeted newspapers only.

Internet Research

Because the Internet is so large—estimated to contain over 11.5 billion Web pages—we want to caution you about the potential for wasting time if you start browsing with one of the common search engines such as Yahoo! or Google. However, there are some ways to use search engine features to narrow your search. One of those ways is to limit your search to certain domains.

Domains

Every Internet address or URL (Uniform Resource Locator) has certain components; it helps to know a little about them. What is known as the "top level domain name" tells you something about who put the site on the Web. For Web sites from the United States, the following are the four most common top level domain names. Web sites from other nations typically have instead an abbreviation of the country's name.

www.mhhe.com/crusius

For further advice on using the Internet to conduct research, go to:

Research > Using the Internet

Commercial (.com) "Dot com" sites include businesses and their publications—such as the real estate newsletter at <http://www.teardowns.com>—other commercial publications, such as magazines; and personal Web pages and blogs, such as those created on Blogger.com. The example, www.teardowns.com, is a site assisting builders who want to construct on the sites of torn-down houses. Although you will find magazine and newspaper articles through search engines like Yahoo! and Google, a better way to ensure that you get them in full text for free is to find them through your library's licensed databases, as described on page 110. Because so much of the Web is commercial sites, you will probably want to use the advanced search options explained in the next section to filter "dot com" sites from your search.

Nonprofit Organizations (.org) "Dot org" sites include organizations and advocacy groups, such as the National Trust for Historic Preservation at <http://www.nationaltrust.org/teardowns/>. Their purpose is to raise awareness of, participation in, and donations to their causes.

Educational Institutions (.edu) "Dot edu" sites contain research and course materials of public and private schools, colleges, and universities. The URL <http://sciencepolicy.colorado.edu/> is a site for a center at University of Colorado at Boulder doing research on science, technology, and public policy. Although mostly what you find at these sites is the work of professors, some of the material may be by graduate and undergraduate students, so as always, check out the author's credentials.

Government Agencies (.gov) "Dot gov" sites are useful for getting the latest information about any aspect of American government or about government agencies and policies. The URL <http://www.census.gov/> leads to articles published by the U.S. Census Bureau.

Advanced Features for Searching the Web

Search engines provide a variety of ways to focus your search, and Google has some that are especially useful for students.

Advanced Searches Search engines will let you customize your search, allowing you to limit your search to just one or two of the domains listed above, or to exclude one. Filtering out the "dot com" sites is like turning on a spam blocker, so you will get fewer hits by writers with no academic or professional credentials. Figure 6.9 shows how to filter Web searches.

Google Specialized Searches Google offers an ever-increasing number of specific kinds of searches, such as News Archives, Books, Images, and Earth. Many link you to materials that you will have to pay for. However, you can probably find many of these for free through your school library, which

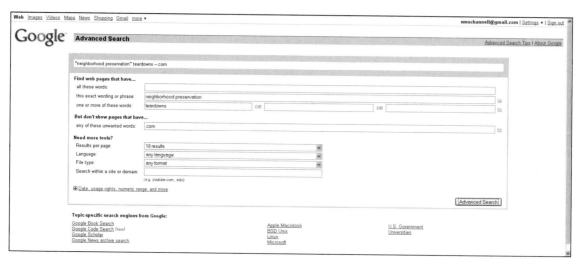

Figure 6.9

Narrow your Google searches by using the advanced search window to combine terms and exclude Web sites in specific domains, like .com.

subscribes to the archives of many magazines and newspapers. See the earlier section, "Your Library's Online Resources," on page 110.

Google Scholar Google Scholar is where your library and the Internet intersect. Google Scholar is an index to scholarly articles and book reviews, many of them available at your university library. If you open Google Scholar from a computer on campus or if your home computer connects to your school's network (or if you have a password that will grant you off-campus access to your school's network), you will be able to access full texts of materials available from your school's library.

Subject Directories to the Web

You can narrow your search for Web sites by going first to a subject directory that organizes Web sites by topic (Figure 6.10). Some examples are

Google

Yahoo!

Exalead

Infomine (assembled by librarians, not machines)

About.com

Other Web Resources: Blogs, Listservs, Message Boards, and Chat Groups

Don't overlook the potential of interactive sites on the Internet. Many authors of your sources have blogs and personal Web pages where they try

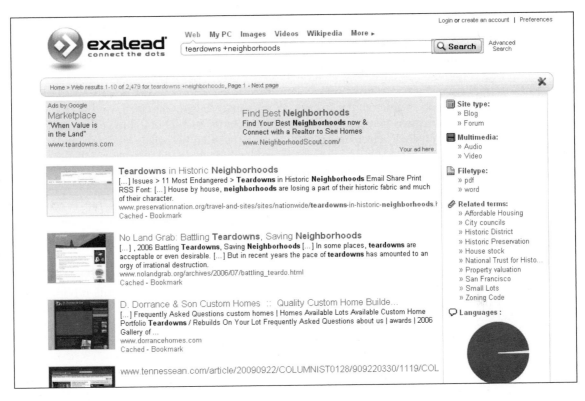

Figure 6.10
Exalead is a new competitor to Google that you may want to try.

out new ideas and get feedback from others interested in their topics. As a student, you may not feel ready to join these conversations, but you can learn a lot by lurking—that is, just reading them. You can find them by using "blogs," "listservs," "message board," or "chat room" as a search term in your browser.

www.mhhe.com/**crusius**   For more online research resources, go to:
Research > Additional Links on Research

EVALUATING SOURCES

Before beginning to read and evaluate your sources, you may need to reevaluate your issue. If you have been unable to find many sources that address the question you are raising, consider changing the focus of your argument.

Once you are sure that sources are available on your topic, use the following method to record and evaluate them.

www.mhhe.com/**crusius**

For a tutorial on evaluating sources, go to:

Research > Source Evaluation Tutor: CARS

Eliminate Inappropriate Sources

You may find that some books and articles are intended for audiences with more specialized knowledge than you have. If you have trouble using a source, put it aside, at least temporarily.

Also, carefully review any electronic sources you are using. Although search engines make it easy to find material on the Web, online documents often have met no professional standards for scholarship. Material can be "published" electronically without review by experts, scholars, and editors that must occur in traditional publishing. Nevertheless, you will find legitimate scholarship on the Internet—news reports, encyclopedias, government documents, and even scholarly journals appear online. The freedom of electronic publishing creates an exciting and democratic arena, but it also puts a much heavier burden on students and researchers to ensure that the sources they use are worthy of readers' respect.

Carefully Record Complete Bibliographic Information

For every source you consider using, be sure to record full bibliographic information (Figure 6.11). Take this information from the source itself, not from an index, which may be incomplete or inaccurate. If you make a record of this information immediately, you will not have to go back later to fill in omissions.

Read the Source Critically

As discussed in Chapter 2, critical reading depends on having some prior knowledge of the subject and the ability to see a text in context. As you research a topic, your knowledge naturally becomes deeper with each article you read. But your sources are not simply windows, giving you a clear view; whether argumentative or informative, they have bias. Before looking through them, you must look *at* your sources. Know the answers to the following questions.

Who Is the Writer, and What Is His or Her Bias?

Is there a note that tells about the writer's professional title or institutional affiliation? If not, search the Internet for the writer's personal home page or university Web site. Do an author search in your library's catalog and online databases to find other books and articles by the writer.

How Reliable Is the Source?

Again, checking for credibility is particularly important when you are working with electronic sources. For example, one student found two sites on the Web, both through a keyword search on "euthanasia." One, entitled "Stop

Print Sources	Electronic Sources
Book • Author's full name (or authors' names) • Title of book, including subtitle • City where published • Publisher • Year published	**Document found on the Internet:** • Author's full name (or authors' names) • Title of the work • Original print date, if applicable • Title of the database or Web site • URL • Date you accessed the document
Article or essay in a collection • Author's full name (or authors' names) • Title of article or essay • Title of book • Editor's name (or editors' names) • City where published • Publisher • Year published • Inclusive page numbers of the article.	**Web site, listserv, or blog:** • Author's full name (or authors' names) • Title of post or subject line • Title of Web site or blog • Date of the posting • URL • Date you accessed the site
Article in a periodical • Author's full name (or authors' names) • Title of the article • Title of the periodical • Date of the issue • Volume number, if given • Library database if retrieved online (example, Academic OneFile) and date you retrieved it • Page numbers on which article appears	

Figure 6.11

Working bibliography entries

the Epidemic of Assisted Suicide," was posted by a person identified only by name, the letters MD, and the affiliation "Association for Control of Assisted Suicide." There was no biographical information, and the "snail mail" address was a post office box. The other Web site, "Ethics Update: Euthanasia," was posted by a professor of philosophy at the University of San Diego whose home page included a complete professional biography detailing his education, titles, and the publishers of his many books and articles. The author gave his address at USD in the Department of Philosophy. The student decided that, although the first source had some interesting information—including examples of individual patients who were living with pain rather than choosing suicide—it was not a source that skeptical readers would find credible. Search engines often land you deep within a Web site, and you have to visit the site's home page to get any background information about the source and its author. Be suspicious of sites that do not contain adequate source information; they probably aren't reliable.

"I just feel fortunate to live in a world with so much disinformation at my fingertips."

When Was This Source Written?

If you are researching a current issue, decide what sources are too old. Arguments on current issues often benefit from earlier perspectives.

Where Did This Source Appear?

If you are using an article from a periodical, be aware of the periodical's readership and editorial bias. For example, *National Review* is conservative, *The Nation* liberal. An article in the *Journal of the American Medical Association* will usually defend the medical profession. Looking at the table of contents and scanning editorial statements will give you a feel for the periodical's politics. Also look at the page that lists the publisher and editorial board. You will find, for example, that *New American* is published by the ultra-right-wing John Birch Society. If you need help determining bias, ask a librarian. A reference book that lists periodicals by subject matter and explains their bias is *Magazines for Libraries*.

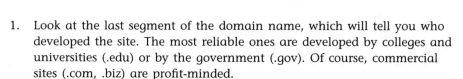

Additional Guidelines for Evaluating Internet Sources

1. Look at the last segment of the domain name, which will tell you who developed the site. The most reliable ones are developed by colleges and universities (.edu) or by the government (.gov). Of course, commercial sites (.com, .biz) are profit-minded.

2. Does the site have a link to information about the person or organization that put it on the Internet? What can you find out about the education and professional credentials of the author or sponsor?

3. If the site is run by an organization, how is it funded? On the site or elsewhere, look for information about funding and donations. Look for conflict of interest or bias in, for example, a site that publishes about the environment but whose corporate donors have been charged with violating environmental protection laws.

4. Check whether the source includes a bibliography, a sign of scholarly work.

5. A tilde (~) indicates a personal page; these pages must be evaluated with special care.

What Is the Author's Aim?

First, determine whether the source informs or argues. Both are useful and both will have some bias. When your source is an argument, note whether it aims primarily to inquire, to convince, to persuade, or to mediate.

How Is the Source Organized?

If the writer doesn't use subheadings or chapter titles, break the text into parts yourself and note what function each part plays in the whole.

Special Help with Evaluating Web Sites

The Internet is a dangerous place for researchers in a hurry. If you are not careful to look closely at what you find on the Web, you could embarrass yourself badly. For example, why would a college student want to cite a paper written for a high school class? Many high school teachers put their best student papers on class sites—good papers, but nevertheless, not exactly the kind of authority a college student should be citing. So before choosing to use something from the Web, go through the following checklist:

1. **Know the site's domain.** See pages 112–113 for how to read a Web address and what the various domain suffixes tell you about the site. Note if the site is commercial, educational, governmental, or some

kind of advocacy group. Advocacy groups are usually indicated by *.org* in the domain name. Commercial sites may be advertising something—they are not disinterested sources.

2. **Find the home page.** A search engine or online directory may take you to a page deep within the site; always look for links back to the home page because that is where you can find out more about the bias of the site and the credentials of the people behind it.

3. **Read about the bias and mission of the site.** At the home page, you should see a link to more information about the site—often the link is called "About Us" or "Mission Statement." Follow it and learn about the ideology of the site and how it compares with your own bias and that of other sources you are using.

4. **Read about the credentials of the site's creators.** The creators' degrees and professional affiliations should be easy to find. Regard any site as bogus if the only link to finding more about the authors is an e-mail address. Also, note whether the credentials of its board of directors or trustees are in the fields of specialization for your topic. For example, many writers for some Web sites on global warming dispute scientific findings, but are not scientists. They may be economists or historians.

5. **Note if the site reports on its funding and donors.** The rule of "follow the money" becomes important when you are using sources outside of the academic world. Think tanks and advocacy groups receive money from large corporations. Consider how the funding might influence their research and reported findings. There should be a link to material about funding, corporate sponsors, and the group's annual tax reports.

6. **Note how current the site is.** Near the beginning or the end of any Web site or part of a Web site, you should be able to find a note about when the site was last updated. You will need this information in order to cite the site—a site that has not been updated in years is not a good choice.

The Web site for the National Trust for Historic Preservation (Figure 6.12), where Julie found a speech about the effects of teardowns on neighborhoods, checks out as a credible site. From the home page, Julie was able to link to a page titled "About the National Trust" (Figure 6.13), where she learned that it is a private, nonprofit organization founded in 1949 and dedicated to saving historical places. It advocates for legislation to protect communities and places of cultural heritage. The home page also provides a link titled "Funding," with information about donations, corporate sponsors, and tax returns. A link to the organization's "Management" gave the credentials of its trustees and its executive staff, including Richard Moe, the author of the speech. Julie learned that Moe graduated from

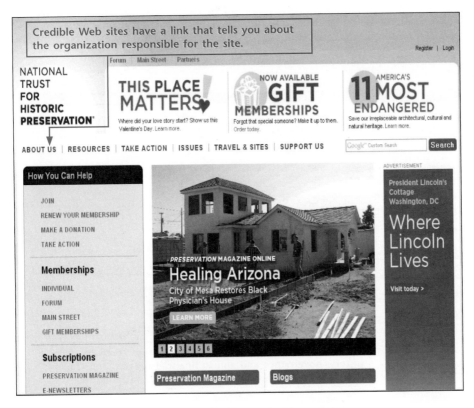

Figure 6.12

The home page of the Web site of the National Trust for Historic Preservation

Williams College in 1959 and from the University of Minnesota Law School in 1966. He has been president of the National Trust since 1993. He is an honorary member of The American Institute of Architects and coauthor of a book titled *Changing Places: Rebuilding Community in the Age of Sprawl*, published in 1997. Clearly, this source from a Web site passed the test.

USING SOURCES

The first way to use your sources is to familiarize yourself with viewpoints on your topic. Your thesis will grow out of your research; you do not do research to find information to support a position you have not investigated. In high school, you may have grabbed quotations or facts from a source; in college you must know the source itself, including something about the author and the author's argument, unless your source is an encyclopedia or

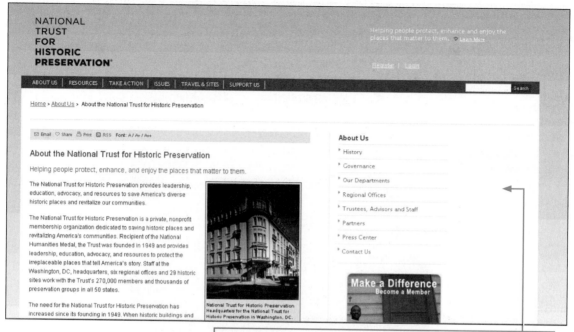

Figure 6.13
"About Us" page on Web site

The organization should provide information about its purpose, history, governance and annual financial reports, and leaders. Reject Web sites that do not provide such information.

almanac or other reference work. For more on getting to know sources, read Chapter 2, "Reading an Argument," and the preceding section in this chapter, "Evaluating Sources," pages 116–121.

When you have gathered and evaluated some sources, you should next spend some time with each one, reading it, marking it up, and writing about it in your notebook or on a notepad. This essential step will help you use your sources confidently and accurately in a paper with your own angle and voice. One teacher calls this step "writing in the middle" because it bridges the gap between the sources you have found and the paper you will turn in. If you skip this step, you risk misrepresenting your source, taking material out of context, plagiarizing (see Chapter 7, "Ethical Writing and Plagiarism"), or, more commonly, letting your sources take over with too much of their voice and wording, resulting in a paper that sounds patched together.

Because you should not use a source that you have not read in its entirety, we reproduce below one of Julie Ross's sources for her argument on neighborhood preservation. We will demonstrate various kinds of informal writing about this source.

Note that we have annotated this reading, an important step you should perform for every source you plan to use.

Battling Teardowns, Saving Neighborhoods

RICHARD MOE, president of the National Trust for Historic Preservation

Speech given to the Commonwealth Club, San Francisco, CA; June 28, 2006.

Note author's credentials

A growing disaster is tearing apart many of America's older neighborhoods. They're being devoured, one house at a time, here in the Bay Area, across California, and in scores of communities from coast to coast.

I'm talking about teardowns—the practice of purchasing and demolishing an existing house to make way for a new, much bigger house on the same site. Teardowns wreck neighborhoods. They spread through a community like a cancer, destroying the character and livability that are a neighborhood's lifeblood. I believe teardowns represent the biggest threat to America's older neighborhoods since the heyday of urban renewal and interstate highway construction during the 1950s and 60s.

Quotable passage here

Claim

Here's how it works: Developers and home-buyers look through desirable neighborhoods for a building lot that can lawfully accommodate a much bigger house than that which currently stands on it. The property is acquired, the existing house is torn down and a bigger house is constructed in its place. There are variations: Sometimes a large estate is leveled and subdivided to accommodate several new houses; in others, several smaller houses are cleared to make way for a single, massive new one.

Extent of the problem

It's a simple process, but it can totally transform the streetscape of a neighborhood and destroy its character. It's especially destructive in older and historic communities.

5   Teardowns are occurring all over America—from fashionable resorts such as Palm Beach and Palm Springs to the inner-ring suburbs around Washington and Chicago and the Richmond District here in San Francisco. The trend has become so alarming that the National Trust included "Teardowns in Historic Neighborhoods" on our list of America's 11 Most Endangered Historic Places in 2002. Back then, we identified 100 communities in 20 states that were having major problems with teardowns. That statistic was troubling in 2002—but four years later, the news is much worse: Today we can document the impact of teardowns in more than 300 communities in 33 states. The National Association of Home Builders says that 75,000 houses are razed and replaced with larger homes each year. . . .

Background information

This disaster goes by many names. In New Jersey, the practice is often called "bash-and-build." In Colorado, teardowns are known as "scrape-offs." In Oregon, the new houses are sometimes called "snout houses" because of the big, protruding garages that dominate their facades. In other places they're known simply—and aptly—as "bigfoots" or "monster homes."

Extent of the problem

Whatever you call it, one teardown usually sparks others. A New Jersey builder says, "It's a trend that keeps on rolling. Builders used to be afraid to be the first person in a neighborhood to tear a house down. Now they're looking around and saying they don't mind taking the risk."

Why is this happening?

Three factors are at work in the spread of teardowns.

10

More background

One reason for teardowns

Other reasons for teardowns

Reason against tearing down: effect on neighborhood

15

Another reason against teardowns

The first is the rise in real-estate prices. In some areas, home values have doubled or tripled over the past decade, and this leads developers to look for "undervalued" properties—many of which exist in older neighborhoods.

The second factor is the trend toward bigger houses. In 1950, the average American home incorporated less than 1,000 sq. ft. By 2005, the average new home had more than doubled in size, to 2,412 sq. ft. According to the National Association of Home Builders, almost 40% of new homes have four or more bedrooms; that's more than twice as many as in the early 1970s—despite the fact that the average family size decreased during that same period. Subdivisions of luxury homes of 5,000 sq. ft. and more are becoming commonplace. Clearly, burgers and french fries aren't the only things in America being "super-sized."

The final factor is that many people are looking for an alternative to long commutes or are simply fed up with the soulless character of sprawling new subdivisions. For these people, older in-town neighborhoods and inner-ring suburbs are enormously appealing because of their attractive architecture, mature landscaping, pedestrian orientation, easy access to public transportation and amenities such as local shopping districts, libraries and schools.

The problem is that too many people try to impose their preference for suburban-style mini-mansions on smaller-scale neighborhoods where they just don't fit. And since most of these older areas offer few vacant lots for new construction, the pressure to demolish existing houses can be intense. A modest cottage gets torn down and hauled off to the landfill, and what goes up in its place is "Tara" on a quarter-acre lot.

Neighborhood livability is diminished as trees are removed, backyards are eliminated, and sunlight is blocked by bulky new structures built right up to the property lines. Economic and social diversity are reduced as costly new "faux chateaux" replace more affordable houses—including the modest "starter homes" that our parents knew and that first-time homebuyers still search for today. . . .

While the destruction of historic houses is wasteful, environmentally unsound and unnecessary, it's often just the beginning of the problems caused by teardowns.

It's not uncommon for a demolished older home to be replaced with a new one that is three times as big as any other house on the block. These structures loom over their neighbors and break the established building patterns of the area. Front yards are often given over to driveways, and three- or four-car garages are the dominant elements in the façade. Floor plans are often oriented to private interior spaces, making the new houses look like fortresses that stand totally aloof from their surroundings. . . .

Apart from their visual impact, teardowns can profoundly alter a neighborhood's economic and social environment. A rash of teardowns can cause property taxes to rise—and while this may be a good thing for communities in search of revenue, it can drive out moderate-income or fixed-income residents. Those who remain start to feel they've lost control of their neighborhood to developers and speculators. A house that once might have been praised as "charming and historic" now gets marketed as "older home on expansive lot"—which is realtor language for "teardown." Once that happens—once the value of an older house is perceived to be less than that of the land it's built on—the house's days are probably numbered. And sadly, the neighborhood's days as a viable historic enclave may be numbered too.

It doesn't have to be this way. There are alternatives to teardowns.

First of all, prospective builders should realize that most older, established neighborhoods simply can't accommodate the kind of sprawling new mini-mansion that is appropriate on a suburban cul-de-sac. People who want to move into the city can often find development opportunities in underused historic buildings and vacant land in older areas. Even in areas where vacant land is scarce, existing older houses can be enlarged in sensitive ways: A new zoning ordinance in Coronado, California, for example, gives homebuilders "bonus" square footage if they incorporate design elements that maintain the historic character of the community.

20   No one is saying that homebuyers shouldn't be able to alter or expand their home to meet their needs, just as no one is saying that older neighborhoods should be frozen in time like museum exhibits. A neighborhood is a living thing, and change is both inevitable and desirable. The challenge is to manage change so that it respects the character and distinctiveness that made these neighborhoods so appealing in the first place.

Let me mention a few things that people and communities can do.

First and most important, communities must realize that they aren't helpless in the face of teardowns. They have choices: They can simply take the kind of community they get, or they can go to work to get the kind of community they want. They have to decide what they like about the community and don't want to lose. They must develop a vision for the future of their community, including where and how to accommodate growth and change. Then they must put in place mechanisms to ensure that their vision is not compromised.

Ideally, this consensus-building should take place as part of a comprehensive planning process—but that can take time, and sometimes the pressure of teardowns calls for immediate action. In those situations, some communities have provided a "cooling-off" period by imposing a temporary moratorium on demolition. This moratorium prevents the loss of significant structures while allowing time for residents and city officials to develop effective means of preserving neighborhood character.

One of those means is local historic district designation. Notice that I said "local historic district." Many people believe that listing a property in the National Register of Historic Places is enough to protect it, but that isn't true. The only real protection comes through the enactment of a local ordinance that regulates demolition, new construction and alteration in a designated historic area. More than 2,500 communities across the country have enacted these ordinances. Most of them require that an owner get permission before demolishing or altering a historic building; many also offer design guidelines to ensure that new buildings will harmonize with their older neighbors.

25   If historic district designation isn't feasible or appropriate, other forms of regulation may work. Conservation districts or design-review districts can address issues such as demolition and new construction with less administrative burden than

Alternatives to tearing down

Qualification of his argument

Solutions to the problem

More solutions

historic districts. Floor-area ratios or lot-coverage formulas can remove the economic incentive for teardowns by limiting the size of new buildings. In the same way, setback requirements, height limits and open-space standards can help maintain traditional neighborhood building patterns. At least two communities in San Mateo County have recently adopted regulations of this sort to limit the height and floor area of newly built homes.

Not all approaches require government involvement. Local preservation organizations or neighborhood groups can offer programs to educate realtors and new residents about the history of older neighborhoods and provide guidance in rehabbing or expanding older houses. They can acquire easements to ensure that the architectural character of historic buildings is permanently protected. They can provide low-interest loans to help encourage sensitive rehabilitation. Incentives such as these are particularly effective when combined with technical assistance and some form of tax abatement from state or local government.

Opposing view and rebuttal

Some people go so far as to claim that teardowns actually support smart growth by directing new-home construction to already-developed areas, thereby increasing density and offering an alternative to suburban sprawl. Again, I disagree.

Tearing down a smaller house to build a bigger one simply adds square footage, not population density. In addition, teardowns affect neighborhood livability, reduce affordability, consume energy, and send thousands of tons of demolition debris to landfills. That doesn't sound like smart growth to me.

Equally important, teardowns exact too high a price in the wasteful destruction of our nation's heritage. Of course we need to encourage investment in existing communities as an alternative to sprawl—but not at the expense of the historic character that makes older neighborhoods unique, attractive and livable. Some say that change is simply the price of progress—but this kind of change isn't progress at all; it's chaos.

30

The National Trust is committed to helping local residents put the brakes on teardowns. It will be a huge job—but it's eminently worthy of our best efforts.

America's older neighborhoods are important chapters in the story of who we are as a nation and a people. Working together, we can keep that story alive. Working together, we can keep America's older and historic communities intact so that generations to come can live in them, learn from them, be sheltered and inspired by them—just as we are today.

Writing Informally to Gain Mastery over Your Sources

The more you engage your sources with informal "talk-back" such as annotations, notebook responses to the ideas in the sources, notebook entries that make connections between and among ideas in sources, and paraphrases and summaries that make you really think about the key points and passages, the easier it will be for you to assume the voice of authority when it is time to start drafting your paper. Here are some suggestions for writing in the middle zone between researching and drafting.

1. Annotate the Source

Use the advice in Chapter 2, "Reading an Argument," which suggests things to look for in sources that are arguments. If a source is not an argument, annotate to comment on the author's angle, bias, and main points.

2. Respond to the Source in Your Notebook

After annotating, write more in your notebook about how you might use the source. If you have roughed out a case, note which reason or reasons of your own case this source could help you develop. If you find a new reason for your case, note it and think how you could develop it with your own observations and other sources you have found.

If you think the source will be mainly useful for facts, make a note about what kind of facts it has and the page numbers, so that when you start drafting, you can find them quickly.

If the author is an expert or authority, note the credentials or at least where you can go to find these as you start drafting—perhaps the author's Web page or a biographical note at the end of the book or article.

If this will be a major source for your paper, you should be sure you grasp the most important concepts in it. Look for the passages that pose a challenge; to use the source with authority, you need to own, not borrow, these ideas. That means instead of just dropping them in as quotations, you will have to work them in, explaining them in your own words. Try out *paraphrases* (see more on paraphrases in item 3 in this list) to make these points completely clear to you and then respond to the major ideas with what you think about them: If it's a good idea, why do you think so? What in your own experiences (field research) confirms it? What can you add of your own as you discuss this idea in your paper?

Look for memorable passages that are worth *direct quotations* (see more on direct quotations in this chapter's section on incorporating source material). The best quotes are strongly worded opinions and writing that cannot be paraphrased without losing its punch.

Think about how additional research might help you develop an idea given to you by this source.

The box on page 128 shows some notes Julie put in her notebook after deciding to use the National Trust source.

3. Paraphrase Important Ideas from the Source

Although you will use paraphrases as you incorporate material from your sources into your essay, consider paraphrase as a study skill that helps you understand key ideas by putting them into your own words. It helps you to "own" the key ideas rather than simply borrowing the author's words to insert into your paper. Here are some suggestions for paraphrasing:

- Read the entire source or section in which the passage appears. You cannot write a good paraphrase of a passage you have taken out of

Notes on Moe, Richard. "Battling Teardowns."

- *Perfect source for my paper. I need to mention the National Trust for Historic Preservation. This source supports my "preserve the neighborhood character" reason. Good description of the garages—"snout houses." Also mention the way these new houses block the sunlight. Good on the economic impact on the older people in my neighborhood. Many can't afford to stay. This source helps explain why.*

- *I also hadn't thought about how these homebuyers are destroying the very thing that makes them want to live here. Old charm won't last if everybody does what they are doing. This could appeal to their interest—restore, not tear down.*

- *I like the part about allowing for change. I'll use this quote:* <u>*"A neighborhood is a living thing. Change is both inevitable and desirable."*</u> *What kinds of changes would I consider OK? Could a new house of different architectural style actually add character to the neighborhood? Maybe look for a source that describes some kind of acceptable change.*

- *He mentions the other part of my case, the environment, but not enough to use this source for that part.*

context. Surrounding sentences will provide information essential for understanding the material you are paraphrasing, and to make the idea clear to yourself, you may need to add some of that information to your paraphrase. Later, if you use the paraphrase in your paper, you will need to provide enough context so that your readers will understand the idea as well.

- Read the passage several times through, including surrounding text, until you think you understand it. Annotate it. Look up any words that are even slightly unfamiliar to you.

- Put the text away so that you will not be tempted to look at it. Then think of the main ideas and try to put each one into your own words and your own wording. A paraphrase must not be an echo of the original's sentence patterns with synonyms plugged in. That is really a form of plagiarism because it involves "stealing" the author's sentence pattern. You may want to break up complex sentences into shorter, more simple ones that make the idea easier to comprehend.

- Do not feel that you must find a substitute word for every ordinary word in the passage. For example, if a passage has the word *children*, don't feel you have to say *kids*.

- Go back and check your paraphrase against the original to see if you have accurately represented the full content of the original passage. Make adjustments as needed.

Examples of Adequate and Inadequate Paraphrasing

Original Passage:

> Some people go so far as to claim that teardowns actually support smart growth by directing new-home construction to already-developed areas, thereby increasing density and offering an alternative to suburban sprawl. Again, I disagree. Tearing down a smaller house to build a bigger one simply adds square footage, not population density.

Inadequate Paraphrase: This example borrows too much of the wording and sentence patterns (underlined) from the original text by Moe.

> Some people even claim that tearing down old houses supports smart growth by increasing new-home construction and density in already developed areas. Therefore, teardowns are an alternative to suburban sprawl. Moe disagrees because tearing down small houses and building bigger ones only adds more square footage, not more people.

Inadequate Paraphrase: The paraphrase below doesn't do justice to the idea: It does not include the concept of smart growth; it does not mention the problem of new development in suburban areas versus rebuilding in existing neighborhoods; and it does not give Moe credit for the opinion.

> It's not smart to tear down old houses and replace them with bigger ones because you don't get more population density.

Good Paraphrase: This explains "smart growth," gives Moe credit, and represents all the points in original sentence patterns. It even offers an interpretation at the end.

> Smart growth is an attempt to develop cities while minimizing suburban sprawl. According to Moe, tearing down older, small homes in close-in neighborhoods and replacing them with bigger ones is not really "smart growth" because bigger houses do not necessarily increase population density; they just offer more square footage for the same size household. So they are really a kind of urban sprawl.

4. Write Summaries of Portions of a Source

As a way to help get your own handle on important sections of a source, write a summary of it in your notebook. That means putting just the most important parts of the text into your own words (paraphrase) and joining them into a smooth paragraph. To write a summary, follow these steps.

1. Read and reread the portion of a text you want to summarize, looking up unfamiliar words.
2. Choose the main points.
3. Paraphrase them, using the advice on paraphrasing above.
4. Combine sentences to make the new version as concise as possible.

Guidelines for Summarizing

1. Read and reread the original text until you have identified the claim and the main supporting points. You ought to be able to write an outline of the case, using your own words. Depending on your purpose for summarizing and the amount of space you can devote to the summary, decide how much, if any, of the evidence to include.

2. Make it clear at the start whose ideas you are summarizing.

3. If you are summarizing a long passage, break it down into subsections and work on summarizing one at a time.

4. As with paraphrasing, work from memory. Go back to the text to check your version for accuracy.

5. Maintain the original order of points, with this exception: If the author delayed presenting the thesis, refer to it earlier in your summary.

6. Use your own words.

7. Avoid quoting entire sentences. If you want to quote keywords and phrases, incorporate them into sentences of your own, using quotation marks around the borrowed words.

Here is an example of a portion of Richard Moe's speech that Julie used in her paper by shortening it and presenting it in her own words. The underlined sections are the ones she deemed important enough to go into the summary.

Original Passage:

Three factors are at work in the spread of teardowns.

The first is the rise in real-estate prices. In some areas, home values have doubled or tripled over the past decade, and this leads developers to look for "undervalued" properties—many of which exist in older neighborhoods.

The second factor is the trend toward bigger houses. In 1950, the average American home incorporated less than 1,000 sq. ft. By 2005, the average new home had more than doubled in size, to 2,412 sq. ft. According to the National Association of Home Builders, almost 40% of new homes have four or more bedrooms; that's more than twice as many as in the early 1970s—despite the fact that the average family size decreased during that same period. Subdivisions of luxury homes of 5,000 sq. ft. and more are becoming commonplace. Clearly, burgers and french fries aren't the only things in America being "super-sized."

The final factor is that many people are looking for an alternative to long commutes or are simply fed up with the soulless character of sprawling new subdivisions. For these people, older in-town neighborhoods and inner-ring suburbs are enormously appealing because of their attractive

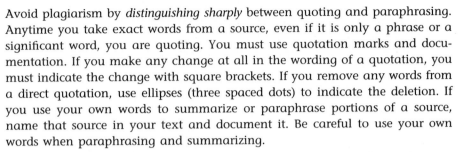

Guidelines for Writing with Sources

Avoid plagiarism by *distinguishing sharply* between quoting and paraphrasing. Anytime you take exact words from a source, even if it is only a phrase or a significant word, you are quoting. You must use quotation marks and documentation. If you make any change at all in the wording of a quotation, you must indicate the change with square brackets. If you remove any words from a direct quotation, use ellipses (three spaced dots) to indicate the deletion. If you use your own words to summarize or paraphrase portions of a source, name that source in your text and document it. Be careful to use your own words when paraphrasing and summarizing.

1. Use an attributive tag such as "According to . . ." to introduce quotations both direct and indirect. Don't just drop them in.

2. Name the person whose words or idea you are using. Provide the full name on first mention.

3. Identify the author(s) of your source by profession or affiliation so that readers will understand the significance of what he or she has to say. Omit this if the speaker is someone readers are familiar with.

4. Use transitions into quotations to link the ideas they express to whatever point you are making.

5. If your lead-in to a quotation is a phrase, follow it with a comma. But if your lead-in can stand alone as a sentence, follow it with a colon.

6. Place the period at the end of a quotation or paraphrase, after the parenthetical citation, except with block quotations. (See page 136 for treatment of block quotations.)

architecture, mature landscaping, pedestrian orientation, easy access to public transportation and amenities such as local shopping districts, libraries and schools.

Julie's Summary:

Moe sees three reasons for the increase in teardowns:

- In the past decade, the value of houses has doubled or tripled, except in some older neighborhoods. Developers look for these "'undervalued' properties" to build on.

- Homebuyers want more space, with the average home size going from 1,000 square feet in 1950 to 2,412 square feet in 2005.

- Some homebuyers desire to move from the "soulless . . . sprawling subdivisions" to close-in neighborhoods that have more character and more amenities, such as public transportation and local shopping.

5. Write Capsule Summaries of Entire Sources

Writers frequently have to summarize the content of an entire source in just a brief paragraph. Such summaries appear in the introduction to a volume of

Sample Entry in an Annotated Bibliography

Here is an annotated bibliography entry for Julie's National Trust source.

> Moe, Richard. "Battling Teardowns, Saving Neighborhoods." *The National Trust for Historic Preservation.* June 28, 2006. Web. Jan. 21, 2007.
>
> In this transcript of a speech given to a San Francisco civic organization, Moe, who is president of the National Trust for Historic Preservation, argues that builders should respect the integrity of older neighborhoods and that local residents should join the Trust's efforts to block the teardown trend, which is fueled by rising real estate values, homebuyers' desire for bigger houses, and fatigue with life in the distant suburbs. Teardowns "wreck neighborhoods" by removing trees and backyards, blocking the sun, ruining historic character, raising taxes so that poorer residents are forced out, and generating environmental waste. Communities can organize to fight teardowns by applying for historical designation or other kinds of government regulations on building as well as offering incentives for realtors and new buyers to respect neighborhood quality.

collected essays, in an opening section of scholarly articles in which the author reviews previously published literature on the topic, and at the end of books or articles in annotated bibliographies or works cited lists. The purpose of these is to let other scholars know about sources they might also want to consult.

If your class is working on a common topic, your instructor may ask the class to assemble a working bibliography of sources all of you have found, including a brief summary of each one to let other students know what the source contains. This is called an "annotated bibliography." Following is some advice on creating capsule summaries and annotated bibliographies.

1. As explained in Chapter 2, "Reading an Argument," read and annotate the entire source, noting claims, reasons, the subdivisions into which the text breaks down, and definitions of words you looked up.

2. Working with one subdivision at a time, write paraphrases of the main ideas in each. Decide how much specific evidence would be appropriate to include, depending on the purpose of your summary. As with any paraphrase, work from memory and recheck the original later for accuracy.

3. You may include brief direct quotations, but avoid quoting whole sentences. That is not efficient.

4. Join your paraphrases into a coherent and smooth paragraph.

5. Edit your summary to reduce repetitions and to combine points into single sentences where possible.

Note that a good capsule summary restates the main points; it doesn't just describe them.

> *Not:* Moe gives three reasons for the rise of the teardown trend.

> *But:* Moe argues that the teardown trend is fueled by rising real estate values, homebuyers' desire for bigger houses, and fatigue with life in the distant suburbs.

6. Dialogue about Sources

Inside or outside of class, any conversations you can have about your research with others researching the same topic will help you get an angle and an understanding of your sources. This is the reason many scholars keep blogs—a blog is a place to converse about ideas. Your instructor may set up an electronic bulletin board for students to chat about their research, or you might make your own blog with friends and start chatting.

INCORPORATING AND DOCUMENTING SOURCE MATERIAL

We turn now to the more technical matter of how to incorporate source material in your own writing and how to document it. You incorporate material through direct quotation or through summary or paraphrase; you document material by naming the writer and providing full publication details of the source—a two-step process. In academic writing, documenting sources is essential, with one exception: You do not need to document sources of factual information that can easily be found in common references, such as an encyclopedia or atlas, or of common knowledge. See page 168 in Chapter 7, "Ethical Writing and Plagiarism," for more explanation of common knowledge.

Different Styles of Documentation

Different disciplines have specific conventions for documentation. In the humanities, the most common style is the Modern Language Association (MLA). In the physical, natural, and social sciences, the American Psychological Association (APA) style is most often used. We will illustrate both in the examples that follow. Both MLA and APA use parenthetical citations in the text and simple, alphabetical bibliographies at the end, making revision and typing much easier. (For a detailed explanation of these two styles, visit the Web sites for the MLA and the APA.)

In both MLA and APA formats, you provide some information in the body of your paper and the rest of the information under the heading "Works Cited" (MLA) or "References" (APA) at the end of your paper. The following summarizes the essentials of both systems.

www.mhhe.com/**crusius**

For Web sites with information on documentation styles, go to:

Research > Annotated Links to Documentation Sites

www.mhhe.com/**crusius**

You can find more documentation information at:

Research > Links to Documentation Sites

www.mhhe.com/**crusius**

For a student sample of a paper
in MLA format, go to:

Research > Sample Paper
in MLA Style

MLA Style

In parentheses at the end of both direct and indirect quotations, supply the last name of the author of the source and the exact page number(s) where the quoted or paraphrased words appear. Online sources often have no page numbers. If an online source is a PDF file, it should have page numbers. You need to use them. If the name of the author appears in your sentence that leads into the quotation, omit it in the parentheses.

Direct quotation with source identified in the lead-in:

> According to Jessie Sackett, a member of the U.S. Green Building Council, home ownership is "the cornerstone of the American dream. Recently, however, we've realized that keeping that dream alive for future generations means making some changes to how we live today" (36).

Indirect quotation with source cited in parenthetical citation:

> A spokesperson for the U.S. Green Building Council reminds us that home ownership is fundamental to the American dream; however, in order to preserve that dream for the generations to come, we need to develop more energy efficient houses and lifestyles today (Sackett 36).

APA Style

www.mhhe.com/**crusius**

For a student sample of a paper
in APA format, go to:

Research > Sample Paper
in APA Style

In parentheses at the end of direct or indirect quotations, place the author's last name, the date published, and the page number(s) where the cited material appears. If the author's name appears in the sentence, the date of publication should follow it in parentheses; the page number still comes at the end of the sentence. Unlike MLA, the APA style uses commas between the parts of the citation and "p." or "pp." before the page numbers.

Direct quotation with source cited in the lead-in:

> Jessie Sackett (2006), a member of the U.S. Green Building Council, writes, "Owning a home is the cornerstone of the American dream. Recently, however, we've realized that keeping that dream alive for future generations means making some changes to how we live today" (p. 36).

Indirect quotation with source cited in parenthetical citation:

> A spokesperson for the U.S. Green Building Council reminds us that home ownership is fundamental to the American dream; however, in order to preserve that dream for the generations to come, we need to develop more energy efficient houses and lifestyles today (Sackett, 2006, p. 36).

Direct Quotations

Direct quotations are exact words taken from a source. The simplest direct quotations are whole sentences worked into your text, as illustrated in the following excerpt. Any citations in the text of your paper must match up with an entry on the works cited or reference list.

MLA Style

> Richard Moe of the National Trust for Historic Preservation explains, "The problem is that too many people try to impose their preference for suburban-style mini-mansions on smaller scale neighborhoods where they just don't fit."

This source will be listed in the MLA Works Cited list as follows:

> Moe, Richard. "Battling Teardowns, Saving Neighborhoods." *The National Trust for Historic Preservation.* 28 June 2006. Web. 15 Jan. 2007.

APA Style

> Richard Moe (2006) of the National Trust for Historic Preservation explains, "The problem is that too many people try to impose their preference for suburban-style mini-mansions on smaller scale neighborhoods where they just don't fit."

This source will be listed in the APA reference list as follows:

> Moe, R. (2006, June 28). Battling teardowns, saving neighborhoods. Retrieved Jan. 15, 2007, from *The National Trust for Historic Preservation* Web site: http://www.nationaltrust.org/news/2006/20060628_speech_sf.html

Altering Direct Quotations with Ellipses and Square Brackets

Although there is nothing wrong with quoting whole sentences, it is often more economical to quote some words or parts of sentences from the original in your own sentences. When you do this, use *ellipses* (three evenly spaced periods) to signify the omission of words from the original; use square *brackets* to substitute words, to add words for purposes of clarification, and to change the wording of a quotation so that it fits gracefully into your own sentence. (If ellipses already appear in the material you are quoting and you are omitting additional material, place your ellipses in square brackets to distinguish them.)

The following passages illustrate quoted words integrated into the sentence, using ellipses and square brackets. The citation is in MLA style.

Square Brackets Use square brackets to indicate any substitutions or alterations to a direct quotation.

Original passage:

> Teardowns wreck neighborhoods. They spread through a community like a cancer, destroying the character and livability that are a neighborhood's lifeblood.

Passage worked into the paper: Part of the quotation has been turned into paraphrase.

> Moe compares the teardown trend to a cancer on the community: "Teardowns wreck neighborhoods. They [destroy] the character and livability that are a neighborhood's lifeblood."

Ellipses Use three spaced periods to indicate where words have been removed from a direct quotation.

Original passage:

> Almost every one of these new, large homes is made out of wood—roughly three-quarters of an acre of forest. Much of the destructive logging around the world is fueled by our demand for housing. But homebuilding doesn't have to translate into forest destruction. By using smart design and forest-friendly products, builders can create new homes that save trees and money.
>   Many houses today are still built using outdated, inefficient construction methods. About one-sixth of the wood delivered to a construction site is never used, but simply hauled away as waste.

Passage worked into the paper: Two entire sentences have been removed, replaced with ellipses, because they were not relevant to the point Julie was making. There are no quotation marks because this will be a blocked quotation in the paper.

> Almost every one of these new, large homes is made out of wood—roughly three-quarters of an acre of forest. Much of the destructive logging around the world is fueled by our demand for housing. . . . Many houses today are still built using outdated, inefficient construction methods. About one-sixth of the wood delivered to a construction site is never used, but simply hauled away as waste.

Using Block Quotations

In MLA style, if a quoted passage runs to more than four lines of text in your essay, indent it one inch (ten spaces of type) from the left margin, double-space it as with the rest of your text, and omit quotation marks. In block quotations, a period is placed at the end of the final sentence, followed by one space and the parenthetical citation.

> In a consumer society, when people see their neighbors driving a new car, they think they need to buy a new one too. This is called "keeping up with the Joneses." Gregg Easterbrook has coined a new phrase, "call and raise the Joneses." He explains his new term this way:

> > In call-and-raise-the-Joneses, Americans feel compelled not just to match the material possessions of others, but to stay ahead. Bloated

> houses, for one, arise from a desire to call-and-raise-the-Joneses—
> surely not from a belief that a seven-thousand-square-foot house that
> comes right up against the property setback line would be an ideal
> place in which to dwell. (140)

In APA style, use the block form for quotations of more than forty words. Indent the block five spaces from the left margin. Double-space all blocked quotations.

Indirect Quotations

Indirect quotations are paraphrases or summaries of a source. Here is how this quotation might be incorporated in a paper as an indirect quotation.

MLA Style

> A spokesperson for the U.S. Green Building Council reminds us that home ownership is fundamental to the American dream; however, in order to preserve that dream for the generations to come, we need to develop more energy efficient houses and lifestyles today (Sackett 36).

The entry in the Works Cited list would appear as follows:

> Sackett, Jessie. "The Green American Dream: LEED for Homes Is Currently Being Piloted." *The LEED Guide: Environmental Design & Construction.* 9.6 (2006): 36+. *Academic OneFile.* Web. 18 Oct. 2006.

APA Style

> A spokesperson for the U.S. Green Building Council reminds us that home ownership is fundamental to the American dream; however, in order to preserve that dream for the generations to come, we need to develop more energy efficient houses and lifestyles today (Sackett, 2006, p. 36).

The entry in the References list would appear as follows:

> Sackett, J. (2006). The green American dream: LEED for homes is currently being piloted. *The LEED Guide: Environmental Design & Construction.* 9.6 (2006): 36+. Retrieved from Academic OneFile.

In-Text References to Electronic Sources

The conventions just described apply to print sources. Adapt the examples to Internet and other electronic sources. Because you must include the electronic sources in your works-cited or reference list, your in-text citations should connect the material quoted or paraphrased in your text to the matching work or posting on the list. Therefore, your in-text citation should begin with the author's name or, lacking that, the title of the work or posting. The APA format requires that you also include the posting date.

Leading into Direct Quotations

Direct quotations need to be set up, not dropped into your paper. Setting up a quotation means leading into it with words of your own. A lead-in may be a short introductory tag such as "According to Smith," if you have already introduced Smith, but lead-ins usually need more thought. You need to connect the quotation to the ideas surrounding it in the original source.

Provide enough of the original context to fit the quotation coherently into your paragraph. You may need to paraphrase some of the surrounding sentences from the original source from which the quotation was taken. If you have not done so already, you may need to introduce the speaker of the words, along with his or her credentials if the speaker is an important writer or authority.

Here is an example of a quotation that does not fit coherently into the student's paper.

Quotation dropped in:

> Affluent Americans are buying new super-sized homes in older, urban residential areas. These lots were once occupied by historic and humble homes. "Teardowns wreck neighborhoods. They [destroy] the character and livability that are a neighborhood's lifeblood" (Moe).

Here is how Julie Ross led into the same quotation so that her readers would know more about the speaker and his point.

Quotation worked in:

> Affluent Americans are buying new super-sized homes in older, urban residential areas. These lots were once occupied by historic and humble houses. The older houses are now known as "teardowns." In their place, towering "McMansions" dominate the street. Richard Moe, President of the National Trust for Historic Preservation, reports that teardowns affect over 300 U.S. cities, with a total of 75,000 older houses razed each year. Moe compares the teardown trend to a cancer on the community: "Teardowns wreck neighborhoods. They [destroy] the character and livability that are a neighborhood's lifeblood."

Introduces the speaker.

Provides context for the quotation.

Parenthetical citation of author's name not needed because author is cited in text.

CREATING WORKS CITED AND REFERENCE LISTS

At the end of your paper, include a bibliography of all sources that you quoted, paraphrased, or summarized. If you are using MLA style, your heading for this list will be *Works Cited;* if you are using APA style, it will be *References.* In either case, the list is in alphabetical order based on either the author's (or editor's) last name or—in the case of unidentified authors—the first word of the title, not counting the articles *a, an, the.* The entire list is double-spaced both within and between entries. See the Works Cited page of the sample student paper at the end of this chapter for the correct indentation and spacing.

www.mhhe.com/crusius

For an electronic tool that helps create properly formatted works-cited pages, go to:

Research > Bibliomaker

Note that MLA format requires that the first line of each entry be typed flush with the left margin; subsequent lines of each entry are indented half an inch (five spaces on a keyboard). The APA recommends the same indentation.

The following examples illustrate the correct MLA and APA style for the types of sources you will most commonly use.

MLA Style for Entries in the Works Cited List

The following pages show examples of how to cite the most commonly used kinds of sources in papers for first-year writing assignments. When putting entries into the Works Cited list,

- Put all entries, regardless of their genres and media, in alphabetical order according to the first word in each entry. This will usually be the lead author's or editor's last name or—if no author is named—the first word in the title that is not an article (*a, an, the*). See page 140 for an example.

- Do not number the entries.

- Double-space within and between entries; the list should look like the spacing in the rest of the paper.

- Begin each entry at the left margin and indent all subsequent lines by five spaces (one-half inch).

- Italicize titles of books, periodicals like magazines and journals, films, and other major works like Web sites and blogs.

- Put quotation marks around titles of articles and essays contained in periodicals or books of collected works, and around pages or posts found on a Web site.

- Capitalize all words in titles and subtitles except for articles (*a, an, the*), coordinating conjunctions (*and, or, but*) and prepositions. Always capitalize the first and last word of a title, regardless of its part of speech.

- Include subtitles of works; separate them from the title with a colon.

Books

The first word in each entry on the Works Cited list must match the in-text citation. The essential items are the

1. author's or editor's name, followed by a period (unless no author or editor is listed);

2. title of the work, followed by a period;

3. place of publication, followed by a colon;

4. publisher, followed by a comma; and

5. date of publication.

Do not cite page numbers for chapters or portions of entire books. Do cite page numbers for items in an anthology or collected set of works.

Book by a Single Author

> Urrea, Luis Alberto. *The Devil's Highway: A True Story.* New York: Little,
> 2004. Print.

Two or More Books by the Same Author Instead of repeating the author's name in your Works Cited list, give the name in the first entry only. For subsequent works, use three hyphens in place of the name, followed by a period. Arrange the works in alphabetical order according to the first word in the title of the work, excluding articles (*a, an, the*).

> Obama, Barack. *The Audacity of Hope: Thoughts on Reclaiming the
> American Dream.* New York: Crown, 2006. Print.
>
> ———. *Dreams from My Father: A Story of Race and Inheritance.* 1995.
> New York: Three Rivers, 2004. Print.

Note: For republished works, include the original date of publication immediately after the book's title.

Book by Two or Three Authors Put the name of the principal author (first author) first, beginning with his or her last name. Place a comma after the first author's name. Put the names of second and third authors in the regular order from first name to last name.

> Small, Gary, and Gigi Vorgan. *iBrain: Surviving the Technological
> Alteration of the Modern Mind.* New York: HarperCollins, 2008.
> Print.
>
> Booth, Wayne, Gregory G. Colomb, and Joseph Williams. *The Craft of
> Research.* 2nd ed. Chicago: U of Chicago P, 2003. Print.

Book by Four or More Authors You can use only the first author's name and the Latin abbreviation et al., meaning "and others." It is also correct to list all the authors in order, as with two or three authors.

> Bellah, Robert N., et al. *Habits of the Heart: Individualism and
> Commitment in American Life.* New York: Harper, 1958. Print.

Book with No Author or Editor Begin the citation with the title. In the Works Cited list, ignore articles *a, an,* and *the* when placing in alphabetical order.

> *The New York Times Guide to Essential Knowledge: A Desk Reference for
> the Curious Mind.* New York: St. Martin's, 2004. Print.

Book by a Corporate Author or Government Agency Treat the corporation or agency as an author.

> Modern Language Association. *MLA Handbook for Writers of Research
> Papers.* 7th ed. New York: Modern Language Association of
> America. 2009. Print.

Anthology or Edited Compilation Place a comma after the editor's name and add the abbreviation for editor.

> Shreve, Susan Richards, ed. *Dream Me Home Safely: Writers on Growing Up in America.* Boston: Houghton, 2003. Print.

Work in an Anthology For works in collections of essays, poetry, and short stories, put the author of the individual work first, followed by its title in quotation marks, then the title of the collection in italics. The editor's name follows in normal order. Note that entries for works in anthologies do include the inclusive page numbers of the selection.

> Nguyen, Bich Minh. "Toadstools." *Dream Me Home Safely: Writers on Growing Up in America.* Ed. Susan Richards Shreve. Boston: Houghton, 2003. 129–132. Print.

Two or More Works from the Same Anthology If you are using more than one selection from an anthology, you will need three entries in your Works Cited list, one for the entire work, opening with the name of its editor, and one for each of the items, opening with the name of its author. Following the title of the work, you simply put the last name of the editor to refer your readers to the entire book, followed by the inclusive page numbers of each selection. Place each entry in its alphabetically determined spot on the Works Cited list, as illustrated below.

> Griffith, Patricia. "The Spiral Staircase." Shreve 73–81.

> MacDonald, Michael Patrick. "Spitting Image." Shreve 112–122.

> Shreve, Susan Richards, ed. *Dream Me Home Safely: Writers on Growing Up in America.* Boston: Houghton Mifflin, 2003. Print.

Translation

> Eco, Umberto. *The Name of the Rose.* Trans. William Weaver. San Diego: Harcourt, 1983. Print.

Later Edition of a Book Directly after the title, abbreviate the edition number without italics.

> Williams, Joseph M. *Style: Ten Lessons in Clarity and Grace.* 9th ed. New York: Pearson, 2007. Print.

Preface, Introduction, Foreword or Afterword Not by the Book's Author or Editor Open the entry with the name of the author of the part of the book; then provide the name of the section, followed by title of the book. If the book is a reprint, follow the title with the original date of publication. Use the word *by* before the author of the book. Indicate the inclusive page numbers for the part of the book you used as your source.

> Brogan, D. W., Introduction. *The Education of Henry Adams: An Autobiography.* 1918. By Henry Adams. Boston: Houghton, 1961. v–xviii. Print.

Reprinted Book   Directly after the title, include the original date of publication.

> Adams, Henry. *The Education of Henry Adams: An Autobiography.* 1918. Boston: Houghton, 1961. Print.

One Volume of a Multivolume Work   Directly after the title of the work, indicate the volume number you used.

> Churchill, Winston. *A History of the English-speaking Peoples.* Vol. 3. London: Cassell, 1956–58. Print.

More than One Volume of a Multivolume Work   After the title, indicate the total number of volumes in the work.

> Churchill, Winston. *A History of the English-speaking Peoples.* 4 vols. London: Cassell, 1956–58. Print.

Book That Is Part of a Series   After the medium (print) put the name of the series and a series number for the work if available. Do not italicize the series title.

> Horning, Alice, and Anne Becker, eds. *Revision: History, Theory, and Practice.* Lafayette, IN: Parlor Press, 2006. Print. Reference Guides to Rhetoric and Composition.

Signed Article in a Reference Book   Cite the name of the author, the title of the entry, the title of the reference work, name of the editor, and publication information. Do not include page numbers if entries appear in alphabetical order.

> Zangwill, O. L. "Hypnotism, History of." *The Oxford Companion to the Mind.* Ed. Richard L. Gregory. New York: Oxford UP, 1987. Print.

Unsigned Article in a Reference Book   Open with the title of the entry. Include page numbers if entries do not appear in alphabetical order.

> "A Technical History of Photography." *The New York Times Guide to Essential Knowledge: A Desk Reference for the Curious Mind.* New York: St. Martin's, 2004. 104–112. Print.

Religious Text Italicize the title and provide names of editors and/or translators and the publication information.

> *The Holy Bible.* Revised Standard Version. Cleveland: World, 1962. Print.

> *The Bhagavad Gita: According to Paramhansa Yogananda.* Ed. Swami Kriyananda. Nevada City, CA: Crystal Clarity, 2008. Print.

Articles in Periodicals

The essential items in entries for articles in periodicals are the

1. author's name, followed by a period;
2. title of the article, followed by a period, all in quotation marks;
3. title of the publication, italicized;
4. volume number (if given);
5. date (if given), followed by a colon;
6. inclusive page numbers followed by a period; and
7. medium (print).

Article in a Weekly Magazine In the following example, the magazine was dated both July 6 and July 13. In such a case, use a comma between the two dates.

> Levy, Ariel. "Nora Knows What to Do." *The New Yorker* 6, 13 July 2009: 60–69. Print.

Article in a Monthly Magazine Abbreviate all months except May, June, and July.

> Mooney, Chris. "Climate Repair Made Simple." *Wired* July 2008: 128–133. Print.

Article in a Print Newspaper Give the day, month, year, and edition, if specified; use abbreviations. Give section and page number. If pages are not consecutive, put a plus sign after the first page number.

> Yoon, Carol Kaesuk. "Reviving the Lost Art of Naming the World." *New York Times* 11 Aug. 2009, natl. ed.: D1+. Print.

Review Open with name of reviewer and title of review, if there is one. Add abbreviation for "review of," not italicized, followed by the title of the work being reviewed, and its author or performer.

> Hofferth, Sandra. "Buying So Children Belong." Rev. of *Longing and Belonging: Parents, Children, and Consumer Culture,* by Allison J. Pugh. *Science* 324 (26 June 2009): 1674. Print.

Editorial in a Newspaper—No Named Author

> "Disfigured Democracy: Health Care Extremism Exposes Our Uglier Side."
> Editorial. *Dallas Morning News* 13 Aug. 2009: A14. Print.

Letter to the Editor of a Newspaper or Magazine

> Reed, Glenn. "Not Enough Fish in the Sea." Letter. *Harper's* Aug. 2009: 5.
> Print.

Article in a Journal with Volume Numbers   Put the volume number, a period, and the issue number after the title of the article. Put the month (if given) and the year in parentheses.

> Bracher, Mark. "How to Teach for Social Justice: Lessons from *Uncle
> Tom's Cabin* and Cognitive Science." *College English* 71.4 (March
> 2009): 363–388. Print.

Other Genres as Sources

Advertisement in Print Medium   Open with the name of the item or service being advertised.

> Daedalus Books. Advertisement. *Harper's* Aug. 2009: 6. Print.

Art Reproduction   Treat art found in books in the same way you treat essays found in edited collections. Open the entry with the artist's name, followed by the title of the work and the date it was created, if available. Before the publication information, include where the original work of art may be found.

> O'Keefe, Georgia. *Light/17: Evening Star, No. V.* 1917. The Marion Koogler
> McNay Art Museum. *O'Keefe and Texas.* By Sharyn R. Udall. San
> Antonio: The Marion Koogler McNay Art Museum, 1998. Print.

Personal Interview   Give the name of the person interviewed, the kind of interview (personal, telephone), and the date it took place.

> Coman, Carolyn. Telephone interview. 15 Aug. 2009.

Sources on the Internet

The essential items in entries for electronic sources are as follows (as available):

1. Name of author, editor (ed.), performer (perf.), or translator (trans.)
2. Title of work
3. Version or edition
4. Publisher or sponsor of the site
5. Date last updated (or n.d.)
6. Medium (Web)
7. Date you accessed the site

Web Site or Independent Online Work

It is not necessary to include the URL of a Web site unless your reader would have difficulty finding the site through a search engine.

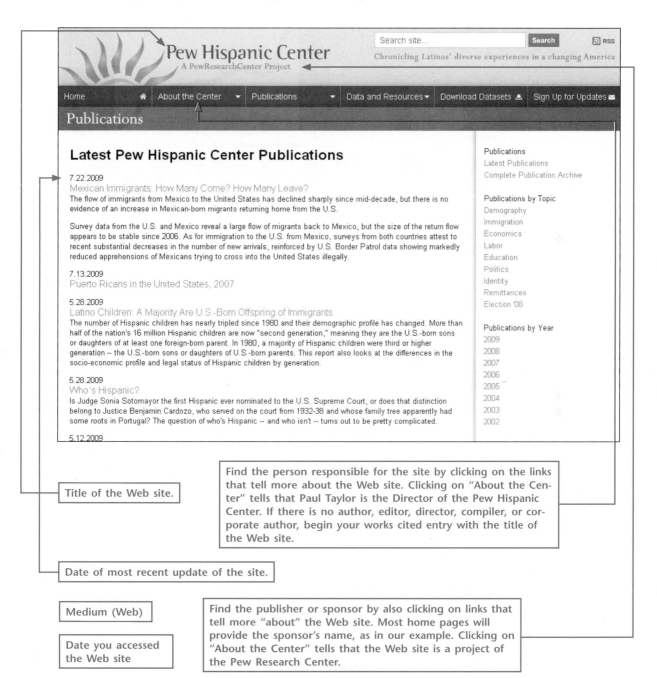

Title of the Web site.

Find the person responsible for the site by clicking on the links that tell more about the Web site. Clicking on "About the Center" tells that Paul Taylor is the Director of the Pew Hispanic Center. If there is no author, editor, director, compiler, or corporate author, begin your works cited entry with the title of the Web site.

Date of most recent update of the site.

Medium (Web)

Find the publisher or sponsor by also clicking on links that tell more "about" the Web site. Most home pages will provide the sponsor's name, as in our example. Clicking on "About the Center" tells that the Web site is a project of the Pew Research Center.

Date you accessed the Web site

Example Entry for Entire Web Site

> Taylor, Paul, dir. *Pew Hispanic Center.* Pew Research Center, 22 July 2009. Web. 20 Aug. 2009.

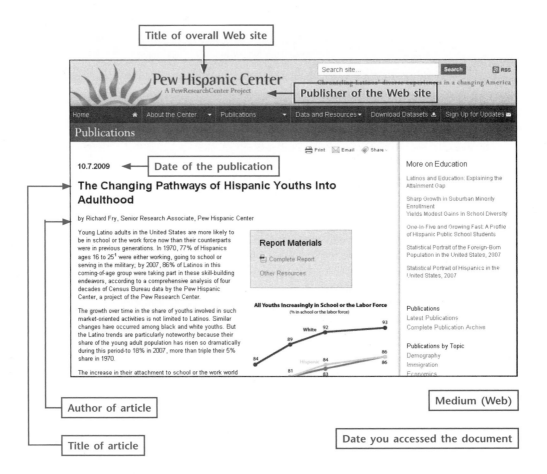

Title of overall Web site

Publisher of the Web site

Date of the publication

Author of article

Title of article

Medium (Web)

Date you accessed the document

Example Entry for Document Found on a Web Site

> Fry, Richard. "The Changing Pathways of Hispanic Youths into Adulthood." *Pew Hispanic Center.* Pew Research Center, 7 Oct. 2009. Web. 15 Oct. 2009.

Personal Web Site   If the site has no title, use "home page" or other descriptive title. If there is no sponsoring organization, use N.p. to indicate no publisher.

> Langer, Ellen. Home page. N.p. 2009. Web. 28 July 2009.

Article in an Online Newspaper   Put the Web site in italics; follow with the name of the sponsor or publisher, not italicized.

> Hotz, Robert L. "Creative Destruction on a Cosmic Scale: Scientists Say Asteroid Blasts, Once Thought Apocalyptic, Fostered Life on Earth by Carrying Water and Protective Greenhouse Gas." *Wall Street Journal*. Wall Street Journal, 14 Aug. 2009. Web. 15 Aug. 2009.

Article in an Online Magazine

> MacFarquhar, Larissa. "Who Cares If Johnny Can't Read? The Value of Books Is Overstated." *Slate*. 17 April 1997. Web. 12 April 2009.

Article in an Online Scholarly Journal   After the author and article title, include the volume and issue number (if given) and the inclusive page numbers (if given.) The following periodical is published annually, so it has a volume number only.

> O'Dwyer, Kathleen. "Nietzsche's Reflections on Love." *Minerva—An Internet Journal of Philosophy* 12 (Nov. 2008): 37–77. Web. 12 Oct. 2009.

Article Accessed through a Library Subscription Database   Italicize the name of the subscription database as well as the title of the publication containing the article.

> Wolf, Maryanne, and Mirit Barzillai. "The Importance of Deep Reading." *Educational Leadership*. 66: 6 March 2009: 32–37. *Academic Search Complete*. Web. 6 March 2009.

Government Document on the Web

> United States. National Endowment for the Arts. *To Read or Not to Read: A Question of National Consequence*. Nov. 2007. Web. 8 April 2009.

Article in an Online Reference Work   If unsigned, open with the title of the article. When alphabetizing, ignore opening article (*a, an, the*).

> "The Biological Notion of Individual." *Stanford Encyclopedia of Philosophy*. 9 Aug. 2007. The Metaphysics Research Lab, Stanford U. Web. 26 Mar. 2009.

Blog Entry Put the title of the post in quotation marks and the blog title in italics.

> Postrel, Virginia. "Naomi Wolf and the Phenomenology of Angelina Jolie."
> *Dynamist*. 19 June 2009. Web. 8 July 2009.

Broadcast or Published Interview Open with the names of the interviewee or interviewees; then provide the interviewer's name and the title of the interview, followed by the publisher, a comma, and the date it was published or put on the Web.

> Ganguly, Sumit, and Minxin Pei. Interview by Jayshree Bajoria.
> "Balancing India and China." Council on Foreign Relations, 6 Aug.
> 2009. Web. 13 Aug. 2009.

Student Sample of a Research Paper in MLA Style

See pages 157–166 for a student's paper using MLA documentation.

Using APA Documentation Style

The American Psychological Association style of documentation is used not only in the field of psychology but also in education, anthropology, social work, business, and other behavioral and social sciences. The conventions of APA style aim to achieve an objective and impersonal tone. In the text, authors are usually referred to by last name only, and direct quotations are rare.

Like MLA, the APA system requires that a writer acknowledge the source of all direct quotations, paraphrased and summarized ideas from sources, and information that is not common knowledge. Citing is a two-step process: a brief in-text reference to the author and date of publication, and a longer entry with complete bibliographical information in the References list at the end of the article or book. Citing page numbers is required for direct quotations and highly specific data but not for summarizing or paraphrasing ideas found throughout a text.

In-text Citations

For both direct and indirect quotations, including paraphrased information that is not common knowledge, the basic in-text citation provides the last name of the author of the source, directly followed by the year the source was published. The following examples show options for citing in-text.

Paraphrased Reference to Source by One Author Named in the Sentence

> The playground is a space where gender identities are constructed.
> Paechter (2007) argues that boys who are physically passive on the
> playground move into the marginal spaces occupied by girls and younger
> children, and thus become stigmatized by other boys as effeminate.

Paraphrased Reference to Source by One Author Cited Only in Parenthetical Citation

> The playground is a space where gender identities are constructed. Boys who are physically passive on the playground move into the marginal spaces occupied by girls and younger children, and thus become stigmatized by other boys as effeminate (Paechter, 2007).

Direct Quotation with Author Named in the Sentence

> According to Yoon (2009) anthropologists have found that people around the world create remarkably similar categories when labeling plants and animals, a phenomenon known as folk taxonomy. Yoon finds consensus about such categories as trees, vines, and bushes especially interesting "since there is no way to define a tree versus a bush" (p. D4). In naming the world around them, people appear "unconsciously to follow a set of unwritten rules" (p. D1).

Direct Quotation with Author Named in Parenthetical Citation

> Anthropologists have found that people around the world create remarkably similar categories when labeling plants and animals, a phenomenon known as folk taxonomy (Yoon, 2009). Consensus about such categories as trees, vines, and bushes is especially interesting "since there is no way to define a tree versus a bush" (p. D4). In naming the world around them, people appear "unconsciously to follow a set of unwritten rules" (p. D1).

Source with Two Authors Give both authors' last names each time you refer to the source. If you name them as part of your sentence, use *and* to join them: Wolf and Barzillai (2009). If you name them in parentheses, use an ampersand as shown in the example below.

> Reading is far from our other natural human functions of seeing, moving, speaking, and thinking. Reading is an invented cognitive function, and understanding how it works illustrates the amazing plasticity of the brain (Wolf & Barzillai, 2009).

Source with Three or More Authors In your in-text citation, give all authors' last names in your first reference to the work. Write out *and* when the list is part of your sentence. Subsequent references should give only the first author's name followed by et al. (not in italics).
First reference:

> Radeloff, Hammer, and Stewart (2005) studied the impact of housing density on forests in the Midwestern United States.

Later references:

> Radeloff et al. (2005) argue that rural sprawl has more impact on forests than urban sprawl because even though rural sprawl is less dense, its effects are spread over larger areas that once were forests.

Two Authors with the Same Last Name   Include identifying initials before each last name.

> S. Young (2007) complains that scientists study earth-eating, or geophagia, only from the standpoint of their own disciplinary interests. Thus, there is no "global perspective of all the possible benefits and all the possible negative consequences of geopaghia" (p. 67).

Citations within Quotations   You will often find that your source cites other sources. Do not put these sources on your References list unless you also read them and used them in your paper. When quoting, include the citations as they appear in the passage you are quoting.

> Cantarero (2007) notes that moral, political, and economic factors enter in to what people think is good to eat. He offers the example of advertising:
>
>> By associating values with products, producers seek to increase their sales. According to the principle of incorporation (Rozin and Nemeroff, 1989; Fischler, 1992) subjects acquire the symbolic qualities of ingested food. Thus, ingestion goes beyond the satisfaction of hunger, deep into the sphere of mentalities and internalizes an ideological language which is "artificially" built. (p. 207)

If you have more than one source for the same point or information, you put both in the parenthetical citation.

With blocked quotations, place final period before the parenthetical citation.

Long Quotations   For direct quotations of forty or more words, omit quotation marks and display the quotation as a block of text set in from the left margin by about one-half inch (in the same place as a new paragraph's opening). Double-space the entire quotation. See the example above on Citations within Quotations.

Work with No Author or Editor   If no author or editor is named, you will use the title of the work in both in-text citations and Reference entries. If the title is long, you should abbreviate it. Use double quotation marks around the title of an article, a chapter, or a Web page. Italicize the title of a periodical, book, or report. The example below shows a Web site.

> The Law School Aptitude Test (LSAT) measures ability to read and comprehend in-depth texts with insight, to draw "reasonable inferences" from readings, and to analyze and evaluate the reasoning of others' arguments ("About the LSAT," 2009).

Personal Communications   Personal communications such as letters and interviews are cited in text only, as in the following example.

> Carolyn Coman described her use of storyboarding to focus on the emotional impact of significant scenes in her fiction (C. Coman, personal communication, August 15, 2009).

Reference List Examples

Below are examples of how to cite the most commonly used kinds of sources in papers using the APA style of documentation. First, some general advice:

- Begin the list on a new page and center the word "References" at the top. (Do not enclose it in quotation marks.)
- Put all entries, regardless of their genres and media, in alphabetical order according to the author's (or editor's) last name, followed by the initials of the author's given name or names.
- If no author is named, use the first word in the title that is not an article (*a, an, the*). See page 183 for an example.
- Put the year, month, and date of publication immediately after the author's (or editor's) name, in parentheses.
- Do not number the entries.
- Double-space within and between entries; the list should look like the spacing in the rest of the paper.
- Begin each entry at the left margin and indent all subsequent lines by five spaces (one-half inch).
- Italicize titles of books and periodicals like magazines and journals.
- Do not enclose titles of articles in quotation marks.
- Capitalize only the first words of titles and subtitles, unless they are proper nouns (names).
- Capitalize the full names of periodicals, journals, and newspapers.

See the following list of examples for more help with citing specific kinds of sources.

Books

Book by a Single Author

> Paechter, C. F. (2007). *Being boys, being girls: Learning masculinities and femininities.* New York: McGraw-Hill.

Two or More Books by the Same Author   List the works in order of publication, with the earliest first.

> Obama, B. (2004). *Dreams from my father: A story of race and inheritance.* New York: Three Rivers. (Original work published 1995)

Obama, B. (2006). *The audacity of hope: Thoughts on reclaiming the American dream.* New York: Crown.

Book by Two or More Authors　List all authors by last name and initials. Put commas between items in this list. Use an ampersand (&) before the final name.

Small, G., & Vorgan, G. (2008). *iBrain: Surviving the technological alteration of the modern mind.* New York: HarperCollins.

Booth, W., Colomb, G., & Williams, J. (2003). *The craft of research* (2nd ed.). Chicago: U of Chicago Press.

Book by a Corporate Author or Government Agency　Treat the corporation or agency as an author. If the author and publisher are the same, put "author" after the place of publication.

American Psychological Association. (2010). *Publication manual of the American Psychological Association* (6th ed.). Washington DC: Author.

Edited Compilation　Between the editor's name and the date, put the abbreviation for editor(s).

MacClancy, J., Henry, J., & Macbeth, H. (Eds.). (2007). *Consuming the inedible: Neglected dimensions of food choice.* New York: Berghahn Books.

Selection in an Edited Compilation　For articles in edited works, put the author of the individual work first, followed by the year of publication, and then the title of the article, followed by the word "In" and the editor or editors' names and the title of the collected work. The inclusive pages of the selection follow the title of the book, in parentheses. End the citation with place and name of publisher.

Young, S. (2007). A vile habit? The potential biological consequences of geophagia, with special attention to iron. In J. MacClancy, J. Henry, & H. Macbeth (Eds.), *Consuming the inedible: Neglected dimensions of food choice* (pp. 67–79). New York: Berghahn Books.

Edition Other than the First　Put the edition number in parentheses after the title.

Williams, J. M. (2007). *Style: Ten lessons in clarity and grace* (9th ed.). New York: Pearson Longman.

Translation　Put the translator's initials and last name, followed by the abbreviation for translator in parentheses, after the book's title.

Durkheim, E. (1984). *The division of labor in society.* (W. D. Halls, Trans.). New York: Free Press. (Original work published 1933)

Preface, Introduction, Foreword or Afterword Not by the Book's Author or Editor   Open the entry with the name of the author of the part of the book; then put the date in parentheses and write out the name of the section written by this author. Follow with publication information for the rest of the book. Do not give page numbers in the References list.

> Coser, L. A. (1984). Introduction. In E. Durkheim, *The division of labor in society.* (W. D. Halls, Trans.). New York: Free Press. (Original work published 1933)

Reprinted Book   Indicate original date of publication in parentheses.

> Obama, B. (2004). *Dreams from my father: A story of race and inheritance.* New York: Three Rivers. (Original work published 1995)

Note: The in-text citation should include both dates. (2004/1995).

One Volume of a Multivolume Work   Directly after the author, indicate the inclusive dates of the volumes. After the title of the work, indicate in parentheses the volume number you used.

> Churchill, W. (1956–58). *A history of the English-speaking peoples* (Vol. 3). London: Cassell.

Article in a Reference Book   Include inclusive page numbers for the entry after the title of the book. Put parentheses around page number or numbers.

> Zangwill, O. L. (1987). "Hypnotism, history of." In R. L. Gergory (Ed.), *The Oxford companion to the mind* (pp. 330–334.) New York: Oxford University Press.

Unsigned Article in a Reference Book   Open with the title of the entry. Put parentheses around page numbers.

> A technical history of photography. (2004). *The New York Times guide to essential knowledge: A desk reference for the curious mind* (pp. 104–112). New York: St. Martin's.

Articles in Periodicals

For newspaper articles, use p. and pp. before page number. For magazine and journal articles, do not use p. or pp. Instead, put volume # in italics followed by the page numbers, separated with a comma.

Article in a Newspaper   Give the day, month, year, and edition if specified. List all page numbers if the article appeared on discontinuous pages.

Yoon, C. K. (2009, August 11). Reviving the lost art of naming the world. *The New York Times,* pp. D1, D4.

Article in a Monthly Magazine

Mooney, C. (2008, July). Climate repair made simple. *Wired,* 128–133.

Article in a Weekly Magazine   Include the day as well as the month and year.

Gladwell, M. (2009, October 19). "Offensive play: How different are dogfighting and football?" *The New Yorker,* 50–59.

Article in a Journal Paginated by Volume   Put the volume number, a period, and the issue number after the title of the article. Put the month (if given) and the year in parentheses. Include inclusive page numbers for the article.

Bracher, M. (2009, March). How to teach for social justice: Lessons from *Uncle Tom's Cabin* and cognitive science. *College English 71*(4), 363–388.

Article in a Journal Paginated by Issue   Put the issue number in parentheses after the volume. The volume number is italicized. The issue number is not.

Wolf, M., & Barzillai M. (2009, March). The importance of deep reading. *Educational Leadership, 66*(6), 32–37.

Newspaper Article with an Anonymous Author   Open citation with title of the article. When alphabetizing, ignore opening articles (*a, an, the*).

Moon travel uncertain. (2009, August 14). *Dallas Morning News,* p. 12A.

Review   Open with name of reviewer and title of review, if there is one. Put "Review of," followed by the item being reviewed, all in square brackets. Note that the volume number of the magazine is in italics, followed by a comma and the page number, not italicized.

Hofferth, S. (2009, June 26). Buying so children belong. [Review of the book *Longing and belonging: Parents, children, and consumer culture].* Science, 324, 1674.

Editorial in a Newspaper—No Author Given   Put the genre (editorial) in square brackets.

Disfigured democracy: Health care extremism exposes our uglier side. (2009, August 13). [Editorial]. *Dallas Morning News,* p. A14.

Letter to the Editor of a Newspaper or Magazine Put the genre (letter to the editor) in square brackets.

> Meibers, R. (2009, July). Thou shall kill. [Letter to the editor]. *Harper's,* 4.

Advertisement in Print Medium

> Daedalus Books. (2009, August). [Advertisement]. *Harper's,* 6.

Sources on the Internet

Article in an Online Newspaper Put the title of the newspaper in italics, followed by the URL of the paper's Web site.

> Hotz, R. L. (2009, August 14). Creative destruction on a cosmic scale: Scientists say asteroid blasts, once thought apocalyptic, fostered life on earth by carrying water and protective greenhouse gas. *Wall Street Journal.* Retrieved from http://online.wsj.com/home-page

Article in a Journal Accessed through Library Subscription Database Include the name of the database only if you think it unlikely that multiple databases would carry the article or that the article would be difficult to find.

Online Journal Article with Digital Object Identifier (DOI) Because uniform resource locators (URLs) often change, a new method of locating online materials has been developed. Increasingly, you will find that articles have an alphanumeric identification string, usually located near the copyright date in the article. You can also find it in the bibliographic information in the library's full record display. Use the DOI, if available, instead of the URL from which you retrieved the online article. Include the issue number in italics after the journal title. Conclude the entry with inclusive page numbers and the DOI.

> McGrevey, M., & Kehre, D. (2009). Stewards of the public trust: Federal laws that serve servicemembers and student veterans. *New Directions for Student Services, 126,* 89–94. doi: 10.1002/ss.320

Article in an Online Magazine without a DOI If there is no DOI, conclude the entry with "retrieved from" and the URL.

> MacFarquhar, L. (1997, April 17). Who cares if Johnny can't read? The value of books is overstated. *Slate.* Retrieved from http://www.slate.com/id/3128/

Article in an Online Scholarly Journal without DOI Volume number follows the journal title. If there is an issue number, it goes in parentheses after the volume number. In this case, there is no issue number because the journal is published annually.

> O'Dwyer, K. (2008). Nietzsche's reflections on love. *Minerva—An Internet Journal of Philosophy, 12*, 37–77. Retrieved from http://www.mic .ul.ie/stephen/vol12/Nietzsche.pdf

Article in an Online Encyclopedia or Reference Work If the entry is unsigned, open with its title, as in the second example below.

> Botstein, L. (2005). Robert Maynard Hutchins and the University of Chicago. In J. Reiff, A. D. Keating, & J. R. Grossman (Eds.), *Encyclopedia of Chicago*. Retrieved from http://www.encyclopedia .chicagohistory.org

> The biological notion of individual. (2007, August 9). In E. N. Zalta (Ed.), *Stanford Encyclopedia of Philosophy*. Retrieved from http://plato.stanford.edu/

Blog Post Give the URL but not the title of the blog.

> Postrel, V. (2009, June 19). Naomi Wolf and the phenomenology of Angelina Jolie. [Web log message]. Retrieved from http://www.dynamist.com/weblog/

Other Genres as Sources

Published or Broadcast Interview Include the medium in which the interview was published.

> Ganguly, S., & Pei, M. (2009, August 6). Interview by J. Bajoria. Balancing India and China [Audio podcast.] Council on Foreign Relations. Retrieved from http://www.cfr.org/

Personal Interviews Personal communication such as interviews and letters are not included in the list of references in APA style. However, you need to cite them in the text as described on page 151.

Student Sample of a Research Paper in APA Style

See pages 181–184 for an article using APA documentation.

STUDENT SAMPLE: A RESEARCH PAPER (MLA STYLE)

Ross 1

Julie Ross

ENGL 1301, Section 009

April 20, 2007

Professor Channell

Why Residential Construction Needs to Get a Conscience

Home ownership is a significant part of the American dream. Americans take great pride in putting down roots and raising a family in a good neighborhood. And, if a recent boom in residential construction is any indication, more Americans are realizing that dream. In addition to the number of new homes being built, the average home size has also grown significantly, almost twice as large as in the 1960s ("How to Build"). The question is: what is the impact of super-sized houses on our neighborhoods and our environment?

In big cities like Dallas, huge new houses are springing up in the outer-ring suburbs like Frisco and Flower Mound. The National Association of Homebuilders reports that the average size of a single-family home has grown from 983 square feet in 1950 to 2,434 square feet in 2005, "even as the average household shrunk from 3.4 to 2.6 people" (Brown 23). This desire for more living space keeps cities sprawling outward as developers look for open land. However, urban residential areas are also now impacted by new building. Affluent Americans are buying new super-sized homes in older, urban residential areas. These lots were once occupied by historic and humble houses. The older houses are now known as "teardowns." In their place, towering "McMansions" dominate the street. Richard Moe, President of the National Trust for Historic Preservation, reports that

Standard heading

Title centered

Entire essay is double-spaced

Introduction announces topic

Poses issue the argument will address

No word breaks at end of lines

Author's last name and page number in MLA style

Full name and credentials of authors who have expertise

Ross 2

teardowns affect over 300 U.S. cities, with a total of 75,000 older houses razed each year.

Moe compares the teardown trend to a cancer on the community: "Teardowns wreck neighborhoods. They [destroy] the character and livability that are a neighborhood's lifeblood." He sees three reasons for the rise in teardowns:

- In the past decade, the value of houses has doubled or tripled, except in some older neighborhoods. Developers look for these "'undervalued' properties" to build on.

- Homebuyers demand more space.

- Some homebuyers want to move from the "soulless . . . sprawling subdivisions" to close-in neighborhoods that have more character and more amenities, such as public transportation and local shopping.

Moe explains, "The problem is that too many people try to impose their preference for suburban-style mini-mansions on smaller scale neighborhoods where they just don't fit."

My neighborhood in Dallas, known as Lakewood Heights, has been plagued by more than its share of tearing down and building up. Once famous for its 1920s Craftsman and Tudor architecture, my quiet residential street is now marred by rows of McMansions, bustling traffic, and noisy, new construction. These colossal residences vary little in outward appearance from one to the next. "Starter mansions" as they are often called, have no particular architectural style and only remotely resemble Tudor or Craftsman styles. No matter where you look, these giants tower over their single-story neighbors, blocking the sunlight and peering into once-private backyards from their tall, garish peaks.

Paraphrases for information from source, quotations for opinions

Colon after full-sentence as introductory tag

Reasons against teardowns begin

Personal observation as support for this reason

Another reason against tearing down

Ross 3

A super-sized new home towers over its older next-door neighbor.

The builders and buyers of these giant homes are callous to community and environmental concerns. Preserving an old Dallas neighborhood's rich architectural history and green landscape is of little importance to them. For example, most McMansions occupy an extremely large footprint, leaving little or no yard space. Original homes in my neighborhood occupied about a third of their rectangular lot. This design permitted a sizable back yard with room for a small one-car garage as well as an inviting front lawn where children could play. By contrast, mega homebuilders show no appreciation for conventional site planning. They employ bulldozers to flatten the lot and uproot native trees. Their goal is to make room for as much house as possible, raking in more profit with each square foot. Furthermore, each tall fortress has a wide cold, concrete driveway leading to the grandiose two-Tahoe garage, equivalent to nearly half the size of my one-story house.

Ross 4

What was once a grassy lawn is now paved with concrete.

Only ten years ago pecan trees, the official state tree of
Texas, and flowering magnolias graced every lawn on my
block. These beautiful native trees, some over a century old,
shaded our homes from the harsh Texas sun and our
sidewalks from the triple-digit, summer heat. There is no
way the new home owners' landscaping can replace what is
lost. The charm of the neighborhood is being destroyed.

Aside from changing the face of my neighborhood, these
monster houses, many selling for half a million or more,
have skyrocketed property taxes and pushed out many older,
lower-income, long-time residents. As a result, several senior
citizens and other long-time residents of Lakewood have been
forced to sell their homes and move to apartments. Many
custom homeowners argue that more expensive, larger
homes positively contribute to a neighborhood by increasing
the resale value of smaller, older homes. This may be true
to a certain extent. However, from a wider perspective,

Transition into
another reason

Ross 5

short-term gains in resale prices are no compensation for the irreversible harm done to our neighborhoods.

But the destruction of a neighborhood is only half the story. These over-sized homes, and others like them everywhere, are irresponsible from a larger environmental perspective. According to Peter Davey, editor of the *Architectural Review,* "Buildings [residential and commercial combined] take up rather more than half of all our energy use: they add more to the pollution of the atmosphere than transport and manufacture combined." Not only is pollution a consequence of this surge in residential structure size, but also the building of larger homes drains our natural resources, such as lumber. The National Resource Defense Council notes that forested areas, necessary for absorbing greenhouse gas emissions, are being depleted by the super-sizing trend in residential building:

> Almost every one of these new, large homes is made out of wood—roughly three-quarters of an acre of forest. Much of the destructive logging around the world is fueled by our demand for housing. . . . Many houses today are still built using outdated, inefficient construction methods. About one-sixth of the wood delivered to a construction site is never used, but simply hauled away as waste. And much of the wood that goes into the frame of a house is simply unnecessary. ("How to Build")

Obviously, residential construction must "go green" in an effort to save valuable resources and conserve energy. But what does it mean to "go green"? As Earth Advantage, a green building certification organization, explains: "Green building entails energy efficiency, indoor air quality, durability and minimal site impact" (Kaleda). However, whether a home can be designated as "green" depends on more than just

Double-space blocked quotations; use no quotation marks

Period ends sentence. Ellipses of three dots indicates material omitted

With block form, period goes before parenthetical citation

Ross 6

energy-efficient construction methods and materials. According to Martin John Brown, an ecologist and independent consultant, green homebuilding is being used to describe a wide range of residential construction, and not all homes should qualify. Essentially, while some homebuilders are selling "environmentally-friendly" design, the epic scale of these new homes outweighs any ecological benefits provided through materials and construction methods. So, size does matter. A recent article in the *Journal of Industrial Energy*, published by M.I.T. Press, reports that a 1,500 square foot house with "mediocre energy-performance standards" will consume far less energy than a 3,000 square foot house with all the latest energy-saving materials and details (Wilson 284). In Boston, a house rated "poor" in terms of energy standards used 66% less energy than one rated "good" but twice the size (Wilson 282).

For articles by reporters or staff writers, rather than experts and authorities, their names can be cited parenthetically only

Brown argues that practically minded, ecologically conscious homebuilding should be part of our overall effort to decrease our consumption of limited resources and energy. Evidence from the Department of Energy supports his claim: "From 1985 to 2002, total residential energy consumption per capita climbed eight percent, and residential consumption for the nation—the figure most relevant to global effects like carbon dioxide (CO_2) emissions—climbed 32 percent" (Brown 23).

Unfortunately, many Americans who can afford it won't stop buying environmentally irresponsible, un-humble abodes. Their motives may stem from the competitive nature of consumer society. When people see their neighbors driving a new car, they think they need to buy a new one too. This is called "keeping up with the Joneses." Discussing the super-sized house, best-selling author Gregg Easterbrook has coined a new phrase, "call and raise the Joneses." As he explains it,

Ross 7

In call-and-raise-the-Joneses, Americans feel compelled
not just to match the material possessions of others,
but to stay ahead. Bloated houses . . . arise from a
desire to call-and-raise-the-Joneses—surely not from a
belief that a seven-thousand-square-foot house that
comes right up against the property setback line
would be an ideal place in which to dwell. (140)

Daniel Chiras, the author of *The Natural House: A Complete
Guide to Healthy, Energy-Efficient, Environmental Homes,*
warns: "People tell themselves that if they can afford a
10,000-square-foot house, then that's what they should have
. . . but I wonder if the earth can afford it" (qtd. in Iovine).

Fortunately, other Americans are starting to recognize
the folly of buying more space than they need. A survey by
Lowe's and Harris Interactive found that "46% of
homeowners admit to wasting up to half of their home"
("Are McMansions Giving Way"). Felicia Oliver of
Professional Builder magazine suggests that the marriage of
conservation and construction is the next natural step in the
evolution of residential building. One example of a builder
taking this step is the Cottage Company in Seattle, which
specializes in "finely detailed and certified-green" houses of
between 1,000 and 2,000 square feet. Company co-owner
Linda Pruitt says Cottage Company houses "'live as big' as
McMansions because they're better designed, with features
like vaulted ceilings and abundant built-ins. 'It's kind of like
the design of a yacht,' she says. The theme is quality of
space, not quantity" (qtd. in Brown 24).

Even Richard Moe of the National Trust for Historic
Preservation admits that responsible new construction has a
place in older neighborhoods:

Cite author of
article, not speaker.
Use "qtd." to
indicate quotation
appeared in the
source

If no author, use
shortened form of
title
Shows possible
solution to problem

Ross 8

Trees tower over this stretch of original modest-scale homes in
Lakewood Heights, reminding us of what is being lost.

No one is saying that homebuyers shouldn't be able to
alter or expand their home to meet their needs, just as
no one is saying that older neighborhoods should be
frozen in time like museum exhibits. A neighborhood is a
living thing, and change is both inevitable and desirable.
The challenge is to manage change so that it respects
the character and distinctiveness that made these
neighborhoods so appealing in the first place.
This is the challenge that must be met in my own
neighborhood. If new construction and additions are as
architecturally interesting as the older homes and
comparable with them in size and footprint, preserving lawns
and trees, the neighborhood can retain its unique character.

Jessie Sackett, a member of the U.S. Green Building
Council, writes: "Owning a home is the cornerstone of the

Conclusion returns
to idea used in
introduction

Ross 9

American dream. Recently, however, we've realized that keeping that dream alive for future generations means making some changes to how we live today" (36). We must ensure that the American Dream doesn't translate into a horrific nightmare for our planet or future generations. Therefore, I ask would-be homebuyers to consider only the more conscientious construction in both urban and suburban areas. When we demand more modest and responsible homebuilding, we send a clear message: younger generations will know that we value our planet and our future more than we value excessive personal living space.

- - - - - - - - - - - - - [separate page] - - - - - - - - - - - - - -

Works Cited

"Are McMansions Giving Way to Smaller, Cozier Homes?"
  Coatings World. Aug. 2004: 12. *Academic OneFile.* Web.
  12 Jan. 2007.

Brown, Martin John. "Hummers on the Homefront: At 4,600
  Square Feet, Is It an Eco-House?" *E, The Environmental
  Magazine.* Sept–Oct 2006: 23–24. *Academic OneFile.* Web.
  6 Oct. 2006.

Davey, Peter. "Decency and Forethought: It Is Foolish to
  Behave As If We as a Race Can Go on Treating the
  Planet As We Have Been Doing Since the Industrial
  Revolution." *The Architectural Review* 213.1281 (2003):
  36–37. *Academic OneFile.* Web. 18 Oct. 2006.

Easterbrook, Gregg. *The Progress Paradox: How Life Gets
  Better While People Feel Worse.* New York: Random
  House, 2003. Print.

"How to Build a Better Home: A New Approach to

Use alphabetical order according to author's last name or if no author, according to first word in title, ignoring articles (a, an, the)

Double-space in and between entries

Ross 10

Homebuilding Saves Trees and Energy—and Makes for Economical, Comfortable Homes." *National Resources Defense Council.* 22 July 2004. Web. 22 Oct. 2006.

Iovine, Julie V. "Muscle Houses Trying to Live Lean; Solar Panels on the Roof, Five Cars in the Garage." *The New York Times.* 30 Aug. 2001: B9. *Academic OneFile.* Web. 18 Oct. 2006.

Kaleda, Colleen. "Keeping It 'Green' with Panels and More." *The New York Times.* 15 Oct. 2006: 11. *Academic OneFile.* Web. 22 Oct. 2006.

Moe, Richard. "Battling Teardowns, Saving Neighborhoods." *The National Trust for Historic Preservation.* 28 June 2006. Web. 23 Jan. 2007.

Oliver, Felicia. "The Case for Going Green." *Professional Builder* (1993). 2.5 (2006): 38. *Academic OneFile.* Web. 6 Oct. 2006.

Sackett, Jessie. "The Green American Dream: LEED for Homes Is Currently Being Piloted." *The LEED Guide: Environmental Design & Construction.* 9.6 (2006): 36+. *Academic OneFile.* Web. 18 Oct. 2006.

Wilson, Alex, and Jessica Boehland. "Small Is Beautiful: U.S. House Size, Resource Use, and the Environment." *Journal of Industrial Energy.* 9.1 (Winter/Spring 2005): 277–287. *Academic Search Complete.* Web. 17 Feb. 2007.

CHAPTER 7

Ethical Writing and Plagiarism

WHY ETHICS MATTER

To write well, you need to be informed about your topic, which means doing research into what others have already said about it. You will want to put some of these ideas into your papers, but it is unethical to do so in a way that does not give credit to the source.

By citing your sources, you also earn your reader's respect. Readers are more likely to accept your views if you project good character, what the ancient rhetoricians called *ethos*. Honesty is part of good character. Part of writing honestly is distinguishing your ideas from the ideas of others.

The news has been filled in recent years with stories about unethical writers, people who have been caught using other writers' words and ideas without citing the source. One university president who borrowed too freely in a convocation speech was forced to resign. Recently, some history professors' books were found to contain long passages taken word-for-word from sources, the result—they claimed—of careless note-taking. Whether deliberate or accidental, such mistakes can destroy a person's career.

Plagiarism by students also has become an increasing problem, partly as a result of the Internet. Students may plagiarize by accident, not realizing

www.mhhe.com/**crusius**

For more information on plagiarism, go to:

Research > Plagiarism

that material that is so easy to copy and paste from the Web must be treated as a quotation and cited as a source. The Internet has also become part of the solution to this problem: Professors using programs like Turnitin.com can check submitted work for originality. At schools using this software, plagiarism dropped by 82%.[*]

For students, the consequences of plagiarizing are severe, ranging from failure on the writing project to failure in the course and even to suspension or expulsion from the university. Many universities will indicate on a student's transcript if there has been an honor violation, something that potential employers will see.

The purpose of this chapter is to help you avoid plagiarizing.

WHAT PLAGIARISM IS

We like the definition of plagiarism on Fairfield University's online honor tutorial because it includes the various kinds of media that count as sources and must be acknowledged when you draw from them. See Concept Close-Up, on the next page, to read this definition.

As we explain in Chapter 6, "Writing Research-Based Arguments," you must document the sources of all direct quotations, all paraphrased ideas taken from sources, and even information paraphrased from sources, unless it is "common knowledge."

A good definition of *common knowledge* comes from Bruce Ballenger's excellent book *The Curious Researcher:* "Basically, common knowledge means facts that are widely known and about which there is no controversy."[†] If you already knew something that shows up in your research, that is a good indication that it is common knowledge, but you also have to consider whether your *readers* would already know it. If your readers know less about your topic than you do, it is good to cite the source, especially if the information might surprise them.

THE ETHICS OF USING SOURCES

There are five major kinds of violations of ethics in using sources.

Purchasing a Paper

A simple Internet browser search for most topics will turn up services that offer pre-written essays for sale. These services claim that the essays are merely "examples" of what could be written on the topic, but we all know better. In almost every arena of life, people are ruthlessly trying to make a

---

[*]"Largest Study of Cheating in the World Reveals 82% Drop in Plagiarism After Using Turnitin.com for Five or More Years." *PR Newswire.* Oct. 4, 2006.

[†]Bruce Ballenger, *The Curious Researcher: A Guide to Writing Research Papers,* 3rd ed. (Boston: Allyn and Bacon, 2001), 236.

Plagiarism: The Presentation or Submission of Another's Work as Your Own

Plagiarism includes summarizing, paraphrasing, copying, or translating words, ideas, artworks, audio, video, computer programs, statistical data, or any other creative work, without proper attribution.

Plagiarism can be deliberate or accidental. It can be partial or complete. No matter which, the penalties are often similar. Understanding what constitutes plagiarism is your first step to avoiding it.

SOME ACTS OF PLAGIARISM:

- Copying and pasting from the Internet without attribution
- Buying, stealing, or ghostwriting a paper
- Using ideas or quotations from a source without citation
- Paraphrasing an author too lightly

"What Constitutes Plagiarism?" by Ramona Islam, Senior Reference Librarian and Instruction Coordinator at Fairfield University. Reprinted with permission.

---

buck off the gullible or the desperate. These services are counting on college students to take the bait. It's a bad idea for all these reasons:

- You learn nothing about writing, so you are cheating yourself.
- College professors can find the same essays by searching the Internet and by using more sophisticated search engines designed by textbook publishers to help them find plagiarism.
- The paper will be a poor fit with the prompt your teacher has given you, and the style of the writing will not match previous examples of your own voice and style—red flags professors easily detect.
- Some of these papers are poorly written, often filled with generalizations, bad thinking, and errors of grammar and punctuation.

Using a Paper Found Online

Many college professors and high school teachers have class Web sites where they post the best work of their students. These papers will often turn up in online searches. Do not be tempted to use these papers or parts of them without citing them, and that includes giving the qualifications of the author.

Using Passages from Online Sources without Citing the Source

It is easy to copy and paste material from the Internet, and much of it is not protected by copyright. Nevertheless, to take passages, sentences, or even

Understanding the Ethics of Plagiarism

A student who plagiarizes faces severe penalties: a failing grade on a paper, perhaps failure in a course, even expulsion from the university and an ethics violation recorded on his or her permanent record. Outside of academe, in the professional world, someone who plagiarizes may face public humiliation, loss of a degree, rank, or job, perhaps even a lawsuit. Why is plagiarism such a serious offense?

Plagiarism is theft. If someone takes our money or our car, we rightly think that person should be punished. Stealing ideas or the words used to express them is no less an act of theft.

Plagiarism is a breach of ethics. In our writing, we are *morally obligated* to distinguish between our ideas, information, and language and somebody else's ideas, information, and language. Human society cannot function without trust and integrity—hence the strong condemnation of plagiarism.

Plagiarism amounts to taking an unearned and unfair advantage. You worked hard to get that "B" on the big paper in your political science class. How would you feel if you knew that another student had simply purchased an "A" paper, thereby avoiding the same effort? At the very least, you would resent it. You should report it. Plagiarism is not just a moral failure with potentially devastating consequences for an individual. *Plagiarism, like any form of dishonesty, damages human society and hurts everyone.*

---

phrases or single significant words from another text is plagiarism. Significant words express strong judgment or original style, such as metaphors.

Compare the source text below with the uses of it. It comes from an interview with Al Gore about his film *An Inconvenient Truth*. The interview appeared in *Sierra* magazine, found on the Sierra Club Web site.*

> **Sierra:** In your movie, you cite U.S. determination in World War II as an example of the kind of resolve we need to confront global warming. But it took the attack on Pearl Harbor to galvanize the country. Are we going to have a similar moment in this crisis?
>
> **Gore:** Obviously, we all hope it doesn't come to that, but for hundreds of thousands of people in New Orleans, that moment has already been reached. And for millions of people in Africa's Sahel, that moment has already been reached with the disappearance of Lake Chad. For an untold number of species, it has been reached. The challenge for the rest of us is to connect the dots and see the picture clearly. H. G. Wells

---

*Pat Joseph, "Start by Arming Yourself with Knowledge: Al Gore Breaks Through with His Global-Warming Message." *Sierra*. Sept.-Oct. 2006. Oct. 21, 2006 <http://www.sierraclub.org/sierra/200609/interview.asp>.

wrote that "history is a race between education and catastrophe." And this is potentially the worst catastrophe in the history of civilization. The challenge now is to seize our potential for solving this crisis without going through a cataclysmic tragedy that would be the climate equivalent of wartime attack. And it's particularly important because, by the nature of this crisis, when the worst consequences begin to manifest themselves, it will already be too late.

Unethical use of source:

> It will take an environmental crisis to galvanize the country into confronting the problem of global warming, and for hundreds of thousands of people in New Orleans, that moment has already been reached. The challenge for the rest of us is to connect the dots and see the picture clearly. H. G. Wells wrote that "history is a race between education and catastrophe." And this is potentially the worst catastrophe in the history of civilization, so we must step up our efforts to learn about global warming and the means to keep it in check.

In this example, the writer has made no reference to the source of the words or ideas. This is wholesale theft of another's words and ideas. This kind of borrowing from sources is every bit as unethical as buying a paper online and turning it in as your own writing.

Ethical use of source:

> There are two routes to discovering the need to confront the problem of global warming, as Al Gore explained to *Sierra* magazine. We can wait for catastrophes like Hurricane Katrina, or we can learn from other environmental crises that are occurring around the globe and take action now. Quoting H. G. Wells, who said that "history is a race between education and catastrophe," Gore argues that we need to get educated because global warming is "potentially the worst catastrophe in the history of civilization. . . ." (Joseph).

The ethical way to use a source is

- to integrate paraphrase and direct quotation into a paragraph of your own, and
- to cite the source.

Notice that good paraphrasing does not borrow either the language or the sentence pattern of the original text. The source is cited and the style of the sentences is the student's own.

Inadequate Paraphrasing

Paraphrasing is tricky because paraphrases must be *entirely* your own words, not a mixture of your words and the words of the source. Even if you cite the source, it is plagiarism to borrow words and phrases from another author.

Therefore, you must put quotation marks around sentences, parts of sentences, and even significant words taken directly from another text.

Here is a source text, and on page 173 is the picture, to which the examples of paraphrase that follow refer:

> Subversive masculine modes in the second half of this century began with the tee-shirts and blue jeans of rural laborers, later adopted by rebellious urban youth.
>
> —Anne Hollander, *Sex and Suits* (New York: A. A. Knopf, 1994)

Unethical use of source:

> Marlon Brando symbolizes the subversive masculine mode of the second half of the twentieth century with the tee-shirts and blue jeans of rural laborers (Hollander 186).

Even though the student cited his source, this is plagiarism because his sentence contains words from the source without quotation marks. This example illustrates the most common kind of unintentional plagiarism. This passage also fails to identify Hollander as the interpreter of the image.

To avoid this accidental plagiarism:

- When taking notes, highlight in color any wording that you copy directly from a source.
- When paraphrasing, study the original passage but then put it aside when you write your paraphrase, so that you will not be tempted to use the wording of the source. Then go back and check your paraphrase for accuracy and for originality of expression. As the ethical version below shows, any quoted parts must be treated as quotations.

Ethical use of source:

> According to art historian Anne Hollander, Marlon Brando's tee-shirt and blue jeans illustrate a rebellious kind of late-twentieth-century masculinity, a look originally associated with "rural laborers" (186).

This version has reworded the sentence into an adequate paraphrase and used quotation marks around a phrase taken word for word from Hollander. It also identifies Hollander as an art historian, which establishes her credibility. When you tell your readers something about your source, you increase the credibility of your own writing.

Paraphrasing Ideas or Information without Naming the Source

Although it is not necessary to cite sources of commonly available information, such as the percentage of high school graduates who go to college, you must give credit when a source presents someone's idea, interpretation, or opinion, or when the information would be difficult for your readers to

Marlon Brando in A Streetcar Named Desire, *1951.*

verify on their own. If in doubt, it is always better to cite. The source text below comes from a book about the college experience:

> Many [college] seniors single out interdisciplinary classes as the courses that meant the most to them. As a corollary, they cite faculty members who, while expert in their own fields, are able to put the fields in proper perspective. Students find this important. They believe that the real world, and the way people think about the world, does not divide neatly into categories called history, chemistry, literature, psychology, and politics.
>
> —Richard J. Light, *Making the Most of College: Students Speak Their Minds* (Cambridge: Harvard UP, 2001)

Unethical use of source:

> Studies have shown that college students find interdisciplinary courses the most meaningful. They also prefer professors who can think outside the box of their own areas of academic specialization.

Richard Light's research led him to this information; he deserves credit for his work.

Ethical use of source:

> In interviews with seniors at Harvard, where he teaches, Richard Light found that college students say that interdisciplinary courses are the most meaningful. They also prefer professors who can think outside the box of their own areas of academic specialization (126).

By citing Light as the source of this information, the writer has also added credibility to his or her own essay.

When Opinions Coincide

Students often ask what to do when they have an idea, opinion, or interpretation and then encounter that same idea, opinion, or interpretation as they are doing research. For example, after looking into the problem of global warming, a student could easily come to the conclusion that rising temperatures and ocean levels could become a threat to civilization. Reading the *Sierra* interview with Al Gore, that student sees that she and Gore share the opinion that global warming "is potentially the worst catastrophe in the history of civilization." If the student doesn't use Gore's exact words, is it plagiarism to use the opinion without citing him? A classic book on the subject of research, *The Craft of Research,* advises the cautious approach: "In the world of research, priority counts not for everything, but for a lot. If you do not cite that prior source, you risk having people think that you plagiarized it, even though you did not."* You do not have to check to see that all of your own ideas are not already out there; however, if you encounter one of your own in a source, you should acknowledge that source.

THE ETHICS OF GIVING AND RECEIVING HELP WITH WRITING

Writing is not a solitary act. Most professional writers seek feedback from colleagues, editors, family, and friends, and they thank those who have contributed in the acknowledgments section of the book. Students benefit from help with their projects—in conferences with their instructors, peer exchanges with other students in class, and visits to their campus's tutorial services. Whether you are giving help or receiving it, you need to realize that inappropriate help is also plagiarism because it involves using someone else's ideas and language. If someone tells you what to write, rewrites your work for you, or even proofreads or "edits" your work, that is plagiarism, because you are using someone else's work as if it were your own. Likewise, it is

---

*Wayne C. Booth, Gregory Colomb, and Joseph M. Williams, *The Craft of Research.* (Chicago: University of Chicago Press, 2003), 203.

unethical for you to provide such help to anyone else, a practice known as "facilitating plagiarism" and equally punishable at most schools.

The following list describes three unethical ways of giving and receiving help.

1. **Having someone "ghostwrite" your paper.** College campuses attract unscrupulous people who offer to "help" students with their writing. It is dangerous to use an off-campus tutor because his or her primary interest is income, not education.

2. **Having someone edit your paper for style.** It is plagiarism to have someone else change your wording and word choices for you. Your instructor will teach you about elements of style and illustrate principles of editing. This textbook covers such material in Appendix A.

   After you have used this advice to edit your own paper, it is okay to ask someone else to point out passages that need more attention and even to explain why those passages are wordy or unclear. But it is up to you to improve the expression.

3. **Having someone proofread your paper for grammar and punctuation.** As with editing for style, proofreading is your responsibility. You

B. Smaller

"My parents didn't write it—they just tweaked it."

plagiarize if you hand your paper to someone else to "clean it up," whether as a favor or for money. Many students need help with proofreading, and your instructor or on-campus tutorial service can offer instruction that will help you catch errors in the future.

ETHICAL WRITING AND GOOD STUDY HABITS

Good study habits are central to ethical writing.

- **Do not procrastinate.** Students who procrastinate are more likely to make the kind of careless errors that lead to accidental plagiarism. They are also more likely to use intentional plagiarism as the only way to meet a deadline.

- **Take careful notes.** Use your notebook or notecards to write about your sources, being sure to distinguish your own ideas from the material you copy directly or paraphrase. Use quotation marks around any words you take directly from a source.

- **Ask your instructor about proper sources of help with your writing.** Avoid using untrained family members and friends as tutors. If your school has a writing center, take advantage of the tutors there.

- **Work on improving your reading skills.** Good reading skills will empower you to use sources more confidently. Read Chapter 2, "Reading an Argument," for advice on how to improve your comprehension and analysis of texts.

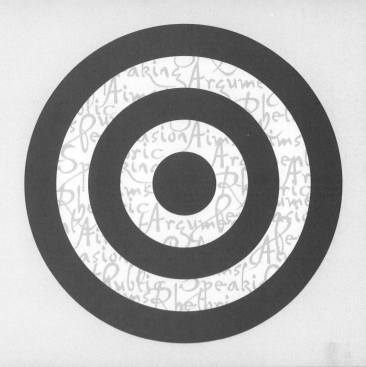

The Aims of
Argument

THE AIMS OF ARGUMENT

CHAPTER 8

Joining the Conversation: Arguing to Inquire

In Chapter 2, "Reading an Argument," and Chapter 3, "Analyzing an Argument," we offered what you need to respond critically to any argument you encounter. Chapter 4 took you through the process of writing a critique, an application of what you learned in Chapters 2 and 3.

What you learned in these chapters applies to arguing to inquire. However, inquiry is different from responding to single arguments. **Inquiry is** *joining a conversation, an ongoing exchange of opinions about some controversial topic,* and therefore involves many arguments advanced by many people.

To join any conversation, you have to know already or become familiar with what is going on. This is the case whether you are talking in a group, posting on a blog, working on a term paper, drafting a business proposal, or composing a letter to your mayor or city council. In short, *having something to say depends on knowing what others have said.* It depends on *comparing perspectives,* analyzing and evaluating existing viewpoints.

What Is Synthesis?

All the genres that use comparisons *synthesize*—a Greek word that means "putting together." Typically the views you encounter in comparing perspectives are at odds with one another enough to make point-by-point reconciliation impossible. In other words, no one could fashion a single, consistent view out of everything they say. Therefore, aim for a *partial synthesis,* selecting what you consider the best insights from each, combining them with your own insights, thereby creating a new perspective. The result is your viewpoint, matured and refined by open and thoughtful engagement with the viewpoints of others.

WHAT IS COMPARING PERSPECTIVES?

Many situations call for written comparisons of people's perspectives on a problem, issue, or question. Money managers compare stock analysts' reports; land developers compare architectural concepts for a new building; government administrators compare reports from advocacy groups; a consumer compares product reviews. Among many others, genres that compare perspectives include

- Book reviews that evaluate two or three recently published books on the same topic
- Market research that analyzes the results of in-depth interviews to find patterns and commonalities in consumers' preferences and attitudes
- Introductions to articles in the sciences that provide overviews of past research
- Exploratory essays that question and evaluate the viewpoints of other people writing on the same topic

WHY WRITE TO COMPARE PERSPECTIVES?

All researched writing begins with reading and comparing other people's perspectives on a topic. Writing out this exploration helps us to

- Sort out the specific points being discussed
- See where opinions intersect and diverge
- Pin down, point by point, the differences and similarities
- Reflect on the points under debate
- Formulate our own view

Put another way, what do you do *after* you find sources for a paper? The answer is, compare perspectives, without which you cannot make sense out of them or use them to say anything yourself. Comparing perspectives, then, is an essential part of doing research for anything you write.

HOW DOES COMPARING PERSPECTIVES WORK?

Writing that compares perspectives usually proceeds by asking and answering a series of questions about the readings selected for comparison.

The Art of Questioning: What to Ask When Comparing Perspectives

1. What is the central question addressed in all the readings?

2. What are the key terms or concepts used in discussing this question, and how do the writers define these terms? Is there disagreement about the meaning of key terms?

3. What do the authors have to say about the question, and where do their answers agree or disagree on points in common? When perspectives disagree, how do you assess the arguments of each author? Whose views have more validity, and why?

4. What conclusions or insights into the central question have you been able to reach as a result of comparing perspectives on it?

Of these four questions, the third is especially important. Locate the points of agreement; they will reveal the *current state of informed opinion.* Locate the points where there is disagreement; they will reveal the *live issues,* what is currently in dispute. We must know both to join a conversation—what is accepted as true, and what people are arguing about.

The Writer as Inquirer

In addition to the perspectives you read, you will probably have a perspective of your own on the central question you are investigating. Acknowledge it, but keep an open mind as you read through others' opinions. Read all perspectives with an equally critical stance. You will be reading arguments, but *you will be arguing to inquire, writing an exploration.* Your paper should open with the central question to explore, not with your own thesis on the question.

It is important to keep the central question open and to present all views fairly and accurately. Use your own thinking to evaluate the views. Keeping a question open does not mean accepting everything you read. Give reasons for saying what you accept as the better perspective as you work through the points of agreement and disagreement. Expect your exploration to lead you to a more informed viewpoint than you had before writing.

Which Character Should Sports Develop?

ANDY RUDD

Andy Rudd is a psychologist on the faculty at Florida State University. The following selection is the opening from a much longer article on the relationship of sports and character. It is widely assumed that participation in sports builds character in young people. If it does, Rudd asks, what kind of character does it build? As you read, identify the differing informed opinions Rudd presents. Where do you stand on this issue, and what might you add to the conversation?

ABSTRACT

For years, strong claims have been made that sport builds character. Despite such claims, a "winning at all cost" mentality can frequently be seen within all of sport. The reason for this paradox may relate to confusion around what it means to demonstrate character. The purpose of this article is to show that there are indeed two distinct types of character that are espoused in the sport milieu. One type is related to social values (social character) the other related to moral values (moral character). Following an explication and comparison of these types of character, a recommendation is made for a needed emphasis towards the development of moral character.

INTRODUCTION

In his *A Way Out of Ethical Confusion,* Zeigler (2004) asks the question: "What character do we seek for people?" He refers to Commager's 1966 list of 12 traits—i.e., "common denominators"—that can be attributed to Americans. In this list are many traits, some of which apply directly to the topic of sport's relationship to character. These are self-confidence; materialism; complacency bordering occasionally on arrogance; cultivation of the competitive spirit; and indifference to, and exasperation with laws, rules, and regulations" (p. 7). Zeigler believes that the situation deteriorated further by the end of the 20th century. In the dedication to this work, he states: "I believe there is an urgent need to challenge the underlying human values and norms that have determined the direction the United States is heading in the 21st century" (p. iii). This comment, if true, has significance in a search for an answer to the topic at hand. Which "character" should sport develop?

Typically when an athlete or team at any level of sport is considered to have displayed character, the word "character" is associated with a host of values such as teamwork, loyalty, self-sacrifice, perseverance, work ethic, and mental toughness. As a specific example, a high school athletic director defined an athlete's character as "a willingness to try no matter what the situation. An attempt to continually improve; a willingness to give all up for the cause; and sacrificing without expectations." In another example, a high school coach asserted: "Character is the belief in self-worth and your own work ethic. . . ." (Rudd, 1999).

In professional sport, character has been defined similarly. For instance, consider a newspaper article that headlined, "The Arizona Diamondbacks Attribute Their Success to Character." Specifically, the article highlighted the Diamondbacks as players who work hard and don't complain about salaries (Heyman, 2000). Consider also an issue of *Sports Illustrated* in which New England Patriots' Troy Brown commented on former teammate Drew Bledsoe's ability to play with a broken finger and lead his team to victory. Brown stated, "It showed a lot of character" (Zimmerman, 2001, p. 162).

Margin notes:

A convention in science articles, abstracts help researchers decide whether an article is relevant to their research without having to read the article itself.

First paragraph "frames" the article by answering key questions: What is character as Americans understand and value it? How does character relate to sports? How does character developed by sports relate to the future of American values?

This article uses APA notational conventions. Use it as a model for papers you write that require APA style.

Specifies what character means in sports, as generally understood by athletic directors and coaches. Author must establish this understanding of character to serve as a contrast with "moral character" in paragraph 4.

4   However, in contrast to the notion that an athlete of character is one who displays values such as teamwork, loyalty, self-sacrifice, perseverance, work ethic, and mental toughness, sport scholars in the area of character development have defined character with a different set of values. Sport scholars, including sport philosophers and sport psychologists, more commonly define an athlete of character as one who is honest, fair, responsible, respectful, and compassionate (Arnold, 1999; Beller & Stoll, 1995; Gough, 1998; Shields & Bredemeier, 1995). For example, Arnold (1999) states, "In terms of moral goodness, or what I refer to as moral character, it involves a life that complies with such virtues as justice, honesty, and compassion" (p. 42).

> Specifies what author means by "moral character" and contrasts it with "social character." This is the second perspective the article develops.

5   It does indeed seem, therefore, that there are two distinct definitions of character maintained by two camps. The first camp consists of coaches, administrators, and players who may typically define character with social values such as teamwork, loyalty, self-sacrifice, and perseverance. This could be designated as "social character." The second camp consists of sport scholars, and people of earlier generations still alive, who typically define character with moral values such as honesty, fairness, responsibility, compassion, and respect. This is commonly referred to by many of them as "moral character." The existence of these two camps, each with their respective definitions of character, suggests that there is confusion and disagreement concerning the definition of character in sport. (Of course, there may be some "in the middle" who accept an overlapping, possibly conflicting set of values to describe the term "character.")

> Summarizes the social versus moral character contrast. It is weighted to favor moral character.

> Anticipates objection: That the contrast between social and moral character is too sharp, as if there is no middle ground. Author concedes that the values can be combined.

6   As a result of the above, the differences in the way character is defined may provide strong evidence why many feel there is a lack of sportsmanship in competitive sport today. Similarly, these same people decry the "winning-at-all-cost" mentality that seems to prevail in athletics (see, for example, "A Purpose," 1999; Hawes, 1998; Spencer, 1996). Many coaches, athletic administrators, and parents may indeed place such a premium on social values such as teamwork, loyalty, self-sacrifice, and work ethic that they forget, or at least downplay, any emphasis on time-honored moral values such as honesty, fairness, responsibility, and respect.

> Points to a commonly recognized problem in contemporary sports that makes the author's research and conclusions relevant, worth reading and studying.

7   The purpose of this paper is to define and discuss in detail two types of character (moral and social) that are espoused by two distinct groups in the sport milieu. The ramifications of the "social character view" in sport are explained below. At the same time, what the author feels is the need for greater emphasis on the development of moral character in sport and physical education will also be discussed.

> Prepares the reader for the rest of the article by stating what the author is doing and why.

REFERENCES

Arnold, P. (1994). Sport and moral education. *The Journal of Moral Education, 23*(1), 75–89.

Beller, J. M., & Stoll, S. K. (1995). Moral reasoning of high school student athletes and general students: An empirical study versus personal testimony. *Pediatric Exercise Science, 7*(4), 352–363.

Gough, R. (1998). A practical strategy for emphasizing character development in sport and physical education. *Journal of Physical Education, Recreation, & Dance, 69*(2), 18–23.

Hawes, K. (1998). Sportsmanship: Why should anybody care? *NCAA news*, pp. 1, 18.

Heyman, J. (2000, May 22). They're 'good guys, good players.' *Statesman Journal*, p. 3B.

A purpose pitch. (1999, May 17). *Sports Illustrated, 90*, 24.

Rudd, A. (1999). [High school coaches' definitions of character]. Unpublished raw data.

Shields, D., & Bredemeier, B. (1995). *Character development and physical activity.* Champaign, IL: Human Kinetics.

Spencer, A. F. (1996). Ethics in physical and sport education. *Journal of Physical Education, Recreation & Dance, 67*(7), 37–39.

Zeigler, E. F. (2004). *A way out of ethical confusion.* Victoria, Canada: Trafford.

Zimmerman, P. (2001, September 3). New England Patriots. *Sports Illustrated, 95*(9), 162–163.

Note APA "References" section, rather than the MLA "Works Cited" list. See Chapter 6, pages 148–156 for more on APA conventions.

QUESTIONS FOR DISCUSSION

1. Notice that the Rudd reading is organized around questions addressed by various writers rather than around what each writer says, taken up one by one. Why does organizing around questions work so well?

2. One of the keys to responding to anything we read, including exploratory writing, is to evaluate it according to our own experience. What have you learned from participating in sports or from observing sports events? Does your experience mirror what this article says?

READINGS

To demonstrate the process of exploring perspectives, we present three readings with different views on whether narcissism is increasing in Western culture, particularly among young people.

See Chapter 2, "Reading an Argument," pages 15–30, for more on preparing to read any challenging text.

Take time to consider the topic and your first response to it. In this case, what is narcissism? A good place to find in-depth definitions is the *Oxford English Dictionary (OED).* As defined by the *OED, narcissism* is:

1. Excessive self-love or vanity; self-admiration, self-centredness.

2. *Psychol.* The condition of gaining emotional or erotic gratification from self-contemplation, sometimes regarded as a stage in the normal

Figure 8.1
Narcissus contemplating his own image
Bridgeman Art Library/Getty Images

psychological development of children which may be reverted to in adulthood during mental illness.

The term *narcissism* alludes to a character in Greek mythology. (See Figure 8.1.) The *OED* defines Narcissus as:

> *Greek Mythol.* (The name of) a beautiful youth who fell in love with his own reflection in water and pined to death. Hence (allusively): a person characterized by extreme self-admiration or vanity; a narcissist.

◎◎ FOLLOWING THROUGH

What examples of excessive self-love have you observed, either in your own life or in the media? What kind of behavior do you consider narcissistic? What conditions might contribute to such behavior?   •

The Paradox of Narcissism

JOHN F. SCHUMAKER

This selection comes from *In Search of Happiness: Understanding an Endangered State of Mind.* John F. Schumaker is a clinical psychologist who lives in Australia and has published nine books on issues of culture and mental health. As you read, consider the concepts of self-esteem, happiness, and consumer culture Schumaker introduces and how he uses them to compare perspectives on narcissism.

1   While walking through the local Botanical Gardens recently, a woman wearing a "Love Yourself" T-shirt jogged past me. T-shirts like that were non-existent in the 1960s, when they all read "Love" or "Love One Another." But preachers of self-love are everywhere today. There are even numerous books extolling the virtues of self-love, including Peter McWilliams's *Love 101: To Love Oneself Is the Beginning of a Lifelong Romance.* The subtitle of that book is actually a tongue-in-cheek comment once made by Oscar Wilde. But it seems that many people have come to take that idea literally.

2   Today the self-esteem movement is in full swing. As an arm of feel-good culture, this movement has persuaded us that it is not good enough to feel good within ourselves. We must also feel good *about* ourselves. It has grown in force to the extent that it has reshaped childhood education. Teachers in recent years have been trained that a high level of self-esteem is the child's passport to happiness and success in life, as well as to a good education. Less and less emphasis is being paid to self-discipline, hard work, integrity, and helping students gain realistic appraisals of themselves. Instead, young people are being told automatically that they are infinitely talented, phenomenally creative, and erupting with potential in any area that takes their fancy. One zealous school in Alabama went so far as placing banners over all bathroom mirrors that read "You are now looking at one of the most special people in the whole world."

3   Young people find themselves in a culture that tells us to feel good about ourselves regardless of what we are as people. It does not matter if we are spoiled, selfish, indifferent, wasteful, or cruel. We have done our best to make self-esteem unconditional. But many education theorists are now conceding that the self-esteem extravaganza is proving to be a dismal failure in terms of education and personality development.

4   For instance, it was once thought that high self-esteem was crucial for effective leadership, social skills, and cooperation. The same was said about the ability to resist risky, anti-social, and self-destructive behaviours such as drug taking, smoking, drinking, and unsafe sex. But in all the cases, high self-esteem offers no advantages. In fact, research shows that high self-esteem increases people's likelihood to experiment and to take chances, which can make them more vulnerable to certain problems.

5   Once considered to be essential for advanced social skills and interpersonal effectiveness, high self-esteem has been shown to give no additional edge in these areas as well. It can even impair social judgement and conscience development. Recent research has found that "self-enhancers" with highly favourable views of themselves were more prone to acts of aggression such as bullying. They were also more inclined toward irritating behaviour patterns such as bragging, being overly opinionated, and interrupting others in conversation.

6   Those with high self-esteem appear to have their trumped-up pride hurt more easily, which can trigger in them hostility and other reactions that turn people off. High self-esteem individuals find themselves even more alienated from others when they are not able to conceal their elevated perception of themselves. While high self-esteem leads people to perceive themselves to be more popular and socially adept than other people, this does not correspond to reality when others are asked to rate them. While it is still promoted as a happiness helper, it has become clear that high self-esteem is not all that it was once cracked up to be.

7   . . . The notion that we are not worthy of being happy unless we are big, and full of ourselves, is a thoroughly Western one. Happiness in modern Western culture unfolds in the context of individualism. So it follows that our perceptions of ourselves would be crucial in judging our own degree of happiness. If we are self-satisfied, we are likely to say that we are satisfied with life. This contrasts with collectivist cultures where happiness is tied to cooperation and social harmony, and to being a worthwhile and valued member of the group. In such settings, less effort would be put into self-enhancement, and more into group-enhancement, as a pathway to happiness.

8   The worst problem comes when self-esteem becomes completely blown out of proportion to the extent that it gives way to narcissism. Unwarranted self-esteem may in many respects be a forerunner of the modern type of "unwarranted happiness" that has been criticised because it is not founded on anything substantial. In this regard, the type of narcissism and unjustified self-esteem that prevails today is quite interesting in light of the history of the self-esteem movement, which many say was begun by Los Angeles psychotherapist and corporate consultant

Dr Nathaniel Branden. While he tried to soften our negative connotations about self-centredness, he was careful to distinguish between healthy and unhealthy types of self-attention. He professed self-esteem that was built on the recognition of the need for love, healthy relationships, and spiritual awareness that he called "soulfulness." Since its origins, the self-esteem movement has given way to unbridled me-ism that lacks much scope for a meaningful shared happiness.

9   The ego has become so artificially inflated in today's cultural climate that the idea of being famous is seen as a requirement for happiness. Local fame is no longer enough. Fame seekers want the whole world as their audience, which may in part be a reaction to the absence of true carers in their local environments. If nobody around me cares, maybe I can get the whole world to care. As our need for affection has been relocated to the public sphere, wooing the mass media has become a popular form of courtship. Ignored people of every description are coming out of the woodwork to set world records or be the first to unicycle blindfolded across the Utah salt flats or leapfrog a thousand beer barrels in less than fifteen minutes.

10   The familiar cry "Look at me!" of the neglected child begging for parental attention has spread across the entire Western world as people have become increasingly invisible. For many, fame is imagined to be the only touch that can soothe their gnawing separation anxiety. The problem from a happiness standpoint is that there are very few winners in the fame game. As desperate as we are to be seen and recognised, getting anonymous fans is no easy task. Yet the quest for fame has become inseparable from the quest for happiness.

11   This trend is eating away at people's prospects for happiness by way of condemning them to almost certain disappointment. They become slaves to a public that is largely a fiction propagated by Hollywood-style hype. The lucky few who make it into the limelight often fall prey to their anxieties about the fickleness of their unknown worshippers, not to mention the loss of privacy and the relationship breakdowns that are part of the package. Despite this, the desire for public fame grows more powerful as our local worlds continue to weaken as a source of recognition. Mixed in with our own ambitions for fame is a trend to bow down further and further to those who have already become famous.

12   Consumer culture has a large investment in narcissism, just as it does with fame. A lot has been said about today's culture of narcissism, but almost always from a negative point of view. The upside of narcissism is that it is always associated with a high degree of entitlement that sways people to think that they deserve to have things—lots of things. The advertising industry is geared toward selling on the back of rising narcissism. Some of it is blatant, such as commercials that blurt out various messages to the effect ". . . because you deserve it." Others are subtler at selling things as part of people's growing desire to romance themselves. As narcissism becomes a dominant personality trait, the person gradually becomes shallower and loses the ability to feel deeply for other people. This too increases consumption potential by making people more accepting of the fictionalised world of objects.

13   The perfect psychological incubator for narcissism is a combination of overindulgence and neglect, which is the story for so many people growing up under modern cultural conditions. It is also the classic condition for the emergence of sociopaths whose main attribute is an absence of social conscience. Narcissists, like sociopaths, experience little guilt, or sense of sin. But sin is not good for the economy. As the cult of the individual has gradually made narcissism acceptable, the sense of sin has been overtaken by the feeling that one has the right to do whatever it takes to satisfy oneself and to feel good.

14   The sins that remain in our culture of narcissism are largely sins against oneself. We feel that we have done something wrong if we have not gotten the most for ourselves, done the most, or made the most of our opportunities. Other than that, the old-fashioned sins that stemmed from offending others or God are virtually obsolete. The worst sin today is to deprive oneself, which once again is music to the ears of a consumer economy. While feelings of being a sinful person can tarnish happiness, the wholesale erasure of social responsibility can be even more destructive to one's prospects for happiness.

15   An unceasing preoccupation with personal happiness is in many ways an expression of narcissism. Or at least this is the case with a large percentage of happiness seekers who are looking for happiness by way of what they can draw toward themselves, rather than what they can share with others. Jean-Jacques Rousseau once alluded to narcissism in saying that "man's nature is not fully mature until it becomes social." One could say the same thing about happiness; that is, happiness is not fully mature until it becomes social.

16   The myth of Narcissus is a tragic one. Because he will not surrender himself, Narcissus blows his chances with the beautiful nymph Echo, only to be cursed by an unrelenting self-devotion that robs him of his vigour and beauty. His beloved self never returns his affections, and finally he pines to death, leaving in his place only a lonely flower to preserve his memory. Fittingly, the tale lacks a happy ending. Yet it could be argued that narcissism is not a bad plan of attack. Put yourself first at all times and devote your full energies to feeling good. But narcissism has little to offer by way of happiness, or even self-love. Societies that generate narcissism among their members are dysfunctional ones that have lost sight of the reciprocal nature of human happiness.

17   The unofficial labels "middle-class narcissism" and "normal narcissism" have been used to describe the garden variety of narcissism that is generated by modern consumer culture, which has removed all taboos on selfishness in order to stimulate consumption. As a personality structure, collective narcissism has some advantages since it allows people in a hyper-competitive environment to exploit others without guilt. At the same time, it promotes a low tolerance for frustration that destroys relationships. People often end up fluctuating between expressions of hostility and ungainly attempts to get the approval of others.

Changes in Narcissism

JEAN M. TWENGE

> Jean M. Twenge is Associate Professor of Psychology at San Diego State University. This selection is from *Generation Me: Why Today's Young Americans Are More Confident, Assertive, Entitled—and More Miserable Than Ever Before* (Free Press, 2006). Notice the number and variety of sources Twenge cites. What do the number and variety of sources Twenge cites reveal about her position on the prevalence of narcissism in today's society?

1 Narcissism is one of the few personality traits that psychologists agree is almost completely negative. Narcissists are overly focused on themselves and lack empathy for others, which means they cannot see another person's perspective. (Sound like the last clerk who served you?) They also feel entitled to special privileges and believe that they are superior to other people. As a result, narcissists are bad relationship partners and can be difficult to work with. Narcissists are also more likely to be hostile, feel anxious, compromise their health, and fight with friends and family. Unlike those merely high in self-esteem, narcissists admit that they don't feel close to other people.

2 All evidence suggests that narcissism is much more common in recent generations. In the early 1950s, only 12% of teens aged 14 to 16 agreed with the statement "I am an important person." By the late 1980s, an incredible 80%—almost seven times as many—claimed they were important. Psychologist Harrison Gough found consistent increases on narcissism items among college students quizzed between the 1960s and the 1990s. GenMe students were more likely to agree that "I would be willing to describe myself as a pretty 'strong' personality" and "I have often met people who were supposed to be experts who were no better than I." In other words, those other people don't know what they're talking about, so everyone should listen to me.

3 In a 2002 survey of 3,445 people conducted by Joshua Foster, Keith Campbell, and me, younger people scored considerably higher on the Narcissistic Personality Inventory, agreeing with items such as "If I ruled the world it would be a better place," "I am a special person," and "I can live my life anyway I want to." (These statements evoke the image of a young man speeding down the highway in the world's biggest SUV, honking his horn, and screaming, "Get out of my way! I'm important!") This study was cross-sectional, though, meaning that it was a one-time sample of people of different ages. For that reason, we cannot be sure if any differences are due to age or to generation; however, the other studies of narcissism mentioned previously suggest that generation plays a role. It is also interesting that narcissism scores were fairly high until around age 35, after which they decreased markedly. This is right around the cutoff between GenMe and previous generations.

4 Narcissism is the darker side of the focus on the self, and is often confused with self-esteem. Self-esteem is often based on solid relationships with others, whereas narcissism comes from believing that you are special and more important than other people. Many of the school programs designed to raise self-esteem probably raise narcissism instead. Lillian Katz, a professor of early childhood

education at the University of Illinois, wrote an article titled "All About Me: Are We Developing Our Children's Self-Esteem or Their Narcissism?" She writes, "Many of the practices advocated in pursuit of [high self-esteem] may instead inadvertently develop narcissism in the form of excessive preoccupation with oneself." Because the school programs emphasize being "special" rather than encouraging friendships, we may be training an army of little narcissists instead of raising kids' self-esteem.

5   Many young people also display entitlement, a facet of narcissism that involves believing that you deserve and are entitled to more than others. A scale that measures entitlement has items like "Things should go my way," "I demand the best because I'm worth it," and (my favorite) "If I were on the *Titanic,* I would deserve to be on the *first* lifeboat!" A 2005 Associated Press article printed in hundreds of news outlets labeled today's young people "The Entitlement Generation." In the article, employers complained that young employees expected too much too soon and had very high expectations for salary and promotions.

Teachers have seen this attitude for years now. One of my colleagues said his students acted as if grades were something they simply deserved to get no matter what. He joked that their attitude could be summed up by "Where's my A? I distinctly remember ordering an A from the catalog." Stout, the education professor, lists the student statements familiar to teachers everywhere: "I need a better grade," "I deserve an A on this paper," "I *never* get B's." Stout points out that the self-esteem movement places the student's feelings at the center, so "students learn that they do not need to respect their teachers or even earn their grades, so they begin to believe that they are entitled to grades, respect, or anything else . . . just for asking."

6   Unfortunately, narcissism can lead to outcomes far worse than grade grubbing. Several studies have found that narcissists lash out aggressively when they are insulted or rejected. Eric Harris and Dylan Klebold, the teenage gunmen at Columbine High School, made statements remarkably similar to items on the most popular narcissism questionnaire. On a videotape made before the shootings, Harris picked up a gun, made a shooting noise, and said "Isn't it fun to get the respect we're going to deserve?" (Chillingly similar to the narcissism item. "I insist upon getting the respect that is due me.") Later, Harris said, "I could convince them that I'm going to climb Mount Everest, or I have a twin brother growing out of my back. I can make you believe anything" (virtually identical to the item "I can make anyone believe anything I want them to"). Harris and Klebold then debate which famous movie director will film their story. A few weeks after making the videotapes, Harris and Klebold killed thirteen people and then themselves.

7   Other examples abound. In a set of lab studies, narcissistic men felt less empathy for rape victims, reported more enjoyment when watching a rape scene in a movie, and were more punitive toward a woman who refused to read a sexually arousing passage out loud to them. Abusive husbands who threaten to kill their wives—and tragically sometimes do—are the ultimate narcissists. They see everyone and everything in terms of fulfilling their needs, and become very angry and aggressive when things don't go exactly their way. Many workplace shootings occur after an employee is fired and decides he'll "show" everyone how powerful he is.

8   The rise in narcissism has very deep roots. It's not just that we feel better about ourselves, but that we even think to ask the question. We fixate on self-esteem, and unthinkingly build narcissism, because we believe that the needs of the individual are paramount. This will stay with us even if self-esteem programs end up in the dustbin of history.

QUESTIONS FOR DISCUSSION

1. How would you summarize Twenge's perspective on the topic of narcissism? How does it compare with Schumaker's?

2. Twenge is a psychology professor—a teacher and researcher. How might her profession affect her purpose and audience?

Generation Y and the New Myth of Narcissus

DUNCAN GREENBERG

At the time he wrote this column for his campus newspaper, the *Yale Herald,* Duncan Greenberg was a senior.

1   In our 10 or 20 years of existence as an age group, we've been called a lot of things, but "narcissistic" is the slur *du jour.* A controversial study at San Diego State University, which trickled down to papers this week, found that "30 percent more college students showed 'elevated narcissism' in 2006 compared with 1982." The study was authored by Jean Twenge, the cynic behind the book *Generation Me: Why Today's Young Americans Are More Confident, Assertive, Entitled—and More Miserable Than Ever Before.* Twenge consolidated data from 25 years of surveys and found—or claimed to find—that the Millennials had reached unhealthy heights of self-esteem.

2   To you and me, narcissism remains an elusive term. But words have different meanings in common parlance than in academic jargon, and there is a general consensus in the psychology community as to the symptoms of "narcissism." Some of the more familiar characteristics, as defined by the Mayo Clinic, include a "need for constant praise," a "grandiose sense of one's own abilities or achievements," a "lack of empathy for other people," and an "expectation of special treatment."

3   Twenge's study hasn't been published yet, but newspaper articles give us glimpses of her methodology: In an annual poll conducted for 25 years, students were asked if they agreed with statements like, "If I ruled the world, it would be a better place," "I think I am a special person," and "I can live my life any way I want to." Each student's answers were ranked on a scale from egocentric to empathetic.

4   Having circumscribed the malady, though, we are left with the problem of diagnosis. You can't just flat-out ask people if they're narcissistic (a true narcissist will never admit it); your only hope is to trick your subject into signing off on

statements that indirectly expose his inflated ego. That's why psychologists use oblique and ambiguous statements like, "I think I am a special person." The downside of obliquity, however, is questionable results.

5   Take the second question for example: if someone thinks he's special, does that make him a narcissist? Isn't everyone "special," in the etymologically related sense of "species," implying a unique combination of color, shape, and size? And where exactly is the line between narcissism and self-confidence? Given our high achievement and low rates of violence, maybe we Millennials are entitled to some self-esteem. Remember, surveys are like a house of mirrors: You can appear fat or thin, tall or short, depending on which study you happen to be looking at. UCLA's annual report, "The American Freshman National Norms for 2006," for example, paints a radically different picture. Its finding? "A record number [of college freshmen]—83 percent— say they volunteered at least occasionally during their senior year of high school."

6   Either we're narcissistic, or we're compassionate—we can't be both. But rather than reconcile the two studies, Twenge dismisses the redeeming evidence, arguing that more and more high schools require students to meet a not-for-profit quota— the drive to do community service, she suggests, is coming from without, not from within. Admittedly, as university acceptance rates have fallen, students have turned increasingly to volunteer work to gild their applications. But if you eliminate competitive pressure from the equation, two-thirds of college freshman still believe it is "essential or very important to help others who are in difficulty, the highest percentage in a quarter century." I'm not calling Twenge a quack, but for every study that supports her point, there's another that contradicts it. And the fact of the matter is that when it comes to giving back, we've more than done our part.

7   "Okay," the critics say, "maybe you're not selfish, but you're self-absorbed." True, Millennials have been known to flaunt their lives on YouTube and MySpace. But it's not as if our predecessors didn't get attention other ways—you're telling me the hippie and grunge movements weren't attempts to attract eyeballs by raising eyebrows. Besides, while there's no denying that YouTube and MySpace are perfect outlets for the world's narcissists, vanity is not the only trait those websites cater to. Would YouTube be worth $1.65 billion to Google if users only posted videos of themselves without so much as a glance at others' postings? Critics get hung up on the egotism of the prefixes "my" and "you," but these sites are only successful because they're about other people—about meeting other people, about seeing what hidden talents other people have. Social networking, whether virtual or in person, is always going to entail a little window-dressing; the quasi-narcissistic practice of putting one's best foot forward in social settings is hardly confined to cyberspace.

8   In a recent *Los Angeles Times* editorial, William Strauss and Neil Howe ["Will the Real Gen Y Please Stand Up?" 2 March 2007] hit upon a baffling phenomenon: "Whenever youth behavior seems clearly positive, critics cynically find a way to dismiss it." Maybe these critics begrudge us our youth, maybe they mistake young-looking bodies for immature minds—your guess is as good as mine. For not only do we care about what other people think, seeking the approval of our peers through YouTube ratings and FaceBook friend requests, but we care about how other people feel, volunteering for heroic causes on unprecedented scale. Yes, we

feel entitled—to a world without terrorism and global warming and to politicians who will take these scourges seriously. And, no, we don't need constant praise—but a little positive feedback, when we deserve it, would be nice.

QUESTIONS FOR DISCUSSION

1. Greenberg was prompted to write this column by a news story about research by Jean Twenge into the topic of narcissism. How does his description of the research compare to Twenge's perspective?

2. What arguments and evidence does Greenberg give to refute Twenge's conclusions? Which author do you find more credible?

CLAIMING VOICE IN COMPARING PERSPECTIVES

Voice must adapt to convention, the norms certain genres typically observe. For example, the reading, "Which Character Should Sports Develop?" by Andy Rudd comes from a science journal. Convention dictates that authors avoid the first person—that is, the use of "I"—because science writing wants to sound objective, as if the judgments made are free of bias and passion.

Nevertheless, authors do express their point of view in scientific writing. For example, in the Rudd reading, the author points out that

> Sport scholars, including sport philosophers and sport psychologists, more commonly define an athlete of character as one who is honest, fair, responsible, respectful, and compassionate (Arnold, 1999; Beller & Stoll, 1995; Gough, 1998; Shields & Bredemeier, 1995).

The voice sounds neutral and objective, but actually the author is favoring what he calls "moral character" over what he calls "social character" by identifying the first with "sports scholars" rather than the coaches with which he associates "winning at all costs." He also cites in parenthesis names and professional publications associated with the moral view of character, which he does not provide for the social view of character. There are subtle ways of expressing your point of view, then, even when convention prevents you from saying "I think that . . ." or "This view is dangerous and that view is healthy."

Because the objective voice is a common convention for writing in many college courses and professional settings, learning how to make this voice work for you is important.

THE ASSIGNMENT

Read at least two perspectives addressing a topic you care about. In an essay explore the perspectives by noting where different authors address the same or similar questions, and compare their answers. Decide which views seem most valid and which have deepened your own understanding of the topic and its relevance to your life.

Topic and Focus

Pick a topic of current interest on which many people are expressing their views. The point is to explore the views, examine and question them carefully. Keep your mind open until you have explored the viewpoints, then draw your conclusions.

Audience

Think of your audience as people interested in your topic but who have not read what you have read. Consequently, you will need to tell your readers enough about each view for them to know who says what, using quotations and paraphrases as needed.

Voice and Style

Imagine that you are participating in a conversation with your readers about the perspectives and your opinions of them. You should sound fair, thoughtful, and receptive, willing to ponder points of view you do not find persuasive but which may contain valuable points or insights. Be willing also to look for problems in perspectives you do find persuasive.

Writing Assignment Suggestions

Comparing perspectives is a common occurrence in our everyday lives. For a film you have seen or a performance you have attended, find two or more reviews of substantial length, and compare the reviewers' interpretations and evaluations. Conclude by explaining how reading the perspectives added to your ideas about the film. If your library has a collection of history textbooks, find ones from different time periods and compare their treatments of events or people. Have "the facts" changed? How has interpretation of the facts changed?

CHOOSING A TOPIC

Your instructor may assign a topic and readings arguing from different perspectives about it. If not, here are some possibilities for finding topics.

- *Reading and research.* Most authors will mention the names of people who agree and disagree with their point of view. For example, a news article about Jean Twenge also mentioned a psychologist whose work disputed Twenge's conclusions. To bring that perspective into your comparison, do an Internet or library database search of that person's name.

- *Library databases.* Research the topic in an index to periodicals, such as Academic OneFile (see Chapter 6, pages 110–112). The advantage is that you will find readings grouped according to topic and time, some of which will likely refer to each other.

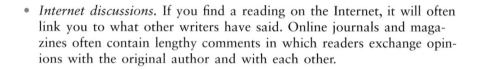

Strategies for Comparing Perspectives

With each reading

1. Paraphrase or summarize the main points
2. Find the questions each point answers
3. Write down your response to each point
4. Keep track of connections across perspectives
5. Maintain an exploratory stance

We take you through these five steps, showing why they are worth doing and how they work with the narcissism topic.

- *Internet discussions.* If you find a reading on the Internet, it will often link you to what other writers have said. Online journals and magazines often contain lengthy comments in which readers exchange opinions with the original author and with each other.

EXPLORING YOUR TOPIC

Before reading, begin by clarifying key definitions as we did with narcissism, using a good dictionary. Write to record your own viewpoints on the topic. Then, move on to explore the perspectives through your selection of readings.

Paraphrase or Summarize the Main Points

Paraphrasing or summarizing will help you digest the ideas and talk about them in your own voice. Mark the major subdivisions (paragraphs that discuss the same point) as you read. For each subdivision, put the main point in your own words. Reread the first two paragraphs of the Schumaker reading, "The Paradox of Narcissism," reproduced below and compare them with our student, Ian Fagerstrom's, paraphrase.

See Chapter 6, pages 127–133, for guidance on paraphrasing and summarizing.

I. Schumaker, Paragraphs 1–2

> While walking through the local Botanical Gardens recently, a woman wearing a "Love Yourself" T-shirt jogged past me. T-shirts like that were non-existent in the 1960s, when they all read "Love" or "Love One Another." But preachers of self-love are everywhere today. There are even numerous books extolling the virtues of self-love, including Peter McWilliams's *Love 101: To Love Oneself Is the Beginning of a Lifelong Romance.* The subtitle of that book is actually a tongue-in-cheek comment once made by Oscar Wilde. But it seems that many people have come to take that idea literally.
>
> Today the self-esteem movement is in full swing. As an arm of feel-good culture, this movement has persuaded us that it is not good

enough to feel good within ourselves. We must also feel good about ourselves. It has grown in force to the extent that it has reshaped childhood education. Teachers in recent years have been trained that a high level of self-esteem is the child's passport to happiness and success in life, as well as to a good education. Less and less emphasis is being paid to self-discipline, hard work, integrity, and helping students gain realistic appraisals of themselves. Instead, young people are being told automatically that they are infinitely talented, phenomenally creative, and erupting with potential in any area that takes their fancy. One zealous school in Alabama went so far as placing banners over all the bathroom mirrors that read "You are now looking at one of the most special people in the whole world."

Ian's Paraphrase of Schumaker's Paragraphs 1–2

Schumaker compares self-love now to the 1960's to show a change in focus. He also makes the point that the schools have worked too hard to bring up kids' self esteem at the expense of old-fashioned values like hard work.

◎◎ FOLLOWING THROUGH

Mark up the text of one of the readings to indicate its subdivisions. For each subdivision, write a paraphrase of its main point or points. As a class, discuss what students selected as main points and compare your paraphrases.   •

Turn Main Points into Questions

Turn the main points into questions by asking, What question is this an answer to? Turning the main points into questions will help you in two ways: (1) *to connect the readings*, because writers will address the same questions; and (2) *to organize your paper*, because exploratory writing is structured around questions. These are the questions the main points in Ian's paraphrase of Paragraphs 1–2 answer:

- Has there been an increase in narcissism? Schumaker says yes.
- What has caused this increase? Schumaker says a cause is the self-esteem movement in the schools.

◎◎ FOLLOWING THROUGH

In groups of two or three, take paraphrases or quotations that the group agrees represent key points in the reading. As we have illustrated, rephrase the point to show what question the author is addressing.   •

Paraphrase and Comment

Write informally, such as in your notebook or on a class discussion board, to respond to the main points in each reading. Draw on your own experiences to test the merit of the author's ideas.

Here is an example of a notebook entry in response to Schumaker's reading. Notice how Ian moves back and forth between quoted and paraphrased passages in the text and his own response to the passages. To show the texture of moving from what the text says to what Ian says back, we have bolded the references to Schumaker's text.

> Shumaker seems to be very cynical about self-esteem, without pointing out that self-esteem in moderation is actually not a bad thing. **He says that "high self-esteem is not all that it was once cracked up to be" (169) and shows a correlation between people with high self-esteem and negative traits like risky sexual behavior, bragging, and hostility when they think they have been slighted.** Yes, I agree that too-high self-esteem is detrimental to happiness, but he could at least say that moderate self-esteem isn't bad. Without some self-esteem, I would not push myself to take on new challenges. Sure, **Western culture says that we always need to feel good about ourselves (169),** but he could at least admit that positive self-worth doesn't automatically lead to narcissism. He says, **"Societies that generate narcissism among their members are dysfunctional ones that have lost sight of the reciprocal nature of human happiness" (173).** This is a good point because individualism won't ever result in true happiness, but why can't he talk about people who balance self-worth with respect and love for others?

As you read other perspectives, write more comparative notebook entries. In a notebook entry responding to more than one reading, show how both provide answers to a single question, either agreeing or disagreeing. If you organize these informal comparisons around questions in common, you will be creating material to use in the rough draft.

◎◎ FOLLOWING THROUGH

As you read and reread each of the perspectives, record key points in a reading and interact with them by stating your own evaluations of the text, connections with the topic, and comparisons to other readings.

Create a comparative grid to map your comparisons. When reading to compare what different authors have to say on similar topics, focus on where they agree and disagree on the same points. If you look at the list of questions raised in the first reading, you will see whether the second reading addresses any of the same questions. A comparative grid makes these connections easier to see. Review the following comparative grid to get a sense of how the points made about narcissism in the Schumaker and Twenge essays compare.   •

Question	Schumaker	Twenge
What is narcissism? How does it compare with self-esteem?	Paragraph 8	Paragraphs 1, 4
Is narcissism greater today than in the past?	Paragraphs 1, 3, 9	Paragraphs 2–3, 5–6
Is high self-esteem a good thing or a bad thing?	Paragraphs 3–6	Paragraph 4
If narcissism is increasing, what is contributing to this change?	Paragraphs 2, 9–13	Paragraphs 4, 9
What effects does narcissism have on personality and behavior?	Paragraphs 5–6, 9, 11, 15, 17	Paragraphs 1, 7–8

FOLLOWING THROUGH

Print out the online worksheet in Connect to make an idea grid of the passages and ideas that connect across the readings as the answers address similar questions. This will also serve as an aid in organizing your draft.

Keep Track of Connections across Perspectives

As you read a second or third person's perspective, try one or more of these suggestions to help keep control over your sources:

- Annotate each reading with references to page numbers in other sources that address the same questions.
- Use color-coded highlighters to mark passages addressing the same questions in different readings.
- Consult previous informal writings often to recall ideas already responded to. Add quotes and paraphrases from new sources as they relate to points already explored.
- Add to your idea grid if you prefer this way of tracking ideas across sources.

Maintain an Exploratory Stance

It is important not to limit your observations to personal experience; doing this will limit your ability to compare effectively. For example, on the question of what causes narcissism, Twenge says that elementary schools praise kids who have done nothing to deserve praise. Some students said, "She's wrong; that didn't happen at my school. We had to work for our A's." A more exploratory stance would be to say, "While some schools may give kids false praise, in my experience I haven't seen it." And then you could go on to say more about how your schools did not have grade inflation, allowed students to fail, and so on. But you might also ask other students what their experiences have been at their schools. Inquiry, comparing perspectives, is all about opening your mind to the way others see the world. Doing so will enhance your own point of view.

DRAFTING YOUR PAPER

Drafting the essay for this project should not be difficult if you have been doing informal writing as you explored the sources. Read through your material again, and then consider the following advice.

Planning the Draft

Before you start drafting you need a plan to give your paper focus, purpose, and organization. For your introduction, you could

- open with your own view before reading. In the body and conclusion, indicate how your thinking changed.
- open with the question that is the focus of your exploration. State it clearly and explain its importance.
- open with one of the main questions that cut across the readings, such as "Some people think narcissism is a growing problem. Is it?" You could move directly into your paper this way.

You also need to mention the writers whose viewpoints you are exploring. You could devote one paragraph to background for all of them, citing full names, credentials, titles of the works you read, and main points. Or you could save this information for the body of your paper, introducing the authors as you bring them into your discussion.

The Art of Questioning: Planning the Body

Do not try to cover every point that comes up in the readings. *Be selective;* explore a few questions in depth. Choose ones you wrote most about in the informal writing you did.

Take up the general questions first and then more specific ones. It wouldn't make sense to look at the role of schools in creating narcissists before taking up the questions "What is narcissism?" and "Is it increasing?"

Bear in mind that you need not agree with a viewpoint to explore interesting questions it raises. You could say, "While I see Greenberg's position on my generation as more realistic than Twenge's, is there anything valid in her idea that American culture encourages self-absorption?" Once you have worked out your answers to these questions, start drafting your paper.

Organizing around Questions

A paper that synthesizes ideas from multiple authors needs to be organized around the questions that cut across the readings, *not around the readings themselves.* If you devote the first part of your paper to just one author's views, the second to the second author's views, and so on, your paper will read like a summary rather than an exploration. Here are some suggestions for organizing around questions.

- Check the lists of questions you have made for each perspective. Put these lists together now and identify questions that appear in multiple readings.

- Consider whether narrowing the focus of your exploration might help. An exploration of narcissism, for instance, might deal only with the difference between healthy self-esteem and genuine narcissism.

- Based on length requirements for the paper and how much you have to say about the questions, select the ones you intend to address.

- Order the questions logically. For example, a definition question makes more sense at the paper's beginning. Discuss causes, then effects.

- Plan on multiple paragraphs for each question. You could, for instance, devote one paragraph to one source's answer, and another to what the others say on the same question.

- Create transitions so that your reader will know when discussion of one question is over and another is beginning.

Development and Organization

The Best Practices box above summarizes a key point about structure in comparing perspectives.

REVISING YOUR DRAFT

Revising this kind of paper usually involves improving the organization, looking more closely at the perspectives to make your exploration more specific, and including more of your own reactions to the authors' views. The Best Practices box on page 201 provides a checklist to help you revise your paper.

When you have limited time to revise a paper, you have to prioritize. Take care of the bigger problems first, the ones that alter your essay substantially. If smaller problems remain, solve as many as you can in the time you have.

The following excerpts from Ian Fagerstrom's draft focus on three problems his peer reviewers found, common problems your draft also may have.

1. One large paragraph addressed two questions rather than one.

> Does narcissism create unhappiness, and more important, is narcissism a growing problem? Schumaker, concerned that happiness is an

The paragraph answers two questions: about effects of narcissism and whether there has been an increase in narcissism. This causes loss of focus and makes the paragraph too long.

Revision Checklist for Comparing Perspectives

The checklist moves in descending order, from the major challenges of the project to concerns in every piece of formal writing.

1. *How much did you explore?* Exploring means entertaining a question. To entertain a question is to hold it open and consider it thoughtfully. If you disputed a point before considering its merits, revise and give it a chance.

2. *How well did you represent the ideas of all the authors?* Did you draw on the sources enough to represent their views accurately and fully?

3. *How well did you work quotations into your paper?* Set them up rather than drop them in, and follow up with explanation and commentary about context as needed.

4. *How well did you organize the paper?* Check to see that you are focusing on one question at a time.

5. *How well did you respond to the sources?* Use specifics to show exactly what you agreed or disagreed with and why.

6. *How smoothly did the sentences flow?* Each sentence sets up the reader's expectations for the one coming next. Read your draft aloud, listening for places where flow could be improved.

7. *Did you introduce the authors adequately?* Provide full name on first mention and something about their credentials.

"endangered state of mind," does well to show that narcissism will lead to a false sense of happiness. Coming from the belief that you must surround yourself with good people to be happy, I completely agree with his point that "happiness is almost impossible if one is unable to escape the prison of self-interest" (175). Considering that happiness is typically the goal of one's life, Schumaker has effectively proved that narcissism ends any chances of that. He does not make any convincing points about it being a significant problem, though—just illustrating with an example of a woman wearing a "love yourself" T-shirt. What does that prove? Twenge says in an interview with National Public Radio that if you are narcissistic, "you may be happy—probably very happy—with how you feel about yourself, but you're going to end up in the long run alienating other people" ("Study"). So they would agree that narcissism really leads to a false kind of happiness that would not be satisfying. In fact, Twenge shows the even darker side of narcissism. Much more than just unhappiness, she believes that in extreme cases narcissism can lead to hostility and aggression of the worst kind, including murder (70–71).

Addresses first question.

Addresses second question.

Addresses first question.

The paragraph was too long and not unified. In the revised version, Ian uses three focused paragraphs: 4, 5, and 6.

2. Ian did not mention Twenge's use of the NPI (Narcissistic Personality Inventory). In this excerpt, Ian refers to data misinterpretation, but he does not say what the data are.

> Jean M. Twenge, an Associate Professor of Psychology at San Diego State University and author of *Generation Me,* also tends to put the young generation in a negative light, accusing us of being obsessed with ourselves and putting the blame for it on the schools, media, and parents. She believes narcissism is on the rise, almost an epidemic. To put things back in perspective, Duncan Greenberg, an undergraduate student at Yale, wrote an editorial in his campus newspaper, "Generation Y and the New Myth of Narcissus." He would confront both Schumaker and Twenge and say that narcissism is actually not a problem at all, instead a misinterpretation of data. He takes the opposition and points out that our generation is actually more empathetic than most. So, on most issues, the two psychologists would agree, and Greenberg would disagree.

Ian hasn't mentioned what data he is referring to. In the revised version, he added what he needed. See paragraph 2 in the revised version.

3. In many places, Ian needed to refer to the texts more specifically.

> There are many perspectives on the topic, some more critical than others. John F. Schumaker, a clinical psychologist and author of *In Search of Happiness,* has a very negative view on it all, arguing that American society is basically going down the drain because of narcissism, saying that it "is an unfulfilling experience that sets the stage for rage and eventual despair" (175).

The cliché about "going down the drain" doesn't get at Schumaker's real concern. See paragraph 2 for a better paraphrase.

REVISED STUDENT EXAMPLE
Comparison of Perspectives on Narcissism

IAN FAGERSTROM

> You will notice that Ian added a fourth reading, a National Public Radio interview with Twenge. Multiple readings can represent the same perspective so long as a participant in the conversation does not change his or her position. Twenge was interviewed about new research supporting her views on narcissism.

Living in a bustling city like Dallas, going to a college with many affluent students, and watching the TV every once in a while, I see self-absorbed people everywhere I turn. Many students get caught up in the appealing idea of being special. It's a good feeling to be at the top of the class, or the one with the newest iPod. So strong is the desire to be special that self-absorption or narcissism has become a much-discussed topic.

Ian leads into his exploration with a natural voice and shows his connection to the topic.

There are many perspectives on it, some more critical than others. John Schumaker, a clinical psychologist and author of *In Search of Happiness,* has a very negative view, arguing that Americans are much less happy than they could be because of their focus on themselves. He says that narcissism "is an unfulfilling experience that sets the stage for rage and eventual despair" (175). While he may acknowledge the positives of healthy self-esteem based in relationships, he is more interested in the downside of high self-esteem.

3   Jean M. Twenge, an Associate Professor of Psychology at San Diego State University and author of *Generation Me,* also tends to put the young generation in a negative light, accusing us of being obsessed with ourselves and putting the blame for it on the self-esteem movement in the schools, media, and parents. She believes narcissism is on the rise, almost an epidemic, as indicated by college students' responses over the years to a psychological survey known as the Narcissistic Personality Inventory (NPI). To put things back in perspective, though, Duncan Greenberg, an undergraduate student at Yale, wrote an editorial in his campus newspaper, "Generation Y and the New Myth of Narcissus." He would confront both Schumaker and Twenge and say that narcissism is actually not a problem at all, instead a misinterpretation of the NPI data. He points out that our generation is actually more empathetic than most. So, on most issues, the two psychologists would agree, and Greenberg would disagree.

4   To fully understand what these authors are saying, we must first know how they are defining narcissism. For Schumaker, narcissism consists of "self-esteem . . . completely blown out of proportion" as well as "unwarranted self-esteem" (170). Although he does not necessarily equate high self-esteem with narcissism, he mentions that certain types of high self-esteem are potentially dangerous. His definition leaves room for misinterpretation and could be used to label many people as narcissists.

5   Twenge describes narcissists as "overly focused on themselves"; they are people who "feel entitled to special privileges and believe that they are superior . . ." (*Generation,* 68). She carefully makes the distinction between high self-esteem and narcissism. She notes that people with high self-esteem feel close to others; narcissists, on the other hand, do not (69). Greenberg wisely uses the Mayo Clinic's definition to define it; traits such as "a need for constant praise" in addition to an "expectation of special treatment" succinctly embody narcissistic tendencies. Instead of trying to make his own definition, he goes with a well-known and respected authority. Still, the Mayo Clinic definitions in Greenberg are similar to the traits Twenge describes; their definitions are the same but they reach different conclusions about the existence of narcissism as a problem.

6   So with these definitions in mind, is narcissism becoming increasingly problematic? Schumaker does not really give evidence to show that rising narcissism is a serious problem. He doesn't have any evidence; he just makes good points that it is a negative trait. While Twenge may have some hard evidence with her survey, saying that 30 percent more college students score above average on the NPI than in 1982 ("Study"), Greenberg makes some compelling points to challenge her findings. He argues that the survey tricks people with "oblique and ambiguous" statements most people would agree with. What's wrong with feeling that you are special? As Greenberg asks, "if someone thinks he's special, does that make him a narcissist? Isn't everyone 'special,' in the etymologically related sense of 'species,' implying a unique combination of color, shape, and size?" He actually goes to the other end of the spectrum by saying that our generation may be "entitled to some

---

This wording is more specific than the cliché "going down the drain."

Ian realized that he had to refer to the survey here to make his later references to it clear.

The second paragraph introduces all three perspectives, one option for introducing them.

Ian leads into his first point of comparison: How do the authors define narcissism?

This paragraph synthesizes definitions and compares similarities.

This section of the paper will address the question: Is narcissism really becoming more prevalent?

Ian revised paragraph 2 to include information about Twenge's research, so he can refer to it again here without confusing his readers.

self-esteem." Greenberg is savvy enough about surveys to realize that for every Twenge argument, there is probably another survey to refute it with. He does this by citing the UCLA survey of first-year students, which shows that they are volunteering "in record numbers" for community service. I agree with Greenberg: young people cannot be both empathetic and narcissistic.

7

The focus of this section of the exploration is: What are the consequences or effects of narcissism on a person?

Whether narcissism is increasing or not, these authors do show that it will lead to a false sense of happiness or worse. Coming from the belief that you must surround yourself with good people to be happy, I completely agree with Schumaker's point that "happiness is almost impossible if one is unable to escape the prison of self-interest" (175). Considering that happiness is typically the goal of one's life, Schumaker has effectively proved that narcissism ends any chances of that. Twenge says in an interview with National Public Radio that if you are narcissistic, "you may be happy—probably very happy—with how you feel about yourself, but you're going to end up in the long run alienating other people" ("Study"). So they would agree that narcissism really leads to a false kind of happiness that would not be satisfying.

8

This paragraph is further development of Twenge's answer to the question about the effects of narcissism.

In fact, Twenge shows the even darker side of narcissism. Much more than just unhappiness, she believes that in extreme cases narcissism can lead to hostility and aggression of the worst kind, including murder (*Generation* 70–71). She uses the example of the Columbine shooters and their video where they make comments about getting the respect they deserve. While this is certainly scary to think about, I would disagree with her here and say that these boys actually had very little self-esteem to begin with. It was their lack of an ego rather than an inflated one that led them to kill thirteen people and commit suicide. Twenge bases her conclusion on the similarities between what the boys said on their video and what some of the items on the NPI say. But that is not enough evidence to make a diagnosis. It simply shows their desire for power after being bullied by other students. Twenge may scare people away from narcissism here, which is not a bad intention, but I believe that her reasoning is flawed.

Ian clearly explains Twenge's point but shows why he reaches a different conclusion.

Whatever definition of narcissism is used, everyone will agree that it is in no way a healthy behavior and will lead to unhappiness, just as in the myth of Narcissus. The main question still remains: Is narcissism on the rise? With many interpretations of data, people refute each other using the same evidence, and given the persistent bickering, the question may never be answered. Personally, at first I was inclined to accept Twenge's argument that schools, media, and parents are going too far in telling children they are the best, most special kids ever ("Study"). And Schumaker is right that some societies encourage narcissistic tendencies, very true in the consumer-society of the United States. But I am not so pessimistic as Twenge and Schumaker about the future, based on my generation's values.

10

I tend to agree with Greenberg that Generation Y is not as narcissistic as generations before us. He makes a valid point when he says that older generations often dismiss positive youth behavior. Whenever a younger generation is praised for something, the older generations put us down, call us spoiled and scoff at us. I have met my fair share of narcissists, but it is hard to prove that it is such a big problem that we need to name my generation "Generation Me."

WORKS CITED

Greenberg, Duncan. "Generation Y and the New Myth of Narcissus." Editorial. *The Yale Herald,* 8 Mar. 2007. Web. 20 Feb. 2007. Print.

Schumaker, John F. *In Search of Happiness: Understanding an Endangered State of Mind.* Westport, CT: Praeger, 2007. Print.

Twenge, Jean M. *Generation Me: Why Today's Young Americans Are More Confident, Assertive, Entitled—and More Miserable Than Ever Before.* New York: Free Press, 2006. Print.

"Study Sees Rise of Narcissism among College Students." Interview by Alex Chadwick and Luke Burbank. *Day to Day.* Natl. Public Radio. WNYC, New York, 27 Feb. 2007. *NPR.org.* Web. 19 Feb. 2008.

CHAPTER SUMMARY

This chapter has given you practice in essential skills for other writing assignments in this course and others. You learned that people's perspectives are answers to questions, and that careful reading uncovers the questions that serve as threads, weaving the conversation together, even if authors do not refer to each other directly. Finding the questions at issue is essential to any research project and to making your own arguments.

CHAPTER 9

Making Your Case:
Arguing to Convince

The last chapter ended where inquiry ends—with the attempt to formulate a position, an opinion that we can assert with some confidence. When our aim shifts from inquiring to convincing, everything changes.

The most significant change is in audience. In inquiry, our audience consists of our fellow inquirers—friends, classmates, and teachers we can talk with face to face. We seek assurance that our position is at least plausible and defensible. In convincing, however, our audience consists of readers whose positions differ from our own or who have no position at all. The audience changes from a small, inside group that helps us develop our argument to a larger, public audience who will either accept or reject it.

As the audience changes, so does the situation or need for argument. Inquiry is a cooperative use of argument; convincing is more competitive. We pit our cases against the cases of others to win the assent of readers who will compare the various arguments and ask, Who makes the best case?

From Inquiry to Convincing

Inquiry ⟶	Convincing
Intimate audience	Public readership
Cooperative	Competitive
Earns a conviction	Argues a thesis
Seeks a case convincing *to us*	Makes a case convincing *to them,* the readers

We take the position we discovered through inquiry and turn it into a thesis supported by a case designed to gain the assent of a specific group of readers.

Because of the change in audience and situation, our thinking becomes more strategic, calculated to influence readers. In inquiry, we find out what we can believe in; in convincing, we make a case readers can believe in. What we find compelling in inquiry will sometimes also convince readers, but *in convincing we must adapt our reasoning to appeal to their beliefs, values, and self-interest.* Convincing, however, does not mean abandoning the work of inquiry. Our version of the truth, our conviction, gained through inquiry, is what we argue for.

WHAT IS A CASE?

A *case* develops your opinion about a controversial issue or question. The result is an argument with three levels of assertion:

1. A central contention or **claim,** also called a thesis.

     Example: College costs are unjustifiably high.

2. One or more reasons that explain or justify the claim.

     Example: They have increased much more than inflation over the last thirty years.

3. Appropriate evidence to back up each reason.

     Example: Data comparing the cost of living in general with increases in tuition and fees over the last thirty years.

WHY MAKE A CASE?

We make cases to do the following:

1. *Influence the thinking of others.* CEOs make cases for decisions they have made to their Board of Directors and stockholders; lawyers make cases to convince judges or a jury; special interest groups make cases to bring their causes to the attention of communities and civic leaders.

Visualizing the Structure of a Case

The **thesis** answers the question, *What are you asserting or claiming?*

Reasons explain or justify the thesis; they answer the question, *Why do you hold this thesis?*

Evidence backs up each reason; it answers the question, *What information confirms your reasoning?*

2. *Avoid violence.* Reason together or fight: these are the alternatives—hence, the Chinese proverb, "He who strikes the first blow has lost the argument." Nothing less than peaceful resolution of differences is at stake in arguing well.

3. *Learn what we really think.* In college, making cases is part of the learning process. We all have casual opinions we have never thought through. How good are they? Do they stand up to what is known about a subject in dispute? If not, we need to modify our opinion or alter what we think entirely. Reasoning is a way of learning that can change us profoundly.

HOW DOES MAKING A CASE WORK?

Cases combine structure with strategy. The structure is the three-part division of reasoning: thesis, reasons, and evidence. The strategy is what you do to *connect with your readers,* to make what you have to say convincing to other

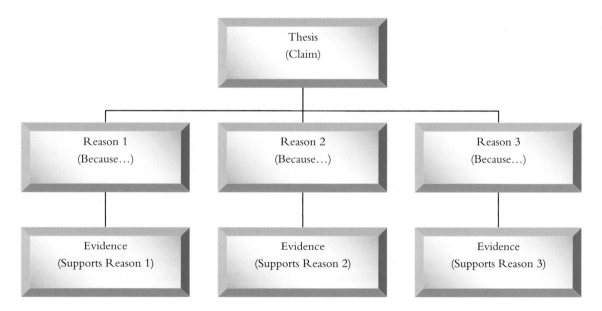

CONCEPT CLOSE-UP

Key Questions for Case-Making

1. Who is your target audience?
2. What preconceptions and biases might they hold about your topic?
3. What claim do you want your readers to accept?
4. What reasons are likely to appeal to this audience?
5. How should you arrange these reasons for maximum impact on your target audience?
6. How might you introduce your case?
7. How might you conclude it?
8. How can you gain the trust and respect of your audience?

Convincing is audience centered. Every choice we make must be made with the target audience in mind.

people. See the Concept Close-Up, "Key Question for Case-Making" to understand the concerns of strategic thinking in general. The following example should also help.

Many people, including some college presidents, are in favor of lowering the drinking age from twenty-one to eighteen. The concern is binge drinking, which they partly blame on the current drinking age. Breaking the law is part of the appeal of underaged drinking. Universities cannot advocate responsible drinking when many undergraduates are not supposed to drink at all.

Organizations such as MADD, Mothers against Drunk Driving, support the twenty-one legal age. They point to thousands of people who die each year in traffic accidents caused by drunk drivers. Lower the drinking age, they say, and you will only make a serious problem worse.

Given the range of opinion, how could you make a good case favoring legal access to alcohol at eighteen? The most common reason offered is based on consistency. If young adults are old enough to fight in Afghanistan or Iraq, shouldn't they be old enough to drink legally?

In making your case, you can offer reasons like this one. However, they will not have much impact on people who support the current law. Reaching them requires strategy, *thinking as the other side thinks.*

Here is one way to cross the divide. All agree that abusing alcohol is a big problem. They differ on how to reduce the problem. Legalize and educate is one way; prohibit by law and strictly enforce the law is the other. In making a case in favor of the lower drinking age, stress the shared goal—reducing alcohol abuse.

You could argue that age is not the issue but rather moderation and responsibility whenever people drink. After all, most drunk drivers are not under legal drinking age. But moderation and responsibility is exactly what the current law cannot promote. Prohibition hardly encourages moderation and responsibility; on the contrary, it drives underaged drinking underground, out of sight but hardly out of common practice. You could go on to support MADD's well-developed measures for preventing drunk driving, such as encouraging designated drivers. You could advocate that universities devote more effort and time to educating college students about drinking. Such is strategy in case-making, without which any case you make can only strengthen the adherence of people who already share your position.

The Art of Questioning: Examining Your Audience's Beliefs

You cannot reach everyone. But you can reach many people, at least enough to get them to reconsider what they think. The problem is not that reasoning lacks power but that its power depends on coming up with ways to appeal to people who do not already agree with you.

Begin by asking these two questions:

- What are the opinions of people who differ from me?
- Why do they hold these opinions?

Based on this understanding, then ask,

- Are there goals, values, attitudes, or beliefs that I share with those who differ from me?
- Can I agree with at least some of what they say?
- What exactly do I need to change in their viewpoint to move them toward my position?

In short, *you need to find the common ground you share with those you want to convince.* In this way you can reduce the "us versus them" mentality that makes reasoning seem so frustrating and pointless.

READINGS

We begin with a recent contribution to a long-standing dispute—teaching evolution in public schools—that remains controversial enough in the United States to result in court cases.

Optimism in Evolution

OLIVIA JUDSON

Educated at Stanford and Oxford, Olivia Judson is a biologist at Imperial College, in London. She's best known for her book, *Dr. Tatiana's Sex Advice to All Creation,* an international best-seller that deals in an engaging way with the role of sex in evolution. She writes a weekly blog on evolutionary biology called "The Wild Side," accessible on the *New York Times* Web site.

The following column appeared in the *New York Times,* August 13, 2008. As you read, note how well Judson structures her case for teaching evolution in all beginning biology classes.

When the dog days of summer come to an end, one thing we can be sure of is that the school year that follows will see <u>more fights over the teaching of evolution and whether intelligent design, or even Biblical accounts of creation, have a place in America's science classrooms.</u>

In these arguments, evolution is treated as an abstract subject that deals with the age of the earth or how fish first flopped onto land. It's discussed as though it were an optional, quaint and largely irrelevant part of biology. <u>And a common consequence of the arguments is that evolution gets dropped from the curriculum entirely.</u>

3   This is a travesty.

4   It is also dangerous.

5   <u>Evolution should be taught—indeed, it should be central to beginning biology classes—for at least three reasons.</u>

<u>First,</u> it provides a powerful framework for investigating the world we live in. Without evolution, biology is merely a collection of disconnected facts, a set of descriptions. <u>The astonishing variety of nature, from the tree shrew that guzzles vast quantities of alcohol every night to the lichens that grow in the Antarctic wastes, cannot be probed and understood.</u> Add evolution—and it becomes possible to make inferences and predictions and (sometimes) to do experiments to test those predictions. All of a sudden patterns emerge everywhere, and apparently trivial details become interesting.

The second reason for teaching evolution is that the subject is immediately relevant here and now. The impact we are having on the planet is causing other organisms to evolve—and fast. And I'm not talking just about the obvious examples: <u>widespread resistance to pesticides among insects; the evolution of drug resistance in the agents of disease, from malaria to tuberculosis; the possibility that, say, the virus that causes bird flu will evolve into a form that spreads easily from person to person.</u> The impact we are having is much broader.

<u>For instance,</u> we are causing animals to evolve just by hunting them. The North Atlantic cod fishery has caused the evolution of cod that mature smaller and younger than they did 40 years ago. Fishing for grayling in Norwegian lakes has caused a similar pattern in these fish. Human trophy hunting for bighorn rams has caused the population to evolve into one of smaller-horn rams. (All of which, incidentally, is in line with evolutionary predictions.)

Conversely, hunting animals to extinction may cause evolution in their former prey species. Experiments on guppies have shown that, without predators, these fish evolve more brightly colored scales, mature later, bunch together in shoals less and lose their ability to suddenly swim away from something. Such changes can happen in fewer than five generations. If you then reintroduce some predators, the population typically goes extinct.

<u>Thus,</u> a failure to consider the evolution of other species may result in a failure of our efforts to preserve them. And, perhaps, to preserve ourselves from

---

Reminds readers of the conflict of opinion.

Indicates what's at stake, why this topic matters.

States thesis or central claim, signals reader to expect three-part defense of the thesis.

Numbers reasons to help readers identify them.

Note use of specific examples of "astonishing variety."

Makes first point forcefully: that nature cannot be understood without evolution.

Reminds readers of well-known examples of evolution caused by human activity.

Use of transitional phrase.

Another use of a transitional word or phrase.

diseases, pests and food shortages. In short, evolution is far from being a remote and abstract subject. A failure to teach it may leave us unprepared for the challenges ahead.

11   The third reason to teach evolution is more philosophical. It concerns the development of an attitude toward evidence. <u>In his book, "The Republican War on Science," the journalist Chris Mooney argues persuasively that a contempt for scientific evidence—or indeed, evidence of any kind—has permeated the Bush administration's policies, from climate change to sex education, from drilling for oil to the war in Iraq.</u> A dismissal of evolution is an integral part of this general attitude.

Cites authority to back up her reason.

12   Moreover, since the science classroom is where a contempt for evidence is often first encountered, it is also arguably where it first begins to be cultivated. A society where ideology is a substitute for evidence can go badly awry. <u>(This is not to suggest that science is never distorted by the ideological left; it sometimes is, and the results are no better.)</u>

Acknowledges that distortion of science is not limited to the political right.

13   But for me, the most important thing about studying evolution is something less tangible. It's that the endeavor contains a profound optimism. It means that when we encounter something in nature that is complicated or mysterious, such as the flagellum of a bacteria or the light made by a firefly, we don't have to shrug our shoulders in bewilderment.

Good conclusion that stresses the author's personal view and refutes the notion that evolution takes away from the wonder and beauty of nature.

14   Instead, we can ask how it got to be that way. And if at first it seems so complicated that the evolutionary steps are hard to work out, we have an invitation to imagine, to play, to experiment and explore. To my mind, this only enhances the wonder.

QUESTIONS FOR DISCUSSION

1. When you took your first biology class, was evolution taught as the foundation of the discipline, or as "an optional, quaint, and largely irrelevant part of biology" (paragraph 2)? How did you feel about evolution then? What is your view now?

2. Judson calls the failure to teach evolution a "travesty"—that is, a gross misrepresentation of something. Does she establish that leaving evolution out of biological instruction distorts the discipline? How?

3. She also calls the failure to teach evolution "dangerous." What in her article confirms that statement?

Strategies Used in Case-Making: Structure and Readership

There could not be a clearer example of how to structure an effective case, one easy for a reader to follow:

Thesis: Evolution should be central to beginning biology classes

> *Reason 1:* It provides a powerful framework for investigation.

>> *Evidence:* moving beyond "disconnected facts" to "inferences and predictions"

Reason 2: Evolution is relevant to the here and now.

Evidence: drug resistance in microbes, the impact of hunting, evolution in species whose prey goes extinct, and so on

Reason 3: Teaching evolution encourages a respect for evidence.

Evidence: reference to *The Republican War on Science,* the ignoring or suppression of scientific evidence

You can learn much about how to structure a case from Judson's article, including how to develop individual reasons in support of a thesis. Note that the second reason takes four paragraphs (7–10) to explain and support and that she devotes two paragraphs (11–12) to her third reason. *Follow her example, and don't think of each reason as corresponding to a single paragraph.* Reasons often require more than one paragraph to explain and support.

Another feature of the article worth your attention is how to *frame* (provide a context for) a case and how to *close* or conclude a case. Note that Judson has a four-paragraph introduction that precedes her thesis, stated in paragraph 5. The opening paragraphs explain why she is making her case for teaching evolution—because too often it either is not taught or not taught well. Readers need to know *why* you are making a case, the context that makes a case worth making.

Her two-paragraph conclusion (13–14) is a good example of something much better than a summarizing "in conclusion" close. She says that evolution "contains a profound optimism" and "enhances the wonder" of studying nature. It is these positive attitudes that opponents of evolution say teaching evolution destroys. Her conclusion, therefore, addresses an objection the other side has raised.

In addition to its structure, the Judson article offers an important insight into *selecting an appropriate readership* for any case you make. On one hand, Judson is not writing for her fellow biologists. With very few exceptions, they agree with her already. On the other hand, she also makes no effort to convince those unalterably opposed to teaching evolution. Instead, she is making her case for those who may think teaching evolution does not matter much or for those who support equal time for evolution and creationism.

You should do likewise in conceiving readers for the cases you make. Depending on the topic and your position on it, there will always be a segment of readers unalterably opposed to what you have to say. Ignore them and address an audience capable of responding to your reasoning.

CLAIMING VOICE IN ARGUING A CASE

Traditionally, the voice of arguing a case has been linked to **middle style,** in contrast to the plain style of informing and the passionate style of some public speaking, designed to arouse emotions in an audience. What does middle style sound like? Here it is in a passage from the reading that follows, an argument advocating prison reform:

> Prison has a role in public safety, but it is not a cure-all. Its value is limited, and its use should be limited to what it does best: isolating young criminals long enough to give them a chance to grow up and get a grip on their impulses.

Read these sentences aloud and you can hear the voice of middle style: It states its position clearly, directly, and forcefully. It is more formal than relaxed chatting with a friend, but not as formal as a speech from President Obama or an emotional sermon from the pulpit on Sunday.

You can miss middle style in two ways. On one hand, you may have been taught to keep your opinions out of your writing. Clearly the advice does not apply to arguing a case because the thesis you are defending *is* your opinion. On the other hand, resist being influenced by the phony, overheated sensationalism of much talk radio and TV. Argument is not name-calling, insults, outrageous claims, or partisan bickering—all designed to increase ratings. Argument is the calm voice of reason, of opinions stated precisely and defended well. It is one of the voices most admired and respected at universities, in business meetings, in community gatherings, and wherever productive interaction among people occurs.

Why Prisons Don't Work

WILBERT RIDEAU

> Wilbert Rideau was convicted of murder at age nineteen, and spent over forty years of his life in Louisiana State Penitentiary at Angola. He edited the prison newspaper and became an award-winning journalist and one of the best-known convicts ever in the United States.
>
> As you read his article, pay special attention to how Rideau depicts the problem of how we deal with criminals in the United States and to the solution he proposes. Note also his use of cause-and-effect reasoning, common in case-making.

1   I was among thirty-one murderers sent to the Louisiana State Penitentiary in 1962 to be executed or imprisoned for life. We weren't much different from those we found here, or those who had preceded us. We were unskilled, impulsive, and uneducated misfits, mostly black, who had done dumb, impulsive things—failures, rejects from the larger society. Now a generation has come of age and gone since I've been here, and everything is much the same as I found it. The faces of the prisoners are different, but behind them are the same impulsive, uneducated, unskilled minds that made dumb, impulsive choices that got them into more trouble than they ever thought existed. The vast majority of us are consigned to suffer and die here so politicians can sell the illusion that permanently exiling people to prison will make society safe.

2   Getting tough has always been a "silver bullet," a quick fix for the crime and violence that society fears. Each year in Louisiana—where excess is a way of

life—lawmakers have tried to outdo each other in legislating harsher mandatory penalties and in reducing avenues of release. The only thing to do with criminals, they say, is get tougher. They have. In the process, the purpose of prison began to change. The state boasts one of the highest lockup rates in the country, imposes the most severe penalties in the nation, and vies to execute more criminals per capita than anywhere else. This state is so tough that last year, when prison authorities here wanted to punish an inmate in solitary confinement for an infraction, the most they could inflict on him was to deprive him of his underwear. It was all he had left.

3   If getting tough resulted in public safety, Louisiana citizens would be the safest in the nation. They're not. Louisiana has the highest murder rate among states. Prison, like the police and the courts, has a minimal impact on crime because it is a response after the fact, a mop-up operation. It doesn't work. The idea of punishing the few to deter the many is counterfeit because potential criminals either think they're not going to get caught or they're so emotionally desperate or psychologically distressed that they don't care about the consequences of their actions. The threatened punishment, regardless of its severity, is never a factor in the equation. But society, like the "incorrigible" criminal it abhors, is unable to learn from its mistakes.

4   Prison has a role in public safety, but it is not a cure-all. Its value is limited, and its use should also be limited to what it does best: isolating young criminals long enough to give them a chance to grow up and get a grip on their impulses. It is a traumatic experience, certainly, but it should be only a temporary one, not a way of life. Prisoners kept too long tend to embrace the criminal culture, its distorted values and beliefs; they have little choice—prison is their life. There are some prisoners who cannot be returned to society—serial killers, serial rapists, professional hit men, and the like—but the monsters who need to die in prison are rare exceptions in the criminal landscape.

5   Crime is a young man's game. Most of the nation's random violence is committed by young urban terrorists. But because of long, mandatory sentences, most prisoners here are much older, having spent fifteen, twenty, thirty, or more years behind bars, long past necessity. Rather than pay for new prisons, society would be well served by releasing some of its older prisoners who pose no threat and using the money to catch young street thugs. Warden John Whitley agrees that many older prisoners here could be freed tomorrow with little or no danger to society. Release, however, is governed by law or by politicians, not by penal professionals. Even murderers, those most feared by society, pose little risk. Historically, for example, the domestic staff at Louisiana's Governor's mansion has been made up of murderers, hand-picked to work among the chief-of-state and his family. Penologists have long known that murder is almost always a once-in-a-lifetime act. The most dangerous criminal is the one who has not yet killed but has a history of escalating offenses. He's the one to watch.

6   Rehabilitation can work. Everyone changes in time. The trick is to influence the direction that change takes. The problem with prisons is that they don't do more to rehabilitate those confined in them. The convict who enters prison illiterate will

probably leave the same way. Most convicts want to be better than they are, but education is not a priority. This prison houses 4,600 men and offers academic training to 240, vocational training to a like number. Perhaps it doesn't matter. About 90 percent of the men here may never leave this prison alive.

7   The only effective way to curb crime is for society to work to prevent the criminal act in the first place, to come between the perpetrator and crime. Our youngsters must be taught to respect the humanity of others and to handle disputes without violence. It is essential to educate and equip them with the skills to pursue their life ambitions in a meaningful way. As a community, we must address the adverse life circumstances that spawn criminality. These things are not quick, and they're not easy, but they're effective. Politicians think that's too hard a sell. They want to be on record for doing something now, something they can point to at reelection time. So the drumbeat goes on for more police, more prisons, more of the same failed policies.

8   Ever see a dog chase its tail?

QUESTIONS FOR DISCUSSION

1.   According to Rideau, why doesn't the possibility of prison deter criminal acts?

2.   What does he say prisons do best? What roles should they play in our society's effort to cope with criminals? Do his proposals make sense, given his analysis of cause and effect? Why or why not?

3.   What does Rideau contend would truly be effective in reducing crime, especially the violent crime we fear most? What would have to change to pursue the course of action he favors?

◎◎ FOLLOWING THROUGH

In groups of two or three, look over Rideau's argument with an eye to **case structure**. Write up an outline of its claim and reasons. Beneath each reason, jot down something about the evidence that he uses to support it. Compare your group's decisions about Rideau's case structure with the outline of at least one other group. Where did you find consensus about the argument's structure? If you found disagreement about structure, how might that be explained or reconciled?   •

Strategies Used in Case-Making: Problem-Solution, Cause-and-Effect Reasoning

The difficulty in solving any problem resides in understanding it, which is why cause-and-effect reasoning dominates problem-solution cases. Fail to grasp the causes of a problem and you will also fail to solve it. It sounds simple, but of course it is not.

Rideau shows us clearly why understanding a problem can be so difficult. First, there is prejudice, often rooted in common sense. Get tough with crime?—certainly, we say. It seems so reasonable that our politicians outdo each other trying to be the toughest. But as Rideau explains, getting tough is only a "mop-up operation" (paragraph 3) after the criminal has been caught and convicted. Do we feel safer when violent criminals receive long prison terms and, in some cases, life without parole? We do, yet murder and other violent crimes are daily news items, and the cost of locking up so many people for so long imposes a huge burden on taxpayers.

With most problems, understanding depends on getting beyond gut reactions and common sense. Ask, *What is really going on?* Answering it requires cool, dispassionate analysis of the information we have. Drawing on his own long experience, Rideau sees a pattern: "Crime is a young man's game," especially the violent crime we fear most (paragraph 5). If this is so, prisons should "[isolate] young criminals long enough to give them a chance to grow up and get a grip on their impulses" (paragraph 4). If this is so, rehabilitation requires more effort; otherwise, paroled prisoners will not be equipped to rejoin society as productive, law-abiding citizens. If this is so, it makes no sense to keep older prisoners in jail for so long, well past their impulsive youth. If this is so, "coming between the perpetrator and the crime"—that is, working with young people in the neighborhoods where so much of the violent crime occurs—is about the only effective way to *prevent* crime, as opposed to reacting to it after it occurs.

The Rideau article shows how problem-solution, cause-and-effect case-making works: Analyze what you know to identify the cause or causes of a problem. The solution, then, follows from understanding the cause: If crime is a young man's game, everything Rideau proposes makes sense.

A Plan for Reducing American Dependence on Foreign Oil

T. BOONE PICKENS

T. Boone Pickens is an internationally prominent Texas oil man, investor, and philanthropist, who recently used his money and influence to bring the following proposal to the attention of all Americans through newspaper spreads and Internet postings.

We took the following argument from his Web site. The selection preserves the formatting of the Web site. As you read, pay special attention to the use of graphics as an efficient way of presenting evidence and to the use of font size and bold print as a way of calling attention to key points.

THE PLAN

1   America is addicted to foreign oil.

2   It's an addiction that threatens our economy, our environment and our national security.

3   It touches every part of our daily lives and ties our hands as a nation and a people.

4   The addiction has worsened for decades and now it's reached a point of crisis.

5   **In 1970, we imported 24% of our oil. Today it's nearly 70% and growing.**

6   Oil prices have come down from the staggering highs of last summer, but lower prices have not reduced our dependence on foreign oil or lessened the risks to either our economy or our security.

7   If we are depending on foreign sources for nearly 70% of our oil, we are in a precarious position in an unpredictable world.

8   In addition to putting our security in the hands of potentially unfriendly and unstable foreign nations, we spent $475 billion on foreign oil in 2008 alone. That's money taken out of our economy and sent to foreign nations, and it will continue to drain the life from our economy for as long as we fail to stop the bleeding.

9   Projected over the next 10 years the cost will be $10 trillion—it will be the greatest transfer of wealth in the history of mankind.

10   Can't we just produce more oil?

11   America uses a lot of oil. Every day 85 million barrels of oil are produced around the world.

12   And 21 million of those are used here in the United States.

13   That's 25% of the world's oil demand. Used by just 4% of the world's population.

14   Consider this: America imports 12 million barrels a day, and Saudi Arabia only produces 9 million a day. Is there really more undiscovered oil here than in all of Saudi Arabia?

15   World oil production peaked in 2005. Despite growing demand and an unprecedented increase in prices, oil production has fallen over the last three years. Oil is getting more expensive to produce, harder to find and there just isn't enough of it to keep up with demand.

16   The simple truth is that cheap and easy oil is gone.

17   **But America is focused on another crisis: The economy.**

18   All Americans are feeling the effects of our recent downturn. And addressing this problem is the top priority of our nation. This is more than bailing out a bank, an insurance firm or a car company. The American economy is huge and has many facets.

19   To make a real and lasting impact we must seek do more than create new jobs and opportunities today, we must build the platform on which our economy can continue to grow for decades to come.

20   There is nothing more important to the present and future of our economy than energy. Any effort to address our economic problems will require a thorough understanding of this issue and willingness to confront our dependence on foreign oil and what domestic resources we can use.

21   It is a crisis too large to be addressed by piecemeal steps. We need a plan of action on scale with the problems we face. That is the spirit in which the Pickens Plan was conceived. The Pickens Plan is a collection of steps that together form a comprehensive approach to America's energy needs.

The Pickens Plan

22 There are several pillars to the Pickens Plan:

- Create millions of new jobs by building out the capacity to generate up to 22 percent of our electricity from wind. And adding to that with additional solar capacity.
- Building a 21st century backbone electrical grid.
- Providing incentives for homeowners and the owners of commercial buildings to upgrade their insulation and other energy saving options.
- Using America's natural gas to replace imported oil as a transportation fuel.

23 While dependence on foreign oil is a critical concern, it is not a problem that can be solved in isolation. We have to think about energy as a whole, and that begins by considering our energy alternatives and thinking about how we will fuel our world in the next 10 to 20 years and beyond.

New Jobs from Renewable Energy and Conservation

24 Any discussion of alternatives should begin with the 2007 Department of Energy study showing that building out our wind capacity in the Great Plains—from northern Texas to the Canadian border—would produce 138,000 new jobs in the first year, and more than 3.4 million new jobs over a ten-year period, while also producing as much as 20 percent of our needed electricity.

25 Building out solar energy in the Southwest from western Texas to California would add to the boom of new jobs and provide more of our growing electrical needs—doing so through economically viable, clean, renewable sources.

26 To move that electricity from where it is being produced to where it is needed will require an upgrade to our national electric grid. A 21st century grid which will, as

5km Global Wind   3TIER.

5km Wind Map at 80m
Wind speed
3   6   9 m/s

technology continues to develop, deliver power where it is needed, when it is needed, in the direction it is needed, will be the modern equivalent of building the Interstate Highway System in the 1950's.

27 Beyond that, tremendous improvements in electricity use can be made by creating incentives for owners of homes and commercial buildings to retrofit their spaces with proper insulation.

28 Studies show that a significant upgrading of insulation would save the equivalent of one million barrels of oil per day in energy by cutting down on both air conditioning costs in warm weather and heating costs in winter.

A Domestic Fuel to Free Us from Foreign Oil

29 Conserving and harnessing renewable forms of electricity not only has incredible economic benefits, but is also a crucial piece of the oil dependence puzzle. We should continue to pursue the promise of electric or hydrogen powered vehicles, but America needs to address transportation fuel today. Fortunately, we are blessed with an abundance of clean, cheap, domestic natural gas.

30 Currently, domestic natural gas is primarily used to generate electricity. It has the advantage of being cheap and significantly cleaner than coal, but this is not the best use of our natural gas resources.

31 By generating electricity from wind and solar and conserving the electricity we have, we will be free to shift our use of natural gas to where it can lower our need for foreign oil—helping President Obama reach his goal of zero oil imports from the Middle East within ten years—by replacing diesel as the principal transportation fuel for heavy trucks and fleet vehicles.

32 Nearly 20% of every barrel of oil we import is used by 18-wheelers moving goods burning imported diesel. An over-the-road truck cannot be moved using current battery technology. Fleet vehicles like buses, taxis, express delivery trucks, and municipal and utility vehicles (any vehicle which returns to the "barn" each night

2010 Civic GX Sedan

The Honda Civic GX Natural Gas Vehicle is the cleanest internal-combustion vehicle in the world according to the EPA.

US sources of
electrical generation

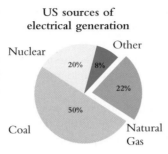

where refueling is a simple matter) should be replaced by vehicles running on clean, cheap, domestic natural gas rather than imported gasoline or diesel fuel.

A Plan that Brings It All Together

33 Natural gas is not a permanent or complete solution to imported oil. It is a bridge fuel to slash our oil dependence while buying us time to develop new technologies that will ultimately replace fossil transportation fuels. Natural gas is the critical puzzle piece that will help us keep more of the $350 to $450 billion every year at home, where it can power our economy and pay for our investments in wind energy, a smart grid and energy efficiency.

34 It is this connection that makes The Pickens Plan not just a collection of good ideas, but a plan. By investing in renewable energy and conservation, we can create millions of new jobs. New alternative energies allow us to shift natural gas to transportation; securing our economy by reducing our dependence on foreign oil, and keeping more money at home to pay for the whole thing.

How Do We Get It Done?

35 The Pickens Plan is a bridge to the future—a blueprint to reduce foreign oil dependence by harnessing domestic energy alternatives, and to buy us time to develop even greater new technologies.

36 Building new wind generation facilities, conserving energy and better utilizing our natural gas resources can replace more than one-third of our foreign oil imports in 10 years. But it will take leadership.

37 We're organizing behind the Pickens Plan now to ensure our voices will be heard.

38 Together with President Obama and the new Congress, we can take down the old barriers and provide energy security for generations to come, while helping dig out of the recession we are in today.

39 As our new President has said, "Yes, we can." And together, as never before, we will.

QUESTIONS FOR DISCUSSION

1. Cases made online or in other popular, mass media like television and newspapers usually observe special conventions. Describe the conventions in this Web site posting. In your view do they work well to communicate the message? Why or why not?

2. This short article uses five graphics, including several types—photographs, a map, and a pie graph. In case-making, graphics present evidence efficiently and memorably. What evidence do the graphics in this piece provide? What statements in the article do they support?

3. The T. Boone Pickens Web site makes no effort to conceal his personal stake in the plan. He is heavily invested in natural gas and wind power. In your view, does being up front strengthen or weaken his case?

Strategies in Case-Making: Lines of Reasoning

Compare the structure of this case with Judson's in "Optimism in Evolution" (pages 211–213). Judson's is the typical case: State a thesis; defend it with three or four reasons; support each reason with evidence. It works well when your thesis is a single claim, such as "Evolution should be central to beginning biology classes."

In contrast, the Pickens Plan is an example of a case composed of two or more claims or theses, each requiring explanation and evidence. The Pickens Plan makes three claims:

-   We must reduce our dependence on foreign oil. (claim 1)
-   We can do this by exploiting domestic wind power for generating electricity. (claim 2)
-   We can also substitute domestic supplies of natural gas for the gasoline and diesel we are currently using in vehicles. (claim 3)

The three claims are linked together by the contrast between *foreign* crude oil and *domestic* wind energy and natural gas.

Each part of the Pickens Plan also develops differently from Judson's single-thesis case. Think of it as answers to your questions as you read, and the logic is easy to follow. Here is the logic for claim 1, which establishes the problem:

> *What is the problem your plan would solve?*
>
> > Answer: America's addiction to foreign oil.
>
> *Is that really such a big problem?*
>
> > Answer: Yes. We import 70% of our oil. It threatens our economy, environment, and national security.
>
> *Why not just produce more oil domestically?*
>
> > Answer: There is not enough to satisfy the current demand. The era of cheap and easy oil is gone.

This way of arguing a point works by anticipating your readers' questions and answering them one by one. The secret to arguing this way is *to imagine what your readers will think based on what you have just said*. If you say that America is addicted to foreign oil, your reader will think, So what? Where's the harm? Then, when you answer that question, your reader will think, Why not produce more domestic oil? When you indicate that doing so will not solve the problem, that brings one line of reasoning to a close, and you are ready to move on to the solutions you advocate.

◉◉ FOLLOWING THROUGH

In class do with the rest of the Pickens case what we did above with claim 1, establishing the problem. What sequence of questions is being answered in the solution parts of the case?

Then address this question: Is the reasoning as a whole convincing? Why or why not?   •

◉◉ FOLLOWING THROUGH

Each of the topics addressed in the readings in this chapter—teaching evolution, prison reform, and the energy crisis—is debated vigorously online, especially in blogs and in e-mail responses to Web postings and print publications. Why not weigh in on the subject that interests you the most? If you have a blog, post a response to one of the readings, or make your own short case on the subject. If you do not maintain a blog, compose an e-mail response to one of the authors, or get a conversation going online with other members of your class via e-mail or Blackboard or any other online means for exchanging viewpoints and ideas.

The best way to learn to make cases is to get involved in real arguments on genuine issues. You also may find your topic for this chapter's assignment this way.   •

THE ASSIGNMENT

Make a case that seeks to convince readers to accept your central claim or thesis about any controversial topic, problem, issue, or question. "Controversial" means that various positions or stances are possible—not necessarily that the subject has received media attention. It can address anything from something as personal and local as a family dilemma or a campus concern to something as impersonal and global as U.S. relations with China.

Topic and Focus

Whatever your topic is, avoid thinking in pro–con, us versus them ways. Despite how they are depicted in the media, even highly polarized issues like abortion are not simply "pro-life" versus "pro-choice." Strongly antiabortion cases, for instance, usually allow abortion in instances of rape, incest, or when the woman's life is in danger, and many people labeled "pro-choice" don't oppose reasonable restrictions on abortion after the first trimester. *Think in terms of many possible stances.*

Most topics also consist of many controversial issues. Consider limiting your case to one of them. For instance, standardized testing in public schools raises many issues, including what subject areas should be tested, how standardized testing affects coverage of a subject, what to do about schools that do not meet standards, and how to control cheating. You can easily locate many other areas for debate in newspapers and Web searches.

Audience

Cases aim at two audiences: people weakly inclined to agree and those tending toward another stance but open to reason. Your case should strengthen the adherence of those favorably disposed to your thesis by giving them good reasons and strong evidence they may have lacked before. Those good reasons and strong evidence also may appeal to readers entertaining other positions, but reaching them requires strategy (see pages 210–211).

Voice and Style

Cases aim for assent to a thesis. They want to secure agreement by advancing good reasons based on current, accurate information about the topic.

Your voice should be dispassionate, calm, and fair. Treat other positions and arguments with respect, even as you show that your evidence and reasons are more compelling.

Writing Assignment Suggestions

The paper could be written in many possible genres: an editorial, a posting on a Web site, a magazine article, a text for a speech, an open letter to some group of people, a personal letter, and so on. You might consider writing in one of these genres if your topic and readership seem appropriate and your instructor approves.

A wide range of topics are of interest to college students: college costs, living conditions on campus, and avoiding excessive debt in personal finances; cultural and social issues, such as the impact of electronic communication on how people live and relate to other people, computer gaming, rap music, the behavior of people at sporting events, controversial films, TV shows, and advertisements; political issues, such as counterterrorism policy, the use of torture in interrogating persons suspected of terrorist activity, health care, energy policy, global warming, and immigration. Perhaps your topic can be one of these or related to one of them.

CHOOSING A TOPIC

Often the best topics come from problems and issues you have experienced directly as a student, voter, friend, parent, resident in a foreign country, participant in a sport or other activity—in short, something you have lived. Maybe you are involved in a club, volunteer organization, or student activity that deserves more recognition or support. Maybe you attended a campus event and heard a controversial speaker with a viewpoint you responded to strongly. Civic activities, internships, and jobs can also be rich sources of topics for case-making. Here are some possibilities for finding topics.

- *Class readings*. Class readings can suggest topics for case-making, especially if the readings themselves are cases, like the examples in this chapter. For instance, after reading the Pickens Plan, you may have your own ideas about how to reduce American dependence on foreign oil.

- *Local news or observation.* Read your local and campus newspapers for issues and problems of concern to your community. Take a walk around your neighborhood or campus with an eye for problems that need solutions, such as wasted energy in offices, dorms, and classrooms.

- *Internet discussions.* If you keep a blog, you probably have a store of observations about issues that concern you, things you would like to convince others to see as you do. Also try visiting blogs concerned with public issues, such as National Public Radio's "Blog of the Nation," based on topics from its radio program *Talk of the Nation.*

EXPLORING YOUR TOPIC

The best approach to exploring a topic depends on many variables: how much you know about the topic already, whether you have participated in debates or discussions about it previously, how much time you have to produce the paper, and so on. Let's assume the situation many students face in their classes: an assigned topic about which you know little or nothing.

The Art of Questioning: Find the Issues

An **issue** is a point of controversy always or frequently discussed when a particular topic arises. For any topic, begin by asking, What are the questions that people disagree about when discussing this topic? For instance, the primary purpose of prisons is always an issue when prison reform is discussed. Some see prisons primarily as punishment for crime; others see them primarily as institutions that should rehabilitate criminals.

◎◎ FOLLOWING THROUGH

Relying on general knowledge, list the issues connected with the topic. The key question is, *What do people argue about whenever this topic is discussed?*

Assign each issue to a group of between two and four students for research and further exploration. Each group should report its results to the class. Here are some key questions class discussion might address:

Did you encounter issues in your group that you were not aware of before research?

What knowledge about the issues struck you as most important?

Given what you know now, what would you like to know more about?

After the discussion is over, consider your view of the topic now. If you had no opinion before discussing the issues, are you beginning to form one now? If you had a strong opinion, is it changing significantly? •

Order the Issues (Stasis)

Discussing the issues is an important step in exploring a controversial topic. Ordering them can help as well, beginning with the most elementary of questions and moving through to subsequent issues. As an example, here is one way of ordering the issues involved in committing American troops to a foreign country:

- Are vital American interests at stake?

   If you say no, make a case against committing the troops. If you say yes, move on to the next question.

- Have nonmilitary alternatives been exploited fully?

   If you say no, make a case for increased diplomatic effort or some other measure not requiring American troops on the ground. If you say yes, move on to the next question.

- Do the announced objectives make sense?

   If you say no, make a case for changing the objectives. If you say yes, move on to the next question.

- Can we realize our objectives in a reasonable amount of time with minimal loss of lives?

   If you say yes, make a case for military intervention. If you say no, make a case against it based on impracticality.

Ordering the issues in this way is sometimes called **stasis,** a word that means "stop" or "stay." That is, if you think a proposed military intervention would not secure vital national interests, you stop with the first question and make a case against it. If you think nonmilitary options have not been pursued far enough, you argue for more diplomacy, economic sanctions, or some other alternative. You stay with the second question—and so on, through the whole list.

   You can order the issues connected with any controversial topic this way. Doing so can help you see how the issues relate to one another and on what key questions opinion divides. It can clarify your own thinking as you work toward an opinion or assess the one you have.

◎◎ FOLLOWING THROUGH

Cases require a *considered opinion*—that is, an opinion *thought through carefully.* Consequently, after finding and ordering the issues, you need to decide what your opinion is on the issue you chose to address. Your opinion may change as you write and assess your first draft, but you cannot write a draft at all without committing to an opinion.

   In a blog post or notebook entry, state your opinion and the reasons you have for holding it.

Doing Team Research

Sometimes instructors want you to do research on your own. When that is part of the assignment, do not use the team approach suggested here. Otherwise a team approach is best because there is so much information on nearly all topics.

Here are the steps in a team approach to research:

1. Form small groups based on sharing the same opinion.

2. Share all information you have already, so that everyone in the group has the same knowledge base.

3. Make a list of the information you lack.

4. Divide the items on the needed information list among group members and set a deadline for getting the research done.

5. Get together to share and discuss the implications of the new research materials.

The team approach to research is the norm in business settings, community organizations, government, and often in advanced academic work. The advantages are obvious: sharing the work burden and having people with whom to discuss the results.

Do More Research

The amount of research needed to argue a case depends on such variables as the nature of the topic, how much you know about it already, and what the assignment requires.

Even thought-through opinions need to confront "the facts," current, reliable knowledge about a topic. For controversial topics, the problem is rarely lack of sources. If you use the resources for finding information discussed in Chapter 6, "Writing Research-Based Arguments," you can count on finding much more than you will have time to read.

Therefore, let the opinion you formed after considering the issues dictate the direction for further research. You can then look only for sources relevant to it and take notes (see pages 127–128 for how to do this) only on those sources that provide the best information. You can pass over many articles and book chapters because the titles alone indicate they will not be relevant. Others you can eliminate with a quick, partial reading; the title turns out to be more promising than the content. You can concentrate on what is left, the articles that are most relevant, and among these, the few that are outstanding, most authoritative, recent, and detailed in offering reliable information. (See pages 116–121 for estimating how reliable a source is.)

The Best Practices box offers an approach to research that can make it more efficient yet.

Analyze Your Sources: Information versus Interpretation

Research materials on controversial topics typically are arguments backed by information used as evidence. Consequently, you need to distinguish information from the "spin" or interpretation the writer and his or her sources supply. For example, it is a fact that in a recent year about 6,200 people died in Mexico as a result of the traffic in narcotics. Citing this figure, some writers argue that American tourists should avoid Mexico. There is no reason to doubt the 6,200 figure, but the interpretation is far from certain—drug-related violence seldom involves American tourists, and many destinations in Mexico are no more risky than some of our own cities.

It is also important to distinguish information from speculation. Facts are uncontested, established pieces of data. How the stock market performed over the last month is a matter of fact, as measured, for example, by the Dow Jones average. Speculations are at most probabilities and possibilities. How the stock market will perform over the next year is anyone's guess. When relevant to your opinion, you *must* engage the facts; speculation you can ignore or use if it supports your opinion.

In general, despite what people sometimes say, the facts cannot speak for themselves. *Facts have to be interpreted, put into a context where they have meaning.* For example, newspapers are in significant financial trouble in the United States. Does this mean, as some people claim, that Americans are less well informed about current events than they were thirty years ago, when papers were in much better shape? Or does it mean that people are getting the news from other sources—online, for instance? It is hard to say, but in any case the decline of newspapers, a fact beyond dispute, must be interpreted to have meaning and significance.

Finally, above all, *strive to maintain intellectual independence from the view your source has of the subject.* Avoid distorting or misrepresenting the information in a source to fit what you want to believe, but feel free to interpret the information your own way, as you see the subject. For instance, you may support screening passengers before boarding commercial airliners as a necessary counterterrorism measure. If so, you cannot ignore considerable evidence that screening often fails to detect prohibited items that could be used for a terrorist act. Instead of ignoring or denying the evidence, argue instead that screening technology must improve.

Start Your Working Bibliography

As you do research, maintain a complete list of your sources, including all information you will need for the concluding bibliography or works cited page. (See examples of the various types of entries for these pages on pages 139–148.) Doing this as you work can save having to relocate the sources later.

Keep the bibliographical information with your drafts, bearing in mind that revision and rewriting usually result in dropping and adding source material.

Ponder a Key Question: Is My Opinion Defensible?

You are about to make your case, so address the following question coolly and apart from how strongly you are committed to the opinion you had before research: Given what I know now, can I make a good case for my opinion?

One outcome is that current knowledge makes your opinion impossible or very difficult to defend. Change your opinion to accord with the evidence.

More commonly, research yields another result. Your opinion is still defensible, but you need to modify it some to allow for information you lacked prior to research. Perhaps you did not know that the flu vaccine developed each year is never 100% effective. You could still make a case in favor of a more aggressive vaccination campaign. You need only admit that the inoculation is not uniformly reliable. There is still overwhelming evidence of its benefit to public health—of the approximately 36,000 Americans who die from the flu each year, a high percentage did not receive the vaccine.

The Art of Questioning: Assessing Your Opinion from Research Results

Cases are public arguments and therefore must respect what is known about a topic. Ask these questions as you adjust your opinion to the evidence you have gathered:

1. What facts and expert opinion best support my position?
2. What did I learn from research that challenges my position? Do I need to rethink or modify it?
3. What further information should I seek?

Some people believe that arguments require that they take a stand and hold it regardless of what the available evidence says. They elevate saying what they think over responding to the evidence, and often they appeal to honesty to justify their behavior.

We urge a sharply different attitude. Case-making is a rational process, and part of being rational is changing your mind or modifying your opinion as you learn more about a subject. This process is not dishonest. On the contrary, admitting that "I used to believe this, but now that I know more I believe that instead" requires not only being honest with yourself and other people but also being open to experience, which is necessary for intellectual growth and maturity.

PREPARING TO WRITE

Some writers prefer to go straight to drafting, working out their cases in several drafts. We recommend going through the following steps first, which most writers find helpful:

1. State your opinion as a claim or thesis.
2. "Unpack" (analyze) the thesis to determine what you must argue to defend it adequately.
3. State the reasons you will use to explain or justify your thesis.
4. Select and order the evidence you will use to back up each reason.

These steps, described in more detail below, yield a **brief,** an outline of your case. Add ideas for an introduction and a conclusion and you have all you need to guide your first draft.

State Your Opinion as a Thesis

You are still exploring your opinion when your write a first draft of your case because the ultimate test of any opinion is how strong a case you can make for it. However, your first draft will be stronger if you attempt to state your opinion as a thesis before you begin drafting. An opinion is a general stance or point of view. For instance, in the second reading in this chapter (pages 215–217), Wilbert Rideau believes that our prison system is not working because politics rather than reason and an adequate understanding of crime and criminals controls it. That is his opinion. In contrast, his thesis is much more specific: "Society would be well served by releasing some of its older prisoners who pose no threat and using the money to catch young street thugs" (paragraph 5).

In preparing to write a case, the advantage of a thesis over an opinion is a *sharper focus, with carefully selected key terms.* It is worth your time and effort to work toward a thesis before you draft.

Writing Defensible Claims

- Your claim is a statement you'll defend, not just a description of something that is factual.

  Not a claim: Student debt for government loans has grown to over $20,000 for the average graduate, a heavy burden for young people just entering the workplace.

  Claim: The economy as a whole would benefit if the federal government would forgive student debts for higher education, which now average over $20,000 per graduate.

The first in this pair describes a problem. The second proposes a solution for doing something about the problem.

- The claim should be focused and specific, and directed at a readership.

  Too general: Many professors do not know how to make effective use of technology in teaching.

  Better: Professors who use presentation technology such as PowerPoint too often stifle creativity and student involvement in the class.

The second example in this pair is more refined, indicating specific directions that the argument will take. The more specific your claim, the easier it will be to decide what your paper will include.

- Some claims may need to be qualified.

  Too absolute: Professors should openly state their opinions on political issues in classes where such opinions are relevant to course content.

Qualified: Provided that students are encouraged to discuss their own opinions freely, professors should be able to openly state their opinions on political issues so long as the issue is relevant to course content.

Think of objections your readers might have to your claim and revise it to eliminate the possible objection.

FOLLOWING THROUGH

Any opinion can be expressed in many thesis statements. If you are having difficulty formulating yours or hesitating between or among two or more possibilities, post a blog entry or send an e-mail to your instructor or to some other appropriate person that lays out your thought process and asks for feedback. Just writing the blog or e-mail can help you think things through and make a good decision. Any feedback you receive can help you even more. •

Unpack Your Thesis

To "unpack" a thesis means to detect the key terms that make the assertion. Judson's thesis, "Evolution should be central to beginning biology classes," contains terms that demand that the argument show why evolution is *central*, rather than a theory one can explain and discuss at one meeting and then ignore. It will also show why biology classes must start with evolution as a foundation.

As another example, consider the thesis: "*Huckleberry Finn* should be required reading in all American high schools." To defend the thesis adequately requires addressing all the key terms: why this *particular book* should be a *required* title on American literature lists and why *high school* is the best place to teach it.

The Art of Questioning: Thinking about Reasons

The reasoning that led you to your claim will supply the reasons you will offer to explain and justify it to your reader. In listing your reasons, however, you can avoid potential problems by thinking carefully about the following questions:

- Does the statement of each reason say exactly what I mean to say? The wording of your reason or reasons matters as much as the wording of your thesis.

- Do I need all the reasons I am thinking of using? As a general rule, two or three reasons are better than four or five because they are easier for the reader to remember. *Concentrate on developing your best reasons well rather than offering all the reasons you can think of.*

- Does each reason clearly connect to the thesis by either explaining or justifying it? Imagine your reader asking this question, "Why do you believe your thesis?" Each reason should answer this question.

- Are there advantages in developing my reasons in a particular order? In general, begin and end your argument with your strongest reasons. But also consider the possibility that one reason will lead naturally to another, and therefore should come first.

- If you have more than one reason, are they consistent with each other? Make sure, for instance, that your first reason does not contradict your third reason.

Arrange Your Evidence under Each Reason

Just as the reasons that led you to your thesis are the reasons you will develop to convince your readers, so the information you found in research that led you to your reasons or confirmed them will supply the evidence. Arrange the evidence you have under each reason.

The Art of Questioning: Thinking about Evidence

Select and order your evidence in response to the following questions:

- What kind of evidence does each reason require? For example, if you are arguing for making cell phone use by drivers illegal, one of your main reasons will be the link of cell phone use with accidents. You will need data, facts and figures, to back it up. If you also argue that such a law would not restrict personal freedom unduly, you will need other kinds of evidence, such as pointing out that banning cell phones is no more restrictive than laws against driving while intoxicated.

- How much evidence do I need? The answer is, *Enough to overcome the degree of resistance your reader is likely to have.* Many Americans, for instance, assume that the federal government is already too big, too intrusive, and too expensive. Defending any proposal that would increase its role requires significant evidence for both need and positive results.

- Have I mixed evidence types when I can? For example, when a reason requires hard data, you must supply it. But if you also have a statement from a respected expert confirming your reason, consider using it as well. Some readers are convinced more by authoritative statements than by hard data. You could also offer anecdotes, stories from people involved in an event, to confirm a reason. Stories from wounded soldiers who have served in Afghanistan or Iraq, for example, can be used to argue for improvements in Veteran Administration hospitals. Many people find testimony more convincing than any other kind of evidence.

- Have I selected the best pieces of evidence from all that I could use? Just as it is better to develop two or three reasons well than four or five poorly, so it is better to offer two or three strong pieces of evidence than four or five that vary in quality. More is not necessarily better, and too much evidence can confuse and overburden your reader.

1. A position or general outlook on a topic is not a thesis. A **thesis** is a carefully worded claim that your entire essay backs up with reasons and evidence. Experiment with various ways of stating your thesis until it says *exactly* what you want it to say and creates the least resistance in your readers.

2. Be willing to give up or modify significantly a thesis you find you cannot support with good reasons and strong evidence that appeal *to your readers*. We must argue a thesis that fits the available **evidence.**

3. Create a specific audience profile. We are always trying to convince some definite group of possible readers. What are the age, gender, and economic status of your target audience? What interests, beliefs, and values might they bring to your topic and thesis?

4. Unpack your thesis to discover what you must argue. If you say, for instance, that *Huckleberry Finn* should be *required* reading in high school, you must show why *this particular novel* should be an experience shared by all American high school students. It will not be enough to argue that it is a good book.

5. Select your reasons based on what you must argue to defend your thesis combined with what you should say given your audience's prior knowledge, preconceptions, prejudices, and interests.

6. Be prepared to try out different ways of ordering your reasons. The order that seemed best in your brief might not work best as you draft and redraft your essay.

Student Example: Noelle Alberto's Brief

See Best Practices, "The Brief in Sum" for a checklist of the thinking that needs to go into preparing a brief.

Here is an example of a brief from a student urging her fellow students to stop multitasking when they study. Note its three-level structure: the claim is the thesis or statement your paper defends; each reason is subordinate to the thesis because it explains why you hold your thesis; each piece of evidence is subordinate to the reason it supports.

Claim: **Multitasking between recreational technology and studying impairs students' learning and does not prepare them for the real world of work.**

> *Reason: Multitasking increases the amount of time spent studying.*

>> *Evidence:* Homework takes twice as long to complete with multitasking. (Source: Tugend)

>> *Evidence:* Switching tasks makes you have to relearn information to get back on track. (Source: Hamilton)

Reason: Multitasking impairs the brain's abilities to learn and store information.

> *Evidence:* It prevents students from being able to store information learned through studying. (Sources: Rosen, Jarmon)

Reason: Multitasking is poor preparation for the workplace.

> *Evidence:* Businesses don't want people who multitask; they want people who prioritize. (Source: LPA)

> *Evidence:* Multitasking decreases production ability of workers. (Source: Rosen)

Reason: *Multitasking promotes shallow rather than deep thinking.*

> *Evidence:* Ability to pay attention to one thing at a time is a mark of mature thinking. (Source: Rosen)

DRAFTING YOUR PAPER

Using your brief as a guide, write your first draft.

Development and Organization

Start by orienting your reader, providing what she or he needs to know to understand your topic and why it is significant. Establish the point of view toward the topic you have and want your reader to share. Make your own position clear. The Best Practices box offers suggestions to help you as you write.

Student Example: Excerpts from Noelle's Draft

The introduction from Noelle's first draft illustrates a common problem with arguments. It opens with generalizations that do not grab the reader's attention and show how the topic of the paper will matter to them.

> Long before the computer, people have always needed to multitask. Mothers dressed their children while getting ready for work and making breakfast. Men drank their morning coffee and ate breakfast on their drive to work. Multitasking has long been a part of our society, and now, technology has granted us new means of multitasking. This multitasking is now crucial to the younger generation's way of life, but it may be hurting them academically.

Noelle did a good job of creating a context for her case against multitasking, and her thesis is clearly stated in the last sentence. However, she could have used a specific example to connect with her intended audience, college and high school students. By using a source, she was able to revise her introduction (see page 238) to engage her readers better immediately.

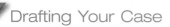

Drafting Your Case

1. Openers are important. Start your essay by putting your case in context. For example, Judson (page 211) opens hers by referring to the beginning of a school year, when how to teach biology is immediately relevant.

2. Your reader may need background information to understand your case. Part of this will come from establishing the context in the opening, but sometimes additional information your reader lacks or may not remember will be necessary. Pickens (page 219) provides a good example of needed background information in developing his first claim: "America is addicted to foreign oil." Most of his readers are aware of our dependence on foreign crude, but probably not of its full consequences: $700 billion going out of the country to feed our habit every year, $10 trillion over the next ten years, "the greatest transfer of wealth in the history of mankind." Information like this not only provides needed background but also catches reader attention.

3. Cases do not have to deal with opposing points of view. However, if there is an obvious objection to your case you think most readers will think of, better mention it and show why the objection does not hold. Pickens provides good examples of anticipating and responding to objections. For instance, he explains why we cannot overcome our addiction to foreign oil by pumping more domestically (page 219).

4. Consider using visuals as an efficient way to convey evidence. Again, Pickens provides a good example of how effective photos, maps, and graphs can be.

5. Avoid summary, "in conclusion," conclusions. Strive instead for a memorable "parting shot," something with impact. Rideau's "Ever see a dog chase its tail?" is a good example, but you can use, for instance, a well-worded quotation followed by commentary of your own.

6. Strive to maintain throughout your essay the voice described in the assignment—dispassionate, calm, and fair—and the middle style case-making favors: simple, forceful statements that allow the thesis and its supporting reasons and evidence to stand out for your reader.

Another common problem in arguments is using sources to support and develop points, but not using enough from the source to make the evidence clear and convincing. Here is an example that is not easy to follow.

> David Meyer, a professor at University of Michigan, found that when you switch to a new task, the parts of the brain that are no longer being used "start shutting things down—like neural connections to important information" (Hamilton). The work you were focusing on isn't as understandable, and when you finally get back to it you "will have to repeat much of the process that created [the information] in the first place" (Hamilton).

Revision Checklist for Arguing a Case

1. Who is the target audience? How is the case framed—introduced—to reach that audience? Does the writer keep this audience in mind throughout the essay?

2. Locate the claim as stated or implied. Is it held consistently throughout the essay?

3. Locate the reasons that explain and justify the claim. Does the writer focus on one reason at a time, staying with it until it is completely developed? How effectively does each reason appeal to the audience? Is each reason clearly connected to the thesis it defends?

4. Do you detect a logical progression in the ordering of the reasons, so that the first reason leads to the second, the second to the third, and so on? Is there a better way to order the reasons? Can you find weak reasons that should be cut? Can you suggest reasons not included that would make the case stronger?

5. How much will the audience resist each reason? Is there sufficient evidence to overcome the resistance? Is the evidence for each reason clear and relevant to the reason it supports?

6. Do you see a better way to order the evidence for any of the reasons?

7. Look at the conclusion. How does it clinch the case, leaving the reader with something memorable? Can you see a way to make the conclusion more forceful?

The source actually gave a much more detailed description of the problem Noelle describes above. See the revised version of this passage (paragraph 3 on page 238).

To catch this kind of revision problem, ask a friend to read your draft and to be completely honest about where you may not have been clear enough in explaining evidence from a source.

REVISING YOUR DRAFT

Write a brief assessment of your first draft. Exchange your draft and assessment with at least one other student and help each other decide what needs improvement.

The revision questions in the Best Practices box should help you assess your own and your partner's draft.

Formulate a Plan to Guide Your Revision

The plan can be a single sentence or two: "I'll cut this, rearrange that, and add a section here." The important thing is to have a definite, clear idea of what you want to do and what moves you will make to get the results you want.

REVISED STUDENT EXAMPLE
Multitasking: A Poor Study Habit

NOELLE ALBERTO

1   A recent National Public Radio program described the study habits of a modern teenager, Zach Weinberg of Chevy Chase, Maryland. On a typical evening, he worked on French homework while visiting his e-mail and Facebook, listening to iTunes, messaging a friend, and playing an online word puzzle (Hamilton). According to the story, Zach is a successful student, but many studies of multitasking suggest that he could be better if he focused on one thing at a time. While human beings are capable of doing two things at once if one of those things does not require much attention, like driving and drinking your morning coffee, there are some things that require a single focus, like school work. Multitasking between studies and recreational technology is not an effective way to study.

2   One misconception that students may have about their multitasking is that they are saving time. Some say that they feel they get more done in a shorter amount of time, but they are actually not doing two things at once. They are switching from one task to another, and constant task switching takes more time. Gloria Mark of the University of California, Irvine conducted a study in which business workers were interrupted while working on a project. Each time, it took them about 25 minutes to return their attention to the original project (Turgend). In study terms, if you interrupt yourself to check your e-mail, a chapter that would take thirty minutes to read straight through could take much longer.

Paragraph gives more evidence for the first reason.

3   What happens when people shift from one demanding task to another? David Meyer, a professor at University of Michigan, found that when you switch to a new task, the parts of the brain that are no longer being used "start shutting things down—like neural connections to important information." If a student is studying French and stops to shop online, the neural connections to the French homework start to shut down. To restore full understanding, Meyer says the student "will have to repeat much of the process that created [the connections] in the first place" (qtd. in Hamilton).

A transitional paragraph wrapping up the first reason.

4   This frequent reconnecting to prior levels of focus and understanding is a waste of time. It is time lost that could be used more efficiently. If students eliminated technological distractions during study time, they would be able to complete more work in a shorter amount of time with greater understanding. There is always time to socialize after homework and studying has been completed.

Second reason.

Another misconception is that multitasking prepares you for the business world. "Able to multitask" used to be considered a positive on employee résumés. However, the researchers found that "extreme multitasking—information overload—costs the U.S. economy $650 billion a year in lost productivity" (Rosen 106). A study conducted at the University of London found that "workers distracted by e-mail and phone calls suffer a fall in IQ more than twice that found in marijuana smokers" (qtd. in Rosen 106). Employers, therefore, do not value multitasking. Now, according to the U.S. Departments of Labor and Education, businesses want an employee who "selects goal-relevant activities, ranks them, allocates time, and prepares and follows schedules" ("Skills and Competencies"). If multitasking is difficult and harmful in the business world, it has no place in university work either.

6   Besides wasted time and money, another unfortunate effect of multitasking is serious damage to students' ability to learn. Studies by psychology professor Russell Poldrack show that multitasking makes "learning . . . less flexible and more special-ized, so you cannot retrieve the information as easily" (qtd. in Rosen 107). Studies of blood flow in the brain show why. When people are task-switching, they use the "striatum, a region of the brain involved in learning new skills" (Rosen 107). In contrast, people who are not multitasking "show activity in the hippocampus, a region involved in storing and recalling information" (Rosen 108). Amy Jarmon, Dean at Texas Tech's School of Law, recalls a study comparing two groups of students in a large lecture class. One group of students was allowed to use laptops in class; they performed much more poorly on a memory quiz of lecture content than students not permitted to use laptops. Students who checked their e-mail and updated their Web pages during class did not recall information as well because they were not using the hippocampus.

Third reason.

7   Finally, if students get into the habit of multitasking, they could miss out on developing a personality trait prized by highly successful people. Christine Rosen calls the trait "a finely honed skill for paying attention" (109). The great British scientist Sir Isaac Newton said his discoveries owed "more to patient attention than to any other talent." The American psychologist William James wrote that the ability to pay attention marked the difference between a mature and an immature person: "The faculty of voluntarily bringing back a wandering attention, over and over again . . . is the very root of judgment, character, and will" (qtd. in Rosen 109). Maturity means recognizing that there is "a time and place for everything." When I go to the library to study, I leave my computer behind so that I will not be tempted to multitask. After an hour of focused school work, I have accomplished a great deal.

Fourth reason. This is the last reason because it has weight in showing how multitasking undermines intel-lectual potential.

Brings personal experience into the paper.

8   Multitasking is now part of every student's life. The facts indicate that we need to resist it more. It is not as helpful as many people think, and its very appeal is part of the problem. It is inefficient, reduces intelligence, and impairs recall. To think deeply rather than shallowly, we need to concentrate. Therefore, the best approach is to divide study time from social time. Focusing on one thing at a time will produce better outcomes now and in the future.

WORKS CITED

Hamilton, Jon. "Multitasking Teens May Be Muddling Their Brains." *NPR.* National Public Radio, 9 Oct. 2008. Web. 7 Apr 2009.

Jarmon, Amy L. "Multitasking: Helpful or Harmful? Multitasking Has Been Shown to Slow Learning and Reduce Efficiency." *Student Lawyer* 36.8 (April 2008): 30(5). *Academic OneFile.* Web. 23 Mar. 2009.

Rosen, Christine. "The Myth of Multitasking," *The New Atlantis* 20 (Spring 2008) 105–110. Print.

"Skills and Competencies Needed to Succeed in Today's Workplace." North Central
   Regional Education Laboratory, Learning Point Associates. N.d. Web. 7 April 2009.
Tugend, Alina. "Multitasking Can Make You Lose . . . Um . . . Focus." *The New York
   Times.* 25 Oct. 2008. Web. 23 Mar. 2009.

CHAPTER SUMMARY

Go back and review the steps you went through in writing this paper, concentrating on what happened when you were preparing to write. Pay special attention to testing your opinion. No matter what the subject or whether you are writing an argument or not, the method and attitude always apply. Internalize it. Make it a part of how you encounter new information and new experience. It boils down to this: Take time to form an opinion on controversial issues you hear and read about. But be constantly open to revising your opinion when you encounter anything new and relevant. Only in this way can your understanding of life and the world deepen and mature.

You know people who seem to gain almost instant respect from others, people who are listened to—part of this special quality is knowing what you think while remaining open to changing what you think. The impact of such people is not surprising at all: When people offer considered and well-informed opinions, they influence others who lack them. That is not only how it is but how it should be.

CHAPTER 10

Motivating Action: Arguing to Persuade

We can define persuasion as "convincing plus" because, in addition to reason, three other forms of appeal receive conscious attention: appeals to the writer's character, to the emotions of the audience, and to style, the artful use of language. These three forms of appeal usually are present in case-making but in need of development for full persuasive impact, which means everything you learned in Chapter 9 remains relevant. We are building on Chapter 9 to help you understand and control persuasion's wider range of appeals.

WHAT IS PERSUASION?

Have you ever advocated change in an existing policy or way of doing something at school, in your dormitory or apartment complex, on your job, or at a community meeting? If so, you know about the potential power of persuasion. *Persuasion asks us to do something*—spend money, give money, join a demonstration, recycle, vote, enlist, convict, or acquit. For this reason, we call persuasion "appealing for action."

Persuasion joins a case to other ways of moving people to act, especially by gaining their trust and confidence and by arousing emotions favorable to the action advocated. In a moment, we will look at the means of persuasion,

When Should You Persuade?

Pay close attention to what your course assignments call for because the full range of persuasive appeal is not always appropriate. The more purely intellectual your topic and the more academic your audience, the more you should emphasize logical appeal, or making a good case. A clear thesis, supported by good reasons and backed by solid evidence, is usually what professors want.

When the issue is public, matters of policy or right and wrong, persuasion's fuller range of appeal is appropriate. Making an argument for the creation of a homeless shelter in your community requires establishing your good character and personal involvement with the project as well as appealing to the emotions of your readers. *Persuasion appeals to the whole person:* mind, emotion, the capacity for trust and cooperation, even the virtue of saying things well.

College assignments calling for persuasion will often ask you to take knowledge gained from a course and use it to persuade others who lack it. For example, using what you learned from a course in environmental science, you might write an article urging Americans to buy smaller, fuel-efficient automobiles to reduce carbon dioxide emissions and consumption of oil.

often called forms of appeal. First, consider the issue of appropriateness, when to convince and when to persuade, especially in college writing.

WHY WRITE TO PERSUADE?

Persuasion brings about change in the world, whether in national or local politics, in neighborhoods, on campus, in the workplace, or in personal relationships. For example, persuasion can:

- Sway elected officials to favor one policy over another
- Induce people and nations to resolve conflicts peacefully rather than by violent means
- Affect business decisions of all kinds, including how to promote a product or service
- Influence college officials who set tuition rates and housing costs on campus

No other kind of writing has more practical impact. If you want to make a difference in a world that needs to change in many ways, learning how to persuade other people is the key.

HOW DOES PERSUASION WORK?

Getting people to take action requires more than a good case. That's why the ancient Greek philosopher Aristotle identified three kinds of appeal: to reason (*logos*); to the character of the speaker (*ethos*); and to the emotions

The Four Forms of Appeal

Form	Function	Presence in Text
Reason	Logical cogency	Your case; any supported contention
Character	Personal appeal	Indications of author's status and values
Emotion	Appeals to feelings	Concrete descriptions, moving images
Style	Appeals through language	Word choice, sentence structure, metaphor

Essentially, persuasion differs from convincing in seeking action, not just agreement; it integrates rational appeal with other ways to influence people.

of the listeners (*pathos*). In all three, you adapt what you are advocating to the interests, beliefs, and values of a target audience.

In the readings that follow this section, you will see the appeals at work in an ad and two articles, all finished texts. Let us consider them at the other end of the writing process, as a *heuristic* (learning device) for coming up with something to say.

To save money and for other reasons, Americans are looking for alternatives to cars. One of these alternatives is the motorcycle or scooter. Suppose you were writing an essay with the title, "Getting Around on Two Wheels." What might you say?

Starting with logos, or the appeal to reason, you could argue that

- Motorcycles cost far less than cars to buy and maintain.
- They use on average about one-third as much gas.
- They take up only about half as much parking space.
- With proper training and equipment, they are not as dangerous to operate as many people think.

Motorcycles could help solve many problems, including reduction in traffic, greenhouse gas emissions, and American dependence on foreign crude oil.

How could you use pathos, or emotional appeal? The main value here is the fun of motorcycling. Motorcycles are the mechanical horse—you do not drive them, you ride them—and it should be fairly easy to appeal to the American love for freedom and adventure.

Finally, how could you appeal to ethos, or character? If you are a motorcyclist yourself, you could draw on your own experience. If not, interview friends who ride and cite what they say: you can borrow ethos from others.

The Art of Questioning: What Really Persuades Us?

Many people say they are persuaded by reasons and evidence. That is, logos matters most. Aristotle thought that ethos might be more powerful: if we think that a writer is intelligent, well informed, trustworthy, and has genuine concern for our needs, we will tend to believe most of what that person says. Look at advertising and you will probably conclude that pathos is the prime persuader. Nearly all ads appeal to emotions and attitudes most of all.

What do you think? Consider the last important decision you made. How did you persuade yourself to do one thing rather than another? If someone tried to persuade you, what kinds of appeal did they use? Which of these appeals had the most impact on the decision you made?

READINGS

The following readings will help you see in more detail how persuasion works and what you can do when you encounter a situation that calls for persuasion.

Subaru Advertisement

1 | Advertising is one of the most common examples of moving people to action. We can learn a great deal about persuasion by studying advertisers' creative use of

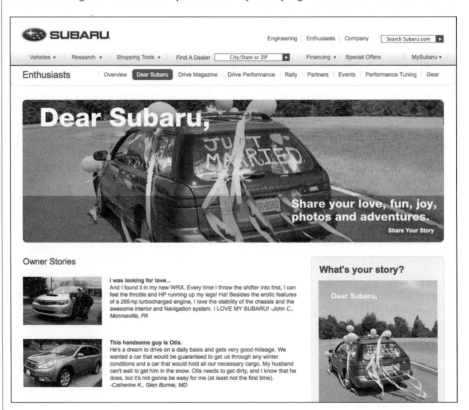

http://www.subaru.com/dearsubaru/index.html

rhetorical appeals, both verbal and visual, to targeted audiences. This advertisement from Subaru's Web site illustrates all of the appeals Aristotle identified as contributing to effective persuasion.

2   Although Subaru also advertises in print magazines, appealing to specific readerships like mountain-bike riders, this advertisement is well designed for people who use the Internet to investigate possible automobile choices. The links in the menu across the top enable readers to see the range of vehicles, specifics about Subaru cars, pricing, and dealerships—all good basic information. However, this particular page moves beyond informing to persuading because of its emotional and ethical appeals aimed at people accustomed to the social networking and collaboration made possible by Web 2.0.

3   The ad invites owners and potential buyers to interact personally with the company and with each other by posting pictures of themselves with their cars and brief testimonials about why they love their Subaru. It is an emotional appeal to be part of a group of happy and fun-loving people swapping their stories. Sharing is emphasized in the text: "Share your love. . . ." "Share your story."

4   The ad also appeals logically to Internet shoppers who routinely check out other consumers' reviews and opinions about a product. Buyers' testimonials about good mileage, safety, and performance are good reasons and evidence that would also move the reader to choose this line of cars.

5   Subaru also displays its corporate ethos, or character, in this promotion by showing that it cares about its customers and the pleasure they get from driving their cars. The corporate image is friendly and unpretentious, a company for sporty, adventurous, outdoor lovers. "Share the love" is a theme in Subaru advertisements, referring to Subaru's philanthropic efforts on behalf of five major national charities. Market research told Subaru that its customers are likely to be committed to charitable causes.

6   Finally, the visuals and layout of the advertisement contribute to the message of personal connection, fun, and adventure. The featured visual looks like a letter with its salutation, "Dear Subaru." The letter's message is the car itself with its balloons, flowing streamers, and "Just Married" sign. These details visually depict the words in the caption at the lower right. The compilation of pictures and stories are a slightly less cluttered version of a Facebook page, completing the appeal to a targeted audience of connected, fun-loving people.

◎◎ FOLLOWING THROUGH

Find an advertisement that you think is effective for its target audience. Who is the audience? Analyze how the ad appeals to ethos, pathos, and logos. Describe the visual and verbal appeals to style.   •

Consuming Faith

TOM BEAUDOIN

> "Consuming Faith" was published in *Tikkun,* the journal of a socially progressive orga-
> nization that publishes interfaith perspectives on issues of justice, preservation of the
> environment, and political freedom.
>
> Tom Beaudoin is professor of theology at Santa Clara University in California. The
> essay comes from his book, *Consuming Faith: Integrating Who We Are with What We
> Buy* (Sheed and Ward, 2004). As you read this essay, think about your own consumer
> behavior and your relationship to the people who produce the items you purchase.

1   In December, several Honduran women came to Boston College. They were on a
speaking tour of New England universities, talking about their work back home
sewing shirts for a major brand that many of my students wore.

2   These women told stories that anyone familiar with the global sweatshop workforce will find painfully predictable: verbal abuse, beastly wages, forbidden unions,
forced overtime, no holidays, no health insurance or other benefits, the inability to
save money so their children can break out of this life, and transportation and food
costs that ate up four hours' wages every day. And the workforce consisted entirely
of young women, aged 15 to 30.

3   I was outraged, because these women worked for a company that I knew had
turned enormous profits. It was not as if the company was going to go broke if it
had even minimally met the meager requests of these women. I was outraged
because many of my students wore this clothing brand and I hated that they were
paying this corporation to brand themselves at these women's expense [. . .] . And
I was outraged because I was reminded that this corporation got away with it
because I myself spent so many years not doing my part to stop such practices. I
had paid lots of money to be a foot soldier for my favorite brands of shoes, jeans,
and shirts—even coffee.

4   For me, the turning point came when I started seeing the faces of the women
making my favorite brands. I had read a story several years ago about impoverished
coffee farmers who harvest coffee beans for wealthy American coffee companies,
and saw a picture of one of their faces on the Web or in the paper. I ended up
pulling my favorite brands out of my closet and tracking down who made "my"
brands, where they were produced, and the conditions under which they were put
together. With the exception of my branded sport coat produced in Toronto under
Canadian labor laws, the rest of my favorite brands were assembled by non-American
faces that were forbidden to join unions, had to submit to pregnancy tests, and
were kept in poverty by American companies that had almost eliminated the cost
of labor, while avoiding paying any taxes at all due to breaks from the host countries
where the factories were placed. Not that any of them volunteered this information.
Most of the companies gave me public relations blowback and legal-speak and some
outright lied to me. I had to turn to independent reportage to find out exactly what
I was supporting, and whose faces I was affecting, by my purchase of my favorite
brands. When I called the corporate headquarters of my local outpost of a coffee

chain to see if I could travel—at my own expense—to South America to take pictures of the farmers who harvested my coffee and post them in the store, I got a firm and unequivocal "no." Why did so many of my favorite coffee and clothing brands want to hide the faces of those who made my stuff?

5   I was beginning to see that there were relationships in which I was an involved but irresponsible partner—economic relationships. Just as any other common relationship we have has both pleasures and responsibilities (whether as spouse, friend, or co-worker), so do my economic relationships, I was beginning to see. By enjoying my branded jeans, I was necessarily in relationship with the women who made them. They had done their part by making clothes that protected me and brought me pleasure. What was my obligation to them? What was my part of the relationship?

6   This raised the question for me: how central are economic relationships to faith? Are my economic relationships secondary to who I am before God, or central? The popular picture of Christianity today, unfortunately, does not show the best face of my faith on this issue. As a Catholic Christian, I notice the way Christianity is portrayed in the media, and how it portrays itself in its own advertising, and what I see lately is a religion too often indifferent to war, over interested in individual morality, and defensive about its own institutional abuses. One would almost think that this public image of religiosity was mandated by the Christian scriptures. However, when I turned back to scripture to see how Jesus of Nazareth dealt with economics, I was shocked at what I found. Jesus very seldom talks about God's final judgment, about "heaven" and "hell," but when he does, as his way of talking about what is most important in a life of spiritual maturity before God, he does something interesting. He almost always talks about intimacy with God in the next life as bound up with one's economic relationships in this life. He speaks of a wealthy man who ignores a poor man at his gate finding himself later in hell, crying out to the poor man for help. He talks about those who use their resources of time and money to visit prisoners and clothe the naked as going on to a final happiness with God, and those who do not as having failed to love God and live a truly human life. Jesus was not focused on whom one is sleeping with, whether one has properly obeyed religious authorities, or how religious institutions can preserve themselves. He saw economic relationships as ultimate expressions of one's true faith. Responsibility for the other is where and how one ought to live in relationship to that gracious and mysterious power that sustains us, which he intimately called his "Father."

7   For me, the Jewishness of Jesus' concern for the other is present in a more recent idiom in the philosophy of Emmanuel Levinas. For Levinas, we are everywhere and in each moment dependent on and responsible to others. To be human is to be responsible for the other, whose well-being my very existence may be threatening. This obligation to others is encountered and symbolized in the face-to-face relationship. The faces of others represent persons genuinely different from us, exposed to us. The vulnerability of the human face presents us with the claim: do not kill me. In a sense, Levinas says, the face says to us "do not deface me"; allow me, it says, my otherness and exposure without violation, shame, or indifference.

8   But what if we are systematically excluded, in a brand economy, from seeing the faces of the others who inhabit our lives? What if your local branded coffee shop does not want you to even see the faces of those who harvest your coffee? Would we not think of our brands differently if we had in view the faces of those who make our stuff?

9   A more human brand economy would be a more holy one, one in which we take responsibility for our economic relationships, for the well-being of the faces who make our stuff. In a better world, the brands themselves will better manage the economic relationships between producers and consumers that they steward. In a better world, we will each think and even pray about our obligations to our economic relationships. In a better world, brands will try to talk us into purchasing them because they give their workers in China, Indonesia, or El Salvador a living wage, holidays, overtime pay, child care, and health insurance. Whether you are more with Jesus of Nazareth or Levinas of Lithuania, this better world is possible. If only we made economics a part of the discourse of spiritual maturity today, it would begin to happen.

QUESTIONS FOR DISCUSSION

1. Beaudoin uses word pattern repetition to appeal to the readers' emotions. Reread the selection and locate some examples. Why does he employ this strategy in those places rather than others? How effective is it for his intended audience?

2. The article attempts to overcome a common dissociation: probably most people see religion and economics as separate and at most weakly related. Does it succeed? Are you persuaded to pull them together? Why or why not?

Strategies Used for Appealing for Action

Beaudoin wants to persuade his readers to see their consumer choices as part of their religious practice. He tailors his argument to his audience (1) by giving them religious reasons for knowing more about the conditions in which goods are produced and (2) by refusing to buy from companies that exploit and abuse their workers.

We can learn something about strategy in appealing for action by examining how Beaudoin arranged the parts of his essay. Like many persuasive writers, he does not present his claim and reasons at the start of the essay but leads the readers gradually to the argument, which does not begin until about the midpoint. Beaudoin's essay falls into three parts:

1. The introductory narrative about the Honduran women. (paragraphs 1–3)

> Stories based on personal experience are often good openings. Beaudoin connects with his readers by assuming that they already know and disapprove of sweatshop conditions. But they are still buying the products, not "doing [their] part."

2. The story of his attempts to find out more about his brand-name goods. (paragraph 4)

> This section, also a narrative, builds up Beaudoin's ethos because it shows his long-term concern for and dedication to finding out about the workers.

3. The argument that responsible economic relationships are central to living a spiritual life. (paragraphs 5–9)

> This section is a case based on reasons and evidence. Paragraph 5 gives his first reason: Economic relationships entail responsibility just like other relationships. Then, in paragraphs 6–9, he argues that this relationship is religious. He asks, "[H]ow central are economic relationships to faith?" He answers this question by showing that economic relationships are central to religious identity (*the claim*). He justifies the claim with this reason: Both Christianity and Judaism see economic responsibility for others as integral to faith. He supports the reason with evidence from two sources, the Bible and the writings of the Jewish philosopher Emmanuel Levinas.

The Factories of Lost Children

KATHARINE WEBER

> Katharine Weber's subject matter and claim are similar to Beaudoin's in the previous essay, but she bases her argument on tragic incidents involving child labor. It was originally published in the *New York Times*.
>
> How does Weber's use of persuasion differ from that found in the Beaudoin essay? As you read, consider which argument is more appealing to you and why.

1 Ninety-five years ago, March 25 also fell on a Saturday. At 4:40 p.m. on that sunny afternoon in 1911, only minutes before the end of the workday, a fire broke out on the eighth floor of the Asch Building, a block east of Washington Square in Manhattan.

2 The Triangle Waist Company occupied the top three floors of the 10-story building. There, some 600 workers were employed in the manufacture of ladies' shirtwaists, most of them teenage girls who spoke little English and were fresh off the boat from Russia, the Austro-Hungarian Empire and Italy. The fire, probably caused by a carelessly tossed match or cigarette butt (there were perhaps 100 men working at the Triangle), engulfed the premises in minutes.

3 The factory owners and the office staff on the 10th floor, all but one, escaped onto the roof and climbed to an adjacent building on Waverly Place. But on the eighth and ninth floors, the workers were trapped by a deadly combination of highly combustible materials, workrooms crowded by dense rows of table-mounted sewing machines, doors that were locked or opened inward, inadequate fire escapes, and the lack of any plan or instruction.

4   Before the first horse-drawn fire engines arrived at the scene, girls—some holding hands, in twos and threes—had already begun to jump from the windows. The hundred-foot drop to the cobbled street was not survivable. The firemen deployed their nets, but the force of gravity drove the bodies of the girls straight through to the pavement, and they died on impact.

5   The ladders on the fire trucks were raised quickly, but the New York City Fire Department of 1911 was not equipped to combat fires above six stories—the limit of those ladders. The top floors of the Asch Building, a neo-Renaissance "fireproof" warehouse completed in 1901 in full compliance with building codes, burned relentlessly.

6   The workers trapped near the windows on the eighth and ninth floors made the fast and probably instinctive choice to jump instead of burning or suffocating in the smoke. The corpses of the jumpers, by some estimates as many as 70, could at least be identified. But the bodies of most of those who died inside the Triangle Waist Company—trapped by the machinery, piled up on the wrong side of doors, heaped in the stairwells and elevator shafts—were hideously charred, many beyond recognition.

7   Before 15 minutes had elapsed, some 140 workers had burned, fallen from the collapsing fire escapes, or jumped to their deaths. Several more, critically injured, died in the days that followed, putting the official death toll at 146.

8   But what happened to the children who were working at the Triangle Waist Company that afternoon?

9   By most contemporary accounts, it was common knowledge that children were usually on the premises. They were hidden from the occasional inspectors, but underage girls, as young as 9 or 10, worked in most New York garment factories, sewing buttons and trimming threads. Where were they on this particular Saturday afternoon?

10   There are no descriptions of children surviving the fire. Various lists of those who died 95 years ago today—140 named victims plus six who were never identified (were some of those charred remains children?)—include one 11-year-old, two 14-year-olds, three 15-year-olds, 16 16-year-olds, and 14 17-year-olds. Were the ages of workers, living and dead, modified to finesse the habitual violation of child labor laws in 1911? How many children actually died that day? We will never know. And now 1911 is almost beyond living memory.

11   But we will also never know how many children were among the dead on May 10, 1993, in Thailand when the factory of the Kader Industrial Toy Company (a supplier to Hasbro and Fisher-Price) went up in flames. Most of the 188 workers who died were described as teenage girls.

12   We will never know with any certainty how many children died on Nov. 25, 2000, in a fire at the Chowdhury Knitwear and Garment factory near Dhaka, Bangladesh (most of the garments made in Bangladesh are contracted by American retailers, including Wal-Mart and the Gap), where at least 10 of the 52 trapped in the flames by locked doors and windows were 10 to 14 years old.

13   And we will never know how many children died just last month, on Feb. 23, in the KTS Composite Textile factory fire in Chittagong, Bangladesh. The official

death toll has climbed into the 50's, but other sources report that at least 84 workers lost their lives. It's a familiar story: crowded and unsafe conditions, locked exits, hundreds of undocumented female workers as young as 12, a deadly fire. There may never be another tragic factory fire in America that takes the lives of children. We don't lock them into sweatshops any more. There are child labor laws, fire codes.

14   But as long as we don't question the source of the inexpensive clothing we wear, as long as we don't wonder about the children in those third world factories who make the inexpensive toys we buy for our own children, those fires will occur and young girls and boys will continue to die. They won't die because of natural catastrophes like monsoons and earthquakes; they will die because it has become our national habit to outsource, and these days we outsource our tragedies, too.

Strategies Used for Appealing for Action

Detailed arguments are not the only way of being persuasive. Weber shows us how effective narrative can be. It serves the following persuasive purposes:

- It establishes her credibility and ethos with a wealth of detailed information. Readers feel she knows what she is talking about and has the welfare of other people foremost in her concerns.

- In paragraphs 4, 6, and 7, she appeals to pathos well, drawing her readers into this tragic incident with powerful images of brutal, unnecessary deaths.

- In these same paragraphs, she also appeals to the readers' ethics, knowing they would not tolerate such conditions in New York today.

Effective narratives depend on *telling detail,* on statements of fact that imply the writer's judgments without stating them. For instance,

- Many of the workers "were fresh off the boat from Russia, the Austrio-Hungarian Empire and Italy."

  Implication: They were expendable. There was a ready supply of labor on the next boat.

- "The factory owners and the office staff on the 10th floor, all but one, escaped."

  Implication: The people that mattered survived. The bosses would not lock themselves or valued employees inside, where they could not escape.

- "The New York City Fire Department of 1911 was not equipped to combat fires above six stories. . . . The top floors of the Asch Building [were] completed in 1901 in full compliance with building codes."

  Implication: You cannot depend on authorities to prevent tragedies or respond to unfolding disasters adequately.

Tell your readers what they need to know and they will draw the conclusions you want them to make.

In the concluding paragraph, Weber makes a summarizing case, stating her claim and her reason in one sentence: "As long as we don't question the source of the inexpensive clothing we wear, as long as we don't wonder about the children in those third world factories who make the inexpensive toys we buy for our own children, those fires will occur and young girls and boys will continue to die." The case brings her general point home, linking her narrative of a past event to present concerns.

◎◎ FOLLOWING THROUGH

Using the analysis of Beaudoin as a model (pages 248–249), break up into small groups, assign the roles of recorder and reporter, and investigate the following questions:

- Why do you think the author organized her material the way she did?
- In paragraphs 11–13 Weber shifts attention from the past to the present. Does the shift work; that is, do you find the connections to the present persuasive? If so, why? If not, why not?

Share the results of your work with the class and discuss how each group's answers differed. Address this question at some point in your class dialogue: What strategies does Weber use that we can use in our own way?

CLAIMING VOICE IN APPEALING FOR ACTION

Appealing for action or persuasion is in part the calm voice of reason described in Chapter 9: your opinion stated clearly, directly, forcefully, with confidence. To this persuasion adds the *controlled passion* of emotional appeal, designed to arouse *appropriate* feelings in your readers.

Look at paragraphs 10–14 in Katharine Weber's "The Factories of Lost Children." Here is the voice of controlled passion:

> We will never know with any certainty how many children died on Nov. 25, 2000, in a fire at the Chowdhury Knitwear and Garment factory near Dhaka, Bangladesh (most of the garments made in Bangladesh are contracted by American retailers, including Wal-Mart and the Gap), where at least 10 of the 52 trapped in the flames by locked doors and windows were 10 to 14 years old. (paragraph 12)

She gives the reader the terrible facts, including the role of American companies in allowing the conditions that result in tragic loss of children's lives. She does not have to say, "This is outrageous, intolerable"; the facts say it for her.

Furthermore, she cites several tragic instances in paragraphs 10–14, all linked together by the repeated statement, "We will never know how many children died." This is how you arouse appropriate emotions in readers and how the voice of controlled passion should sound. Moving people to act requires using this voice as well as the calm voice of reasoning.

THE ASSIGNMENT

Write an essay on any controversial topic that asks your readers to take action. "Controversial" for this assignment means that various courses of action are possible, genuine choice exists. In some cases, you might advocate doing nothing when other people want to take action or stop doing something that causes more harm than benefit.

Topic and Focus

Your topic may grow out of readings or discussion of current events in your class, or your instructor may have you choose your own topic. Whatever happens, distinguish topics from possible focuses within them. For instance, "illegal immigration" is a highly controversial topic, ideal for persuasion because so many courses of action are possible. However, illegal immigration covers too much ground for anything less than a book. You might focus, for example, on the fences being constructed along the U.S.–Mexico border. Or, because many people here illegally overstay their visas, you might focus on the visa process itself. *Find some part of the topic you can handle in the space you have.*

Audience

Think of your audience as people weakly inclined toward your position, weakly opposed, or uncommitted. Within these possibilities, consider two questions: Who can take action? Which audience can I relate to best? Choose your audience based on how you answer these questions.

Voice and Ethos

Persuasion favors middle style, neither ultra-formal (as in a legal brief) nor informal and off-hand (like an e-mail to a friend). You should sound like someone talking about a serious topic to people you do not know well. The readings provide good examples of middle style and the voice that goes with it.

Good character, or ethos, always matters in writing, but especially in persuasion because you are asking your readers to trust you enough to take action. Be sincere. Project confidence. Show respect for your audience.

Writing Assignment Suggestions

This paper could be written in many possible genres: an editorial, a personal letter, a magazine article, a text for a speech, and so on. You might consider one of these genres, especially if your topic and audience seem appropriate and your instructor approves.

Our students have written on the following topics: U.S. policy in Iraq and Afghanistan; immigration issues, especially border control; all issues connected with "going green"; and many issues connected with consumer society. Be sure to consider local issues as well, including what is going on where you work, where you live, and in organizations to which you belong.

CHOOSING A TOPIC

Persuasive topics arise from *exigency;* that is, *the need for action.* If you are choosing your own topic, pick one you care about and are personally invested in enough to take action yourself. You can then draw on what moves you to motivate your readers to act as you do. Here are some possible places to find topics.

- *Class readings.* Class readings can suggest topics for persuasion, especially if the readings themselves are persuasive, like the examples in this chapter. For instance, if the sweatshop problem interests you, begin by finding out about the labor practices of the companies that make the clothing you and your friends wear.

- *Reading in other classes.* In a political science class, for example, you might study how presidential candidates are selected by the Democratic and Republican parties. The process is highly controversial and many proposals for reform have been advanced. Perhaps one of the reforms struck you as especially desirable. Do some more reading about it; perhaps you have found your topic.

- *Local news or observation.* Read your local and campus newspapers for issues and problems of concern to your community. Take a walk around your neighborhood or campus, looking for problems that need solutions, such as wasted energy in offices, dorms, and classrooms.

- *Internet discussions.* If you keep a blog, you probably have a store of observations about issues that concern you, things you would like to see changed. Or visit blogs on issues of public concern, such as "The Opinionator" at the *New York Times,* which gathers opinions from publications all over the world.

EXPLORING YOUR TOPIC

Whether your topic is assigned or you chose your own, all or some of the following activities can help you gain a better initial sense of your paper.

The Art of Questioning: Focus, Audience, and Need

Consider these questions:

- Can you handle the topic in the space you have? If not, how might you limit the topic?

- What audience do you wish to reach? Usually there are several appropriate choices. Consult the Concept Close-Up, "Audience Analysis," when you have identified your audience.

- How can you establish a need for taking action? See the next section to grasp the importance of need in persuasive writing.

Your answers to these questions may change as you work on your paper. Asking them now, however, can help you gain a sense of focus, audience, and purpose, always important in writing well.

Audience Analysis

To understand any audience we hope to persuade, we must know *both* what separates us from them *and* what common ground we share.

We may **differ** from our audience in:

Kind of Difference	Example
Assumptions	Western writers assume that separation of church and state is normal; some Muslim audiences do not make the distinction.
Principles	Most conservative writers believe in the principle of the open market; labor audiences often believe in protecting American jobs from foreign competition.
Value rankings	Some writers value personal freedom over duty and obligation; some audiences place duty and obligation above personal freedom.
Ends and means	Writer and audience may agree about purpose (for example, making America safe from terrorism) but disagree about what policies will best accomplish this end.
Interpretation	Some writers understood the September 11, 2001, attacks as acts of war; some audiences saw them as criminal acts that demanded legal rather than military measures.
Consequences	Some writers think making divorce harder would keep more couples together; some audiences think it would only promote individual unhappiness.

We may **share** with our audience:

Kind of Identification	Example
Local identity	Students and teachers at the same university
Collective identity	Citizens of the same state or the same nation
Common cause	Improving the environment
Common experience	Pride in the success of American Olympic athletes
Common history	Respect for soldiers who have died defending the United States

Essentially, we must understand differences to discover how we need to argue; we must use the resources of identification to overcome differences separating us from our readers.

Establishing Need

Sometimes the need for action is so widely and well understood that it is hardly necessary to mention it. We need a cure for cancer, for instance. Usually, however, need cannot be taken for granted. Consider global warming: Attitudes toward it range from casual dismissal to taking it as the biggest long-term problem we face. If you are trying to persuade an audience to take action to reduce global warming, you must devote a significant portion of your paper to establishing the damage global warming has done already and will do in the next decade or so.

In contrast, sometimes people think that a need to act exists when you think the best course is to do nothing or postpone taking action. When you face such a situation, your entire paper will be devoted to showing that no compelling need to act exists or that no immediate action is required.

In any case, thinking about need—the motivation for action—matters. The temptation is to imagine that everyone sees the need as you do, which is rarely the case.

◎◎ FOLLOWING THROUGH

Jot down your first ideas about topic, focus, audience, and need. If you have the beginnings of a case in mind—your claim, reasons, and evidence—write them down as well. Include whatever insights you have gained from personal experience. These entries will help shape your first ideas. •

Doing Research

If the assignment calls for research, use the techniques for finding and evaluating sources (pages 99–121) to find articles, books, and online materials about or related to your topic. Arguments require evidence, and research will help with this as well as with refining and developing your thinking.

◎◎ FOLLOWING THROUGH

Break out into pairs or groups of three to discuss your ideas for the persuasive paper. Assess each other's choice of topics, focus within the topics, choice of audience, and your ideas for moving the audience to take action. At the end of your discussion, evaluate the comments made about your ideas and use them to refine your topic. •

PREPARING TO WRITE

Exploring your topic is a good first step in preparing to write. Some writers go straight to drafting, preferring to work out what they have to say in chunks that they eventually piece together to form a complete first draft. Most, however, need more preparation before drafting. We suggest beginning with the key questions listed in the Best Practices box, "Key Questions for Preparing to Write."

◎◎ FOLLOWING THROUGH

Write answers to the seven questions in the Best Practices box. Exchange them with a partner via e-mail or in small group sessions in or out of class to help refine and develop your ideas for and approaches to the first draft. •

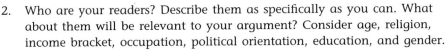

Key Questions for Preparing to Write

1. What do you want your readers to do?

2. Who are your readers? Describe them as specifically as you can. What about them will be relevant to your argument? Consider age, religion, income bracket, occupation, political orientation, education, and gender.

3. Reader awareness is important: How much will they know about the problem, question, or issue you intend to address? What is their likely attitude?

4. Why do you care about this topic? What makes you a credible writer on behalf of your position?

5. What is the best reason you can give your readers for doing what you want them to do? State it as a sentence. Do you have a second reason in mind?

6. What additional ideas do you have for appealing to your readers? What values and beliefs can you appeal to?

7. If your topic requires more than general knowledge and personal experience, what sources have you found to support your argument? What additional material might you need?

Thinking More about Persuasive Appeals

Dig deeper into the appeals to logic, character, and emotion. Thinking them through now helps many writers build up confidence, energy for drafting, and a more detailed plan to guide the first draft.

The Appeal through Logos: Deciding on a Claim and Reasons

You know what you want your readers to do; try formulating it as a claim. These suggestions will help.

1. Your claim is a statement you will defend, not just a description of something factual.

   Not a claim: Students are choosing majors based on future income instead of interests and abilities.

   Claim: Students should find a major that excites their desire to learn rather one that promises only financial rewards.

2. The claim should be focused and specific, and directed at a readership.

   Too general: Parents need to be stricter.

   Better: Parents need to teach children to be sensitive to other people when they are in restaurants, stores, and other public places.

3. The claim uses concrete nouns and verbs, rather than vague and indirect wording, to make its point.

   Vague: One's natural abilities cannot grow into an established intelligence unless a person learns how to control his or her attention and concentration.

Better: Even highly talented people need to learn to control attention and concentration to develop their full potential.

4. Some claims may need to be qualified.

Too absolute: High schools need a vocational track.

Qualified: Except for high schools where all students go on to college, a high-quality vocational track should exist.

◎◎ FOLLOWING THROUGH

Share several versions of the claim you have in mind by an e-mail exchange with one or several other students. Ask for feedback using questions taken from the peer review questions in the Best Practices box on page 263. Modify the claim as you draft and revise using this feedback.

Developing Reasons for Your Claim

Once you have a working version of the claim, begin to formulate reasons for it—why your readers should take the action you are arguing for. Focus on the fit between reasons and the values and beliefs of your readers.

The Best Practices box, "Places to Find Audience-Based Reasons" (page 259), provides some places to look for reader-oriented reasons.

Making a Brief of Your Case

The brief is a concise version of a logical argument. It has three levels:

1. The claim, what you want your readers to do.
2. A reason or reasons explaining why.
3. Evidence to support each reason.

Briefs can help in preparing to write, but keep in mind that new ideas will come to you as you draft. Also bear in mind that a brief is not a plan for the whole paper, only its logical appeal. Beaudoin postponed his argument until the midpoint of his essay (pp. 247–248, paragraphs 6–9); Weber presented her evidence first (p. 251, paragraph 14), then the claim and reasons.

Student Example: Natsumi Hazama's Brief

A student in one of our classes, Natsumi Hazama, wrote a persuasive paper urging Asian parents not to push their children so hard in school. Here is the brief she developed for her argument:

Claim: Asian-American parents need to moderate their demands for high career goals and obedience to parents, allowing their children to find goals and challenges that are right for them.

Reason: Too much pressure can lead to depression and even suicide.

- In the audience's *beliefs and values.* Think about their politics and the values of their culture or subculture.

- In *traditions* and traditional texts. What books, ceremonies, ideas, places, and people do they revere?

- In *expert opinion and data.* Draw on the reasoning of qualified experts your audience will respect—mention them by name and cite their credentials. Construct reasons from information and statistics taken from sources your readers will know and trust.

- In comparisons or *analogies* your audience would accept. Analogies work because they liken the less familiar to the more familiar and known. Those who oppose genetic engineering, for example, often reason that altering human genes is like altering nature—it has bad side effects.

- In establishing *cause and effect.* If you can show that the action you would like the audience to take will lead to positive consequences, you have a good reason. Of course, you will need evidence to show that the cause-and-effect relationship exists.

> *Evidence:* CNN.com article on college student suicides; *Chronicle of Higher Education* online article about depression and suicide at Cornell

Reason: Over-protective parenting does not prepare children for the independence of college life.

> *Evidence:* Asian Outlook Web site quotes

Reason: Students will be more successful at careers they prefer, not the limited choices of engineering and medicine preferred by their parents.

> *Evidence:* My personal experience

Reason: Constant pressure to do better rather than praise for what has been accomplished leads to low self-esteem.

> *Evidence:* Class reading by Csikszentmihalyi.

Note that Natsumi's brief "blocks out" (separates into clear, distinct points) what she intends to say. No matter how closely related they are, *do not allow your reasons to run together.* Note also that she uses both statements from experts and personal experience as evidence. The experts lend authoritative support for her argument, whereas personal experience makes it more concrete and demonstrates firsthand knowledge.

FOLLOWING THROUGH

In your notebook, outline the logical case you will make. If possible, include supporting evidence for each reason.

The Appeal through Ethos: Presenting Good Character

Ethos is self-presentation. In general, you should

- Sound informed and engaged with your topic
- Show awareness of your readers' views
- Treat competing courses of action with respect, but show that yours is better
- Refer to your values and beliefs, your own ethical choices
- When appropriate, reinforce your ethos by citing information and expert testimony from sources your readers respect and trust

A more specific list of ideas for establishing good ethos follows.

The Art of Questioning: Establishing Ethos with Your Readers

1. Do you have a shared local identity—as members of the same organization, the same institution, the same town or community, the same set of beliefs?

2. Can you get your audience to see that you and they have a common cause or perspective?

3. Are there experiences you might share? These might include dealing with siblings, helping friends in distress, caring for ailing family members, struggling to pay debts, or working hard for something.

4. Can you connect through a well-known event or cultural happening, perhaps a movie, book, a political rally, something in the news?

FOLLOWING THROUGH

Write about what attitudes you could convey in your paper that will show your good character and values. What can you talk about that will get these appeals across to your readers?

The Appeal through Pathos: Using Emotional Appeals

Sharing your own emotions is the most honest way to appeal to your audience's feelings. However, simply saying what your feelings are will not arouse emotion in others. How can you arouse emotions?

Show the audience the *concrete images and facts* that aroused the feelings in you. Beaudoin listed the indignities suffered by the Honduran women he interviewed. Likewise, Weber described the bodies of the burned workers in the Triangle fire, "trapped by the machinery, piled up on the wrong side of doors, heaped in the stairwells and elevator shafts . . . hideously charred, many beyond recognition."

In short, give your readers a verbal picture. You can often give them visual images as well, such as photographs.

FOLLOWING THROUGH

Do a free writing of ideas for specifics details and images that moved you. Make lists of what you recall. Visit or revisit places relevant to your topic and take notes or pictures.

DRAFTING YOUR PAPER

By now you have generated many ideas for appealing to your readers. As you move toward drafting, focus attention on two main concerns:

- Voice, how you want to sound to your reader
- A plan to guide the draft

Voice

Voice is always important in writing because people react subconsciously to the "sound" of your prose. In persuasion it is especially important because voice helps to create ethos.

Write with passion and conviction, but also sound reasonable, mature, courteous, and responsible. The readings at the beginning of this chapter are good examples of voice in persuasion. Read aloud the first page or two of the Beaudoin and Weber essays, concentrating only on the impression you have of the writer's character. Then join in the following discussion.

FOLLOWING THROUGH

In small groups of two or three people, explore these questions:

1. How is Weber's voice like Beaudoin's? How are they different?

2. Beaudoin wrote in first person (uses "I"), whereas Weber favors third person. Is your sense of the author's presence different in Beaudoin? If so, how would you describe the difference?

Development and Organization

Here are answers to some common questions that will help you with both development and organization of your paper.

1. *How might I open the paper?*

Here are some possibilities:

- An anecdote (short narrative) based on your own experience or something you found in a source
- A surprising fact or opinion relevant to your topic
- A question that will stimulate reader interest
- A description of a person or place relevant to your claim
- A memorable quotation, with commentary from you

Introductions are often more than one paragraph, and your claim can appear anywhere in the paper.

2. *What background material should I provide?*

Here are two principles:

- Offer *only* what your readers need
- Place it just before the section or sections of your essay where the background is relevant

3. *Where will I show my connection to the topic?*

The introduction is often a good place. Beaudoin's first four paragraphs (p. 246) describe his awakening to a sense of economic responsibility. He wanted his readers to see his personal commitment to the topic.

4. *Will I present opposing views, and, if so, where?*

How you handle opposing views depends on your reader's relationship to them. If you think your readers will believe them, the best strategy is to engage the opposing views first in several paragraphs. Otherwise handle them after your case and with less space devoted to them.

5. *How will I order my reasons?*

If your case has three or more reasons, starting and ending with your stronger ones is good strategy. In developing your reasons, remember that multiple paragraphs are often necessary to develop a reason.

6. *What visuals might I use, and where should they go?*

For example, a student who wrote against wearing fur added much to the pathos of her argument by including photographs of animals injured by trappers.

7. *How will I conclude my paper?*

Try one of these ending strategies:

- Look back at your introduction. Perhaps some idea you used there to attract your reader's attention could come into play again—a question you posed has an answer, or a problem you raised has a solution.
- Think about the larger context of your argument. For example, Beaudoin puts his argument about responsible consuming into the larger context of a more humane world.
- End with a well-worded quotation, and follow it up with comments of your own.
- Repeat an idea you used earlier in the essay, but with a twist. Weber took the word "outsource" and used it in a new way: people "will die because it has become our national habit to outsource, and these days we outsource our tragedies, too."

REVISING YOUR DRAFT

Writing is revising. Most first drafts need big changes on the way to completion. They need parts taken out, new parts added, and parts rearranged.

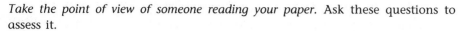

Revision Checklist for Appealing for Action

Take the point of view of someone reading your paper. Ask these questions to assess it.

1. Is it clear what the author wants the readers to do? Where is it stated most clearly? Is this the best place to state it?

2. Does the paper have a shape and sense of direction? Does it have parts that clearly play their individual roles in making the argument? Could you make any suggestions for arranging the parts to make it easier to follow?

3. Do the reasons for taking this action stand out as reasons? Are they good reasons for the intended audience? Is there a better way to order the reasons?

4. Has the author given enough evidence to support each reason?

5. Has the author shown awareness of and sympathy for the audience's perspective?

6. Are the individual paragraphs unified, and is their contribution to the section in which they appear clear?

7. Can you hear the author's voice in this paper? Do you think the readers would find it appealing? Does the author show personal connection with the topic?

8. Where do you see the author using emotional appeals? Are they appropriate? Do they move you?

9. Do you have suggestions to improve the introduction and the conclusion?

10. Has the author smoothly integrated the sources used or just dropped them in?

The strongest revisions begin with assessing the draft yourself. Put it aside for a day or two. Then go back and give it a critical reading.

Getting Feedback from Others

It always helps to have someone else look at your draft. Be sure that the person understands the assignment and the target audience before they read. Share the Revision Checklist in the Best Practices box with your reader.

◎◎ FOLLOWING THROUGH

After getting a second opinion, formulate a revision strategy:

1. Decide what you think the useful criticisms and comments are. Reassess your self-criticisms—do you still see the same problems?

2. Make a list of specific items you intend to work on. "The first point on page 3 needs more development" is an example of what we mean by specific.

3. Divide your list into two categories: big revisions that will change all or much of the paper and smaller revisions requiring only adding, deleting, or rewriting a paragraph or two.

4. Ponder the best order for doing big revisions. For example, suppose that you need to rearrange the order of your reasons and improve your tone throughout. Rearrange first because attending to tone will require changing many sentences, and each sentence revision can have an impact on the flow of ideas from sentence to sentence.

5. Finalize your plan with a step-by-step list. Usually the spot revisions can be done in any order, but tackle the ones requiring most work first, leaving the easier ones for last.   •

Practicing Revision

A revised draft of Natsumi Hazama's paper appears on pages 266–268. To see how revision improved it, read the following excerpts from her first draft.

Paragraph 1

One night in 1990, Eliza Noh got off the phone with her sister in college. Eliza knew her sister was depressed and something bad might happen. She sat down to write a letter to support and encourage her. But it was too late. By the time the letter arrived, her sister was dead. She had taken her own life. Eliza believed that too much pressure to succeed contributed to her sister's death. This tragedy led Noh to pursue a career in studying the effects of pressure on Asian-American students.

Paragraph 7

Low self-esteem can be a result of too much pressure to be at the top. According to Mihaly Csikszentmihalyi, goals can determine a person's level of self-esteem. Because Asian-Americans' goals are set so high by parents, these students tend to have lower self-esteem (Csikszentmihalyi, 23). A 24-year-old Korean rock star named Jeong-Hyun Lim has turned into a global phenomenon from his rock rendition of Pachelbel's Canon (Lam). Some call him a second Jimi Hendrix and his YouTube video has been viewed more than 24 million times (Lam). But when interviewers ask him to rate himself he said 50 or 60 out of 100 and is always thinking that he needs to improve (Lam). This is an example of a stereotypical Asian.

Compare the first draft's introduction with the introduction to the final version of the paper (page 266). Do you agree that opening with Natsumi's own story is more effective? The original opening was moved to paragraphs 12–13; do you think this arrangement is better?

◎◎ FOLLOWING THROUGH

Look at the opening of your own draft. Why did you choose to open the paper as you did? If you are not happy with the opening, do you see material elsewhere in the draft that might work better? If not, review the opening strategies discussed on page 261 and try one of those instead.　　•

Revising to Bring Out the Structure of the Argument

Here is a body paragraph from Natsumi's first draft, offering a reason and evidence in support of her claim:

> Dr. Henry Chung, assistant vice president for student health at New York University and executive director of the NYU student Health Center, says "Asian-American/Asian students, especially males, are under unique pressures to meet high expectations of parents by succeeding in such traditional predetermined careers as medicine and engineering" (qtd. in Ramanujan). Asian students feel that even though they aren't interested in these fields they must major in them and they end up stressing themselves out. Because students major in fields that they aren't interested in they end up not doing as well in school as they could. If you don't have a passion for your job you feel like you are working twice as hard with loads of work on your shoulders.

This paragraph was revised to become paragraph 10 in the final version (page 267). Compare them. In the revised version, how has the argument emerged better in the opening sentence? How has it been better supported?

◎◎ FOLLOWING THROUGH

Look over the body paragraphs of your draft. Open with a point of your own; use your sources to support and develop it. Look over your entire draft. How could revising make your reasons stand out more?　　•

Revising to Improve Incorporation of Quoted Material

Using sources responsibly means not only citing the source but also identifying the source by name. Natsumi noticed that she was not always clear about whose words were in quotation marks. Here is an example of the problem:

See Chapter 6, "Writing Research-Based Arguments," for more on this important research skill.

Draft Version

> Also when kids come to college they receive conflicting messages. "The message at home is that their priority should be to look after their parents and take care of their families" ("Mental"). But the message you get at college and from your friends is that you need to learn to think for yourself and be who you are and do what is best for you. This is a different value than the Asian culture so Asian students feel guilty for not doing what they are supposed to be doing ("Mental").

Revised Version

As the underlined phrases show, identifying your sources by name and qualifications not only helps your reader understand who is saying what but also increases the authority of the quoted statements.

<u>According to Diem Nguyen, a UC Davis student affairs officer,</u> when Asian-American students come to college, they sometimes end up partying too much because they are not used to this freedom (qtd. in "Mental"). Also, when kids come to college they receive conflicting messages. <u>Nadine Tang, a psychotherapist who has counseled students at UC Berkeley,</u> says they get the message at home that family is their top priority, but the message at college is "to be who you are, learn to be yourself and do what is best for you. . . . You feel guilty for not doing what you're supposed to and not fulfilling your obligations" (qtd. in "Mental").

◎◎ FOLLOWING THROUGH

If you are using the words of someone quoted in your source, are you *identifying the actual speaker of the words* as well as citing the source? If not, identify them as Natsumi did in the revised version above.   •

REVISED STUDENT EXAMPLE
Is Too Much Pressure Healthy?

NATSUMI HAZAMA

1   Growing up in an Asian-American family, I was raised to stay close to my family and always to strive to be number one in my class. My parents were both born in Japan and came to America for my father's work. My father was a very intelligent man who wanted me to go into either medicine or engineering. My parents also made me go to Japanese School every Saturday to learn to read and write my native tongue. Going to school six days a week left no time for a social life. The girls at my English school would always have sleepover parties on Friday nights, but I was studying for my next Japanese test. I excelled in school, but that wasn't good enough. Even if I scored a 98 on my math test, my parents would say, "Why didn't you get a 100?"

2   When I was in 8th grade, my father was diagnosed with colon cancer. He grew very ill, and my parents actually knew that he was dying but didn't tell my sister and me. One week, all my relatives from Japan flew in; at the end of that week he passed away. It was a horrible experience, but my mother, sister, and I helped each other, and with the support of all of our family and friends we got through it.

3   Starting high school was completely different. Because my mother knew growing up without a father was hard enough, she just wanted me to be happy. Coming home with a few B's on my report card was okay now. My mother didn't pressure me to get good grades; she basically let me do whatever I wanted. I wasn't in the top 10% of my class, didn't get straight A's, or take all AP courses. However, I was completely satisfied with my high school experience. I was part of the nationally

ranked cheerleading team. I had higher self-esteem. I would give anything to have my father still alive, but I have learned to think for myself and to set my own goals.

4   My situation before the death of my father is common among Asian-American families. I understand it is part of my culture, which I value. However, Asian-American parents need to moderate their demands and allow their children to find goals and challenges that are right for them.

5   Wenju Shen and Weimin Mo, experts on educating Asian-Americans, describe our ways as rooted in Confucianism: "The Confucian ethical code . . . holds that the first loyalty is to the family, even above their allegiance to their country and religion."

6   This closeness to family can bring pressures. In an Asian family the most important thing is to always keep your "face." "Face" means family pride. "Family" means not only immediate relatives, extended relatives, dead ancestors, but also anyone with my last name. To fail in any obligation to the family is to "lose face" and bring shame to myself, my parents, my relatives, and all my ancestors.

7   While family should be important, this cultural pressure to succeed helps to create harmful stereotypes. As Shen and Mo point out, the "whiz kid" stereotype of Asian-American students encourage their parents to maintain practices "not compatible with the values and beliefs of American society." Asian-American parents need to learn how to balance obligations to the family with the more individual values of Americans.

8   A more balanced approach to parenting will lead children to more fulfilling lives. Mihaly Csikszentmihalyi, a psychologist at the University of Chicago, is noted for his work on happiness, creativity, and subjective well-being. His book, *Finding Flow*, describes the kind of family that leads children to develop their full potential: "they combine discipline with spontaneity, rules with freedom, high expectations with unstinting love. An optimal family system is complex in that it encourages the unique individual development of its members while uniting them in a web of affective ties" (88). Asian-American parents should raise their children more like this. Too much parental pressure hinders what Csikszentmihalyi calls "flow," a state of mind where the person is fully engaged in what he or she is doing for its own sake (29–32).

9   For most Asian students, college is their first significant time away from home. Because they aren't used to the freedom of college life, they sometimes end up partying too much.

10   They also receive conflicting messages. Nadine Tang, a psychotherapist who has counseled students at UC Berkeley, says the message at home is that family matters most, but the message at college is "be who you are, learn to be yourself and do what is best for you. . . . You feel guilty for not doing what you're supposed to and not fulfilling your obligations" (qtd. in "Mental").

11   That is what life is all about, fulfilling your own potential, as Csikszentmihalyi says. Unfortunately, even if Asian-American students receive excellent grades in school, they tend to have lower self-esteem than other students (Csikszentmihalyi 24). I think this is so because their parents never praise them. Asian-American parents see success as a duty, so children should not receive praise; instead they are told to do even better and aim still higher (Shen).

12   Along with bringing home straight "A's," parents also urge their children to major in a subject that they see as respectable. Dr. Henry Chung, assistant vice president

for student health at New York University and executive director of the Health Center, points out that "Asian-American/Asian students, especially males, are under unique pressures to meet high expectations of parents by succeeding in such traditional predetermined careers as medicine and engineering" (qtd. in Ramanujan). Even if these fields are not areas of strength or interest, Asian-American students feel that they must major in them. Their grades may start to slip, but as Nguyen at Berkeley says, "Some stay in these majors because they think that they need to. They're reluctant to leave because their parents don't understand: 'If you're not a doctor or engineer, then what are you?'" (qtd. in "Mental").

13　　The result can be destructive to a student's mental health, often leading to anxiety and depression. These problems are more common in Asian-American students than in the general population ("Mental"). When Asian-American students are unhappy, they usually don't seek help, even though the best way to recover is to get counseling. Chung at NYU explains that in Asian culture "suffering and working hard are accepted as part of life, a cultural paradigm" (Ramanujan). Asian-American students don't get counseling because discussing emotional problems is a sign of weakness ("Mental"). They also do not tell their parents about their problems. A psychologist at Baylor University, Dr. Dung Ngo, says, "The line of communication in an Asian culture goes one way. It's communicated from the parents downward" (qtd. in Cohen). If students can't express their anger and frustration, it turns into helplessness; they feel like there is no way out.

14　　Suicide is therefore common among Asian-American students. According to CNN, Asian American women age 15–24 have the highest suicide rate of any ethnic group. Suicide is the second-leading cause of death (Cohen). At Cornell University between 1996 and 2006 there were 21 suicides; 13 of these were Asian or Asian-American students (Ramanujan).

15　　CNN tells the story of how Eliza Noh, a professor of Asian-American studies at California State University at Fullerton, decided to devote her studies to depression and suicide among Asian-American women. One night in 1990, she had been talking to her sister, a college student, on the telephone. She knew her sister was depressed. She sat down to write a letter to encourage her. It was too late. By the time the letter arrived, she had taken her life. Noh believes that the pressure to succeed contributed to her sister's death (Cohen).

16　　I have lived both sides, with pressure and without. Living without pressure has enabled me think for myself and be happier. Asian-American parents need to give their children support and encouragement, allow them to make their own decisions about goals, and most of all, stop pressuring them so much.

WORKS CITED

Cohen, Elizabeth. "Push to Achieve Tied to Suicide in Asian-American Women." *CNN.com Health*. 16 May 2007. Web. 1 April 2008.

Csikszentmihalyi, Mihaly. *Finding Flow: The Psychology of Engagement with Everyday Life*. New York City: Basic Books, 1997. Print.

"Mental Health of Asian Youth a Growing Concern." *Asian Outlook—Challenges for Today's Asian American Students*. Asian Pacific Fund. Fall/Winter 2007. Web. 15 April 2008.

Ramanujan, Krishna. "Health Expert Explains Asian and Asian-American Students' Unique Pressures to Succeed." *Chronicle Online.* The Chronicle of Higher Education. 19 March 2006. Web. 22 Feb. 2008.

Shen, Wenju, and Weimin Mo. "Reaching Out to Their Cultures: Building Communication with Asian American Families." N. p. (1990) ERIC. Web. 15 April 2008.

CHAPTER SUMMARY

In this assignment, you learned to combine logical appeal (logos) with ethos, pathos, and style to move an audience to action. You will use what you have learned over and over, in college, at work, and in the community.

What you learn from persuasion applies to other kinds of writing. For instance, how you present yourself—your ethos—makes a difference. We are always writing to reach others even when moving readers to act is not on our mind.

CHAPTER 11

Resolving Conflict: Arguing to Mediate

Private citizens can avoid the big conflicts that concern politicians and activist groups: debates over gay marriage, abortion, taxes, foreign policy, and so on. However, we cannot hide from all conflict. Family members have different preferences about budgeting, major purchases, where to go on vacation, and much else. Furthermore, if you care about what goes on beyond your front door, you will find conflict close to home. The school down the street, for example, wants to expand its athletic stadium. Some parents support the decision because their children play sports at the school. Others oppose it because they think the expansion will bring more traffic, noise, and bright lights to the neighborhood.

One way to resolve conflict is through reasoned arguments. The chapters on convincing and persuading show how appeals to logic and emotion can change minds. But what if we cannot change someone's mind or impose our will in other ways?

Some conflicts do not have to be resolved. The Republican husband can live happily with the Democratic wife. Other conflicts are resolved by compromise. We can go to the mountains this year, the seashore the next. Compromise is better than shouting matches, but it does not result in a common understanding.

Characteristics of Mediation

1. Aims to resolve conflict between opposing and usually hardened positions, often because action of some kind must be taken.
2. Aims to reduce hostility and promote understanding between or among conflicting parties; preserving human relationships and promoting communication are paramount.
3. Like inquiry, mediation involves dialogue and requires that one understand all positions and strive for an open mind.
4. Like convincing, mediation involves making a case that appeals to all parties in the controversy.
5. Like persuasion, mediation depends on the good character of the negotiator and on sharing values and feelings.
6. Mediation depends on conflicting parties' desire to find solutions to overcome counterproductive stalemates.

Essentially, mediation comes into play when convincing and persuading have resulted in sharply differing viewpoints. The task is first to understand the positions of all parties involved and second to uncover a mediating position capable of producing consensus and a reduction in hostility.

This chapter presents mediation as argument whose aim is to resolve conflict by thinking more critically about it. People too often see disputes uncritically by simplifying them to their extreme positions, pro and con. *Mediation aims to move disputants beyond the polarized thinking that makes conflicts impossible to resolve.*

MEDIATION AND THE OTHER AIMS OF ARGUMENT

Mediation uses the other three aims of argument: inquiry, convincing, and persuading. Like inquiry, it examines the range of positions on an issue. Mediation requires knowledge of case structure. The mediator scrutinizes the arguments offered by all sides. A mediatory essay must also present a well-reasoned case of its own. Finally, like persuasion, mediation considers the values, beliefs, and assumptions of the people who hold the conflicting positions. Mediators must appeal to all sides and project a character all sides will trust and find attractive.

In short, mediation requires the mediator to rise above a dispute, including his or her own preferences, to see what is reasonable and right in conflicting positions. The mediator's best asset is wisdom.

THE PROCESS OF MEDIATION

Mediation takes place more often in conversation, through dialogue with the opposing sides, than in writing. But essays can mediate by attempting to argue for middle ground in a conflict. Mediation begins where all arguments should—with inquiry.

MEDIATION AND ROGERIAN ARGUMENT

Arguing to mediate resembles an approach to communication developed by a psychologist, Carl Rogers (1902–1987). In "Communication: Its Blocking and Its Facilitation," he urged people in conflict to listen carefully and with empathy to each other as a first step toward resolving differences. The second step is to go beyond listening in an effort to understand one another's background. Finally, a third step is for each person involved in a dispute to state the position of his or her opponents in a way the opponents agree is accurate and fair. The total approach reduces misunderstanding and helps to clarify what the genuine points of difference are, thus opening up the potential to resolve conflict.

In their textbook *Rhetoric: Discovery and Change* (1970), Richard Young, Alton Becker, and Kenneth Pike outlined four stages for Rogerian argument:

1. An introduction to the problem and a demonstration that the opponent's position is understood

2. A statement of the contexts in which the opponent's position may be valid

3. A statement of the writer's position, including the contexts in which it is valid

4. A statement of how the opponent's position would benefit if he were to adopt elements of the writer's position. If the writer can show that the positions complement each other, that each supplies what the other lacks, so much the better.[1]

Our approach to mediation draws on Rogerian argument. As a mediator, rather than a participant in a dispute, you need to consider the validity of opposing positions, including the personal backgrounds of the people involved. In light of these backgrounds, you look for what is good and right in each position.

Rather than face-to-face oral arguments, in this chapter you will be reading written arguments on a controversial issue and exploring them to uncover

---

[1]This summary of the four stages comes from Douglas Brent, "Rogerian Rhetoric: An Alternative to Traditional Rhetoric," *Argument Revisited, Argument Redefined: Negotiating Meaning in the Composition Classroom,* ed. Barbara Emmel, Paula Resch, and Deborah Tenney (Thousand Oaks, CA: Sage, 1996) <http://www.acs.ucalgary.ca/~dabrent/art/rogchap.html>.

exactly how and why their authors disagree. Instead of sitting around a table with parties in conflict as mediators do, you will write a mediatory essay proposing a point of view designed to appeal to both sides.

A Conflict to Mediate

The United States is a nation of immigrants, but recently the immigrant population includes a wider array of races, ethnicities, religions, and cultures than in the past. The result is a population less white and less Protestant. Should we become a multicultural nation or maintain a single culture based on the original northern European settlers?

Some people argue that the influx of diverse people should have no impact on the traditional Eurocentric identity of America. According to this position, America has a distinctive and superior culture, traceable to the Puritan settlers and based more broadly on Western civilization. This culture is the source of our nation's strength. To keep it strong, newcomers need to assimilate, adopting its values and beliefs. In other words, people holding this position advocate the melting-pot metaphor. Because they believe cultural differences should dissolve as new immigrants become "true Americans," they oppose multiculturalism. We have chosen a recent essay by Roger Kimball, an art critic and editor at the conservative journal *The New Criterion,* to represent the assimilationist position.

Opponents argue that newcomers should preserve their distinctive cultures, taking pride in being Mexican, Chinese, African, and so on. Their metaphor is the mosaic, with each culture remaining distinct but contributing to the whole. We have chosen an essay by Elizabeth Martínez to represent the multiculturalist perspective. Martínez is a Chicana writer and an activist on issues of social justice, including racism and women's rights.

Understanding the Positions

Any attempt to mediate positions requires an understanding of opposing cases. Printed below are the two arguments, followed by our analyses.

Institutionalizing Our Demise: America vs. Multiculturalism

ROGER KIMBALL

The following abridged article appeared in *The New Criterion* (June 2004). Roger Kimball's books include *The Long March: How the Cultural Revolution of the 1960s Changed America* (Encounter, 2000) and *Tenured Radicals: How Politics Has Corrupted Our Higher Education* (HarperCollins, 1990).

There is no room in this country for hyphenated Americanism. When I refer to hyphenated Americans, I do not refer to naturalized Americans. Some of the very best Americans I have ever known were naturalized Americans, Americans born abroad. But a hyphenated American is not an American at all. This is just as true of the man who puts "native" before the hyphen as of the man who puts German or Irish or English or French before the hyphen.

—Theodore Roosevelt, 1915

1   It is often said that the terrorist attacks of September 11 precipitated a new resolve throughout the nation. There is some truth to that. Certainly, the extraordinary bravery of the firefighters and other rescue personnel in New York and Washington, D.C., provided an invigorating spectacle—as did Todd "Let's roll" Beamer and his fellow passengers on United Airlines Flight 93. Having learned from their cell phones what had happened at the World Trade Center and the Pentagon, Beamer and his fellows rushed and overpowered the terrorists who had hijacked their plane. As a result, the plane crashed on a remote Pennsylvania farm instead of on Pennsylvania Avenue. Who knows how many lives their sacrifice saved?

2   The widespread sense of condign outrage—of horror leavened by anger and elevated by resolve—testified to a renewed sense of national purpose and identity after 9/11. Attacked, many Americans suddenly (if temporarily) rediscovered the virtue of patriotism. At the beginning of his remarkable book *Who Are We? The Challenges to America's National Identity* (2004), the Harvard political scientist Samuel Huntington recalls a certain block on Charles Street in Boston. At one time, American flags flew in front of a U.S. Post Office and a liquor store. Then the Post Office stopped displaying the flag, so on September 11, 2001, the flag was flying only in front of the liquor store. Within two weeks, seventeen American flags decorated that block of Charles Street, in addition to a huge flag suspended over the street close by. "With their country under attack," Huntington notes, "Charles Street denizens rediscovered their nation and identified themselves with it."

3   Was that rediscovery anything more than a momentary passion? Huntington reports that within a few months, the flags on Charles Street began to disappear. By the time the first anniversary rolled around in September 2002, only four were left flying. True, that is four times more than were there on September 10, 2001, but it is less than a quarter of the number that populated Charles Street at the end of September 2001.

4   There are similar anecdotes from around the country—an access of flag-waving followed by a relapse into indifference. Does it mean that the sudden upsurge of patriotism in the weeks following 9/11 was only, as it were, skin deep? Or perhaps it merely testifies to the fact that a sense of permanent emergency is difficult to maintain, especially in the absence of fresh attacks. Is our sense of ourselves as Americans patent only when challenged? "Does it," Huntington asks, "take an Osama bin Laden . . . to make us realize that we are Americans? If we do not experience recurring destructive attacks, will we return to the fragmentation and eroded Americanism before September 11?"

5   One hopes that the answer is No. . . . But I fear that for every schoolchild standing at attention for the National Anthem, there is a teacher or lawyer or judge or politician or ACLU employee militating against the hegemony of the dominant

culture, the insupportable intrusion of white, Christian, "Eurocentric" values into the curriculum, the school pageant, the town green, etc., etc. . . .

6   The threat shows itself in many ways, from culpable complacency to the corrosive imperatives of "multiculturalism" and political correctness. . . . In essence, as Huntington notes, multiculturalism is "anti-European civilization. . . . It is basically an anti-Western ideology.". . . [W]herever the imperatives of multiculturalism have touched the curriculum, they have left broad swaths of anti-Western attitudinizing competing for attention with quite astonishing historical blindness. Courses on minorities, women's issues, the Third World proliferate; the teaching of mainstream history slides into oblivion. "The mood," Arthur Schlesinger wrote in *The Disuniting of America* (1992), his excellent book on the depredations of multiculturalism, "is one of divesting Americans of the sinful European inheritance and seeking redemptive infusions from non-Western cultures."

7   A profound ignorance of the milestones of American culture is one predictable result of this mood. The statistics have become proverbial. Huntington quotes one poll from the 1990s showing that while 90 percent of Ivy League students could identify Rosa Parks, only 25 percent could identify the author of the words "government of the people, by the people, for the people." (Yes, it's the Gettysburg Address.) In a 1999 survey, 40 percent of seniors at fifty-five top colleges could not say within half a century when the Civil War was fought. Another study found that more high school students knew who Harriet Tubman was than knew that Washington commanded the American army in the revolution or that Abraham Lincoln wrote the Emancipation Proclamation. Doubtless you have your own favorite horror story.

8   But multiculturalism is not only an academic phenomenon. The attitudes it fosters have profound social as well as intellectual consequences. One consequence has been a sharp rise in the phenomenon of immigration without—or with only partial—assimilation: a dangerous demographic trend that threatens American identity in the most basic way. These various agents of dissolution are also elements in a wider culture war: the contest to define how we live and what counts as the good in the good life. Anti-Americanism occupies such a prominent place on the agenda of the culture wars precisely because the traditional values of American identity—articulated by the Founders and grounded in a commitment to individual liberty and public virtue—are deeply at odds with the radical, de-civilizing tenets of the "multiculturalist" enterprise.

9   To get a sense of what has happened to the institution of American identity, compare Robert Frost's performance at John F. Kennedy's inauguration in 1961 with Maya Angelou's performance thirty-two years later. As Huntington reminds us, Frost spoke of the "heroic deeds" of America's founding, an event, he said, that with "God's approval" ushered in "a new order of the ages." By contrast, Maya Angelou never mentioned the words "America" or "American." Instead, she identified twenty-seven ethnic or religious groups that had suffered repression because of America's "armed struggles for profit," "cynicism," and "brutishness.". . .

10   A favorite weapon in the armory of multiculturalism is the lowly hyphen. When we speak of an African-American or Mexican-American or Asian-American these

days, the aim is not descriptive but deconstructive. There is a polemical edge to it, a provocation. The hyphen does not mean "American, but hailing at some point in the past from someplace else." It means "only provisionally American: my allegiance is divided at best.". . . The multicultural passion for hyphenation is not simply a fondness for syntactical novelty. It also bespeaks a commitment to the centrifugal force of anti-American tribalism. The division marked by the hyphen in African-American (say) denotes a political stand. It goes hand-in-hand with other items on the index of liberal desiderata—the redistributive impulse behind efforts at "affirmative action," for example. . . .

11   Multiculturalism and "affirmative action" are allies in the assault on the institution of American identity. As such, they oppose the traditional understanding of what it means to be an American—an understanding hinted at in 1782 by the French-born American farmer J. Hector St. John de Crèvecoeur in his famous image of America as a country in which "individuals of all nations are melted into a new race of men." This crucible of American identity, this "melting pot," has two aspects. The negative aspect involves disassociating oneself from the cultural imperatives of one's country of origin. One sheds a previous identity before assuming a new one. One might preserve certain local habits and tastes, but they are essentially window-dressing. In essence one has left the past behind in order to become an American citizen.

12   The positive aspect of advancing the melting pot involves embracing the substance of American culture. The 1795 code for citizenship lays out some of the formal requirements.

> I do solemnly swear (1) to support the Constitution of the United States; (2) to renounce and abjure absolutely and entirely all allegiance and fidelity to any foreign prince, potentate, state, or sovereignty of whom or which the applicant was before a subject or citizen; (3) to support and defend the Constitution and the laws of the United States against all enemies, foreign and domestic; (4) to bear true faith and allegiance to the same; and (5) (A) to bear arms on behalf of the United States when required by law, or (B) to perform noncombatant service in the Armed Forces of the United States when required by law. . . .

For over two hundred years, this oath had been required of those wishing to become citizens. In 2003, Huntington tells us, federal bureaucrats launched a campaign to rewrite and weaken it.

13   I shall say more about what constitutes the substance of American identity in a moment. For now, I want to underscore the fact that this project of Americanization has been an abiding concern since the time of the Founders. "We must see our people more Americanized," John Jay declared in the 1780s. Jefferson concurred. Teddy Roosevelt repeatedly championed the idea that American culture, the "crucible in which all the new types are melted into one," was "shaped from 1776 to 1789, and our nationality was definitely fixed in all its essentials by the men of Washington's day."

14   It is often said that America is a nation of immigrants. In fact, as Huntington points out, America is a country that was initially a country of *settlers*. Settlers

precede immigrants and make their immigration possible. The culture of those mostly English-speaking, predominantly Anglo-Protestant settlers defined American culture. Their efforts came to fruition with the generation of Franklin, Washington, Jefferson, Hamilton, and Madison. The Founders are so denominated because they founded, they inaugurated a state. Immigrants were those who came later, who came from elsewhere, and who became American by embracing the Anglophone culture of the original settlers. The English language, the rule of law, respect for individual rights, the industriousness and piety that flowed from the Protestant work ethic—these were central elements in the culture disseminated by the Founders. And these were among the qualities embraced by immigrants when they became Americans. "Throughout American history," Huntington notes, "people who were not white Anglo-Saxon Protestants have become Americans by adopting America's Anglo-Protestant culture and political values. This benefited them and the country."

15   Justice Louis Brandeis outlined the pattern in 1919. Americanization, he said, means that the immigrant "adopts the clothes, the manners, and the customs generally prevailing here . . . substitutes for his mother tongue the English language" and comes "into complete harmony with our ideals and aspirations and cooperate[s] with us for their attainment." Until the 1960s, the Brandeis model mostly prevailed. Protestant, Catholic, and Jewish groups, understanding that assimilation was the best ticket to stability and social and economic success, eagerly aided in the task of integrating their charges into American society.

16   The story is very different today. In America, there is a dangerous new tide of immigration from Asia, a variety of Muslim countries, and Latin America, especially from Mexico. The tide is new not only chronologically but also in substance. First, there is the sheer matter of numbers. More than 2,200,000 legal immigrants came to the U.S. from Mexico in the 1990s alone. The number of illegal Mexican immigrants is staggering. So is their birth rate. Altogether there are more than 8 million Mexicans in the U.S. Some parts of the Southwest are well on their way to becoming what Victor Davis Hanson calls "Mexifornia," "the strange society that is emerging as the result of a demographic and cultural revolution like no other in our times." A professor of Chicano Studies at the University of New Mexico gleefully predicts that by 2080 parts of the Southwest United States and Northern Mexico will join to form a new country, "La Republica del Norte."

17   The problem is not only one of numbers, though. Earlier immigrants made—and were helped and goaded by the ambient culture to make—concerted efforts to assimilate. Important pockets of these new immigrants are not assimilating, not learning English, not becoming or thinking of themselves primarily as Americans. The effect of these developments on American identity is disastrous and potentially irreversible.

18   Such developments are abetted by the left-wing political and educational elites of this country, whose dominant theme is the perfidy of traditional American values. Hence the passion for multiculturalism and the ideal of ethnic hyphenation that goes with it. This has done immense damage in schools and colleges as well as in

the population at large. By removing the obligation to master English, multiculturalism condemns whole subpopulations to the status of permanent second-class citizens. . . .

19 As if in revenge for this injustice, however, multiculturalism also weakens the social bonds of the community at large. The price of imperfect assimilation is imperfect loyalty. Take the movement for bilingualism. Whatever it intended in theory, in practice it means *not* mastering English. It has notoriously left its supposed beneficiaries essentially monolingual, often semi-lingual. The only *bi* involved is a passion for bifurcation, which is fed by the accumulated resentments instilled by the anti-American multicultural orthodoxy. Every time you call directory assistance or some large corporation and are told "Press One for English" and "Para español oprime el numero dos" it is another small setback for American identity. . . .

20 We stand at a crossroads. The future of America hangs in the balance. Huntington outlines several possible courses that the country might take, from the loss of our core culture to an attempt to revive the "discarded and discredited racial and ethnic concepts" that, in part, defined pre-mid-twentieth century America. Huntington argues for another alternative. If we are to preserve our identity as a nation we need to preserve the core values that defined that identity. This is a point that the political philosopher Patrick, Lord Devlin made in his book *The Enforcement of Morals* (1965):

> [S]ociety means a community of ideas; without shared ideas on politics, morals, and ethics no society can exist. Each one of us has ideas about what is good and what is evil; they cannot be kept private from the society in which we live. If men and women try to create a society in which there is no fundamental agreement about good and evil they will fail; if having based it upon a common set of core values, they surrender those values, it will disintegrate. For society is not something that can be kept together physically; it is held by the invisible but fragile bonds of common beliefs and values. . . . A common morality is part of the bondage of a good society, and that bondage is part of the price of society which mankind must pay.

What are those beliefs and values? They embrace several things, including religion. You wouldn't know it from watching CNN or reading *The New York Times,* but there is a huge religious revival taking place now, affecting just about every part of the globe except Western Europe, which slouches towards godlessness almost as fast as it slouches towards bankruptcy and demographic collapse. (Neither Spain nor Italy are producing enough children to replace their existing populations, while the Muslim birthrate in France continues to soar.)

21 Things look different in America. For if America is a vigorously secular country—which it certainly is—it is also a deeply religious one. It always has been. Tocqueville was simply minuting the reality he saw around him when he noted that "[o]n my arrival in the United States the religious aspect of the country was the first thing that struck my attention." As G. K. Chesterton put it a century after Tocqueville, America is "a nation with the soul of a church." Even today, America is a country where an astonishing 92 percent of the population says it believes in God and 80 to 85 percent of the population identifies itself as Christian. Hence Huntington's call for a return to America's core values is also a call to embrace the religious

principles upon which the country was founded, "a recommitment to America as a deeply religious and primarily Christian country, encompassing several religious minorities adhering to Anglo-Protestant values, speaking English, maintaining its cultural heritage, and committed to the principles" of political liberty as articulated by the Founders. . . . Huntington is careful to stress that what he offers is an "argument for the importance of Anglo-Protestant culture, not for the importance of Anglo-Protestant people." That is, he argues not on behalf of a particular ethnic group but on behalf of a culture and set of values that "for three and a half centuries have been embraced by Americans of all races, ethnicities, and religions and that have been the source of their liberty, unity, power, prosperity, and moral leadership."

22   American identity was originally founded on four things: ethnicity, race, ideology, and culture. By the mid-twentieth century, ethnicity and race had sharply receded in importance. Indeed, one of America's greatest achievements is having eliminated the racial and ethnic components that historically were central to its identity. Ideology—the package of Enlightened liberal values championed by the Founders—[is] crucial but too thin for the task of forging or preserving national identity by themselves. ("A nation defined only by political ideology," Huntington notes, "is a fragile nation.") Which is why Huntington, like virtually all of the Founders, explicitly grounded American identity in religion. . . .

23   Opponents of religion in the public square never tire of reminding us that there is no mention of God in the Constitution. This is true. Neither is the word "virtue" mentioned. But both are presupposed. For the American Founders, as the historian Gertrude Himmelfarb points out, virtue, grounded in religion, was presumed "to be rooted in the very nature of man and as such . . . reflected in the *moeurs* of the people and in the traditions and informal institutions of society." It is also worth mentioning that if the Constitution is silent on religion, the Declaration of Independence is voluble, speaking of "nature's God," the "Creator," "the supreme judge of the world," and "divine Providence.". . . Benjamin Rush, one of the signers of the Declaration of Independence, summed up the common attitude of the Founders toward religion when he insisted that "[t]he only foundation for a useful education in a republic is to be laid in religion. Without it there can be no virtue, and without virtue there can be no liberty, and liberty is the object of all republican governments." George Washington concurred: "Reason and experience both forbid us to expect that national morality can prevail in exclusion of religious principles."

24   No nation lasts forever. An external enemy may eventually overrun and subdue it; internal forces of dissolution and decadence may someday undermine it, leaving it prey to more vigorous competitors. Sooner or later it succumbs. The United States is the most powerful nation the world has ever seen. Its astonishing military might, economic productivity, and political vigor are unprecedented. But someday, as Huntington reminds us, it too will fade or perish as Athens, Rome, and other great civilizations have faded or perished. Is the end, or the beginning of the end, at hand?

25   So far, the West—or at least the United States—has disappointed its self-appointed undertakers. How do we stand now, at the dawn of the twenty-first

century? It is worth remembering that besieged nations do not always succumb to the forces, external or internal, that threaten them. Sometimes, they muster the resolve to fight back successfully, to renew themselves. Today, America faces a new external enemy in the form of militant Islam and global terrorism. That minatory force, though murderous, will fail in proportion to our resolve to defeat it. Do we still possess that resolve? Inseparable from resolve is self-confidence, faith in the essential nobility of one's regime and one's way of life. To what extent do we still possess, still practice that faith?

Reinventing "America": Call for a New National Identity

ELIZABETH MARTÍNEZ

> Elizabeth Martínez has written six books, including one on Chicano history. This essay comes from her 1998 book, *De Colores Means All of Us: Latina Views for a Multi-Colored Century.*

1   For some 15 years, starting in 1940, 85 percent of all U.S. elementary schools used the Dick and Jane series to teach children how to read. The series starred Dick, Jane, their white middle-class parents, their dog Spot and their life together in a home with a white picket fence.

2   "Look, Jane, look! See Spot run!" chirped the two kids. It was a house full of glorious family values, where Mom cooked while Daddy went to work in a suit and mowed the lawn on weekends. The Dick and Jane books also taught that you should do your job and help others. All this affirmed an equation of middle-class with whiteness with virtue.

3   In the mid-1990s, museums, libraries and 80 Public Broadcasting Service (PBS) stations across the country had exhibits and programs commemorating the series. At one museum, an attendant commented, "When you hear someone crying, you know they are looking at the Dick and Jane books." It seems nostalgia runs rampant among many Euro-Americans: a nostalgia for the days of unchallenged White Supremacy—both moral and material—when life was "simple."

4   We've seen that nostalgia before in the nation's history. But today it signifies a problem reaching a new intensity. It suggests a national identity crisis that promises to bring in its wake an unprecedented nervous breakdown for the dominant society's psyche.

5   Nowhere is this more apparent than in California, which has long been on the cutting edge of the nation's present and future reality. Warning sirens have sounded repeatedly in the 1990s, such as the fierce battle over new history textbooks for public schools, Proposition 187's ugly denial of human rights to immigrants, the 1996 assault on affirmative action that culminated in Proposition 209, and the 1997 move to abolish bilingual education. Attempts to copycat these reactionary measures have been seen in other states.

6   The attack on affirmative action isn't really about affirmative action. Essentially it is another tactic in today's war on the gains of the 1960s, a tactic rooted in

Anglo resentment and fear. A major source of that fear: the fact that California will almost surely have a majority of people of color in 20 to 30 years at most, with the nation as a whole not far behind.

7   Check out the February 3, 1992, issue of *Sports Illustrated* with its double-spread ad for *Time* magazine. The ad showed hundreds of newborn babies in their hospital cribs, all of them Black or brown except for a rare white face here and there. The headline says, "Hey, whitey! It's your turn at the back of the bus!" The ad then tells you, read *Time* magazine to keep up with today's hot issues. That manipulative image could have been published today; its implication of shifting power appears to be the recurrent nightmare of too many potential Anglo allies.

8   Euro-American anxiety often focuses on the sense of a vanishing national identity. Behind the attacks on immigrants, affirmative action and multiculturalism, behind the demand for "English Only" laws and the rejection of bilingual education, lies the question: with all these new people, languages and cultures, what will it mean to be an American? If that question once seemed, to many people, to have an obvious, universally applicable answer, today new definitions must be found. But too often Americans, with supposed scholars in the lead, refuse to face that need and instead nurse a nostalgia for some bygone clarity. They remain trapped in denial.

9   An array of such ostriches, heads in the sand, began flapping their feathers noisily with the publication of Allan Bloom's 1987 best-selling book, *The Closing of the American Mind.* Bloom bemoaned the decline of our "common values" as a society, meaning the decline of Euro-American cultural centricity (shall we just call it cultural imperialism?). Since then we have seen constant sniping at "diversity" goals across the land. The assault has often focused on how U.S. history is taught. And with reason, for this country's identity rests on a particular narrative about the historical origins of the United States as a nation.

THE GREAT WHITE ORIGIN MYTH

10   Every society has an origin narrative that explains that society to itself and the world with a set of stories and symbols. The origin myth, as scholar-activist Roxanne Dunbar Ortiz has termed it, defines how a society understands its place in the world and its history. The myth provides the basis for a nation's self-defined identity. Most origin narratives can be called myths because they usually present only the most flattering view of a nation's history; they are not distinguished by honesty.

11   Ours begins with Columbus "discovering" a hemisphere where some 80 million people already lived but didn't really count (in what became the United States, they were just buffalo-chasing "savages" with no grasp of real estate values and therefore doomed to perish). It continues with the brave Pilgrims, a revolution by independence-loving colonists against a decadent English aristocracy and the birth of an energetic young republic that promised democracy and equality (that is, to white male landowners). In the 1840s, the new nation expanded its size by almost one-third, thanks to a victory over that backward land of little brown people called Mexico. Such has been the basic account of how the nation called the United States of America came into being as presently configured.

12   The myth's omissions are grotesque. It ignores three major pillars of our nationhood: genocide, enslavement and imperialist expansion (such nasty words, who wants to hear them?—but that's the problem). The massive extermination of indigenous peoples provided our land base; the enslavement of African labor made our economic growth possible; and the seizure of half of Mexico by war (or threat of renewed war) extended this nation's boundaries north to the Pacific and south to the Rio Grande. Such are the foundation stones of the United States, within an economic system that made this country the first in world history to be born capitalist.

13   Those three pillars were, of course, supplemented by great numbers of dirt-cheap workers from Mexico, China, the Philippines, Puerto Rico and other countries, all of them kept in their place by White Supremacy. In history they stand alongside millions of less-than-supreme white workers and sharecroppers.

14   Any attempt to modify the present origin myth provokes angry efforts to repel such sacrilege. In the case of Native Americans, scholars will insist that they died from disease or wars among themselves, or that "not so many really did die." At worst it was a "tragedy," but never deliberate genocide, never a pillar of our nation-hood. As for slavery, it was an embarrassment, of course, but do remember that Africa also had slavery and anyway enlightened white folk finally did end the practice here.

15   In the case of Mexico, reputable U.S. scholars still insist on blaming that country for the 1846–48 war. Yet even former U.S. President Ulysses Grant wrote in his memoirs that "[w]e were sent to provoke a fight [by moving troops into a disputed border area] but it was essential that Mexico should commence it [by fighting back]" (*Mr. Lincoln's General: Ulysses S. Grant, an illustrated autobiography*). President James Polk's 1846 diary records that he told his cabinet his purpose in declaring war as "acquiring California, New Mexico, and perhaps other Mexican lands" (*Diary of James K. Polk 1845–49*). To justify what could be called a territorial drive-by, the Mexican people were declared inferior; the U.S. had a "Manifest Destiny" to bring them progress and democracy.

16   Even when revisionist voices expose particular evils of Indian policy, slavery or the war on Mexico, they remain little more than unpleasant footnotes; the core of the dominant myth stands intact. PBS's eight-part documentary series of 1996 titled "The West" is a case in point. It devoted more than the usual attention to the devastation of Native Americans, but still centered on Anglos and gave little attention to why their domination evolved as it did. The West thus remained the physically gorgeous backdrop for an ugly, unaltered origin myth.

17   In fact, "The West" series strengthens that myth. White Supremacy needs the brave but inevitably doomed Indians to silhouette its own inevitable conquest. It needs the Indian-as-devil to sustain its own holy mission. Remember Timothy Wight, who served as pastor to Congress in the late 1700s and wrote that, under the Indians, "Satan ruled unchallenged in America" until "our chosen race eternal justice sent." With that self-declared moral authority, the "winning of the West" metamorphosed from a brutal, bloody invasion into a crusade of brave Christians marching across a lonely, dangerous landscape.

RACISM AS LINCHPIN OF THE U.S. NATIONAL IDENTITY

18   A crucial embellishment of the origin myth and key element of the national identity has been the myth of the frontier, analyzed in Richard Slotkin's *Gunfighter Nation,* the last volume of a fascinating trilogy. He describes Theodore Roosevelt's belief that the West was won thanks to American arms, "the means by which progress and nationality will be achieved." That success, Roosevelt continued, "depends on the heroism of men who impose on the course of events the latent virtues of their 'race.'" Roosevelt saw conflict on the frontier producing a species of virile "fighters and breeders" who would eventually generate a new leadership class. Militarism thus went hand in hand with the racialization of history's protagonists.

19   No slouch as an imperialist, Roosevelt soon took the frontier myth abroad, seeing Asians as Apaches and the Philippines as Sam Houston's Texas in the process of being seized from Mexico. For Roosevelt, Slotkin writes, "racial violence [was] the principle around which both individual character and social organization develop." Such ideas have not remained totally unchallenged by U.S. historians, nor was the frontier myth always applied in totally simplistic ways by Hollywood and other media. (The outlaw, for example, is a complicated figure, both good and bad.) Still, the frontier myth traditionally spins together virtue and violence, morality and war, in a convoluted, Calvinist web. That tortured embrace defines an essence of the so-called American character—the national identity—to this day.

20   The frontier myth embodied the nineteenth-century concept of Manifest Destiny, a doctrine that served to justify expansionist violence by means of intrinsic racial superiority. Manifest Destiny saw Yankee conquest as the inevitable result of a confrontation between enterprise and progress (white) versus passivity and backwardness (Indian, Mexican). "Manifest" meant "God-given," and the whole doctrine is profoundly rooted in religious conviction going back to the earliest colonial times. In his short, powerful book *Manifest Destiny: American Expansion and the Empire of Right,* Professor Anders Stephanson tells how the Puritans reinvented the Jewish notion of chosenness and applied it to this hemisphere so that territorial expansion became God's will. . . .

MANIFEST DESTINY DIES HARD

21   The concept of Manifest Destiny, with its assertion of racial superiority sustained by military power, has defined U.S. identity for 150 years. Only the Vietnam War brought a serious challenge to that concept of almightiness. Bitter debate, moral anguish, images of My Lai and the prospect of military defeat for the first time in U.S. history all suggested that the long-standing marriage of virtue and violence might soon be on the rocks. In the final years of the war the words leaped to mind one day: this country is having a national nervous breakdown.

22   Perhaps this is why the Vietnam War continues to arouse passions today. Some who are willing to call the war "a mistake" still shy away from recognizing its immorality or even accepting it as a defeat. A few Americans have the courage to conclude from the Vietnam War that we should abandon the idea that our identity rests on being the world's richest, most powerful and indeed *best* nation. Is it possible that the so-called Vietnam syndrome might signal liberation from a crippling

self-definition? Is it possible the long-standing belief that "American exceptionalism" had made freedom possible might be rejected someday?

23   The Vietnam syndrome is partly rooted in the fact that, although other societies have also been based on colonialism and slavery, ours seems to have an insatiable need to be the "good guys" on the world stage. That need must lie at least partially in a Protestant dualism that defines existence in terms of opposites, so that if you are not "good" you are bad, if not "white" then Black, and so on. Whatever the cause, the need to be seen as virtuous, compared to someone else's evil, haunts U.S. domestic and foreign policy. Where on earth would we be without Saddam Hussein, Qaddafi, and that all-time favorite of gringo demonizers, Fidel Castro? Gee whiz, how would we know what an American really is?

24   Today's origin myth and the resulting concept of national identity make for an intellectual prison where it is dangerous to ask big questions about this society's superiority. When otherwise decent people are trapped in such a powerful desire not to feel guilty, self-deception becomes unavoidable. To cease our present falsification of collective memory should, and could, open the doors of that prison. When together we cease equating whiteness with Americanness, a new day can dawn. As David Roediger, the social historian, has said, "[Whiteness] is the empty and therefore terrifying attempt to build an identity on what one isn't, and on whom one can hold back."

25   Redefining the U.S. origin narrative, and with it this country's national identity, could prove liberating for our collective psyche. It does not mean Euro-Americans should wallow individually in guilt. It does mean accepting collective responsibility to deal with the implications of our real origin. A few apologies, for example, might be a step in the right direction. In 1997, the idea was floated in Congress to apologize for slavery; it encountered opposition from all sides. But to reject the notion because corrective action, not an apology, is needed misses the point. Having defined itself as the all-time best country in the world, the United States fiercely denies the need to make a serious, official apology for anything. . . . To press for any serious, official apology does imply a new origin narrative, a new self-image, an ideological sea change.

26   Accepting the implications of a different narrative could also shed light on today's struggles. In the affirmative-action struggle, for example, opponents have said that that policy is no longer needed because racism ended with the Civil Rights Movement. But if we look at slavery as a fundamental pillar of this nation, going back centuries, it becomes obvious that racism could not have been ended by 30 years of mild reforms. If we see how the myth of the frontier idealized the white male adventurer as the central hero of national history, with the woman as sunbonneted helpmate, then we might better understand the dehumanized ways in which women have continued to be treated. A more truthful origin narrative could also help break down divisions among peoples of color by revealing common experiences and histories of cooperation.

27   A new origin narrative and national identity could help pave the way to a more livable society for us all. A society based on cooperation rather than competition, on the idea that all living creatures are interdependent and that humanity's goal

28   should be balance. Such were the values of many original Americans, deemed "savages." Similar gifts are waiting from other despised peoples and traditions. We might well start by recognizing that "America" is the name of an entire hemisphere, rich in a stunning variety of histories, cultures and peoples—not just one country.

28   The choice seems clear, if not easy. We can go on living in a state of massive denial, affirming this nation's superiority and virtue simply because we need to believe in it. We can choose to believe the destiny of the United States is still manifest: global domination. Or we can seek a transformative vision that carries us forward, not backward. We can seek an origin narrative that lays the groundwork for a multicultural, multinational identity centered on the goals of social equity and democracy. We do have choices.

29   There is little time for nostalgia. Dick and Jane never were "America," they were only one part of one community in one part of one country in one part of one continent. Yet we have let their image define our entire society and its values. Will the future be marked by ongoing denial or by steps toward a new vision in which White Supremacy no longer determines reality? When on earth will we transcend the assumptions that imprison our minds?

30   At times you can hear the clock ticking.

Analysis of the Writers' Positions

The first step in resolving conflict is to understand what the parties are claiming and why. Below is our paraphrase of Kimball's and Martínez's arguments.

Kimball's Position He opposes multiculturalism and wants to preserve an American identity based in Anglo-Protestant culture.

> *Thesis:* Multiculturalism weakens America by keeping people of different cultures from assimilating to the core values of America's Anglo-Protestant identity.
>
> > *Reason:* Educational multiculturalism degrades traditional American values and ignores mainstream history and culture.
> >
> > > *Evidence:* Opinions of Samuel Huntington and Arthur Schlesinger Jr. Examples of college students' ignorance about history. Maya Angelou's speech at Clinton's inauguration.
> >
> > *Reason:* Multiculturalism "weakens the social bond" by denying that immigrants need to assimilate to the language and values of the dominant culture.
> >
> > > *Evidence:* Rise of hyphenization. Rise of non-English-speaking communities. Calls for affirmative action, which violates the idea of success based on merit.
> >
> > *Reason:* America should be defined by one culture and nationality, not many.
> >
> > > *Evidence:* Quotations from de Crèvecoeur on the "new race of men." Quotations from Theodore Roosevelt, John Jay, Thomas

Jefferson, Benjamin Franklin. The 1795 oath of allegiance for citizenship.

Reason: The single, unifying identity of America should be based in Anglo-Saxon Protestant Christianity.

Evidence: Religious beliefs of original settlers. Historian Himmelfarb on American virtue as deeply rooted in religion. Quotes from Founding Fathers on relation of virtue to religion. Huntington on the need for national identity based in religion.

Martínez's Position   She wants to replace traditional Anglo-American identity with a multicultural one.

Thesis: The United States needs to discard its "white supremacist" identity.

Reason: It's based on racism, genocide, and imperialist expansion.

Evidence: The "origin myth" in common accounts of U.S. history. The historical record of slavery, takeover of Native American land, wars of expansion. Primary sources such as Presidents Grant and Polk. Theodore Roosevelt's statements about racial superiority. Historian Richard Slotkin's analysis of frontier myth.

Reason: It's based on a false sense of moral superiority and favor in the eyes of God.

Evidence: Professor Anders Stephanson on the concept of Manifest Destiny. Protestant moral dualism—seeing the world in terms of good and evil. Social historian David Roediger on the Anglo sense of superiority.

Reason: America will be a more fair and democratic country if we revise our identity to acknowledge Anglo faults and adopt the values of non-Anglo cultures.

Evidence: Racism and sexism not eliminated. The valuable gifts of other cultures, such as cooperation over competition.

◎◎ FOLLOWING THROUGH

If you and some of your classmates have written arguments taking opposing views on the same issue, prepare briefs of your respective positions to share with one another. (You might also create briefs of your opponents' positions to see how well you have understood one another's written arguments.)

Alternatively, write briefs summarizing the opposing positions offered in several published arguments as a first step toward mediating these viewpoints.   •

Locating the Areas of Agreement and Disagreement

Differences over Facts

Most conflicts result from interpreting facts differently rather than disagreement about the facts themselves. For example, in the arguments of Kimball and Martínez, we see agreement on many factual points:

- Whites are becoming the minority in some parts of the United States.
- Assimilation has meant conformity to a culture defined by Anglo-Protestant values.
- Christianity has played a large role in America's sense of identity.

If a mediator finds disagreement over facts, he or she needs to look into them and provide evidence from credible sources that would resolve the disagreement.

FOLLOWING THROUGH

For the arguments you are mediating, make a list of facts that the authors both accept. Note facts offered by one side but denied or not considered by the other. Where your authors do not agree on the facts, do research to decide how valid the facts cited on both sides are. Explain the discrepancies. If your class is mediating the same conflict, compare your findings.

Differences over Interests, Values, and Interpretations

Facts alone cannot resolve entrenched disputes such as the debate over multiculturalism. For example, a history lesson about white settlers' treatment of Native Americans would not change Kimball's mind. Nor would a lesson in Enlightenment philosophy alter what Martínez thinks. When we attempt to mediate, *we have to look into why people hold the positions they do.* Like persuasion, mediation looks at the contexts of a dispute.

To identify these differences, we can ask questions similar to those that are useful in persuasion for identifying what divides us from our audience (see the Best Practices box, "Questions for Understanding Difference," page 289). We apply below the questions about difference to Kimball's and Martínez's positions.

Is the Difference a Matter of Assumptions? Every argument has assumptions—unstated assertions that the audience must share to find the reasoning valid and persuasive. Kimball assumes that Anglo-Protestant culture is moral; therefore, he does not show how Christianity has made America a moral nation. Martínez disputes the very assumption that America is moral. But she also makes assumptions. She assumes that the "origin narrative" of the white man's conquest and exploitation is the sole basis for the nation's past and present identity. This assumption allows her to argue that the culture of the United States is simply white supremacist.

Questions for Understanding Difference

1. Is the difference a matter of *assumptions?*
2. Is the difference a matter of *principle?*
3. Is the difference a matter of *values* or a matter of having the same values but giving them different *priorities?*
4. Is the difference a matter of *ends* or *means?*
5. Is the difference a matter of *implications* or *consequences?*
6. Is the difference a matter of *interpretation?*
7. Is the difference a result of *personal background, basic human needs,* or *emotions?*

To our list of questions about difference in persuasive writing, we add this last question because mediators must look not just at the arguments but also at the disputants as people with histories and feelings. Mediators must take into account such basic human needs as personal security, economic well-being, and a sense of belonging, recognition, and control over their lives.

These two assumptions show polarized thinking—one assumes that Anglo-Protestant values are all good, the other that Anglo-Protestant values are all evil. Such polarized assumptions are common in disputes because, as philosopher of ethics Anthony Weston explains, we polarize not just to simplify but to justify: "We polarize . . . to be able to picture ourselves as totally justified, totally right, and the 'other side' as totally unjustified and wrong."[2] It is precisely this tactic that mediation must resist and overcome.

Is the Difference a Matter of Principle? By principles, we mean informal rules that guide our actions, like the "rule" in sales: "The customer is always right." Kimball's principle is patriotism: Americans should be undivided in loyalty and allegiance to the United States. Martínez's principle is fairness and justice for all, which means rewriting the origin narrative, admitting past mistakes, and recognizing the richness and morality of all the cultures that make up America. A mediator might ask, Can we be patriotic *and* self-critical? Must we repudiate the past entirely to fashion a new national identity?

Is the Difference a Matter of Values or Priorities? The principles just discussed reflect differing priorities. In the post–9/11 world, Kimball is concerned with America's strength on the world stage, whereas Martínez concentrates more on America's compassion in its domestic policies. This is a significant difference because Martínez supports programs like affirmative

---

[2]Anthony Weston, *A Practical Companion to Ethics* (New York: Oxford, 2005) 50.

action and multicultural education, the very policies Kimball claims weaken our social bonds. Once we see this difference, we can see the dispute in the context of liberal and conservative opinion in general. Kimball is arguing for a national identity acceptable to conservatives, Martínez for one acceptable to liberals. But what we need, obviously, is something that can cross this divide and appeal to most Americans.

Is the Difference a Matter of Ends or Means?   Martínez and Kimball have different ends in mind, so they also have different means to achieve the ends. For Martínez, a multicultural identity is the means to a more fair and livable society for all. For Kimball, a common identity in Anglo-Protestant culture is the means to remaining "the most powerful nation the world has ever seen." A mediator could reasonably ask: Couldn't we have both? Couldn't the United States be a powerful nation that is also fair and livable for all its citizens?

Is the Difference a Matter of Implications or Consequences?   The mediator has to consider what each side fears will happen if the other side prevails. Kimball fears that multiculturalism will lead Americans to self-doubt, loss of confidence. He also forecasts a large population of "permanent second-class citizens" if subgroups of the population do not assimilate. Martínez fears continuing oppression of minorities if our national self-conception does not change to fit our country's actual diversity. The mediator must acknowledge the fears of both sides while not permitting either to go unquestioned. Fear is a powerful motivator that must be confronted squarely.

Is the Difference a Matter of Interpretation?   A major disagreement here is over how to interpret the values of Anglo-Protestant culture. To Kimball, these values are "individual liberty and public virtue" (paragraph 8), "the rule of law" (paragraph 14), "respect for individual rights" (paragraph 14), devotion to God and a strong work ethic (paragraph 14). In contrast, Martínez interprets Anglo-Protestant values as a belief in whites' moral superiority and favor in the eyes of God (paragraph 20) that enabled them to see their own acts of "genocide, enslavement, and imperialist expansion" (paragraph 12) as morally acceptable and even heroic (paragraph 19). These interpretations stem from the different backgrounds of the writers, which we consider next.

Is the Difference a Matter of Personal Background, Basic Human Needs, or Emotions?   When mediating between positions, it is a good idea to go to the library or an online source for biographical information about the authors. It will pay off with insight into why they disagree.

Kimball and Martínez obviously come from very different backgrounds that are representative of others who hold the same positions they do. For example, as a white male with the financial means to have attended Yale, Kimball represents the group that has benefited most from the traditional national identity. His conservative views have pitted him against liberal academics and social activists.

Martínez identifies herself as a Chicana, an American woman of Mexican descent (her father was an immigrant). She is an activist for social justice and heads the Institute for MultiRacial Justice in San Francisco and has taught women's studies and ethnic studies in the California State University system. She knows the burden of discrimination from personal experience and from her work and research. As a proponent of bilingual and multicultural education, she sees people like Kimball as the opposition.

FOLLOWING THROUGH

If you are mediating among printed arguments, write an analysis based on applying the questions in the Best Practices box on page 289 to two or more arguments. Write out your analysis in list form, as we did in analyzing the differences between Kimball and Martínez.   •

Finding Creative Solutions: Exploring Common Ground

Using critical thinking to mediate means looking closely at what people want and why they want it. It also means seeing the dispute in larger contexts. For example, the dispute over national identity is part of a larger debate between liberals and conservatives over social policy and education.

Mediation cannot reach everyone. Some people hold extreme views that reason cannot touch. An example would be the professor Kimball cites who predicts that the southwestern United States and northern Mexico will eventually become a new and separate country. Mediation between this person and Kimball is about as likely as President Obama and Osama bin Laden having dinner together. But mediators can bring reasonable people closer together by trying to arrive at creative solutions that appeal to some of the interests and values of all parties.

The ethicist Anthony Weston suggests trying to see conflict in terms of what each side is right about.[3] He points to the debate over saving owls in old-growth forests versus logging interests that employ people. Preserving the environment and endangered species is good, but so is saving jobs. If jobs could be created that use wood in craft-based ways, people could make a living without destroying massive amounts of timber. This solution is possible if the parties cooperate—but not if corporations are deadlocked with radical environmentalists, neither willing to concede anything or give an inch.

Mediators should aim for "win-win" solutions, which resolve conflict by dissolving it. The challenge for the mediator is keeping the high ground and looking for the good and reasonable in what each side wants.

---

[3]Weston, *Practical Companion* 56.

Exploring Common Ground
in the Debate over National Identity

To find solutions for the national identity–multiculturalism dispute, we used our list of questions for understanding difference to find interests and values Kimball and Martínez might share or be persuaded to share. Here, in sum, is what we found.

Both want Americans to know their history. Kimball is right. It is a disgrace that college students cannot recognize a famous phrase from the Gettysburg Address. But they need to know that *and* the relevance of Harriet Tubman to those words. Martínez is right also that history should not be propaganda for one view of events. The history of all nations is a mix of good and bad.

Neither Kimball nor Martínez wants a large population of second-class citizens, living in isolated poverty, not speaking English, not seeing themselves as Americans, and not having a say in the democratic process. Martínez's multiculturalism would "break down divisions among peoples of color by revealing common experiences and histories of cooperation" with the goal of "social equity and democracy." She would be more likely, however, to achieve her goal if she considered white men and women *as participants* in this multicultural discussion. To exclude whites keeps people of color where they too often are—on the margins, left out. Kimball needs to be reminded that failure to assimilate is not typically a choice. As in the past, assimilation works only when educational and economic opportunities exist. Kimball needs to look into solutions to the problem of poverty among immigrants.

There is agreement too on the need for a national identity. Martínez calls for "a new identity." But asking what culture should provide it is the wrong question. Concentrating on the values themselves will help everyone see that most values are shared across races and cultures. For example, Martínez takes Anglo-Protestant culture as competitive, not cooperative. We need to recall that early Protestant settlers also valued community. The Puritans tried to establish utopian communities devoted to charity. Kimball's "Protestant" work ethic can be found in every ethnic group—for example, in the predominantly Catholic Mexican laborers who do backbreaking work in agriculture and construction.

Finally, what agreement could be reached about assimilation? Kimball suggests that immigrants follow Justice Louis Brandeis's advice—adopting "the clothes, the manners, and the customs generally prevailing here." But would such advice mean that what "prevails" here is based in Protestantism and Anglo-Saxon culture? A more realistic idea of "Americanization" comes from our third writer, Bharati Mukherjee, who suggests in her mediatory essay that "assimilation" is a two-way transformation, with immigrants and mainstream culture interacting, influencing each other. Such a conception *requires* both the preservation of tradition Kimball wants and the respect for diversity Martínez wants.

◎◎ FOLLOWING THROUGH

Either in list form or as an informal exploratory essay, find areas of agreement between the various positions you have been analyzing. End your list or essay with a summary of a position that all sides might accept.　　•

THE MEDIATORY ESSAY

The common human tendency in argument is to polarize—to see conflict as "us" versus "them." That is why mediation is necessary: to move beyond polarized thinking. An example of mediation in the multiculturalism debate appears below. The essay's author is the novelist Bharati Mukherjee. She was born into a wealthy family in Calcutta but became an American citizen. She is now Distinguished Professor of English at the University of California at Berkeley.

There is no single model for a mediatory essay. In this case, Mukherjee's essay mediates by making a case against both radical extremes, one way of seeking to bring people together on the remaining middle ground.

Beyond Multiculturalism: A Two-Way Transformation

BHARATI MUKHERJEE

1 The United States exists as a sovereign nation with its officially stated Constitution, its economic and foreign policies, its demarcated, patrolled boundaries. "America," however, exists as image or idea, as dream or nightmare, as romance or plague, constructed by discrete individual fantasies, and shaded by collective paranoias and mythologies.

2 I am a naturalized U.S. citizen with a certificate of citizenship; more importantly, I am an American for whom "America" is the stage for the drama of self-transformation. I see American culture as a culture of dreamers, who believe material shape (which is not the same as materialism) can be given to dreams. They believe that one's station in life—poverty, education, family background—does not determine one's fate. They believe in the reversal of omens; early failures do not spell inevitable disaster. Outsiders can triumph on merit. All of this happens against the backdrop of the familiar vicissitudes of American life.

3 I first came to the United States—to the state of Iowa, to be precise—on a late summer evening nearly thirty-three years ago. I flew into a placid, verdant airport in Iowa City on a commercial airliner, ready to fulfill the goals written out in a large, lined notebook for me by my guiltlessly patriarchal father. Those goals were unambiguous: I was to spend two years studying Creative Writing at Paul Engle's unique Writers Workshop; then I was to marry the perfect Bengali bridegroom selected by my father and live out the rest of a contented, predictable life in the city of my birth, Calcutta. In 1961, I was a shy, pliant, well-mannered, dutiful young daughter from a very privileged, traditional, mainstream Hindu family that believed women should be

protected and provided for by their fathers, husbands, sons, and it did not once occur to me that I might have goals of my own, quite distinct from those specified for me by my father. I certainly did not anticipate then that, over the next three decades, Iowans—who seemed to me so racially and culturally homogeneous—would be forced to shudder through the violent paroxysms of a collective identity in crisis.

4   When I was growing up in Calcutta in the fifties, I heard no talk of "identity crisis"—communal or individual. The concept itself—of a person not knowing who she or he was—was unimaginable in a hierarchical, classification-obsessed society. One's identity was absolutely fixed, derived from religion, caste, patrimony, and mother tongue. A Hindu Indian's last name was designed to announce his or her forefathers' caste and place of origin. A Mukherjee could *only* be a Brahmin from Bengal. Indian tradition forbade inter-caste, inter-language, inter-ethnic marriages. Bengali tradition discouraged even emigration; to remove oneself from Bengal was to "pollute" true culture.

5   Until the age of eight, I lived in a house crowded with forty or fifty relatives. We lived together because we were "family," bonded by kinship, though kinship was interpreted in flexible enough terms to include, when necessary, men, women, children who came from the same *desh*—which is the Bengali word for "homeland"—as had my father and grandfather. I was who I was because I was Dr. Sudhir Lal Mukherjee's daughter, because I was a Hindu Brahmin, because I was Bengali-speaking, and because my *desh* was an East Bengal village called Faridpur. I was encouraged to think of myself as indistinguishable from my dozen girl cousins. Identity was viscerally connected with ancestral soil and family origins. I was first a Mukherjee, then a Bengali Brahmin, and only then an Indian.

6   Deep down I knew, of course, that I was not quite like my girl cousins. Deeper down, I was sure that pride in the purity of one's culture has a sinister underside. As a child I had witnessed bloody religious riots between Muslims and Hindus, and violent language riots between Bengalis and Biharis. People kill for culture, and die of hunger. Language, race, religion, blood, myth, history, national codes, and manners have all been used, in India, in the United States, are being used in Bosnia and Rwanda even today, to enforce terror, to "otherize," to murder.

7   I do not know what compelled my strong-willed and overprotective father to risk sending us, his three daughters, to school in the United States, a country he had not visited. In Calcutta, he had insisted on sheltering us from danger and temptation by sending us to girls-only schools, and by providing us with chaperones, chauffeurs, and bodyguards.

8   The Writers Workshop in a quonset hut in Iowa City was my first experience of coeducation. And after not too long, I fell in love with a fellow student named Clark Blaise, an American of Canadian origin, and impulsively married him during a lunch break in a lawyer's office above a coffeeshop.

9   That impulsive act cut me off forever from the rules and ways of upper-middle-class life in Bengal, and hurled me precipitously into a New World life of scary improvisations and heady explorations. Until my lunchtime wedding, I had seen myself as an Indian foreign student, a transient in the United States. The five-minute ceremony in the lawyer's office had changed me into a permanent transient.

10   Over the last three decades the important lesson that I have learned is that in this era of massive diasporic movements, honorable survival requires resilience, curiosity, and compassion, a letting go of rigid ideals about the purity of inherited culture.

11   The first ten years into marriage, years spent mostly in my husband's *desh* of Canada, I thought myself an expatriate Bengali permanently stranded in North America because of a power surge of destiny or of desire. My first novel, *The Tiger's Daughter,* embodies the loneliness I felt but could not acknowledge, even to myself, as I negotiated the no-man's-land between the country of my past and the continent of my present. Shaped by memory, textured with nostalgia for a class and culture I had abandoned, this novel quite naturally became my expression of the *expatriate consciousness.*

12   It took me a decade of painful introspection to put the smothering tyranny of nostalgia into perspective, and to make the transition from expatriate to immigrant. I have found my way back to the United States after a fourteen-year stay in Canada. The transition from foreign student to U.S. citizen, from detached onlooker to committed immigrant, has not been easy.

13   The years in Canada were particularly harsh. Canada is a country that officially—and proudly—resists the policy and process of cultural fusion. For all its smug rhetoric about "cultural mosaic," Canada refuses to renovate its national self-image to include its changing complexion. It is a New World country with Old World concepts of a fixed, exclusivist national identity. And all through the seventies when I lived there, it was a country without a Bill of Rights or its own Constitution. Canadian official rhetoric designated me, as a citizen of non-European origin, one of the "visible minority" who, even though I spoke the Canadian national languages of English and French, was straining "the absorptive capacity" of Canada. Canadians of color were routinely treated as "not real" Canadians. In fact, when a terrorist bomb, planted in an Air India jet on Canadian soil, blew up after leaving Montreal, killing 329 passengers, 90 percent of whom were Canadians of Indian origin, the prime minister of Canada at the time, Brian Mulroney, cabled the Indian prime minister to offer Canada's condolences for India's loss, exposing the Eurocentricity of the "mosaic" policy of immigration.

14   In private conversations, some Canadian ambassadors and External Affairs officials have admitted to me that the creation of the Ministry of Multiculturalism in the seventies was less an instrument for cultural tolerance, and more a vote-getting strategy to pacify ethnic European constituents who were alienated by the rise of Quebec separatism and the simultaneous increase of non-white immigrants.

15   The years of race-related harassments in a Canada without a Constitution have politicized me, and deepened my love of the ideals embedded in the American Bill of Rights.

16   I take my American citizenship very seriously. I am a voluntary immigrant. I am not an economic refugee, and not a seeker of political asylum. I am an American by choice, and not by the simple accident of birth. I have made emotional, social, and political commitments to this country. I have earned the right to think of myself as an American.

17   But in this blood-splattered decade, questions such as who is an American and what is American culture are being posed with belligerence and being answered with violence. We are witnessing an increase in physical, too often fatal, assaults on Asian Americans. An increase in systematic "dot-busting" of Indo-Americans in New Jersey, xenophobic immigrant-baiting in California, minority-on-minority violence during the south-central Los Angeles revolution.

18   America's complexion is browning daily. Journalists' surveys have established that whites are losing their clear majority status in some states, and have already lost it in New York and California. A recent *Time* magazine poll indicated that 60 percent of Americans favor limiting *legal* immigration. Eighty percent of Americans polled favor curbing the entry of undocumented aliens. U.S. borders are too extensive and too porous to be adequately policed. Immigration, by documented and undocumented aliens, is less affected by the U.S. Immigration and Naturalization Service, and more by wars, ethnic genocides, famines in the emigrant's own country.

19   Every sovereign nation has a right to formulate its immigration policy. In this decade of continual, large-scale diasporic movements, it is imperative that we come to some agreement about who "we" are now that the community includes oldtimers, newcomers, many races, languages, and religions; about what our expectations of happiness and strategies for its pursuit are; and what our goals are for the nation.

20   Scapegoating of immigrants has been the politicians' easy instant remedy. Hate speeches fill auditoria, and bring in megabucks for those demagogues willing to profit from stirring up racial animosity.

21   The hysteria against newcomers is only minimally generated by the downturn in our economy. The panic, I suspect, is unleashed by a fear of the "other," the fear of what Daniel Stein, executive director of the Federation for American Immigration Reform, and a champion of closed borders, is quoted as having termed "cultural transmogrification."

22   The debate about American culture has to date been monopolized by rabid Eurocentrists and ethnocentrists; the rhetoric has been flamboyantly divisive, pitting a phantom "us" against a demonized "them." I am here to launch a new discourse, to reconstitute the hostile, biology-derived "us" versus "them" communities into a new *consensual* community of "we."

23   All countries view themselves by their ideals. Indians idealize, as well they should, the cultural continuum, the inherent value system of India, and are properly incensed when foreigners see nothing but poverty, intolerance, ignorance, strife, and injustice. Americans see themselves as the embodiments of liberty, openness, and individualism, even when the world judges them for drugs, crime, violence, bigotry, militarism, and homelessness. I was in Singapore when the media was very vocal about the case of an American teenager sentenced to caning for having allegedly vandalized cars. The overwhelming local sentiment was that caning Michael Fay would deter local youths from being tempted into "Americanization," meaning into gleefully breaking the law.

24   Conversely, in Tavares, Florida, an ardently patriotic school board has legislated that middle school teachers be required to instruct their students that American

culture—meaning European-American culture—is inherently "superior to other foreign or historic cultures." The sinister, or at least misguided, implication is that American culture has not been affected by the American Indian, African American, Latin American, and Asian American segments of its population.

25   The idea of "America" as a nation has been set up in opposition to the tenet that a nation is a collection of like-looking, like-speaking, like-worshiping people. Our nation is unique in human history. We have seen very recently, in a Germany plagued by anti-foreigner frenzy, how violently destabilizing the traditional concept of nation can be. In Europe, each country is, in a sense, a tribal homeland. Therefore, the primary criterion for nationhood in Europe is homogeneity of culture, and race, and religion. And that has contributed to blood-soaked balkanization in the former Yugoslavia and the former Soviet Union.

26   All European Americans, or their pioneering ancestors, gave up an easy homogeneity in their original countries for a new idea of Utopia. What we have going for us in the 1990s is the exciting chance to share in the making of a new American culture, rather than the coerced acceptance of either the failed nineteenth-century model of "melting pot" or the Canadian model of the "multicultural mosaic."

27   The "mosaic" implies a contiguity of self-sufficient, utterly distinct culture. "Multiculturalism" has come to imply the existence of a central culture, ringed by peripheral cultures. The sinister fallout of official multiculturalism and of professional multiculturalists is the establishment of one culture as the norm and the rest as aberrations. Multiculturalism emphasizes the differences between racial heritages. This emphasis on the differences has too often led to the dehumanization of the different. Dehumanization leads to discrimination. And discrimination can ultimately lead to genocide.

28   We need to alert ourselves to the limitations and the dangers of those discourses that reinforce an "us" versus "them" mentality. We need to protest any official rhetoric or demagoguery that marginalizes on a race-related and/or religion-related basis any segment of our society. I want to discourage the retention of cultural memory if the aim of that retention is cultural balkanization. I want to sensitize you to think of culture and nationhood *not* as an uneasy aggregate of antagonistic "them" and "us," but as a constantly re-forming, transmogrifying "we."

29   In this diasporic age, one's biological identity may not be the only one. Erosions and accretions come with the act of emigration. The experiences of violent unhousing from a biological "homeland" and rehousing in an adopted "homeland" that is not always welcoming to its dark-complected citizens have tested me as a person, and made me the writer I am today.

30   I choose to describe myself on my own terms, that is, as an American without hyphens. It is to sabotage the politics of hate and the campaigns of revenge spawned by Eurocentric patriots on the one hand and the professional multiculturalists on the other, that I describe myself as an "American" rather than as an "Asian-American." Why is it that hyphenization is imposed only on non-white Americans? And why is it that only non-white citizens are "problematized" if they choose to

describe themselves on their own terms? My outspoken rejection of hyphenization is my lonely campaign to obliterate categorizing the cultural landscape into a "center" and its "peripheries." To reject hyphenization is to demand that the nation deliver the promises of the American Dream and the American Constitution to *all* its citizens. I want nothing less than to invent a new vocabulary that demands, and obtains, an equitable power-sharing for all members of the American community.

31   But my self-empowering refusal to be "otherized" and "objectified" has come at tremendous cost. My rejection of hyphenization has been deliberately misrepresented as "race treachery" by some India-born, urban, upper-middle-class Marxist "green card holders" with lucrative chairs on U.S. campuses. These academics strategically position themselves as self-appointed spokespersons for their ethnic communities, and as guardians of the "purity" of ethnic cultures. At the same time, though they reside permanently in the United States and participate in the capitalist economy of this nation, they publicly denounce American ideals and institutions.

32   They direct their rage at me because, as a U.S. citizen, I have invested in the present and the future rather than in the expatriate's imagined homeland. They condemn me because I acknowledge erosion of memory as a natural result of emigration; because I count that erosion as net gain rather than as loss; and because I celebrate racial and cultural "mongrelization." I have no respect for these expatriate fence-straddlers who, even while competing fiercely for tenure and promotion within the U.S. academic system, glibly equate all evil in the world with the United States, capitalism, colonialism, and corporate and military expansionism. I regard the artificial retentions of "pure race" and "pure culture" as dangerous, reactionary illusions fostered by the Eurocentric and the ethnocentric empire builders within the academy. I fear still more the politics of revenge preached from pulpits by some minority demagogues. . . .

33   As a writer, my literary agenda begins by acknowledging that America has transformed *me.* It does not end until I show that I (and the hundreds of thousands of recent immigrants like me) am minute by minute transforming America. The transformation is a two-way process; it affects both the individual and the national cultural identity. The end result of immigration, then, is this two-way transformation: that's my heartfelt message.

34   Others often talk of diaspora, of arrival as the end of the process. They talk of arrival in the context of loss, the loss of communal memory and the erosion of an intact ethnic culture. They use words like "erosion" and "loss" in alarmist ways. I want to talk of arrival as gain. . . .

35   What excites me is that we have the chance to retain those values we treasure from our original cultures, but we also acknowledge that the outer forms of those values are likely to change. In the Indian American community, I see a great deal of guilt about the inability to hang on to "pure culture." Parents express rage or despair at their U.S.-born children's forgetting of, or indifference to, some aspects of Indian culture. Of those parents, I would ask: What is it we have lost if our children are acculturating into the culture in which we are living? Is it so terrible that our children are discovering or inventing homelands for themselves? Some first-generation Indo-Americans, embittered by overt anti-Asian racism and by

unofficial "glass ceilings," construct a phantom more-Indian-than-Indians-in-India identity as defense against marginalization. Of them I would ask: Why not get actively involved in fighting discrimination through protests and lawsuits?

36   I prefer that we forge a national identity that is born of our acknowledgment of the steady de-Europeanization of the U.S. population; that constantly synthesizes—fuses—the disparate cultures of our country's residents; and that provides a new, sustaining, and unifying national creed.

Analyzing Mukherjee's Essay

Let's see what we can learn about how to appeal to audiences in mediatory essays. We'll look at ethos (how Mukherjee projects good character), pathos (how she arouses emotions favorable to her case), and logos (how she wins assent through good reasoning).

Ethos: Earning the Respect of Both Sides

Mediatory essays are not typically as personal as this one. But the author is in an unusual position, which makes the personal relevant. By speaking in the first person and telling her story, Mukherjee seeks the goodwill of people on both sides. She presents herself as patriotic, a foreigner who has assimilated to American ways, clearly appealing to those on Kimball's side. But she is also a "person of color," who's been "tested" by racial prejudices in the United States, clearly appealing to Martínez's side. She creates negative ethos for the radical extremists in the identity debate, depicting them as lacking morality and/or honesty. That is why she cites the violence committed by both whites and minorities, the scapegoating by politicians pandering to voter fears, the hypocrisy of professors who live well in America while denouncing its values. She associates her own position with words like *commitment, compassion, consensus, equality,* and *unity.*

By including her own experiences in India and Canada and her references to Bosnia, Rwanda, Germany, and the former Soviet Union, Mukherjee is able to place this American debate in a larger context—parts of the world in which national identity incites war and human rights violations.

Pathos: Using Emotion to Appeal to Both Sides

Appealing to the right emotions can help to move parties in conflict to the higher ground of consensus. Mukherjee displays a range of emotions, including pride, anger, and compassion. In condemning the extremes on both sides, her tone becomes heated. She uses highly charged words like *rabid, demagogues, scapegoaters, fence-straddlers,* and *reactionaries* to describe them. Her goal is to distance the members of her audience who are reasonable from those who are not, so her word choice is appropriate and effective.

Patriotism is obviously emotional. Mukherjee's repeated declaration of devotion to her adopted country stirs audience pride. So does the contrast with India and Canada and the celebrating of individual freedom in the United States.

Her own story of arrival, nostalgia, and transformation arouses compassion and respect because it shows that assimilation is not easy. She understands the reluctance of Indian parents to let their children change. This shows her ability to empathize.

Finally, she appeals through hope and optimism. Twice she describes the consensus she proposes as *exciting*—and also fresh, new, vital, alive—in contrast to the rigid and inflexible ethnic purists.

Logos: Integrating Values of Both Sides

Mukherjee's thesis is that the opposing sides in the national identity debate are two sides of the wrong coin: the mistaken regard for ethnic purity. Making an issue of one's ethnicity, whether it be Anglo, Chicano, Indian-American, or whatever, is not a means to harmony and equality. Instead, America needs a unifying national identity that blends the ever-changing mix of races and cultures that make up our population.

Mukherjee offers reasons to oppose ethnic "purity":

Violence and wars result when people divide according to ethnic and religious differences. It creates an "us" versus "them" mentality.

The multicultural Canadian program created second-class, marginal populations.

Hyphenization in America makes a problem out of non-whites in the population.

We said that mediation looks for the good in each side and tries to show what they have in common. Mukherjee shows that her solution offers gains for both sides, a "win-win" situation. She concedes that her solution would mean some loss of "cultural memory" for immigrants, but these losses are offset by the following gains:

The United States would be closer to the strong and unified nation that Kimball wants because *everyone's* contributions would be appreciated.

The cultural barriers between minorities would break down, as Martínez wants. This would entail speaking to each other in English, but being free to maintain diverse cultures at home.

The barriers between "Americans" and hyphenated Americans would break down, as both Kimball and Martínez want. In other words, there would be assimilation, as Kimball wants, but not assimilation to one culture, which Martínez strongly resists.

By removing the need to prove one's own culture superior, we could all recognize the faults in our past as well as the good things. We would have no schools teaching either the superiority or the inferiority of any culture.

Emphasizing citizenship instead of ethnicity is a way of standing up for and demanding equal rights and equal opportunity, helping to bring about the social justice and equality Martínez seeks.

The new identity would be "sustaining," avoiding future conflicts
because it would adapt to change.

Mukherjee's essay mediates by showing that a definition of America based
on either one ethnic culture or many ethnic cultures is not satisfactory. By
dropping ethnicity as a prime concern, both sides can be better off and freer
in pursuit of happiness and success.

QUESTIONS FOR DISCUSSION

Look over the essays by Elizabeth Martínez and Roger Kimball. Do you think
either of them would find Bharati Mukherjee's essay persuasive? What does
Mukherjee say that might cause either of them to relax their positions about
American identity? Do you think any further information might help to bring
either side to Mukherjee's consensus position? For example, Kimball mentions the
"Letter from an American Farmer" by de Crèvecoeur, who describes Americans as
a new "race" of blended nationalities, leaving behind their ties and allegiances to
former lands. How is Crèvecouer's idea of the "new race" similar to Mukherjee's?

Writing a Mediatory Essay

Prewriting

In preparing to write a mediatory essay, you should work through the steps
described on pages 286–293. Prepare briefs of the various conflicting positions,
and note areas of disagreement; think hard about the differing interests of the
conflicting parties, and respond to the questions about difference on page 289.

Give some thought to each party's background—age, race, gender, and
so forth—and how it might contribute to his or her viewpoint on the issue.

Describe the conflict in its full complexity, not just its polar opposites.
Try to find the good values in each position: You may be able to see that
people's real interests are not as far apart as they might seem. You may be
able to find common ground.

At this point in the prewriting process, think of some solutions that
would satisfy at least some of the interests on all sides. It might be necessary
for you to do some additional research. What do you think any of the opposing parties might want to know more about in order to accept your solution?

Finally, write up a clear statement of your solution. Can you explain how
your solution appeals to the interests of all sides?

Drafting

There is no set form for the mediatory essay. As with any argument, the
important thing is to have a plan for arranging your points and to provide
clear signals to your readers. One logical way to organize a mediatory essay
is in three parts:

Overview of the conflict. Describe the conflict and the opposing
positions in the introductory paragraphs.

Discussion of differences underlying the conflict. Here your goal is to make all sides more sympathetic to one another and to sort out the important real interests that must be addressed by the solution.

Proposed solution. Here you make a case for your compromise position, giving reasons why it should be acceptable to all—that is, showing that it does serve at least some of their interests.

Revising

When revising a mediatory essay, you should look for the usual problems of organization and development that you would be looking for in any essay to convince or persuade. Be sure that you have inquired carefully and fairly into the conflict and that you have clearly presented the cases for all sides, including your proposed solution. At this point, you also need to consider how well you have used the persuasive appeals:

The appeal to character. Think about what kind of character you have projected as a mediator. Have you maintained neutrality? Do you model open-mindedness and genuine concern for the sensitivities of all sides?

The appeal to emotions. To arouse sympathy and empathy, which are needed in mediation, you should take into account the emotional appeals discussed on pages 299–300. Your mediatory essay should be a moving argument for understanding and overcoming difference.

The appeal through style. As in persuasion, you should put the power of language to work. Pay attention to concrete word choice, striking metaphors, and phrases that stand out because of repeated sounds and rhythms.

For suggestions about editing and proofreading, see Appendix A.

www.mhhe.com/**crusius**

For help editing your essay, go to:

Editing

AN ESSAY ARGUING TO MEDIATE

The following mediatory essay was written by Angi Grellhesl, a first-year student at Southern Methodist University. Her essay examines opposing views on the institution of speech codes at various U.S. colleges and its effect on freedom of speech.

Mediating the Speech Code Controversy

ANGI GRELLHESL

1   The right to free speech has raised many controversies over the years. Explicit lyrics in rap music and marches by the Ku Klux Klan are just some examples that test the power of the First Amendment. Now, students and administrators are questioning if, in fact, free speech ought to be limited on university campuses. Many schools have instituted speech codes to protect specified groups from harassing speech.

2   Both sides in the debate, the speech code advocates and the free speech advocates, have presented their cases in recent books and articles. Columnist Nat Hentoff argues strongly against the speech codes, his main reason being that the codes violate students' First Amendment rights. Hentoff links the right to free speech with the values of higher education. In support, he quotes Yale president Benno Schmidt, who says, "Freedom of thought must be Yale's central commitment. . . . [U]niversities cannot censor or suppress speech, no matter how obnoxious in content, without violating their justification for existence . . . " (qtd. in Hentoff 223). Another reason Hentoff offers against speech codes is that universities must teach students to defend themselves in preparation for the real world, where such codes cannot shield them. Finally, he suggests that most codes are too vaguely worded; students may not even know they are violating the codes (216).

3   Two writers in favor of speech codes are Richard Perry and Patricia Williams. They see speech codes as a necessary and fair limitation on free speech. Perry and Williams argue that speech codes promote multicultural awareness, making students more sensitive to the differences that are out there in the real world. These authors do not think that the codes violate First Amendment rights, and they are suspicious of the motives of those who say they do. As Perry and Williams put it, those who feel free speech rights are being threatened "are apparently unable to distinguish between a liberty interest on the one hand and, on the other, a quite specific interest in being able to spout racist, sexist, and homophobic epithets completely unchallenged—without, in other words, the terrible inconvenience of feeling bad about it" (228).

4   Perhaps if both sides trusted each other a little more, they could see that their goals are not contradictory. Everyone agrees that students' rights should be protected. Hentoff wishes to ensure that students have the right to speak their minds. He and others on his side are concerned about freedom. Defenders of the codes argue that students have the right not to be harassed, especially while they are getting an education. They are concerned about opportunity. Would either side really deny that the other's goal had value?

5   Also, both sides want to create the best possible educational environment. Here the difference rests on the interpretation of what benefits the students. Is the best environment one most like the real world, where prejudice and harassment occur? Or does the university have an obligation to provide an atmosphere where potential victims can thrive and participate freely without intimidation?

6   I think it is possible to reach a solution that everyone can agree on. Most citizens want to protect constitutional rights; but they also agree that those rights have limitations, the ultimate limit being when one person infringes on the rights of others to live in peace. All sides should agree that a person ought to be able to speak out about his or her convictions, values, and beliefs. Most people can see a difference between that protected speech and the kind that is intended to harass and intimidate. For example, there is a clear difference between expressing one's view that Jews are mistaken in not accepting Christ as the son of God, on the one hand, and yelling anti-Jewish threats at a particular person on the other. Could a code not be worded in such a way as to distinguish between these two kinds of speech?

7   Also, I don't believe either side would want the university to be an artificial world. Codes should not attempt to ensure that no one is criticized or even offended. Students should not be afraid to say controversial things. But universities do help to shape the future of the real world, so shouldn't they at least take a stand against harassment? Can a code be worded that would protect free speech and prevent harassment?

8   The current speech code at Southern Methodist University is a compromise that ought to satisfy free speech advocates and speech code advocates. It prohibits hate speech at the same time that it protects an individual's First Amendment rights.

9   First, it upholds the First Amendment by including a section that reads, "[D]ue to the University's commitment to freedom of speech and expression, harassment is more than mere insensitivity or offensive conduct which creates an uncomfortable situation for certain members of the community" (*Peruna* 92). The code therefore should satisfy those, like Hentoff, who place a high value on the basic rights our nation was built upon. Secondly, whether or not there is a need for protection, the current code protects potential victims from hate speech or "any words or acts deliberately designed to disregard the safety or rights of another, and which intimidate, degrade, demean, threaten, haze, or otherwise interfere with another person's rightful action" (*Peruna* 92). This part of the code should satisfy those who recognize that some hurts cannot be permitted. Finally, the current code outlines specific acts that constitute harassment: "Physical, psychological, verbal and/or written acts directed toward an individual or group of individuals which rise to the level of 'fighting words' are prohibited" (*Peruna* 92).

10   The SMU code protects our citizens from hurt and from unconstitutional censorship. Those merely taking a position can express it, even if it hurts. On the other hand, those who are spreading hatred will not be protected. Therefore, all sides should respect the code as a safeguard for those who use free speech but a limitation on those who abuse it.

www.mhhe.com/crusius

For an electronic tool that helps create properly formatted works cited pages, go to:

Research > Bibliomaker

WORKS CITED

Hentoff, Nat. "Speech Codes on the Campus and Problems of Free Speech." *Debating P.C.* Ed. Paul Berman. New York: Bantam, 1992. 215–24.

Perry, Richard, and Patricia Williams. "Freedom of Speech." *Debating P.C.* Ed. Paul Berman. New York: Bantam, 1992. 225–30.

Peruna Express 1993–1994. Dallas: Southern Methodist U, 1993.

CHAPTER SUMMARY

We often must deal as constructively as we can with sharp differences of opinion, where people taking opposing positions seem unable or unwilling to explore ways to reduce or eliminate conflict. Sometimes efforts at mediation fail, no matter how skillful the mediator is. However, as you have seen in this chapter, mediation is possible and can result in agreement on a course of action satisfactory to all parties. Mediating involves understanding the positions of all sides, finding common ground, defusing hostilities among the contending sides, and making a good case for the course of action the mediator advocates. It involves, that is, everything you have learned in this book about using argument to inquire, convince, and persuade.

Two Casebooks for Argument

TWO CASEBOOKS FOR ARGUMENT

CHAPTER 12

Consumer Society: The Urge to Splurge

PHOTO MONTAGE: BLACK FRIDAY EVE

Dedicated consumers waited in line for the 5:00 a.m. opening of Best Buy on the day after Thanksgiving.

GENERAL INTRODUCTION: WHAT IS A CONSUMER SOCIETY?

When we say we live in a consumer society, we commonly mean that we live with more products and services than our parents and grandparents did; more choices within a product category, including premium labels at the high-priced end; and more information about it all in the form of advertising, media images, and product placement in music, movies, and TV. Even people who would never buy a pair of Manolo Blahnik shoes have heard of them because of the show *Sex and the City*. This casebook takes a close and critical look at how consumerism affects our sense of identity and quality of life.

Scholars who observe consumer societies describe not just the amount of goods available but the importance people place on them. Says Paul Elkins: "A consumer society is one in which the possession and use of an increasing number and variety of goods and services is the principal cultural aspiration and the surest perceived route to personal happiness, social status, and national success."[1]

The readings in this chapter focus on the United States, but the consumer society is really a global village, including the middle- and upper-class populations of developing nations whose workers supply most of the products we buy. In China, for example, parts of Shanghai and other booming cities epitomize the consumer society. A serious problem for China, however, is the disparity of income between rich and poor. The United States also has a vast disparity between rich and poor. Although not as great as Brazil's, the income gap in the United States is larger than that of any other advanced industrialized country, as illustrated in Figure 12.1.

Some other statistics to bear in mind: According to the U.S. Census Bureau, the median household income in the United States in 2005 rose to $46,326, while the poverty rate in that year remained unchanged, at 12.6% of the population, about 37 million people. However, the rich are getting much, much richer:

> According to Emmanuel Saez of the University of California, Berkeley, and Thomas Piketty of the École Normale Supérieure in Paris, the share of aggregate income going to the highest-earning 1% of Americans has doubled from 8% in 1980 to over 16% in 2004. That going to the top tenth of 1% has tripled from 2% in 1980 to 7% today. And that going to the top one-hundredth of 1%—the 14,000 taxpayers at the very top of the income ladder—has quadrupled from 0.65% in 1980 to 2.87% in 2004.[3]

---

[1]Paul Elkins, qtd. in Neva R. Goodwin, "Overview Essay," *The Consumer Society,* ed. Neva R. Goodwin, Frank Ackerman, and David Kiron (Washington, D.C.: Island Press, 1997), 2.
[2, 3]From "Inequality in America: The Rich, the Poor, and the Growing Gap between Them," *The Economist,* June 15, 2006. Copyright 2006 by Economist Newspaper Group. Reproduced with permission of Economist Newspaper Group in the format Textbook via Copyright Clearance Center.

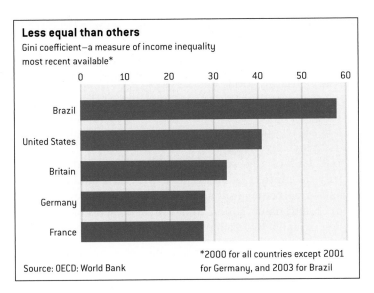

Less equal than others

Gini coefficient—a measure of income inequality
most recent available*

Source: OECD: World Bank

*2000 for all countries except 2001 for Germany, and 2003 for Brazil

Figure 12.1[2]

These statistics are worth remembering as you read the arguments in this chapter. Some of the authors address the problem of those excluded from the consumer society; others do not. And, as Juliet Schor argues, even those who can afford to participate at some level feel inadequate because they constantly compare themselves to the biggest spenders at the top. Thanks to the media, the "lifestyles of the rich and famous" are highly visible while the lives of the poor can easily be ignored by those who choose not to look.

SECTION 1: THE MEANING OF SPENDING
Overview

This section opens with two arguments about why people buy what we might call "unnecessary" things: goods and services that are upscale, stylish, and in some cases, over-the-top luxurious. America has clearly changed since the 1950s. Americans used to have modest goals for houses, cars, and lifestyles, but today, it is not enough to just be comfortable. People want more. The question is, Is this change for the better?

The second half of this section provides three readings that illustrate more concretely the motives of consumers. We visit a suburban Home Depot where Dad buys a barbeque grill, a strip of transient stores in a ghetto where teenagers buy brand-name shoes, and a cyberspace community of young people making friends by exchanging information about their personal possessions.

The Aesthetic Imperative

VIRGINIA POSTREL

> Virginia Postrel, whose degree from Princeton is in English literature, has made a career writing on the subjects of economics, progress, and design. She writes regular columns for *The Atlantic* and *Forbes* magazines and has published two books, *The Future and Its Enemies* (Free Press 1998) and *The Substance of Style: How the Rise of Aesthetic Value Is Remaking Commerce, Culture, and Consciousness* (HarperCollins 2003), from which this selection is excerpted.

1   The twenty-first century isn't what the old movies imagined. We citizens of the future don't wear conformist jumpsuits, live in utilitarian high-rises, or get our food in pills. To the contrary, we are demanding and creating an enticing, stimulating, diverse, and beautiful world. We want our vacuum cleaners and mobile phones to sparkle, our bathroom faucets and desk accessories to express our personalities. We expect every strip mall and city block to offer designer coffee, several different cuisines, a copy shop with do-it-yourself graphics workstations, and a nail salon for manicures on demand. We demand trees in our parking lots, peaked roofs and decorative façades on our supermarkets, auto dealerships as swoopy and stylish as the cars they sell.

2   Aesthetics has become too important to be left to the aesthetes. To succeed, hard-nosed engineers, real estate developers, and MBAs must take aesthetic communication, and aesthetic pleasure, seriously. We, their customers, demand it.

3   "We are by nature—by deep, biological nature—visual, tactile creatures," says David Brown, the former president of the Art Center College of Design in Pasadena, California, and a longtime observer of the design world. That is a quintessential turn-of-our-century statement, a simultaneous affirmation of biological humanity and aesthetic power. Our sensory side is as valid a part of our nature as the capacity to speak or reason, and it is essential to both. Artifacts do not need some other justification for pleasing our visual, tactile, emotional natures. Design, says Brown, is moving from the abstract and ideological—"this is good design"—to the personal and emotional—"I *like* that." In this new age of aesthetics, we are acknowledging, accepting, and even celebrating what a design-museum curator calls our "quirky underside."

4   This trend doesn't mean that a particular style has triumphed or that we're necessarily living in a period of unprecedented creativity. It doesn't mean everyone or everything is now beautiful, or that people agree on some absolute standard of taste. The issue is not *what* style is used but rather *that* style is used, consciously and conscientiously, even in areas where function used to stand alone. Aesthetics is more pervasive than it used to be—not restricted to a social, economic, or artistic elite, limited to only a few settings or industries, or designed to communicate only power, influence, or wealth. Sensory appeals are everywhere, they are increasingly personalized, and they are intensifying.

5   Of course, saying that aesthetics is pervasive does not imply that look and feel trump everything else. Other values have not gone away. We may want mobile phones to sparkle, but first we expect them to work. We expect shops to look good, but we also want service and selection. We still care about cost, comfort,

and convenience. But on the margin, aesthetics matters more and more. When we decide how next to spend our time, money, or creative effort, aesthetics is increasingly likely to top our priorities.

6   In this context, "aesthetics" obviously does not refer to the philosophy of art. Aesthetics is the way we communicate through the senses. It is the art of creating reactions without words, through the look and feel of people, places, and things. Hence, aesthetics differs from entertainment that requires cognitive engagement with narrative, word play, or complex, intellectual allusion. While the sound of poetry is arguably aesthetic, the meaning is not. Spectacular special effects and beautiful movie stars enhance box-office success in foreign markets because they offer universal aesthetic pleasure; clever dialogue, which is cognitive and culture-bound, doesn't travel as well. Aesthetics may complement storytelling, but it is not itself narrative.

7   Aesthetics shows rather than tells, delights rather than instructs. The effects are immediate, perceptual, and emotional. They are not cognitive, although we may analyze them after the fact. As a mid-century industrial designer said of his field, aesthetics is "fundamentally the art of using line, form, tone, color, and texture to arouse an emotional reaction in the beholder."

8   Whatever information aesthetics conveys is prearticulate—the connotation of the color and shapes of letters, not the meanings of the words they form. Aesthetics conjures meaning in a subliminal, associational way, as our direct sensory experience reminds us of something that is absent, a memory or an idea. Those associations may be universal, the way Disney's big-eyed animals play on the innate human attraction to babies. Or they may change from person to person, place to place, moment to moment.

9   Although we often equate aesthetics with beauty, that definition is too limited. Depending on what reaction the creator wants, effective presentation may be strikingly ugly, disturbing, even horrifying. The title sequence to *Seven*—whose rough, backlit type, seemingly stuttering film, and unsettling sepia images established a new style for horror films—comes to mind. Or aesthetics may employ novelty, allusion, or humor, rather than beauty, to arouse a positive response. Philippe Starck's fly swatter with a face on it doesn't represent timeless beauty. It's just whimsical fun.

10   Aesthetic effects begin with universal reactions, but these effects always operate in a personal and cultural context. We may like weather-beaten paint because it seems rustic, black leather because it makes us feel sexy, or fluffy pop music because it reminds us of our youth. Something novel may be interesting, or something familiar comforting, without regard to ideal beauty. The explosion of tropical colors that hit women's fashion in 2000 was a relief from the black, gray, and beige of the late 1990s, while those neutrals looked calm and sophisticated after the riot of jewel tones that preceded them. Psychologists tell us that human beings perceive changes in sensory inputs—movement, new visual elements, louder or softer sounds, novel smells—more than sustained levels.

11   Because aesthetics operates at a prerational level, it can be disquieting. We have a love-hate relationship with the whole idea. As consumers, we enjoy sensory appeals but fear manipulation. As producers, we'd rather not work so hard to keep up with the aesthetic competition. As heirs to Plato and the Puritans, we suspect

sensory impressions as deceptive, inherently false. Aesthetics is "the power of pro-vocative surfaces," says a critic. It "speaks to the eye's mind, overshadowing matters of quality or substance."

12   But the eye's mind is identifying something genuinely valuable. Aesthetic plea-sure itself has quality and substance. The look and feel of things tap deep human instincts. We are, as Brown says, "visual, tactile creatures." We enjoy enhancing our sensory surroundings. That enjoyment is real. The trick is to appreciate aesthetic pleasure without confusing it with other values.

13   Theorist Ellen Dissanayake defines art as "making special," a behavior designed to be "sensorily and emotionally gratifying and more than strictly necessary." She argues that the instinct for "making special" is universal and innate, a part of human beings' evolved biological nature. Hers may or may not be an adequate definition of art, but it does offer a useful insight into our aesthetic age. Having spent a century or more focused primarily on other goals—solving manufacturing problems, lowering costs, making goods and services widely available, increasing convenience, saving energy—we are increasingly engaged in making our world special. More people in more aspects of life are drawing pleasure and meaning from the way their persons, places, and things look and feel. Whenever we have the chance, we're adding sensory, emotional appeal to ordinary function.

14   "Aesthetics, whether people admit it or not, is why you buy something," says a shopper purchasing a high-style iMac, its flat screen pivoting like a desk lamp on a half-spherical base. He likes the computer's features, but he particularly likes its looks. A computer doesn't have to be a nondescript box. It can express its owner's taste and personality.

15   "Deciding to buy an IBM instead of a Compaq simply because you prefer black to gray is absolutely fine as long as both machines meet your other significant criteria," a writer advises computer shoppers on the female-oriented iVillage Web site. "Not that color can't or shouldn't be a significant criterion; in truth, the mar-ket is filled with enough solid, affordable machines that you finally have the kind of freedom of choice previously reserved only for the likes of footwear." Computers all used to look pretty much the same. Now they, too, can be special.

16   A Salt Lake City grocery shopper praises her supermarket's makeover. Gone are the gray stucco exterior, harsh fluorescent lighting, and tall, narrow aisles. In their place are warm red brick, spot and track lighting, and low-rise departments of related items. The "crowning glory" is the Starbucks in the front, which provides both a welcoming aroma and a distinctive look and feel. "The experience is a lot more calm, a lot more pleasant," she says, "an extraordinary change, and a welcome one." Grocery shopping is still a chore, but at least now the environment offers something special.

17   A political writer in Washington, D.C., a city noted for its studied ignorance of style, says he pays much more attention to his clothes than he did ten or fifteen years ago, and enjoys it a lot more. "One thing I try to do is not to wear the same combination of suit, shirt, and tie in a season," he says. "It's another way of saying every day is special." Once seen as an unnecessary luxury, even a suspect indul-gence, "making special" has become a personal, social, and business imperative.

NOTES

315 *"We are by nature"* David Brown, interview with the author, November 9, 2000.

315 *"quirky underside"* Martin Eidelberg, quoted in Linda Hales, "When Designs Delight," *The Washington Post,* November 12, 1998, p. T12.

316 *As a midcentury industrial designer* Harold Van Doren, *Industrial Design: A Practical Guide to Product Design and Development,* 2nd ed. (New York: McGraw-Hill, 1954), p. 166.

317 *"The power of provocative surfaces"* Stuart Ewen, *All Consuming Images: The Politics of Style in Contemporary Culture* (New York: Basic Books, 1988), p. 2.

317 *"making special"* Ellen Dissanayake, *Homo Aestheticus: Where Art Comes From and Why* (Seattle: University of Washington Press, 1992, 1995), p. 56.

317 *"Aesthetics, whether people admit it . . . "* Dave Caldwell, quoted in Vikas Bajaj, "Electronic Manufacturers Emphasize Form with Function," *The Dallas Morning News,* April 4, 2002, p. 5D.

317 *"Deciding to buy an IBM"* Heidi Pollock, "How to Buy a Computer, Part I," iVillage, http://www.iVillage.com/click/experts/goodbuygirl/articles/0,5639,38862,00.html.

317 *"A Salt Lake City grocery shopper"* Deborah Moeller, e-mail to the author, December 27, 2001, and interview with the author, April 8, 2002.

317 *A political writer* Michael Barone, interview with the author, April 8, 2002.

Needing the Unnecessary

JAMES B. TWITCHELL

> James B. Twitchell is an English professor at the University of Florida who also teaches advertising. His interests range from Romanticism to popular commercial culture, especially shopping. Among his most recent books are *Branded Nation: The Marketing of Megachurch, College, Inc., and Museumworld* (Simon & Schuster, 2005) and *Living It Up: Our Love Affair with Luxury* (Columbia, 2002), from which the following selection was originally excerpted and published in *Reason* magazine.

THE DEMOCRATIZATION OF LUXURY

1 If you want to understand material culture at the beginning of the 21st century, you must understand the overwhelming importance of unnecessary material. If you are looking for the one unambiguous result of modern capitalism, of the industrial revolution, and of marketing, here it is. In the way we live now, you are not what you make. You are what you consume. And most of what you consume is totally unnecessary yet remarkably well made.

2 The most interesting of those superfluous objects belong in a socially constructed and ever-shifting class called luxury. Consuming those objects, objects as rich in meaning as they are low in utility, causes lots of happiness and distress. As well they should. For one can make the argument that until all necessities are had by all members of a community, no one should have luxury. More complex still is that, since the 1980s, the bulk consumers of luxury have not been the wealthy but the middle class, your next-door neighbors and their kids. And this is happening not just in the West but in many parts of the world.

3 When I was growing up in the middle class of the 1950s, luxury objects were lightly tainted with shame. You had to be a little cautious if you drove a Cadillac, wore a Rolex, or lived in a house with more than two columns out front. The rich could drip with diamonds, but you should stay dry. Movie stars could drive convertibles; you should keep your top up. If you've got it, don't flaunt it. Remember, the people surrounding you had lived through the Depression, a time that forever lit the bright lines between have-to-have, don't-need-to-have, and have-in-order-to-show-off.

4 The best definition of this old-style off-limits luxury came to me from my dad. I was just a kid, and it was my first trip to a cafeteria: Morrison's Cafeteria in Pompano Beach, Florida, February 1955. When I got to the desserts, I removed the main course from my tray and loaded up on cake and Jell-o. My dad told me to put all the desserts back but one. I said that wasn't fair. To me the whole idea of cafeteria was to have as much as you want of what you want. My dad said no, that was not the idea of cafeteria. The idea of cafeteria is that you can have just one of many choices.

LUXURIFICATION

5 Look around American culture, and you will see how wrong he was. Almost every set of consumables has a dessert at the top. And you can have as much of it as you can get on your tray or as much of it as your credit card will allow. This is

true not just for expensive products like town cars and McMansions but for every-day objects. In bottled water, for instance, there is Evian, advertised as if it were a liquor. In coffee, there's Starbucks; in ice cream, Häagen-Dazs; in sneakers, Nike; in whiskey, Johnnie Walker Blue; in credit cards, American Express Centurian; in wine, Chateau Margaux; in cigars, Arturo Fuente Hemingway; and, well, you know the rest.

6   Name the category, no matter how mundane, and you'll find a premium or, better yet, a super-premium brand at the top. And having more than you can conceivably use of such objects is not met with opprobrium but with genial accep-tance. This pattern persists regardless of class: The average number of branded sneakers for adolescent males? It's 4.8 pairs. And regardless of culture: A favorite consumer product in China? Chanel lipstick dispensers sans lipstick.

7   Basil Englis and Michael Solomon, professors of marketing in the School of Business at Rutgers University, have studied the effects of brand consumption, particularly how college students cluster around top-brand knowledge. They drew guinea pigs from undergraduate business majors at their institution and presented them with 40 cards, each containing a description of a different cluster of consumers.

8   The professors sifted the clusters to make four groups—lifestyles, if you will—representative of undergraduate society. They were Young Suburbia, Money & Brains, Smalltown Downtown, and Middle America. Then Englis and Solomon gathered images of objects from four product categories (automobiles, magazines/newspapers, toiletries, and alcoholic beverages) that fit into each group. The students were asked to put the various images together into coherent groups; they were also to state their current proximity to, or desire to be part of, each group in the future.

9   As might be expected, the Money & Brains cluster was the most popular aspirational niche. What Englis and Solomon did not expect was how specific and knowledgeable the students were about the possessions that they did not have but knew that members of that cluster needed.

10   When asked what brand of automobile they would drive, here's what they said: BMWs (53.6 percent), Mercedes (50.7), Cadillacs (30.4), Volvos (23.2), Porsches (21.7), Acuras (17.4), and Jaguars (15.9). They knew what they wanted to read: travel magazines (21.7 percent), *Vogue* (21.7), *BusinessWeek* (20.3), *Fortune* (17.9), and *GQ* (15.9). Again, this is not what they did read but what they took to be the reading material of the desired group. What they were actually reading (or so they said) were *Forbes, Barron's, The New Yorker,* and *Gourmet.* No mention of *Rolling Stone, Playboy, Spin,* or *Maxim* for this group. They certainly knew what to drink: Heineken beer (33.3 percent), expensive wines (26.1), scotch (18.8), champagne (17.4), and Beck's beer (15). They also knew what to sprinkle on their bodies: Polo (27.5 percent), Obsession (15.9), and Drakkar (15.9).

11   What the professors found was not just that birds of a feather had started to flock together, but that these young birds already knew what flock to shy away from. They were not ashamed of smoking, for instance, but of smoking the wrong brand. Their prime avoidance group corresponded to the Smalltown Downtown cluster.

12   The Money & Brainers knew a lot about the Smalltowners. They knew about favored pickup trucks, Chevys (23.2 percent) and Fords (18.8). They knew that this group reads *People* (30.4), *Sports Illustrated* (26.1), *TV Guide* (24.6), *Wrestling* (21.7), fishing magazines (20.3), and *The National Enquirer* (18.8). They assumed that Smalltowners preferred Budweiser (59.4), followed by Miller (24.6) and Coors (18.8). Essentially, the Money & Brainers had learned not just what to buy but what to avoid (or at least what to say to avoid).

13   Such shared knowledge is the basis of culture. This insight was, after all, the rationale behind a liberal arts education. John Henry Newman and Matthew Arnold argued for state-supported education in the 19th century precisely because cultural literacy meant social cohesion. No one argued that it was important to know algebraic functions or Latin etymologies or what constitutes a sonnet because such knowledge allows us to solve important social problems. We learn such matters because it is the basis of how to speak to each other, how we develop a bond of shared history and commonality. This is the secular religion of the liberal arts and sciences, what French sociologist Pierre Bourdieu calls cultural capital.

14   In our postmodern world we have, it seems, exchanged knowledge of history and science (a knowledge of production) for knowledge of products and how such products interlock to form coherent social patterns (a knowledge of consumption). Buy this and don't buy that has replaced make/learn this, don't make/learn that. After all, in the way we live now, everyone is a consumer, but not everyone is a worker. As Marcel Duchamp, sly observer of the changing scene, said, "Living is more a question of what one spends than what one makes." Thus a new denomination of cultural capital.

15   A shift in currency has clear ramifications. A producer culture focuses on the independent self of the worker: self-help, self-discipline, self-respect, self-control, self-reliance, self-interest. Responsibility is situated in the individual: Can she get work? A consumer culture, however, focuses on community: Fit in, don't stand out. Be cool. The standard of judgment becomes the ability to interact effectively with others, to win their affection and admiration—to merge with others of the same lifestyle. Can he consume the right brands? . . .

OVER THE TOP

16   I must say that I found most of the luxury objects that I've looked at, from Patek Philippe watches to Porsche Turbos to the men's room of the Bellagio Hotel, to be a little over the top. But I am not so oblivious to the world around me that I can't appreciate how important the new luxury has become. And I can't overlook how high-end consumption promises to do exactly what critics of the stuff have always yearned for, namely, to bring us together, often traumatically. Yes, indeed, the transgenerational poor are excluded, as the bottom fifth of our population has not budged an inch in the luxe explosion. Yet more people than ever are entering the much-vaunted global village because of consumption, not despite it.

17   In fact, one could argue, as Dinesh D'Souza, Virginia Postrel, and W. Michael Cox and Richard Alm have recently done, that the aspiration of the poor to get at

these unnecessary goods has done more than any social program to motivate some of the disenchanted to become enfranchised. While one may be distressed at seeing a dish antenna atop a ramshackle house or a Caddie out front, the yearning to have superfluous badges of affluence may promise a more lasting peace around the world than any religion or political system has ever delivered. I don't mean to overlook the complexities here.

18   This is not a universal phenomenon, as the al Qaeda have wickedly demonstrated. Some of the world's poor are most certainly not becoming better off in absolute or relative terms. I only want to say that, given a choice between being mugged for your sneakers or having your ethnic or religious heritage cleansed, the lust for sneakers may prove a more lasting way to improve the general lot of humanity.

19   Let's face it. In the world that I grew up in, your religion, your family name, the color of your skin, your language skills, your gender, where you went to school, your accent, and your marriage partner were doing the work that luxury consumption does now. My dad went to Exeter, Williams, and Harvard Med, and he never drove anything fancier than a Plymouth. He never had to. Today I wouldn't go to a doctor who drove a Plymouth. I would figure that if she doesn't drive a Lexus, she is having trouble with her practice.

20   So I admit the ugly truth. After spending the last few years trying to understand the pull of the material world, I am far more sympathetic to its blandishments and far more forgiving of its excesses. The democratization of luxury has been the single most important marketing phenomenon of modern times. And it has profound political implications. It may not be as bad as some lifestyle scolds make it out to be. In its own way it is a fair, albeit often wasteful, system, not just of objects but of meaning. Don't get me wrong: It's not that I came to mock and stayed to pray, but I do feel that getting and spending has some actual worth. Nobody checks the number of vowels in your name, or the color of your skin, or whether you know the difference between *like* and *as* when you are buying your Prada parka—that's got to mean something.

21   Although luxury has become a mallet with which one pounds the taste of others, this misses some essential points. One is that humans are consumers by nature. We are tool users because we like to use what tool using can produce. In other words, tools are not the ends but the means. So too materialism does not crowd out spiritualism; spiritualism is more likely a substitute when objects are scarce. When we have few things, we make the next world luxurious. When we have plenty, we enchant the objects around us.

22   Second, consumers are rational. They are often fully aware that they are more interested in consuming aura than objects, sizzle than steak, meaning than material. In fact, if you ask them—as academic critics are usually loath to do—they are quite candid in explaining that the Nike swoosh, the Polo pony, the Guess? label, the DKNY logo are what they are after. They are not duped by advertising, packaging, branding, fashion, and merchandising. They actively seek and enjoy the status that surrounds the object, especially when they are young.

23   Third, we need to question the standard argument that consumption of opu-luxe almost always leads to disappointment. Admittedly, the circular route from desire to purchase to disappointment to renewed desire is never-ending, but we may follow it because the other route—from melancholy to angst—is worse. In other words, in a world emptied of inherited values, consuming what looks to be overpriced fripperies may be preferable to consuming nothing.

24   Finally, we need to rethink the separation between production and consumption, for they are more alike than separate and occur not at different times and places but simultaneously. Instead of wanting less luxury, we might find that just the opposite—the paradoxical luxury for all—is a suitable goal of communal aspiration. After all, luxury before all else is a social construction, and understanding its social ramifications may pave the way for a new appreciation of what has become a characteristic contradiction of our time, the necessary consumption of the unnecessary.

The Grill-Buying Guy

DAVID BROOKS

> David Brooks, a graduate of University of Chicago, is a regular columnist for the *New York Times,* writing with what he describes as a "Hamiltonian or Giuliani" conservative viewpoint. His two books of social commentary are *Bobos in Paradise: The New Upper Class and How They Got There* (Touchstone, 2000) and *On Paradise Drive: How We Live Now (And Always Have) in the Future Tense* (Simon & Schuster, 2004). Although he pokes fun at consumers' behavior, Brooks reveals a deep appreciation for Americans' work ethic, ingenuity, and tireless pursuit of their dreams. This selection is from *On Paradise Drive.*

1   I don't know if you've ever seen the expression of a man who is about to buy a first-class barbecue grill. He walks into Home Depot or Lowe's or one of the other mega-hardware complexes, and his eyes are glistening with a faraway visionary zeal, like one of those old prophets gazing into the promised land. His lips are parted and twitching slightly.

2   Inside the megastore, the man adopts the stride American men fall into when in the presence of large amounts of lumber. He heads over to the barbecue grills, just past the racks of affordable house-plan books, in the yard-machinery section. They are arrayed magnificently next to the vehicles that used to be known as riding mowers but are now known as lawn tractors, because to call them riding mowers doesn't fully convey the steroidized M1 tank power of the things. The man approaches the barbecue grills with a trancelike expression suggesting that he has cast aside all the pains and imperfections of this world and is approaching the gateway to a higher dimension. In front of him is a scattering of massive steel-coated reactors with names like Broilmaster P3, Thermidor, and the Weber Genesis, because in America it seems perfectly normal to name a backyard barbecue grill after a book of the Bible.

3   The items in this cooking arsenal flaunt enough metal to survive a direct nuclear assault. Patio Man goes from machine to machine comparing their various features—the cast-iron/porcelain-coated cooking surfaces, the 328,000-BTU heat-generating capacities, the 2,000-degree tolerance linings, multiple warming racks, lava-rock containment dishes, or built-in electrical meat thermometers. Certain profound questions flow through his mind. Is a 542-cubic-inch grilling surface enough, considering he might someday get the urge to roast a bison? Can he handle the TEC Sterling II grill, which can hit temperatures of 1,600 degrees, thereby causing his dinner to spontaneously combust? Though the matte-steel overcoat resists scratching, doesn't he want a polished steel surface so he can glance down and admire his reflection while performing the suburban manliness rituals such as brushing tangy teriyaki sauce on meat slabs with his right hand while clutching a beer can in an NFL foam insulator in his left?

4   Pretty soon a large salesperson in an orange vest—looking like an SUV in human form—comes up to him and says, "Howyadoin'," which is "May I help you?" in

Home Depot talk. Patio Man, who has so much lust in his heart, it is all he can do to keep from climbing up on one of these machines and whooping rodeo-style with joy, still manages to respond appropriately. He grunts inarticulately and nods toward the machines. Careful not to make eye contact at any point, the two manly suburban men have a brief exchange of pseudo-scientific grill argot that neither of them understands, and pretty soon Patio Man comes to the reasoned conclusion that it would make sense to pay a little extra for a grill with V-shaped metal baffles, ceramic rods, and a side-mounted smoker box.

5   But none of this talk matters. The guy will end up buying the grill with the best cup holders. All major purchases of consumer durable goods these days ultimately come down to which model has the most impressive cup holders.

6   Having selected his joy machine, Patio Man heads for the cash register, Visa card trembling in his hand. All up and down the line are tough ex-football-playing guys who are used to working outdoors. They hang pagers and cell phones from their belts (in case a power line goes down somewhere) and wear NASCAR sunglasses, mullet haircuts, and faded T-shirts that they have ripped the sleeves off of to keep their arm muscles exposed and their armpit hair fully ventilated. Here and there are a few innately Office Depot guys who are trying to blend in with their more manly Home Depot brethren, and not ask Home Depot inappropriate questions, such as "Does this tool belt make my butt look fat?"

7   At the checkout, Patio Man is told that some minion will forklift the grill over to the loading dock around back. He is once again glad that he's driving that Yukon XL so he can approach the loading-dock guys as a co-equal in the manly fraternity of Those Who Haul Things.

8   As he signs the credit-card slip, with its massive total price, his confidence suddenly collapses, but it is revived as wonderful grill fantasies dance in his imagination:

9   There he is atop the uppermost tier of his multilevel backyard dining and recreational area. This is the kind of deck Louis XIV would have had if Sun Gods had had decks. In his mind's eye, Patio Man can see himself coolly flipping the garlic-and-pepper T-bones on the front acreage of his new grill while carefully testing the citrus-tarragon trout filets simmering fragrantly on the rear. On the lawn below, his kids Haley and Cody frolic on the weedless community lawn that is mowed twice weekly courtesy of the people who run Monument Crowne Preserve, his townhome community.

10   Haley, the fourteen-year-old daughter, is a Travel-Team Girl who spends her weekends playing midfield against similarly ponytailed, strongly calved soccer marvels such as herself. Cody, ten, is a Buzz-Cut Boy whose naturally blond hair has been cut to lawnlike stubble, and the little that's left is highlighted an almost phosphorescent white. Cody's wardrobe is entirely derivative of fashions he has seen watching the X Games. Patio Man can see the kids playing with child-safe lawn darts alongside a gaggle of their cul-de-sac friends, a happy gathering of Haleys and Codys and Corys and Britneys. It's a brightly colored scene—Abercrombie & Fitch pink spaghetti-strap tops on the girls and ankle-length canvas shorts and laceless Nikes on the boys. Patio Man notes somewhat uncomfortably that in

America today the average square yardage of boyswear grows and grows, while the square inches in the girls' outfits shrinks and shrinks. The boys carry so much fabric they look like skateboarding Bedouins, and the girls look like preppy prostitutes.

11   Nonetheless, Patio Man envisions a Saturday-evening party—his adult softball-team buddies lounging on his immaculate deck furniture, watching him with a certain moist envy as he mans the grill. They are moderately fit, sockless men in Docksiders, chinos, and Tommy Bahama muted Hawaiian shirts. Their wives, trim Jennifer Aniston lookalikes, wear capris and sleeveless tops, which look great on them owing to their countless hours on the weight machines at Spa Lady. . . .

12   They are wonderful people. Patio Man can envision his own wife, Cindy, the Realtor Mom, circulating among them serving drinks, telling parent-teacher-conference stories and generally stirring up the hospitality; he, Patio Man, masterfully wields his extra-wide fish spatula while absorbing the aroma of imported hickory chips— again, to the silent admiration of all. The sun is shining. The people are friendly. The men are no more than twenty-five pounds overweight, which is the socially acceptable male-paunch level in upwardly mobile America, and the children are well adjusted. This vision of domestic bliss is what Patio Man has been shooting for all his life.

False Connections

ALEX KOTLOWITZ

Alex Kotlowitz is best known as a journalist concerned with issues of race and poverty in America. His book *There Are No Children Here: The Story of Two Boys Growing Up in the Other America* (Knopf, 1992) won many prizes for journalism and was selected by the New York Public Library as one of the 150 most important books of the century. His more recent books are *The Other Side of the River* (Knopf, 1999) and a book about Chicago, *Never a City So Real* (Crown, 2004). Kotlowitz has been a writer-in-residence at Northwestern University and a visiting professor at University of Notre Dame. The selection below was originally published in Roger Rosenblatt's anthology *Consuming Desires: Consumption, Culture, and the Pursuit of Happiness* (Island Press, 1999).

1   A drive down Chicago's Madison Street, moving west from the lake, is a short lesson in America's fault lines of race and class. The first mile runs through the city's downtown—or the Loop, as it's called locally—past high-rises that house banks and law firms, advertising agencies and investment funds. The second mile, once lined by flophouses and greasy diners, has hitched onto its neighbor to the east, becoming a mecca for artists and new, hip restaurants, a more affordable appendage to the Loop. And west from there, past the United Center, home to the Chicago Bulls, the boulevard descends into the abyssal lows of neighborhoods where work has disappeared. Buildings lean like punch-drunk boxers. Makers of plywood do big business here, patching those same buildings' open wounds. At dusk, the gangs claim ownership to the corners and hawk their wares, whatever is the craze of the moment, crack or smack or reefer. It's all for sale. Along one stretch, young women, their long, bare legs shimmering under the lamplight, smile and beckon and mumble short, pithy descriptions of the pleasures they promise to deliver.

2   Such is urban decay. Such are the remains of the seemingly intractable, distinctly American version of poverty, a poverty not only "of the pocket" but also, as Mother Teresa said when she visited this section of the city, "of the spirit."

3   What is most striking about this drive down Madison, though, is that so few whites make it. Chicago's West Side, like other central-city neighborhoods, sits apart from everything and everyone else. Its inhabitants have become geographically and spiritually isolated from all that surrounds them, islands unto themselves. Even the violence—which, myth has it, threatens us all—is contained within its borders. Drug dealers shoot drug dealers. Gang members maul gang members. And the innocents, the passersby who get caught in the crossfire, are their neighbors and friends. It was that isolation which so struck me when I first began to spend time at the Henry Horner Homes, a Chicago public housing complex that sits along that Madison Street corridor. Lafeyette and Pharoah, the two boys I wrote about in my book *There Are No Children Here,* had never been to the Loop, one mile away. They'd never walked the halls of the Art Institute of Chicago or felt the spray from the Buckingham Fountain. They'd never ogled the sharks at the John G. Shedd Aquarium or stood in the shadow of the stuffed pachyderms at the Field Museum. They'd never been to the suburbs. They'd never been to the countryside. In fact, until we stayed at a hotel one summer on their first fishing trip, they'd never felt the steady

steam of a shower. (Henry Horner's apartments had only bathtubs.) At one point, the boys, so certain that their way of life was the only way of life, insisted that my neighborhood, a gentrified community on the city's North Side, had to be controlled by gangs. They knew nothing different.

4   And yet children like Lafeyette and Pharoah do have a connection to the American mainstream: it is as consumers that inner-city children, otherwise so disconnected from the world around them, identify themselves not as ghetto kids or project kids but as Americans or just plain kids. And they are as much consumers as they are the consumed; that is, they mimic white America while white America mimics them. "Inner-city kids will embrace a fashion item as their own that shows they have a connection, and then you'll see the prep school kids reinvent it, trying to look hip-hop," says Sarah Young, a consultant to businesses interested in tapping the urban market. "It's a cycle."[1] A friend, a black nineteen-year-old from the city's West Side, suggests that this dynamic occurs because the inner-city poor equate classiness with suburban whites while those same suburban whites equate hipness with the inner-city poor. If he's right, it suggests that commercialism may be our most powerful link, one that in the end only accentuates and prolongs the myths we have built up about each other.

5   Along Madison Street, halfway between the Loop and the city's boundary, sits an old, worn-out shopping strip containing small, transient stores. They open and close almost seasonally—balloons mark the openings; "Close-Out Sale" banners mark the closings—as the African American and Middle Eastern immigrant owners ride the ebb and flow of unpredictable fashion tastes. GQ Sports. Dress to Impress. Best Fit. Chic Classics. Dream Team. On weekend afternoons, the makeshift mall is thronged with customers blithely unaware that store ownership and names may have changed since their last visit. Young mothers guiding their children by the shoulders and older women seeking a specific purchase pick their way through packs of teenagers who laugh and clown, pulling and pushing one another into the stores. Their whimsical tastes are the subject of intense curiosity, longing, and marketing surveys on the part of store owners and corporate planners.

     On a recent spring afternoon, as I made my way down Madison Street toward Tops and Bottoms, one of the area's more popular shops, I detected the unmistakable sweet odor of marijuana. Along the building's side, two teenage boys toked away at cigar-sized joints, called blunts. The store is long and narrow; its walls are lined with shoes and caps and its center is packed with shirts, jeans, and leather jackets. The owner of the store, a Palestinian immigrant, recognized me from my previous visits there with Lafeyette and Pharoah. "You're a probation officer, right?" he asked. I told him what my connection was with the boys. He completed a sale of a black Starter skullcap and then beckoned me toward the back of the store, where we could talk without distraction.

7   Behind him, an array of nearly 200 assorted shoes and sneakers lined the wall from floor to ceiling. There were the predictable brands: Nike, Fila, and Reebok, the shoes that have come to define (and nearly bankrupt) a generation. There were the heavy boots by Timberland and Lugz that have become popular among urban teens. But it was the arrangement of shoes directly in front of me that the proprietor

pointed to, a collection of Hush Puppies. "See that?" he asked. "It's totally white-bread." Indeed, Hush Puppies, once of earth tones and worn by preppies, have caught on among urban black teens—and the company has responded in kind, producing the shoes in outrageous, gotta-look-at-me colors such as crayon orange and fire-engine red. I remember the first time Pharoah appeared in a pair of lime green Hush Puppies loafers—I was dumbfounded. But then I thought of his other passions: Tommy Hilfiger shirts, Coach wallets, Guess? jeans. They were the fashions of the economically well heeled, templates of those who had "made it." Pharoah, who is now off at college, ultimately found his path. But for those who are left behind, these fashions are their "in." They give them cachet. They link them to a more secure, more prosperous world, a world in which they have not been able to participate—except as consumers.

8   Sarah Young, whose clients include the company that manufactures Hush Puppies, suggests that "for a lot of these kids, what they wear is who they are because that's all they have to connect them to the rest of the larger community. It marks their status because there's not a lot else."[2]

9   It's a false status, of course. They hold on to the idea that to "make it" means to consume at will, to buy a $100 Coach wallet or an $80 Tommy Hilfiger shirt. And these brand-name companies, knowing they have a good thing going, capitalize on their popularity among the urban poor, a group that despite its economic difficulties represents a surprisingly lucrative market. The companies gear their advertising to this market segment. People such as Sarah Young nurture relationships with rap artists, who they lure into wearing certain clothing items. When the company that makes Hush Puppies was looking to increase their presence in the urban market, Young helped persuade Wyclef Jean, a singer with the Fugees, to wear powder blue Bridgeport chukkas, which bear a sneaking resemblance to the Wallabee shoes familiar to members of my generation. In a recent issue of *Vibe,* a magazine aimed at the hip-hop market, rappers Beenie Man and Bounty Killer are pictured posing in Ralph Lauren hats and Armani sweaters, sandwiched between photographs of other rappers decked out in Calvin Klein sunglasses and Kenneth Cole shoes. The first three full-page advertisements in that same issue are for Hilfiger's athletic line, Coach handbags (with jazz singer Cassandra Wilson joyfully walking along with her Coach bag slung over her shoulder), and Perry Ellis casual wear (with a black man and three young boys lounging on the beach). This, as Pharoah told me, represents class—and, as Young suggested, the one connection that children growing up amid the ruins of the inner city have to a more prosperous, more secure world. It is as consumers that they claim citizenship. And yet that Coach handbag or that Tommy Hilfiger or Perry Ellis shirt changes nothing of the cruel realities of growing up poor and black. It reminds me of the murals painted on abandoned buildings in the South Bronx: pictures of flowers, window shades, and curtains, and the interiors of tidy rooms. As Jonathan Kozol observes in his book *Amazing Grace,* "the pictures have been done so well that when you look, the first time, you imagine that you're seeing into people's homes—pleasant-looking homes, in fact, that have a distinctly middle-class appearance."[3]

10   But the urban poor are more than just consumers. They help drive fashions as well. The Tommy Hilfiger clothing line, aimed initially at preppies, became hot in the inner city, pushed in large part by rap artists who took to the clothing maker's stylish, colorful vestments. A 1997 article in *Forbes* magazine suggests that Hilfiger's 47 percent rise in earnings over the first nine months of its fiscal year 1996–1997 had much to do with the clothing line's popularity among the kinds of kids who shop Chicago's Madison Street.[4] Suddenly, Tommy Hilfiger became cool, not only among the urban teens but also among their counterparts in the suburbs. "That gives them a sense of pride, that they're bringing a style to a new height," Sarah Young suggests.[5] Thus, those who don't have much control over other aspects of their life find comfort in having at least some control over something—style.

11   There's another facet to this as well: the romanticization of urban poverty by some white teens. In St. Joseph, Michigan, a nearly all-white town of 9,000 in the state's southwestern corner, a group of teens mimicked the mannerisms and fashions of their neighbors across the river in Benton Harbor, Michigan, a nearly all-black town that has been economically devastated by the closing of the local factories and foundries. This cadre of kids called themselves "wiggers." A few white boys identified themselves with one of the Benton Harbor gangs, and one small band was caught carrying out holdups with a BB gun. A local police detective laughingly called them "wannabes." At St. Joseph High School, the wiggers greeted one another in the hallways with a high five or a twitch of the head. "Hey, Nigger, wha's up?" they'd inquire. "Man, just chillin'."

12   But it was through fashions—as consumers—that they most clearly identified themselves with their peers across the way. They dressed in the hip-hop fashion made popular by M. C. Hammer and other rap artists, wearing blue jeans big enough for two, the crotch down at their knees. (The beltless, pants-falling-off-hips style originated, many believe, in prison, where inmates must forgo belts.) The guys wore Starter jackets and hats, the style at the time. The girls hung braided gold necklaces around their necks and styled their hair in finger waves or braids. For these teens, the life of ghetto kids is edgy, gutsy, risky—all that adolescents crave. But do they know how edgy, how gutsy, how risky? They have never had to comfort a dying friend, bleeding from the head because he was on the wrong turf. They have never sat in a classroom where the desks are arranged so that no student will be hit by falling plaster. They have never had to say "Yes, Sir" and "No, Sir," as a police officer, dripping with sarcasm, asks, "Nigger, where'd you get the money for such a nice car?" From a safe distance—as consumers—they can believe they are hip, hip being defined as what they see in their urban counterparts. With their jeans sagging off their boxer shorts, with their baseball caps worn to the side, with their high-tops unlaced, they find some connection, though in the end it is a false bond.

13   It is as consumers that poor black children claim membership to the larger community. It is as purchasers of the talismans of success that they can believe they've transcended their otherwise miserable situation. In the late 1980s, as the drug trade began to flourish in neighborhoods such as Chicago's West Side, the vehicle of choice for these big-time entrepreneurs was the Chevrolet Blazer, an icon

of suburban stability. As their communities were unraveling, in part because of their trade, they sought a connection to an otherwise stable life. And they sought it in the only way they knew how, the only way available to them: as consumers. Inner-city teens are eager to participate in society; they want to belong.

14   And for the white teens like those in St. Joseph, who, like all adolescents, want to feel that they're on the edge, what better way than to build some connection—however manufactured—to their contemporaries across the river who must negotiate that vertical drop every day? By purchasing, in complete safety, all the accoutrements associated with skirting that fall, they can believe that they've been there, that they've experienced the horrors and pains of growing up black and poor. Nothing, of course, could be further from the truth. They know nothing of the struggles their neighbors endure.

15   On the other hand, fashions in the end are just that—fashions. Sometimes kids yearn for baggy jeans or a Tommy Hilfiger shirt not because of what it represents but because it is the style of their peers. Those "wiggers," for example, may equate the sagging pants with their neighbors across the river, but kids a few years younger are mimicking them as much as their black counterparts. Fashions grow long limbs that, in the end, are only distantly connected to their roots.

16   Take that excursion down Madison Street—and the fault lines will become abundantly clear. One can't help but marvel at the spiritual distance between those shopping at Tops and Bottoms on the blighted West Side and those browsing the pricey department stores in the robust downtown. And yet many of the children have one eye trained down Madison Street, those on each side watching their counterparts and thinking they know the others' lives. Their style of dress mimics that of the others. But they're being cheated. They don't know. They have no idea. Those checking out the array of Hush Puppies at Tops and Bottoms think they have the key to making it, to becoming full members of this prosperous nation. And those trying on the jeans wide enough for two think they know what it means to be hip, to live on the edge. And so, in lieu of building real connections—by providing opportunities or rebuilding communities—we have found some common ground as purchasers of each other's trademarks. At best, that link is tenuous; at worst, it's false. It lets us believe that we are connected when the distance, in fact, is much farther than anyone cares to admit.

NOTES

1. Sarah Young, telephone interview with the author, January 1998.
2. Ibid.
3. Jonathan Kozol, *Amazing Grace: The Lives of Children and the Conscience of a Nation* (New York: HarperPerennial, 1996).
4. Joshua Levine, "Baad Sells," *Forbes* 159, no. 8 (April 21, 1997): 142.
5. Sarah Young, telephone interview with the author, January 1998.

A Sense of Belonging among Belongings

STEPHANIE ROSENBLOOM

> The following selection is an informative article about Zebo, a Web site that describes itself as The World's Largest Repository of What People Own. Members, who are mostly in their teens and early twenties, socialize by posting lists of what they own or hope to own. Rosenbloom's article appeared in the *New York Times* in September 2006.

1 Baxter C., 13, owns a Yamaha dirt bike. Hayley J., 19, has pink Converse sneakers. Laurie H., 16, amassed a sizable Pez dispenser collection.

2 All of them have profiles on Zebo.com, a new Web site devoted to lists of everyday possessions of young consumers, with postings from the United States, Canada, Britain and Ireland and as far across the globe as the Philippines, Australia and New Zealand.

3 If the Internet encourages people to share with the world the contents of their souls, Zebo encourages them to share the contents of their homes. It is "MTV Cribs" for the masses. Minimalists need not log in.

4 "It was so different and interesting," said Kara Valeriano, 19, a student at the University of San Francisco, who is a member. "It was kind of fun just listing your own things."

5 Zebo.com, which went live last Tuesday, is neither salacious nor gossipy. The lists of strangers' possessions is about as interesting as a FreshDirect order. Yet some four million people have joined the free site since January, during its private beta test, according to Roy de Souza, Zebo's founder and chief executive. Most of them are 16 to 25, he said. "The older generation find it a bit odd," said Mr. de Souza, who is based in San Francisco. "The younger people are very keen to display this stuff for their friends."

6 But why? People don't normally compile a list of their possessions for reasons other than to file an insurance claim or to compose a rap song—unless they are extreme materialists on the level of Veruca Salt, the spoiled rich girl in "Charlie and the Chocolate Factory."

7 The youngest generations of consumers are going even further and making those lists public. It is almost a declaration of the maxim "He who has the most toys wins."

8 Mr. de Souza, though, sees it somewhat differently. "For the youth, you are what you own," he said. "They list these things because it defines them." Compare it to gleaning something about someone's personality by reviewing their book or music collection.

9 Some Zebo members said they like to list what they own because they enjoy maintaining an evolving inventory of what they have and what they crave; the site allows users to do both. Karly Mossberg, 18, a student at the San Francisco Art Institute, said she likes to make notes in her online profile about the things she desires. "I'm obsessed with shopping and I'm also really organized," she said. "It's like my daily planner."

10 But even more interesting for this first crop of site users is seeing what other people list and want. And because of that, Zebo is in many ways a social networking

site, with several of the same features as MySpace. There are member profiles that include each user's relationship status, interests and location, along with photographs and links to their friends. Members can also fill in blanks on their profiles about their "celebrity style" and the shopping areas in which they feel they need improvement.

11   But while visitors to MySpace are greeted with the saccharine "a place for friends" tagline, visitors to Zebo are greeted with a brusque: "Hi. What do you own?" That is to be expected, as Zebo, after all, is also a business. While billing itself as "the world's largest repository of what people own," it is designed to be a shopping community and e-commerce site. Mr. de Souza plans to add more product links, sell advertising and regularly publish data about the habits and preferences of the young people who use the site.

12   But the first goal was to build an online community, said Mr. de Souza, who has put his marketing and advertising expertise to use for companies like Hewlett-Packard and Charles Schwab. And in doing that, he is preparing for the future. Zebo's profiles already have spaces for members to describe how they like to shop. (There is a box for them to blog about shopping, too.) And the site enables them to search for items they want and to solicit advice from one another.

13   Kris Browning, 26, of Jackson, Mich., said she likes to check out whether her friends have purchased anything new and to peruse their wish lists. "It's great," she said. "You can see what your friends like and you can get them birthday presents or Christmas presents." One member, Julianna E., 17, wants an engagement ring ("eventually"), a greenhouse full of orchids and rooms of Crate & Barrel furniture. Hector E., 18, wants an Xbox 360. Michael B., 20, wants hydraulics for his car so it will bounce.

14   Some people just want a girlfriend. And perhaps one day Zebo will give Match .com a run for its money. A man with a 42-inch plasma television could fall for a woman with a Panasonic DVD recorder and live materialistically ever after. . . .

15   Zebo (the name was chosen in part because it is a short, catchy Web address) is owned by Zedo Inc., an Internet and advertising technology company based in San Francisco. The site's first members were enlisted by advertisements on Google and invitations that members of a former e-commerce Web site sent to their friends.

16   In their profiles, many users explain why they joined. Some were attracted by Zebo's theme, citing "product advice"— or, as 11-year-old Reina G. put it, "Shopping duhh!" But many said they joined Zebo for the same reasons a person might join MySpace: making friends and networking.

17   So far, Zebo is almost wholesome. Its members' primary vice is coveting. It is like MySpace, Ms. Mossberg said, but "without the creepy part."

QUESTIONS FOR DISCUSSION

1. Virginia Postrel argues in paragraph 4 that the aesthetic imperative is not limited to the "social, economic, or artistic elite . . ." but pervades our consumer society at all levels. What examples of style does she give in this selection, and how well do they support her argument? How would you describe the relationship between "the aesthetic imperative" and a society's standard of living?

2. Discuss Virginia Postrel's definition of aesthetics as presented in paragraphs 6–12. What possible criticisms might people have about the increased importance of aesthetics in "people, places, and things" these days? What criticisms can you think of that are not mentioned here? How does Virginia Postrel answer the critics of aesthetics?

3. James Twitchell shows that materialism has taken the place of the things that used to give meaning to life in an earlier day, such as in the lifetime of his father: family, religion, education, work. How compatible are materialistic values with these older ways of building a meaningful life?

4. What is Alex Kotlowitz's complaint about rich and poor teenage subcultures borrowing each other's styles?

5. The Zebo Web site encourages a kind of community based on shared knowledge, such as James Twitchell describes in his essay in paragraphs 13–15. Visit the Web site at <www.zebo.com>. How would you describe the community that forms there? If you are familiar with MySpace or Facebook, how would you compare those online communities with what you find at Zebo? Would you agree with Stephanie Rosenbloom's assessment that Zebo is "almost wholesome" compared to MySpace?

SUGGESTIONS FOR WRITING

For Inquiry and Convincing (or Mediating)

James Twitchell and Alex Kotlowitz have contrasting views about whether buying similar brands and products is a unifying force in society. Does poor people's desire for high-end products bring them into mainstream culture, or does it offer them a false sense of belonging? Make your own case for the viewpoint you think holds the most truth, or write a mediatory essay showing how each writer's position holds some truth. You may want to do additional research, such as, How fluid is the economic status of the poor population in America? What causes people to remain in conditions such as Kotlowitz describes?

For Inquiry and Persuasion

Virginia Postrel and James Twitchell do not mention the impact of consumer spending on the environment. Look into some particular aspect of the consumer society to determine its impact on the Earth's environment. If you can see a need for people to reduce their consumption in some area that is not often discussed in the media, write a persuasive essay to raise people's awareness and move them to change their spending.

SECTION 2: THE MESSAGES OF ADVERTISING
Overview

In the first section of this chapter, writers talked about the meaning of products in a consumer society. Consumers buy a product for its meaning, for what it says to them and about them. And much of the meaning of products comes from advertising, the focus of the readings in this section. Advertisements tell us very little about the product itself; instead, they associate the product with a targeted audience's values, emotions, and aspirations. Some people deny the power of advertising, saying they are not influenced by it, but evidence of its power is undeniable. In the United States, over $150 billion is spent on advertising each year, as much as the total national expenditure on higher education.

One issue connected with advertising in a consumer society is the question, "Does advertising manipulate people into buying things against their better judgment?" It uses emotional appeals, suggesting that a product will help us find love, success, and personal fulfillment. But what happens when people buy the product and find that the ads made false promises? Critics argue that repeatedly discovering the broken promises of advertising, people become depressed and cynical.

Another issue addressed in this section is the impact of advertising on values and behavior. Besides showing us products, ads show us images of the good life. Some would argue that those images simply reflect values already present in a society; others would argue that the images affect the society, influencing people to accept the values implied in the ads. Jean Kilbourne argues that advertising both reflects and affects dangerous attitudes toward girls and women, leading to mental health problems and eating disorders. But men are no longer immune from media-induced body-image dissatisfaction. Now they compare themselves to the buff guys in commercial messages and engage in their own risky behavior to achieve perfection, the topic of Alissa Quart's essay "X-Large Boys."

How I Bought My Red Miata

JAMES B. TWITCHELL

You have already met James Twitchell if you read the preceding section of this case-book where his essay "Needing the Unnecessary" appears. If you have not already, read the headnote about Twitchell on page 319. The following selection comes from another of his books, *Lead Us into Temptation: The Triumph of American Materialism* (Columbia University Press, 1999).

All our wants, beyond those which a very moderate income will supply, are purely imaginary.

—Henry St. John, 1743

Things, as such, become goods as soon as the human mind recognizes them as means suitable for the promotion of human purposes.

—Carl Menger, 1871

1   . . . When my daughters were little they would go with me to the grocery store. We would start as friends, and before a few aisles had passed we would be at each other's throats. "Gimme this, I want that, can we have these?"—it would go on and on until, by the vegetables, I would lose control and things would degenerate into Kmart Khaos. "No, no, a thousand nos," I would yell at them. "No, you can't have that. No, I won't buy you that." This didn't work, and by the time we had reached the checkout line, they had gotten much of what they had sought.

2   To stop the demoralizing defeat I tried to teach them about consumption. I developed The Nerminological Laws of Consumption, and I drilled these so-called laws into them so that I could later say, "What Nerminological law have you just broken?" whenever they asked for anything.

3   Here are the rules. First, isolate the need. Do you need this thing or do you just want it? Don't let *needs* be confused with *wants*. Next, shop around. Check out the competition. Do your research. Third, can you afford this? Check current and anticipated cash flow. And last, once you have decided, can you read the instructions on how to use it properly? Why buy a toy you can't assemble? The success of such a system was not so much that it was logical but that it took so long to go through that once they had come to the instruction part, we were out the door. I would live to regret my explanation of what goes on in the Land of the Nermies ruled by the inexorable Nerminological Laws.

4   It happened about ten years ago. I bought a Mazda Miata. This is a snappy little red sports car that twelve-year-old boys really like, but chubby, balding fifty-year-olds usually buy. My daughters like driving it, but better, they like asking me which of the Nerminological Laws I followed when I bought it. Did I need a car when I biked to work? Did I need a car that seats only two? Did I really shop around? Could I afford it on my schoolteacher salary? Did I even know how to drive it properly? If so, why did I brake during cornering instead of accelerating? Could I fix it? Did I even know where the battery was hidden? Clearly, they enjoyed seeing me hoisted by my own petard.

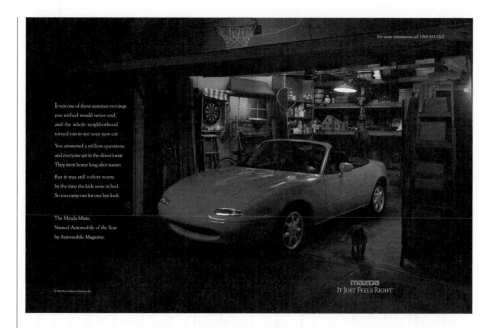

5   Although this car has given me much pleasure, I still can't figure out exactly why I bought it. I know how to buy stuff. I'm fully mature. I have a 401(k) plan. When I was growing up my parents subscribed to *Consumer Reports,* and I learned how to read all the little bulls-eye symbols telling you if this was a good deal or a so-so one. So what happened?

6   I bought the car because of an advertisement. The ad itself is not complex. In fact, it is the standard "product as hero" ad that we have all seen a thousand times. There stage center, lit from behind like a haloed angel, is this thing in your garage. If you are middle-aged, the garage is clearly from your early adolescence, when you were moving out of your room and mixing your toys with the stuff of your parents. But wait! That stuff in the pictured garage is not your dad's stuff—those are not his toys, they are yours. Dad didn't grow up with a whiffle ball, a dart board, the teddy bear, the metronome (aargh!), the dollhouse, that bike.

7   The maudlin text below the icon makes it clear. All this is/was yours:

> It was one of those summer evenings you wished would never end, and the whole neighborhood turned out to see your new car. You answered a million questions, and everyone sat in the driver's seat. They went home long after sunset.

8   In an interesting kind of temporal dislocation the "you" is in the past tense. This is the "you" of your childhood, the you who rushed downtown each September to see what the new cars looked like, the you who dreamed about getting an MG, an Austin Healey 3000, or maybe a Triumph. It would be red, or maybe English

racing green. When someone had a car like that what could you do but just stand there and look at it? There was really nothing you could say.[1]

9   The last line in the copy pulls the plug. "But it was still T-shirt warm by the time the kids were in bed. So you came out for one last look." The "you" as observer has become the "you" as owner. It's yours now. This missing part of your past, this thing that always belonged to someone else, is yours. Little wonder the car is positioned and lit like a holy relic. It's coming at you. All you have to do is grasp it.

10   What separates this ad from the usual automotive pitch is its claim on memory. The more usual claim for sports cars is sexual: Get this car, get that girl. So the sports car is usually photographed out in the rugged countryside, the sport himself is young and virile, and the chick by his side just can't stop looking at him. In advertising lingo this is called the aspirational sell: use the product and everyone will see what a real man you are.

11   What is important about the Miata ad is that there is no one at the wheel and no dreamy chick flapping her lashes at him. This driver's seat is vacant. You've always wanted to sit there. Now you can. Here as my colleagues might say, is nostalgic onanism.[2]

12   Although I had "new-car fever" (a common enough strain of affluenza), the object was difficult to consume. Here's why. I teach school. I wear khaki pants. I had a green book bag in graduate school. I am a company man. I buy my cars from Volvo or Saab, not because I like these cars—I don't. They are built to be ugly and are no fun. But they are part of the uniform. They are from Sweden, for goodness' sake, the Valhalla of academic liberalism. If I bought the Miata I was not just going to lose my affiliation with my PRIZM group. I was going over to a different group, to a group I abhorred. If I bought this car I was going to become . . . a yuppie!

13   At the time I was making my decision, yuppies were the group du jour of marketers and the group de résistance for all the rest of us. Yuppies were disgusting. What made them disgusting was their lack of reticence in the displaying of commercial badges. More interesting still was that no one ever would admit to being one of them. In fact, in retrospect, the real sign of being

[1]I still remember being in the parking lot in Stowe, Vermont at the base of Mt. Mansfield after a day of skiing. Someone from New York City had left his Aston Martin idling while he was in the warming hut. There must have been fifteen teenage boys who stopped in their tracks and just listened to that car. No one dared get near it. It was as holy as any object I had ever seen. Later at Christmas I remember thinking that I could understand how the wise men felt as they beheld the Christ child in Bethlehem. I knew it was sacrilegious to make such a comparison but I also knew it was true.

[2]Larry Kapold, executive creative director of Foote, Cone & Belding in Los Angeles, which made the ad, has a slightly different explanation. He says he was able to tease this ad from various focus groups.

> Early on, whenever we'd show a picture of the car to anyone, we'd get one of two reactions. Either, it's beautiful or you know what it reminds me of. . . . We wanted to tap that feeling of a car evoking warm memories without hitting people over the head with something like a 1950s sock-hop. (Goldrich 6)

a yuppie was that you tried hard to disassociate from them while all along displaying their badges.[3]

14 Yuppies were unique in that they were the first consumption community that I can think of known *only* by their badges. No one came forward like Marlon Brando, Abbie Hoffman, John Wayne, or Elton John to personify the group. Richard Gere laying out his clothes on the bed in the movie *American Gigolo* might have been the yuppie archetype, but he seemed a little too moody about his stuff. Still, rather like Eagle Scouts, yuppies had no distinct personality other than their merit (or demerit, it's up to you) badges worn almost Pancho Villa style around their vacuous lifestyles.

15 Here are just a few of the yuppie badges: yellow ties and red suspenders, Merlot, marinated salmon steaks, green-bottle beer, Club Med vacations, stuff with ducks on it, Gaggenau stoves, Sub-Zero refrigerators, latte, clothing from Ann Taylor or Ralph Lauren, designer water, Filofax binders, Cuisinarts, kiwi fruit, Ben & Jerry's ice cream, ventless Italian suits, pasta makers, bread makers, espresso-cappuccino makers, cellphones, home fax machines, air and water cleaners, laptop computers, exercise machines, massage tables, and remote controls for the television, the VCR, the CD player, the stereo receiver, the garage door, the child. More than anything, of course, the car—especially the BMW, the infamous beemer—was the yuppie badge nonpareil.

16 The yuppie and his German or Japanese car were academic anathema. If a colleague were to see me in such a car he would surely think I had gone over to the other side. My cousin with the pricy condo, the Jenn-Air gas grill, Biggest Bertha Ever golf club, and the Suburban could be a yuppie. But not me. I only bought just the things I absolutely needed . . . like a red Miata? And that, of course, was precisely my problem. When I bought this car, I became one of them.

17 I dilate on my Miata decision because it shows the dynamic of pressures in the commercial world. Two generations ago maybe choosing what denomination of the Congregational church to attend would have caused me such distress. Do I dare be seen with Unitarians? At the turn of this century what musical instrument you played would have been important. "They laughed when I sat down at the piano, but when I started to play!" describes a Horatio Alger experience we have trouble understanding. Maybe status would have been derived from what I read. Could I be seen reading Walt Whitman? What about what I ate? Our grandparents read etiquette books detailing the shame you should feel if you ordered the same meal too often. "Again she orders—A chicken salad, please!" is the headline of an

[3]The original definition was a young urban professional, but at some point this became corrupted to young upwardly mobile professional. From there meaning spread to define an entire generation of affluent and selfish twenty-somethings who were hot on the heels of us baby boomers. Demographically, yuppies were part of the 76 million people born between 1946 and 1964. Their number was small (the only definitive estimate of the yuppie population found just four million of them, representing a mere 5 percent of late baby boomers [see "The Big Chill Revisited," and entire issue of *American Demographics,* September 1985]), but their impact on the rest of us was huge—reverse magnetism.

ad for such an etiquette book. It is presumably spoken by an exasperated young man about his date. What if I coughed? Would that be a social blunder? Perhaps what I wore. Could I be seen wearing a gold stickpin in my tie? The way we live now, I worry that I might be mistaken for a yuppie.

18   While I certainly went through the modern version of the "agonies of the damned" buying a Japanese internal-combustion engine advertised through nostalgia and wrapped in red plastic, I never once was duped, misled, waylaid, or reified. In fact, I loved the process. They offered me my dream and I gladly bought it. I never liked that dreary Volvo to begin with. Now I'm wondering about a Jaguar, perhaps something from the early '80s, not too ostentatious but still flashy, if you know what I mean.

19   Let's face it, the idea that consumerism creates artificial desires rests on a wistful ignorance of history and human nature, on the hazy, romantic feeling that there existed some halcyon era of noble savages with purely natural needs. Once fed and sheltered, our needs have always been cultural, not natural. Until there is some other system to codify and satisfy those needs and yearnings, capitalism—and the culture it carries with it—will continue not just to thrive but to triumph.

20   In the way we live now, it is simply impossible to consume objects without consuming meaning. Meaning is pumped *and* drawn everywhere throughout the modern commercial world, into the farthest reaches of space and into the smallest divisions of time. Commercialism is the water we all swim in, the air we breathe, our sunlight and shade. Currents of desire flow around objects like smoke in a wind tunnel. The complications of my Miata purchase are the norm. . . .

21   To some degree, the triumph of consumerism is the triumph of the popular will. You may not like what is manufactured, advertised, packaged, branded, and broadcast, but it is far closer to what most people want most of the time than at any other period of modern history. . . .

22   We have not been led into this world of material closeness against our better judgment. For many of us, especially when young, consumerism is our better judgment. And this is true regardless of class or culture. We have not just asked to go this way, we have demanded. Now most of the world is lining up, pushing and shoving, eager to elbow into the mall. Woe to the government or religion that says no.

23   Getting and spending has been the most passionate, and often the most imaginative, endeavor of modern life. We have done more than acknowledge that the good life starts with the material life, as the ancients did. We have made stuff the dominant prerequisite of organized society. Things "R" Us. Consumption has become production. While this is dreary and depressing to some, as doubtless it should be, it is liberating and democratic to many more.

REFERENCE

Goldrich, Robert. "Go West, Creatives . . . ." *Back Stage,* August 11, 1989, p. 6B.

Out-of-Body Image

Self-objectification—seeing ourselves through others' eyes—impairs women's body image, mental health, motor skills and even sex lives

CAROLINE HELDMAN

Caroline Heldman, PhD, is an assistant professor of politics at Occidental College in Los Angeles. Her work centers primarily on issues of gender and race.

1 On a typical day, you might see ads featuring a naked woman's body tempting viewers to buy an electronic organizer, partially exposed women's breasts being used to sell fishing line, or a woman's rear—wearing only a thong—being used to pitch a new running shoe. Meanwhile, on every newsstand, impossibly slim (and digitally airbrushed) cover "girls" adorn a slew of magazines. With each image, you're hit with a simple, subliminal message: Girls' and women's bodies are objects for others to visually consume.

2 If such images seem more ubiquitous than ever, it's because U.S. residents are now exposed to anywhere from 3,000 to 5,000 advertisements a day—up from 500 to 2,000 a day in the 1970s. The Internet accounts for much of this growth, and young people are particularly exposed to advertising: 70 percent of 15- to 34-year-olds use social networking technologies such as MySpace and Facebook, which allow advertisers to infiltrate previously private communication space.

3 Although mass media has always objectified women, it has become increasingly provocative. More and more, female bodies are shown as outright objects (think Rose McGowan's machine-gun leg in the recent horror movie *Grindhouse*), are literally broken into parts (the disembodied woman's torso in advertisements for TV's *The Sarah Connor Chronicles*) or are linked with sexualized violence (simulated crime scenes on *America's Next Top Model* featuring seemingly dead women).

4 A steady diet of exploitative, sexually provocative depictions of women feeds a poisonous trend in women's and girls' perceptions of their bodies, one that has recently been recognized by social scientists as self-objectification—viewing one's body as a sex object to be consumed by the male gaze. Like W.E.B. DuBois' famous description of the experience of black Americans, self-objectification is a state of "double consciousness . . . a sense of always looking at one's self through the eyes of others."

5 Women who self-objectify are desperate for outside validation of their appearance and present their bodies in ways that draw attention. A study I did of 71 randomly selected female students from a liberal arts college in Los Angeles, for example, found that 70 percent were medium or high self-objectifiers, meaning that they have internalized the male gaze and chronically monitor their physical appearance. Boys and men experience self-objectification as well, but at a much lower rate—probably because, unlike women, they rarely get the message that their bodies are the primary determination of their worth.

6 Researchers have learned a lot about self-objectification since the term was coined in 1997 by University of Michigan psychology professor Barbara Fredrickson and Colorado College psychology professor Tomi-Ann Roberts. Numerous studies since then have shown that girls and women who self-objectify are more prone to

depression and low self-esteem and have less faith in their own capabilities, which can lead to diminished success in life. They are more likely to engage in "habitual body monitoring"—constantly thinking about how their bodies appear to the outside world—which puts them at higher risk for eating disorders such as anorexia and bulimia. And they are prone to embarrassment about bodily functions such as menstruation, as well as general feelings of disgust and shame about their bodies.

7   Self-objectification has also been repeatedly shown to sap cognitive functioning, because of all the attention devoted to body monitoring. For instance, a 1998 study asked two groups of women to take a math exam—one group in swimsuits, the other in sweaters. The swimsuit-wearers, distracted by body concerns, performed significantly worse than their peers in sweaters.

8   Several of my own surveys of college students indicate that this impaired concentration by self-objectifiers may hurt their academic performance. Those with low self-objectification reported an average GPA of 3.5, whereas those with high self-objectification reported a 3.1. While this gap may appear small, in graduate-school admissions it represents the difference between being competitive and being out of the running for the top schools.

9   Another worrisome effect of self-objectification is that it diminishes political efficacy—a person's belief that she can have an impact through the political process.

In another survey of mine, 33 percent of high self-objectifiers felt low political efficacy, compared to 13 percent of low self-objectifiers. Since political efficacy leads to participation in politics, having less of it means that self-objectifiers may be less likely to vote or run for office.

10   The effects of self-objectification on young girls are of such growing concern that the American Psychological Association published an investigative report on it last year. The APA found that girls as young as 7 years old are exposed to clothing, toys, music, magazines and television programs that encourage them to be sexy or "hot"—teaching them to think of themselves as sex objects before their own sexual maturity. Even thong underwear is being sold in sizes for 7- to 10-year-olds. The consequence, wrote Kenyon College psychology professor Sarah Murnen in the journal *Sex Roles,* is that girls "are taught to view their bodies as 'projects' that need work before they can attract others, whereas boys are likely to learn to view their bodies as tools to use to master the environment."

11   Fredrickson, along with Michigan communications professor Kristen Harrison (both work within the university's Institute for Research on Women and Gender), recently discovered that self-objectification actually impairs girls' motor skills. Their study of 202 girls, ages 10 to 17, found that self-objectification impeded girls' ability to throw a softball, even after differences in age and prior experience were factored out. Self-objectification forced girls to split their attention between how their bodies looked and what they wanted them to do, resulting in less forceful throws and worse aim.

12   One of the more stunning effects of self-objectification is its impact on sex. Nudity can cause great anxiety among self-objectifiers, who then become preoccupied with how their bodies look in sexual positions. One young woman I interviewed described sex as being an "out of body" experience during which she viewed herself through the eyes of her lover, and, sometimes, through the imaginary lens of a camera shooting a porn film. As a constant critic of her body, she couldn't focus on her own sexual pleasure.

13   Self-objectification can likely explain some other things that researchers are just starting to study. For instance, leading anti-sexist male activist and author Jackson Katz observes, "Many young women now engage in sex acts with men that prioritize the man's pleasure, with little or no expectation of reciprocity." Could this be another result of women seeing themselves as sexual objects, not agents? . . .

14   It would be encouraging if these choices reflected the sexual agency for women that feminists have fought so hard for, but they do not. The notion of objectification as empowering is illogical, since objects are acted upon, rather than taking action themselves. The real power in such arrangements lies with boys and men, who come to feel entitled to consume women as objects—first in media, then in real life.

15   At the root of this normalization of self-objectification may lie new consumer values in the U.S. Unlike the "producer citizen" of yesteryear—invoked in the 1960s by John F. Kennedy's request to "ask not what your country can do for you, ask what you can do for your country"—the more common "consumer citizen" of today asks what the country, and everyone else, can do for him or her. Consumer

citizens increasingly think of relationships with others as transactions in which they receive something, making them more comfortable consuming other human beings, visually or otherwise.

16   Self-objectification isn't going anywhere anytime soon. So what can we do about it? First, we can recognize how our everyday actions feed the larger beast, and realize that we are not powerless. Mass media, the primary peddler of female bodies, can be assailed with millions of little consumer swords. We can boycott companies and engage in other forms of consumer activism, such as socially conscious investments and shareholder actions. We can also contact companies directly to voice our concerns (see *Ms.'* backpage No Comment section, for example) and refuse to patronize businesses that overtly depict women as sex objects.

17   An example of women's spending power, and the limits of our tolerance for objectification, can be found in the 12-percent dip in profits of clothing company Victoria's Secret this year—due, according to the company's CEO, to its image becoming "too sexy." Victoria's Secret was not the target of an organized boycott: rather, its increasingly risque "bra and panty show" seems to have begun alienating women, who perhaps no longer want to simply be shown as highly sexualized window dressing.

18   Another strategy to counter one's own tendency to self-objectify is to make a point of buying products, watching programs and reading publications that promote more authentic women's empowerment. This can be difficult, of course, in a media climate in which companies are rarely wholeheartedly body-positive. For instance, Dove beauty products launched a much-lauded advertising campaign that used "real women" (i.e., not super-skinny ones) instead of models, but then Dove's parent company, Unilever, put out hypersexual ads for Axe men's body spray that showed the fragrance driving scantily clad women into orgiastic states.

19   Locating unadulterated television and film programming is also tough. Even Lifetime and Oxygen, TV networks created specifically for women, often portray us as weak victims or sex objects and present a narrow version of thin, white "beauty." Action films that promise strong female protagonists (think of the women of *X-Men,* or Lara Croft from *Tomb Raider*) usually deliver these characters in skintight clothes, serving the visual pleasure of men.

20   Feminist media criticism, at least, is plentiful. *Ms., Bitch* and others, along with publications for young girls such as *New Moon Magazine,* provide thoughtful analyses of media from various feminist perspectives. NOW's Love Your Body website (http://loveyourbody.nowfoundation.org) critiques offensive ads and praises body-positive ones. Blogs, both well-known and lesser-known, provide a platform for women and girls to vent about how the media depicts them. And there's some evidence that criticizing media helps defuse its effects: Murnen's study found that grade-school girls who had negative reactions to pictures of objectified women reported higher self-esteem.

21   A more radical, personal solution is to actively avoid media that compels us to self-objectify—which, unfortunately, is the vast majority of movies, television programs and women's magazines. My research with college-age women indicates that the less women consume media, the less they self-objectify, particularly if they

avoid fashion magazines. By shutting out media, girls and women can create mental and emotional space for true self-exploration. What would our lives look like if we viewed our bodies as tools to master our environment, instead of projects to be constantly worked on? What if our sexual expressions were based on our own pleasure as opposed to a narrow, consumerist idea of male sexual pleasure? What would disappear from our lives if we stopped seeing ourselves as objects? Painful high heels? Body hatred? Constant dieting? Liposuction? Unreciprocated oral sex?

22   It's hard to know. Perhaps the most striking outcome of self-objectification is the difficulty women have in imagining identities and sexualities truly our own. In solidarity, we can start on this path, however confusing and difficult it may be.

X-Large Boys

ALISSA QUART

> Alissa Quart, a graduate of Columbia School of Journalism, has written two critically acclaimed books: *Branded: The Buying and Selling of Teenagers* (Basic Books, 2003), from which the selection below is excerpted, and *Hothouse Kids: The Dilemma of the Gifted Child* (Penguin, 2006). She also writes for the *New York Times* and *Atlantic Monthly.*

1   "Supersize your superset" proclaims one teen weightlifter, echoing female teens' urges to augment their breasts.

2   The term *superset* refers to an extraordinary number of exercises, or weightlifting sets, performed with little or no rest between them. The hope for the boys who do supersets is to grow big—bigger than their classmates, as big as male models, professional wrestlers, and bodybuilders. In a sense, teen superset obsessions result from branding efforts . . .—the selling of nutritional-supplement companies and preppy clothing manufacturers such as Abercrombie & Fitch. In just five years, these firms have created a greater sense of inadequacy among boys about their bodies than ever before. Not so coincidentally, this has produced a whole new market for underwear and powdered drinks that teen boys now buy in an attempt to end this inadequacy. An astronomical and younger-than-ever use of steroids accompanies it all, along with a trade in dubious, over-the-counter nutritional supplements. The drive to grow big, like the drive for youthful plastic surgery, goes beyond becoming big or becoming perfect; it's the sort of self-construction that Generation Y understands. It's self-branding as an emotional palliative.

3   According to a Blue Cross-Blue Shield 2001 survey of ten-to-seventeen-year-olds, half of the 785 children interviewed said they were "aware" of sports supplements and drugs, and one in five take them. Forty-two percent did it to build muscle and 16 percent just to look better (i.e., "built"). These numbers are way up: In contrast, the 1999 BCBS survey found that no sample of kids under fourteen had taken products.

4   The push began in 1999 with the emergence of products such as Teen Advantage Creatine Serum, which made appearances on the shelves of vitamin chain stores. The marketing shows a kind of malignant genius: The formula was developed, according to the label, "especially for young aspiring athletes 8–19 years of age." (It also carries the necessary but misleadingly low-key caveat that excess dosage of creatine is not a "wise decision.") Not surprisingly, the products took off; there's nothing like a new teen-specific product that claims to alleviate a new teen-specific pathology.

5   The campaign worked so well that 52 percent of young users of performance-enhancing supplements said they had tried creatine (only 18 percent of adults surveyed used these supplements). Other supplements popular with kids—kids as young as ten—include ephedrine (which ostensibly increases endurance) and "andro," or androstenedione, an over-the-counter alternative to anabolic steroids (like steroids, androstenedione increases testosterone in the body—in fact, it also increases production of estrogen). These supplements, experts agree, range from

suspect to dangerous, and even deadly, as ephedra turned out to be. In fact, some of these supplements, says Charles Yesalis, author of *The Steroids Game,* are permitted to be called supplements only because of legal loopholes and are in fact drugs that are virtually unregulated by the FDA.

6   All this supplement use does not, unfortunately, mean that kids are staying away from steroids: In the 2001 Monitoring the Future study, 2.8 percent of eighth graders, 3.5 percent of tenth graders, and 3.7 percent of twelfth graders said they had taken steroids, meaning they had "cycled" on the drugs from eight to twelve weeks at least once (only 1.7 percent of high school sophomores had taken steroids in 1992). Why? Because steroids change body fat by adding muscle and thus decrease body fat proportionally. The possible side effects of steroids include stunted bone growth, liver damage, and shrunken testicles. A cycle is also costly, ranging from a few hundred to a few thousand dollars. But, as happens with a new ward-robe or a new pair of breasts, that's not seen as much of a price for looking more attractive. Allowances are up, working hours are up; kids can afford to juice. In such an environment, the decision not to use steroids but to depend instead on supplements can seem both cautious and economical. The no-worries attitude toward supplements, and dependence on them, can be seen in Sam, a thoughtful, quiet, dedicated prep school sophomore. Sam is also a prize-winning sixteen-year-old bodybuilder who writes for teen bodybuilding sites on which he proudly posts photos of his rippling and massive physique. Every day, Sam takes ephedrine mixed with caffeine along with 5 milligrams of creatine. He's been lifting weights since he was seven, and his punishing regimen now takes two hours of lifting daily.

7   Sam's passion for weightlifting started when he was exploring a hotel where he was staying with his family and he saw an adult lifting in the weight room. This weightlifter was his version of Edgar Allan Poe's Annabel Lee—he would never forget the image of the strong older man lifting the barbells. As soon as he got home, he bought some weights at a discount store and began working on getting big. Sam is not alone in starting so early. It's a trend that echoes the other ways in which kids are getting older younger in the market economy: Thirty-five percent of 60,000 weightlifting injuries in 1998 were for those aged from fifteen to twenty-four, and 12 percent were suffered by *children* aged from five to fourteen.

8   Today, he weighs 225 pounds, and has 6 percent body fat. He says that lifting helps him "stay healthy, look good, and feel confident," but acknowledges that for some of his peers, "exposed to weightlifting at first by popular culture," the reasons for their passions are not as hale and hearty. Some use steroids, for instance. (His own practice of taking ephedrine—an herbal supplement that can lead to heart attacks, seizures, psychoses, and death—to lose weight is arguably not such a great way of "staying healthy" either.) "There is definitely undue pressure on teen boys to look good and be big," Sam says. There is also undue pressure not to be fat given the commercial pressure to eat and the rising rates of obesity spurred on by com-mercials for fattening and sugary foods. In the stories of adolescents, childhood and teen obesity is a recurring theme. "The fat child is more abused than the muscled one; look at Piggy in *Lord of the Flies,*" explains Sam. "The big boy with the glasses—nobody listens to him. Teens now start lifting because they are overweight."

9   For sure, teen male body culture is a response to the now ubiquitous over-weight childhoods of American boys; a fat child may put a hard body between the self that was ostracized and emasculated flesh and his new adolescent self. The teen muscle boys, like the breast augmentation girls, exchange one supersized consumerism for another: They trade family-sized packages of branded food bought in bulk at discount stores for giant, branded adult-male-looking bodies and large vats of powdered supplements.

10   Juan, a Cuban American sixteen-year-old bodybuilder who lives in New Jersey, used weightlifting to go from 225 pounds to 165 pounds in one year. He says he started weightlifting because he "got a lot of prejudice" when he was fat. "That's why I did it [weightlifting], so they wouldn't make fun of me." Now his classmates respect him, he says, and girls talk to him, although he doesn't care about girls; he's more interested in the company of other high school weightlifters. "I want to get big, really big, but natural. I wanna be feared," Juan says. Like Sam, Juan doesn't consider the supplements unnatural—he takes from 5 to 10 milligrams of creatine a day, as well as whey for protein and glutamine for joint strength.

11   The desire of adolescents to leave behind the scrawny or husky teaseable boy for the hard, well-packaged man is not a new one, of course. The virtues of the well-developed man are extolled in the writings of the Greeks and in Shakespeare's *Measure for Measure:* "O, it is excellent / To have a giant's strength; but it is tyrannous / To use it like a giant." The wish to become big in puberty, for reasons of both dominance over one's peers and of display, can be seen in the twentieth-century in the fifty years of Charles Atlas magazine advertisements. The Atlas ads famously promised pubescents bodybuilding courses that would "make you a new man in just 15 minutes a day," that could "'RE-BUILD' skinny rundown weaklings" into creatures with "a coat of muscle straight across your stomach." In addition, bodybuilding magazines aimed at boys have a long history (and so do complementary homoerotic physique magazines). The 1977 film *Pumping Iron* also gave encouragement to boys to build themselves up.

12   However, the omnipresent gymmed-out, almost-naked male body began to make the rounds only in the late 1980s. A big force for this was a new advertising culture—the giant billboards for Calvin Klein underwear flaunting well-built models, the denuded male torsos in that same designer's perfume ads, helped to change the shape of men, literally. It is no coincidence that this was a period when the teen members of Generation Y were toddlers.

13   "When you hear girls gawking at Abercrombie & Fitch about how hot the guy is on the bag—that makes an impression," one teen bodybuilder told the *New York Times Magazine* in 1999. One of Abercrombie's countless bare-chested and buff youths had clearly been seared on that teen's mind; perhaps he still thinks of him every time he makes yet another andro shake.

14   The rise of teen male bigorexia, as media wags have called it, has also been spurred on by a new strain of magazines as well. There's the abdomen-mania of the men's magazines that these boys have grown up with, from *Men's Health* to *GQ.* In 2000, for instance, *Men's Health* even launched a magazine in celebration

of the teen male abdomen called *MH-17*. According to its initial press release, *MH-17* was "aimed at the 'rapidly growing' market of male teenagers in the United States."

15   *MH-17* and its ideology of male teen "fitness" (read: male bodily self-hatred) flopped. But the tyranny of taut, ripped, and dieted teen male bodies on screen and in advertisements still rules. Teen films, for example, almost entirely lack the sloppy, scrawny, or plumpish boys of yesteryear, boys who were blissfully oblivious of the body obsession of their female counterparts. Now even those who play geeks, actors such as Jason Biggs of *American Pie 2,* are forced to have washboard stomachs or "six-packs" and to bare them constantly.

16   To achieve the required body, teen boys are willing to put in time and painful effort that many of their fathers couldn't have imagined—becoming a branded boy body takes just as much labor and pain as becoming a branded girl body. For instance, teen boy bodybuilders tend to engage in spartan, highly structured eating patterns. On the teenbodybuilder.com Web site, one boy describes the ten austere meals on his daily menu for the months when he prepares for competition. The meals are austere, obsessively observed, and protein-filled fare, one consisting of one scoop of egg white protein, one scoop of casein, half a scoop of Optimum's whey, four slices of turkey, and two pieces of whole wheat bread.

In their urge to build themselves into commercially approved hypermasculine specimens, the boys of Generation Y are in solidarity with their long-suffering female peers. Once there was a hope among feminists that girls could be taught to escape their oppressive body project. This has not occurred. Now, boys partake in it as well. Weightlifting, enthusiasts say, is a form of self-construction. For the teen weightlifters, however—boys shooting steroids and eating egg whites for breakfast; shaving their chests and backs and legs—the line between self-betterment and a morphic pathology is a blurry one.

QUESTIONS FOR DISCUSSION

1. James Twitchell admits that he bought his Miata because of an advertisement (paragraph 6). What was the promise of the ad, as he describes it in paragraphs 6–11? As the ad's creator describes it in footnote 2? Why does Twitchell not see the ad as manipulative or exploitative (see paragraphs 18 and 19)?

2. In telling the story of his Miata purchase, James Twitchell discusses his own struggle with what he calls the "dynamic of pressures in the commercial world" (paragraph 17). The Miata was not one of the brands of his consumption community, "liberal academics." What products are badges of the "liberal academic" group? Why is a Miata not acceptable to the "liberal academic" group? Have you experienced similar conflicts when considering a purchase your friends might disapprove of?

3. Alissa Quart discusses the pressure on boys to conform to commercial messages about supersized male bodies, and Caroline Heldman, in

"Out-of-Body Image," outlines the perils of self-objectification for girls. Both writers suggest that commercial messages exploit teens' insecurities about values, roles, and identity. What do advertisements tell teenagers about gender roles? What is harmful about these images of masculinity and femininity? In what ways does advertising undermine girls' development as women? What are boys learning about masculinity? Men used to think it was effeminate to be too concerned about looks. Is the image of the "new man" liberating or entrapping?

4. Read Virginia Postrel's definition of aesthetics in paragraphs 6–9 in "The Aesthetic Imperative" (Section One, page 316). Why is aesthetic communication "emotional" rather than "cognitive"? In one issue of any magazine, examine the ads. Would you say that ads themselves have been affected by what Postrel calls "the aesthetic imperative"? If so, how might that affect the ways that ads appeal to their target audiences?

SUGGESTIONS FOR WRITING

For Persuasion and Visual Rhetoric

Look at advertisements aimed at you and your peers. Do you see the same kinds of messages that either Caroline Heldman (regarding females) or Alissa Quart (regarding males) sees? Or do you see other harmful messages about values or gender roles? One of the writers in Section Three of this casebook, John F. Schumaker, suggests that the economic interests of consumer societies are best served by making citizens feel anxious and inadequate. If you see evidence of this, select representative ads to illustrate a persuasive essay helping readers to understand how the ads are harmful to them.

For Convincing with Visual Rhetoric

James Twitchell analyzes the rhetoric of the Miata ad that persuaded him to buy his red Miata. He claims that the ad "worked" on his memories of childhood, but did not manipulate him. Read Chapter 5 of this text on visual arguments, especially the material on advertising on pages 65–66. Then choose an advertisement that you find persuasive and that makes you want to buy the advertised product. Write an analysis of the rhetoric of the ad and make a case as to whether the ad manipulates or does not manipulate.

SECTION 3: THE PURSUIT OF HAPPINESS
Overview

The readings in this section all deal with the question of how happy people are in consumer societies. A problem arises, first of all, with the key term *happiness*. What is happiness? If you look up *happy* in a dictionary, the definitions range all the way from "lucky" to "cheerful" to "showing joy," and even to "having enthusiasm" for something. Social scientists often use a testing instrument called the "Satisfaction with Life Scale," developed by Ed Diner in 1985. The test asks people to respond to items like these:

> In most ways my life is close to my ideal.
>
> The conditions of my life are excellent.
>
> I am satisfied with my life.
>
> So far I have gotten the important things I want in life.
>
> If I could live my life over, I would change almost nothing.

Our first reading in this section reports on the efforts of a Dutch sociologist to measure the relationship between a country's per capita income and its happiness in terms of life satisfaction. The results of his surveys have been positive: People report being happy more than you might expect. The surprise in his findings is that beyond a certain level, satisfaction with life does not increase with more income.

However, clinical psychologist John F. Schumaker, in his essay "The Happiness Conspiracy: What Does It Mean to Be Happy in a Modern Consumer Society?" questions the measurement and definition of happiness in terms of self-satisfaction. Schumaker points out that this scale "mirrors the supreme value that consumer culture attaches to the romancing of desire and the satiation of the self." Therefore, although they may claim to be happy, people in consumer societies suffer more depression and other mental health problems. Schumaker suggests that we would be healthier if we thought of happiness in less self-centered and materialistic ways.

In the final essay, psychologist Mihaly Czikszentmihalyi offers "Enjoyment as an Alternative to Materialism." Although shopping may give us pleasure, he suggests that a more lasting satisfaction comes from being so involved in a challenging and outwardly directed activity that you lose awareness of self.

Does Money Buy Happiness?

DON PECK AND ROSS DOUTHAT

In the following selection, which appeared originally in the *Atlantic Monthly*, Peck and Douthat report on research into the connection between per capita income and self-reported happiness in various countries around the world. Some of the findings may surprise you.

1   Historically the province of philosophers and theologians, the relationship between wealth and happiness has recently been taken up by a cadre of social scientists seeking to quantify and compare levels of well-being worldwide.

2   The results of their research, thus far, are clear: money does buy happiness—but only to a point. Study after study shows that the inhabitants of richer countries are, on average, significantly happier than those of poorer ones. This is true even controlling for other variables that rise with income and that may influence personal happiness: education, political freedom, women's rights, and so forth. National income appears to be one of the best single predictors of overall well-being, explaining perhaps 40 percent of the difference in contentment among nations. For individual countries, with few exceptions, self-reported happiness has increased as incomes have risen.

3   The chart on pages 354–355 shows survey data on happiness for fifty-four countries, compiled throughout the 1990s by the Dutch sociologist Ruut Veenhoven.

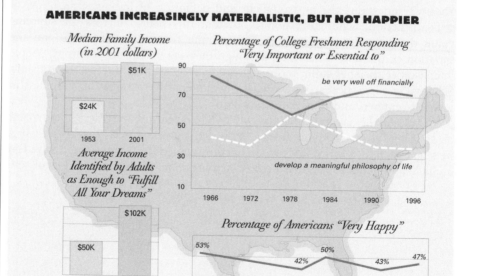

AMERICANS INCREASINGLY MATERIALISTIC, BUT NOT HAPPIER

Median Family Income (in 2001 dollars)

$51K — 2001
$24K — 1953

Average Income Identified by Adults as Enough to "Fulfill All Your Dreams"

$102K — 1994
$50K — 1987

Percentage of College Freshmen Responding "Very Important or Essential to"

be very well off financially

develop a meaningful philosophy of life

1966 1972 1978 1984 1990 1996

Percentage of Americans "Very Happy"

53% 1957
42% 1977
50% 1982
43% 1992
47% 2000

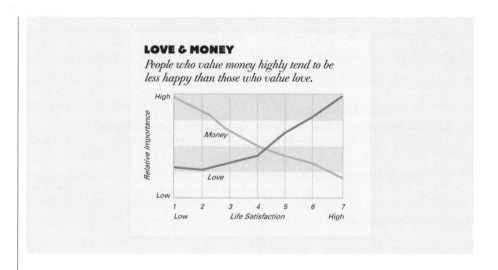

LOVE & MONEY

People who value money highly tend to be less happy than those who value love.

These data indicate a robust, if inexact, relationship between per capita income and "life satisfaction." Veenhoven's findings provide an unexpectedly sunny view. First, they indicate that most people worldwide say they are fairly happy. It is debatable whether most people have ever viewed life as nasty, brutish, and short; but on balance, they don't now. (Even citizens of impoverished or politically star-crossed countries, such as the Philippines and Romania, or of countries with high levels of income inequality, such as Brazil and the United States, report being at least somewhat happy on average.) Moreover, though the fact that richer countries are in general happier than poorer ones may not seem terribly surprising, it does suggest that continuing economic development will generate rising happiness worldwide.

4 That said, there are clear limits to what money can buy. Although improvements in income produce large improvements in happiness for poor countries—gains that continue to rise with income well above the level where basic food, shelter, and sanitation needs have been met—the law of diminishing returns takes effect at higher income levels. Above about $20,000 per capita, increases in wealth yield at best minimal increases in happiness. This effect takes place at both the individual and the societal level. In poor societies those at the top of the socioeconomic ladder are significantly happier than those at the bottom; in highly developed societies there is little class difference in happiness. (In fact, oddly, in wealthy nations both those in the top 10 percent of the socioeconomic spectrum and those in the bottom 50 percent appear to be slightly happier, on average, than those in between.)

5 Robert E. Lane, a political scientist at Yale, argues that the leveling off of happiness in wealthy societies reflects more than just diminishing returns. Lane suggests that happiness is derived largely from two sources—material comfort, and social and familial intimacy—that are often incompatible. Economic development increases material comfort, but it systematically weakens social and familial ties by

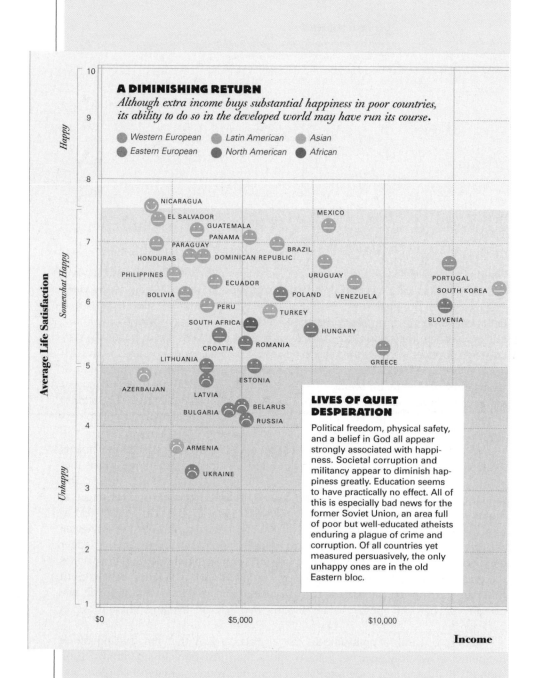

A DIMINISHING RETURN

Although extra income buys substantial happiness in poor countries, its ability to do so in the developed world may have run its course.

- Western European
- Eastern European
- Latin American
- North American
- Asian
- African

LIVES OF QUIET DESPERATION

Political freedom, physical safety, and a belief in God all appear strongly associated with happiness. Societal corruption and militancy appear to diminish happiness greatly. Education seems to have practically no effect. All of this is especially bad news for the former Soviet Union, an area full of poor but well-educated atheists enduring a plague of crime and corruption. Of all countries yet measured persuasively, the only unhappy ones are in the old Eastern bloc.

Average Life Satisfaction

Happy · Somewhat Happy · Unhappy

Income

$0 · $5,000 · $10,000

NICARAGUA · EL SALVADOR · GUATEMALA · PANAMA · MEXICO · PARAGUAY · BRAZIL · HONDURAS · DOMINICAN REPUBLIC · PHILIPPINES · URUGUAY · PORTUGAL · BOLIVIA · ECUADOR · POLAND · VENEZUELA · SOUTH KOREA · PERU · TURKEY · SOUTH AFRICA · SLOVENIA · CROATIA · ROMANIA · HUNGARY · LITHUANIA · GREECE · AZERBAIJAN · ESTONIA · LATVIA · BULGARIA · BELARUS · RUSSIA · ARMENIA · UKRAINE

SWITZERLAND

DENMARK LUXEMBOURG

ICELAND CANADA

SWEDEN

IRELAND NETHERLANDS

FINLAND

BELGIUM NORWAY U.S.A.

U.K. AUSTRALIA

ITALY

GERMANY

SPAIN

FRANCE

JAPAN

AUSTRIA

WHY ARE LATIN AMERICANS HAPPIER THAN THE JAPANESE?

Neither income nor any other quantifiable variable has fully explained cross-cultural differences in perceptions of well-being. The Japanese, for example, are far less happy than Japan's national income would suggest; life satisfaction in that country has not risen dramatically since the 1950s, despite strong income growth. Latin Americans, on the other hand, seem predisposed to happiness in spite of economic and political hardship. (The Japanese, for their part, seldom admit to being "very" anything in surveys, perhaps reflecting a cultural bias against standing out.) Thus, although social or economic changes can push happiness up or down, perceptions of well-being appear to be at least somewhat determined by a society's cultural norms.

THE MYTH OF THE CONTENTED VILLAGER

Idyllic visions notwithstanding, there is little evidence to show that the residents of traditional villages and farming communities are particularly happy. In poor countries city-dwellers report themselves to be markedly happier than villagers. And surveys show these same villagers to be far more materialistic than urbanites, valuing money and material goods above friendship and family. Though rural residents in the United States say they are happy overall, they rate themselves as lonelier than suburbanites.

| $15,000 | $20,000 | $25,000 | $30,000 |

Per Person

encouraging mobility, commercializing relationships, and attenuating the bonds of both the extended and the nuclear family. In less developed countries, where social ties are often strong and money is scarce, this tradeoff works overwhelmingly to society's advantage—the gains in material comfort more than outweigh the slight declines in social connectedness. At some point, however, the balance tips and the happiness-diminishing effects of reduced social stability begin to outweigh the happiness-increasing effects of material gain. Lane believes that the United States has passed this tipping point, and that we will actually become unhappier as incomes rise further.

6   Lane's argument is controversial. It is unclear that happiness is actually falling in the United States. Clinical depression is rising, which Lane cites as one basis for his argument, but it still afflicts only a small percentage of the population. Nonetheless, it is true that happiness in the United States has not risen over the past fifty years, despite an average increase of more than 85 percent in the real value of family income. And although the weakening of the relationship between money and contentment perhaps ought to have induced Americans to look elsewhere for sources of happiness, that hasn't happened. Indeed, as the graphs on pages 352 and 353 show, Americans have become *more* materialistic over the past three decades.

7   The Western notion of progress was shaped during a centuries-long period when rising wealth almost certainly bought rising happiness. Only recently have we left that era behind—and our society has not yet adjusted. Conditioned to value financial achievement, we may cling to materialism even as it makes the contentment we seek more elusive.

The Happiness Conspiracy: What Does It Mean to Be Happy in a Modern Consumer Society?

JOHN F. SCHUMAKER

John F. Schumaker, a clinical psychologist, was born in Wisconsin but now lives and practices in New Zealand. He has published nine books and many articles on culture and mental health. His most recent book is *In Search of Happiness: Understanding an Endangered State of Mind* (Penguin, 2006). Schumaker's essay "The Happiness Conspiracy" appeared in the magazine *New Internationalist,* July 2006.

1   "The trouble with normal is it always gets worse," sang the Canadian guitarist Bruce Cockburn back in 1983. Seems he was on to something. Normal doesn't seem to be working any longer. The new Holy Grail is happiness. At every turn are "how-to" happiness books, articles, TV and radio programs, videos, and websites. There are happiness institutes, camps, clubs, classes, cruises, workshops, and retreats. Universities are adding courses in Happiness Studies. Fast-growing professions include happiness counseling, happiness coaching, "life-lift" coaching, "joyology," and happiness science. Personal happiness is big business and everyone is selling it.

2   Being positive is mandatory, even with the planet in meltdown. Cynics and pessimists are running for cover while the cheerleaders are policing the game with an iron fist. Only the bravest are not being bullied into cheering up or at least shutting up.

3   But a society of "happichondriacs" isn't necessarily a healthy sign. No one is less able to sustain happiness than someone obsessed with feeling only happiness. A happy and meaningful existence depends on the ability to feel emotions other than happiness, as well as ones that compete with happiness.

4   "Happiness never appeared to me as an absolute aim," said Einstein. "I am even inclined to compare such moral aims to the ambitions of a pig. The ideals that have lighted my way are Kindness, Beauty and Truth."

5   If we've become pigs at the happiness trough, it's understandable. As higher systems of meaning have withered, life purpose has dwindled to feeling good. Innocence, the lifeblood of happiness, is obsolete. We live on cultural soil perfectly suited for depression.

6   Other happiness blockers include materialism, perpetual discontent, overcomplication, hypercompetition, stress, rage, boredom, loneliness, and existential confusion. We're removed from nature, married to work, adrift from family and friends, spiritually starved, sleep deprived, physically unfit, dumbed down, and enslaved to debt.

7   Health professionals face new epidemics of "hurry sickness," "toxic success syndrome," the "frantic family," the "over-commercialized child," and "pleonexia" or out-of-control greed.

8   Too much is no longer enough. Many are stretching themselves so far that they have difficulty feeling anything at all. At its heart the happiness boom is a metaphor for the modern struggle for meaning.

9   We laugh only a third as often as we did 50 years ago—hence the huge popularity of laughter clubs and laughter therapy. We make love less frequently

and enjoy it less, even though sex is now largely deregulated and available in end-less guilt-free varieties. Yet we're the least happy society in history if we measure happiness in terms of mental health, personal growth, or general sense of aliveness.

10   A society's dominant value system dictates how happiness is measured. The native Navajos in the southwest of the U.S. saw happiness as the attainment of universal beauty, or what they called Hozho. Their counterpart of "Have a nice day" was "May you walk in beauty."

11   Personal satisfaction is the most common way of measuring happiness today (via something called the Life Satisfaction Scale). This mirrors the supreme value that consumer culture attaches to the romancing of desire and the satiation of the self. When measured this way, almost everyone seems pretty happy—even if it's primarily false needs being satisfied. A high percentage of depressed people even end up happy when "personal satisfaction" is the yardstick.

12   By the middle of the 19th century, social critics were already noticing how happiness was losing its social, spiritual, moral, and intellectual anchors and becoming a form of emotional masturbation. In his classic 1863 work, *Utilitarianism,* John Stuart Mill scorned this trend: "Better to be Socrates dissatisfied than a fool satisfied," he opined.

13   Total satisfaction can actually be a major obstacle to happiness. Artist Salvador Dali lamented: "There are days when I think I'm going to die from an overdose of satisfaction." To preserve the "rarity value" of life one must resist wrapping heaven around oneself. Keeping paradise at a distance, yet within reach, is a much better way of staying alive. People who have it all must learn the art of flirting with deprivation.

14   The highest forms of happiness have always been experienced and expressed as love. But happiness is being wooed in increasingly autistic ways that lack this vital dimension. In a recent survey only one percent of people indicated "true love" as what they wanted most in life. Our standard of living has increased but our standard of loving has plummeted.

15   The backlash against today's narcissistic happiness is rekindling interest in the ancient Greek philosophers who equated happiness with virtue. Especially celebrated by them were loyalty, friendship, moderation, honesty, compassion, and trust. Research shows that all these traits are in steep decline today—despite being happiness boosters. Like true love and true happiness, they have become uneconomic.

16   When author John Updike warned, "America is a vast conspiracy to make you happy," he was referring to the superficial mass happiness that prevails when economics successfully conspires to define our existence. I profit, therefore I am. To be happy, gulp something. Pay later.

17   Novelist J. D. Salinger was so unnerved by the happiness conspiracy that he confessed: "I'm a kind of paranoiac in reverse. I suspect people are plotting to make one happy." The wrong type of happiness is worse than no happiness at all.

18   Governments are the biggest players in the happiness conspiracy. Any political action aimed at a more people-friendly or planet-friendly happiness is certain to be met with fierce resistance. The best consumers are itchy narcissists who hop, skip,

and jump from one fleeting desire to the next, never deeply satisfied, but always in the process of satisfying themselves. Our entire socioeconomic system is designed to spew out this type of "ideal citizen." Contentment is the single greatest threat to the economics of greed and consumer happiness.

19   Our ignorance of happiness is revealed by the question on everyone's lips: "Does money make us happy?" The head of a U.S. aid agency in Kenya commented recently that volunteers are predictably dumbstruck and confused by the zest and jubilance of the Africans. It's become a cliché for them to say: "The people are so poor, they have nothing—and yet they have so much joy and seem so happy."

20   I never knew how measly my own happiness was until one day in 1978 when I found myself stranded in a remote western Tanzanian village. I saw real happiness for the first time—since then I have learned that it has vastly more to do with cultural factors than genetics or the trendy notion of personal "choice."

21   So it didn't surprise me that an African nation, Nigeria, was found recently to be the world's happiest country. The study of "happy societies" is awakening us to the importance of social connectedness, spirituality, simplicity, modesty of expectations, gratitude, patience, touch, music, movement, play, and "down time."

22   The small Himalayan nation of Ladakh is one of the best-documented examples of a "happy society." As Helena Norberg-Hodge writes in *Ancient Future,* Ladakhis were a remarkably joyous and vibrant people who lived in harmony with their harsh environment. Their culture generated mutual respect, community-mindedness, an eagerness to share, reverence for nature, thankfulness, and love of life. Their value system bred tenderness, empathy, politeness, spiritual awareness, and environmental conservation. Violence, discrimination, avarice, and abuse of power were nonexistent while depressed, burned-out people were nowhere to be found.

23   But in 1980 consumer capitalism came knocking with its usual bounty of raised hopes and social diseases. The following year, Ladakh's freshly appointed Development Commissioner announced: "If Ladakh is ever going to be developed, we have to figure out how to make these people more greedy." The developers triumphed, and a greed economy took root. The issues nowadays are declining mental health, family breakdown, crime, land degradation, unemployment, a widening gap between rich and poor, pollution, and sprawl.

24   Writer Ted Trainer says before 1980 the people of Ladakh were "notoriously happy." He sees in their tragic story a sobering lesson about our cherished goals of development, growth, and progress. For the most part these are convenient myths that are much better at producing happy economies than happy people.

25   When normality fails, as it has today, happiness becomes a form of protest. Some disillusioned folks are resorting to "culture jamming" and "subvertisements" to expose the hollow core of commercial society. Others are seeking refuge in various forms of primitivism and eco-primitivism. Spurring this on is intriguing evidence from the field of cognitive archaeology suggesting that our Paleolithic ancestors were probably happier and far more alive than people today. The shift toward "Paleo" and "Stone Age" diets also reflects the belief that they had happier bodies.

26   There is an exquisite line by the philosopher Friedrich Nietsche which touches on one of the keys to happiness: the need to appreciate "the least, the softest,

lightest, a lizard's rustling, a breath, a moment." Paradoxically, happiness is closer when we kneel than when we soar. Our own nothingness can be a great source of joy.

27   We usually hitch our emotional wagons to ego, ambition, personal power, and the spectacular. But all of these are surprising flops when it comes to happiness. Today's "success" has become a blueprint for failure.

28   Visionaries tell us that the only happiness that makes sense at this perilous juncture in Earth's history is "sustainable happiness." All worthwhile happiness is life-supporting. But so much of what makes us happy in the age of consumerism is dependent upon the destruction and over-exploitation of nature. A sustainable happiness implies that we take responsibility for the wider contexts in which we live and for the well-being of future generations.

29   Sustainable happiness harks back to the classical Greek philosophies in viewing ethical living as a legitimate vehicle for human happiness. Compassion in particular plays a central role. In part it rests on the truth that we can be happy in planting the seeds of happiness, even if we might miss the harvest.

30   Some argue that as a society we are too programmed to selfishness and over-consumption for a sustainable happiness to take root. Democracy itself is a problem when the majority itches for the wrong things. But if we manage to take the first few steps, we may rediscover that happiness resonates most deeply when it has a price.

31   The greatest irony in the search for happiness is that it is never strictly personal. For happiness to be mature and heartfelt, it must be shared—whether by those around us or by tomorrow's children. If not, happiness can be downright depressing.

"I didn't do anything on my summer vacation—
should I write about what I bought?"

Enjoyment as an Alternative to Materialism

MIHALY CSIKSZENTMIHALYI

Mihaly Csikszentmihalyi directs the Quality of Life Research Center at Claremont's Peter F. Drucker and Masatoshi Ito Graduate School of Management. Through his research and writing on the experience of "flow" as a state of mind, Csikszentmihalyi has earned recognition in the fields of education, business, and positive psychology. An extended version of the selection below appeared in the collection *Psychology and Consumer Culture: The Struggle for a Good Life in a Materialistic World,* edited by Tim Kasser and Allen D. Kramer.

1   Evolution has built two contradictory motivations into our nervous system: *pleasure,* which is the well-being we feel when eating, resting, and procreating; and *enjoyment,* which is the exhilarating sensation we feel when going beyond the requirements of survival (Csikszentmihalyi, 1993; Ryan & Deci, 2000; Waterman, 1993). Pleasure is a powerful source of motivation, but it does not produce change; it is a conservative force that makes us want to satisfy existing needs and to achieve comfort and relaxation. It is the motivation that makes us look for material resources to improve the quality of life—after all, these are scarce and everyone wants them, so they must be valuable. The concreteness of material goals also makes them seem more real than more complex goals. However, the improvement that money,

power, and comfort produce is often simply that of removing momentarily the anxiety we all experience when confronting mortality and finitude. "More stuff" promises security and comfort, even when the benefits are short-lived and we need ever more stuff to regain equanimity in the face of the slings and arrows inherent in living. There is nothing wrong with seeking pleasure in material goals, but individuals for whom it becomes the main reason for living are not going to grow beyond what the genes have programmed them to desire.

2   Enjoyment, on the other hand, is not always pleasant, and it can be very stressful at times. A mountain climber may be close to freezing, utterly exhausted, in danger of falling into a bottomless crevasse, yet she would not want to be anywhere else. Sipping a cocktail under a palm tree at the edge of the turquoise ocean is nice, but it just does not compare to the exhilaration she feels on that freezing ridge. At the moment it is experienced, enjoyment may be physically painful and mentally taxing; but because it involves a triumph over the forces of entropy and decay, it nourishes the spirit. Enjoyment builds memories that enrich lives in retrospect, and it gives confidence for facing the future.

3   Because enjoyable activities usually require more effort than those that provide pleasure, and their rewards are often delayed, all too often the short-term logic is to choose pleasure over enjoyment. For instance, in our studies using the experiential sampling method (Csikszentmihalyi & Larson, 1984; Csikszentmihalyi & Schneider, 2000), we often show individuals the results of the week during which they reported what they were doing and how they felt about it, and we ask: "Look, this is how happy you reported being when the pager signaled while you were watching television. And here is how much more happy you reported being while playing basketball or playing the piano. Can you tell me then why you spent 15 times as many hours last week watching TV than doing active leisure?"

4   Confronted with such questions, most people hem and haw, and admit that yes, it's much more enjoyable to do some active form of leisure, but it also requires more energy to get organized for it. Turning on a TV set, by contrast, is very easy and therefore attractive when one feels tired.

5   However, it would be a mistake to assume that opting for enjoyment over pleasure is tantamount to delaying gratification. What we find in our studies is that growth-producing, complex activities not only build the ability to enjoy a richer life later, but they are actually enjoyed more in the present compared with more glamorous and heavily advertised pleasurable activities.

6   For instance, many entrepreneurs and professionals find that their work provides a sense of adventurous growth that produces enjoyment greater than any money could buy. One of the business leaders we interviewed describes his attitude toward work:

> It's an enormous responsibility and it's an enormous challenge. And it's the most fun job in the world! I love coming to work every morning. I can't wait to get here. I can't wait, because everyday something else is going to happen.

7   One finds the same enthusiasm for work—although less often—among salaried and even assembly-line workers. Again, the issue is not so much *what* one does

but *how* one does it. As Studs Terkel (1974) and many others who study work have noted, if one is proud of one's job and tries to do one's best at it, it can become as fun and interesting as that of any executive.

8   Among successful scientists, artists, physicians, lawyers, and business leaders, one finds that they express the same sort of enthusiasm about their work. Unfortunately, most jobs do not have enough challenges or enough variety to provide that level of enjoyment. There are also many wealthy and well-known professionals or business persons whose work has become routine. Such people then look for enjoyment outside work or to the pleasures provided by material experiences. The more boring and routine everyday life becomes, the more likely that the number of those seeking substitutes for enjoyment will increase. But what does it mean that a person enjoys something?

9   In the last few decades, studies conducted around the world have shown that whenever people feel a deep sense of enjoyment they describe their experience in very similar terms. Regardless of age, gender, or education, they report very similar mental states. What they actually do at the time is wildly different—they may be meditating, running a race, playing chess, or doing a surgical operation, but what they feel when they really enjoy what they are doing sounds remarkably the same. I have given the name of *flow* to this common experience, because so many of the people used the analogy of being carried away by an outside force, of moving effortlessly with a current of energy, at the moments of highest enjoyment (Csikszentmihalyi, 1975, 1990, 1996).

10   Here are three quotes from among the close to 8,000 interviews collected over the years in our laboratory, as well as by colleagues around the world, providing some glimpses of how the flow experience feels. The first is from an expert rock-climber who describes his mental state when climbing:

> The task at hand is so demanding and rich in its complexity and pull. . . . one tends to get immersed in what is going on around him, in the rock, in the moves that are involved . . . search for handholds . . . proper position of the body—so involved he might lose consciousness of his own identity and melt into the rock.

11   Compare his quote with that from an inner-city African American teenager who plays basketball after school:

> The court—that's all that matters . . . sometimes on court I think of a problem, like fighting with my steady girl, and I think that's nothing compared to the game. You can think about a problem all day but as soon as you get in the game, the hell with it! . . . When you are playing basketball, that's all there is on your mind.

Or with the account from a surgeon describing why his job is so enjoyable:

> In good surgery everything you do is essential, every move is excellent and necessary; there is elegance, little blood loss, and a minimum of trauma. . . . This is very pleasant, particularly when the group works together in a smooth and efficient manner.

12   These individuals describe some of the basic elements of flow: The task at hand draws people in with its complexity to such an extent that they become completely

involved in it. There is no distinction between thought and action, between self and environment. The important thing is to do each move as well as possible, because even lives may depend on it. Other elements of the experience are a sense of control, a loss of the sense of time, and a good fit between what a person can do and what the opportunities of the situation are. When these conditions are present, we feel a sense of exhilaration that is rare in life.

13   However, flow does not require a life-and-death setting to be enjoyable. The most widely reported flow activity the world over is reading a good book, when one gets immersed in the characters and the vicissitudes of their fictional lives to the point of forgetting oneself. Remarkably often flow is experienced when at work, as told by this 76-year-old woman who still farms in the Italian Alps:

> It gives me a great satisfaction to be outdoors, to talk with people, to be with my animals. . . . I talk to everybody—plants, birds, flowers, and animals. Everything in nature keeps you company, you see nature progress each day. You feel clean and happy: Too bad you get tired and have to go home. . . . Even when you have to work a lot it is very beautiful.

14   This woman describes her work as though it were a romantic idyll. In fact, she gave this account after walking several miles down mountain meadows carrying on her back a bale of hay twice as tall as she is. Nevertheless, by paying attention to the complexity of the natural world around her, she was able to become at one with it and to enjoy the experience. Often the experience is the result of spending time with others in a close interaction. Here is a mother describing her most precious moments:

> When I'm working with my daughter, when she is discovering something new. A new cookie recipe that she has accomplished, that she has made herself, an artistic work that she has done that she's proud of. Her reading is one thing that she's really into, and we read together. She reads to me, and I read to her, and that's a time when I sort of lose touch with the rest of the world, I'm totally absorbed in what I am doing.

15   Paying attention to one's daughter, watching her grow and discover new things, and appropriately responding to her changing self requires as much psychic energy as it takes to be a good rock-climber, farmer, or surgeon. By getting immersed in such a complex activity, one's own self becomes more complex and stronger.

MATERIALISM AS A SUBSTITUTE FOR ENJOYMENT

16   I propose that when a person cannot build a self based on flow, he or she tries to build a self with the help of material goals and material experiences. These include competitive striving for wealth and power and seeking pleasure in its various forms, such as passive leisure and consumer behavior. The saying that "nature abhors a vacuum" is true of the human psyche as well: During waking hours, we need a constant stream of experiences to keep the mind working properly. In everyday life, people often find themselves in an existential vacuum where no clear need suggesting a specific goal presents itself to consciousness. Normal American

teenagers, for instance, when paged at random moments of the day, report 30% of the time that what they are doing is not what they want to do but that they can't think of anything else they would rather be doing instead. Although this pattern is strongest when teenagers are in school, it is also typical of responses at home (Csikszentmihalyi & Schneider, 2000). We have less data from adults, but what there is suggests that they also spend quite a large part of their days in a state where, as far as they are concerned, "there is nothing to do."

17   This pattern is significant because when a person feels that there is nothing to do, the quality of experience tends to decline. One feels less alert, active, strong, happy, and creative. Self-esteem declines. Contrary to what one might expect, such a negative experiential state is more likely to occur at home during free time than at work, where goals are usually clear and attention is more readily engaged (Csikszentmihalyi & LeFevre, 1989).

18   This suggests that, in addition to the existential needs described by Maslow (e.g. Maslow, 1968) and others, we also have an *experiential* need—perhaps peculiar to human beings—to keep consciousness in an organized state, focused on some activity that requires attention. When there is nothing to do, attention starts to turn inward, we begin to ruminate, and, frequently, get depressed. By and large, when we start thinking about ourselves rather than about what we need to accomplish, attention turns to deficits: We are getting old and fat, we are losing our hair, our children are getting in trouble, we have not accomplished much in life. As a result, our mood begins to turn sour (Csikszentmihalyi, 1993, 1996; Csikszentmihalyi & Figurski, 1982). The downward spiral of rumination is interrupted only when attention is again engaged by some need that suggests a goal: preparing dinner, taking the dog for a walk, or if all else fails, watching a show on TV. Yet trying to fill unstructured time with passive entertainment does not work well; the quality of experience while watching TV is barely more positive than that of the slough of despond that awaits the unfocused mind (Kubey & Csikszentmihalyi, 1990).

19   The experiential need to keep entropy from overwhelming consciousness is responsible for a great deal of material values and consumer behavior. It could be said of shopping, as McLuhan (1964) said of television, that "the medium is the message." In other words, it often does not matter what we are shopping *for*—the point is to shop for anything, whatever. Shopping is a goal-directed activity and thus fills the experiential vacuum that leads to depression and despair. That we have to pay, that is, expend the equivalent of psychic energy, for what we acquire lends an additional importance to the activity. If we spend money, it must be worthwhile. As Linder (1970) pointed out, the value of the goods we consume in leisure becomes a measure of the value of our time: If in one hour's time I drink $20 worth of a single-malt Scotch, while listening to a stereo that depreciates at the rate of $5 an hour, in an apartment whose rent pro-rates at $10 an hour, then it means that my time is worth at least $35 an hour—even without counting the cost of clothing, furniture, girlfriend, and so forth that may also be contributing to the value of my time.

20   Thus, consuming is one of the ways we respond to the void that pervades consciousness when there is nothing else to do. Shopping and surrounding ourselves

with possessions is a relatively easy way to forestall the dread of nonbeing, even though this does not improve the quality of our lives because no psychological capital is accumulated in the process. Of course, reliance on materialist coping mechanisms is encouraged by the huge economic apparatus of advertising and merchandising, which has become so ingrained in our society. A particularly egregious example of such dependence on purchasing as a pabulum for terror was the reaction of so many political leaders after the September 11 attack. The advice one heard most often in the aftermath of that tragedy was to go out and shop. Buying an extra car or refrigerator was supposed to be an act of patriotic defiance against the enemies, an act that confirmed the meaningfulness of our lives.

21   Material resources beyond a rather low threshold contribute little to a positive experience, a fact that is by now fairly well established. The first line of evidence concerning the futility of expecting material well-being to produce happiness is based on a variety of surveys conducted over several decades (Csikszentmihalyi, 1999; Diener, 2000; Myers, 2000). For instance, although the average income for Americans measured in constant dollars has doubled in the last 40 years, the level of happiness they report has not changed. Winning the lottery creates a small blip of happiness that lasts a few months, after which the lucky winner's happiness returns to what it was before (Brickman, Coates, & Janoff-Bulman, 1978). In a current longitudinal study tracking more than 800 American teenagers through high school and beyond, we find that teenagers from the most affluent suburbs tend to be less happy and have lower self-esteem than those from middle-class communities and even than those living in inner city slums (Csikszentmihalyi & Schneider, 2000). Several researchers have shown that excessive concern with financial success and material values is associated with lower levels of life satisfaction and self-esteem, presumably because such concerns reflect a sense of "contingent worth" predicated on *having* rather than *being* (Kasser & Ryan, 1993; Richins & Dawson, 1992). . . .

ENJOYMENT AS AN ALTERNATIVE TO MATERIALISM

22   Almost half a century ago, the social philosopher Hannah Arendt warned that advances in technology and the increase in free time were providing us with the opportunity to consume the whole world.

> That . . . consumption is no longer restricted to the necessities but, on the contrary, mainly concentrates on the superfluities of life . . . harbors the grave danger that eventually no object of the world will be safe from consumption and annihilation through consumption. (Arendt, 1956, p. 133)

This outcome is made even more likely by people's increasing reliance on material experiences to construct their lives. To the extent that flow in everyday life is rare and that material success has achieved a hegemony relative to other forms of success, an increasing amount of psychic energy is likely to be devoted to the pursuit of material goals. This then would accelerate the "annihilation through consumption" of the world Arendt (1956) foresaw half a century ago.

23   Looking at the impact of humankind on the planet, one of three scenarios is likely to play out in the coming decades. One is a coming to pass of the danger

Arendt and many others have warned us about: a quick deterioration of the planetary environment, an exhaustion of such basic resources as water and fossil fuels, followed by warfare and civil discord for the possession of the dwindling resources. The second possibility is that technology saves us despite our greed. Practical use of renewable energy, new agricultural practices, and desalinization of seawater could do the trick. It would be nice if this came to pass, but it would not be wise to bet the farm on it.

24   Finally, there is the possibility of a steady transformation of our lifestyles from one built around material experiences to one rich in transcendent experiences. This may be the hardest and least likely scenario, but in the long run it would be the most promising. If instead of pleasure and the false security of material goals we built our lives around investments of psychic energy in complex activities that provide flow, we would be happier as well as more likely to survive on a planet freed from the threat of terminal depletion.

25   To achieve such a goal, many habits engrained in our lifestyles have to change and many of the institutions that have arisen to supply our habits and then exploit them have to be regulated or transformed. Parents have to learn that buying a car as a graduation present is not the best way to express love for their children—teaching them to enjoy life is a far better gift. Schools have to realize that learning without joy is useless in the long run. Politics have to focus on the goal held foremost by the Declaration of Independence—the pursuit of happiness—not just by facilitating material goals, but by striving to support the evolution of psychological complexity in its various forms. To achieve all this, however, we need to agree on a new covenant—a set of nonmaterial goals that in the past religions have taught and which science has been unable to formulate thus far.

26   Such changes are not easy for two simple reasons: The genetic instructions we carry are still set to a survival mode in an environment of material scarcity, and the social institutions that have developed over time depend in large part on being able to exploit our material goals. When 2,000 years ago the Christians introduced a new lifestyle into the Roman Empire, one that dispensed with pomp and power, the stakeholders in the old regime realized the danger this posed to the institutions that protected their privileges. Thus, Christians were fed to lions and burned at the stake. How would the World Bank, the Enrons, Savings-and-Loans, and their political allies react if a new worldview based on voluntary simplicity really gained ground? Human nature has not had a chance to change that much in two millennia, and technology can be more potent than lions and stakes.

REFERENCES

Arendt, H. (1956). *The human condition.* Chicago: University of Chicago Press.
Brickman, P., Coates, D., & Janoff-Bulman, R. (1978). Lottery winners and accident victims: Is happiness relative? *Journal of Personality and Social Psychology, 36,* 917–927.
Csikszentmihalyi, M. (1975). *Beyond boredom and anxiety.* San Francisco: Jossey-Bass.
Csikszentmihalyi, M. (1990). *Flow: The psychology of optimal experience.* New York: HarperCollins.
Csikszentmihalyi, M. (1993). *The evolving self.* New York: HarperCollins.
Csikszentmihalyi, M. (1996). *Finding flow: The psychology of engagement with everyday life.* New York: Basic Books.

Csikszentmihalyi, M. (1999). If we are so rich, why aren't we happy? *American Psychologist, 54,* 821–827.

Csikszentmihalyi, M., & Figurski, T. (1982). Self-awareness and aversive experience in everyday life. *Journal of Personality, 50,* 15–28.

Csikszentmihalyi, M., & Larson, R. (1984). *Being adolescent: Conflict and growth in the teenage years.* New York: Basic Books.

Csikszentmihalyi, M., & LeFevre, J. (1989). Optimal experience in work and leisure. *Journal of Personality and Social Psychology, 56,* 15–22.

Csikszentmihalyi, M., & Schneider, B. (2000). *Becoming adult: How teenagers prepare for the world of work.* New York: Basic Books.

Diener, E. (2000). Subjective well-being: The science of happiness and a proposal for a national index. *American Psychologist, 55,* 34–43.

Kasser, T., & Ryan, R. M. (1993). A dark side of the American dream: Correlates of financial success as a central life aspiration. *Journal of Personality and Social Psychology, 65,* 410–422.

Kubey, R., & Csikszentmihalyi, M. (1990). *Television and the quality of life.* Hillsdale, NJ: Erlbaum.

Linder, S. (1970). *The harried leisure class.* New York: Columbia University Press.

Maslow, A. (1968). *Toward a psychology of being.* New York: Van Nostrand.

McLuhan, M. (1964). *Understanding media.* New York: Signet.

Myers, D. G. (2000). The funds, friends, and faith of happy people. *American Psychologist, 55,* 56–67.

Richins, M. L., & Dawson, S. (1992). A consumer values orientation for materialism and its measurement: Scale development and validation. *Journal of Consumer Research, 19,* 303–316.

Ryan, R. M., & Deci, E. L. (2000). On happiness and human potentials: A review of hedonic and eudaimonic well-being. *Annual Review of Psychology, 52,* 141–166.

Terkel, S. (1974). *Working.* New York: Pantheon.

Waterman, A. S. (1993). The conception of happiness: Contrasts of personal expressiveness (eudaimonia) and hedonic enjoyment. *Journal of Personality and Social Psychology, 64,* 678–691.

QUESTIONS FOR DISCUSSION

1. From the article "Does Money Buy Happiness?" paraphrase Robert Lane's explanation of why happiness "levels off" as incomes rise (paragraph 5). What can you find in John Schumaker's argument about the "happiness conspiracy" that corroborates Lane's interpretation?

2. According to Mihaly Csikszentmihalyi, what is the difference between pleasure and enjoyment? What is wrong with choosing TV or shopping to occupy free time? What are some activities that he labels enjoyment? What are the benefits of the more challenging activities?

3. According to Mihaly Csikszentmihalyi, why do people turn to shopping when they are depressed? What is causing the depression in the first place? (See paragraphs 16–20).

4. There is some overlap in this section with an important theme in some of the earlier sections: the comparison between spiritual and material routes to happiness. For instance, James Twitchell claims (paragraph 21, page 322) that people today find their happiness through consumer goods because it is our nature to be materialistic, not spiritual; "spiritualism is more likely a substitute when objects are scarce," he writes. How do you respond to his claim?

SUGGESTIONS FOR WRITING

For Analysis and Convincing

Examine some popular advertising campaigns aimed at young people today. What values are displayed in advertising? Do you agree with Schumaker that the values of consumer culture are not compatible with mental well-being? Arrive at a claim on the issue and defend it in an argument to convince.

For Persuasion

Because of the stress of college life, students often choose the kinds of leisure activities that Mihaly Csikszentmihalyi describes as pleasure rather than enjoyment. What sorts of activities do you choose? If you have known the benefits of "enjoyment" over "pleasure," write an argument to persuade other students that enjoyment is worth the effort. If you have experienced the "flow" state, you could describe that experience as part of your evidence.

For Convincing

Using John Schumaker and Mihaly Csikszentmihalyi as sources but adding any additional reasons and evidence you wish, make a case against the commonly held idea of happiness in mainstream American society. Be sure to define happiness as your readers would see it; then give reasons and evidence why they should not seek it.

For Mediation

Drawing from readings in all three sections of this casebook, sum up some of the major objections to the consumer society. Sum up some of the benefits. Propose suggestions for living meaningfully and well in a materialistic culture.

FOR FURTHER READING AND RESEARCH

Berger, Arthur Asa. *Shop 'Til You Drop.* Lanham, MD: Rowman & Littlefield, 2005.

Brooks, David. *On Paradise Drive: How We Live Now (And Always Have) in the Future Tense.* New York: Simon & Schuster, 2004.

Csikszentmihalyi, Mihaly. "If We Are So Rich, Why Aren't We Happy?" *American Psychologist* Oct. 1999:821–27.

Easterbrook, Gregg. *The Progress Paradox: How Life Gets Better While People Feel Worse.* New York: Random House, 2004.

———. "The Real Truth about Money." *Time* 17 Jan. 2005:32–34. Ebsco Academic Host. Dallas, TX, Fondren Library, Southern Methodist University.

Milner, Murray, Jr. *Freaks, Geeks, and Cool Kids: American Teenagers, Schools, and the Culture of Consumption.* New York: Routledge, 2004.

Rosenblatt, Roger, ed. *Consuming Desires: Consumption, Culture, and the Pursuit of Happiness.* Washington, D.C.: Island Press, 1999.

Schor, Juliet. *Born to Buy: The Commercialized Child and the New Consumer Culture.* New York: Scribner, 2004.

———. *The Overspent American: Why We Want What We Don't Need.* Basic Books, 1992.

———. *The Overworked American. The Unexpected Decline of Leisure.* HarperPerennial, 1998.

Schumaker, John F. *In Search of Happiness: Understanding an Endangered State of Mind.* Auckland: Penguin New Zealand, 2006.

———. "Dead Zone." *New Internationalist* July 2001.

Twitchell, James B. *Adcult USA: The Triumph of Advertising in American Culture.* New York: Columbia, 1997.

———. *Lead Us Into Temptation: The Triumph of American Materialism.* New York: Columbia, 1999.

———. *Living It Up: America's Love Affair with Luxury.* New York: Simon & Schuster, 2003.

Romantic Relationships: Sex, Love, and Maybe Marriage

GENERAL INTRODUCTION: LOVE TODAY

In the twenty-first century, there is no decline in the patterns and habits that make us less connected as a society: families see each other less because of the demands of school and jobs; neighbors move in and out without our knowing much about them; marriages continue to break up at the rate of about 50%; and more and more people live alone. But one connection persists—the romantic relationship based in love. Our love lives are often the defining factor in personal happiness today.

Whether you call the person a husband or wife, girlfriend or boyfriend, partner or significant other, we seem highly invested in finding love. Surveys of young adults indicate the desire to find a soul mate and stay married for life. While some people resist conventional marriage, the vast majority still seek lifelong commitment.

And yet none of this comes easily. The writers who appear in this casebook describe Americans trying to navigate in a sea of conflicting ideas and social pressures:

1. We have unrealistic ideas about what love is. Popular culture depicts love as romantic infatuation between beautiful people, usually young. Portrayals of love as long-term attachment between real-life, mature people are rare.

2. We have high expectations for what we want in a mate. Whoever invented the term "soul mate" hit a chord with people's needs today; both sexes want deep emotional intimacy with their partner. We want mates who will anticipate and satisfy all our needs.

3. We want intimacy, and yet we fear it. College students go out in groups because they want to protect themselves from intimacy. But avoiding personal relationships for years makes the search for the right partner more serious than fun. Dating services and publishers of advice books feed off of people's anxiety about finding the right partner and women's fears that it will not happen in time for them to bear children.

SECTION 1: ATTRACTING AND CHOOSING A MATE

Overview

When people are powerfully attracted to one another, they talk about having "chemistry," which turns out to be more than a metaphor. The research Lauren Slater discusses in the first selection shows that certain powerful chemicals in our bodies, especially dopamine, serotonin, and oxytocin, stimulate both the "high" of early romance and the less exciting but more stable feelings of long-term attachment. It also shows something else we could predict: that certain parts of our brain are involved much more than others in passionate attraction. Our brains began to evolve for mating hundreds of millions of years ago, when animals started reproducing sexually. In short, it is hardly surprising that desire and devotion have deep and complicated biological foundations, strong enough to take over and drive our behavior. We sometimes say that being in love is like addiction to a drug. And so it is—more than we realize.

But the chemistry of love helps us understand only a little of the mystery of love—basically why people are drawn to other people and why love can be so overwhelming. It does not help us grasp why we are attracted to some people and not to others. The second selection, from Helen Fisher's influential book, *Why We Love,* exposes the largely unconscious motivations involved. Many of these evidently developed to ensure that people would mate with genetically appropriate partners, produce many and healthy children, and tie parents together long enough to raise their offspring.

So, is romantic love in the final analysis all genetics, chemistry, brain structures, and evolution? Are we learning more about love only to take the wonderful mystery out of it? No, on both counts. As Slater and Fisher both recognize in different ways, human love is as much cultural as it is biological. When our species originated in Africa about 200,000 years ago, we were already tool-users with complex social arrangements. Our behavior has always been a combination of nature and nurture, biology and culture. So intertwined are the two that we cannot disentangle them. As far as the mystery of love is concerned, we will never understand everything involved in one person loving another, much less everything the relationship reveals to two people who love each other. But perhaps we can grow wiser, learn to love better, and free ourselves from delusions that lead to disappointment.

Love: The Chemical Reaction

LAUREN SLATER

Lauren Slater is a freelance writer. The following article appeared in *National Geographic* in February 2006.

1   My husband and I got married at eight in the morning. It was winter, freezing, the trees encased in ice and a few lone blackbirds balancing on telephone wires. We were in our early 30s, considered ourselves hip and cynical, the types who decried the institution of marriage even as we sought its status. During our wedding brunch we put out a big suggestion box and asked people to slip us advice on how to avoid divorce; we thought it was a funny, clear-eyed, grounded sort of thing to do, although the suggestions were mostly foolish: Screw the toothpaste cap on tight. After the guests left, the house got quiet. There were flowers everywhere: puckered red roses and fragile ferns. "What can we do that's really romantic?" I asked. . . . Benjamin suggested we take a bath. I didn't want a bath. He suggested a lunch of chilled white wine and salmon. I was sick of salmon.

2   What can we do that's really romantic? The wedding was over, the silence seemed suffocating, and I felt the familiar disappointment after a longed-for event has come and gone. We were married. Hip, hip, hooray. I decided to take a walk. . . . I came to our town's tattoo parlor. Now I am not a tattoo type person, but for some reason, on that cold silent Sunday, I decided to walk in. "Can I help you?" a woman asked.

3   "Is there a kind of tattoo I can get that won't be permanent?" I asked.

4   "Henna tattoos," she said.

5   She explained that they lasted for six weeks, were used at Indian weddings, were stark and beautiful and all brown. She showed me pictures of Indian women with jewels in their noses, their arms scrolled and laced with the henna markings. Indeed they were beautiful, sharing none of the gaudy comic strip quality of the tattoos we see in the United States. . . . And because I had just gotten married, and because I was feeling a post wedding letdown, and because I wanted something really romantic to sail me through the night, I decided to get one.

6   "Where?" she asked.

7   "Here," I said. I laid my hands over my breasts and belly.

8   She raised her eyebrows. "Sure," she said.

9   I am a modest person. But I took off my shirt, lay on the table, heard her in the back room mixing powders and paints. She came to me carrying a small black-bellied pot inside of which was a rich red mush, slightly glittering. She adorned me. She gave me vines and flowers. She turned my body into a stake supporting whole new gardens of growth, and then, low around my hips, she painted a delicate chain-linked chastity belt. An hour later, the paint dry, I put my clothes back on, went home to find [Benjamin]. This, I knew, was my gift to him, the kind of present you offer only once in your lifetime. I let him undress me.

10   "Wow," he said, standing back.

11   I blushed, and we began.

12   We are no longer beginning. . . . This does not surprise me. Even back then, wearing the decor of desire, the serpentining tattoos, I knew they would fade, their red-clay color bleaching out until they were gone. On my wedding day I didn't care.

13   I do now. Eight years later, pale as a pillowcase, here I sit, with all the extra pounds and baggage time brings. And the questions have only grown more insistent. Does passion necessarily diminish over time? How reliable is romantic love, really, as a means of choosing one's mate? . . .

14   In the Western world we have for centuries concocted poems and stories and plays about the cycles of love, the way it morphs and changes over time, the way passion grabs us. . . and then leaves us for something saner. . . . We have relied on stories to explain the complexities of love, tales of jealous gods and arrows. Now, however, these stories—so much a part of every civilization—may be changing as science steps in to explain what we have always felt to be myth, to be magic. For the first time, new research has begun to illuminate where love lies in the brain, the particulars of its chemical components.

15   Anthropologist Helen Fisher may be the closest we've ever come to having a doyenne of desire. . . . She has devoted much of her career to studying the biochemical pathways of love in all its manifestations: lust, romance, attachment, the way they wax and wane. . . . "A woman unconsciously uses orgasms as a way of deciding whether or not a man is good for her. If he's impatient and rough, and she doesn't have the orgasm, she may instinctively feel he's less likely to be a good husband and father. Scientists think the fickle female orgasm may have evolved to help women distinguish Mr. Right from Mr. Wrong."

16   One of Fisher's central pursuits in the past decade has been looking at love, quite literally, with the aid of an MRI machine. Fisher and her colleagues Arthur Aron and Lucy Brown recruited subjects who had been "madly in love" for an average of seven months. Once inside the MRI machine, subjects were shown two photographs, one neutral, the other of their loved one.

17   What Fisher saw fascinated her. When each subject looked at his or her loved one, the parts of the brain linked to reward and pleasure—the ventral tegmental area and the caudate nucleus—lit up. What excited Fisher most was not so much finding a location, an address, for love as tracing its specific chemical pathways. Love lights up the caudate nucleus because it is home to a dense spread of receptors for a neurotransmitter called dopamine. . . . In the right proportions, dopamine creates intense energy, exhilaration, focused attention, and motivation to win rewards. It is why, when you are newly in love, you can stay up all night, watch the sun rise, run a race, ski fast down a slope ordinarily too steep for your skill. . . .

18   I first fell in love when I was only 12, with a teacher. His name was Mr. McArthur, and he wore open-toed sandals and sported a beard. I had never had a male teacher before, and I thought it terribly exotic. Mr. McArthur did things no other teacher dared to do. He explained to us the physics of farting. He demonstrated how to make an egg explode. He smoked cigarettes at recess, leaning languidly against the side of the school building, the ash growing longer and longer until he casually tapped it off with his finger. . . .

19   Sound familiar? . . . Donatella Marazziti is a professor of psychiatry at the University of Pisa in Italy who has studied the biochemistry of lovesickness. Having been in love twice herself and felt its awful power, Marazziti became interested in exploring the similarities between love and obsessive-compulsive disorder.

20   She and her colleagues measured serotonin levels in the blood of 24 subjects who had fallen in love within the past six months and obsessed about this love object for at least four hours every day. Serotonin is, perhaps, our star neurotransmitter, altered by our star psychiatric medications: Prozac and Zoloft and Paxil, among others. Researchers have long hypothesized that people with obsessive-compulsive disorder (OCD) have a serotonin "imbalance." Drugs like Prozac seem to alleviate OCD by increasing the amount of this neurotransmitter available at the juncture between neurons.

21   Marazziti compared the lovers' serotonin levels with those of a group of people suffering from OCD and another group who were free from both passion and mental illness. Levels of serotonin in both the obsessives' blood and the lovers' blood were 40 percent lower than those in her normal subjects. Translation: Love and obsessive-compulsive disorder could have a similar chemical profile. Translation: Love and mental illness may be difficult to tell apart. Translation: Don't be a fool. Stay away.

22   Of course that's a mandate none of us can follow. We do fall in love, sometimes over and over again, subjecting ourselves, each time, to a very sick state of mind. There is hope, however, for those caught in the grip of runaway passion—Prozac. There's nothing like that bicolored bullet for damping down the sex drive. . . . Helen Fisher believes that the ingestion of drugs like Prozac jeopardizes one's ability to fall in love—and stay in love. By dulling the keen edge of love and its associated libido, relationships go stale. Says Fisher, "I know of one couple on the edge of divorce. The wife was on an antidepressant. Then she went off it, started having orgasms once more, felt the renewal of sexual attraction for her husband, and they're now in love all over again.". . .

23   Psychiatrists such as Thomas Lewis from the University of California at San Francisco's School of Medicine hypothesize that romantic love is rooted in our earliest infantile experiences with intimacy, how we felt at the breast, our mother's face, these things of pure unconflicted comfort that get engraved in our brain and that we ceaselessly try to recapture as adults. According to this theory we love whom we love not so much because of the future we hope to build but because of the past we hope to reclaim. Love is reactive, not proactive, it arches us backward, which may be why a certain person just "feels right." Or "feels familiar." He or she is familiar. He or she has a certain look or smell or sound or touch that activates buried memories.

24   When I first met my husband, I believed this psychological theory was more or less correct. My husband has red hair and a soft voice. A chemist, he is whimsical and odd. One day before we married he dunked a rose in liquid nitrogen so it froze, whereupon he flung it against the wall, spectacularly shattering it. That's when I fell in love with him. My father, too, has red hair, a soft voice, and many eccentricities. He was prone to bursting into song, prompted by something we never saw.

25 However, it turns out my theories about why I came to love my husband may be just so much hogwash. Evolutionary psychology has said good riddance to Freud and the Oedipal complex and all that other transcendent stuff and hello to simple survival skills. . . . It hypothesizes that we tend to see as attractive, and thereby choose as mates, people who look healthy. . . .

26 It all seems too good to be true, that we are so hardwired and yet unconscious of the wiring. . . . We say, "I married him (or her) because he's intelligent, she's beautiful, he's witty, she's compassionate." But we may just be as deluded about love as we are when we're in love. . . .

27 Why doesn't passionate love last? How is it possible to see a person as beautiful on Monday, and 364 days later, on another Monday, to see that beauty as bland? Surely the object of your affection could not have changed that much. She still has the same shaped eyes. Her voice has always had that husky sound, but now it grates on you—she sounds like she needs an antibiotic. Or maybe you're the one who needs an antibiotic, because the partner you once loved and cherished and saw as though saturated with starlight now feels more like a low-level infection, tiring you, sapping all your strength.

28 Studies around the world confirm that, indeed, passion usually ends. Its conclusion is as common as its initial flare. No wonder some cultures think selecting a lifelong mate based on something so fleeting is folly. Helen Fisher has suggested that relationships frequently break up after four years because that's about how long it takes to raise a child through infancy. Passion, that wild, prismatic insane feeling, turns out to be practical after all. We . . . need enough passion to start breeding, and then feelings of attachment take over as the partners bond to raise a helpless human infant. . . .

29 Biologically speaking, the reasons romantic love fades may be found in the way our brains respond to the surge and pulse of dopamine that accompanies passion and makes us fly. . . . Maybe it's a good thing that romance fizzles. Would we have railroads, bridges, planes, faxes, vaccines, and television if we were all always besotted? In place of the ever evolving technology that has marked human culture from its earliest tool use, we would have instead only bonbons, bouquets, and birth control. More seriously, if the chemically altered state induced by romantic love is akin to a mental illness or a drug-induced euphoria, exposing yourself for too long could result in psychological damage. . . .

30 Once upon a time, in India, a boy and a girl fell in love without their parents' permission. They were from different castes, their relationship radical and unsanctioned. Picture it: the sparkling sari, the boy in white linen, the clandestine meetings on tiled terraces with a fat, white moon floating overhead. Who could deny these lovers their pleasure, or condemn the force of their attraction?

31 Their parents could. In one recent incident a boy and girl from different castes were hanged at the hands of their parents as hundreds of villagers watched. A couple who eloped were stripped and beaten. Yet another couple committed suicide after their parents forbade them to marry.

32 Anthropologists used to think that romance was a Western construct, a bourgeois by-product of the Middle Ages. Romance was for the sophisticated, took

place in cafes, with coffees and Cabernets, or on silk sheets, or in rooms with a flickering fire. It was assumed that non-Westerners, with their broad familial and social obligations, were spread too thin for particular passions. How could a collectivist culture celebrate or in any way sanction the obsession with one individual that defines new love? Could a lice-ridden peasant really feel passion?

33   Easily, as it turns out. Scientists now believe that romance is panhuman, embedded in our brains since Pleistocene times. In a study of 166 cultures, anthropologists William Jankowiak and Edward Fischer observed evidence of passionate love in 147 of them. In another study men and women from Europe, Japan, and the Philippines were asked to fill out a survey to measure their experiences of passionate love. All three groups professed feeling passion with the same searing intensity.

34   But though romantic love may be universal, its cultural expression is not. To the Fulbe tribe of northern Cameroon, poise matters more than passion. Men who spend too much time with their wives are taunted, and those who are weak-kneed are thought to have fallen under a dangerous spell. Love may be inevitable, but for the Fulbe its manifestations are shameful, equated with sickness and social impairment.

35   In India romantic love has traditionally been seen as dangerous, a threat to a well-crafted caste system in which marriages are arranged as a means of preserving lineage and bloodlines. Thus the gruesome tales, the warnings embedded in fables about what happens when one's wayward impulses take over. Today love marriages appear to be on the rise in India, often in defiance of parents' wishes.

36   The triumph of romantic love is celebrated in Bollywood films. Yet most Indians still believe arranged marriages are more likely to succeed than love marriages. In one survey of Indian college students, 76 percent said they'd marry someone with all the right qualities even if they weren't in love with the person (compared with only 14 percent of Americans). Marriage is considered too important a step to leave to chance.

37   Renu Dinakaran is a striking 45-year-old woman who lives in Bangalore, India . . . . [She] was born into a traditional Indian family where an arranged marriage was expected. She was not an arranged kind of person, though, emerging from her earliest days as a fierce tennis player, too sweaty for saris, and smarter than many of the men around her. Nevertheless at the age of 17 she was married off to a first cousin, a man she barely knew, a man she wanted to learn to love, but couldn't. Renu considers many arranged marriages to be acts of "state-sanctioned rape."

38   Renu hoped to fall in love with her husband, but the more years that passed, the less love she felt, until, at the end, she was shrunken, bitter, hiding behind the curtains of her in-laws' bungalow, looking with longing at the couple on the balcony across from theirs. "It was so obvious to me that couple had married for love, and I envied them. I really did. It hurt me so much to see how they stood together, how they went shopping for bread and eggs."

39   Exhausted from being forced into confinement, from being swaddled in saris that made it difficult to move, from resisting the pressure to eat off her husband's plate, Renu did what traditional Indian culture forbids one to do. She left. By this time she had had two children. She took them with her. In her mind was an old

movie she'd seen on TV, a movie so strange and enticing to her, so utterly confounding and comforting at the same time, that she couldn't get it out of her head. It was 1986. The movie was *Love Story*. "Before I saw movies like *Love Story*, I didn't realize the power that love can have," she says.

40 Renu was lucky in the end. In Mumbai she met a man named Anil, and it was then, for the first time, that she felt passion. "When I first met Anil, it was like nothing I'd ever experienced. He was the first man I ever had an orgasm with. I was high, just high, all the time. And I knew it wouldn't last, couldn't last, and so that infused it with a sweet sense of longing, almost as though we were watching the end approach while we were also discovering each other."

41 When Renu speaks of the end, she does not, to be sure, mean the end of her relationship with Anil; she means the end of a certain stage. The two are still happily married, companionable, loving if not "in love," with a playful black dachshund they bought together. Their relationship, once so full of fire, now seems to simmer along at an even temperature, enough to keep them well fed and warm. They are grateful.

42 "Would I want all that passion back?" Renu asks. "Sometimes, yes. But to tell you the truth, it was exhausting."

43 From a physiological point of view, this couple has moved from the dopamine-drenched state of romantic love to the relative quiet of an oxytocin-induced attachment. Oxytocin is a hormone that promotes a feeling of connection, bonding. It is released when we hug our long-term spouses, or our children. It is released when a mother nurses her infant. . . . In long-term relationships that work—like Renu and Anil's—oxytocin is believed to be abundant in both partners. In long-term relationships that never get off the ground, like Renu and her first husband's, or that crumble once the high is gone, chances are the couple has not found a way to stimulate or sustain oxytocin production.

44 "But there are things you can do to help it along," says Helen Fisher. "Massage. Make love. These things trigger oxytocin and thus make you feel much closer to your partner."

45 Well, I suppose that's good advice, but it's based on the assumption that you still want to have sex with that boring windbag of a husband. Should you fake-it-till-you-make-it?

46 "Yes," says Fisher. "Assuming a fairly healthy relationship, if you have enough orgasms with your partner, you may become attached to him or her. You will stimulate oxytocin.". . .

47 Arthur Aron, a psychologist at Stony Brook University in New York, conducted an experiment that illuminates some of the mechanisms by which people become and stay attracted. He recruited a group of men and women and put opposite sex pairs in rooms together, instructing each pair to perform a series of tasks, which included telling each other personal details about themselves. He then asked each couple to stare into each other's eyes for two minutes. After this encounter, Aron found most of the couples, previously strangers to each other, reported feelings of attraction. In fact, one couple went on to marry.

48 Fisher says this exercise works wonders for some couples. Aron and Fisher also suggest doing novel things together, because novelty triggers dopamine in the

brain, which can stimulate feelings of attraction. In other words, if your heart flutters in his presence, you might decide it's not because you're anxious but because you love him. Carrying this a step further, Aron and others have found that even if you just jog in place and then meet someone, you're more likely to think they're attractive. So first dates that involve a nerve-racking activity, like riding a roller coaster, are more likely to lead to second and third dates. That's a strategy worthy of posting on Match.com. Play some squash. And in times of stress—natural disasters, blackouts, predators on the prowl—lock up tight and hold your partner.

49   In Somerville, Massachusetts, where I live with my husband, our predators are primarily mosquitoes. That needn't stop us from trying to enter the windows of each other's soul. When I propose this to Benjamin, he raises an eyebrow.

50   "Why don't we just go out for Cambodian food?" he says.

51   "Because that's not how the experiment happened."

52   As a scientist, my husband is always up for an experiment. But our lives are so busy that, in order to do this, we have to make a plan. We will meet next Wednesday at lunchtime and try the experiment in our car.

53   On the Tuesday night before our rendezvous, I have to make an unplanned trip to New York. My husband is more than happy to forget our date. I, however, am not. That night, from my hotel room, I call him.

54   "We can do it on the phone," I say.

55   "What am I supposed to stare into?" he asks. "The keypad?"

56   "There's a picture of me hanging in the hall. Look at that for two minutes. I'll look at a picture I have of you in my wallet."

57   "Come on," he says.

58   "Be a sport," I say. "It's better than nothing."

59   Maybe not. Two minutes seems like a long time to stare at someone's picture with a receiver pressed to your ear. My husband sneezes, and I try to imagine his picture sneezing right along with him, and this makes me laugh.

60   Another 15 seconds pass, slowly, each second stretched to its limit so I can almost hear time, feel time, its taffy-like texture, the pop it makes when it's done. Pop pop pop. I stare and stare at my husband's picture. It doesn't produce any sense of startling intimacy, and I feel defeated.

61   Still, I keep on. I can hear him breathing on the other end. The photograph before me was taken a year or so ago, cut to fit my wallet, his strawberry blond hair pulled back in a ponytail. I have never really studied it before. And I realize that in this picture my husband is not looking straight back at me, but his pale blue eyes are cast sideways, off to the left, looking at something I can't see. I touch his eyes. I peer close, and then still closer, at his averted face. Is there something sad in his expression, something sad in the way he gazes off?

62   I look toward the side of the photo, to find what it is he's looking at, and then I see it: a tiny turtle coming toward him. Now I remember how he caught it after the camera snapped, how he held it gently in his hands, showed it to our kids, stroked its shell, his forefinger moving over the scaly dome, how he held the animal out toward me, a love offering. I took it, and together we sent it back to the sea.

"That First Fine Careless Rapture": Who We Choose

HELEN FISHER

> Helen Fisher is a research professor in anthropology at Rutgers. The following selection comes from her celebrated book, *Why We Love: The Nature and Chemistry of Romantic Love.*

1   Love can be triggered when you least expect it—by pure chance. The perfect partner can sit right next to you at a party and you might not notice him or her if you are exceptionally busy at work or school, enmeshed in another relationship, or otherwise emotionally preoccupied.

2   But if you just entered college or moved to a new city by yourself, recently recovered from an unsatisfactory love affair, began to make enough money to raise a family, are lonely or suffering through a difficult experience, or have too much spare time, you are ripe to fall in love.[1] In fact, people who are emotionally aroused, be it by joy, sadness, anxiety, fear, curiosity, or *any* other feeling, are more likely to be vulnerable to this passion.[2]

3   I suspect this is because all agitated mental states are associated with arousal mechanisms in the brain, as well as with elevated levels of stress hormones. Both systems elevate levels of dopamine—thus setting up the chemistry for romantic passion. . . .

4   Many other hidden forces play a role in whom you choose. Among them: mystery.

MYSTERY

5   Both sexes are often attracted to those they find mysterious. As Baudelaire wrote, "We love women in proportion to their degree of strangeness to us." The sense that one has a slippery grip on an elusive, improbable treasure can trigger romantic passion.

6   The reverse is also true. Familiarity can deaden thoughts of romantic love—as life on one Israeli kibbutz has shown. Here children grew up together in a common house where they lived, slept, and bathed with other youths of all ages. Boys and girls touched and lay together playfully. By age twelve, however, they became tense with one another. Then as teenagers, they developed strong brother-sister bonds. But none of those who started life in this common cradle married a fellow kibbutznik.[3] So scientists now think that at a critical time in childhood, sometime between ages three and six, boys and girls who live in close proximity and get to know each other well lose the ability to fall in love with one another. . . .

7   You and I inherited this natural repulsion for copulation with close family members and other individuals we know well, a distaste that undoubtedly evolved to discourage in-breeding—the destructive act of mixing one's DNA with close kin. As a result, we are more likely to become attracted to someone from outside our family or the group in which we were raised—someone with a touch of mystery. . . .

DO OPPOSITES ATTRACT?

8 Nevertheless, "that first fine careless rapture," as Robert Browning called romantic love, is generally directed toward someone much like one's self. Most people around the world do feel that amorous chemistry for unfamiliar individuals of the *same* ethnic, social, religious, educational, and economic background, who have a similar amount of physical attractiveness, a comparable intelligence, and similar attitudes, expectations, values, interests, and social and communication skills.[4]

9 In fact, in a new study of mate selection in America, evolutionary biologists Peter Buston and Stephen Emlen report that young men and women think of themselves as particular types of marriage partners and choose people with the same traits, ranging from financial and physical assets to intricacies of personality.[5] If a woman is blessed with a trust fund, for example, she seeks another from the upper class. Handsome men seek beautiful women. And those devoted to family and sexual fidelity select someone with these attributes. . . . Men and women also gravitate to lovers who share their sense of humor, to those with similar social and political values, and to individuals with much the same beliefs about life in general.[6] . . .

SYMMETRY: THE "GOLDEN MEAN"

10 Another biological taste we have inherited from the animal kingdom is our tendency to choose well-proportioned mates. . . . Almost twenty-five hundred years ago Aristotle maintained that there were some universal standards of physical beauty. One, he believed, was balanced bodily proportions, including symmetry. This accorded with his high respect for what he called the golden mean, or moderation between extremes.

11 Modern science supports Aristotle's notion. Symmetry is beautiful—to insects, birds, mammals, all of the primates, and people around the world.[7] Female scorpion flies seek mates with uniform wings. Barn swallows like partners with well-proportioned tails. Monkeys are partial to consorts with symmetrical teeth. If you walk into a village in New Guinea and point to the most beautiful man or woman sitting around the campfire, the natives will agree with you.[8] And when researchers used computers to blend many faces into a composite "average" face, both men and women liked the average face better than any of the individual ones.[9] It was more balanced. Even two-month-old infants gaze longer at more symmetrical faces.[10] . . .

12 The beauty of symmetry does tell a basic truth. Creatures with balanced, well-proportioned ears, eyes, teeth, and jaws, with symmetrical elbows, knees, and breasts, have been able to repel bacteria, viruses, and other minute predators that can cause bodily irregularities. By displaying symmetry, animals advertise their superior genetic ability to combat diseases.[11]

13 So our human attraction to symmetrical suitors is a primitive animal mechanism designed to guide us to select genetically sturdy mating partners.[12]

14 And nature has taken no chances; the brain naturally responds to a beautiful face. When scientists recorded the brain activity of heterosexual men ages twenty-one

to thirty-five as they looked at women with beautiful faces, the ventral tegmental area (VTA) "lit up."[13] A similar response occurred in our scanning study: those subjects who gazed at photos of better-looking partners showed more activity in the VTA. And the VTA is rich with dopamine—the neurotransmitter that provides the energy, elation, focussed attention, and motivation to win a reward. . . .

15   Because symmetry enhances one's choices in the mating game, women go to extraordinary lengths to achieve it or at least a semblance of it. With powders they make the two sides of the face more similar. With mascara and eyeliner, they make their eyes appear more alike. With lipstick they enhance one lip to match the other. And with plastic surgery, exercise, belts, bras, and tight jeans and shirts, they mold their forms to create the symmetrical proportions men prefer.

16   Nature helps. Scientists have found that women's hands and ears are more symmetrical during monthly ovulation—a time when it is reproductively important to attract a man.[14] Women's breasts become more symmetrical during ovulation too.[15] Moreover, young men and young women are often quite symmetrical; we become more and more lopsided as we age.

"WAIST TO HIP" RATIO

17   The golden mean of balance also applies to other bodily proportions. To a group of American men, psychologist Devendra Singh displayed an array of line drawings of young women and asked which body types they found most attractive.[16] Most chose women whose waist circumference was about 70 percent of their hips. This experiment was then redone in Britain, Germany, Australia, India, Uganda, and several other countries. Responses varied, but many informants favored this same general waist-to-hip ratio.

18   When Singh measured the waist-to-hip ratio of 286 ancient sculptures from several African tribes, as well as from ancient India, Egypt, Greece, and Rome, he found that all favored a ratio that was smaller for women than for men. And in a study of 330 artworks of Europe, Asia, the Americas, and Africa, some of which date back thirty-two thousand years, scientists found that most women were depicted with a waist-to-hip ratio of these same general proportions.[17] Interestingly, *Playboy* centerfolds display these proportions, too, as do American "supermodels.". . .

19   A woman's waist-to-hip ratio is largely inherited; it is produced by genes. Moreover, although it clearly varies from one woman to the next, this ratio adjusts during ovulation to come closer to 70 percent. Why has nature gone to such extraordinary lengths to produce curvaceous women? And why do men around the world appreciate this particular waist-to-hip ratio in women?

20   Most likely for an evolutionary reason. Women with a waist-to-hip ratio of around 70 percent are more likely to bear babies, Singh reports. They possess the right amount of fat in the right places—due to high levels of bodily estrogen in relation to testosterone. Women who vary substantially from these proportions find it harder to get pregnant; they conceive later in life; and they have more miscarriages. . . .

21   So Singh theorizes that male attraction to a specific female waist-to-hip ratio is a natural preference for healthy, fertile partners. . . . Of course, men prefer other things in women, too.

WHO MEN CHOOSE

22 In a classic study of some ten thousand people in thirty-seven societies, scientists asked men and women to rank eighteen characteristics in order of their importance in choosing a spouse.[18] Both sexes ranked love or mutual attraction first. A dependable character came next, followed by emotional stability and maturity, and a pleasing disposition. Both men and women also said they would choose someone who was kind, smart, educated, sociable, healthy, and interested in home and family.

23 But this study also showed a distinct gender difference in romantic tastes. When it came to sizing up potential romantic partners, men were more likely to choose women who displayed *visual* signs of youth and beauty.

24 These masculine predilections are documented across millennia and cultures.[19] Osiris, the legendary ruler of predynastic Egypt, was overwhelmed by the physical beauty of his beloved wife, Isis. As he wrote over four thousand years ago, "Isis has cast her net, / and ensnared me / in the noose of her hair / I am held by her eyes / curbed by her necklace / imprisoned by the scent of her skin."[20]

25 A Tiv tribesman of Nigeria was swept away by the shapeliness of a woman, exclaiming, "When I saw her dance she took my life away and I knew I must follow her."[21]

26 American men who place courtship ads in newspapers and magazines are three times more likely than women to mention that they seek beauty in a partner.[22]

27 And on average, men around the world marry women who are three years younger than themselves.[23] In the United States, men who remarry usually choose a woman about five years younger; if they wed a third time, they often take a bride about eight years their junior.[24]

28 When asked why people desire physical beauty, Aristotle replied: "No one that is not blind could ask that question." Men unquestionably find good-looking women aesthetically pleasing to look at. They also like to impress friends and colleagues with their dazzling girlfriends or trophy wives. In fact, people in general tend to regard beautiful women (and good-looking men) as warm, smart, strong, giving, friendly, polite, sexy, interesting, financially secure, and socially popular.[25]

29 But evolutionary psychologists now believe that men subconsciously also prefer youth and beauty because it gives them reproductive payoffs.[26] Young women with smooth skin, snow-white teeth, sparkling eyes, gleaming hair, taut muscles, a lithe body, and a lively personality are more likely to be healthy and energetic—good qualities for bearing and rearing babies. Smooth, clear skin and babylike facial features also signal elevated levels of estrogen that can aid in reproduction. . . .

THE MALE BRAIN IN LOVE

30 Our fMRI study on the brain circuitry of people in love turned up some unexpected results: we found several gender differences.[27] These findings were complex and varied. Men did not fit neatly in one category and women in another. . . . But there were statistically significant differences between the sexes. No one knows exactly what these findings mean. But I will speculate about men for the moment and theorize about women later.

31   In our sample, men tended to show more activity than women in brain regions associated with *visual* processing, particularly of the face.

32   Could this have evolved to enhance men's ability to fall in love when they *saw* a woman who was young, symmetrical, and a good reproductive bet? Maybe. This brain activity could also help explain why men generally fall in love faster than women.[28] When the time is right and a man *sees* an attractive woman, he is anatomically equipped to rapidly associate attractive *visual* features with feelings of romantic passion. What an effective courtship device.

33   Indeed, we found another gender difference that could have evolved to help men court efficiently. . . . When our subjects looked at their beloveds, men tended to show more positive activity in a brain region associated with penile erection. . . . This male response directly links romantic passion with a brain region associated with sexual arousal.

34   Although this may be far-fetched, this male brain response may also shed light on why men so avidly support the worldwide trade in *visual* pornography; why women are more likely than men to regard their personal appearance as an important component of their self-esteem;[29] and why women go to such extraordinary lengths to advertise their assets *visually,* with all manner of clothing, makeup, and ornaments. . . .

MALE "MATING EFFORT"

35 Another male penchant interests me because it also comes, I think, directly from deep history. Psychologists report that men want to help women, to solve their problems, to be useful by *doing* something.[30] Men feel manly when they rescue a damsel in distress.

36   No doubt millions of years of protecting and providing for women has bred into the male brain this tendency to choose women they feel they need to save. In fact, the male brain is well built to assist women. Men are, on average, more skilled at all sorts of mechanical and spatial tasks than women are. Men are problem solvers.[31] And many of men's particular skills are fashioned in the womb by high levels of fetal testosterone. Perhaps men evolved this biological machinery, at least in part, to attract, assist, and save women.

37   Men are also more single-minded than women when they love. Only 40 percent of the young women in my survey agreed with the statement: "Having a good relationship with _____ is more important than having a good relationship with my family," whereas a solid 60 percent of young men reported that their love relationship came first. Moreover, although most people think women are the ones who wait by the phone, change their schedules, and hang around the office or the gym to be available to a beloved, my questionnaire showed that American men reorder their priorities more frequently than women do. . . .

38   This male penchant may be due to the fact that men have fewer intimate connections with their natal families and friends than women. But deep evolutionary forces probably contribute. Women are custodians of the egg—a valuable commodity. And women expend much more time rearing infants and small children, a vital job. For millions of years men needed to make themselves available to potential mating partners, even risk their lives to save these precious reproductive vessels. . . .

THE FEMALE BRAIN IN LOVE

39 | Much of the psychological literature reports that both sexes feel passionate romantic love with roughly the same intensity.[32] I suspect this is true; their responses are just somewhat different. For example, my questionnaire on this passion showed that more American and Japanese women than men reported feeling "lighter than air" when they were certain their beloved felt passionately about them. Women also experienced slightly more obsessive thinking about an amor.

40 | Our fMRI experiment also showed several ways in which our female subjects responded differently than our male participants. When women looked at the photo of their beloved, they tended to show *more* activity in the body of the caudate nucleus and the septum—brain regions associated with motivation and attention. Parts of the septum are also associated with the processing of emotion. Women also showed activity in some different brain regions, including one associated with retrieval and recall of memories and some associated with attention and emotion.[33]

41 | Once again, no one knows what these results mean. But as you recall memories and register your emotions, you inform yourself about your feelings[34] and assemble information into patterns; both activities help you make decisions. And for millions of years, women needed to make appropriate decisions about a potential mating partner. If an ancestral woman became pregnant during a romance, she was obliged to incubate the embryo for nine months, then deliver the child. These were (and remain) metabolically costly, time-consuming, uncomfortable, and physically dangerous tasks. Moreover, a woman had to raise her helpless infant through a long childhood and adolescence.

42 | While a man can *see* many of a woman's assets for bearing and rearing babies, a woman cannot see a man's "mate value" just by looking. She must compute a partner's ability to protect and provide. And these gender differences suggest that when a woman gazes at her lover, natural selection has given her specific brain responses that enable her to recall the details and emotions she needs to assess her man.

43 | "Heredity is nothing but stored environment," wrote the great botanist Luther Burbank. The vicissitudes of rearing helpless infants in a hostile ancestral environment have unquestionably bred into women other mechanisms they use to choose a mate.

WHO WOMEN CHOOSE

44 | In a survey of eight hundred personal advertisements placed in newspapers and magazines, American women sought partners who offered financial security twice as frequently as men did.[35] Many female doctors, lawyers, and very wealthy women are interested in men with even more money and status than themselves.[36] In fact, women everywhere in the world are more attracted to partners with education, ambition, wealth, respect, status, and position—the kinds of assets their prehistoric predecessors needed in a parenting partner. As scientists sum this up: men look for sex objects and women look for success objects.

45 | Women are also attracted to tall men, perhaps because towering men are more likely to acquire prestige in business and politics and provide more bodily defense.[37] Women like men who sit in a carefree position, a sign of dominance, as well as

men who are self-confident and assertive. Women are somewhat more likely to choose a long-term partner who is smart.[38] And women respond to men who are well-coordinated, strong, and courageous—as world literature and legend attest. . . .

46   No wonder a man's self-respect is more tightly linked to his general status at work and in the community.[39] No wonder men are also more likely to jeopardize their health, safety, and spare time to achieve rank. . . .

47   Women also prefer men with distinctive cheekbones and a strong jaw—for another unconscious reason. Masculine cheekbones and a rugged jawline are built with testosterone—and testosterone suppresses the immune system. Only exceedingly healthy teenage boys can tolerate the effects of this and build a rugged face.[40] Not surprisingly, around the time of monthly ovulation women become even more interested in men with these signs of testosterone. Now they can get pregnant, so they unconsciously seek males with superior genes. . . .

CASUAL PASSION

48   The sexes become more flexible in their romantic choices when they are looking for short-term love, such as when they are on vacation or seeking a temporary romance while pursuing other interests.

49   Historically, women looking for short-term passion choose free-spending men with resources—bestowers of gifts, lavish vacations, fancy dinners, and social or political connections.[41] Frugality was not acceptable to a woman on a fling. But today's women are wealthier and more independent than in the historical past and those pursuing casual passion are somewhat more eager to choose tall, symmetrical men with chiseled cheekbones and rugged jaws, men who are likely to have sturdy genes.[42]

50   Some of these women are testing their own mate value—seeing what kind of man they can attract.[43] Others use a casual relationship as a form of insurance policy; they want a backup in case their own mate defects or becomes ill and dies. But many women also use casual sex to "try out" a particular person for a longer relationship.

51   Psychologists know this because women are less enthusiastic than men about engaging in a one-night stand with someone who is married or involved in another love relationship. Not only is this lover unavailable but his resources are directed elsewhere. And since he is cheating on his established partner, he is likely to be unfaithful to her as well. Most women don't lower their standards for brief love affairs either. They still seek a partner who is healthy, stable, funny, kind, and generous. For women, casual sex is often not as casual as it is for men.[44] . . .

52   "Tell me where is fancy bred, / Or in the heart, or in the head? / How begot, how nourished? / Reply, reply."[45] We can answer much of Shakespeare's question. A taste for symmetry; men's love of youthfulness and beauty and their need to help women in distress; women's attraction to men's wealth and status: these biological predilections can potentially trigger the brain circuitry for romantic love. An element of mystery, along with similarities of background, education, and beliefs, guide our tastes. Chance, timing, and proximity can also play a part in who we choose.

53   But of all the forces that guide your mate selection, I think the most important is your personal history, the myriad childhood, teenage, and adult experiences that

have shaped and reshaped your likes and dislikes throughout your life. All these combine to create your largely unconscious psychological chart, what is called your "love map."

LOVE MAPS

54 | We grow up in a sea of moments that slowly sculpt our romantic choices. Your mother's wit and way with words; your father's zest for politics and tennis; your uncle's love of boats and hiking; your sister's interests in training dogs; how people in your household use silence, express intimacy and anger; how those around you handle money; the amount of laughter at the dinner table; what your older brother finds challenging; your religious education and intellectual pursuits; the pastimes of your school chums; what your grandmother finds polite; how the community you live in views honor, justice, loyalty, gratitude, and kindness; what teachers admire and deplore; what you see on television and in the movies: these and thousands of other subtle forces build our individual interests, values, and beliefs. So by the teenage years, each of us has constructed a catalogue of aptitudes and mannerisms we are looking for in a mate.

55 | This chart is unique. Even identical twins, who have similar interests and lifestyles, as well as similar religious, political, and social values, tend to develop different styles of loving and choose different types of partners.[46] Subtle differences in their experiences have shaped their romantic tastes.

56 | This idiosyncratic psychological chart is also enormously complex. Some people seek a partner who will agree with what they say; others like a spirited debate. Some love a prank; others want predictability, order, or flamboyance. Some want to be amused; others wish to be intellectually excited. Many need a partner who will support their causes, quell their fears, or share their goals. And some choose a partner for the lifestyle they wish to lead. Søren Kierkegaard, the Danish philosopher, felt that love must be unselfish, filled with devotion for the beloved. But some are uncomfortable with a doting mate. Instead, they want a partner to challenge them to grow intellectually or spiritually.

57 | Love maps are subtle and difficult to read. A good example is a friend of mine who grew up with an alcoholic father. She acclimated to the unpredictability around the house. But she resolved she would never marry a man like dear ol' dad. Indeed, she didn't. She married an unpredictable, chaotic artist instead—a match that suited her largely unconscious love map.

58 | "Love looks not with the eyes, but the mind, / And therefore is winged Cupid painted blind," wrote Shakespeare.[47] This is probably why it is so difficult to introduce single friends to one another and why Internet dating services often fail: matchmakers don't know the intricacies of their clients' love templates. Often men and women don't know their own love map either. . . .

THE LOVER'S PSYCHE

59 | . . . Individual "love maps" probably begin to develop in infancy as we adjust to countless environmental forces that influence our feelings and ideas. As Maurice Sendak wisely noted, childhood is "damned serious business." Then as we enter

school and make new friends, we engage in infatuations that further mold our likes and dislikes. As we develop more durable love affairs as teenagers, we continue to expand this personal psychological chart. And as we ride the waves of life—and experience a few romantic disasters—we trim and enrich this mental template.

60   So as you walk into a room of potential mating partners, you carry within your brain an extraordinary sum of infinitesimal, mostly unconscious biological and cultural preferences that can spoil or spark romantic passion.

61   To make matters even more complex, our suitors are, themselves, enormously varied. Do you know any two people who are alike? I don't. The variety of human personalities is remarkable. Some are brilliant musicians; others can write a touching poem, build a bridge, make the perfect golf shot, perform Shakespearean roles from memory, deliver witticisms to thousands from a bandstand, philosophize coherently about the universe, preach effectively on God or duty, predict economic patterns, or charismatically lead soldiers into battle. And that's just the beginning. Nature has provided us with a seemingly infinite variety of individuals to choose from—even within our social, economic, and intellectual milieu.

62   And here is the focal point of this chapter. It is my belief that along with the evolution of humanity's outstanding variety came the fundamental mechanism with which we choose a mate—the brain circuitry for human romantic love.

THE MATING MIND

63   Why are we all so different from one another? My thinking on this matter stems from Charles Darwin's fascinating idea of sexual selection.

64   Darwin was annoyed by all the ornaments he saw in nature.[48] Crimson ruffs, blue penises, pendulous breasts, whirling dances, melodious trills, particularly the peacock's cumbersome tail feathers: he felt these seemingly superfluous decorations undermined his theory that all traits evolved for a purpose. . . .

65   But with time Darwin came to believe that all these flashy embellishments evolved for an important purpose: to attract mates. Those with the finest courtship displays, he reasoned, attracted more and better mating partners; these dandies disproportionately bred—and passed along to their descendants these seemingly useless decorations. He called this process sexual selection.

66   In a highly original book, *The Mating Mind,* psychologist Geoffrey Miller adds to Darwin's theory of sexual selection. He proposes that human beings have also evolved extravagant traits to impress potential mating partners.

67   As Miller reasons, our human intelligence, linguistic talent, and musical ability, our drive to create visual arts, stories, myths, comedies, and dramas, our taste for all kinds of sports, our curiosity, our ability to solve complex math problems, our moral virtue, our religious fervor, our impulse for charitable giving, our political convictions, sense of humor, need to gossip, creativity, even our courage, pugnacity, perseverance, and kindness are all far too ornate and metabolically expensive to have evolved solely to survive another day.[49] Had our forebears needed these advanced aptitudes simply to live, chimpanzees would have developed these abilities as well. They didn't.

68 Miller believes, therefore, that all these marvelous human capacities evolved to win the mating game. We are "courtship machines," Miller writes.[50] Those ancestors who could speak poetically, draw deftly, dance nimbly, or deliver fiery moral speeches were regarded as more attractive. These talented men and women produced more babies. And gradually these human capacities became inscribed in our genetic code. Moreover, to distinguish themselves, our forebears specialized— creating the tremendous variety in human personalities seen today.

69 Miller acknowledges that in their simple forms, many of these traits were also useful in order to survive on the grasslands of ancient Africa; these talents had *many* purposes. But these aptitudes, he believes, became more and more complex because the opposite sex *liked* them and chose to mate with verbal, musical, or otherwise talented men and women. . . .

70 But Miller offers no concrete suggestion as to what actually enables the display chooser to choose one wooing tactic rather than another, saying only that it is something like "a big pleasure meter" in the brain and that endorphins (the brain's natural painkillers) might be involved.

71 I propose that this pleasure meter is the brain circuitry for romantic love— orchestrated largely by dopamine networks through the caudate nucleus and other reward pathways in the brain. As ancestral men and women sifted through their array of mating opportunities, the primordial brain circuitry for animal attraction evolved into human romantic love—to help the chooser choose a specific mating partner, pursue this beloved avidly, and devote his/her courtship time and energy to this reproductive prize.

NOTES

1. Hatfield 1988, p. 204.
2. Walster and Berscheid 1971; Dutton and Aron 1974; Hatfield and Sprecher 1986; Aron et al.1989.
3. Shepher 1971.
4. Galton 1884; Rushton 1989; Laumann et al.1994; Pines 1999.
5. Buston and Emlen 2003.
6. Byrne, Clore, and Smeaton 1986; Cappella and Palmer 1990.
7. Gangestad and Thornhill 1997.
8. Gangestad, Thornhill, and Yeo 1994; Jones and Hill 1993.
9. Langlois and Roggman 1990.
10. Langlois et al. 1987.
11. Hamilton and Zuk 1982; Thornhill and Gangestad 1993.
12. Gangestad and Thornhill 1997.
13. Aharon et al. 2001.
14. Manning and Scutt 1996.
15. Manning et al. 1996.
16. Singh 1993.
17. Singh 2002.
18. Buss et al. 1990.
19. Ford and Beach 1951; Ellis 1992.
20. Wolkstein 1991, pp. 6–7.
21. Jankowiak 1995, p. 10.
22. Harrison and Saeed 1977.
23. Buss 1994.

24. Guttentag and Secord 1983; Low 1991.
25. Dion, Berscheid, and Walster 1972.
26. Johnston 1999.
27. H. Fisher et al. 2003; Aron et al., in preparation.
28. Kanin, Davidson, and Scheck 1970; Dion and Dion 1985; Peplau and Gordon 1985.
29. Berscheid et al. 1971; Lerner and Karabenick 1974.
30. Tannen 1990; Tavris 1992.
31. Baron-Cohen 2003.
32. Hatfield and Rapson 1996; Tennov 1979.
33. H. Fisher et al. 2003; Aron et al., in preparation.
34. Damasio 1999.
35. Harrison and Saeed 1977.
36. Ellis 1992; Buss 1994.
37. Ellis 1992; Buss 1994.
38. Kenrick et al. 1990.
39. Lerner and Karabenick 1974.
40. Buss 2003, p. 242.
41. Buss 1994.
42. Buss and Schmitt 1993; Kenrick et al. 1993; Gangestad and Thornhill 1997.
43. Buss 2003; Cristiani 2003.
44. Buss 2003.
45. Shakespeare 1936, *The Merchant of Venice,* act III, scene ii, line 63.
46. Waller and Shaver 1994.
47. Shakespeare 1936, *A Midsummer Night's Dream,* act I, scene i, lines 241–42.
48. Darwin (1859/1978, 1871/n.d.). Darwin (1871/n.d.) distinguished between two types of sexual selection: *intra*sexual selection, by which members of one sex evolve traits that enable them to compete directly with one another to win mating opportunities; and *inter*sexual selection or "mate choice," by which individuals of one sex evolve traits because the opposite sex prefers them. The antlers on the male moose are a good example of Darwin's first principle. This appendage developed to enable its wearer to intimidate other males during the breeding season. It is Darwin's second form of sexual selection that is central to this book: mate choice. Human female breasts are a good example. Unlike female teats, these fleshy appendages have no purpose in reproduction; they probably evolved primarily because ancestral males *liked* them. In fact, scientists now call these adornments that evolved by mate choice "fitness indicators," precisely because they are extreme, striking, metabolically expensive, hard to fake, and useless in the daily struggle to survive (Fisher 1915; Zahavi 1975; Miller 2000). Because these traits are "handicaps," only the fittest can build and maintain them (Zahavi 1975). For this reason alone, these traits impress.
49. Miller 2000, p. 35.
50. Ibid., pp. 3, 29.

REFERENCES

Aharon et al. 2001. Beautiful faces have variable reward value: fMRI and behavioral evidence. *Neuron* 32(3):537–51.

Aron, A., D. G. Dutton, E. N. Aron, and A. Iverson. 1989. Experiences of falling in love. *Journal of Social and Personal Relationships* 6:243–57.

Baron-Cohen, S. 2003. *The Essential Difference: The Truth about the Male and Female Brain.* New York: Basic Books.

Berscheid, E., K. K. Dion, E. Walster, and G. W. Walster. 1971. Physical attractiveness and dating choice: a test of the matching hypothesis. *Journal of Experimental Social Psychology* 7:173–89.

Buss, D. M. 1994. *The Evolution of Desire: Strategies of Human Mating.* New York: Basic Books.

———. 2003. *The Evolution of Desire: Strategies of Human Mating.* Rev. and exp. ed. New York: Basic Books.

Buss, D. M., and D. P. Schmitt. 1993. Sexual strategies theory: An evolutionary perspective on human mating. *Psychological Review* 100:204–32.

Buss, D. M., et al. 1990. International preferences in selecting mates: A study of 37 cultures. *Journal of Cross-Cultural Psychology* 21:5–47.

Buston, P. M., and S. T. Emlen. 2003. Cognitive processes underlying human mate choice: The relationship between self-perception and mate preference in Western society. *Proceedings of the National Academy of Sciences* 100(15):8805–10.

Byrne, D., G. L. Clore, and G. Smeaton. 1986. The attraction hypothesis: Do similar attitudes affect anything? *Journal of Personality and Social Psychology* 51:1167–70.

Cappella, J. N., and M. T. Palmer. 1990. Attitude similarity, relational history, and attraction: The mediating effects of kinesic and vocal behaviors. *Communication Monographs* 57: 161–83.

Cristiani, M. 2003. A life history perspective on dating and courtship among Albuquerque adolescents. Ph.D. dissertation, Dept. of Anthropology, University of New Mexico.

Damasio, A. R. 1999. *The Feeling of What Happens: Body and Emotion in the Making of Consciousness.* New York: Harcourt Brace.

Darwin, C. 1859/1978. *The Origins of Species by Means of Natural Selection.* Franklin Center, Pa.: Franklin Library.

———. 1871/n.d. *The Descent of Man and Selection in Relation to Sex.* New York: The Modern Library/Random House.

Dion K. K., E. Berscheid, and E. Walster. 1972. What is beautiful is good. *Journal of Personality and Social Psychology* 24:285–90.

Dion, K. L., and K. K. Dion. 1985. Romantic love: Individual and cultural perspectives. In *The Psychology of Love,* ed. R. J. Sternberg and M. L. Barnes. New Haven: Yale University Press.

Dutton, D. G., and A. P. Aron. 1974. Some evidence of heightened sexual attraction under conditions of high anxiety. *Journal of Personality and Social Psychology* 30(4):510–17.

Ellis, B. J. 1992. The evolution of sexual attraction: Evaluative mechanisms in women. In *The Adapted Mind: Evolutionary Psychology and the Generation of Culture,* ed. J. H. Barkow, L. Cosmides, and J. Tooby. New York: Oxford University Press.

Fisher, H., A. Aron, D. Mashek, G. Strong, H. Li, and L. L. Brown. 2003. Early stage intense romantic love activates cortical-basal-ganglia reward/motivation, emotion and attention systems: An fMRI study of a dynamic network that varies with relationship length, passion intensity and gender. Poster presented at the Annual Meeting of the Society for Neuroscience, New Orleans, November 11.

Fisher, R. A. 1915. The evolution of sexual preference. *Eugenics Review* 7:184–92.

Ford, C. S., and F. A. Beach. 1951. *Patterns of Sexual Behavior.* New York: Harper and Row.

Galton, F. 1884. The measurement of character. *Fortnightly Review* 36:179–85.

Gangestad, S. W., and R. Thornhill. 1997. The evolutionary psychology of extra-pair sex: The role of fluctuating asymmetry. *Evolution and Human Behavior* 18(2):69–88.

Gangestad, S. W., R. Thornhill, and R. A. Yeo. 1994. Facial attractiveness, developmental stability, and fluctuating asymmetry. *Ethology and Sociobiology* 15:73–85.

Guttentag, M., and P. F. Secord. 1983. *Too Many Women: The Sex Ratio Question.* Beverly Hills, Calif.: Sage Publications.

Hamilton, W. D., and M. Zuk. 1982. Heritable true fitness and bright birds: A role for parasites? *Science* 218:384–87.

Harrison, A. A., and L. Saeed. 1977. Let's make a deal: An analysis of revelations and stipulations in lonely hearts advertisements. *Journal of Personality and Social Psychology* 35:257–64.

Hatfield, E. 1988. Passionate and companionate love. In *The Psychology of Love,* ed. R. J. Sternberg and M. L. Barnes. New Haven: Yale University Press.

Hatfield, E., and R. Rapson. 1996. *Love and Sex: Cross-Cultural Perspectives.* Needham Heights, Mass.: Allyn and Bacon.

Hatfield, E., and S. Sprecher. 1986. *Mirror, Mirror: The Importance of Looks in Everyday Life.* Albany, N.Y.: State University of New York Press.

Jankowiak, W. 1995. Introduction. In *Romantic Passion: A Universal Experience?,* ed. W. Jankowiak. New York: Columbia University Press.

Johnston, V. S. 1999. *Why We Feel: The Science of Human Emotions.* Cambridge, Mass.: Perseus Books.

Jones, E., and K. Hill. 1993. Criteria of facial attractiveness in five populations. *Human Nature* 4:271–96.

Kanin, E. J., K. R. Davidson, and S. R. Scheck. 1970. A research note on male-female differentials in the experience of heterosexual love. *Journal of Sex Research* 6(1):64–72.

Kenrick, D. T., G. E. Groth, M. R. Trost, and E. K. Sadalla. 1993. Integrating evolutionary and social exchange perspectives on relationships: Effects of gender, self-appraisal, and involvement level on mate selection. *Journal of Personality and Social Psychology* 64:951–69.

Kenrick, D. T., E. K. Sadalla, G. E. Groth, and M. R. Trost. 1990. Evolution, traits and the states of human courtship: Qualifying the parental investment model. *Journal of Personality* 58(1):97–116.

Langlois, J. H., and L. A. Roggman. 1990. Attractive faces are only average. *Psychological Science* 1:115–21.

Langlois, J. H., L. A. Roggman, R. J. Casey, J. M. Ritter, L. A. Rieser-Danner, and V. Y. Jenkins. 1987. Infant preferences for attractive faces: Rudiments of a stereotype. *Developmental Psychology* 23:363–69.

Laumann, E. O., J. H. Gagnon, R. T. Michael, and S. Michaels. 1994. *The Social Organization of Sexuality: Sexual Practices in the United States.* Chicago: University of Chicago Press.

Lerner, R. M., and S. A. Karabenick. 1974. Physical attractiveness, body attitudes, and self-concept in late adolescence. *Journal of Youth and Adolescence* 3:307–16.

Low, B. S. 1991. Reproductive life in nineteenth-century Sweden: An evolutionary perspective on demographic phenomena. *Ethology and Sociobiology* 12:411–48.

Manning, J. T., and D. Scutt. 1996. Symmetry and ovulation in women. *Human Reproduction* 11:2477–80.

Manning, J. T., D. Scutt, G. H. Whitehouse, S. J. Leinster, and J. H. Walton. 1996. Asymmetry and menstrual cycle in women. *Ethology and Sociobiology* 17:129–43.

Miller, G. F. 2000. *The Mating Mind: How Sexual Choice Shaped the Evolution of Human Nature.* New York: Doubleday.

Peplau, L., and S. Gordon. 1985. Women and men in love: Gender differences in close heterosexual relationships. In *Women, Gender and Social Psychology,* ed. V. O'Leary, R. Unger, and B. Wallston. Hillsdale, N.J.: Erlbaum.

Pines, A. M. 1999. *Falling in Love: Why We Choose the Lovers We Choose.* New York: Routledge.

Rushton, J. P. 1989. Epigenesis and social preference. *Behavioral and Brain Sciences* 12:31–32.

Shakespeare, W. 1936. *The Complete Works of William Shakespeare: The Cambridge Edition Text,* ed. W. A. Wright. New York: Doubleday.

Shepher, J. 1971. Mate selection among second-generation kibbutz adolescents and adults: Incest avoidance and negative imprinting. *Archives of Sexual Behavior* 1:293–307.

Singh, D. 1993. Adaptive significance of waist-to-hip ratio and female physical attractiveness. *Journal of Personality and Social Psychology* 65:293–307.

———. 2002. Female mate value at a glance: Relationship of waist-to-hip ratio to health, fecundity and attractiveness. *Neuroendocrinology Letters* 23(suppl 4):81–91.

Tannen, D. 1990. *You Just Don't Understand: Women and Men in Conversation.* New York: Ballantine Books.

Tavris, C. 1992 *The Mismeasure of Woman.* New York: Simon and Schuster, pp. 15–25.

Tennov, D. 1979. *Love and Limerence: The Experience of Being in Love.* New York: Stein and Day.

Thornhill, R., and S. W. Gangestad. 1993. Human facial beauty. *Human Nature* 4(3):237–69.

Waller, N., and P. Shaver. 1994. The importance of nongenetic influences on romantic love styles: A twin-family study. *Psychological Science* 5(5):268–74.

Walster, E., and E. Berscheid. 1971. Adrenaline makes the heart grow fonder. *Psychology Today,* June, 47–62.

Wolkstein, D. 1991. *The First Love Stories.* New York: HarperPerennial.

Zahavi, A. 1975. Mate selection: A selection for a handicap. *Journal of Theoratical Biology* 53:205–14.

QUESTIONS FOR DISCUSSION

1. Lauren Slater's article begins with an amusing anecdote about getting a henna tattoo. How does her act connect with the chemistry of love she discusses later? How would Helen Fisher explain Slater's unusual choice of a way to be romantic?

2. Clearly love and sexual desire are not just "socially constructed," as some people claim. Biochemistry and the evolution of attraction show that love is not just "made up" by each human society. Yet, Lauren Slater calls attention to how culture strongly shapes passionate love. How does she insist on the importance of culture?

3. At least since Freud, most students of human motivation have stressed the role of the unconscious. What does Helen Fisher reveal about attraction that you were not aware of? What does she discuss that you more or less understood already, but understood more clearly after reading her article?

4. Few people have the "total package" for being attractive as lovers and potential mates. Why, then, is Helen Fisher's discussion of Geoffrey Miller's *The Mating Mind* especially important for understanding how, for instance, a man compensates for not having a jutting jaw or a woman for not having a waist that is 70% the size of her hips? To what extent does the human cultivation of certain talents and abilities make Darwin's notion of sexual selection too simple to account for human mating?

SUGGESTIONS FOR WRITING

For Convincing

It's not hard to see why some people are disturbed by what Lauren Slater and Helen Fisher say. We may resist or refuse to believe that the chemistry of attraction has so much power. Must long-term sexual love eventually lose most of its passion? Or we may feel that a formula such as "men look for sex objects and women look for success objects" is too simple or is insulting to both sexes. Consider both articles in terms of what people are likely to resist or dispute and select a point or several related points that interest you most.

Using additional research or your own experience and knowledge (or both), defend the point or set of related points you have selected. Convince your readers that they should accept the basic truth of the claim (or claims) you are defending.

For Inquiry

Neither Lauren Slater nor Helen Fisher has much to say about current ways that men and women relate. Some selections in Section Two, such as the ones by Grimes, Watters, and Wartik, open up such matters for discussion.

As a class, list and discuss current ways men and women relate. You might consider, for instance, how financial independence for women, which was not common just fifty years ago, has affected mating choices. Or you might ponder the implications of the decline of traditional dating. Or you could investigate how both men and women are now often breaking out of traditional gender roles and attitudes. There's much to talk about because current conditions are in many ways quite different from those in even the recent past.

After the discussion, select one way that men and women relate now that is clearly new and that you find especially interesting. Write an exploratory essay that poses and attempts to answer this question: To what extent do the Slater and Fisher selections shed light on what is going on now?

SECTION 2: GETTING TOGETHER
Overview

It is hard to appreciate how much things have changed in only the last one hundred years. A century ago few people went to college, and the United States was still predominantly rural. Most people were born, lived, and died in the same place, surrounded by friends and relatives. The local community is what mattered to them and what they knew—no television, movies, or Internet. In 1900 the average age at death in the United States was just under fifty.

Many marriages were arranged or were between two people who had known each other from childhood. Men and women married much younger— middle to late teens. Once married, they rarely divorced. Women had many children, partly because they were useful for farm work, partly because infant and child mortality rates were much higher, partly because reliable birth control—the pill—would not come into use for another sixty years.

Now, except that people still want relationships, what has not changed? Probably the biggest change is more years of education, with college almost assumed for middle-class young adults. Consequently, most people are not in a position to marry until at least their middle twenties. Couple this with the earlier onset of puberty, because of improved nutrition, and clearly there can be fifteen years or more between the beginning of sexual development and marriage. Toss in a sex-obsessed media and our urban-centered, intensely competitive, fast-paced economy and you have all the basic ingredients for change in love relationships. It is no wonder that people do not get together in ways common even a generation ago. Traditional dating, for instance, is apparently the exception rather than the rule.

This section focuses on how young adults get together now. There is Jack Grimes on "hooking up"; Ethan Watters on "urban tribes," large bands of friends hanging out together, now a common practice among young singles; and Nancy Wartik on living together, also known as cohabitation.

Sculpture

ANTONIO CANOVA

Psyche Revived by Eros' Kiss

For Discussion

The beautiful and sensual sculpture *Psyche Revived by Eros' Kiss,* by Antonio Canova, is displayed at the Louvre in Paris. The photo of it cannot capture what you see in three dimensions, but still conveys its power. How would you describe its appeal or impact? What are the implications of Eros (passionate love) reviving Psyche (spirit or mind)?

Hook-Up Culture

JACK GRIMES

> Jack Grimes was a senior at Tufts when he wrote this opinion column for the school paper, the *Tufts Daily.*

1   Whatever happened to dating? College students have been asking that question for years. Every once in a while, even a newspaper will pick up the question and interview a few co-eds. The reporter finds dating's departure mostly blamed on what is universally called "the hook-up culture." While there are no (as of yet) proposals for the [student] Senate to take on a Hook-up Culture Rep, I do not think many would deny that the culture is here and thriving at Tufts. But where did it come from? And is it here to stay?

2   The hook-up culture is simply an environment that expects casual sexual encounters that do not necessarily lead to anything further. Common sense would say that people hook-up for basic physical needs. They do not want to get involved in a relationship, but they do have intense desires for a sexual partner. In a word, they are horny. So they hook-up—either with a friend or a stranger. But something makes me think folks hook-up for something more than just the raging hormones.

3   What makes me think horniness cannot fully explain the hook-up culture is this question: Would you hook-up with someone who was fast asleep—totally unresponsive? You could kiss them, touch them, make them touch you, whatever you would like. But they would remain completely oblivious to you and just lay there dead to the world. Not exactly appealing, is it? A bit like eating cold oatmeal. All the physical parts are there, all the same sensations, but something is missing— an energy, a spark, a life. There must then be a pleasure that is not strictly physical. What makes a hook-up more desirable than any pornography or anything you could do to yourself is the one pleasure neither of those could ever provide—the consent of a partner.

4   A lively, animated partner is lively and animated for you and (for the moment at least) you alone. You are special. What your partner does not let the world see, she lets you see. Personal space that is ordinarily walled off from the outside world becomes open to you alone. You are being let in, given privileged access. You become, for a few moments, the center of his attention. The real thrill of a hook-up is not simply what you do with a partner, but the fact that your partner wants to be doing it with you! It is not just "She's so hot," but "She's so hot and she wants me!" Not just "He's so cute," but "He's so cute and he likes me!"

5   The physical pleasure does not, and cannot, exist by itself. It is inextricably tied up with the emotional. The body and soul are one. To give someone your body is to give them all of yourself. A sexual encounter is in its essence an act of deepest intimacy, and so to be considered worthy of that intimacy is powerfully affirming and very exciting. Everyone wants to be loved that much. Consensual sex is an affirmation so powerful that the porno fiend fabricates it and the rapist steals it. It is a feeling of acceptance so intoxicating that it gets pursued weekend after weekend in frat after frat.

6   Is it being found there? Well, how could it be? How can you find love and intimacy in a system that presupposes the meaninglessness of sex? If sex is simply handed out to anyone, then sexual intimacy becomes no big deal. Even if it happens to get handed over to you, you are no longer special. You are just a fling. The premise of the hook-up culture is to receive pleasure without commitment. But the pleasure really being sought can only come from commitment, from someone saying "Yes, I want to give my all to you and no one else." But hooking-up is all about holding back, not giving all of one's self, not committing. The more that commitment gets detached from sex, the less sex means anything. The less it means anything, the less enjoyable it becomes, and so the more hook-ups are made to get the old thrill. And on it goes, spiraling down. Trying to find intimate fulfillment by hooking-up is like trying to dig your way out of a hole in the ground.

7   Some people claim that they are not at all bothered by emotional needs. They get a thrill from the display of independence and sexual virility that serial hook-ups can give. Now this used to be said mostly by men. They do not talk like this much anymore (at least in public), as it seems to hinder their ability to get much play.

8   Appeals to self-determination and sexual empowerment to support hook-ups are now given by women. And this I find strange. I wonder what is so empowering about being, in essence, an unpaid prostitute. The boys may politely clap and publicly congratulate the women for liberating their sexuality and owning their miniskirt and so on, but privately they are having a good laugh and passing the word on who is the easy lay. A woman who embraces the hook-up culture is simply making it easier for guys to treat her as a sex object. Is this women's liberation? Both sexes can use a partner for their own selfish gratification, but more often than not, it is the woman whose hopes of a relationship get tossed in the trash. The real sexual power a woman has is to refuse to give away sex until the man has proved his commitment to her.

9   The hook-up culture is very deceptive. Hooking-up promises to be liberating and strengthening. Yet people find themselves needing more and more "liquid courage" to even make the first move. Hooking-up promises fun and fulfillment and no regrets, but when morning comes it delivers the "walk of shame." The hook-up culture has tricked us. It has led us to believe that our emotions are disconnected from our bodies, that love is divorced from sex.

10   What can we do about it? Well, a culture only lasts as long as people are willing to live it. If we refuse to believe its false promises, then we can build a new culture that says sex is just too good to be thrown around. We can bring back some middle ground between random hook-ups and being joined-at-the-hip. We can bring dating back to life. Or not. We can also make the break between love and sex complete and final. We can become dead to the ache within for intimacy. We can consider ourselves simply people with assets: he has what she wants, she has what he wants. Just a mutual exchange. Just business. Cold, soulless, heartless, loveless business.

Photographs: Couples Past vs. Present

A 1950s couple

A couple on Sex and the City

For Discussion

In the 1950s, the most popular venue for dating was the soda shop, and a standard "couple" photo showed them drinking ice cream sodas, heads together. In contrast, media images today often show the couple in a bar, as in the scene from the popular show *Sex and the City*. What messages about love or "romance" do these two images send?

In My Tribe

ETHAN WATTERS

In *Urban Tribes,* from which this essay is excerpted, Ethan Watters describes his own life prior to marriage, as part of a circle of good friends similar to those depicted in television shows like *Seinfeld* and *Friends.*

1   You may be like me: between the ages of 25 and 39, single, a college-educated city dweller. If so, you may have also had the unpleasant experience of discovering that you have been identified (by the U.S. Census Bureau, no less) as one of the fastest-growing groups in America—the "never marrieds." In less than 30 years, the number of never-marrieds has more than doubled, apparently pushing back the median age of marriage to the oldest it has been in our country's history—about 25 years for women and 27 for men.

2   As if the connotation of "never married" weren't negative enough, the vilification of our group has been swift and shrill. These statistics prove a "titanic loss of family values," according to *The Washington Times.* An article in *Time* magazine asked whether "picky" women were "denying themselves and society the benefits of marriage" and in the process kicking off "an outbreak of 'Sex and the City' promiscuity." In a study on marriage conducted at Rutgers University, researchers say the "social glue" of the family is at stake, adding ominously that "crime rates . . . are highly correlated with a large percentage of unmarried young males."

3   Although I never planned it, I can tell you how I became a never-married. Thirteen years ago, I moved to San Francisco for what I assumed was a brief transition period between college and marriage. The problem was, I wasn't just looking for an appropriate spouse. To use the language of the Rutgers researchers, I was "soul-mate searching." Like 94 percent of never-marrieds from 20 to 29, I, too, agree with the statement "When you marry, you want your spouse to be your soul mate first and foremost." This *über*-romantic view is something new. In a 1965 survey, fully three out of four college women said they'd marry a man they didn't love if he fit their criteria in every other way. I discovered along with my friends that finding that soul mate wasn't easy. Girlfriends came and went, as did jobs and apartments. The constant in my life—by default, not by plan—became a loose group of friends. After a few years, that group's membership and routines began to solidify. We met weekly for dinner at a neighborhood restaurant. We traveled together, moved one another's furniture, painted one another's apartments, cheered one another on at sporting events and open-mike nights. One day I discovered that the transition period I thought I was living wasn't a transition period at all. Something real and important had grown there. I belonged to an urban tribe.

4   I use the word "tribe" quite literally here: this is a tight group, with unspoken roles and hierarchies, whose members think of each other as "us" and the rest of the world as "them." This bond is clearest in times of trouble. After earthquakes (or the recent terrorist strikes), my instinct to huddle with and protect my group is no different from what I'd feel for my family.

5   Once I identified this in my own life, I began to see tribes everywhere I looked: a house of ex-sorority women in Philadelphia, a team of ultimate-frisbee players in

Ethan Watters, center, with his tribe in San Francisco

Boston and groups of musicians in Austin, Tex. Cities, I've come to believe, aren't emotional wastelands where fragile individuals with arrested development mope around self-indulgently searching for true love. There are rich landscapes filled with urban tribes.

6   So what does it mean that we've quietly added the tribe years as a developmental stage to adulthood? Because our friends in the tribe hold us responsible for our actions, I doubt it will mean a wild swing toward promiscuity or crime. Tribal behavior does not prove a loss of "family values." It is a fresh expression of them.

7   It is true, though, that marriage and the tribe are at odds. As many ex-girlfriends will ruefully tell you, loyalty to the tribe can wreak havoc on romantic relationships. Not surprisingly, marriage usually signals the beginning of the end of tribal membership. From inside the group, marriage can seem like a risky gambit. When members of our tribe choose to get married, the rest of us talk about them with grave concern, as if they've joined a religion that requires them to live in a guarded compound.

8   But we also know that the urban tribe can't exist forever. Those of us who have entered our mid-30's find ourselves feeling vaguely as if we're living in the latter episodes of *Seinfeld* or *Friends,* as if the plot lines of our lives have begun to wear thin.

9   So, although tribe membership may delay marriage, that is where most of us are still heading. And it turns out there may be some good news when we get there. Divorce rates have leveled off. Tim Heaton, a sociologist at Brigham Young University, says he believes he knows why. In a paper to be published next year, he argues that it is because people are getting married later.

10   Could it be that we who have been biding our time in happy tribes are now actually grown up enough to understand what we need in a mate? What a fantastic twist—we "never marrieds" may end up revitalizing the very institution we've supposedly been undermining.

11   And there's another dynamic worth considering. Those of us who find it so hard to leave our tribes will not choose marriage blithely, as if it is the inevitable next step in our lives, the way middle-class high-school kids choose college. When we go to the altar, we will be sacrificing something precious. In that sacrifice, we may begin to learn to treat our marriages with the reverence they need to survive.

Web Page

eHARMONY

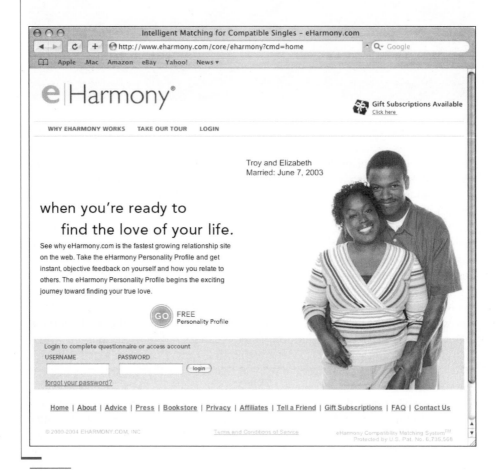

Reprinted with permission.

For Discussion

Computer dating services claim that by studying the personalities and tastes of clients, they can find good matches more effectively and efficiently than people can find for themselves through ads, friends, and the more traditional ways of finding a partner. After reading "Who Wants to Marry a Soul Mate?" (pages 416–420), discuss the eHarmony ad (above) and the service itself. How do the ad and service appeal to people looking for a soul mate?

The Perils of Playing House

NANCY WARTIK

Nancy Wartik is a freelance writer. The following article appeared in *Psychology Today*.

1　Forget undying love or shared hopes and dreams—my boyfriend and I moved in together, a year after meeting, because of a potential subway strike. He lived in Manhattan, and I across the river in Brooklyn. Given New York City taxi rates, we'd have been separated for who knows how long. And so, the day before the threatened strike, he picked me up along with two yowling cats and drove us home. Six years, one wedding and one daughter later, we still haven't left.

2　Actually, if the strike threat hadn't spurred us to set up housekeeping, something else would have. By then, we were 99 percent sure we'd marry some day—just not without living together first. I couldn't imagine getting hitched to anyone I hadn't taken on a test-spin as a roommate. Conjoin with someone before sharing a bathroom? Not likely!

3　With our decision to cohabit, we joined the mushrooming ranks of Americans who choose at some point in their lives to inhabit a gray zone—more than dating, less than marriage, largely without legal protections. Thirty or 40 years ago, cohabitation was relatively rare, mainly the province of artists and other questionable types, and still thought of as "living in sin." In 1970 only about 500,000 couples lived together in unwedded bliss.

4　Now, nearly 5 million opposite-sex couples in the United States live together outside of marriage; millions more have done it at some point. Some couples do choose to live together as a permanent alternative to marriage, but their numbers are only a tiny fraction: More than 50 percent of couples who marry today have lived together beforehand. (At least 600,000 same-sex couples also cohabit, but their situation is different, since most don't have the choice to marry.)

5　"It's not this bad little thing only a few people are doing," says University of Michigan sociologist Pamela Smock. "It's not going away. It's going to become part of our normal, typical life course—it already is for younger people. They think it would be idiotic not to live with someone before marriage. They don't want to end up the way their parents or older relatives did, which is divorced."

6　In my and my husband's case, the pre-matrimonial experiment seems to have worked out well. But according to recent research, our year of shacking up could have doomed our relationship. Couples who move in together before marriage have up to two times the odds of divorce, as compared with couples who marry before living together. Moreover, married couples who have lived together before exchanging vows tend to have poorer-quality marriages than couples who moved in after the wedding. Those who cohabited first report less satisfaction, more arguing, poorer communication and lower levels of commitment.

7　Many researchers now argue that our penchant for combining households before taking vows is undermining our ability to commit. Meaning, the precautions we take to ensure marriage is right for us may wind up working against us.

FROM TOOTHBRUSH TO REGISTRY

8 | Why would something that seems so sensible potentially be so damaging? Probably the reigning explanation is the inertia hypothesis, the idea that many of us slide into marriage without ever making an explicit decision to commit. We move in together, we get comfortable, and pretty soon marriage starts to seem like the path of least resistance. Even if the relationship is only tolerable, the next stage starts to seem inevitable.

9 | Because we have different standards for living partners than for life partners, we may end up married to someone we never would have originally considered for the long haul. "People are much fussier about whom they marry than whom they cohabitate with," explains Paul Amato, a sociologist at Penn State University and one of the theory's originators. "A lot of people cohabit because it seems like a good idea to share expenses and have some security and companionship, without a lot of commitment."

10 | Couples may wind up living together almost by accident. "People move in their toothbrush, their underwear, pretty soon a whole dresser," says Marshall Miller, coauthor with his partner, Dorian Solot, of *Unmarried to Each Other: The Essential Guide to Living Together as an Unmarried Couple*. "Then someone's lease is up and since they're spending all their time together anyhow.". . .

11 | "There's an inevitable pressure that creates momentum toward marriage," says Amato. "I've talked to so many cohabiting couples, and they'll say, 'My mother was so unhappy until I told her we were getting married—then she was so relieved.'" On top of the social pressure, Amato points out, couples naturally start making investments together: a couch, a pet—even a kid. Accidental pregnancies are more common among cohabiting couples than among couples who don't live together.

12 | Once their lives are thoroughly entangled, some couples may decide to wed more out of guilt or fear than love. "I know a lot of men who've been living with women for a couple of years, and they're very ambivalent about marrying them," says John Jacobs, a New York City psychiatrist and author of *All You Need Is Love and Other Lies About Marriage*. "What sways them is a feeling they owe it to her. She'll be back on the market and she's older. He's taken up a lot of her time." Women in particular may be afraid to leave an unhappy cohabiting relationship and confront the dating game at an older age. "If you're 36, it's hard to take the risk of going back into the single world to look for another relationship," says Jacobs. . . .

13 | Some evidence indicates that women have less control over the progress of the cohabiting relationship. She may assume they're on the road to marriage, but he may think they're just saving on rent and enjoying each other's company. Research by sociologist Susan Brown at Bowling Green State University in Ohio has shown there's a greater chance cohabiting couples will marry if the man wants to do so. The woman's feelings don't have as much influence, she found: "The guy has got to be on board. What the woman wants seems to be less pivotal.". . .

THE COHABITING TYPE

14   The inertia theory is not the only way to explain why couples who move in before marriage are less likely to stick it out for the long haul. There may also be something specific about the experience that actually changes people's minds about marriage, making it seem less sacrosanct. "A couple of studies show that when couples cohabit, they tend to adopt less conventional beliefs about marriage and divorce, and it tends to make them less religious," says Amato. That could translate, once married, to a greater willingness to consider options that are traditionally frowned upon—like saying "so long" to an ailing marriage.

15   Nonetheless, there's a heated debate among social scientists about whether the research to date has been interpreted properly or overplayed to some extent. Having a family income below $25,000, for example, is a stronger predictor of divorce in the first 15 years of marriage than having shared a premarital address. "Having money, a sense of an economically stable future, good communication skills, living in a safe community—all of those things are more important," says Smock.

16   Because it's impossible to directly compare the effects of marriage and cohabitation, there's just no way to prove cohabiters' higher divorce rates aren't a side effect of their other characteristics, says psychologist William Pinsof, president of the Family Institute at Northwestern University. They may just be less traditional people—less likely to stay in an unhappy marriage in observance of religious beliefs or for the sake of appearances. "Those who choose to live together before getting married have a different attitude about marriage to begin with. I think cohabiting is a reflection of that, not a cause of higher divorce rates," he says. . . .

17   In short, not everyone buys the idea that cohabitation itself is hazardous to your relationship. For some couples, it may serve a useful purpose—even when it lacks a happy ending. About half of all cohabiters split up rather than marry, and many of those splits save the parties involved from rocky marriages, miserable divorces or both. . . .

18   The debate over cohabitation is partly a rehash of the values and morals conflicts that tend to become political footballs in America today. But on one point, virtually all researchers agree: We need to understand the effects of cohabitation on children. Some 40 percent of all cohabiting households include kids—that's somewhere close to 3.5 million children living in homes with two unmarried opposite-sex grown-ups.

19   Cohabiting relationships, by their nature, appear to be less fulfilling than marital relationships. People who cohabit say they are less satisfied and more likely to feel depressed, Susan Brown has found. While the precarious finances of many cohabiters has something to do with it, Brown also points to the inherent lack of stability. Long-term cohabitation is rare: most couples either break up or marry within five years. "Cohabiters are uncertain about the future of their relationship and that's distressing to them," she says.

20   As a result, cohabitation is not an ideal living arrangement for children. Emotionally or academically, the children of cohabiters just don't do as well, on average, as those with two married parents, and money doesn't fully explain the difference.

The stress of parenting in a shakier living situation may be part of the problem, says Brown. "Stability matters. It matters for the well-being of children and adults alike," she adds. "We're better off with commitment, a sense that we're in it for the long haul."

THE MUST-HAVE DISCUSSION

21 Cohabitation rates may be skyrocketing, but Americans are still entirely enchanted with marriage. That's a sharp contrast with some Western societies—Sweden, France or the Canadian province of Quebec, for example—where cohabitation is beginning to replace marriage. In the United States, 90 percent of young people are still expected to tie the knot at some point.

22 Since most Americans are destined for marriage—and a majority will live together beforehand—how can we protect against the potentially undermining effects of cohabitation? Follow the lead of one subgroup of cohabiters: Those who make a permanent commitment to each other first. One study that tracked 136 couples through the initial months of marriage found that early intentions seem to make a big difference. About 60 of the couples in the study lived together before getting engaged, while the rest waited either until after they were engaged or after they were married to set up housekeeping. Ten months after the wedding, the group that had cohabited before being engaged had more negative interactions, less confidence about the relationship and weaker feelings of commitment than the other two groups. But the marriages of couples who had moved in together after getting engaged seemed just as strong as those who had moved in together after marrying.

23 Miller and Solot don't advise against cohabitation for couples without immediate plans to marry. But they do believe each partner needs to understand clearly what the other is thinking. "The most important thing is for people to treat moving in together as a serious decision, a major life choice," Miller says. "What does it mean to you both for the long and short term? If one person thinks living together means a quick path towards marriage and the other thinks it's just saving on rent and having a friend with benefits, there could be trouble. The important thing is to be on the same page."

QUESTIONS FOR DISCUSSION

1. Do you think Jack Grimes's rejection of hooking up (pages 399–400) raises *moral* objections? If so, what are they? If not, on what grounds does Grimes object?

2. In "The Perils of Playing House," Nancy Wartik cites Pamela Smock, a sociologist who is one of the leading experts on cohabitation. According to Smock, living together is "going to become . . . normal . . . it already is for younger people" (paragraph 5) She explains it as motivated by a desire to avoid divorce. What other motives does Wartik say enter into it? Based on your own experience or that of young adults you know who live

together, what motives not discussed by Wartik might be involved? Considering all the motivations that might be involved, is cohabitation an option you would consider? If you have lived with someone or do so now, what's your assessment of the experience?

SUGGESTIONS FOR WRITING

For Research and Mediation

Jack Grimes is hardly the only person to argue against the practice of "hooking up" and to advocate a return to traditional dating. But traditional dating requires two things that many young adults, especially those attending college, lack: time and money. And dating may sometimes have been just a different way of hooking up that only seems more respectable.

Find out what you can about hooking up from research done on it. Supplement knowledge from research with interviews of people who have experience with it. Then write an essay that mediates between those who, like Grimes, reject hooking up, and those who practice it without seriously considering the potential emotional emptiness.

SECTION 3: ATTACHMENT AND MARRIAGE
Overview

Most of us have romantic relationships, or perhaps the relationships have us. To begin to understand them, we should start as we did in the first section, with attraction. But attraction is not enough. People have to get together somehow—hence the focus in Section Two on hooking up, urban tribes, and living together. Attraction has deep biological foundations, an evolutionary history, and depends on something as natural as brain chemistry. How we get together, however, is largely cultural, varying a great deal from place to place and from era to era.

Most people also want to attach, to form a permanent relationship with one person. Of course, living together is one way of doing this, but in our culture few people choose it *instead of* marriage; for the overwhelming majority, living together is a prelude to marriage. And so this section deals with attachment and marriage, with norms typical of not only our culture but most human cultures in all places and times.

We begin with the crucial question, What is love? The first selection, by Robert and Lisa Firestone, two clinical psychologists who specialize in intimate relationships, and Joyce Catlett, explores the general question insightfully. Then, in the second selection, Barbara Dafoe Whitehead and David Popenoe address the question in a more specific context—the common distinction between people we might have sex with and people we might marry. Presumably, part of the difference is love, love developed over time in a sustained relationship. The question is crucial because our culture routinely tends to equate romance and love, which most cultures, past and present, do not. We need to consider carefully what love is, especially in marriage. And so two reflections on marital love are offered against the backdrop of the attitudes of young adults toward marriage gathered and interpreted by Whitehead and Popenoe in "Who Wants to Marry a Soul Mate?" The ideal encounters the reality, but not with discouraging results. We see Eve LaPlante's successful marriage, despite being the child of divorce, and Helen Fremont's marriage to Donna, made legal in 2004 in Massachusetts. No one thinks love and marriage necessarily go together, but they are not necessarily incompatible either, which offers some basis for hope even in a culture in which about 50% of all marriages end in divorce.

What Is Love?

ROBERT W. FIRESTONE, LISA A. FIRESTONE, AND JOYCE CATLETT

Robert Firestone and Lisa Firestone are prominent clinical psychologists who specialize in treating intimacy problems. Joyce Catlett is an author and lecturer who often collaborates with the Firestones. The following selection is from *Sex and Love in Intimate Relationships* (American Psychological Association, 2006).

The great aim of every human being is to understand the meaning of total love. Love is not to be found in someone else, but in ourselves; we simply awaken it. But in order to do that, we need the other person. The universe only makes sense when we have someone to share our feelings with.

—Paulo Coelho, *Eleven Minutes*, 2004

1   Volumes have been written about the nature of love and how love is manifested in an intimate relationship. The philosopher Singer (2001), in *Sex: A Philosophical Primer,* asserted that

There is no single entity, no discernible sensation or emotion, that is love. . . . Love is a form of life, though often short-lived, a disposition, a tendency to respond in a great variety of ways, many overlapping but none that is necessary and sufficient. . . . (pp. 84–85)

2   In *The Four Loves,* Lewis (1960) wrote about Eros (or what many refer to as passion), describing it as "that state which we call 'being in love'" (p. 91). He observed that "the lover desires the Beloved herself, not the pleasure she can give" (p. 94).

Without Eros sexual desire, like every other desire, is a fact about ourselves. Within Eros it is rather about the Beloved. . . . [It is] entirely a mode of expression. It . . . [is] something outside us, in the real world. . . . One of the first things Eros does is to obliterate the distinction between giving and receiving. (pp. 95–96)

3   In *You Can't Go Home Again,* Wolfe (1934) gave "love" great significance when he eloquently described the basic nature of human beings:

Man loves life, and loving life, hates death, and because of this he is great, he is glorious, he is beautiful, and his beauty is everlasting. He lives below the senseless stars and writes his meanings in them. . . . Thus it is impossible to scorn this creature. For out of his strong belief in life, this puny man made love. At his best, he *is* love. Without him there can be no love. . . no desire. (p. 411)

4   In a conversation with Arnold Toynbee (Gage, 1976), Daisaku Ikeda, former president of Soka Gakkai International, a Buddhist organization, described a version of the Buddhist conception of love:

The word *love* has been highly conceptualized and made very abstract. . . . I believe that the Buddhist concept of compassion . . . defined as removing sorrow and bringing happiness to others . . . gives love substantial meaning. . . .

Yoraku—the second component of compassion in the Buddhist sense—means the giving of pleasure. . . . It is the joy of living. . . the ecstacy of life. It includes both material and spiritual pleasure. Without the deep feelings of fulfillment and the ecstacy generated by the emotions of life, pleasure in the truest sense is impossible. (pp. 357–358)

5   There are also many Judeo-Christian conceptualizations of love. Perhaps the most familiar are the statements attributed to the apostle Paul in I Corinthians 13 (World English Bible):

Love is patient and is kind; love doesn't envy. Love doesn't brag, is not proud, doesn't behave itself inappropriately, doesn't seek its own way, is not provoked, takes no account of evil; doesn't rejoice in unrighteousness, but rejoices with the truth; bears all things, believes all things, hopes all things, endures all things. Love never fails. . . . But now faith, hope, and love remain—these three. The greatest of these is love. (vv. 4–13)

OUR VIEW OF LOVE

6   But what is love, really? What does it mean to love someone?. . . In *Altruism and Altruistic Love,* Post, Underwood, Schloss, and Hurlbut (2002) raised an important question: "What is at the very core of human altruistic love?" Their answer was that love might be conceptualized as "affirmative affection."

We all know what it feels like to be valued in this way, and we remember loving persons who conveyed this affective affirmation through tone of voice, facial expression, a hand on the shoulder in time of grief, and a desire to be with us. . . . Love implies benevolence, care, compassion, and *action.* (p. 4) [italics added]

7   In our view, actions that fit the description of a loving relationship are expressions of affection, both physical and emotional; a wish to offer pleasure and satisfaction to one's mate; tenderness, compassion, and sensitivity to the needs of the other; a desire for shared activities and pursuits; an appropriate level of sharing of one's possessions; an ongoing, honest exchange of personal feelings; and the process of offering concern, comfort, and outward assistance for the love object's aspirations. . . .

8   Our thinking regarding the nature of love is congenial with the words written by Fromm (1956) in *The Art of Loving.* Fromm observed that "There is only one proof for the presence of love: the depth of the relationship, and the aliveness and strength in each person concerned; this is the fruit by which love is recognized" (p. 87). These manifestations of love [are described in] one man's feelings for his wife after 25 years of marriage:

When I first met Annette, I thought that she was attractive and she appeared to be a very nice person. At the time, however, I wasn't especially drawn to her; in fact, she seemed a little boring. Yet for some bizarre reason, a crazy thought came into my mind and it came up repeatedly: "You're going to marry this girl." It was so odd and out of character to the way I usually think that I told my friends about it and we all laughed. . . .

Later on, Annette became involved in my social circle and we actually became friends. One day, on our way to meet friends for a day sail, Annette and I found ourselves alone together. . . . While we were driving to the marina, I suggested that we stop for a moment to look at the ocean conditions. Parked by the breakwater, I leaned toward her and we kissed. From that moment on we were in love.

In our love, a remarkable transformation took place in both of our lives. For one thing, her looks changed radically; indeed, in love, she developed into an exceptionally beautiful woman and I wasn't the only one who noticed the difference. All of our friends commented on it. Now it's close to thirty years later since we first met and she's still beautiful, but it's not just her physical beauty.

For me, my life changed radically. We did get married, my friendships expanded, and I was inspired in my work. I had the courage to forge ahead in many new and creative endeavors.

Annette is an incredibly sensitive, psychologically sophisticated and sweet person, very affectionate and naturally responsive sexually. . . . I love her body and her responsiveness. I know that it's hard to believe, but after all of these years, I'm still as sexually attracted as I was originally.

There are many other qualities in Annette that I discovered as our relationship unfolded. Annette is exceptionally intelligent, free-thinking, creative, and has an incredible sense of humor. She can turn an unfortunate or embarrassing situation into something poignant and special. . . .

In our relationship there has always been a sense of equality and mutual respect. We fully believe in the personal freedom of each other and pose no limits on each other's development. This has been a guiding principle for us even when it caused us inconvenience or pain. I think that's why our relationship is still fresh and exciting. In that respect, we feel different from what we see in so many other couples. They appear to be so much more possessive and intrusive on each other and act different in each other's company than otherwise. I find the company of most couples . . . boring. They seem to cancel out each other's sexuality and appear deadened in each other's presence.

From what I have said, you might think that life for us has always been happy. It has certainly been good overall, but we have had our bad times. When I first suggested that we have children together, Annette became emotionally distraught, even hostile. I had never seen her like that before and it shocked her as well. She had never been defensive and caught on that something was radically wrong with her response. But that didn't change things. We had trouble for months after that. Her feelings were all over the place and it practically ruined us. Luckily she got help and worked out her fears about having children. The result was that we now have four grown daughters who have turned out well.

And the trouble about having children wasn't our only problem. Whenever the issue of death came up—a movie, something on the news or information about the tragedy of someone we knew—she would become cold and unaffectionate. I would be hurt at those times and it was difficult for both of us. . . .

There were occasions when I was shaken up, too, because I had never been so vulnerable in a relationship. But eventually we sweated out these difficult times together because we really cared deeply for one another. To this day, we are lovers and the best of friends, rely on each other for support and companionship, and are a vital part of each other's lives. I know that she knows me and loves me and that I make her happy. She says that her life would be impossibly dull without me. I can barely imagine the horror of living life without her.

9 The relationship between this man and woman was inspirational to all of their friends and acquaintances and was illustrative of what we conceive to be the essence of a loving style of relating. Both parties were kind, generous with one another, independent, self-reliant, warm, respectful, sexually responsive, not restrictive or

intrusive, and nondefensive. Although this example illustrates love between a couple, many of the same qualities apply to love between friends and family members and can be extended to a love for humanity.

WHAT GENUINE LOVE IS NOT

10 To better understand what genuine love is, perhaps we should also describe what it is not. Love is not what we mean when one is told by a family member that "mommy or daddy really loves you but he/she just doesn't know how to show it." Love is not selfish, possessive, or demanding, or a proprietary right over the other. Love is never submission or dominance, emotional coercion, or manipulation. Love is not the desperate attempt to deny aloneness or the search for security that many couples manifest in their desire for a fused identity.

11 Lawrence (1920) stressed this theme in his work:

> Why should we consider ourselves, men and women, as broken fragments of one whole? It is not true. We are not broken fragments of one whole. (p. 271)

> Fusion, fusion, this horrible fusion of two beings, which every woman and most men insisted on, was it not nauseous and horrible anyhow, whether it was a fusion of the spirit or of the emotional body? Why could they not remain individuals, limited by their own limits? Why this dreadful all-comprehensiveness, this hateful tyranny? Why not leave the other being free, why try to absorb, or melt, or merge? One might abandon oneself utterly to the *moments,* but not to any other being. (p. 391)

12 Love is not to be confused with emotional hunger, that is, a desperate, immature need for dependence on another that drains the other person's vitality. Nor is it to be confused with a deep longing to find total confirmation of oneself in the other. In *The Denial of Death,* Becker (1973/1997) described the results of finding such an "ideal" love:

> If you find the ideal love and try to make it the sole judge of good and bad in yourself, the measure of your strivings, you become simply the reflex of another person. You lose yourself in the other, just as obedient children lose themselves in the family. . . . When you confuse personal love and cosmic heroism you are bound to fail in both spheres. . . . How can a human being be a god-like "everything" to another? (p. 166)

13 We have found that many people fail to reach a level of emotional maturity that would allow them to be capable of offering love, and they are also afraid of accepting or receiving love. In working with couples in initial intake sessions, we have observed that one or the other will outline a number of objections that amount to a fairly extensive annihilation of the other's character, only to be followed by an equally denigrating attack by the other partner. As the session progresses, we often notice their mistreatment of one another firsthand and tend to agree with both parties' assessment of each other, as these negative behaviors become more obvious. In other words, they have described each other fairly accurately, as it turns out, and manifest considerable hostility. Yet when we ask these warring couples why they stay together when they find each other so objectionable, they typically respond by saying, "Because we love each other." However, the destructive

behaviors these people manifest toward one another do not fit any acceptable definition of the word love. Why call it "love" when the behavior toward the love object is neither affectionate nor respectful, lacks communication and companionship, violates the personal boundaries of the other, and is often insensitive or outright hostile or abusive?. . .

CONCLUSION

14 Learning to love wholeheartedly is a most worthwhile endeavor but requires considerable devotion, time, and energy. As Rilke (1908/1984) observed,

> It is also good to love: because love is difficult. For one human being to love another human being: that is perhaps the most difficult task that has been entrusted to us, the ultimate task, the final test and proof, the work for which all other work is merely preparation. (p. 68)

15 . . . [W]hen people have been hurt in the past, they are reluctant to trust and be open to being hurt again. They feel self-protective and fear being vulnerable and open to emotional pain. In describing this learning process, Coelho (2004) wrote

> Everyone knows how to love, because we are all born with that gift. Some people have a natural talent for it, but the majority of us have to re-learn, to remember how to love, and everyone, without exception, needs to burn on the bonfire of past emotions, to relive certain joys and griefs, certain ups and downs, until they can see the connecting thread that exists behind each new encounter; because there is a connecting thread. (p. 139)

16 A person who overcomes self-limiting defenses and learns to give and receive love experiences the most satisfaction in life. . . . When love is sincere and real, it reaches spiritual proportions that give value and meaning to life.

REFERENCES

Becker, E. (1997). *The denial of death.* New York: Free Press. (Original work published 1973)

Coelho, P. (2004). *Eleven minutes* (M. J. Costa, Trans.). New York: HarperCollins.

Fromm, E. (1956). *The art of loving.* New York: Bantam Books.

Gage, R. L. (Ed.). (1976). *Choose life: A dialogue: Arnold Toynbee and Daisaku Ikeda.* Oxford, England: Oxford University Press.

Lawrence, D. H. (1920). *Women in love.* London: Penguin Books.

Lewis, C. S. (1960). *The four loves.* New York: Harcourt Brace.

Post, S. G., Underwood, L. G., Schloss, J. P., & Hurlbut, W. B. (2002). General introduction. In S. G. Post, L. G. Underwood, J. P. Schloss, & W. B. Hurlbut (Eds.), *Altruism and altruistic love: Science, philosophy and religion in dialogue* (pp. 3–12). New York: Oxford University Press.

Rilke, R. M. (1984). *Letters to a young poet* (S. Mitchell, Trans.). New York: Vintage Books. (Original work published 1908)

Singer, I. (2001). *Sex: A philosophical primer.* Lanham, MD: Rowman & Littlefield.

Wolfe, T. (1934). *You can't go home again.* New York: Harper and Row.

Who Wants to Marry a Soul Mate?

BARBARA DAFOE WHITEHEAD AND DAVID POPENOE

> The Rutgers National Marriage Project (http://marriage.rutgers.edu/about.htm), headed by Rutgers sociology professors David Popenoe and Barbara Dafoe Whitehead, aims to study the institution of marriage in America and, from a conservative perspective, educate the public about their concerns over the apparent decline of marriage as the foundation for family life. Each year the Project focuses on a different question. In 2001, the Project sociologists surveyed young people on their preferences for choosing a mate.

1   [Who wants to marry a soul mate?] Practically all young adults, according to a national survey of men and women conducted for the National Marriage Project by the Gallup Organization—the first large-scale study to look at attitudes about dating and marriage among married and single people, ages 20–29.

2   Young adults today are searching for a deep emotional and spiritual connection with one person for life. The overwhelming majority (94%) of never-married singles agree that "when you marry you want your spouse to be your soul mate, first and foremost." There is no significant gender gap in this response; similarly high proportions of men and women agree that they want to marry a soul mate. In another measure of the strength of the soul-mate ideal, over 80% of all women, married and single, agree it is more important to them to have a husband who can communicate about his deepest feelings than to have a husband who makes a good living.

3   Among single men and women, a large majority (88%) also agree that "there is a special person, a soul mate, waiting for you somewhere out there." And never-married singles are highly confident that they will be successful in locating that soul mate; a substantial majority (87%) agree that they will find that special someone when they are ready to get married.

4   Along with their ambitions for a spouse who meets their needs for emotional closeness and intimacy, these twentysomething singles also aspire to a marriage that lasts a lifetime. Seventy-eight percent agree that a couple should not get married unless they are prepared to stay together for life. In addition, they are reasonably confident that their own future marriages will be long lasting. Only 6% say it is unlikely that they will stay married to the same person for life.

5   Although young adults are confident that they will be successful in achieving a soul-mate marriage for themselves, they are less confident about the state of marriage in general. A substantial majority (68%) agree that it is more difficult to have a good marriage today than in their parents' generation, and slightly more than half (52%) agree that one sees so few good or happy marriages that one questions it as a way of life. Women, and those with a high-school education or less, are more likely than others to agree that there are very few people who have really good or happy marriages.

6   As one might expect, the generation that grew up in the midst of the divorce revolution also worries about the risks of divorce. Slightly more than half of all single adults (52%)—and an even higher percentage of those in their late twenties (60%)—agree that one of their biggest concerns about getting married is the possibility it will end in divorce.

7 | The high aspirations for a soul mate may be one reason why so many young adults are cohabiting before they take the plunge into marriage. Among the young adults surveyed, 44% had at some time lived with an opposite sex partner outside of marriage. As we reported in *The State of Our Unions, 2000,* single men and women in their twenties see cohabitation as a way to investigate a prospective partner's character, habits and capacity for fidelity before marriage. Many believe that living together yields more useful information about a partner than simply dating for a period of time. . . .

FROM SOCIAL INSTITUTION TO SOUL-MATE RELATIONSHIP

8 | Although young adults express high aspirations for the marital relationship, they see a diminished role for marriage in other domains. Many of the larger social, economic, religious and public purposes once associated with marriage are receding or missing altogether from their portrait of marriage.

9 | Most noteworthy is the weakened link between marriage and child rearing. Only 16% of young adults agree that the main purpose of marriage these days is to have children. The idea that marriage is the principal pathway into parenthood is changing as well. A clear majority of young men (62%) agree that, while it may not be ideal, it's okay for an adult woman to have a child on her own if she has not found the right man to marry. More than four out of ten describe adults who choose to raise a child out of wedlock as "doing their own thing."

10 | The survey also points to some evidence of the declining importance of marriage as an economic institution. Although two-thirds (65%) of singles say that they believe that marriage will improve their economic situation, an even higher percentage say it is extremely important to be economically "set" as individuals before they marry. It is especially noteworthy that young women are as likely as young men to agree that it is important for them to be economically "set" before marriage.

11 | Indeed, this attitude represents a dramatic shift for women. In earlier generations, most women saw marriage as a stepping-stone to achieving economic independence from parents and to gaining economic security. Today, however, women are more likely to look to themselves and to their own educational and career achievements as a source of economic independence and security.

12 | Partly this shift is due to changing patterns of education and work during the young adult years. More women are going on to higher education—now outranking men among college graduates—and also spending more years as working singles before marriage. During this expanded period of early adult singlehood, they acquire credit ratings, debts and assets on their own. For this reason, they tend to think about their economic lives and fortunes in individual terms.

13 | But the shift is also due to fears of the high risk of divorce. Because marriages break up at a high rate, young adults—and especially young women—no longer trust marriage as a reliable economic partnership. A large majority (82%) agree it is unwise for a woman to rely on marriage for financial security. For this reason, young women may prefer to invest in portable assets, like education and career development, rather than to place all their trust and self-investment in marriage.

This pattern may also explain why young women say that they are less interested in having a spouse who makes a good living than in having a spouse who is a soul mate. . . .

14   Along with the diminished importance assigned to marriage as a parental and economic partnership, the role of marriage as a religious institution seems to be fading. Although young adults seek a deep spiritual connection through marriage, they are not necessarily looking to marry someone who shares their own religion. Among singles, less than half (42%) agree that it is important to find a spouse who shares their own religious faith. Indeed, the popular soul-mate ideal may be a substitute for more traditional religious understandings of marriage. In a secular society, where sex has lost its connection to marriage and also its sense of mystery, young people may be attracted to the soul-mate ideal because it endows intimate relationships with a higher spiritual, though not explicitly religious, significance. . . .

15   Taken together, these findings paint a portrait of marriage as emotionally deep but socially shallow. While marriage is losing much of its broad public and institutional character, it is gaining popularity as a SuperRelationship, an intensely private spiritualized union, combining sexual fidelity, romantic love, emotional intimacy and togetherness. Indeed, this intimate couple relationship pretty much defines the sum total of marriage. Other bases for the marital relationship, such as an economic partnership or parental partnership, have receded in importance or disappeared altogether.

SOUL-MATE MARRIAGE IN A HIGH-DIVORCE SOCIETY

16   There is nothing historically new in the desire for lasting friendship in marriage. Indeed, the notion of combining friendship, romantic love and sexual fidelity in marriage is one of the distinctive features, and perhaps most daring experiments, in the Western marriage tradition. (Most societies, past and present, still prefer marriages arranged by kin or parents, and many adhere to the sexual double standard "she's faithful, he's not.") However, the findings in this survey suggest that today's young adults may be reaching even higher in their expectations for marriage. The centuries-old ideal of friendship in marriage, or what sociologists call companionate marriage, may be evolving into a more exalted and demanding standard of a spiritualized union of souls.

17   This development is understandable. Amid the dislocations of today's mobile society, dynamic economy, and frantic pace of life, it is difficult to sustain deep and lasting attachments. What's more, the desire for loving and lasting relationships may be especially strong among members of a generation that has come of age during the divorce revolution. It is not surprising, therefore, that young adults look to a soul mate for the steady emotional support and comfort that may be missing in other parts of their life. And, indeed, this is not an unworthy aspiration. For those who achieve it, a soul-mate relationship can be personally rewarding and deeply satisfying.

18   However, as today's young adults seem to realize, a soul-mate marriage in a high divorce society is difficult to sustain. Perhaps that is why a high percentage (86%) indicate that marriage is hard work and a full-time job. Over eight in ten

young adults (86%) agree that one reason for divorce is too much focus on expectations for happiness and not enough hard work needed for a successful marriage. Women and college-educated young adults are more likely than men and those with fewer years of formal education to agree that marriage is hard work. . . .

IMPLICATIONS FOR CHILDREN

19 | The emphasis on marriage as an intimate couples relationship rather than as a child-rearing partnership has profound implications for children. For one thing, it means that marriages with children are likely to remain at high risk of breakdown and breakup. The soul-mate ideal intensifies the natural tension between adult desires and children's needs. When children arrive, some couples may find it difficult to make the transition between couplehood and parenthood and may become disappointed and estranged from one another during the child-rearing years. This is not to say that couples should neglect each other while they are in the intensive child-rearing years, but it is to suggest that the soul-mate ideal of marriage may create unrealistic expectations that, if unfulfilled, may lead to marital discontent and perhaps a search for a new soul mate.

20 | Moreover, the high expectations for marriage as a couples relationship may also cause parents to leave marriages at a lower threshold of unhappiness than in the past. Indeed, in 1994, a nationally representative survey found only 15% of the population agreeing that "when there are children in the family, parents should stay together even if they don't get along." And, according to one recent study, the meaning of "not getting along" is being defined down. It's been estimated that more than half of recent divorces occur, not because of high conflict, but because of "softer" forms of psychological distress and unhappiness. Unfortunately, these are the marriages that might improve over time and with help. As it turns out, people do change their minds about the level of marital contentment. One recent large-scale study indicates that 86% of people who said they were unhappily married in the late 1980s but stayed married, indicated that they were happier when interviewed five years later. Indeed, three-fifths of the formerly unhappily married couples rated their marriages as either "very happy" or "quite happy."

21 | The central importance assigned to the soul-mate relationship also means that unwed parenthood is likely to remain at high levels. As the survey indicates, a high percentage of young adults, who are in the peak years of fertility, tend to separate sex and parenthood, on the one hand, from marriage, on the other. Put another way, people are pickier about the person they choose for a soul-mate relationship than they are about the people they choose as sexual partners, or as biological parents of their children. This is consistent with findings in other recent surveys. For example, a 1994 survey of University of California undergraduates found both men and women agreeing that a man is financially responsible for his child but not responsible to marry his pregnant girlfriend.

22 | However, these speculations could be wrong. Perhaps today's young adults will be able to reconcile their aspirations for emotional closeness with the realities of parenthood and domestic life. Clearly, they are more strongly committed to avoiding parental divorce than the Baby Boom generation. Indeed, while only 15% of

adults in the general population agree that parents should stay together for the sake of the children, 40% of young adults in the National Marriage Project survey agree. Moreover, our survey indicates that young adults are not cavalier about marriage or marital permanence. They are committed to lifelong marriage and to the idea that it takes constant effort to sustain a happy marriage. These attitudes may offer some glimmer of hope for their future marriages and for the future of marriage itself.

Cartoon

TOM CHENEY

"And do you, Rebecca, promise to make love only to Richard, month after month,
year after year, and decade after decade, until one of you is dead?"

For Discussion

The cartoon gets its humor from its rewording of the standard wedding vows—and the expressions of the couple at the altar, who have apparently never thought of their lifelong monogamous commitment as the preacher's words describe it. The serious point, of course, is that monogamy *does* mean making love to the same person, "month after month, year after year . . . until one of you is dead." You probably have attitudes toward monogamy in long-term relationships. What are they? After reading the Lauren Slater article (pages 375–381) on the chemistry of love, does your view of monogamy change? Why or why not?

18,260 Breakfasts

EVE LAPLANTE

> Eve LaPlante is the author of three books and has written for *The Atlantic,* the *New York Times,* and many other publications. The following essay appeared in *Why I'm Still Married,* a collection of articles by women, edited by Karen Propp and Jean Trounstein (Hudson Street Press, 2006).

1 "That's not Daddy," my daughter Charlotte, who is eight, informs me, pointing to the wedding photo on my dresser. "He doesn't have a beard." In the photo, David and I stand, hand in hand, on a granite headland in bright sunlight. Visible behind us are brambles, the ocean, and a stone pier. Our smiles look frozen. Fear—panic—plays on our faces.

2 At our wedding, a third of our lifetimes ago, David was clean-shaven. The David in the photograph is practically a stranger to me, too, as is the younger-looking version of myself, a blushing innocent who looks more like Charlotte than like me now, at middle age.

3 In fifteen years of marriage, David and I have changed in the usual ways. We've braided together our lives, sharing a bed and tax and mortgage payments, raising children, and, lately, watching our gums start to recede. Every evening after the kids are upstairs, David and I talk together over what have become ritual cups of tea. . . .

4 "So who *is* that guy in the photo?" I ask Charlotte, who ignores me. She doesn't linger over the photo, which is what I would have done as a child. She doesn't need to linger over photos of us, I suppose, because she actually has her father and me.

5 My parents' wedding photos were not displayed when I was a child, nor did anyone ever show them to me. I was three when Mom and Dad separated and five at their divorce, so by Charlotte's age I had no conscious awareness of them as a couple. To me, their interactions consisted of hot exchanges at the door of Mom's apartment, where I lived, before and after my occasional weekend with Dad. So their wedding photos, when I eventually discovered them, became an obsession.

6 I must have been eight when I found the packet of photos tucked away inside the cover of Mom's photograph album. Black and white, with the silvery brilliance of old photographs, they were windows on a past that seemed unreal. Mom and Dad were radiant, shining, glowing with expectation. I pored over their images, my heart pounding, searching for a clue as to who I was. But the photos never helped: I couldn't find myself in them. A few years later, while visting my maternal grandparents, I found some of the same images pasted into a family album with jagged holes replacing my father's face. . . .

7 As a child of divorce, I yearned for marriage, yet the path . . . was a mystery to me. Had I dared to think what marriage really meant, I'd have had to say, marriage is dangerous. It means being embattled and apart, like my parents. The very thing I longed for seemed out of my reach. This quandary was behind some of the panic that still, in the wedding photo, plays on my face.

8   Fifteen years later, I know [the fulfillment of marriage]. There's the abiding warmth of waking up each morning beside David, confident that he'll be there to encourage, critique, and even tease me. There's the exhilaration of knowing another person, deeply and without pretense, and similarly being known. . . . As ordinary as it may seem, David's and my ability to jointly—rather than separately—raise our children thrills me. I savor family life more than I might have if I'd known it as a child. I appreciate special occasions doubly, once because they're fun, and again because they represent the stability I missed. Simply gathering for regular meals as a gang, crowded around the kitchen table, is a delightful contrast to the solitary meals I ate as a girl with Mom or Dad. "Staying together is more important to those of us who come from divorce," a friend in her forties explains. "You really want to work things out."

9   "The ability to be grateful for comparative happiness," as she puts it, comes up often in conversations with adult children of divorce, who comprise a growing segment of the population. The great wave of divorce in the United States began around 1960, the year before my parents split up. A generation later, during the final decade of the twentieth century, a striking social shift occurred: the number of Americans living in single- or stepparent families surpassed the number in traditional families. Today, one in two new marriages includes at least one child of divorce.

10   Like many offspring of divorce, I grew up with a poignant sense of loss. Besides the trauma of the breakup and its aftermath, there's the prolonged pain of missing one parent and the security of an intact family. During my teens, I dreamed of a future happy family, but believed my chances of ever attaining one were infinitesimal. I felt inadequate as a potential marital partner; my parents' divorce served as a scar. As a college senior, with little sense of my prospects or of myself, I watched, amazed, as classmates planned weddings as well as careers.

11   Several years later, I had a series of blind dates that almost turned me off marriage forever. At some point, in hopes of short-circuiting this process, I began trying to figure out what I was looking for in a potential mate. . . . Some time passed before I came up with just one question, the answer to which could determine whether to proceed to a second date. That question is: Can you conceive of wanting to wake up every morning and chat with this person over breakfast for fifty years? The time frame arose from the fact that a couple that weds around age thirty can probably look forward to a half century of mornings together. I assumed that the breakfasts my husband and I would consume through the decades would be neither solitary nor silent; this was my hope. I didn't do the math then, but I have now: a fifty-year marriage entails 18,260 breakfasts.

12   In devising this scheme I was behaving, I believe, like a typical child of divorce. Based on my lengthy if unscientific survey of my peers, we are unlike the children of stable marriages in that we plan for, or rather anticipate, divorce even as we marry. Having learned firsthand that marriage is difficult and precious, we approach commitment with unusual thoughtfulness and practicality.

13   My scheme may not have been romantic, but it was discriminating. It shrank the number of my dates. Once I met David it allowed us a second date. So far

we've been together only fifteen years—that's 5,478 breakfasts—but I remain intrigued by what he may come up with tomorrow over a bowl of cereal and a cup of coffee.

14   Our marriage is not always easy, of course. We find each other exasperating from time to time, and some of our fights get nasty. Early in our marriage we chose to spend several nights apart, one of us at a hotel, and a few times considered divorce. In our early battles of wills, we kept score, brought up old conflicts, and generally played dirty, as many new couples do. To me, our first few years of marriage felt oddly like reenacting the same years of my parents' lives, during which I was not even present. I became uncharacteristically anxious. I could hear my parents' voices slicing the air and see the worn threshold of the kitchen doorway where I huddled as a toddler to escape their rage. I cannot say where I got this material, for it was certainly not in conscious awareness, but I was somehow compelled to replay scenes from their marriage, perhaps in an effort to defuse their emotional power. It was an odd personal challenge: Can I endure marital conflicts like those of my parents and resolve them in a new way?

15   For David and me, marriage gets better every year. . . . The pleasures it brings mitigate the frustrations. On Saturday mornings when David and I would like nothing more than to make love, we are blocked by a four-year-old in snowman pajamas, his limbs splayed between us. He, a result of our having made love, is sweet, too, and warm. A few years ago David surprised me by taking up insight meditation, a Buddhist practice. Seeing its calming effect, I began a practice of Christian meditation based on the writings of Saint Ignatius of Loyola. In our tandem journeys, our differences draw us closer.

16   Marriage is good for my body as well as my soul. I like my physical self more than I did before. David finds me beautiful, which helps me feel beautiful. To be known by him is part of the pleasure: we have nothing to hide. I find every human detail of him delightful, no less so as we age. . . .

17   Even with four children, marriage is good for my work. I recall that when I was single and childless, each day stretched out before me. With few obligations to anyone, I often didn't begin writing until the sun was setting. What did I do all day? I have no idea. Now, with my workweek limited to the hours when my children are at school (which has included preschool and part-time family day care), I get much more accomplished. My first book, composed before I had kids, took years to write. My most recent book, begun when our fourth child was less than two years old, emerged in just nine months. During that period, I should add, David did almost all the child care on weekends so that I could write.

18   This may be the keystone of our marriage: David and I share the work. While he makes more money and works longer hours, we divide the chores. I do more child care during the week, when he has a full-time office job, and he does more child care on the weekend. We divide minor chores by preference: he writes checks; I take care of our cars; he plants in the garden; I rake . . .

19   The really crucial split involved the two big chores besides child care. David cooks. I clean. That is, David shops for and prepares twenty-one meals each week,

while I wash, dry, and put away our clothes, occasionally visit the dry cleaner, and twice a month write a check to a housecleaning crew.

20   You may think I've got the better deal. I would agree. Producing twenty-five bag lunches weekly, which is only part of David's chore, seems herculean to me. But David would disagree. He actually chose the cooking, back when we first divided the household chores, and I—with an eye to the future—was accommodating enough to agree to clean. He enjoys preparing food, and even when it feels onerous, as it can, he believes eating together at home is healthy and economical. An inventive chef, he scans the Food and Dining pages and keeps a growing list of favorite recipes in a loose-leaf binder he shares with the kids. . . .

21   Our arrangement may sound complicated, but it feels simple. One reason it's sustainable is that we each have a separate realm of duty. I never fret about preparing dinner, while David never feels the tug of the stuffed laundry hamper. Dividing the labor is an essential ingredient of our marriage. If I find myself resenting David because he has shirked some chore or other, I remind myself of the delicious meals he routinely prepares. I may even taste one in the midst of my resentment, which might prompt me to do the chore myself. . . .

22   A happy marriage, it seems to me, is filled with compromises of one sort or another. Now and then, one of us is offered a business trip to someplace wonderful like Ireland or Hawaii. We usually try to bring the whole family along. But if a family trip is not feasible, financially or otherwise, David or I go solo. . . .

23   Not long ago, I had business in England. David urged me to go alone, knowing I'd get more work done. Then, to my amazement, he requested that I travel during February school vacation, the sort of week I admit I dread because of the unrelenting family time. Unlike me, who enjoys combining part-time work with part-time child care, David said that in my absence he would rather go whole hog, spending all day every day with the kids. Naturally, I agreed.

24   Thick snowflakes were falling on the morning of my flight to London. Taking a trip unnerves me, which may be another legacy of divorce. As a child I hated the long car or, later, bus ride between my parents' homes. Traveling without my family also arouses a certain amount of guilt. While I finished packing, David baked chocolate zucchini bread with the children. As we ate lunch, the five of them discussed all the places they could go and things they could do during the week. . . .

25   I listened quietly as David and our children planned their week without me, feeling myself relax. When the time came to depart for the airport, everyone boarded the minivan to take me to the trolley station near our house. There I kissed each of them, hoisted my bag, and walked across the tracks. I watched the van drive away, David at the wheel, and our children's hands waving in the windows.

26   Alone in the falling snow, awaiting the trolley that would take me to the airport, I was conscious of having left behind the fear I felt on our wedding day, the fear that persists in the photograph on my dresser. Neither did I feel any guilt about leaving our children at home with David. They would all eagerly await my return. In the meantime, they would be well fed.

Photograph

KIMBERLY WHITE

For Discussion

Officials in California and other states have married same-sex couples in defiance of state laws forbidding such marriages. The photograph shows Joy Galloway and Keltie Jones's ceremony in San Francisco's City Hall in February 2004. What was your first reaction to the photo? What attitude do you have toward lesbians and gays marrying? What in your background or experience helps to explain your attitude?

First Person Plural

HELEN FREMONT

Helen Fremont wrote the national best-seller *After Long Silence.* She works as a public defender. The following essay appeared in the same collection as the previous essay, *Why I Am* Still *Married* (2006).

COMMITMENT

1 Our marriage is based on a fundamental, irrefutable fact: neither of us can bear the trauma of dating. Our own courtship was excruciatingly long. The general rule of thumb in lesbian relationships is that on the second date you move in together. Donna and I held off cohabitation for nearly two months, which is something like a record in the gay community. Having accomplished this feat together, we are not about to venture out on our own again. This basic fear lies at the heart of our relationship, and offers us a sense of stability and security. We are bound to each other because neither of us has the courage to start over again.

THE DANGERS OF MARRIAGE

2 Getting married is a little like sticking your feet in cement: it feels sublimely gooey and sensual now, but you know that it's going to feel constricting in time—stabilizing, yes, but dangerously . . . well . . . *permanent.*

3 And let's face it: marriage is an act of pure arrogance. You are pretending to lay claim to the future, which is a risky business at best. The gods may not like it. They might feel obliged to prove that *they're* in charge, not you. Common ways for gods to get their point across would be to kill your spouse for no good reason at all—by introducing a drunk driver into your lane, or a suicide bomber, or a grade IV glioblastoma. Something like this happens every day, and I think it is a pretty simple matter for the gods to arrange for it to happen to you.

4 And then, of course, there's a statistical reason not to get married: marriage, as any lawyer will tell you, is the first step to divorce.

THE ILLEGAL MARRIAGE

5 So my wife and I were cautious, and we took both of our weddings seriously. Our first marriage—the illegal one—took place in 1996 in our living room. . . . The illegal marriage was the one that really mattered to us. We bought similar white linen dresses and had rings made by a local goldsmith. I wrote our vows, and Donna planned and cooked an elaborate menu for our guests. We got nervous and drank champagne afterward.

HISTORY LESSON

6 My wife had been married before—she was what she called a serial monogamist, having been married to a man for ten years (during her twenties), and then having lived with a woman for the next ten years (there went her thirties). These relationships

had ended badly and therefore she was hardly interested in starting a new one. My history of love was not exactly confidence-inspiring. Until the age of thirty-seven, when I met Donna in my backyard, I had never set up house with anyone. In my twenties, I had gone through the motions of sleeping with boys because that seemed to be what girls did. I had been passionately in love with several of my college and law school roommates, but they were all women, and the Amazing Force of Denial kept me clueless for years. I could not imagine that I might be a pervert or a deviant, so my worshipful feelings must be what all roommates feel for each other. I certainly wasn't queer. My love for these drop-dead gorgeous, sharp-witted women was pure, platonic, and agonizing.

7   After losing roommate after roommate to their fiancés, I finally decided to get my own fiancé in law school. He was adorable. I'd known him since high school, when we'd flirted and played endurance Ping-Pong for hours, progressing over the years to bicycling and distance running, winter camping and ski mountaineering.

8   Now, in my third year of law school, we added sex and big American-style breakfasts to our repertoire of activities and accomplishments. I was crazy about him, and he loved me anyway. We announced our engagement to our parents, and then I backed out of the marriage a few weeks later. I had doubts. What, exactly, was love? And why was my sexual attention span so short? I was no longer keen on being a lawyer, either, and I suspected other surprises lurking in my subconscious—that strange corridor where so many of my feelings have permanent lockers.

9   Sure enough, good old-fashioned introspection (coupled with expensive psychotherapy) led me, within a year, to the epiphany that I was, in fact, a lesbian. For an additional charge, I learned that this was okay. It would take me another five years before I actually tested out my new hunch of homosexuality in the field—I have never been particularly impulsive. And it would be another ten years before I fell for Donna.

COURTSHIP

10   Donna and I were set up by my neighbors, a gang of opera singers who knew Donna from their day jobs in the health-care industry, where Donna worked. These boys decided to throw a Memorial Day barbecue in my backyard. It was supposed to be a team effort, but they had songs to sing and boys to see, so I ended up doing all the cleaning, grocery shopping, preparing, and cooking, and they invited fifty of their closest friends. One of them was Donna. She walked into my backyard Monday afternoon bearing twenty pounds of potato salad. She was wearing an Indian-print skirt and a little black tank top; her toes were painted a honking red. I was wearing my ratty college crew shirt and a pair of giant industrial-strength canary-yellow rubber gloves, because I was carrying the mildewed grill from the backyard to the kitchen sink.

11   "Hi," I said, my hands full of greasy grill.

12   "Hi," she said, tipping the bowl of potato salad in greeting.

13   I was in love. Immediately after washing the grill I went upstairs and changed into a nicer T-shirt.

14 | The next day I called her for a date and we went out to dinner. She invited me home afterward to meet her cat—an auspicious start, I thought. Her cat was a used cat; Donna had gotten him from the local shelter a few months before. He had already broken every lamp in her apartment. He looked at me with suspicion, but I must have passed the test because Donna accepted my invitation to see the Mark Morris Dance Group the following week. She seemed depressed, however, and cried throughout the performance, so I believed my chances might be dwindling.

15 | But I soldiered on. On the advice of my romance counselors (a couple of friends who had met Donna at the barbecue), I asked her over for dinner. Soon after, she asked me to bring my dog to meet her cat. Fortunately, the two seemed to get along, if not in temperament, at least in color. They're both redheads.

16 | In July, we had dinner at a little jazz restaurant. I cried over the loss of my last girlfriend to cancer; she cried over the loss of her last girlfriend to a younger woman. We shared a container of pocket tissues. Within a month my dog and I moved in with her and her cat. I proposed marriage almost immediately. Two years later, she agreed.

MARRIAGE, LEGAL-STYLE

17 | In 2004, everyone was running down to City Hall to register; Massachusetts had legalized same-sex marriages. All our friends were planning their ceremonies, ordering invitations and flowers and dresses and cakes and caterers and musicians. Time was of the essence. There was movement afoot to amend the Constitution to ban same-sex marriages, and our chance to get state recognition was shrinking.

18 | This was both annoying and exhilarating. After all, Donna and I had been married for eight years already, without an ounce of help from the state. Now, in 2004, we had a chance to make our bond legal, albeit at tremendous psychic cost to millions of decent, God-fearing Americans, who considered the sanctity of their own marriages suddenly at risk.

19 | In September, Donna and I went on vacation to Provincetown for a week, and we decided to get married there. Unlike our first marriage at the dinner table, this marriage was a cold, calculated legal move. The week before vacation, we went to get our blood drawn for the medical certificate. It turned out that neither of us had syphilis, and our doctors pronounced us eligible for marriage. We drove to the Cape, checked into our beach cottage, and went to town hall to fill out the application for marriage. The town clerk congratulated us and gave us a list of justices of the peace. We had to wait three days, the legally required cooling-off period, before scheduling the wedding. For a justice of the peace, our innkeeper recommended a friend of his, a Provincetown old-timer who needed the business. I called her up. Judge Millie, as I will call her, was on disability and asked that we pay her in cash, so as not to confuse the authorities. She also pointed out that she was desperately in debt, and that the state-set fees for justices of the peace (seventy-five dollars) didn't begin to cut it. We should feel free to pay whatever additional "donation" we could for her services. We agreed on a time and place. She already had a five o'clock marriage scheduled, but would squeeze us in at four at the rotary in the West End of town, overlooking the marshes. She encouraged us to exchange vows, but very *short ones.*

20   The wedding was exactly what we'd hoped for. It took less than fifteen minutes. . . . Donna and I exchanged two-sentence vows, including promises to be honest with each other, to fail, and to keep trying—goals we believed we could fulfill. There were no witnesses (none are required in Massachusetts), and Judge Millie pronounced us married. . . .

THE CERTAINTY OF ABANDONMENT AND LOSS

21   Throughout our ten-year relationship, Donna and I have been certain that each will be abandoned by the other. Consequently, we remain ever vigilant and . . . well, frankly . . . paranoid.

22   Perhaps due to a failure of imagination, each of us anticipates the other's betrayal according to a precise transcript of what happened in our previous relationships. Donna's former lover left her for a younger woman, so Donna believes I will inevitably do the same. Never mind that I am not the Babe Magnet that her former lover was. . . . Donna does not confine her fears to the rational.

23   Neither do I, of course, but I have good reason for my paranoia. My previous lover died of cancer, so I am convinced that Donna will do the same. To prove my theory, Donna came into our relationship with a solid track record of previous bouts of cancer, three abdominal surgeries, six weeks of radiation, and a year of chemotherapy. And sure enough . . . six years into our relationship, Donna had a recurrence. As I had done with my previous lover, I now went to the hospital with Donna, wrung my hands waiting for the surgeon's report, slept in the chair at her bedside for a week, disobeyed the nurses, ate her food, brought her take-out from McDonald's, and planned to kill myself after she died.

24   For the next ten months, I took Donna to chemotherapy every Monday morning, and we'd cap the day off with a matinee at the multiplex cinema next to the health center. The movies produced in late 2000 and early 2001, by and large, sucked. But we were living our own melodrama, and despite the fact that Donna survived this ordeal, I remain convinced that she will die on me. I believe I'm carcinogenic.

25   This was the year that made our marriage four-dimensional. It had weight and shape and depth, and now *time.*

LOSS, CONTINUED

26   My wife and I are middle-aged. It is our season of mothers and fathers dying. They are dropping like flies, left and right. They ruled our lives, and now—poof—they're gone.

27   In the last three years Donna and I have gone to several funerals: her mother's, my father's, her father's. And we have mourned another sort of death—my own. (Just before dying, my father signed a codicil to his will, disowning me and declaring me dead. This had nothing to do with Donna, whom he had liked, or with our relationship, which seemed to amuse him. It had to do with my having written a memoir revealing my Jewish heritage—an identity far more complicated than lesbianism.)

28   Families are proof that love and loss go hand in hand, but marriage can be a sort of compensation. Donna and I collect our losses and grow closer, like two

stitches pulled more tightly together. We fill the gaps for each other, growing into the holes left behind. . . .

THE MARITAL BED

29 Our lily pad. It sits in the middle of the room, facing the sun. We spend sleepless nights plotting revenge here. We spend hours wondering what went wrong, and then more hours making love, and then more hours floating in our bodies. She tells me her dreams in the morning. We make new ones each night. We snore into each other's ears here, and toss the covers and yank the covers and flop around in the stupidity of sleep. We are most married with our arms and legs flung across each other, unselfconscious, unconscious.

30 We wash the sheets and make the bed, and now that we are Old Marrieds, we sleep less and spend more time watching the years vanish. The city sizzles outside the window, and we wait until it's safe to wake. We are madly in love, and only the solidity of the days that stretch before and behind us give lie to our sense that we are suspended in midair, that all our intentions amount to nothing but ideas, thin and permeable.

THE DAILY GRIND

31 My wife and I snap to attention at the buzz of the alarm. We take turns with the hair dryer, the nail clipper, the cuticle scissors. We reach for the nylons and rub lotion on our elbows and begin the day, and then the next day, and the next, and the next. We share a calendar. We share a tube of toothpaste, a bottle of wine, a cold. We share a joke, a fight, a bank account, an apartment, a dog and a cat who consider us divisible. We share doubts about the dog and cat.

32 She goes to her office, I to mine. And then we call each other in the middle of the day. What's your day like? What are you doing? I miss you. What shall we eat? Who will call the plumber? Who will call our friends? I miss you. Hours go by when we do not think of each other. It happens. I'm sure it happens.

MARRIAGE, THE CREATURE

33 Ten years in, you realize that marriage is a breathing organism that grows with you. Regardless of what you thought you were raising, you now have a preteen on your hands, a restless, rambunctious ten-year-old marriage that thinks it knows everything, but that still has a lot of surprises left. We're watching this kid grow, and it's got a zillion things up its sleeve, delights and disappointments, and every so often, we feel like slapping it around and taking it to Disneyland. Well, maybe not Disneyland, but Provincetown. Or St. Thomas. Or Pitigliano. Sometimes we are sorry. You never know when you travel with a ten-year-old marriage. Sometimes it gets cranky, but it can be so easily distracted!

THE LONG HAUL

34 We don't answer the phone. Who goes there? We pull the covers over our heads and wait it out together. We hibernate.

35 | Months go by. Years. We crawl out of bed to see what's new in the world. We double-park and return all the videos and library books and pay all the late fees. We forgive ourselves our trespasses. We eat our daily bread and chocolate. We pray and hold hands. For ever and ever.

QUESTIONS FOR DISCUSSION

1. As the many definitions of love in "What Is Love?" imply, it is evidently hard to say what love is and easier to say what it is not. The authors say that "love is not selfish, possessive, and demanding," never involves "submission or dominance, emotional coercion, or manipulation," and is "not the desperate attempt to deny aloneness or the search for security that many couples manifest in their desire for a fused identity." Would you say your past or present romantic relationships avoid the negatives entirely? Is it realistic to think that most romantic relationships can avoid them entirely?

2. Barbara Dafoe Whitehead and David Popenoe propose that "the popular soul-mate ideal may be a substitute for more traditional religious understandings of marriage" (paragraph 14). They go on to claim that "sex has lost its connection to marriage and also its sense of mystery," and therefore we need the soul-mate notion as spiritual compensation. What do you think? Is the traditional religious understanding of marriage at odds with, or even markedly different from, the soul-mate ideal? If so, how?

3. The accounts of married love in Eve LaPlante's "18,260 Breakfasts" and Helen Fremont's "First Person Plural" are obviously different. Yet, the love described in both pieces has much in common. Would you say that the relationships described avoid or overcome what the Firestones say love is not? Would you say that the people involved are soul mates?

4. No doubt there are die-hard romantics among us, people who can only be satisfied with that state of affairs we call being "in love." But most people just want a reasonably happy long-term relationship that works, where the two people involved love each other and manage to cope with life together. Yet we often also say that married love means "settling" for something less than what we really want. In your experience, would you say that realistic compromise is an accurate and fair description of long-term love?

SUGGESTIONS FOR WRITING

For Persuasion

The specter of divorce hangs over marriage today. Many young adults today are children of failed marriages and understandably fear repeating the mistakes of their parents.

It is not surprising, then, that many proposals have been offered to make divorce more difficult. Instead of thinking about changing the law, consider reducing divorce from another angle: the private agreement the couple reaches *before* they marry. Decide what you think a couple should recognize as grounds for splitting up, regardless of whether the split ends in permanent separation or divorce. Write an essay persuading your peers to adopt your view of what justifies ending a marriage.

For Inquiry and Convincing

We encounter different explanations for the problems with marriage today in Part Three's selections. Let's focus attention on one of them. Barbara Dafoe Whitehead and David Popenoe see in the views of young adults "a portrait of marriage as emotionally deep but socially shallow." In other words, couples today are conceiving marriage as an intensely private matter between soul mates, without much connection with the social network that used to help sustain married couples—family, faith and church, friends, and so on.

Whitehead and Popenoe require us to change our idea of marriage. Write an essay evaluating Whitehead and Popenoe's view.

FOR FURTHER READING AND RESEARCH

Ackerman, Diane. *The Natural History of Love.* New York: Random House, 1994.

Buss, David M. *The Evolution of Desire: Strategies of Human Mating.* New York: Basic Books, 1994.

Firestone, Robert W., Lisa A. Firestone, and Joyce Catlett. *Sex and Love in Intimate Relationships.* Washington, D.C.: American Psychological Association, 2006.

Fisher, Helen. *Why We Love: The Nature and Chemistry of Romantic Love.* New York: Holt, 2004.

Kipnis, Laura. *Against Love: A Polemic.* New York: Pantheon, 2005.

Mitchell, Stephen A. *Can Love Last? The Fate of Romance over Time.* New York: Norton, 2002.

Propp, Karen, and Jean Trounstein, eds. *Why I'm Still Married: Women Write Their Hearts Out on Love, Loss, Sex, and Who Does the Dishes.* New York: Hudson Street Press, 2006.

Trimberger, E. Kay. *The New Single Woman.* Boston: Beacon Press, 2005.

Whitehead, Barbara Defoe, and David Popenoe. See the annual reports of the Rutgers Marriage Project at <http://www.marriage.rutgers.edu>.

Readings: Issues and Arguments

Global Warming: What Should Be Done?

There's no issue quite like global warming. A strong consensus exists among scientists that the Earth is warming up at an alarming rate. Natural processes are involved, but most of the warming is caused by human activities, especially the burning of fossil fuels, mainly coal and oil. If something is not done and done soon—within the next decade or two—we face a long list of trouble: rising sea levels that will threaten coastal cities, droughts that will make farming difficult or impossible, increasingly destructive weather (such as the hurricane that devastated New Orleans), complete loss of the already stressed coral reefs, widespread extinction of species in the ocean and on land, and so on.

Yet despite repeated warnings from scientists, often reported in the press and television news, the American public as a whole lacks a sense of urgency. The scientific consensus is not having the impact it should, and too many people think questions that have been answered with a high degree of probability are still matters of serious dispute. This chapter attempts to engage the genuine issues, as summed up in its title, What should be done?

What are the genuine issues? Some are technological. We have many "green" sources of power—wind, solar, ethanol produced from corn, biodiesel, and so on. Which should we use and in what combination? We have a 200-year supply of coal—can we use some of it while making the transition to cleaner power sources without releasing the current huge discharge of carbon dioxide (CO_2) into our atmosphere? These and many other technological issues are certainly arguable.

Other questions are economic. What approach to reducing greenhouse gases will prove least expensive to consumers and most profitable for industry and investors, many of whom are increasingly aware of both the wisdom and the money in going green? It is not obvious where economic commitments should be.

Then there are political questions. What will persuade our energy companies to think beyond fossil fuels? How can we secure the cooperation of countries like Saudi Arabia, whose wealth is too dependent on oil exports? While reducing our own greenhouse gas emissions, how can we help developing countries, like China, from becoming polluters as bad as or worse than the United States and Europe currently are? Again, the best political course of action is far from settled.

This chapter explores many facets of the global warming problem, but not all of them. It is meant to encourage you to explore both problems and solutions in greater depth. We think learning to live in harmony with our planet may be *the* most important issue we face.

Text of the American College and University Presidents' Climate Commitment

Established in 2006, the American College and University Presidents' Climate Commitment (ACUPCC) now includes a long list of signatories who have endorsed meaningful steps to make their campuses "climate neutral"—that is, the goal of emitting no more greenhouse gases than they eliminate by such measures as planting trees. The existence of this high-profile organization affirms both the seriousness of global warming and the commitment required to bring it under control.

More than ever, universities must take leadership roles to address the grand challenges of the twenty-first century, and climate change is paramount amongst these.

—Michael M. Crow, President, Arizona State University

American College and University Presidents' Climate Commitment.
www.presidentsclimatecommitment.org

1   We, the undersigned presidents and chancellors of colleges and universities, are deeply concerned about the unprecedented scale and speed of global warming and its potential for large-scale, adverse health, social, economic and ecological effects. We recognize the scientific consensus that global warming is real and is largely being caused by humans. We further recognize the need to reduce the global emission of greenhouse gases by 80% by mid-century at the latest, in order to avert the worst impacts of global warming and to reestablish the more stable climatic conditions that have made human progress over the last 10,000 years possible.

2   While we understand that there might be short-term challenges associated with this effort, we believe that there will be great short-, medium-, and long-term economic, health, social and environmental benefits, including achieving energy independence for the U.S. as quickly as possible.

3   We believe colleges and universities must exercise leadership in their communities and throughout society by modeling ways to minimize global warming emissions, and by providing the knowledge and the educated graduates to achieve climate neutrality. Campuses that address the climate challenge by reducing global warming emissions and by integrating sustainability into their curriculum will better serve their students and meet their social mandate to help create a thriving, ethical and civil society. These colleges and universities will be providing students with the knowledge and skills needed to address the critical, systemic challenges faced by the world in this new century and enable them to benefit from the economic opportunities that will arise as a result of solutions they develop.

4   We further believe that colleges and universities that exert leadership in addressing climate change will stabilize and reduce their long-term energy costs, attract excellent students and faculty, attract new sources of funding, and increase the support of alumni and local communities. Accordingly, we commit our institutions to taking the following steps in pursuit of climate neutrality.

1. Initiate the development of a comprehensive plan to achieve climate neutrality as soon as possible.
    a. Within two months of signing this document, create institutional structures to guide the development and implementation of the plan.
    b. Within one year of signing this document, complete a comprehensive inventory of all greenhouse gas emissions (including emissions from electricity, heating, commuting, and air travel) and update the inventory every other year thereafter.
    c. Within two years of signing this document, develop an institutional action plan for becoming climate neutral, which will include:
        i. A target date for achieving climate neutrality as soon as possible.
        ii. Interim targets for goals and actions that will lead to climate neutrality.
        iii. Actions to make climate neutrality and sustainability a part of the curriculum and other educational experience for all students.
        iv. Actions to expand research or other efforts necessary to achieve climate neutrality.
        v. Mechanisms for tracking progress on goals and actions.

2. Initiate two or more of the following tangible actions to reduce greenhouse gases while the more comprehensive plan is being developed.
    a. Establish a policy that all new campus construction will be built to at least the U.S. Green Building Council's LEED Silver standard or equivalent.
    b. Adopt an energy-efficient appliance purchasing policy requiring purchase of ENERGY STAR certified products in all areas for which such ratings exist.
    c. Establish a policy of offsetting all greenhouse gas emissions generated by air travel paid for by our institution.

   d.   Encourage use of and provide access to public transportation for all faculty, staff, students and visitors at our institution.

   e.   Within one year of signing this document, begin purchasing or producing at least 15% of our institution's electricity consumption from renewable sources.

   f.   Establish a policy or a committee that supports climate and sustainability shareholder proposals at companies where our institution's endowment is invested.

   g.   Participate in the Waste Minimization component of the national RecycleMania competition, and adopt 3 or more associated measures to reduce waste.

3.   Make the action plan, inventory, and periodic progress reports publicly available by providing them to the Association for the Advancement of Sustainability in Higher Education (AASHE) for posting and dissemination.

5   In recognition of the need to build support for this effort among college and university administrations across America, we will encourage other presidents to join this effort and become signatories to this commitment.

Signed,

The Signatories of the American College & University Presidents Climate Commitment

FOR RESEARCH AND DISCUSSION

To save space, we did not include the long list of colleges and universities that have signed the Presidents' Climate Commitment. The list is available online and worth consulting. For instance, in our own state, Texas, some of our most prominent schools are not among the signatories, probably because much of the money that supports higher education comes from fossil fuel interests.

If your school is on the list, find out why it is and what is being done to carry out the promises made in the document. In your view, is the commitment serious and sustained, or just a public relations ploy without much substance? If your school is not on the list, find out why it is not and what could be done to make your school more environmentally aware and responsible. Discuss what you discover from research, including the economic and political forces that have so much to do with a college or university's priorities and decision making.

A Climate Repair Manual

GARY STIX

The September 2006 issue of *Scientific American* focused on global warming and the various technologies for reducing greenhouse gas emissions. The eight articles that constitute "Energy's Future: Beyond Carbon" are well worth reading and careful study. Gary Stix, the Special Projects Editor for *Scientific American,* wrote the introduction to this set of articles.

1   Explorers attempted and mostly failed over the centuries to establish a pathway from the Atlantic to the Pacific through the icebound North, a quest often punctuated by starvation and scurvy. Yet within just 40 years, and maybe many fewer, an ascending thermometer will likely mean that the maritime dream of Sir Francis Drake and Captain James Cook will turn into an actual route of commerce that competes with the Panama Canal.

2   The term "glacial change" has taken on a meaning opposite to its common usage. Yet in reality, Arctic shipping lanes would count as one of the more benign effects of accelerated climate change. The repercussions of melting glaciers, disruptions in the Gulf Stream and record heat waves edge toward the apocalyptic: floods, pestilence, hurricanes, droughts—even itchier cases of poison ivy. Month after month, reports mount of the deleterious effects of rising carbon levels. One recent study chronicled threats to coral and other marine organisms, another a big upswing in major wildfires in the western U.S. that have resulted because of warming.

3   The debate on global warming is over. Present levels of carbon dioxide—nearing 400 parts per million (ppm) in the earth's atmosphere—are higher than they have been at any time in the past 650,000 years and could easily surpass 500 ppm by the year 2050 without radical intervention.

4   The earth requires greenhouse gases, including water vapor, carbon dioxide and methane, to prevent some of the heat from the received solar radiation from escaping back into space, thus keeping the planet hospitable for protozoa, Shetland ponies and Lindsay Lohan. But too much of a good thing—in particular, carbon dioxide from SUVs and local coal-fired utilities—is causing a steady uptick in the thermometer. Almost all of the 20 hottest years on record have occurred since the 1980s.

5   No one knows exactly what will happen if things are left unchecked—the exact date when a polar ice sheet will complete a phase change from solid to liquid cannot be foreseen with precision, which is why the Bush administration and warming-skeptical public-interest groups still carry on about the uncertainties of climate change. But no climatologist wants to test what will arise if carbon dioxide levels drift much higher than 500 ppm.

A LEAGUE OF RATIONS

6   Preventing the transformation of the earth's atmosphere from greenhouse to unconstrained hothouse represents arguably the most imposing scientific and technical challenge that humanity has ever faced. Sustained marshaling of cross-border

THE HEAT IS ON

A U.S. senator has called global warming the "greatest hoax" ever foisted on the American people. But despite persistently strident rhetoric, skeptics are having an ever harder time making their arguments: scientific support for warming continues to grow.

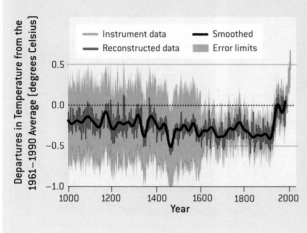

This "hockey stick graph," from one of many studies showing a recent sharp increase in average temperatures, received criticism from warming skeptics, who questioned the underlying data. A report released in June by the National Research Council lends new credence to the sticklike trend line that traces an upward path of temperatures during the 20th century.

engineering and political resources over the course of a century or more to check the rise of carbon emissions makes a moon mission or a Manhattan Project appear comparatively straightforward.

7   Climate change compels a massive restructuring of the world's energy economy. Worries over fossil-fuel supplies reach crisis proportions only when safeguarding the climate is taken into account. Even if oil production peaks soon—a debatable contention given Canada's oil sands, Venezuela's heavy oil and other reserves—coal and its derivatives could tide the earth over for more than a century. But fossil fuels, which account for 80 percent of the world's energy usage, become a liability if a global carbon budget has to be set.

8   Translation of scientific consensus on climate change into a consensus on what should be done about it carries the debate into the type of political minefield that has often undercut attempts at international governance since the League of Nations.[1] The U.S. holds less than 5 percent of the world's population but produces nearly 25 percent of carbon emissions and has played the role of saboteur by failing to ratify the Kyoto Protocol[2] and commit to reducing greenhouse gas emissions to 7 percent below 1990 levels.

[1]The League of Nations was established after World War I, but failed in its mission to prevent further conflicts. The U.S. did not join the League, despite the role of President Woodrow Wilson in establishing it.

[2]The Kyoto Protocol was a 1997 international agreement to limit greenhouse gas emissions. The U.S. Senate rejected the agreement by a 95–0 vote.

GREENHOUSE EFFECT

A prerequisite for life on earth, the greenhouse effect occurs when infrared radiation (heat) is retained within the atmosphere.

| 1 Most solar energy reaching the earth is absorbed at the surface | 2 The warmed surface emits infrared radiation | 3 Like a blanket, atmospheric greenhouse gases absorb and reradiate the heat in all directions, including back to the earth | 4 Human activity has increased the amount of greenhouse gas in the atmosphere and thus the amount of heat returned to the surface. In consequence, global temperatures have risen |

9   Yet one of the main sticking points for the U.S.—the absence from that accord of a requirement that developing countries agree to firm emission limits—looms as even more of an obstacle as a successor agreement is contemplated to take effect when Kyoto expires in 2012. The torrid economic growth of China and India will elicit calls from industrial nations for restraints on emissions, which will again be met by even more adamant retorts that citizens of Shenzhen and Hyderabad should have the same opportunities to build their economies that those of Detroit and Frankfurt once did.

10   Kyoto may have been a necessary first step, if only because it lit up the pitted road that lies ahead. But stabilization of carbon emissions will require a more tangible blueprint for nurturing further economic growth while building a decarbonized energy infrastructure. An oil company's "Beyond Petroleum" slogans will not suffice.

11   Industry groups advocating nuclear power and clean coal have stepped forward to offer single-solution visions of clean energy. But too much devoted too early to any one technology could yield the wrong fix and derail momentum toward a sustainable agenda for decarbonization. Portfolio diversification underlies a plan laid out by Robert H. Socolow and Stephen W. Pacala in this single-topic edition of *Scientific American*. The two Princeton University professors describe how deployment of a basket of technologies and strategies can stabilize carbon emissions by midcentury.

12   Perhaps a solar cell breakthrough will usher in the photovoltaic age, allowing both a steel plant and a cell phone user to derive all needed watts from a single source. But if that does not happen—and it probably won't—many technologies (biofuels, solar, hydrogen and nuclear) will be required to achieve a low-carbon energy supply. All these approaches are profiled by leading experts in this special issue, as are more radical ideas, such as solar power plants in outer space and fusion generators, which may come into play should today's seers prove myopic 50 years hence.

NO MORE BUSINESS AS USUAL

13   Planning in 50- or 100-year increments is perhaps an impossible dream. The slim hope for keeping atmospheric carbon below 500 ppm hinges on aggressive programs of energy efficiency instituted by national governments. To go beyond what climate specialists call the "business as usual" scenario, the U.S. must follow Europe and even some of its own state governments in instituting new policies that affix a price on carbon—whether in the form of a tax on emissions or in a cap-and-trade system (emission allowances that are capped in aggregate at a certain level and then traded in open markets). These steps can furnish the breathing space to establish the defense-scale research programs needed to cultivate fossil fuel alternatives. The current federal policy vacuum has prompted a group of eastern states to develop their own cap-and-trade program under the banner of the Regional Greenhouse Gas Initiative.

14   Fifty-year time frames are planning horizons for futurists, not pragmatic policymakers. Maybe a miraculous new energy technology will simultaneously solve our energy and climate problems during that time, but another scenario is at least as likely: a perceived failure of Kyoto or international bickering over climate questions could foster the burning of abundant coal for electricity and synthetic fuels for transportation, both without meaningful checks on carbon emissions.

15   A steady chorus of skeptics continues to cast doubt on the massive peer-reviewed scientific literature that forms the cornerstone for a consensus on global warming. "They call it pollution; we call it life," intones a Competitive Enterprise Institute advertisement on the merits of carbon dioxide. Uncertainties about the extent and pace of warming will undoubtedly persist. But the consequences of inaction could be worse than the feared economic damage that has bred overcaution. If we wait for an ice cap to vanish, it will simply be too late.

FOR DISCUSSION

1. "The debate on global warming is over," the author says. What does he think is certain, beyond debate? What is not certain? In your view, how important are the questions we cannot answer right now? What effect should they have on taking action?

2. The author has much to say about "translat[ing] scientific consensus on climate change into a consensus on what should be done." What are the barriers to action as he depicts them? Which seem most important to you? Why?

3. Energy efficiency is certainly part of the solution to global warming. One approach is the cap-and-trade approach the author mentions. What does cap-and-trade involve? How might it contribute to both energy efficiency and the development of alternate energy sources (nonfossil fuels)?

FOR RESEARCH, INQUIRY, AND CONVINCING

In 2009 a much-anticipated international climate meeting in Copenhagen proved disappointing to all climate-concerned people. At the last minute, President Obama negotiated an agreement with China, which made it possible to salvage some positive outcome from a meeting that nearly fell apart entirely.

Much has been written and said online about Copenhagen. Find out all you can, including especially what the conflicts were and why greater progress in confronting the greenhouse gas threat did not happen.

Then write an essay defending a stance on international efforts to combat global warming. Should we continue to pursue this avenue for change or not?

15 Ways to Make a Wedge

SCIENTIFIC AMERICAN

This chart comes from the same issue of *Scientific American* as the previous article. It is helpful as a way of envisioning the many routes to reducing global warming and as a reminder that only a multifaceted approach will yield satisfactory results.

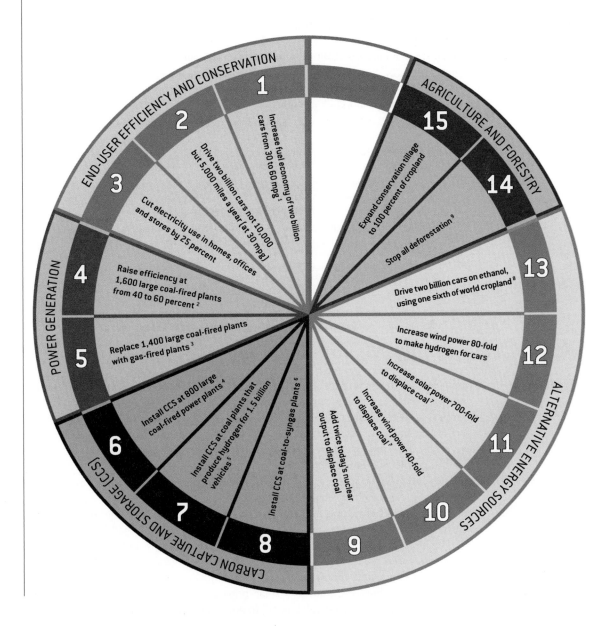

An overall carbon strategy for the next half a century produces seven wedges' worth of emissions reductions. Here are 15 technologies from which those seven can be chosen. Each of these measures, when phased in over 50 years, prevents the release of 26 billion tons of carbon. Leaving one wedge blank symbolizes that this is by no means exhaustive.

NOTES

[1] World fleet size in 2056 could well be two billon cars. Assume they average 10,000 miles a year.

[2] "Large" is one gigawatt (GW) capacity. Plants run 90 percent of the time.

[3] Here and below, assume coal plants run 90 percent of the time at 50 percent efficiency. Present coal power output is equivalent to 800 such plants.

[4] Assume 90 percent of CO_2 is captured.

[5] Assume a car (10,000 miles a year, 60 miles per gallon equivalent) requires 170 kilograms of hydrogen a year.

[6] Assume 30 million barrels of synfuels a day, about a third of today's total oil production. Assume half of carbon originally in the coal is captured.

[7] Assume wind and solar produce, on average, 30 percent of peak power. Thus replace 2,100 GW of 90-percent-time coal power with 2,100 GW (peak) wind or solar plus 1,400 GW of load-following coal power, for net displacement of 700 GW.

[8] Assume 60-mpg cars, 10,000 miles a year, biomass yield of 15 tons a hectare, and negligible fossil-fuel inputs. World cropland is 1,500 million hectares.

[9] Carbon emissions from deforestation are currently about two billion tons a year. Assume that by 2056 the rate falls by half in the business-as-usual projection and to zero in the flat path.

Illustration by Janet Chao from Robert H. Socolow and Stephen W. Pacala, "A Plan to Keep Carbon on Track," *Scientific American,* September 2006. Reprinted by permission of Janet Chao.

FOR DISCUSSION AND RESEARCH

Some of the fifteen wedges are clear enough, such as increasing fuel economy in cars and trucks. The less gasoline and diesel we burn, the less carbon dioxide escapes from exhaust tailpipes into the air. Others may not be so clear, such as carbon capture and storage. In class, discuss all the wedges, listing the ones that are unfamiliar and the ones that are familiar but not understood.

Using the September 2006 issue of *Scientific American* and other quality sources, individuals or groups in the class should find out more about any of the wedges the class knows little about or does not understand. Short oral reports to the class will help bring everyone up to speed on all the existing and developing methods for reducing carbon dioxide emissions.

Another approach is to divide the class into five groups and assign them one of the categories on the outer edge of the circle. Each group should investigate its category in depth and report to the class. The advantage of this approach is that even familiar technologies, such as solar power, are in constant development and need to be grasped in considerable detail to appreciate their potential and limitations.

Contributions to Global Warming

AL GORE

Al Gore was vice president when Bill Clinton was president and was the Democratic presidential candidate in 2000. His commitment to environmental causes goes back many years and has made him the best-known major American politician to raise public awareness about ecology in general and about global warming in particular.

The graphic on the following two pages, from *An Inconvenient Truth* (pp. 250–251), represents the relative amounts of carbon dioxide emissions contributed from various parts of the world.

FOR DISCUSSION

1. What is the principle behind the scale used to represent the various parts of the world? What point does it imply? Is the graphic effective? If so, how?

2. The United States and Europe account for almost 60% of estimated CO_2 emissions worldwide. Clearly, relative prosperity correlates with greenhouse gas generation. But the graphic misleads in some ways. For example, Southeast Asia, China, and India may now contribute only 12.2% of the total, but their share, especially that of China and India, is on the rise. What other aspects of this graphic might mislead?

3. Note the source of the information used to create the graphic—the U.S. Department of Energy. How much credence and authority do you allot to federal government agencies?

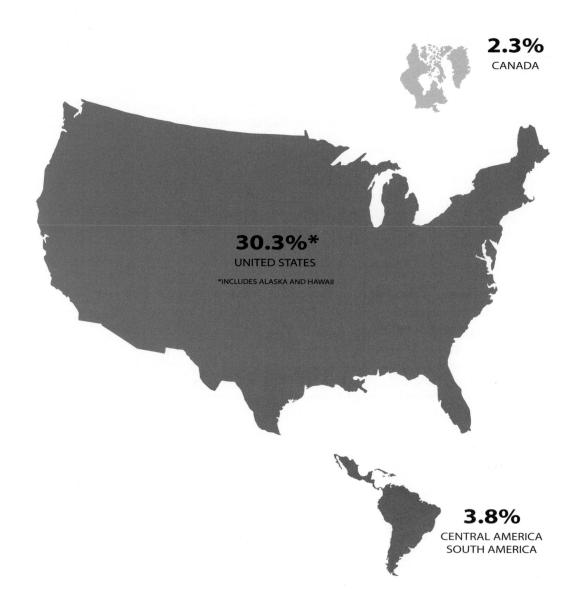

2.3%
CANADA

30.3%*
UNITED STATES
*INCLUDES ALASKA AND HAWAII

3.8%
CENTRAL AMERICA
SOUTH AMERICA

CONTRIBUTIONS TO GLOBAL WARMING

■ United States   ■ Other industrialized nations   ■ Developing nations

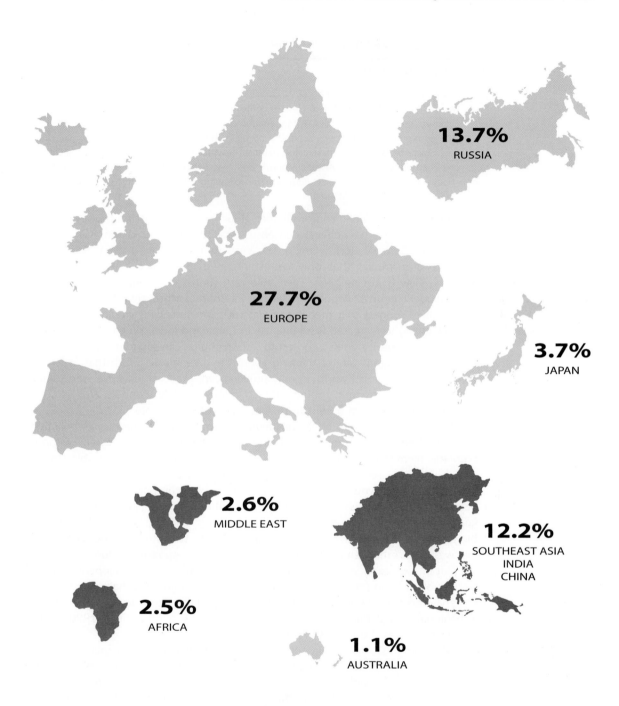

13.7%
RUSSIA

27.7%
EUROPE

3.7%
JAPAN

2.6%
MIDDLE EAST

12.2%
SOUTHEAST ASIA
INDIA
CHINA

2.5%
AFRICA

1.1%
AUSTRALIA

Source: U.S. Department of Energy, Energy Information Administration, Carbon Dioxide Information
Analysis Center.

Some Convenient Truths

GREGG EASTERBROOK

> Obviously playing off the title of Al Gore's controversial book, Gregg Easterbrook argues that both advocates of climate control and those who oppose it are guilty of "gloom and doom" attitudes. A few enlightened government policies that encourage the entrepreneurial spirit will solve the problem, he believes.
>
> Easterbrook is a prominent journalist who writes often about scientific subjects. He is an editor for both *Atlantic Monthly* and *New Republic* and the author of many books, including *The Progress Paradox*. The following article came from the September 2006 issue of *Atlantic Monthly*.

1   If there is now a scientific consensus that global warming must be taken seriously, there is also a related political consensus: that the issue is Gloom City. In *An Inconvenient Truth,* Al Gore warns of sea levels rising to engulf New York and San Francisco and implies that only wrenching lifestyle sacrifice can save us. The opposing view is just as glum. Even mild restrictions on greenhouse gases could "cripple our economy," Republican Senator Kit Bond of Missouri said in 2003. Other conservatives suggest that greenhouse-gas rules for Americans would be pointless anyway, owing to increased fossil-fuel use in China and India. When commentators hash this issue out, it's often a contest to see which side can sound more pessimistic.

2   Here's a different way of thinking about the greenhouse effect: that action to prevent runaway global warming may prove cheap, practical, effective, and totally consistent with economic growth. Which makes a body wonder: Why is such environmental optimism absent from American political debate?

3   Greenhouse gases are an air-pollution problem—and all previous air-pollution problems have been reduced faster and more cheaply than predicted, without economic harm. Some of these problems once seemed scary and intractable, just as greenhouse gases seem today. About forty years ago urban smog was increasing so fast that President Lyndon Johnson warned, "Either we stop poisoning our air or we become a nation [in] gas masks groping our way through dying cities." During Ronald Reagan's presidency, emissions of chlorofluorocarbons, or CFCs, threatened to deplete the stratospheric ozone layer. As recently as George H. W. Bush's administration, acid rain was said to threaten a "new silent spring" of dead Appalachian forests.

4   But in each case, strong regulations were enacted, and what happened? Since 1970, smog-forming air pollution has declined by a third to a half. Emissions of CFCs have been nearly eliminated, and studies suggest that ozone-layer replenishment is beginning. Acid rain, meanwhile, has declined by a third since 1990, while Appalachian forest health has improved sharply.

5   Most progress against air pollution has been cheaper than expected. Smog controls on automobiles, for example, were predicted to cost thousands of dollars for each vehicle. Today's new cars emit less than 2 percent as much smog-forming pollution as the cars of 1970, and the cars are still as affordable today as they were then. Acid-rain control has cost about 10 percent of what was predicted in 1990, when Congress enacted new rules. At that time, opponents said the regulations would cause a "clean-air recession"; instead, the economy boomed.

6   Greenhouse gases, being global, are the biggest air-pollution problem ever faced. And because widespread fossil-fuel use is inevitable for some time to come, the best-case scenario for the next few decades may be a slowing of the rate of greenhouse-gas buildup, to prevent runaway climate change. Still, the basic pattern observed in all other forms of air-pollution control—rapid progress at low cost—should repeat for greenhouse-gas controls.

7   Yet a paralyzing negativism dominates global-warming politics. Environmentalists depict climate change as nearly unstoppable; skeptics speak of the problem as either imaginary (the "greatest hoax ever perpetrated," in the words of Senator James Inhofe, chairman of the Senate's environment committee) or ruinously expensive to address.

8   Even conscientious politicians may struggle for views that aren't dismal. Mandy Grunwald, a Democratic political consultant, says, "When political candidates talk about new energy sources, they use a positive, can-do vocabulary. Voters have personal experience with energy use, so they can relate to discussion of solutions. If you say a car can use a new kind of fuel, this makes intuitive sense to people. But global warming is of such scale and magnitude, people don't have any commonsense way to grasp what the solutions would be. So political candidates tend to talk about the greenhouse effect in a depressing way."

9   One reason the global-warming problem seems so daunting is that the success of previous antipollution efforts remains something of a secret. Polls show that Americans think the air is getting dirtier, not cleaner, perhaps because media coverage of the environment rarely if ever mentions improvements. For instance, did you know that smog and acid rain have continued to diminish throughout George W. Bush's presidency?

10   One might expect Democrats to trumpet the decline of air pollution, which stands as one of government's leading postwar achievements. But just as Republicans have found they can bash Democrats by falsely accusing them of being soft on defense, Democrats have found they can bash Republicans by falsely accusing them of destroying the environment. If that's your argument, you might skip over the evidence that many environmental trends are positive. One might also expect Republicans to trumpet the reduction of air pollution, since it signifies responsible behavior by industry. But to acknowledge that air pollution has declined would require Republicans to say the words, "The regulations worked."

11   Does it matter that so many in politics seem so pessimistic about the prospect of addressing global warming? Absolutely. Making the problem appear unsolvable encourages a sort of listless fatalism, blunting the drive to take first steps toward a solution. Historically, first steps against air pollution have often led to pleasant surprises. When Congress, in 1970, mandated major reductions in smog caused by automobiles, even many supporters of the rule feared it would be hugely expensive. But the catalytic converter was not practical then; soon it was perfected, and suddenly, major reductions in smog became affordable. Even a small step by the United States against greenhouse gases could lead to a similar breakthrough.

12   And to those who worry that any greenhouse-gas reductions in the United States will be swamped by new emissions from China and India, here's a final

reason to be optimistic: technology can move across borders with considerable speed. Today it's not clear that American inventors or entrepreneurs can make money by reducing greenhouse gases, so relatively few are trying. But suppose the United States regulated greenhouse gases, using its own domestic program, not the cumbersome Kyoto Protocol; then America's formidable entrepreneurial and engineering communities would fully engage the problem. Innovations pioneered here could spread throughout the world, and suddenly rapid global warming would not seem inevitable.

13   The two big technical advances against smog—the catalytic converter and the chemical engineering that removes pollutants from gasoline at the refinery stage—were invented in the United States. The big economic advance against acid rain—a credit-trading system that gives power-plant managers a profit incentive to reduce pollution—was pioneered here as well. These advances are now spreading globally. Smog and acid rain are still increasing in some parts of the world, but the trend lines suggest that both will decline fairly soon, even in developing nations. For instance, two decades ago urban smog was rising at a dangerous rate in Mexico; today it is diminishing there, though the country's population continues to grow. A short time ago declining smog and acid rain in developing nations seemed an impossibility; today declining greenhouse gases seem an impossibility. The history of air-pollution control says otherwise.

14   Americans love challenges, and preventing artificial climate change is just the sort of technological and economic challenge at which this nation excels. It only remains for the right politician to recast the challenge in practical, optimistic tones. Gore seldom has, and Bush seems to have no interest in trying. But cheap and fast improvement is not a pipe dream; it is the pattern of previous efforts against air pollution. The only reason runaway global warming seems unstoppable is that we have not yet tried to stop it.

FOR DISCUSSION

1. What reasons are offered to explain the negativism about solving the greenhouse gas problem? Do you find them convincing? Why or why not? Can you think of other reasons why the problem is not being addressed in more positive terms?

2. The author bases his optimism on previous successes with smog, CFCs, and acid rain, arguing that CO_2 emissions are just another air pollution problem, larger in scale but not fundamentally different. Do you agree? How much does the size and global extent of the problem matter?

3. Easterbrook clearly does not put much stock in international agreements, preferring instead national policies to encourage innovation, which he thinks will rapidly cross national borders. "Americans love challenges," he says. Do you find this approach appealing? Why or why not?

FOR PERSUASION

"Some Convenient Truths" is a good model for writing persuasively about environmental problems such as global warming. Using Easterbrook's essay as your inspiration, write an article of similar length for your local or college paper advocating measures ordinary citizens can take to reduce their contribution to greenhouse gases. You may want to look at later articles in this chapter or read about green movements currently under way on many college campuses. Whatever you choose to talk about, remember that taking action depends on believing that action is worthwhile. Overcoming what Easterbrook calls "listless fatalism" is essential.

The Coal Paradox

TIM APPENZELLER

Electricity is clean by the time we use it in homes, offices, and industry but not, at present, in the power plants that generate it. Many of them are coal-powered, and every ton of coal burned produces four tons of CO_2. Yet coal is abundant and relatively cheap—hence the paradox Tim Appenzeller explores in the following *National Geographic* (March 2006) article. We cannot seem to do without coal, but using it contributes significantly to global warming and many other problems, such as the destruction of land where the coal is mined.

Appenzeller is the science editor for *National Geographic* and a winner of the Walter Sullivan Award for Excellence in Science Journalism.

1   On a scorching August day in southwestern Indiana, the giant Gibson generating station is running flat out. Its five 180-foot-high boilers are gulping 25 tons of coal each minute, sending thousand-degree steam blasting through turbines that churn out more than 3,000 mega-watts of electric power, 50 percent more than Hoover Dam. The plant's cooling system is struggling to keep up, and in the control room warnings chirp as the exhaust temperature rises.

2   But there's no backing off on a day like this, with air conditioners humming across the Midwest and electricity demand close to record levels. Gibson, one of the biggest power plants in the country, is a mainstay of the region's electricity supply, pumping enough power into the grid for three million people. Stepping from the sweltering plant into the air-conditioned offices, Angeline Protogere of Cinergy, the Cincinnati-based utility that owns Gibson, says gratefully, "This is why we're making all that power."

3   Next time you turn up the AC or pop in a DVD, spare a thought for places like Gibson and for the grimy fuel it devours at the rate of three 100-car trainloads a day. Coal-burning power plants like this one supply the United States with half its electricity. They also emit a stew of damaging substances, including sulfur dioxide—a major cause of acid rain—and mercury. And they gush as much climate-warming carbon dioxide as America's cars, trucks, buses, and planes combined.

4   Here and there, in small demonstration projects, engineers are exploring technologies that could turn coal into power without these environmental costs. Yet unless utilities start building such plants soon—and lots of them—the future is likely to hold many more traditional stations like Gibson.

5   Last summer's voracious electricity use was just a preview. Americans' taste for bigger houses, along with population growth in the West and air-conditioning-dependent Southeast, will help push up the U.S. appetite for power by a third over the next 20 years, according to the Department of Energy. And in the developing world, especially China, electricity needs will rise even faster as factories burgeon and hundreds of millions of people buy their first refrigerators and TVs. Much of that demand is likely to be met with coal.

6   For the past 15 years U.S. utilities needing to add power have mainly built plants that burn natural gas, a relatively clean fuel. But a near tripling of natural

gas prices in the past seven years has idled many gas-fired plants and put a damper on new construction. Neither nuclear energy nor alternative sources such as wind and solar seem likely to meet the demand for electricity.

7 Meanwhile, more than a quarter trillion tons of coal lie underfoot, from the Appalachians through the Illinois Basin to the Rocky Mountains—enough to last 250 years at today's consumption rate. You hear it again and again: The U.S. is the Saudi Arabia of coal. About 40 coal-burning power plants are now being designed or built in the U.S. China, also rich in coal, could build several hundred by 2025.

8 Mining enough coal to satisfy this growing appetite will take a toll on lands and communities. Of all fossil fuels, coal puts out the most carbon dioxide per unit of energy, so burning it poses a further threat to global climate, already warming alarmingly. With much government prodding, coal-burning utilities have cut pollutants such as sulfur dioxide and nitrogen oxides by installing equipment like the building-size scrubbers and catalytic units crowded behind the Gibson plant. But the carbon dioxide that drives global warming simply goes up the stacks— nearly two billion tons of it each year from U.S. coal plants. Within the next two decades that amount could rise by a third.

9 There's no easy way to capture all the carbon dioxide from a traditional coal-burning station. "Right now, if you took a plant and slapped a carbon-capture device on it, you'd lose 25 percent of the energy," says Julio Friedmann, who studies carbon dioxide management at Lawrence Livermore National Laboratory. But a new kind of power station could change that.

10 A hundred miles up the Wabash River from the Gibson plant is a small power station that looks nothing like Gibson's mammoth boilers and steam turbines. This one resembles an oil refinery, all tanks and silvery tubes. Instead of burning coal, the Wabash River plant chemically transforms it in a process called coal gasification.

11 The Wabash plant mixes coal or petroleum coke, a coal-like residue from oil refineries, with water and pure oxygen and pumps it into a tall tank, where a fiery reaction turns the mixture into a flammable gas. Other equipment removes sulfur and other contaminants from the syngas, as it's called, before it's burned in a gas turbine to produce electricity.

12 Cleaning the unburned syngas is cheaper and more effective than trying to sieve pollutants from power plant exhaust, as the scrubbers at a plant like Gibson do. "This has been called the cleanest coal-fired power plant in the world," says Steven Vick, general manager of the Wabash facility. "We're pretty proud of that distinction."

13 The syngas can even be processed to strip out the carbon dioxide. The Wabash plant doesn't take this step, but future plants could. Coal gasification, Vick says, "is a technology that's set up for total CO_2 removal." The carbon dioxide could be pumped deep underground into depleted oil fields, old coal seams, or fluid-filled rock, sealed away from the atmosphere. And as a bonus, taking carbon dioxide out of the syngas can leave pure hydrogen, which could fuel a new generation of nonpolluting cars as well as generate electric power.

14 The Wabash plant and a similar one near Tampa, Florida, were built or refurbished with government money in the mid-1990s to demonstrate that gasification

FACTS ABOUT COAL

WHO HAS COAL?

The world has more than a trillion tons of readily available coal. The U.S. has the largest share, but other energy-hungry countries, such as China and India, are richly endowed as well.

27%	17%	13%	10%	9%	5%	19%
U.S.	RUSSIA	CHINA	INDIA	AUSTRALIA	SOUTH AFRICA	OTHER

WHO USES COAL NOW?

Global coal consumption is roughly five billion tons a year, with China burning the most. Western Europe has cut coal use by 36 percent since 1990 by using available natural gas from the North Sea and Russia.

MILLIONS OF TONS

1,531	1,117	1,094	431	251	1,016
CHINA	EUROPE*	U.S.	INDIA	RUSSIA	OTHER

WHO WILL USE IT TOMORROW?

China's coal needs will more than double by 2025 to satisfy factories and consumers. The country also plans to convert coal to liquid motor fuels. Worldwide, consumption will rise by 56 percent.

MILLIONS OF TONS

3,242	1,505	853	736	288	1,602
CHINA	U.S.	EUROPE*	INDIA	RUSSIA	OTHER

*Excluding Russia

U.S. ELECTRICITY GENERATION

50%	20%	18%	9%	3%
COAL	NUCLEAR	NATURAL GAS	RENEWABLES	OIL

U.S. POWER PLANT CO_2 EMISSIONS

83%	13%	4%
COAL	NATURAL GAS	OIL

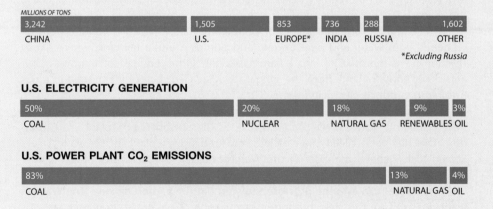

is a viable electricity source. Projects in North Dakota, Canada, the North Sea, and elsewhere have tested the other parts of the equation: capturing carbon dioxide and sequestering it underground. Researchers say they need to know more about how buried carbon dioxide behaves to be sure it won't leak back out—a potential threat to climate or even people. But Friedmann says, "For a first cut, we have enough information to say, 'It's a no-brainer. We know how to do this.'"

WHAT'S IN COAL SMOKE?

Sulfur Dioxide
The sulfur in coal forms this gas, which gives rise to acid rain when it reacts with water in clouds. Many plants control sulfur emissions by burning low-sulfur coal and passing the exhaust through scrubbers, which capture sulfur dioxide.

Nitrogen Oxides
The heat of power-plant burners turns nitrogen from the air into nitrogen oxides, which can contribute to acid rain and ground-level ozone. Pollution controls on many plants limit nitrogen oxide emissions.

Mercury
The traces of mercury in coal escape in power-plant exhaust. Falling hundreds of miles away in rain or snow, the mercury builds up in fish, making some species unsafe for children and pregnant women to eat.

Carbon Dioxide
Coal produces more CO_2 per energy unit than any other fossil fuel. CO_2 is a greenhouse gas, affecting climate by trapping heat that would otherwise escape to space. Power plants today release all their CO_2 into the atmosphere.

Particulates
Particles from coal-burning plants can harm people who have heart and breathing disorders. Soot and ash are captured before they go up the stacks, but finer particles can form later, from oxides of sulfur and nitrogen.

15 | Yet that's no guarantee utilities will embrace the gasification technology. "The fact that it's proved in Indiana and Florida doesn't mean executives are going to make a billion-dollar bet on it," says William Rosenberg of Harvard's Kennedy School of Government. The two gasification power plants in the U.S. are half the size of most commercial generating stations and have proved less reliable than traditional plants. The technology also costs as much as 20 percent more. Most important, there's little incentive for a company to take on the extra risk and expense of cleaner technology: For now U.S. utilities are free to emit as much carbon dioxide as they like.

16 | Cinergy CEO James Rogers, the man in charge of Gibson and eight other carbon-spewing plants, says he expects that to change. "I do believe we'll have regulation of carbon in this country," he says, and he wants his company to be ready. "The sooner we get to work, the better. I believe it's very important that we develop the ability to do carbon sequestration." Rogers says he intends to build a commercial-scale gasification power plant, able to capture its carbon dioxide, and several other companies have announced similar plans.

17   The energy bill passed last July by the U.S. Congress offers help in the form of loan guarantees and tax credits for gasification projects. "This should jump-start things," says Rosenberg, who advocated these measures in testimony to Congress. The experience of building and running the first few plants should lower costs and improve reliability. And sooner or later, says Rogers, new environmental laws that put a price on carbon dioxide emissions will make clean technology look far more attractive. "If the cost of carbon is 30 bucks a ton, it's amazing the kinds of technologies that will evolve to allow you to produce more electricity with less emissions."

18   If he's right, we may one day be able to cool our houses without turning up the thermostat on the entire planet.

FOR DISCUSSION

1. According to Tim Appenzeller, why is coal the choice of so many power-generating plants? Though still producing significant amounts of CO_2, natural gas is a cleaner alternative—why is it falling out of use?

2. What are the advantages of coal gasification? What are the disadvantages?

3. Neither conventional nor coal gasification plants currently capture and sequester the CO_2 they produce, though we are told in the article that research projects have tested this technology. In essence, in this process the gas is liquefied, pumped underground, and stored in such places as played-out oil fields. What is your reaction to such a method of pollution control?

FOR RESEARCH AND CONVINCING

Suppose that carbon sequestration will work and that economic and political forces allow it to come into widespread use. Because coal is a fossil fuel, we still have the problem that the supplies will eventually run out. Furthermore, the damage done by strip-mining will be even greater than it is now. Clearly, we need to find alternatives to coal, and natural gas is not satisfactory because it is in shorter supply, pollutes significantly, and is needed for other industrial processes besides power generation.

There are basically two ways to approach the problem. The first way is to continue to build massive power-generating plants but to power them with something that is cleaner—such as nuclear energy. The other way is to encourage what is already being done in Japan and elsewhere on a significant scale—to have each home and business generate its own power via solar or wind energy. Of course, the two ways can be combined. When the sun is shining or the wind is blowing, a home or business can go off the grid and use its own power, resorting to the centrally generated source only when necessary.

Explore these two approaches. There is much information on both. Then write a paper proposing and defending the approach or combination of approaches that you think will work best in your area.

Existing Technologies for Reducing CO$_2$ Emissions

AL GORE

We need to remind ourselves often that powerful technologies exist for reducing carbon dioxide emissions. The ones pictured here, from *An Inconvenient Truth,* are only a few of many.

Fuel-Cell Hybrid Buses

Green Roof

Hybrid Car

Compact Fluorescent Lightbulbs

Solar Panels

Electric Car Powered by Hydrogen Fuel Cell

Geothermal Power Station

FOR DISCUSSION

In the short term, we need energy conservation, ways to reduce pollution from cars and power-generating plants, and increasing use of power sources that are renewable and clean. Such measures will buy us time for more radical and permanent solutions. In the long term, we need to cease using fossil fuels as an energy source entirely, replacing them with wind, solar, tidal, hydrogen, fusion, and other potentially inexhaustible and nonpolluting sources of energy. As a class, brainstorm the possibilities both short and long term. Don't worry too much about how practical the suggestions are. After the class completes the brainstorming, examine what you have generated. Which suggestions appeal the most? Why?

Selling the Wind

MICHELLE NIJHUIS

The dream is an inexhaustible, inexpensive, and nonpolluting source of energy—a dream right now because, for instance, about 80% of the electricity generated in the United States comes from fossil fuels, but also a reality because of the many kinds of alternate energy sources already in use here and abroad. Many of these are old power sources, such as the wind, revolutionized by new technology. In the following piece from *Audubon,* the freelance writer Michelle Nijhuis discusses some of the pluses and minuses of wind power.

1   On the Emick family ranch in far southeastern Colorado, a row of antique windmills adorn the entrance road, their delicate wooden blades stilled for the moment. These windmills, some more than a century old, once helped prairie homesteaders pump water out of the ground, sustaining both families and farms. Throughout the Great Plains, such windmills are still a proud symbol of survival—of pioneer persistence in a land often too hot or too cold, too dry or too windy.

2   Today a very different sort of windmill is helping the Emick family survive on the blustery western edge of the Great Plains. In every direction, lines of cylindrical steel towers rise from the landscape, each white column topped by three sleek, swooping blades. These modern wind turbines, which measure more than 300 feet from their base to the tips of their blades, are more than 10 times taller than the frontier-era windmills at their feet.

3   The 108 turbines in this neighborhood comprise the Colorado Green project, the largest wind farm in Colorado and among the 10 largest in the nation. The project, a joint venture of Shell Wind Energy and PPM Energy (a subsidiary of Scottish-Power), produces roughly enough electricity each year to supply more than 52,000 average homes.

4   Though the Emicks and other families who lease land to wind-power companies can't divulge the details of their agreements, typical payments range from $3,000 to $6,000 per turbine per year, and generally allow farmers to continue raising crops and livestock among the towers. For agricultural families, which face the vagaries of rainfall and commodity prices, the reliable additional income is welcome. It can help them keep their farms afloat—and keep land relatively undeveloped, in some cases preserving both wildlife habitat and open vistas.

5   Small farmers are far from the only fans of wind energy. Wind farms in the United States now have a combined capacity of more than 9,000 megawatts, generating enough electricity to power approximately 2.3 million homes. . . . While wind currently provides less than 1 percent of the country's total energy needs, many states are looking to increase their supplies of renewable energy, helping to make wind the nation's second-fastest-growing source of electricity (natural gas is tops).

6   Multinationals continue to make significant investments in wind power. GE Energy built well more than half of the new turbines in the United States last year, and Goldman Sachs, one of the world's largest investment banking firms, recently purchased a wind-power development company now called Horizon Wind Energy.

Meanwhile, the U.S. Department of Energy has set a goal of helping at least 30 states increase their wind-power generating capacity to 100 megawatts each by 2010.

7   While consumers have long paid a premium for wind power, high natural gas and coal prices are enhancing wind's appeal. Last year in Colorado and in Austin, Texas, the price of wind power dipped below the price of traditional energy sources, and utility customers of all political stripes flocked to sign up for it.

8   If wind power dilutes our diet of coal and other fossil fuels, it will reduce air pollution, and even cushion the devastating, and increasingly apparent, effects of global warming. "It's critical to have a sense of urgency about dealing with global climate challenge in general, and about displacing coal in particular," says Ralph Cavanagh, an expert on renewable energy at the Natural Resources Defense Council (NRDC). "Wind is a very important part of that equation."

9   For many conservationists, however, wind power remains an uncomfortable subject. It's well known that wind turbines kill both birds and bats, though exactly how often—and why—these deaths occur remains poorly understood. Wildlife advocates hope they can push for more research, better planning, and more stringent oversight of wind farms without sabotaging the industry's hard-won momentum.

10   Much of the current controversy over wind power and wildlife stems from a place called Altamont Pass, a line of golden, oak-studded hills on the eastern outskirts of the San Francisco Bay Area. The Altamont Wind Resource Area, established in the early 1980s, was one of the first modern wind farms in the nation, and a visit to Altamont is a one-stop tour of the history of wind power.

11   On one grassy hillside stands a row of closely spaced "eggbeater" turbines, each with three busily spinning blades mounted on a latticed steel tower. Arrayed on another slope are the smooth, solid towers of newer turbines, much like those on the Emick family ranch in Colorado. Although the blades of these turbines turn more slowly than those of their smaller predecessors, each enormous turbine can generate 1.5 megawatts of power, more than twice that produced by older models. In all, more than 5,000 turbines crowd into Altamont Pass, generating enough electricity to serve some 100,000 homes.

12   But these turbines are believed to kill more birds of prey than any other wind farm in the world. Beginning in the late 1980s biologists reported that large numbers of golden eagles, hawks, and other raptors were flying into the spinning blades at Altamont, and dying as a result. Wind-energy companies tried many measures to limit the damage, such as installing chicken wire on the latticed towers to discourage perching. But a recent five-year study by the California Energy Commission estimated that every year up to 1,300 raptors are killed at Altamont, including more than a hundred golden eagles. . . .

13   The farms and ranches of the West and Midwest are now favored homes for wind turbines, and so far they seem to be relatively safe for both raptors and songbirds. "The bird mortality we're seeing is lower than what's been seen at Altamont," says Tim Cullinan, director of science and bird conservation for Audubon Washington and a wildlife biologist. Cullinan is working with the U.S. Fish and Wildlife Service and other stakeholders such as the American Wind Energy Association

and the International Association of Fish and Wildlife Agencies to strengthen siting standards for wind facilities nationwide. . . .

14   Even if biologists underestimate the number of birds killed by turbines, the damage is surely smaller, in orders of magnitude, than the numbers killed in other ways. While a 2001 study surmised that some 10,000 to 40,000 birds die in wind turbines each year, the U.S. Fish and Wildlife Service contends that these numbers are out of date and that the true mortality figures are much higher. Still, an estimated 100 million birds are killed a year by hunting housecats, and as many as 60 million die from collisions with cars and trucks.

15   Yet if the wind industry continues to boom, turbine numbers multiply, and the gaps in research persist, it is possible that collisions with turbines—and construction associated with wind farms—will become a more widespread and substantial threat, particularly for threatened and endangered species. "The fear is that with all the new wind farms rolling out, there is a new Altamont being created today," says Greg Butcher, National Audubon's director of bird conservation. "But because we don't have the data, we just don't know about it."

16   When wildlife researchers have looked closely at wind farms, disturbing numbers have emerged. One 2003 study spent seven months compiling bat fatalities at a wind-power site in the West Virginia mountains. Researchers found, to their surprise, that the 44 turbines killed as many as 4,000 migratory bats. Similarly grim findings have since been reported at wind farms in Pennsylvania and Tennessee, raising the possibility that significant bat kills are a regional or even national phenomenon.

17   The three wind farms in question stand on forested Appalachian ridges, and Ed Arnett, a conservation scientist for Bat Conservation International, speculates that tree-roosting bats hunt insects in the clearings around the turbines. But because the wind industry has only a handful of bat studies to draw on, the reasons for the kills are unclear, the number of species involved uncertain, and no one is sure how to mitigate the impacts at existing or future sites. "There's a huge dearth of research," Arnett says. "What we do know is that these are long-lived species with low reproductive rates, so a new source of mortality could drive them into serious declines very quickly."

18   Other researchers are concerned that proliferating wind turbines will take a heavy toll on night-migrating songbirds or ground-nesting birds. A 2004 study, led by Robert Robel, a biology professor at Kansas State University, found that roads and other infrastructure disturb ground-nesting species such as the lesser-prairie chicken, a candidate for federal listing as an endangered species. Again, though, the questions far outnumber the answers.

19   In a 2005 Government Accountability Office report to Congress summarizing the research on wind farms and wildlife impacts, the authors describe "significant gaps in the literature" that "make it difficult for scientists to draw conclusions about wind power's impact on wildlife in general.". . .

20   So conservationists find themselves in a tough spot. How can they support and encourage the rapid spread of wind power—our most promising source of clean, renewable energy—while ensuring that the industry minimizes its damage to birds and other wildlife?

21   "We can't lose sight of the larger benefits of wind," says Audubon Washington's Tim Cullinan. "The direct environmental impacts of wind get a lot of attention, because there are dead bodies on the ground. But nobody ever finds the bodies of the birds killed by global warming, or by oil drilling on the North Slope of Alaska. They're out there, but we don't see them.". . .

22   The solution to this dilemma, say many conservationists, begins with early, consistent involvement in project planning. "Once those turbines go in," says biologist Pete Bloom, "they don't come down." To encourage early consideration of wildlife, environmental groups have developed guidelines and policies for wind development. Audubon Washington's guidelines, for instance, call for several seasons of bird surveys and other in-depth wildlife studies at proposed wind-power sites, and support statewide or multi-state planning efforts for wind facilities. . . .

23   By asking the right questions at the right time, conservationists can help wind power continue its growth and fulfill its promise. They can also share in the building enthusiasm for wind's wide-ranging benefits. Farmer and rancher Greg Emick, who grew up on his family's land, guesses that his ancestors—immigrants from Germany who arrived in Colorado nearly 100 years ago—would be pleased by the towering wind turbines that rise from the land they once homesteaded. "They always thought the prairie would be good for more than just raising cattle and growing a little bit of crop," says Emick, as he listens to the steady swoosh of the gigantic turbine blades above his head. "But I don't think they ever imagined we could sell the wind."

FOR DISCUSSION

1. As the author emphasizes, wind energy has developed far past the old windmill on the family farm and become big business. What positive signs do you detect in the significant economic incentives for wind power?

2. When we compare 40,000 birds killed annually by wind turbines with the 100 million that cats kill or the 60 million lost to being hit by vehicles, we may be tempted to dismiss the damage done by the turbines. But other details in the article show that bird and bat mortality may be more significant than the raw numbers indicate. What details indicate this? How can we best reduce this problem?

3. Because the author is writing for conservationists whose concern is wind power's impact on wildlife and habitats, she says little about the main objection to wind turbines: many people consider them unsightly and take the NIMBY (not in my backyard) position. In view of the obvious pluses to wind power, how serious do you feel this objection is?

FOR RESEARCH AND CONVINCING

As "Selling the Wind" shows, no form of energy is without drawbacks, and some of the negatives can be quite serious, such as the radioactive waste from nuclear power plants. Nevertheless, we must give up or greatly reduce our dependence on fossil fuels. For this to happen, the general public must strongly support alternate energy sources.

Choose one of the many alternate sources—wind, water, geothermal, nuclear, hydrogen, biodiesel, ethanol, and so on—and do enough research to understand the advantages and disadvantages. Then write an editorial for your local or school newspaper urging support for the energy source. Be sure to deal with the negatives honestly, arguing either that they must be tolerated or that measures can be taken to remedy or reduce them.

FOR MEDIATION

In practical terms, no way of reducing global warming can work without negotiation among conflicting interests. Even at the personal and private level, individuals have to balance money and convenience against environmental concerns. At the public level are situations like the one Nijhuis discusses—the value of wind power versus the concerns for species loss and aesthetics. The various interests have to be fitted together somehow.

Imagine you are an advocate for wind power and that you are addressing an audience of conservationists and ordinary citizens who oppose wind turbines in their community. Compose the text of a speech that mediates—that firmly advocates increased use of wind power but does so in a way that respects and accommodates, as much as possible, the concerns of your audience. You may need to do research on wind power to find the information and lines of argument you need.

Ten Personal Solutions

UNION OF CONCERNED SCIENTISTS

We tend to think of global warming as a large-scale problem involving public issues such as the generation of electric power. But much of the solution is personal and small-scale, a matter of what you and I choose to do or not do in our daily lives. The suggestions in the following article (see www.ucsusa.org) are only a few of the many choices we can make.

1   Individual choices can have an impact on global climate change. Reducing your family's heat-trapping emissions does not mean forgoing modern conveniences; it means making smart choices and using energy-efficient products, which may require an additional investment up front, but often pay you back in energy savings within a couple of years.

2   Since Americans' per capita emissions of heat-trapping gases is 5.6 tons—more than double the amount of western Europeans—we can all make choices that will greatly reduce our families' global warming impact.

1. **The car you drive: the most important personal climate decision.** When you buy your next car, look for the one with the best fuel economy in its class. Each gallon of gas you use releases 25 pounds of heat-trapping carbon dioxide (CO_2) into the atmosphere. Better gas mileage not only reduces global warming, but will also save you thousands of dollars at the pump over the life of the vehicle. Compare the fuel economy of the cars you're considering and look for new technologies like hybrid engines.

2. **Choose clean power.** More than half the electricity in the United States comes from polluting coal-fired power plants. And power plants are the single largest source of heat-trapping gas. None of us can live without electricity, but in some states, you can switch to electricity companies that provide 50 to 100 percent renewable energy. (For more information go to Green-e.org.)

3. **Look for Energy Star.** When it comes time to replace appliances, look for the Energy Star label on new appliances (refrigerators, freezers, furnaces, air conditioners, and water heaters use the most energy). These items may cost a bit more initially, but the energy savings will pay back the extra invest-ment within a couple of years. Household energy savings really can make a difference: If each household in the United States replaced its existing appli-ances with the most efficient models available, we would save $15 billion in energy costs and eliminate 175 million tons of heat-trapping gases.

4. **Unplug a freezer.** One of the quickest ways to reduce your global warming impact is to unplug the extra refrigerator or freezer you rarely use (except when you need it for holidays and parties). This can reduce the typical family's carbon dioxide emissions by nearly 10 percent.

5. **Get a home energy audit.** Take advantage of the free home energy audits offered by many utilities. Simple measures, such as installing a

programmable thermostat to replace your old dial unit or sealing and insulating heating and cooling ducts, can each reduce a typical family's carbon dioxide emissions by about 5 percent.

6. **Light bulbs matter.** If every household in the United States replaced one regular light bulb with an energy-saving model, we could reduce global warming pollution by more than 90 billion pounds over the life of the bulbs; the same as taking 6.3 million cars off the road. So, replace your incandescent bulbs with more efficient compact fluorescents, which now come in all shapes and sizes. You'll be doing your share to cut back on heat-trapping pollution and you'll save money on your electric bills and light bulbs.

7. **Think before you drive.** If you own more than one vehicle, use the less fuel-efficient one only when you can fill it with passengers. Driving a full minivan may be kinder to the environment than two midsize cars. Whenever possible, join a carpool or take mass transit.

8. **Buy good wood.** When buying wood products, check for labels that indicate the source of the timber. Supporting forests that are managed in a sustainable fashion makes sense for biodiversity, and it may make sense for the climate too. Forests that are well managed are more likely to store carbon effectively because more trees are left standing and carbon-storing soils are less disturbed.

9. **Plant a tree.** You can also make a difference in your own backyard. Get a group in your neighborhood together and contact your local arborist or urban forester about planting trees on private property and public land. In addition to storing carbon, trees planted in and around urban areas and residences can provide much-needed shade in the summer, reducing energy bills and fossil fuel use.

10. **Let policymakers know you are concerned about global warming.** Our elected officials and business leaders need to hear from concerned citizens.

FOR DISCUSSION

1. The piece claims that each American produces 5.6 tons of greenhouse gas emissions each year—double the European amount. In your view, how much of this difference is a matter of circumstances, such as the size of the United States, and how much is the result of lifestyle choices that could be changed?

2. What action have you taken to reduce your personal carbon footprint? What in the list of ten suggestions appeals to you most? What has the least appeal? Do you have resistance to any of the ten items? If there are changes you do not want to make, such as the car you drive, what could you do to reduce carbon emissions in other ways?

FOR INQUIRY AND CONVINCING

Besides taking action at the personal and home or family level, each of us can urge greater concern for the environment in local institutions and workplaces. Universities and colleges, for instance, are not always models of efficient energy use. A growing student movement in the United States aims to address this problem.

As a class project, find out what your university or college is doing and plans to do to use energy more efficiently. As part of this research, walk around campus and tour the buildings. Is the level of heating and cooling appropriate? Are lights left on in rooms that are empty? Take note of anything that seems wasteful to you.

Discuss the results of your research and work together as a class to create a document to present to the central administration, urging whatever improvements the class thinks might make a difference.

Consuming Earth's Gifts

WILLIAM F. RUDDIMAN

> Global warming has gotten so much attention recently that we are apt to forget that it is only one of many environmental problems. William Ruddiman, retired professor of environmental science at the University of Virginia, reminds us of another big problem—exhaustion of the Earth's resources, including water and topsoil. The following essay comes from his influential book, *Plows, Plagues, and Petroleum* (Princeton UP, 2005), which traces human impact on climate back to the invention of agriculture, about 10,000 years ago.

1   Even though I have made the case that future climate change is likely to be large . . . , I do not rank the oncoming global warming as the greatest environmental problem of our time. Other environmental issues seem to me far more immediate and pressing, and in the future I suspect our concerns will focus heavily on the eventual depletion of key resources.

2   . . . Humankind has been steadily transforming Earth's surface for some 8,000 years, initially in Eurasia and later on all continents. Initially, we caused these transformations by clearing land for farming; later, other aspects of civilized life joined farming as important causes of this transformation. Well before the industrial era, the cumulative result over many millennia was an enormous loss of what had been "natural" on this planet.

3   During the 1800s and 1900s, human population increased from 1 billion to 6 billion, an explosion unprecedented in human history. This rise came about because new sanitary standards and medicines reduced the incidence of disease and because human ingenuity led to innovations in agriculture that fed ever-larger numbers of people. As a result, our already sizable impact on Earth's surface increased at a much faster rate. . . .

4   By most estimates, the explosive population increase still under way will end near AD 2050 as global population levels out at some 9–10 billion people, or roughly 50 percent more people than now. A major reason for the predicted stabilization will be the increase in affluence that has historically resulted in fewer children per family. . . .

5   On the other hand, as affluence and technology continue to spread, increased pressures on the environment will occur for that reason alone. If a billion or more people in China and India begin to live the way Americans and Europeans do now, their additional use of Earth's resources will be enormous. Even without population increases, humanity will continue to alter the environment in new ways.

6   The cumulative impact of so many millennia of transforming Earth's surface has inevitably come at a cost to nature. Many of the problems our actions have created have been described elsewhere by ecologists and others knowledgeable about the environment. In the process of transforming Earth's surface, we have fragmented the space that ecosystems require, transported species from the places they belong to regions where their presence is invasive to existing flora and fauna, and caused the extinction of species in numbers that no one really knows. . . .

7   Those with environmental concerns have in recent decades added a new argument to their side of this battle. Ecologists have coined the term "ecosystem services" to describe processes that nature provides for free and that have real economic value. For example, trees and other vegetation on hill slopes trap rainfall that would otherwise flow away and erode soils. As the retained water passes into subsurface layers, the soils slowly filter it and transform it into clean, drinkable water that can be retrieved from wells or springs. Some of the water flows into wetlands and is further cleansed there. Nature gives us a large supply of clean water.

8   But when the trees are cut or the wetlands are filled in, these free services are lost, and society must pick up the cost of doing nature's job. . . . The loss of nature's subsurface cleansing of water requires municipal water treatment plants and home water filters, but these remedies rarely return water of the quality nature once provided. So we buy bottled water shipped from other regions or even other continents. All in all, we pay an economic price to replace ecosystem services. Ecologists rightly argue that the costs incurred from losing ecosystem services must be included in complete "economic" analyses of land-use decisions. . . .

9   Probably as a result of my long interest in Earth's climate history, my own concerns about the future tend to focus on a related set of longer-term problems— "gifts" that nature has provided us through slow-acting processes that took place well back in Earth's past and that cannot be replaced once they are consumed.

10   My concern about these gifts is simple: When these resources run low or run out, how will we find comparably inexpensive replacements? . . . We live today in an era of remarkably cheap oil, gas, and coal. It took nature hundreds of millions of years to create the world's supply of these resources, by burying organic carbon in swamps and inland seas and shallow coastal areas, and by cooking the carbon at just the right temperature and pressure. We only began using these resources in significant amounts in the middle 1800s, and yet the first signs are already at hand that the world will reach the year of peak oil production and consumption in just one or two decades, if not sooner. World supplies of natural gas will last a bit longer, and coal for a few centuries. I wonder whether we will ever find a substitute even remotely as inexpensive as these carbon gifts. We are investigating alternative sources of energy, but as of now none of them seems likely to be as widely available and as inexpensive as the solar energy stored in carbon-based fuels.

11   At some point early in the current century, gradual depletion of this vital commodity will presumably become a major economic issue. Once world oil production begins to decline by 1 percent or so per year, it seems likely to add a measurable cost to the functioning of the global economy, in effect adding a new form of built-in "inflation" on top of the normal kind. Fuel for cars and trucks is not the only concern; a vast array of products made from petrochemicals has become part of the basic fabric of our lives. All of them will cost more.

12   I also wonder about the long-term supply of water. With more than half of the supply of water from surface run-off already in use for irrigation and human consumption, we have for years been pumping water from aquifers deep in the ground, especially in arid and semi-arid regions into which many people are now moving.

The water stored in the deep aquifers of the American West was put there tens to hundreds of thousands of years ago by melt water flowing southward from the margins of the great ice sheets, and by snow and rain water that fell during climatic conditions much wetter than today. In recent decades, the level of those aquifers has been falling as we extract water from depths where it cannot be quickly replenished by nature.

13   Pumping ever deeper will require more carbon fuel, which in turn will become more expensive. Gradually, the water from greater depths will contain ever-larger concentrations of dissolved salts that will be left on irrigated fields, making agriculture more difficult. Eventually, we will exhaust the useable water in these underground reservoirs. Little by little, agriculture will probably retreat from the arid high-plains regions of the West back toward the midcontinent regions nearer the Mississippi River, where natural rainfall supports agriculture. The same retreat will occur in other regions of extensive groundwater use across the globe.

14   I have no idea when these groundwater limits will be reached in each region, but new reports suggest the start of the problem may be close at hand in some regions. To conserve water, the municipal government of Santa Fe, New Mexico, recently began requiring home builders to retrofit six existing houses for improved water economy to offset the added water use in each new house built. In the Oklahoma-Texas panhandle region, oilman and investor T. Boone Pickens has been buying up the rights to groundwater in the glacial-age Ogallala aquifer. When municipal governments put extra burdens on local builders, and when wealthy oil tycoons invest in underground water as a scarce commodity, problems must be looming. . . .

15   I also wonder about topsoil. The most productive farms in the American Midwest can thank the ice sheets for their topsoil. Ice repeatedly gouged bedrock and scraped older soils in north-central Canada and pushed the eroded debris south, where streams of glacial melt water carried it into river valleys, and winds blew it across the western prairies. During the 1800s, farmers began breaking up the tough top layer of prairie sod, which had been held in place by extremely deep-rooted plants, and farming began at a scale the world had never seen. The midwestern American agricultural miracle has been one of the great success stories in human history.

16   But this great success came at a price. Repeated tilling exposed the rich prairie soils to decades of dry winds and floods. Estimates are that half of the original topsoil layer in the American Midwest has been lost, most of it flowing down the Mississippi River to the Gulf of Mexico. In the late 1900s, farmers began adapting new techniques that have reduced, but not stopped, the rapid removal of this precious gift. These methods and other conservation efforts will keep us from losing soil as rapidly as before, but slower rates of loss will continue to deplete soils that no longer have the natural protection provided by prairie vegetation.

17   Farmers and farm corporations now spend enormous sums of money every year on manufactured fertilizers to replenish nutrients lost to crop production and natural erosion. These fertilizers are produced from petrochemical (petroleum) products, which again brings us back to the gradual depletion (and increased

expense) of carbon-based products in the coming decades. Once again, it will be a very long wait indeed until nature gets around to making more topsoil, probably 50,000 to 100,000 years until the next ice sheet bulldozes the next rich load southward. . . .

18   With no wish to be alarmist about the slow depletion of these many gifts, especially carbon-based energy sources, I still wonder: What will humankind do when they grow scarce? Will our resourcefulness as a species open up new avenues? Or will the depletion be a true loss? I have no clue what answers to these vital questions the distant future will bring.

FOR DISCUSSION

1. In your own words, describe what Ruddiman means by "ecosystem services." He points to the economic costs when technology has to replace what nature once provided freely, as "gifts" to us. What other costs are involved?

2. One of the author's concerns is depletion of fossil fuels or prohibitively expensive supplies. He understands the role of such sources of energy in global warming, so why is he concerned?

3. Water is another of nature's "gifts." Why, according to the author, should we be worried about it?

4. Why is topsoil erosion a problem? Are there other ecological problems connected with it? What, for instance, happens when topsoil is washed down a river and deposited in the ocean?

FOR RESEARCH, DISCUSSION, AND PERSUASION

Environmental problems seldom have a single cause. We're losing coral reefs, for example, through a combination of forces: ocean warming, ocean acidification (caused by CO_2 from the atmosphere turning into carbonic acid), topsoil erosion (the soil smothers the reefs), pollution from many other sources, and the carelessness of boaters and divers.

Do research on coral reefs—or on rain forests, which are also in deep trouble. Investigate all the causes of their destruction or degradation, including but not limited to global warming. Then write an article aiming to raise awareness of the value of what we are losing, the complex causes, and the necessity of taking immediate action. Address your U.S. congressperson or senator.

FOR FURTHER READING

Flannery, Tim. *The Weather Makers: How Man Is Changing the Climate and What It Means for Life on Earth*. New York: Atlantic Monthly P, 2005.
Gore, Al. *An Inconvenient Truth*. Emmaus, PA: Rodale, 2006.
Houghton, John. *Global Warming: The Complete Briefing*. Cambridge: Cambridge UP, 1997.
Linden, Eugene. *The Winds of Change: Climate, Weather, and the Destruction of Civilizations*. New York: Simon and Schuster, 2006.

National Aeronautics and Space Administration (NASA) Web site: www.nasa.gov

National Oceanic and Atmospheric Administration Web site: www.noaa.gov

Newell, Peter. *Climate for Change: Non-State Actors and the Global Politics of the Greenhouse.* Cambridge: Cambridge UP, 2000.

Ruddiman, William F. *Plows, Plagues, and Petroleum: How Humans Took Control of Climate.* Princeton: Princeton UP, 2005.

Union of Concerned Scientists Web site: www.ucsusa.org

The Millennials: Issues Facing Young Adults

"The Millennials" refer to people born between 1980 and 2000. Also commonly called Generation Y or Twenty-Something, this group includes a high percentage of students currently enrolled in our colleges and universities. It is difficult to generalize about more than 80 million people—the size of the Millennial generation—but the general opinion is that this younger generation is distinctive and full of promise. In our first selection, Kate Yarrow and Jayne O'Donnell, who have done extensive research in their capacity as retail consultants, claim that

> Having never experienced a world without computers, the Internet, cell phones, and digital cameras, Gen Yers are free of anxiety and full of

playfulness when they interact with the Internet and technology of all sorts. This makes learning easier for them than it is for all but the most tech-savvy parents.

Similar positive assessments abound; in our third selection Russ Linden, a professor who specializes in organizational change, points to "a talent (and preference) for collaboration, a passion for service, [and] a desire to make a (big) difference" as characteristics of the current generation of young people.

Of course, no generation escapes criticism from older generations. You can find recent articles that call attention to an alleged tardiness in growing up among Millennials, doubts about how deep and sound their literacy is, references to being spoiled by a culture of instant gratification, too much parental indulgence, and so on. However, on the whole, the sentiment is that "the kids are alright," as Yarrow and O'Donnell say. The divisive conflict between generations characteristic of the 1960s is not in evidence today.

If Millennials are getting good reviews from older generations, they also face problems their parents did not. The chief problem is economic, as the photograph that opens this chapter dramatizes—a young person with empty pockets. College now costs far more than it did thirty or forty years ago, with students graduating from college on average about $22,000 in debt, not counting an additional $7,000 on credit cards. In other words, too many young people start their lives after college significantly in debt. For those who pursue graduate degrees, the debt could double or triple.

Perhaps starting in a deep hole would not be so bad if job prospects were better. But as Tamara Drout and Anya Kamenetz point out in the last two articles in this chapter, the employment situation is not favorable. There are too many college graduates pursuing too few positions, the result being unemployment, underemployment, and jobs that do not pay well and offer few benefits that an older generation took for granted. College loans are therefore hard to repay, and we should not be surprised that many young people are forced to live with their parents for several years after college. Of course, the situation has gotten worse since Drout and Kamenetz wrote, before the great recession that started in 2007. About 40% of graduating seniors once reported having a job waiting for them; now the percentage is about 20%.

In sum, then: Your generation is promising, but circumstances, especially economic ones, are holding you back.

In this chapter we invite you to assess yourself and your generation against the information and viewpoints about your "cohort," the term social scientists use for a particular group of people they are studying. How are you like and unlike the Millennials as our authors depict them? After that, we hope to increase awareness of the challenges your generation must confront, which Drout and Kamenetz explore so well. They suggest ways of coping better as well as needed changes in the way our society does things so that young people are not so hamstrung by lack of opportunity. This realistic combination of self-assessment and sizing up what is "out there" should prepare you to be even more creative in making a better life and world.

Gen Y Is from Mercury

KIT YARROW AND JAYNE O'DONNELL

Kit Yarrow is a consumer psychologist, chair of the psychology department at Golden Gate University, and consultant for such companies as General Electric, Del Monte, and Nokia. Jayne O'Donnell is a prominent journalist at *USA Today,* who has done important work on product safety, especially relating to air bags and teenaged drivers. They coauthored *Gen BuY: How Tweens, Teens, and Twenty-Somethings Are Revolutionizing Retail* (Jossey-Bass, 2009), from which the following excerpt comes.

1   This generation, the product of a transformed world, is to previous generations as man is to woman and Mars is to Venus. Which is to say: basically the same, but entirely different. Generation Y is unquestionably unique, and some say potentially one of the most powerful and influential generations ever.

2   Gen Y is diverse, adaptive, and confident. Fewer than two-thirds of them are white, over 25 percent are raised in single parent households, and three-quarters have working moms. Their generation's size—almost eighty-four million members— helps give them unprecedented influence; their confidence and their ability to connect with others guarantee it. . . .

THE TWO GREATEST INFLUENCES

3   Though some may point to social or political events such as the Columbine shootings, the Bill Clinton–Monica Lewinsky scandal, the fall of the Soviet Union, and even the death of Princess Diana as the forces that have shaped Gen Y, there are two profoundly influential factors that outweigh the rest: *their adoring parents* and *the digital world.*

Adoring Parents

4   Gen Y children are considered to be the most wanted children of all time, and they've grown up in an era of exploding interest in and knowledge about child development and psychology. Unlike previous generations of parents—who certainly wanted and loved their children, but also saw them as responsibilities—or even earlier generations, who felt the same way but saw them as potential laborers— today's parents prize their children as more equal and central members of the household. Additionally, no society in history has had a greater focus on, interest in, and understanding of the child.

5   And even though nearly half of Gen Y children have divorced parents, and one-third come from single-parent households, those parents still spent more focused time with their Gen Y kids than any previous generation. The greater attention and parental involvement of fathers as central figures in parenting has also had a great effect on the sense of Gen Yers that they are important and central. Additionally, technology brings families even closer, thanks to the frequent contact between kids and parents that cell phones afford.

6   Gen Y parents have been criticized for coddling, for impairing their child's independence by hovering like helicopters, for being enmeshed in or overly

dependent on their kid's approval. These characteristics are generally more true of this generation than of previous ones, and in the course of our research we certainly did see examples of just the sort of behavior that's inspired these descriptions (including moms who know who's asking whom to the prom before their kids do), and also *plenty* of parents dependent on their kids' success for their own egos. But what we also saw were "helicopters" who might also have been described as simply interested, involved parents; "coddlers" who could have been called warm, nurturing parents; and "overly dependent parents" who might have been seen as folks who value their kid's minds and opinions. . . .

7   We found it most helpful to view Gen Y parents on a normally distributed curve, with those clearly overinvolved, coddling helicopters at one end; some relatively dis-engaged parents at the other end; and most of the group in the middle—registering more kid-centric than the last generation of parents, but not 'coptering coddlers either.

8   Being a wanted kid in a child-centered household adds to your clout, of course. Gen Y households are the most egalitarian of all time, and Gen Y parents tend to be nonauthoritarian and to value their friendships with their kids. This is one of the primary reasons behind Gen Y's confidence and power. . . .

Their Digital World

9   The second most important factor that's shaped the uniqueness of this generation is their enmeshment with technology and their ability to harness the power of the Internet. This sophistication has increased their influence in their households, added a pedal-to-the-metal element to their cognitive and social styles, reinforced and equipped a team mentality, and empowered them.

10   ***Household Clout.*** In addition to their kid-centric clout, Gen Yers typically provide in-house tech support for their parents, which has reinforced their stature as equals—or even superiors, at least in the IT department. It's also made them *the* great force to be reckoned with by electronics marketers. When they have prized knowledge and expertise, it becomes pretty hard to discount the thoughts and abilities of a kid. Previous generations had to pretend or humor their kids ("Let's frame your Picasso!"), but in the case of this generation, their intuitive ease with technology and their ability to adapt to technological shifts is a genuine asset to any family. Having never experienced a world without computers, the Internet, cell phones, and digital cameras, Gen Yers are free of anxiety and full of playfulness when they interact with the Internet and technology of all sorts. This makes learning easier for them than it is for all but the most tech-savvy parents. . . .

11   ***Speed, Power, and Self-Reliance.*** Put simply, they want what they want when they want it. As the first generation raised from day one under the influence of the Internet, the world, as they know it, means speed; multitasking; instant answers; always available friends, parents, teachers, and experts; a connection to others that defies geography and hierarchy; less necessity for face-to-face (or voice-to-voice) human interaction; and free access to information for everyone.

12   Kit noticed, during a recent guest lecture at UC Berkeley, that at least half of her students were typing. A quick cruise around the room revealed about half of those typists were looking up her articles, an international student was checking a word definition, and the rest were on Facebook. In other words: multitasking, available to their friends no matter where they were, and instantly accessing free information.

13   "They are a very different generation," says Jenny Floren, founder and CEO of Experience, which helps recruits students from nearly four thousand colleges and universities for its business clients. Because they've been online often since they were toddlers, they process information very differently. "That's where their friends are, where they shop, and where they study," says Floren. "In many regards, being in person is the same as being online."

14   The digital world that Gen Y inhabits is credited with shortening their attention spans, increasing their need for immediate gratification, and helping them to become super speedy at processing visual data—Gen Yers live in a faster world than anything previous generations have known.

15   Gen Yers are also proactive and empowered when it comes to information. They seek out only the information that's relevant (or that they perceive to be relevant) to them. Previous generations, unaided by the power of search engines, acquired information in a more passive way. For example, most boomers wouldn't have had a way to learn more about a physical symptom or health malady—those answers were in the hands of physicians and households lucky enough to have a set of encyclopedias. There was no such thing as an instant answer. Not to mention that the answers available had been edited and vetted prior to publication. So when we say "empowered" we truly do mean power. From the information (though not the wisdom) of a physician to the latest Van's hoodie available to a skater living 350 miles from a mall, Gen Yers have known only one world—one in which they can get what they want when they want it.

16   Consequently, there has been an important social shift toward a mentality of self-reliance and the flattened hierarchy that accompanies democratized information. Contributing to this is a disappointment in social institutions ranging from our schools and religious institutions to our political leaders and even athletes and celebrities—all widely (and sometimes hysterically) reported through an increasingly competitive media. Businesses, in particular, have taken a big hit in confidence. Once the most likely villain in the movies was a Communist, monster, or alien—today it's a white businessman.

17   ***My Posse.*** Gen Yers, already trained in school to work as teams, have embraced technology as a way to facilitate group connections. They can and do unite with likeminded (physical) strangers from around the world to champion causes, play computer games such as World of Warcraft, stay in touch with school and business friends and colleagues indefinitely through social networking sites such as LinkedIn and Facebook, and text their moms' group about sales at Baby Gap. Whatever the interest, connections—already the social DNA of Gen Y—are enabled through technology. Gen Yers between thirteen and twenty-four tell an average of eighteen

people about a website or TV show that they enjoy, whereas older adults tell an average of only ten people.

18   Although older folks sometimes struggle to learn and adapt to technological advances, they've also had the opportunity to weigh consequences and compare outcomes. Some of the anxiety we've seen in older generations regarding Gen Y is due, in part, to their fear that Gen Y won't know what they're missing or losing by relying on technology. Will all that speed and multitasking result in superficiality? Will Gen Yers have the patience to think deeply about things? Will online relating replace or diminish intimacy? Will shorthand communication, like text messaging and Twittering, and the highly portable nature of technology result in social rudeness (like loud cell phone chats in elevators) and poor formal writing and communication skills?

19   We all know the answer to the social rudeness question—and it's certainly not just the younger members of our community who are at fault. As to the other questions, some of the answer resides in the asker: it's a time-honored tradition of every senior generation to ask, "What's with these kids?" And though our Gen Yers shared some serious struggles and concerns—many of which are related to technology and even more to the high expectations they have for themselves and the world—we found overall that the kids are alright. They'll have their own set of problems to solve, just as every generation before them, but they'll also have powerful gifts and new tools to help—namely confidence, teamwork, technology, and their desire to make a positive contribution to the world. . . .

FOR DISCUSSION

1. The Millennial generation is "unquestionably unique," Yarrow and O'Donnell say. What are the characteristics that make them unique?

2. "Gen Y's parents have been criticized for coddling, for impairing their child's independence by hovering like helicopters." Do you think this criticism has merit? How important in your view is independence and how does it relate to being *inter*dependent, connected to a network of people via electronic communications?

3. One characteristic that Millennials and the parent generation may share is "a disappointment in social institutions," certainly widespread in the 1960s and 1970s. Are you disappointed in American social institutions? If so, did you acquire this attitude from your parents or from other sources?

FOR RESEARCH, DISCUSSION, AND PERSUASION

According to Yarrow and O'Donnell, older generations pose these questions about Millennials:

Will all that speed and multitasking result in superficiality? Will Gen Yers have the patience to think deeply about things? Will online relating replace or diminish intimacy? Will shorthand communication, like text messaging and Twittering, and the highly portable nature of technology result in social rudeness . . . and poor formal writing?

All these questions have been much debated and researched, both online and in print sources. Choose one of them or a related question you would like to investigate and read what you can find on it. (Consult Chapter 6, pages 99–115 for help in doing the research.)

After discussion of research results in class, write a persuasive essay directed at the older generation urging them not to be overly concerned about your question, or directed at a Millennial audience urging them to take steps to resist or counteract the impact of electronic communication.

This Year's Freshmen at 4-Year Colleges: A Statistical Profile

CHRONICLE OF HIGHER EDUCATION

The data below came from an article in the *Chronicle of Higher Education,* but the information was gathered by the UCLA Higher Education Research Institute (HERI), widely considered the most comprehensive and reliable source of data about college students and faculty. As you read through the data, see if you can discover patterns in it and ask, What does it add up to or mean? Does the profile fit your own experience and the other students you see around you?

1 | Racial and ethnic background

White/Caucasian	71.9%
African-American/Black	11.3
Asian-American/Asian	8.8
Mexican-American/Chicano	5.7
Puerto Rican	1.4
Other Latino	4.2
American Indian/Alaska Native	2.6
Native Hawaiian/Pacific Islander	1.3
Other	4.0

2 | College attended is student's

First choice	60.7%
Second choice	26.1
Third choice	8.6
Less than third choice	4.6

3 | Top reasons noted as very important in selecting college attended

	All	Men	Women
College has a very good academic reputation	64.7%	59.5%	68.9%
Graduates get good jobs	54.2	50.5	57.3
Was offered financial assistance	43.0	38.1	47.0
A visit to the campus	41.4	35.7	46.1
The cost of attending	39.9	35.8	43.3

4 | Concern about financing college

	All	Men	Women
None (I am confident that I will have sufficient funds)	35.9%	42.8%	30.2%
Some (but I probably will have enough funds)	53.2	48.7	56.9
Major (not sure I will have enough funds to complete college)	10.9	8.4	12.9

5 | Intended majors

Business	16.7%
Professional	13.8
Arts and humanities	13.5
Social sciences	11.5
Biological sciences	9.3
Engineering	9.3
Education	8.3
Physical sciences	3.2
Technical	1.0
Other fields	7.0
Undecided	6.2

6 | Estimated parental income

Less than $10,000	3.7%
$10,000 to $14,999	2.8
$15,000 to $19,999	2.5
$20,000 to $24,999	3.4
$25,000 to $29,999	3.3
$30,000 to $39,999	6.3
$40,000 to $49,999	7.3
$50,000 to $59,999	8.3
$60,000 to $74,999	11.0
$75,000 to $99,999	14.2
$100,000 to $149,999	17.6
$150,000 to $199,999	8.0
$200,000 to $249,999	4.1
$250,000 or more	7.4

7 | Students rated self above average or highest 10 percent in

	All	Men	Women
Drive to achieve	75.2%	72.6%	77.3%
Cooperativeness	73.7	72.8	74.4
Academic ability	69.5	73.4	66.2
Writing ability	47.5	45.5	49.2
Mathematical ability	44.9	55.0	36.5

8 | Political views

Conservative	20.7%
Far right	1.8
Middle of the road	43.3
Liberal	31.0
Far left	3.2

9 | Agree strongly or somewhat that

	All	Men	Women
The federal government is not doing enough to control environmental pollution	79.0%	75.6%	81.9%
The federal government should do more to control the sale of handguns	72.2	63.7	79.3
A national health-care plan is needed to cover everybody's medical costs	70.3	65.2	74.4
Same-sex couples should have the right to legal marital status	66.2	58.8	72.4
Wealthy people should pay a larger share of taxes than they do now	60.4	59.5	61.2
Abortion should be legal	58.2	59.1	57.6
Affirmative action in college admissions should be abolished	47.6	53.3	42.7
Undocumented immigrants should be denied access to public education	47.2	52.6	42.7
Marijuana should be legalized	41.3	46.7	36.8
Colleges have the right to ban extreme speakers from campus	40.5	43.9	37.6
Students from disadvantaged social backgrounds should be given preferential treatment in college admissions	39.5	41.1	38.1
The death penalty should be abolished	34.9	31.2	38.0
The federal government should raise taxes to reduce the deficit	28.3	33.0	24.4
Federal military spending should be increased	28.0	32.2	24.4
Realistically, an individual can do little to bring about changes in our society	27.3	31.3	24.0
Racial discrimination is no longer a major problem in America	20.1	25.1	16.0

10 | During the past year, did you frequently

	All	Men	Women
Take notes in class	65.8%	51.0%	78.0%
Support your opinions with a logical argument	57.9	60.7	55.6
Ask questions in class	63.9	49.9	57.2
Seek solutions to problems and explain them to others	51.7	50.9	52.3
Accept mistakes as part of the learning process	51.6	50.3	52.7
Seek feedback on your academic work	47.7	41.1	53.2
Revise your papers to improve your writing	46.6	36.9	54.7
Seek alternative solutions to a problem	44.3	45.7	43.1
Take a risk because you feel you have more to gain	40.0	43.6	37.0
Evaluate the quality or reliability of information you received	37.0	36.9	37.1

	All	**Men**	**Women**
Explore topics on your own, even though it was not required for a class	31.4	34.8	28.5
Look up scientific research articles and resources	22.1	24.0	20.6

NOTE: The statistics are based on survey responses of 240,580 first-year students entering 340 baccalaureate colleges and universities in the fall of 2008. The figures were statistically adjusted to represent the total population of approximately 1.4 million first-time, full-time students at four-year institutions. Because of rounding or multiple responses, figures may add up to more than 100 percent.

SOURCE: "The American Freshman: National Norms for Fall 2008, published by the U of California at Los Angeles Higher Education Research Institute.

FOR DISCUSSION

1. Surveys by nature are self-reports—that is, the data are not independent of subjective perceptions, biases, guesses about what the "right" response is, and the like. How do you view survey results?

2. When you look at the information under "racial and ethic background," "concern about financing college," and "estimated parental income," do you see any patterns? What does the information suggest?

3. Politically, 2009 first-year college students seem center-tending-left to a significantly higher degree than Americans in general, with over 74% identifying themselves as either "middle of the road" or "liberal." How would you classify the responses to the statements of policy under "agree strongly or somewhat that"? Do the responses seem consistent with the middle-of-the-road or liberal classifications?

FOR RESEARCH AND INQUIRY

1. The HERI has been conducting surveys of college students for more than forty years now. Choose a year that corresponds to about the time your parents were your age and look up the survey results online. Write an essay exploring the comparative data and offering explanations for the similarities and differences.

2. The HERI survey is relatively large—nearly a quarter of a million students—but also not representative of all students because many students attend junior and community colleges rather than four-year institutions. Find information on students attending junior and community colleges. Write an essay exploring the comparative data and offering explanations for the similarities and differences.

The Promise of the Millennial Generation

RUSS LINDEN

> Russ Linden is a management educator who runs Russ Linden and Associates, a consulting firm that has worked extensively with many U.S. government agencies and departments as well as foreign governments. The author of four books and numerous articles, he is an expert on improving organizational performance.

1   Millennials may be problematic, but consider their potential for radically improving government.

2   With good reason, Tom Brokaw coined the term "the greatest generation," in his book of the same name, to describe those who grew up during the Great Depression and went on to persevere through WWII. I was raised by two members of this remarkable group and I'm continually astonished by both the accomplishments of their generation and their mental fortitude. These people faced one enormous challenge after another, handled those challenges beautifully and without complaint, and did so with humility and a positive spirit.

3   It's just possible that we're about to witness another great generation.

4   That's my take after reading the intriguing book *Generations,* by William Strauss and Neil Howe. The authors identify a pattern of four generations that have repeated sequentially throughout American history since 1584 (the only period in which a generation was skipped was during the Civil War).

5   The four generational types they discovered are:

> Adaptives: They tend to be risk averse, like to conform to existing norms, and try to live up to the high standards of the powerful generation that preceded them. The most recent Adaptive cohort includes those born from 1925–1946.

> Idealists: They often inspire a "spiritual awakening." Their strengths include visionary leadership and their shortcomings can include a tendency toward narcissism. The most recent Idealistic cohort was the baby boom generation, born 1946–1964.

> Reactives: They tend to be alienated and highly individualistic and are skeptical of existing institutions and of the Idealists who preceded them. The most recent Reactive cohort, commonly referred to as Generation X, was born between 1964 and 1980.

> Civics: This group is called an "institution building" generation. Like the Idealists, they tend to set the social agenda for the country. They respect authority, are comfortable working within the system, and set very high goals. The most recent Civic cohort was born between 1980 and 2000.

6   The Idealist and Civic cohorts are change-oriented generations, the other two reflect a more stable and conservative orientation. The 20-somethings now entering the workplace are a Civic generation, often referred to as Millennials. And, if you believe Strauss and Howe's premise, they offer enormous promise for our organizations and our society.

WHAT THE NEXT GENERATION HAS TO OFFER

7   My wife and I have two adult "Millennial" children. They and their friends reflect most of the characteristics that Civics have historically demonstrated. Moreover, the research on Millennials who are now in the workplace suggests that this group's strengths align beautifully with government's most pressing needs. Consider the following list of traits exhibited by Millennials:

- a great facility for technology
- an eagerness for change
- an assumption that information is to be shared, not hoarded
- a lack of patience with bureaucracy
- a talent (and preference) for collaboration
- a passion for service, and
- a desire to make a (big) difference

8   Wouldn't you want such people working for you?

9   Yes, this group can be problematic. Their impatience with bureaucracy can get them in trouble, and their expectations for immediate change can leave them easily disappointed. As a result of their early life experiences (e.g., being carted by parents from one structured activity to another) many Millennials need more adult attention and supervision than managers may choose to give. But, consider this group's potential for radically improving government.

10   At a time when most government agencies need to find new ways to engage their citizen-customers as active partners, Millennials are able and eager to redefine citizen engagement by harnessing the power of Web 2.0. In a "discontinuous" age of incredible global changes, Millennials aren't unsettled by the turbulence; on the contrary, they are energized by it. In an era when we must tear down organizational walls, collaborate, and share information, this generation has been doing exactly that since they were given group projects in elementary school (and were graded for how well they worked in a group).

11   These are all generalizations, of course, and you'll no doubt find many exceptions. But my experience with a number of Millennials tells me that this generation does share the characteristics described in recent research. Moreover, they reflect the fundamental nature of Civic generations discovered by Howe and Strauss.

12   The next time you're truly despondent about your own team, or division, or agency, just reflect on this fact: Most of America's founding fathers were members of a Civic generation (Jefferson, Madison, Hamilton, Monroe, John Marshall, John Jay, and many other founders were born 1742–1766). The Civics are, indeed, an institution-building generation. The real challenge is ours: Will we be farsighted and smart enough to put today's Civic cohort into appropriate positions of leadership so they can build tomorrow's government?

FOR DISCUSSION

1. Linden refers to "impatience with bureaucracy" as a characteristic of Millennials, together with "expectations for immediate change." What is the relation between these alleged characteristics and Yarrow and O'Donnell's description of Millennials in the first selection as accustomed to getting "what they want when they want it"?

2. Linden clearly believes that Millennials are a significant asset for government agencies, yet Yarrow and O'Donnell say that Millennials are critical of our social institutions, and so presumably government institutions as well. How do you assess this apparent conflict? Do you agree with Linden that Millennials are an "institution-building generation"?

FOR RESEARCH, DISCUSSION, AND CONVINCING

Linden's view of Millennials is heavily indebted to a highly influential book he refers to, William Strauss and Neil Howe's *Generations*. Get a copy of this book and study it, especially everything in it relating to the Civics, supposedly the generation type Millennials represent. In what ways are they like past Civic generations? In what ways are they unique or different? What characteristics of the other three generation types do you see also among Millennials?

Write an article making a case for Millennials as another Civic generation, or arguing that they really do not fit the type, or advocating perhaps a combination of types as the only way to characterize them adequately. Conceive your essay as an editorial for a campus newspaper or as a well-developed blog entry for an online audience.

The Economic Crunch

TAMARA DRAUT

The following is an excerpt from the introduction to *Strapped: Why America's 20- and 30-Somethings Can't Get Ahead* (Doubleday, 2005). We supplied the full title to emphasize the author's main point, that money problems have reached crisis proportion for young adults.

Tamara Draut is director of the Economic Opportunity Program at Demos, a think tank in New York City. A young adult herself, she has experienced the economic crunch she depicts with such authority in *Strapped*.

1   They say music feeds the soul. When you're flat broke, it can also feed your stomach. Several years ago, my husband and I found ourselves sitting in the middle of our living-room floor, our entire CD collection spread out before us. We had not a dollar between us and payday was three long days away. It wasn't the first time we'd been strapped for cash, but we never imagined we'd be peddling our wares for food money at the age of 30.

2   By the time of our CD purge, becoming adults had left us with $57,000 in student loan debt and $19,000 in credit card debt.

3   We were so far behind in fulfilling our own expectations, our parents' expectations, and society's expectations, we didn't know whether to laugh or cry. We weren't clothes hounds, we didn't take vacations, and we seldom went out to dinner. Most of our economic woes could be traced back to eight years of start-up costs (pots, sheets, a bed), flights for family visits and friends' weddings, unstable incomes from shoestring salaries, three bouts of unemployment, a gig at graduate school, and one major career change.

4   And we weren't alone. When we talked to people our age from all walks of life, it became clear that we weren't the only ones who were strapped. While my husband and I were dismantling our CD collection to make some cold hard cash, other young adults were facing tougher decisions and making bigger sacrifices. Across the country, young adults of different cultural, social, and economic backgrounds were confronting brick walls on their path to adulthood.

- Cecilia graduated from a California high school in 1999. It was the height of the tech boom and many of her classmates were dreaming of fast money and early retirement. Cecilia had a different dream: this second-generation Latina wanted to go to college and become a teacher. Despite a good grade-point average and athletic awards in several sports, Cecilia didn't earn the much-needed scholarship money to pay for school. So she did what millions of graduating seniors do each year: she applied for financial aid. But her working-class parents earned too much money to qualify her for aid, yet not enough to afford the state university where Cecilia was accepted. And so with her heart still set on becoming a teacher, she enrolled in the local community college, worked part-time, and lived at home to save money. Three years later, Cecilia has her associate's degree and is working at the mall. She still wants to be a teacher. She still wants to be the first person in her family to graduate from college.

- Rob and Laura, a white couple now in their mid-thirties, are further along in their journey to adulthood. When they first got married, they thought they were on sound financial footing. Though neither finished college, Rob became trained as a heating and air-conditioning technician while Laura got a job working in the accounts-receivable department at the local plastics plant. They made $50,000 between them, which enabled them to live comfortably, but not extravagantly. When Laura became pregnant with their first child, Rob's parents gave them the down payment to buy a house. Their "first child" turned out to be twins—and, overnight, comfortable became very uncomfortable. Without the option of affordable child care, Laura had little choice but to quit her job and take care of the twins. Just then her husband's business took a dive. With their savings dwindling, credit cards went from occasional aids to lifelines. Today, the couple have three young children and $40,000 in credit card debt. They never dreamed that starting a family would plunge them into such deep financial and emotional straits.

- Wanda and Jerome seem like the quintessential middle-class African American couple who have captured the American dream. Both aged thirty-two, they are a dynamic duo with multiple college degrees. Wanda has a master's in human relations and Jerome has an M.B.A. Getting these credentials also got them $30,000 in student loan debt. Thankfully the couple resides in Montgomery, Alabama, where the cost of living is low. But with a five-month-old baby, a six-year-old son, and a twelve-year-old daughter, this family of five is living paycheck to paycheck. They are unable to afford child care, so Wanda's mother has been living with them for five months, and they don't know what they'll do when she leaves. After Jerome was laid off from his account-manager position at a Fortune 100 company, they ran up a couple of thousand dollars in credit card debt. His layoff was an especially bitter pill, since it was this job that brought them to Alabama in the first place. They would like to move out of Montgomery because the educational system is poor, but right now they're biding their time and trying to pay down their debts.

5   The lives of Cecilia, Rob and Laura, and Wanda and Jerome are at once strikingly different and fundamentally similar. Three different backgrounds. Three different classes. Three different life experiences. They did all the right things, but they're all struggling to make ends meet. And they're not alone. All across the country young adults are sinking economically. The question is, why?

6   Behind each of these individual stories is a broader tale of economic and political changes that have occurred over the last three decades. For our parents, who grew up during the 1950s and early 1960s, establishing oneself as an adult was a fairly straightforward process. Moving out of your parents' house, getting a job, and starting a family—the three major markers of adulthood—unfolded in a rather swift and orderly fashion. There was little time between graduation, landing a well-paying job, getting married, and having kids. But in the late 1960s, the baby boomers, then in their twenties, began charting a different course to adulthood. Driven by social, economic, and political forces, young adults began delaying

definitive "adult" behaviors such as getting married and having kids. As college and career opportunities expanded for women and minorities, more young adults began going to college instead of directly into the labor market after high school. The transition to adulthood was becoming less rigid and more ill defined. A generation later, these trends became more exacerbated. The path to adulthood for today's young adults is a full-blown obstacle course of loop-de-loop turns and jagged-edged hurdles.

7　　When our parents were starting out, three factors helped smooth the transition to adulthood. The first was the fact that there were jobs that provided good wages even for high school graduates. A college degree wasn't necessary to earn a decent living. But even if you wanted to go to college, it wasn't that expensive and grants were widely available. The second was a robust economy that lifted all boats, with productivity gains shared by workers and CEOs alike. The result was a massive growth of the middle class, which provided security and stability for families. Third, a range of public policies helped facilitate this economic mobility and opportunity: a strong minimum wage, grants for low-income students to go to college, a generous unemployment insurance system, major incentives for home ownership, and a solid safety net for those falling on hard times. Simply put, government had your back.

8　　This world no longer exists. The story of what happened is well known. The nation shifted to a service- and knowledge-based economy, dramatically changing the way we lived and worked. Relationships between employers and employees became more tenuous as corporations faced global competitors and quarterly bottom-line pressures from Wall Street. Increasingly, benefits such as health care and pension plans were provided only to well-paid workers. Wages rose quickly for educated workers and declined for those with only high school diplomas, resulting in new demands for college credentials. As most families saw their incomes stagnate or decline, they increasingly needed two full-time incomes just to stay afloat, which created new demands and pressures on working parents. Getting into the middle class now required a four-year college degree, and even that was no guarantee of achieving the American dream.

9　　Although adults of all ages have endured the economic and social changes wrought by the postindustrial era, today's young adults are the first to experience its full weight as they try to start their adult lives. But the challenges facing young adults also reflect the failure of public policy to address the changing realities of building a life in the twenty-first century. Government no longer has our back. . . .

COLLEGE: A LUXURY-PRICED NECESSITY

10　　College students today are graduating on average with close to $20,000 in debt. Those who take the plunge into graduate school can plan on carrying about $45,000 in combined student loan debt.[1] Those who want to be lawyers or doctors will be lucky to escape with less than $100,000 in debt. Back in the 1970s, before college became essential to securing a middle-class lifestyle, our government did a great job of helping students pay for school. Students from modest economic backgrounds received almost free tuition through Pell grants, and middle-class households could still afford to pay for their kids' college.

11   That was before tuition began to spiral ever upward and student aid fossilized. Inflation-adjusted tuition at public universities has nearly tripled since 1980, up from $1,758 in 1980 to $5,132 in 2004.[2] To be fair, the federal government is spending more money than ever before on student aid, over $81 billion in the 2003–04 school year. But 70 percent of this aid is in the form of loans, while grant aid only makes up 21 percent and tax credits the remaining 9 percent.[3] Federal grant funding hasn't kept up with rising enrollments, so what little grant aid is available gets spread more thinly across a greater number of students.

12   As a result of soaring college costs and dwindling financial aid, in 2001 half a million high school graduates who were college-ready either downscaled their dreams by enrolling in community college or skipped college altogether. Congress has responded to this crisis in educational opportunity by merely tinkering with grant and student loan amounts—a bit like the fire department pulling up to a five-alarm fire with a garden hose. Case in point: The maximum Pell Grant award— the nation's premier government program for helping low-income students pay for college—covers about 40 percent of the costs of a four-year college today. It covered nearly three quarters in the 1970s.[4]

13   Thirty years ago, in 1976–77, the average cost of attending a *private* college was $12,837 annually, in inflation-adjusted dollars. Today, the average cost of attending a *public* college is $11,354—which means the burden of affording a state college today is equivalent to that of paying for a private college in the 1970s.[5] These figures include tuition, fees, and room and board. While tuition at four-year public colleges has soared, tuition at private colleges has entered the stratosphere, costing an average of $27,000 per year. Adding to the financial pressures is the new credential craze that all but mandates a master's degree to get out of the entry-level track in business, marketing, social work, teaching, and many other professions. Already in the hole for a bachelor's degree, many young adults find that the demand to get even more education leaves them up against the ropes. They want the better jobs but can't take the risk of going even deeper into debt.

14   Young adults have been given the signal loud and clear that getting a degree is now the only way into the middle class. As the burden of paying for college has shifted to the individual, more students are going into debt, dropping out, or not enrolling at all.

THE REAL "NEW" ECONOMY

15   What does the . . . job market for young adults look like? In a word, depressing. Compared to older workers, young adults are more likely to be unemployed, hold part-time jobs, or work as temps. Almost half of temp agency workers are in the 18-to-34 age group. That's half a million young adults stuck in the temp system, and another 2.2 million who are independent contractors. These job arrangements rarely offer health care or other benefits, such as pensions.

16   For college grads who land a job with an actual firm, it's still far from sure that they'll be offered health or retirement benefits. One out of three young adults—a full 17.9 million 18-to-34-year-olds—don't have health insurance, making this the age group with the largest percentage of uninsured. They're not

going without health-care coverage out of some sense of invincibility either; in fact, only 3 percent of young workers are uninsured because they declined available coverage.

17   In addition to often working in a benefit-free zone, moving up the wage or career ladder in the new economy is more difficult than it was a generation ago. The well-paying middle-management jobs that characterized the workforce up to the late 1970s have been eviscerated. Corporate downsizing in the 1980s and 1990s slashed positions in the middle of the wage distribution, and now outsourcing threatens to take thousands more. Instead of becoming more financially secure with each passing year, many young adults in their late twenties and early thirties find themselves struggling ever harder as they start having children and taking on mortgages. What they're experiencing is paycheck paralysis.

18   Today, America's economy looks like an hourglass. Job growth is concentrated at the top and bottom, while the middle is increasingly whittled away. According to the Bureau of Labor Statistics, jobs requiring a bachelor's degree or higher will account for 29 percent of total job growth from 2000 to 2010. Many of these new jobs are what we think of as "hot jobs"—those clustered in the tech and computer sector. The *largest* job growth, accounting for 58 percent of new jobs, will be those requiring only work-related training. These jobs are primarily in the low-wage retail and food sector, including such jobs as sales associates, food preparation, cashiers, and waitstaff.

19   Young adults who came of age in the mall culture are still trolling the malls—only this time they're looking for work.

20   As the job market has changed, so have the paychecks. Young adults across the board are earning less today than they would have twenty or even thirty years ago. In 1972, the typical earnings for males 25 to 34 years old with a high school diploma was $42,630 (in 2002 dollars). In 2002, the typical earnings for high school grads had dropped to $29,647. Typical earnings for young males with a bachelor's degree or higher have also declined, from $52,087 in 1972 to $48,955 in 2002.[6]

21   Living paycheck to paycheck is the new norm for young adults. College grads may have a better shot of slowly digging their way out of the insecurity, but it most likely will not happen until they hit their forties. Today's paycheck paralysis makes it almost impossible for most young adults to get ahead. Dwindling salaries and rising costs mean less leftover money to put into savings, less to contribute to a 401(k), and less to put into their own kids' college funds. And all the while, they're racking up credit card debt to pay for any additional expenses, like going to the dentist or fixing the car, at exorbitant interest rates that rob them of even more money.

NOTES

1. Sandy Baum and Marie O' Malley, "College on Credit: How Borrowers Perceive Their Education Debt: Results of the 2002 National Student Loan Survey," Nellie Mae Corporation, February 6, 2003, available at http://www.nelliemae.com/library/research_10 .html.
2. College Board, "Trends in College Pricing 2004," available at http://www.collegeboard .com/prod_downloads/press/cost04/041264TrendsPricing2004_FINAL.pdf.

3. College Board, "Trends in Student Aid 2004," available at http://www.collegeboard
   .com/prod_downloads/press/cost04/TrendsinStudentAid2004.pdf.
4. Lawrence E. Gladieux, "Low-Income Students and the Affordability of Higher Education," in Richard D. Kahlenberg, ed., *America's Untapped Resource: Low-Income Students
   in Higher Education* (New York: Century Foundation Press, 2004), p. 29.
5. College Board, "Trends in College Pricing 2004."
6. U.S. Department of Education, National Center for Education Statistics, *The Condition of
   Education 2004,* indicator 14, table 14-1, available at http://nces.gov//programs/
   coe/2004/pdf/14_2004.pdf.

FOR DISCUSSION

1. It is important to realize that the debt and job problems Draut discusses are
   widely distributed in the young adult group. How does she establish that
   the economic crunch is not restricted to an unfortunate few or a particular
   social class? Are you facing or have you seen similar drastic circumstances
   among your friends and acquaintances?

2. One of Draut's key points is that things have changed significantly since the
   1950s and 1960s. What exactly has changed? Why have these changes had
   a greater impact on today's young adults than on their parents' generation?
   In your view, what changes must just be accepted, lived with somehow, and
   what changes can be coped with better by government policy designed to
   help young adults?

3. A college degree, almost any degree in any major, was once virtually a
   guarantee of economic opportunity, and certainly college graduates still earn
   more on average over a lifetime than high school graduates do. However,
   the college degree is not the passport to success it once was. As Draut
   describes the situation, why isn't it? What have you observed about the
   financial value of a college degree from people you know who have
   graduated recently?

FOR RESEARCH AND CONVINCING

The high cost of college is beyond dispute. As Draut points out, a public university
now costs as much as a private one did thirty years ago. People tend to accept
it without asking why, as if escalating costs were inevitable. Are they? Find out
why college expenses have increased faster than inflation over the last few
decades. What causes almost yearly tuition hikes?

Based on what you learn from research, make a case defending what you
think will best contain runaway college costs. Address it to an audience of your
peers and their parents, who need to understand what is driving the rising cost
of higher education before they can hope to do anything about it.

Waking Up and Taking Charge

ANYA KAMENETZ

It is one thing to know we have a problem, quite another to do something to solve it, even when we understand it reasonably well. In the following excerpt from *Generation Debt: Why Now Is a Terrible Time to Be Young* (Riverside Press, 2006), Anya Kamenetz proposes action to promote needed change.

Like Tamara Draut, who offers similar proposals in *Strapped* (see the previous selection), Kamenetz, despite being a recent Yale graduate, has struggled herself with difficult economic conditions. And like Draut, she is helping to lead young adults toward becoming a potent political force.

We aren't particularly interested in "rocking the vote." . . . We're here to represent our generation because decisions are made by the people who show up.
—Virginia21, *the first student-led state political action committee, 2004*

1   If you're like me, you're a little impatient with the political sphere of action. Spend months and years supporting local candidates? Send blast faxes to your congresspeople? Actually read those endless e-mail alerts?

2   Well, look, if 35 million people over fifty can band together to demand respect from Congress, so can we. Unless we're willing to continue being typecast as passive "adultescents," unless we really want to get "rolled over by greedy middle-aged and older people who have been expropriating our earnings for generations," as the economist Laurence Kotlikoff says, it's the only way. Young people urgently need a strong national generational movement—for higher education funding, fairer credit laws, a better-designed school-to-work system, justice system reform, worker protections, a living wage, health care, saving programs, support for young families and homeowners, entitlement reform, and a million other issues.

3   As college gets ever more out of reach, there are signs of a nascent movement. At my alma mater on a freezing day in February 2005, fifteen students sat in at the admissions office until removed by police. The undergraduates were demanding changes to Yale's financial aid policy to bring it in line with several other Ivies, including Harvard, Princeton, and Brown. In the past few years, these schools have all dipped into their multimillion-dollar endowments to make it easier for families to afford college without heavy loans. One week after the sit-in, Yale, too, announced that it would no longer expect any tuition contribution at all from families earning less than $45,000 a year.

4   By all accounts, the financial aid reform issue galvanized the campus. One in five Yalies signed on to the reform platform, including the president of the Yale College Republicans and other campus conservatives. "This is self-interested organizing in a positive way," Phoebe Rounds, a sophomore on financial aid who organized for six months leading up to the sit-in, told me. "The campaign has made people realize the extent to which their individual struggles are shared by a large number of students."

5   The Yale action also demonstrates, however, that without a unified voice, individual protests can make only small ripples. Tuition discounting is possible only at a tiny percentage of well-endowed private schools serving a tiny percentage of students. At selective colleges in 2004, only 10 percent of students came from the bottom half of the income scale.

6   An effective student movement should be organized state by state, to pressure the governors who make decisions about public schools where the vast majority of students are enrolled. When it comes to the broader problems facing young people, only national political organizing will do.

7   The student loan debt explosion could potentially be more amenable to lobbying than any of the other problems facing Generation Debt. The federal government gives out most student financial aid. They say how much you can borrow in guaranteed student loans and how high an interest rate the banks can charge. Given a true reordering of our national priorities—a big given—a few amendments to the Higher Education Act could immediately bring student borrowing down to a manageable level and lower the barriers to access. Increasing the maximum Pell Grant, and making the grant an entitlement that rises automatically from year to year, are obvious first steps. In the words of the National Association of Student Financial Aid Administrators, "If we are serious about reducing student loan debt . . . making the Pell Grant Program a true entitlement, divorced from the vagaries of the appropriations process, is the only way."

8   As this book is going to press, the eighth reauthorization of the Higher Education Act is finally getting under way, a few years overdue. The Bush administration assigned the lion's share of spending cuts for the purpose of deficit reduction to the House and Senate Education committees, and they turned around and passed the pain on to student aid, with $15 billion in cuts and new fees—the biggest cuts since HEA programs were created.

9   Even if legislative reform is years in coming, a vocal activist campaign about the dangers of student loans could accomplish a lot. After all, excessive student debt is not measured by a fixed number of dollars. It's a function of each person's income, other debts, financial management skills, ability to persist in college, and expectations about the value of a diploma. Raising awareness about the long-term dangers of high debt could help all those kids who "just sign on the dotted line as an eighteen-year-old and you don't know what you're getting into," as one interviewee put it.

10   Youth activism could effectively address credit card debt, too. It would be great to reinstate usury laws nationwide and end 29 percent annual interest rates, so that twenty-somethings earning $12,000 a year are no longer profitable customers for $10,000 lines of credit. That would require a morally high-fiber Congress willing to take on one of the fastest-growing profit areas in financial services. Failing that, returning to the norms of the 1980s, when college students without incomes needed a parental cosigner for a card, would keep eighteen-year-olds from charging down that path before they realize the consequences.

11   With credit card debt, just as with student loans, a vocal activist movement could bring the problem out into the open, making kids think twice before signing

up for the free Frisbees and key chains. Universities have a role to play, too, in limiting their students' exposure to credit card marketing. Just as Stella, [a] thirty-one-year-old debtor . . . , says, the next time you see the Discover Card table, RUN the other way!

12   Where is our national student antidebt crusade? Over the past four decades, college students have gained a reputation as the most engaged political activists in the country—except on issues directly affecting them. Each year, for example, *Mother Jones* magazine recognizes the top ten activist campuses in the nation. From 2001 to 2005, the list featured left-wing campaigns on free speech, the war in Iraq, AIDS, the drug war, and living wages. Missing were bipartisan student issues like mounting debt burden, aggressive credit card marketing, the lack of health insurance, and the dearth of solid entry-level jobs.

13   Standing up for world peace is utterly admirable, but the social safety net in this country was woven by people lobbying for their own lives, not fighting for causes a world away. American college students need to experience that "click" moment, as the feminists of the 1970s called it, and realize that our personal problems are also political. If we young people don't march on our own behalf, who will march for us?

14   In other countries, students get it. Many EU and Latin American countries have overwhelmingly public, centralized university systems, making organizing easier (and education cheaper). Around the world, national undergraduate student unions have lobbied forcefully for decades. They address issues like diversity and date rape, along with tuition, books, housing, health care, debt, and jobs. They win battles for their constituencies, keeping young people on the social agenda.

15   The UK's National Union of Students claims 5 million members, nearly all the country's higher education students. In October 2003, an estimated 31,000 of them rallied in London against higher school fees.

16   After huge national budget cuts in the '90s, Canadians' student loans are comparable to Americans', at an average $22,520 ($19,143 U.S.) in 2001. Educational access is worsening for lower-income Canadians, although not quite as badly as in the United States.

17   Canada's two national student lobbying organizations boast combined memberships of 750,000, nearly half the nation's college students. James Kusie, a 2002 university grad from Manitoba, served from 2003 to 2005 as the elected national director of the Canadian Alliance of Student Associations (CASA). His group, founded in 1995, represents 300,000 students at nineteen universities across Canada. Member associations fund CASA's full-time staff of five, which drafts policy in the nation's capital and builds relationships with lawmakers, both elected representatives and bureaucrats. "You can be rallying outside and shouting through the window, and that's an important piece of building public support," Kusie says. "But you also need to be at the table with them, engaging them on the issues."

18   Each year, the presidents and vice presidents of each student council in CASA come to the national capital, Ottawa, and meet in person with their elected

representatives. They also hold media stunts. In November 2003, they built a 120-foot Wall of Debt out of foam blocks, bearing the signatures of 20,000 students along with the debt burdens of each.

19   Throughout the 1990s, Canadian student organizations won tuition freezes and even cuts in several provinces. Kusie glows as he describes the accomplishments of his term as CASA's chair. In 2004, the federal government adopted their proposal for a new grant to low-income students, up to $3,000, modeled on the Pell Grant. They also changed the formulas for expected parental contributions, making up to 50,000 more students eligible for financial aid. These victories came during comparatively good economic times for Canada, but after more than a decade of deep budget cuts that shrank the size of the federal government by a third and while the country was experiencing the same increases in health care and pension costs as in the United States. CASA and the Canadian Federation of Students work to ensure that a government tending to the needs of an aging population does not forget young people.

20   "When Parliament begins a new session following an election, the government gives a 'throne speech,' setting out its priorities for the legislative session," Kusie says. "When it came to the section on education, chunks of it seemed to have come word for word from our pre-budget submission. . . . We were very happy to see that our work had paid off."

21   The United States Student Association, this nation's oldest and largest student organization, contrasts poorly with the muscle flexed abroad. Its exact membership is not available on its seldom updated website. Most students have never heard of it, and the media tend to pass it over. Its lobbying clout is dwarfed by that of the big student loan companies—it spent just $20,000 on lobbying in 2000, compared with $1.5 million spent by Sallie Mae.

22   The 80 percent of students who attend public schools are pitted against the immovable object of state budgets. In the past few years, community college and state university students from California and New York demonstrated against big tuition hikes coupled with budget cuts. Ten thousand students from California's community colleges marched to Sacramento in 2003 to protest a 120 percent rise in fees and budget cuts in the hundreds of millions. They carried paper effigies representing an estimated 200,000 students priced out of the community college system. Public college students backed by the New York Public Interest Research Group rallied strongly against tuition hikes throughout the '90s, marching 561 miles across New York State in 2003. In both cases, despite temporary responses, the budget cuts and tuition increases continued.

23   There is a model here in America of what students could be doing to focus legislators' attention on education. A state political action committee, as powerful and well organized as the student unions in other countries, has taken root in, of all places, placid suburban Virginia.

24   In 2002, students at the public College of William and Mary formed Students PAC to help pass a $900 million state bond issue for higher education. In the summer of 2003, the coalition, now called Virginia21, went statewide. It now boasts

over 14,500 members at all fifteen public four-year colleges and universities in the Commonwealth.

25   VA21, the first student-led state PAC, addresses voters between eighteen and twenty-four on economic issues like tuition, book costs, and education budget cuts. They reject the popular approach of relying on mass media or celebrity to sell young voters on civic involvement. Jesse Ferguson, the twenty-four-year-old executive director, notes that voters of all ages tend to be motivated by concrete self-interest, not abstract ideals.

26   "We're trying to find a way to support mainstream, bipartisan, middle-of-the-road issues that affect all of us on a day-to-day basis," Ferguson says. He cofounded Students of Virginia PAC as a college student. Now he and a small staff work full-time in Virginia's capital to drive home their message about budget priorities. At their website, you can check the status of all the legislation they're working on, from cutting textbook prices, to increasing student financial aid, to reforming absentee voting so college students have an easier time getting to the ballot box. Their rhetoric strikes a determined but not angry note; they remind legislators that education is an investment in Virginia, and they remind students that they don't deserve to be priced out. In June 2004, Virginia21 celebrated passage of a state budget with $275 million more for higher education than the year before, the first such increase in years.

27   VA21 draws on its members for letter-writing campaigns, e-mail blasts, and rallies. They collected and trucked 200,000 pennies to the state capitol in 2004 in support of a one-cent sales tax for education. Meanwhile, Ferguson and his team haunted the halls of the capitol during their first legislative session just as all the other power players did.

28   In a bow to the realities of American politics, VA21, unlike the Canadian groups, depends on corporate contributions. Their 2003–2004 budget was $100,000. Donors included America Online, Bank of America, and Philip Morris's corporate owner. With this backing, it's hard to imagine VA21 addressing issues like unfair credit card marketing. Still, they're getting results, and lawmakers are taking them seriously.

29   Jesse Ferguson says he would seize the chance to take VA21 national if offered the funding. He calls his group a young, wired equivalent of the AARP, for its focus on issues that affect everyone of a certain age, and for its pragmatic, even insider, approach. "There's a change you can see in recent years in eighteen- to twenty-four-year-olds—they would rather have a seat at the table than a rally outside," Ferguson told me, echoing James Kusie of CASA. "It's got to be not just student activism but effective student activism."

FOR DISCUSSION

1. A common charge, which Kamenetz indirectly acknowledges, is that young adults are alienated from politics, too passive in accepting whatever older adults dish out. In your experience, is there any truth in this criticism? If you pay little or no attention to politics and do not vote, how do you explain or justify your behavior?

2. Kamenetz presents VA21 in terms obviously designed to make political action attractive. Do you find the idea for a college student–young adult PAC (political action committee) appealing? Why or why not? If you had a chance to take a role in such a group, would you? Why or why not?

3. Unfortunately, there is too much in American culture that encourages young adults to think that the sky is the limit, that you can achieve anything you want to achieve—"chase your dreams" is an American credo. What is good about such an outlook? How much do you think the credo contributes to college students and their parents taking on too much debt for college expenses? What do you think should be done to encourage young adults to assess themselves and their financial situation with greater realism and practicality?

FOR RESEARCH AND INQUIRY

The great model for an age-specific PAC is AARP (formerly known as the American Association of Retired Persons). Find out all you can about its membership, how it is organized, what it does to create a sense of group identity and purpose, and why it is effective with the political establishment.

Then write a paper exploring the possibility of creating a similar group for young adults, a group that would embrace college students and college graduates as well as the majority of young adults who do not go to or do not finish college. In what ways could such a group follow the AARP model? In what ways should it depart from it? What do you think needs to be done to make young adults a political force to be reckoned with by politicians at all levels of government?

An alternative is to research VA21 instead, the student-led PAC in Virginia that won important concessions from state government. If you take this route, ponder what VA21 accomplished and exactly why and how they managed to get things done. Would a similar PAC work in your state? Would it be better to go national—form a group that takes in all college students—or remain more local, working state by state instead?

FOR FURTHER READING

Apter, Terri. *The Myth of Maturity: What Teenagers Need from Parents to Become Adults.* New York: Norton, 2001.

Arnett, Jeffrey Jensen. *Emerging Adulthood: The Winding Road from the Late Teens through the Twenties.* New York: Oxford UP, 2004.

Draut, Tamara. *Strapped: Why America's 20- and 30-Somethings Can't Get Ahead.* New York: Doubleday, 2005.

Kamenetz, Anya. *Generation Debt: Why Now Is a Terrible Time to Be Young.* New York: Riverside Books, 2006.

Twenge, Jean M. *Generation Me: Why Today's Young Americans Are More Confident, Assertive, Entitled—and More Miserable Than Ever Before.* New York: Free Press, 2006.

Yarrow, Kit, and Jayne O'Donnell. *Gen BuY: How Tweens, Teens, and Twenty-Somethings Are Revolutionizing Retail.* San Francisco: Jossey-Bass, 2009.

CHAPTER 16

Immigration Revisited: A New Look at a Permanent Issue

About a decade ago, we had a chapter on immigration in the second edition of this book. In many important ways, little has changed:

- About 1.2 million immigrants come to the United States each year, the vast majority of whom are Hispanics and Asians.

- Many of them are undocumented aliens.

- Our border with Mexico remains leaky, with perhaps about half a million people crossing it illegally each year since 2000.
- All measures to control the border and significantly reduce illegal immigration have failed.
- Immigrants, both legal and illegal, contribute significantly to our economy while also imposing significant costs, especially on state and local governments.

We could extend this list, but you get the point: as the French proverb says, "The more things change, the more they stay the same."

Yet things have changed. Many recent legal immigrants come from regions and countries that supplied few willing residents in the past—from Africa and India, for instance. In the past, most immigrants were confined to coastal or gateway cities and the Southwest. That is less and less the case; states such as North Carolina and Iowa now receive many new immigrants.

Furthermore, 9/11 led Americans to worry about the country's porous borders more than before. More recently, immigration has been discussed extensively in the news, on talk radio, and on thousands of Web sites, raising awareness of the issue to heights not seen since the 1920s and resulting in efforts to pass new legislation in Congress. Hardly anyone doubts that new laws will eventually pass—but what they will be no one knows for sure, and the actual impact they will have is anyone's guess.

Few issues confronting us are more poorly understood, more emotional, and more up in the air than immigration. Consequently, we need to focus on certain fundamental questions of long-term importance:

- There are now more than 300 million Americans. How long can we continue to absorb so many new people? From the standpoint of population control and ecology, *should we want to reduce the immigration rate?*
- Measures to control immigration are often both ineffective and produce unintended results, some of them clearly negative. Supposing that we want to, *can we reduce the immigration rate?* As the recent recession clearly shows, economic forces drive immigration; perhaps we should let market forces control it. If not, what measures would really work, without producing intolerably bad side effects?
- All data indicate that without immigrants many millions of jobs would go unfilled. Even assuming we would like to reduce immigration and can actually do so, *can we afford to reduce the immigration rate?*
- Finally, until recently, the pressure on new immigrants to "become Americans" was unrelenting and almost unquestioned. But now assimilation itself is an issue. *Do we really want immigrants to lose all sense of connection to their culture of origin?* If, as many people believe, the whole idea of the melting pot belongs to the past, *how much assimilation is desirable?*

The following selections address these questions directly and by implication. How we answer them will determine the nature and future of our country.

Historical Images: Our Contradictory Attitudes toward Immigration

The following posters were printed in popular publications about one hundred years ago, when immigration was highest, as measured by percentage of the total U.S. population. We think they capture in dramatic fashion the conflicting attitudes Americans have always had toward new arrivals. These and several similar drawings appeared in the magazine *Reason*, August–September 2006.

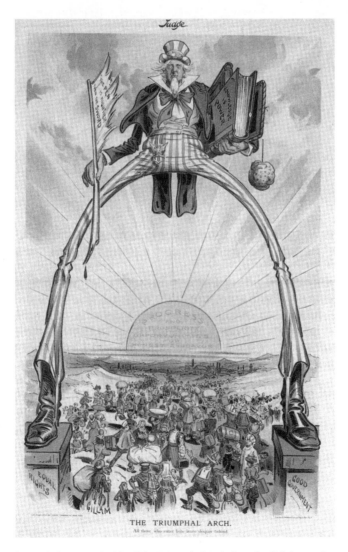

The caption beneath the poster's title, "The Triumphal Arch," reads, "All those who enter here leave despair behind."

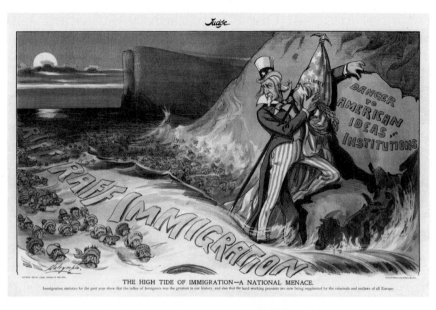

THE HIGH TIDE OF IMMIGRATION—A NATIONAL MENACE.

The caption beneath the poster's title, "The High Tide of Immigration . . . ," reads, "Immigration statistics for the past year show that the influx of foreigners was the greatest in history, and also that the hard-working peasants are now being supplanted by the criminals and outlaws of all Europe."

FOR DISCUSSION

Look carefully at the details in these two posters. What "assertions" are they making by implication? In your view, how do they reflect reality? How do they distort it?

FOR RESEARCH, ANALYSIS, AND INQUIRY

As a class project, collect recent images connected with attitudes toward immigration—photographs, cartoons, anything pictorial. Discuss each image in class, exploring both its conscious and unconscious impact, and comparing it with the posters from a century ago. How much has changed? How much remains the same?

Select two or three recent images you find particularly interesting and write an essay about the attitudes they express. Do they capture your own ideals and fears? If so, how?

The New Immigrants and the Issue of Assimilation

TAMAR JACOBY

One of the better books published on immigration is a collection of essays called *Reinventing the Melting Pot: The New Immigrant and What It Means to Be American* (New York: Basic Books, 2004). The following selection is an excerpt from the first two chapters, both written by Tamar Jacoby, the editor of the volume and a senior researcher at the Manhattan Institute. She provides basic information on the current wave of immigrants and poses the issue of assimilation as we wrestle with it now.

THE BIG PICTURE

1　The immigrant influx of the last forty years is a demographic shift of historic proportions. The percentage of the population that was born abroad is slightly lower than it was when the last great wave of immigrants arrived, at the beginning of the twentieth century: 11 percent now compared to 15 percent then. But the absolute number of newcomers living in the United States today is the highest it has ever been: some 31 million. Roughly 1.2 million arrive on our shores every year. One in nine Americans is an immigrant. And half the laborers entering the American workforce in the 1990s were foreign-born. Add in their families and extended families and the picture grows more dramatic still. Together, immigrants and their children now account for one in five Americans. Hispanics, at nearly 14 percent of the population, are already the largest minority, outnumbering blacks. Asian-Americans are still a relatively small share of the nation—at only 4 percent. But despite their numbers, they, too, are going to play a major part in the country's future: already, they make up between 15 and 20 percent of the students at most Ivy League colleges.

2　Where do these new arrivals come from? Just over half the foreign-born are Hispanic and a little more than a quarter are Asian. They hail from all the corners of the globe, though more from some countries than from others. Mexicans, by far the largest category, account for roughly one in three first-generation immigrants—almost ten times more than any other nationality. The next largest groups are Filipinos and Indians, followed by Chinese, Vietnamese, Koreans, Cubans and Salvadorans—but none of these account for more than 3 or 4 percent of the total.

3　What do the newcomers do for a living? They tend to be clustered at both the top and the bottom of the job ladder. A large percentage work in dirty, demeaning, low-paid jobs that native-born Americans no longer want to do: busboys, chambermaids, farmhands, nurses' aides, sweatshop workers, on the assembly-line in meatpacking plants. But a large number also work at the top of the job pyramid: as scientists, engineers, nurses, high-tech entrepreneurs and the like. Two of the statistics that paint this picture most vividly are the percentage of U.S. farmhands who are foreign-born (an astonishing 80 percent) and the percentage of patents that are held by foreigners (an equally astonishing 26 percent). Social scientists call this a "barbell pattern," and it has some predictable corollaries. Not surprisingly, today's newcomers are either quite rich or quite poor, and they are either very well educated or hardly educated at all. Roughly a quarter have less than nine years of schooling, while an equal percentage have university degrees—a much larger share than the proportion of native-born Americans who have stayed in school that long.

4   Where in the United States do most immigrants settle? Until about ten years ago, they were concentrated in what demographers call "gateway cities": New York, Los Angeles, Miami, Houston, Chicago. But this is changing dramatically and with profound consequences for the country. States such as New York and California and New Jersey are still home to the largest numbers. But the states with the fastest growing immigrant populations are places like North Carolina, Georgia, Arkansas and Tennessee. Even Iowa more than doubled its share in the 1990s. The cities where the immigrant population expanded the most in the past decade are equally surprising: Greensboro, N.C., Charlotte, N.C., Raleigh, N.C., Atlanta and Las Vegas. Still more of a departure, while some of today's new arrivals still gravitate to urban areas, many head straight for the suburbs, and roughly half of all Asians and Latinos now live outside the center city. . . .

5   Most foreigners, whether they arrive legally or illegally, come to the United States to work. Most do not come in the expectation of living on welfare: most are not entitled to most kinds of benefits for at least five years. Thanks to modern technology, they generally know from other immigrants who have preceded them from their regions whether or not work is available. And in economic downturns, when there are fewer jobs to be had, fewer immigrants seem to make the trip. . . .

6   Of course, however hard they work, many poor, ill-educated immigrants who start at the bottom of the ladder remain there throughout their lives. This is not particularly surprising, and it may seem to vindicate those who claim that the United States today is importing a new lower class. But that's part of the point of our immigration policy: America no longer has this kind of working class, and it turns out that we need one. And even this does not necessarily mean the newcomers will not be absorbed into the economy or do well by it. Indeed while most brand-new arrivals make considerably less than the native-born, by the time they have been in the United States for ten or fifteen years, they are usually making more. (Mexicans seem to be an exception—and a troubling one—but despite their overwhelming numbers and the way this weights any statistical measure, the overall immigrant average is still a success story.) By the time they've been in the country for fifteen to twenty years, immigrants are also less likely than the native-born to be living in poverty.

7   The trajectory of high-end immigrants—those who come with some money or an education—is even more impressive. Immigrant entrepreneurship is nothing short of astonishing—in the first and second generation and beyond. Asian and Latino business start-up rates were four times the average American rate in the 1990s. Most of these minority-owned firms were small, and most had no paid employees—but that was also true of the businesses owned by native-born Americans. . . .

8   In some cases, immigrants are not merely assimilating into a regional economy: they dominate it. In Silicon Valley in the 1990s, foreign-born scientists accounted for a third of the scientific workforce, and Chinese and Indian entrepreneurs ran a quarter of the high-tech companies. In New York, by one estimate, Korean

immigrants own 70 percent of the independent groceries, 80 percent of the nail salons and 60 percent of the dry cleaners. In Los Angeles, an increasing share of the banks are Asian-owned, and newcomers—whether from the Middle East, North Africa or Korea—control most of the $22 billion fashion industry. Whatever one calls it, there can be little question, immigrants are finding their place—and generally a productive place—in the American economy. . . .

THE TENSIONS OF ASSIMILATION

9   Like many Asian-Americans of his generation, Eddie Liu* isn't quite sure how to place or describe himself. Born in Taiwan to professional parents who moved to the United States when he was two years old, Eddie grew up in a California suburb, speaking mostly English and absorbing the manners and morals he saw on television, hardly aware of any differences between himself and his mostly Anglo school friends. Going to college changed all that: by the mid–1990s, identity politics had taken over his University of California campus, and Eddie quickly learned to see himself as an Asian-American. He took courses in Asian-American studies, joined several Chinese-American organizations, decided he could date only Asian women and grew more and more skeptical about the United States—the typical trajectory of a young, hyphenated American in the age of multiculturalism.

10   By the time I met him, he was twenty-five, and his life reflected both of these younger selves. He lived in a comfortable Los Angeles suburb, drove an expensive late-model car, dated both Asian and white women and, though he worked for an internet company that targeted Asian-Americans, knew more about American popular culture than I did. A bright and engaging young man, he grew thoughtful and a little tentative when our conversation turned to ethnic identity. Asked whether he saw himself as an excluded minority or a "person of color," he laughed good-naturedly. "Hardly," he said. And yet, when asked about the word "assimilation," he was plainly uncomfortable. "I don't know," he mused, "not if it's a one-way street. Not if you're asking me to give up who I am and fit into some 1950s 'Leave It To Beaver' America. Of course, I'm American. But I'm not sure I'm assimilated—or want to be."

11   Eddie's ambivalence is far from unique. Like most immigrants in the past, the overwhelming majority of today's brand-new arrivals know why they have come to the United States: to make a better life for themselves and their children by becoming American. These newcomers struggle against all odds to fit in—finding jobs, learning the system, picking up the rudiments of the language. And with the exception of a few community leaders who draw their status and livelihood from their separate ethnicity, first-generation immigrants have no trouble with the word "assimilation." "I don't see why people would not want to assimilate," a Chinese-American newcomer said to me recently with a certainty typical of those born in another country.

12   But the second generation, be it Asian or Latino or some other group, is often far less clear about its relationship to the new place. Like Eddie, they know what they don't want. None seek to lose themselves and their cultural heritage in a bland,

*That isn't his real name.

homogenized America—assimilation as defined by the conformist, lily-white suburban neighborhoods of 1950s television and advertising. Multiculturalism combined with the sheer number of newcomers arriving today has laid that dream—if it ever really was anyone's dream—to rest forever. But nor do most voice the oppositional attitudes and color-coded divisiveness associated with identity politics. They are keen to make it in America, yet reject the metaphor of the melting pot—and desperately need a way to understand just who they are and how they fit in. . . .

MAKING IT INTO THE MAINSTREAM—AS HARD IF NOT HARDER THAN EVER

13   The story of immigrant absorption is as old as America, but the new arrivals and the country they are settling in are very different today than in the past. Yesterday's newcomers were ethnically more similar to the nation they were joining: like the native born, virtually all were of European stock. In contrast, today, most immigrants hail from the developing world, more than half of them from Latin-America and a quarter from Asia. Today's newcomers include skilled, middle-class people, but many are poor and uneducated and woefully unprepared to join the knowledge economy. (Some 60 percent of those from India, for example, have completed four years of college, but only 6 percent of refugees from Cambodia have, and the average Mexican arrives with 7.6 years of schooling.) Together, immigrants and their children account for more than 60 million people, or a fifth of all U.S. residents. And by 2050, if today's projections are borne out, a third of all Americans will be either Asian or Latino.

14   The America they come to is also different: at once more prosperous and unequal economically than it was a century ago, often making it harder for newcomers to assimilate into the middle class. The gap between rich and poor is wider than ever, creating what some social scientists call an "hourglass economy." In many cities, well-paid factory jobs have been replaced by service-sector work, and for some time now, real wages at the bottom of the pay scale have been declining rather than growing. On top of this, many newcomers settle in impoverished inner cities, where crime, drugs, gangs and broken families conspire to hinder their climb up the economic ladder. Getting an education—the most critical step in assimilating into the knowledge economy—is no easy matter in the barrios of, say, south central Los Angeles. . . .

15   Some immigrant enclaves are better off: many Asian-Americans in California, for example, live in leafy, upscale suburbs. But pleasant as they are, these neighborhoods can be as insular as any ghetto: their ethnic shopping malls, ethnic restaurants and groceries, in-language newspapers, one-country Rotary Clubs, community banks, ethnic movie theaters and other amenities often make it unnecessary to have much contact with the integrated mainstream. The more newcomers arrive from the old country, the larger and more all-encompassing these enclaves—both rich and poor—grow, reducing incentives to make the difficult transition to a mixed neighborhood. Meanwhile, geographic proximity and cheap air travel allow newcomers to shuttle back and forth to their home countries and, in some cases, to maintain dual citizenship and even vote in both places.

16   Then there are the cultural factors that conspire against assimilation: everything from the internet and niche advertising to color-coded identity politics. The attacks

of September 11, 2001, have sparked new patriotism and a new confidence in what brings us together as Americans. Some forty years after the Black Power movement and the ethnic revival it sparked among people of all backgrounds, the excesses of group chauvinism seem finally to be fading a bit. But no mere swing of the cultural pendulum is going to repeal multiculturalism or erase the profound effect it has had on the way most Americans live and view the world. From the relativism that now reigns in intellectual circles to the way Congress divides up into monolithic ethnic caucuses, multiculturalism has become the civil religion of the United States. . . .

17   The drumbeat of ethnocentric messages can be constant and unavoidable. In an inner city high school, native-born minority classmates tease you for listening and doing your homework—both widely condemned by poor blacks and Latinos as "acting white" or "selling out." If this doesn't deter you, if and when you get to college, you'll be assailed by campus ethnic activists pressing you to question why you want to join the mainstream, racist and exploitative as it is seen to be. By the time you've finished your education, according to one study, you'll be far less likely to consider yourself an American, or even a hyphenated American, than you were as a young teenager. In many cases, by then, you'll see yourself simply as an aggrieved minority or as what some are now calling "ampersand Americans"—as in "Mexican & American." . . .

18   We shouldn't exaggerate the threat. Today, as before in our history when the immigrant tide was rising, nativists peddle a frightening array of grim scenarios: balkanization, civil strife, economic ruin and worse. Very few of these nightmare visions are based in fact, and all are unlikely . . . . The nation is steadily absorbing tens of millions of newcomers: people of all ages and backgrounds who are finding work, learning English, making their way through school and up into more comfortable circumstances than they knew at home or when they first arrived in America. Still, like any wholesale social shift or personal transformation of this magnitude, the integration of today's influx needs watching—and occasional tending. . . .

A NEW INTELLECTUAL CURRENT

19 What about Eddie Liu and his doubts? Is what we as a nation want to encourage really *assimilation?* The very notion is almost a dirty word today. Some who oppose it are plainly extremists: people so taken with multiculturalism that they see being absorbed into a larger America as so much cultural "genocide." Yet Eddie is no activist, and concerns like his are widely felt, particularly in his generation. To young people like him, "assimilation" implies a forced conformity. They feel that it would require them to give up what makes them special, and they dread being reduced to what they see as the lowest common denominator of what it means to be American. As for the melting pot, if anything, that seems even more threatening: who wants to be melted down, after all—for the sake of national unity or anything else?

20   Meanwhile, at the other end of the political spectrum are those who think that, desirable as it is, assimilation is no longer possible in America. Some in this camp are driven by racial concerns: they view today's immigrants as simply too different ethnically ever to fit in in the United States. Others believe that the obstacles are cultural: that America has a distinct national ethos that cannot be

grasped by any but a few newcomers—the better educated, perhaps, or those from Christian Europe. Still others feel that the problem lies less in the foreign influx than in ourselves: that in the wake of multiculturalism and the upheavals of the 1960s, we as a nation have lost the confidence to assert who we are and what we believe in. But whatever their reasoning, all three kinds of pessimists have gained a wider hearing in the wake of 9/11 as the nation has grown ever more anxious about what many imagine are the unassimilated in our midst. And together, these two groups—those who believe assimilation is impossible and those who fear it—have come to dominate most discussion of the issue, leaving little room for those in the middle who take a more positive view. . . .

21   Hemmed in on both sides, hardly heard in the din of an often emotional debate, in fact, many of the thinkers who have thought longest and hardest about immigration believe that assimilation is still possible and indeed desirable, if not inevitable, today. They don't all like or use that word—for some of the same reasons that Eddie has trouble with it. Very few imagine that it should look as it looked in the 1950s: that it requires newcomers to forget their roots or abandon their inherited loyalties. And fewer still believe that it happens automatically—that it needs no tending or attention from the nation as a whole. Still, whatever word they use, these thinkers maintain that we as a nation not only can but must continue to absorb those who arrive on our shores: absorb them economically, culturally, politically and, perhaps most important, give them a sense that they belong.

FOR DISCUSSION

1. Of all the facts about immigration Jacoby provides, which ones surprised you the most? Which seem most important? Why?

2. Recent immigrants cluster at either the top or the bottom of our society—the "barbell pattern" the author refers to. In terms of actual numbers, however, most arrive poor and stay poor for some time. Given what Jacoby tells us and what you know about immigrants in general, is it accurate and fair to say we are importing a new lower class?

3. Summarize the complex view of assimilation Jacoby presents, being sure to include the opinions she characterizes as extreme and between which she seeks a middle ground. Where would you locate your own opinion in this spectrum of outlooks? How did you acquire your opinion?

FOR INQUIRY AND PERSUASION

"As for the melting pot . . . ," Jacoby asks, "who wants to be melted down . . . for the sake of national unity or anything else?" Find out as much as you can about your own background. Where did your family originate? How much of your culture of origin does your family preserve? How much is fading away or lost?

Write an essay defending the proposition that being American ought not to imply loss of our sense of origins and family cultural traditions.

One Nation, Out of Many: Why "Americanization" of Newcomers Is Still Important

SAMUEL HUNTINGTON

A professor of political science at Harvard, Samuel Huntington has been a leading intellectual voice for neoconservative views for many years. In the following article he argues that "Anglo Protestant culture, values, [and] institutions" formed America and must be preserved amid a large influx of immigrants from other traditions, especially from Mexico. Without stronger efforts to "Americanize" this latest wave of immigrants, we are in danger, he believes, of becoming two nations instead of one.

The following article appeared in *The American Enterprise.* It is an excerpt from his book *Who Are We? The Challenges to America's National Identity* (Simon and Schuster).

1   America's core culture has primarily been the culture of the seventeenth and eighteenth century settlers who founded our nation. The central elements of that culture are the Christian religion; Protestant values, including individualism, the work ethic, and moralism; the English language; British traditions of law, justice, and limits on government power; and a legacy of European art, literature, and philosophy. Out of this culture the early settlers formulated the American Creed, with its principles of liberty, equality, human rights, representative government, and private property. Subsequent generations of immigrants were assimilated into the culture of the founding settlers and modified it, but did not change it fundamentally. It was, after all, Anglo Protestant culture, values, institutions, and the opportunities they created that attracted more immigrants to America than to all the rest of the world. . . .

2   One has only to ask: Would America be the America it is today if in the seventeenth and eighteenth centuries it had been settled not by British Protestants but by French, Spanish, or Portuguese Catholics? The answer is no. It would not be America; it would be Quebec, Mexico, or Brazil. . . .

3   During the decades before World War I, the huge wave of immigrants flooding into America generated a major social movement devoted to Americanizing these new arrivals. It involved local, state, and national governments, private organizations, and businesses. Americanization became a key element in the Progressive phase of American politics, and was promoted by Theodore Roosevelt, Woodrow Wilson, and other leaders. . . .

4   The central institution for Americanization was the public school system. Indeed, public schools had been created in the nineteenth century and shaped in considerable part by the perceived need to Americanize and Protestantize immigrants. "People looked to education as the best way to transmit Anglo-American Protestant values and to prevent the collapse of republican institutions," summarizes historian Carl Kaestle. In 1921–22, as many as a thousand communities conducted "special public school programs to Americanize the foreign-born." Between 1915 and 1922, more than 1 million immigrants enrolled in such programs. School

systems "saw public education as an instrument to create a unified society out of the multiplying diversity created by immigration," reports Reed Ueda.

5   Without these Americanizing activities starting in the early 1890s, America's dramatic 1924 reduction in immigration would in all likelihood have been imposed much earlier. Americanization made immigration acceptable to Americans. The success of the movement was manifest when the immigrants and their children rallied to the colors and marched off to fight their country's wars. In World War II in particular, racial, ethnic, and class identities were subordinated to national loyalty, and the identification of Americans with their country reached its highest point in history.

6   National identity then began to fade. In 1994, 19 scholars of American history and politics were asked to evaluate the level of American unity in 1930, 1950, 1970, and 1990. The year 1950, according to these experts, was the "zenith of American national integration." Since then "cultural and political fragmentation has increased" and "conflict emanating from intensified ethnic and religious consciousness poses the main current challenge to the American nation."

7   Fanning all of this was the new popularity among liberal elites of the doctrines of "multiculturalism" and "diversity," which elevate subnational, racial, ethnic, cultural, gender, and other identities over national identity, and encourage immigrants to maintain dual identities, loyalties, and citizenships. Multiculturalism is basically an anti-Western ideology. Multiculturalists argue that white Anglo America has suppressed other cultural alternatives, and that America in the future should not be a society with a single pervasive national culture, but instead should become a "tossed salad" of many starkly different ingredients.

8   In sharp contrast to their predecessors, American political leaders have recently promoted measures consciously designed to weaken America's cultural identity and strengthen racial, ethnic, and other identities. President Clinton called for a "great revolution" to liberate Americans from their dominant European culture. Vice President Gore interpreted the nation's motto, *E pluribus unum* (Out of many, one), to mean "out of one, many." By 1992, even some liberals like Arthur Schlesinger, Jr. were warning that the "ethnic upsurge" which had begun "as a gesture of protest against the Anglocentric culture" had become "a cult, and today it threatens to become a counterrevolution against the original theory of America as 'one people,' a common culture, a single nation."

9   These efforts by members of government to deconstruct the nation they led are, quite possibly, without precedent in human history. And important parts of academia, the media, business, and the professions joined them in the effort. A study by Paul Vitz of 22 school texts published in the 1970s and 1980s for grades three and six found that only five out of 670 stories and articles in these readers had "any patriotic theme." All five dealt with the American Revolution; none had "anything to do with American history since 1780." In four of the five stories the principal person is a girl, in three the same girl, Sybil Ludington. The 22 books lack any story "featuring Nathan Hale, Patrick Henry, Daniel Boone, or Paul Revere's ride." "Patriotism," Vitz concludes, "is close to nonexistent" in these readers.

10   The deconstructionist coalition, however, does not include most Americans. In poll after poll, majorities of Americans reject ideas and measures that would lessen

national identity and promote subnational identities. Everyday Americans remain deeply patriotic, nationalistic in their outlook, and committed to their national culture, creed, and identity. A major gap has thus developed between portions of our elite and the bulk of our populace over what America is and should be. . . .

11   The current wave of immigration to the U.S. has increased with each decade. During the 1960s, 3 million people entered the country. During the 1980s, 7 million people did. In the 1990s it was over 9 million. The foreign born percentage of the American population, which was a bit above 5 percent in 1960, more than doubled to close to 12 percent in 2002.

12   The United States thus appears to face something new in its history: persistent high levels of immigration. The two earlier waves of heavy immigration (1840s and 50s; and 1880s to 1924) subsided as a result of world events. But absent a serious war or economic collapse, over 1 million immigrants are likely to enter the United States each year for the indefinite future. This may cause assimilation to be slower and less complete than it was for past waves of immigration.

13   That seems to be happening with today's immigration from Latin America, especially from Mexico. Mexican immigration is leading toward a demographic "reconquista" of areas Americans took from Mexico by force in the 1830s and 1840s. Mexican immigration is very different from immigration from other sources, due to its sheer size, its illegality, and its other special qualities.

14   One reason Mexican immigration is special is simply because there are now so very many arrivals (legal and illegal) from that one country. Thanks to heavy Mexican inflows, for the very first time in history a majority of U.S. immigrants now speak a single non-English language, Spanish. The impact of today's large flow of Mexican immigrants is reinforced by other factors: the proximity of their country of origin; their geographical concentration within the U.S.; the improbability of their inflow ending or being significantly reduced; the decline of the assimilation movement; and the new enthusiasm of many American elites for multiculturalism, bilingualism, affirmative action, and cultural diversity instead of cultural unity. In addition, the Mexican government now actively promotes the export of its people to the United States while encouraging them to maintain their Mexican culture, identity, and nationality. President Vicente Fox regularly refers to himself as the president of 123 million Mexicans, 100 million in Mexico, 23 million in the United States. The net result is that Mexican immigrants and their progeny have not assimilated into American society as other immigrants did in the past, or as many other immigrants are doing now. . . .

15   Problems in digesting Mexican immigrants would be less urgent if Mexicans were just one group among many. But because legal and illegal Mexicans comprise such a large proportion of our current immigrant flow, any assimilation problems arising within their ranks shape our immigrant experience. The overwhelming influence of Mexicans on America's immigration flow becomes clearly visible if one poses a thought experiment. What if Mexican immigration to the U.S. somehow abruptly stopped, while other immigration continued as at present? In such a case, illegal entries in particular would diminish dramatically. Agriculture and other

businesses in the southwest would be disrupted, but the wages of low-income Americans would rise. Debates over the use of Spanish, and whether English should be made the official language of state and national governments, would fade away. Bilingual education and the controversies it spawns would decline. So also would controversies over welfare and other benefits for immigrants. The debate over whether immigrants are an economic burden on state and federal governments would be decisively resolved in the negative. The average education and skills of the immigrants coming to America would rise to levels unprecedented in American history. Our inflow of immigrants would again become highly diverse, which would increase incentives for all immigrants to learn English and absorb American culture. The possibility of a split between a predominantly Spanish-speaking America and English-speaking America would disappear, and with it a major potential threat to the cultural and possibly political integrity of the United States.

16   A glimpse of what a splintering of America into English- and Spanish-speaking camps might look like can be found in current day Miami. Since the 1960s, first Cuban and then other Latin American immigrants have converted Miami from a fairly normal American city into a heavily Hispanic city. By 2000 Spanish was not just the language spoken in most homes in Miami, it was also the principal language of commerce, business, and politics. The local media and communications are increasingly Hispanic. In 1998, a Spanish language television station became the number one station watched by Miamians—the first time a foreign-language station achieved that rating in a major American city. . . .

17   Is Miami the future for Los Angeles and the southwest generally? In the end, the results could be similar: the creation of a large, distinct, Spanish-speaking community with economic and political resources sufficient to sustain its own Hispanic identity apart from the national identity of other Americans, and also sufficient to significantly influence American politics, government, and society. The process by which this might come about, however, is different. The Hispanization of Miami has been led from the top down by successful Cuban and other Central and South American immigrants. In the southwest, the overwhelming bulk of Spanish-speaking immigrants are Mexican, and have been poor, unskilled, and poorly educated. It appears that many of their offspring are likely to be similar. The pressures toward Hispanization in the southwest thus come from below, whereas those in South Florida came from above. . . .

18   The continuation of high levels of Mexican and Hispanic immigration and low rates of assimilation of these immigrants into American society and culture could eventually change America into a country of two languages, two cultures, and two peoples. This will not only transform America. It will also have deep consequences for Hispanics—who will be in America but not of the America that has existed for centuries.

FOR DISCUSSION

1. In the previous selection, Tamar Jacoby characterized one view of immigration as based on the assumption or fear that many of the new immigrants cannot be "Americanized"—that is, assimilated. Is that Huntington's view? What is the problem with "Americanization" as Huntington sees it?

2. According to Huntington, patriotic values are not being taught much in our schools. Based on your own experience as a high school student or as a parent of high school children, would you agree? If you do, should this change?

3. We all have what Huntington calls "subnational" aspects of identity, dimensions of what we are based on race, ethnicity, culture, class, and gender, among other differences. He believes that these subnational aspects have become too important, even more important than loyalty to the United States. Is he right? That is, do you recognize such attitudes in your own life? In other people you know well?

FOR RESEARCH, DISCUSSION, AND CONVINCING

As a class project, find out all you can about Hispanic immigration in general and immigration from Mexico in particular. Discuss the implications of the various points of view and the information you discover.

Then write an essay that addresses the question Huntington raises: Are we on the way to becoming two countries? Does the large influx of Hispanics pose a serious, long-term threat to U.S. national identity?

Cartoon: Playing POLITICS with the Border

JEFF KOTERBA

Like most political cartoons, this one makes a simple point forcefully: Politics may be the real barrier to handling illegal immigration intelligently.

Jeff Koterba. © North American Syndicate.

FOR DISCUSSION

Most of us get impatient with politics at least sometimes, and the accusation of "playing politics" with some serious issue is a frequent criticism. But in what way are our impatience and that accusation misdirected?

The Border

ROSS DOUTHAT AND JENNY WOODSON

This compact, fact-filled article and graphic appeared in *The Atlantic Monthly* (January–February 2006).

1   More than 1.3 million people were caught trying to enter the United States illegally from Mexico in 2004. Nearly 200,000 were attempting to cross, often concealed in vehicles, at one of the twenty-five U.S.-Mexican Customs stations; most of the rest—those indicated on the map [on pages 522–523]—were apprehended by the U.S. Border Patrol, while making their way across the Rio Grande or the Sonora Desert or through the fences and other barriers separating Tijuana from southern California.

2   The Border Patrol has become much larger and more sophisticated in recent decades. Since the current wave of illegal Mexican immigration began, in the mid-1970s, the number of agents along the southern U.S. border has risen from 2,000 to 11,000. Roadways have been extended into remote areas to give agents better access to smuggling routes; floodlights, motion sensors, and remote video cameras have been installed; and agents have started patrolling in aircraft as well as on the ground. Last year the Border Patrol deployed a "Predator B" unmanned aerial vehicle—the first American UAV put to civilian use. It provides real-time bird's-eye views of previously inaccessible areas, transmitting images that are quickly relayed to agents on the ground.

3   But, of course, the migrants keep slipping through. The Border Patrol will not speculate about how many evade capture and enter the United States; the Pew Hispanic Center recently estimated that, on average, 485,000 Mexicans have crossed the border illegally every year since 2000, and that more illegal than legal aliens have entered the country altogether since 1995.

4   Immigration pressure from Mexico is unlikely to abate anytime soon. Nearly half of all Mexicans asked by Pew said they would come to the United States immediately if they had "the means and opportunity." Twenty-one percent said they would do so even if they had to come illegally. Indeed, many Mexicans seem to have a sense of entitlement regarding the United States: 58 percent surveyed in a 2002 Zogby poll believe that "the territory of the United States' Southwest rightfully belongs to Mexico."

5   Americans are unhappy about this state of affairs: according to recent polls, most favor beefing up the enforcement of immigration laws and using troops to police the border. A majority even voiced support for the Minuteman Project, a group of civilian vigilantes who have begun patrolling the border themselves.

6   However, political leaders in both parties (along with many business organizations, media outlets, and bipartisan interest groups) see the issue differently, believing that restricting immigration is not economically desirable. The immigration proposals currently circulating in Washington seem unlikely to reduce the influx from the south. They are aimed instead at regularizing it, by creating a temporary-visa program for migrant laborers. Although such a "guest worker" program might

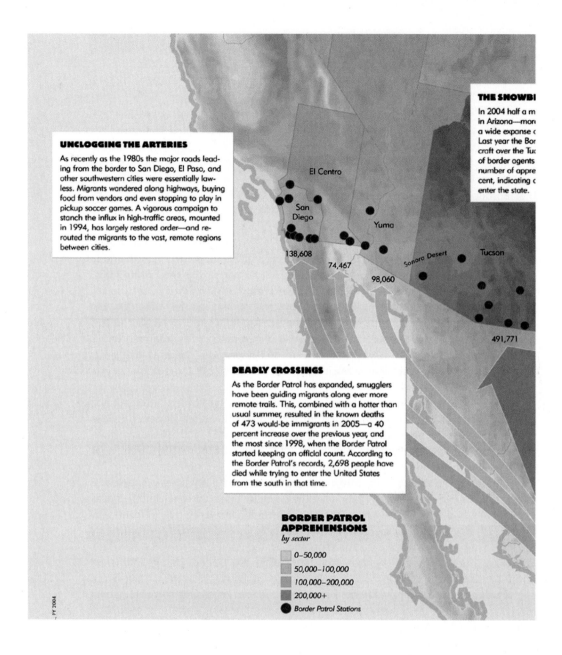

UNCLOGGING THE ARTERIES

As recently as the 1980s the major roads leading from the border to San Diego, El Paso, and other southwestern cities were essentially lawless. Migrants wandered along highways, buying food from vendors and even stopping to play in pickup soccer games. A vigorous campaign to stanch the influx in high-traffic areas, mounted in 1994, has largely restored order—and re-routed the migrants to the vast, remote regions between cities.

THE SNOWBI

In 2004 half a m in Arizona—mor a wide expanse Last year the Bor craft over the Tuc of border agents number of appre cent, indicating enter the state.

DEADLY CROSSINGS

As the Border Patrol has expanded, smugglers have been guiding migrants along ever more remote trails. This, combined with a hotter than usual summer, resulted in the known deaths of 473 would-be immigrants in 2005—a 40 percent increase over the previous year, and the most since 1998, when the Border Patrol started keeping an official count. According to the Border Patrol's records, 2,698 people have died while trying to enter the United States from the south in that time.

BORDER PATROL APPREHENSIONS
by sector

- 0–50,000
- 50,000–100,000
- 100,000–200,000
- 200,000+
- Border Patrol Stations

be paired with legislation to tighten border security and curb the hiring of illegal immigrants, as President Bush suggested in a November policy speech, there's reason to doubt that serious restrictions would actually result. The last major immigration reform, in 1986, was supposed to provide a similar tradeoff—an amnesty program for illegal aliens already in the United States was joined to commitment to crack down on employers of illegal immigrants. The amnesty was

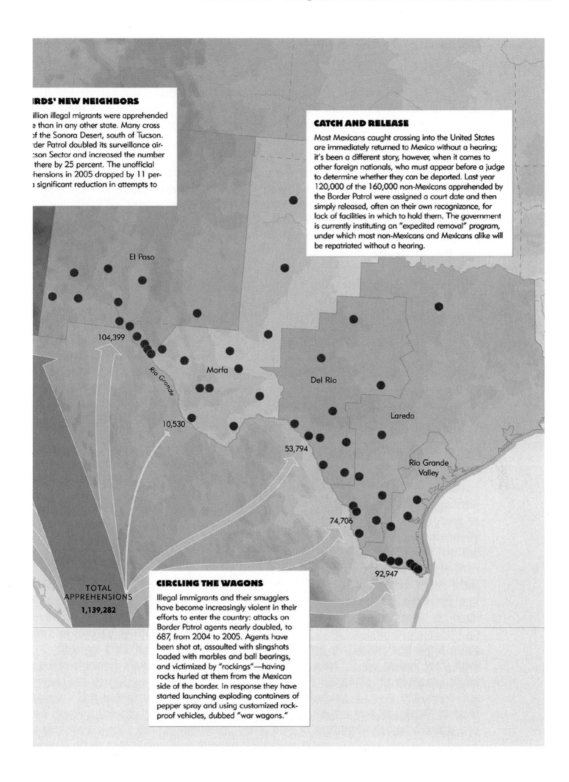

IRDS' NEW NEIGHBORS

illion illegal migrants were apprehended
e than in any other state. Many cross
of the Sonora Desert, south of Tucson.
der Patrol doubled its surveillance air-
son Sector and increased the number
there by 25 percent. The unofficial
hensions in 2005 dropped by 11 per-
a significant reduction in attempts to

CATCH AND RELEASE

Most Mexicans caught crossing into the United States
are immediately returned to Mexico without a hearing;
it's been a different story, however, when it comes to
other foreign nationals, who must appear before a judge
to determine whether they can be deported. Last year
120,000 of the 160,000 non-Mexicans apprehended by
the Border Patrol were assigned a court date and then
simply released, often on their own recognizance, for
lack of facilities in which to hold them. The government
is currently instituting an "expedited removal" program,
under which most non-Mexicans and Mexicans alike will
be repatriated without a hearing.

El Paso

104,399

Rio Grande

Marfa

Del Rio

10,530

Laredo

53,794

Rio Grande
Valley

74,706

92,947

TOTAL
APPREHENSIONS
1,139,282

CIRCLING THE WAGONS

Illegal immigrants and their smugglers
have become increasingly violent in their
efforts to enter the country: attacks on
Border Patrol agents nearly doubled, to
687, from 2004 to 2005. Agents have
been shot at, assaulted with slingshots
loaded with marbles and ball bearings,
and victimized by "rockings"—having
rocks hurled at them from the Mexican
side of the border. In response they have
started launching exploding containers of
pepper spray and using customized rock-
proof vehicles, dubbed "war wagons."

7 implemented; the crackdown fizzled out. And in December of 2004 Congress authorized the addition of 10,000 Border Patrol agents over a five-year period beginning in 2006—but only 210 new positions were funded for this year.

7 This gap between popular and elite opinion means that the porousness of the border is becoming a potent issue, especially for working-class voters, whose jobs may be vulnerable to guest-worker programs. Tom Tancredo, a Republican congressman from Colorado, has threatened to make an insurgent run for the 2008 GOP presidential nomination if no other candidate comes out strongly against illegal immigration, and observers speculate that Democrats might use the issue to try to outflank the GOP on the right. (Last year the governors of New Mexico and Arizona, both Democrats, declared states of emergency because of the influx of illegal immigrants, blaming the federal government for failing to secure the border.)

8 Nativist politics hasn't fared well in recent decades. And securing the border may not be feasible no matter what the public wants—at least absent a heavy military presence and the sorts of barriers used in Cold War Berlin and the Korean DMZ. (Spending on border security rose dramatically during the 1990s, but so did the number of illegal immigrants.) However, unless the gap on this issue between America's leaders and its citizenry is somehow narrowed, whether by stringent reform or by rising economic optimism on Main Street, a populist backlash could ensue—against both illegal immigrants themselves and those many see as their enablers in Washington.

FOR DISCUSSION

1. This article is an example of one kind of slightly disguised argument. It seems to be informative and, of course, is. But the information implies conclusions, arguable contentions, some spelled out, some not. What conclusions both explicit and implicit do you find?

2. What information were you unaware of? What surprised you the most? What conclusions do you draw from the information you now have? Are any of your conclusions different from the viewpoint of the authors?

3. Border control is a topic of much casual, often heated discussion. The graphic depicts the magnitude of the problem well and mentions the vast amount of manpower and money devoted to apprehending undocumented aliens. In your view, is the effort worthwhile?

FOR RESEARCH, DISCUSSION, AND MEDIATION

Many commentators point to the gap between the opinions of many ordinary Americans and those of the so-called elite concerning immigration. All the articles so far allude to it, and "The Border" highlights it. Basically, the popular view is generally anti-immigration and strongly for increased efforts to control the border with Mexico. Elite opinion—professors who study immigration, big business concerns, and many politicians—tend to be more pro-immigration and skeptical of efforts to control the border.

Do research on this rift in opinion, including current legislative proposals in Congress, which reflect the sharp contrast. Discuss the implications of what you turn up, being sure to reflect on *why* popular opinion moves one way and elite opinion another.

Then write an essay proposing an approach to border control designed to give both sides some of what they want. Defend it as a practical, middle-of-the-road way of better coping with this difficult problem.

The Realities of Immigration

LINDA CHAVEZ

Chairperson of the Center for Equal Opportunity in Washington, D.C. and author of *Out of the Barrio* (1991), Linda Chavez is a frequent and perceptive commentator on immigration. She argues here that large-scale immigration from Mexico does not pose the threat some make it out to be, but we need a guest-worker program coupled with other measures to bring our border under greater control.

Her article appeared in *Commentary* (July–August 2006).

1   What to do about immigration—both legal and illegal—has become one of the most controversial public-policy debates in recent memory. But why it has occurred at this particular moment is something of a mystery. The rate of immigration into the U.S., although high, is still below what it was even a few years ago, the peak having been reached in the late 1990's. President Bush first talked about comprehensive immigration reform almost immediately after assuming office, but he put the plan on hold after 9/11 and only reintroduced the idea in 2004. Why the current flap?

2   By far the biggest factor shaping the popular mood seems to have been the almost daily drumbeat on the issue from political talk-show hosts, most prominently CNN's Lou Dobbs and the Fox News Channel's Bill O'Reilly and Sean Hannity (both of whom also have popular radio shows), syndicated radio hosts Rush Limbaugh, Laura Ingraham, Michael Savage, and G. Gordon Liddy, and a plethora of local hosts reaching tens of millions of listeners each week. Stories about immigration have become a staple of cable news, with sensational footage of illegal crossings featured virtually every day.

3   Media saturation has led, in turn, to the emergence of immigration as a wedge issue in the . . . 2008 presidential campaign. Several aspiring Republican candidates—former House Speaker Newt Gingrich, Senate Majority Leader Bill Frist, and Senator George Allen—have worked to burnish their "get tough" credentials, while, on the other side of the issue, Senator John McCain has come forward as the lead sponsor of a bill to allow most illegal aliens to earn legal status. For their part, potential Democratic candidates have remained largely mum, unsure how the issue plays with their various constituencies.

4   And then there are the immigrants themselves, who have shown surprising political muscle, especially in response to legislation passed by the House that would turn the illegal aliens among them into felons. Millions of mostly Hispanic protesters have taken to the streets in our big cities in recent months, waving American flags and (more controversially) their own national flags while demanding recognition and better treatment. Though Hispanic leaders and pro-immigrant advocates point to the protests as evidence of a powerful new civil-rights movement, many other Americans see the demonstrators as proof of an alien invasion—and a looming threat to the country's prosperity and unity.

5   In short, it is hard to recall a time when there has been so much talk about immigration and immigration reform—or when so much of the talk has been misinformed, misleading, and ahistorical. Before policy-makers can decide what to

do about immigration, the problem itself needs to be better defined, not just in terms of costs and benefits but in relation to America's deepest values.

6   Contrary to popular myth, immigrants have never been particularly welcome in the United States. Americans have always tended to romanticize the immigrants of their grandparents' generation while casting a skeptical eye on contemporary newcomers. In the first decades of the 20th century, descendants of Northern European immigrants resisted the arrival of Southern and Eastern Europeans, and today the descendants of those once unwanted Italians, Greeks, and Poles are deeply distrustful of current immigrants from Latin America. Congressman Tom Tancredo, a Republican from Colorado and an outspoken advocate of tighter restrictions, is fond of invoking the memory of his Italian immigrant grandfather to argue that he is not anti-immigrant, just anti-*illegal* immigration. He fails to mention that at the time his grandfather arrived, immigrants simply had to show up on American shores (or walk across the border) to gain legal entry. . . .

7   The modern immigration era commenced in 1965 with the passage of the Immigration and Nationality Act, which abolished all national-origin quotas, gave preference to close relatives of American citizens, refugees, and individuals with certain skills, and allowed for immigrants from the Western hemisphere on a first-come, first-served basis. The act's passage drew a huge wave, much of it from Latin America and Asia. From 1970 to 2000, the United States admitted more than 20 million persons as permanent residents.

8   By 2000, some 3 million of these new residents were formerly illegal aliens who had gained amnesty as part of the 1986 Immigration Reform and Control Act (IRCA). This, Congress's first serious attempt to stem the flow of illegal immigration, forced employers to determine the status of their workers and imposed heavy penalties on those hiring illegal entrants. But from the beginning, the law was fraught with problems. It created huge bureaucratic burdens, even for private individuals wanting to hire someone to cut their lawn or care for their children, and spawned a vast new document-fraud industry for immigrants eager to get hold of the necessary paperwork. The law has been a monumental failure. Today, some 11.5 million illegal aliens reside in the U.S.—quadruple the population of two decades ago, when IRCA was enacted—and the number is growing by an estimated 500,000 a year. . . .

9   The real question is not whether the U.S. has the means to stop illegal immigration—no doubt, with sufficient resources, we could mostly do so—but whether we would be better off as a nation without these workers. Restrictionists claim that large-scale immigration—legal and illegal—has depressed wages, burdened government resources, and acted as a net drain on the economy. The Federation for American Immigration Reform (FAIR), the most prominent of the pressure groups on the issue, argues that, because of this influx, hourly earnings among American males have not increased appreciably in 30 years. As the restrictionists see it, if the U.S. got serious about defending its borders, there would be plenty of Americans willing to do the jobs now performed by workers from abroad. . . .

10   Despite the presence in our workforce of millions of illegal immigrants, the U.S. is currently creating slightly more than two million jobs a year and boasts an

unemployment rate of 4.7 percent, which is lower than the average in each of the past four decades. More to the point perhaps, when the National Research Council (NRC) of the National Academy of Sciences evaluated the economic impact of immigration in its landmark 1997 study *The New Americans: Economic, Demographic, and Fiscal Effects of Immigration,* it found only a small negative impact on the earnings of Americans, and even then, only for workers at lower skill and education levels.

11   Moreover, the participation of immigrants in the labor force has had obvious positive effects. The NRC estimated that roughly 5 percent of household expenditures in the U.S. went to goods and services produced by immigrant labor—labor whose relative cheapness translated into lower prices for everything from chicken to new homes. These price advantages, the study found, were "spread quite uniformly across most types of domestic consumers," with a slightly greater benefit for higher-income households.

12   Many restrictionists argue that if Americans would simply cut their own lawns, clean their own houses, and care for their own children, there would be no need for immigrant labor. But even if this were true, the overall economy would hardly benefit from having fewer workers. If American women were unable to rely on immigrants to perform some household duties, more of them would be forced to stay home. A smaller labor force would also have devastating consequences when it comes to dealing with the national debt and government-funded entitlements like Social Security and Medicare, a point repeatedly made by former Federal Reserve Board Chairman Alan Greenspan. As he told a Senate committee in 2003, "short of a major increase in immigration, economic growth cannot be safely counted upon to eliminate deficits and the difficult choices that will be required to restore fiscal discipline." The following year, Greenspan noted that offsetting the fiscal effects of our own declining birthrate would require a level of immigration "much larger than almost all current projections assume."

13   The contributions that immigrants make to the economy must be weighed, of course, against the burdens they impose. FAIR and other restrictionist groups contend that immigrants are a huge drain on society because of the cost of providing public services to them—some $67 to $87 billion a year, according to one commonly cited study. Drawing on numbers from the NRC's 1997 report, FAIR argues that "the net fiscal drain on American taxpayers [from immigration] is between $166 and $226 a year per native household."

14   There is something to these assertions, though less than may at first appear. Much of the anxiety and resentment generated by immigrants is, indeed, a result of the very real costs they impose on state and local governments, especially in border states like California and Arizona. Providing education and health care to the children of immigrants is particularly expensive, and the federal government picks up only a fraction of the expense. But, again, there are countervailing factors. Illegal immigrants are hardly free-riders. An estimated three-quarters of them paid federal taxes in 2002, amounting to $7 billion in Social Security contributions and $1.5 billion in Medicare taxes, plus withholding for income taxes. They also pay state and local sales taxes and (as homeowners and renters) property taxes.

15   Moreover, FAIR and its ilk have a penchant for playing fast and loose with numbers. To support its assessment of immigration's overall fiscal burden, for instance, FAIR ignores the explicit cautions in a later NRC report about cross-sectional analyses that exclude the "concurrent descendants" of immigrants—that is, their adult children. These, overwhelmingly, are productive members of the workforce. As the NRC notes, when this more complete picture is taken into account, immigrants have "a positive federal impact of about $1,260 [per capita], exceeding their net cost [$680 per capita on average] at the state and local levels." Restrictionists also argue that fewer immigrants would mean more opportunities for low-skilled native workers. Of late, groups like the Minuteman Project have even taken to presenting themselves as champions of unemployed American blacks (a curious tactic, to say the least, considering the views on race and ethnicity of many in the anti-immigrant camp*).

16   But here, too, the factual evidence is mixed. Wages for American workers who have less than a high-school education have probably been adversely affected by large-scale immigration; the economist George Borjas estimates a reduction of 8 percent in hourly wages for native-born males in that category. But price competition is not the only reason that many employers favor immigrants over poorly educated natives. Human capital includes motivation, and there could hardly be two more disparately motivated groups than U.S.-born high-school drop-outs and their foreign-born rivals in the labor market. Young American men usually leave high school because they become involved with drugs or crime, have difficulty with authority, cannot maintain regular hours, or struggle with learning. Immigrants, on the other hand, have demonstrated enormous initiative, reflecting, in the words of President Reagan, "a special kind of courage that enabled them to leave their own land, leave their friends and their countrymen, and come to this new and strange land."

17   Just as important, they possess a strong desire to work. Legal immigrants have an 86-percent rate of participation in the labor force; illegal immigrant males have a 94-percent rate. By contrast, among white males with less than a high-school education, the participation rate is 46 percent, while among blacks it is 40 percent. If all immigrants, or even only illegal aliens, disappeared from the American work-force, can anyone truly believe that poorly skilled whites and blacks would fill the gap? To the contrary, productivity would likely decline, and employers in many sectors would simply move their operations to countries like Mexico, China, and the Philippines, where many of our immigrants come from in the first place.

18   Of equal weight among foes of immigration are the cultural changes wrought by today's newcomers, especially those from Mexico. In his book *Who Are We? The Challenges to National Identity* (2004), the eminent political scientist Samuel P. Huntington warns that "Mexican immigration is leading toward the demographic *reconquista* of areas Americans took from Mexico by force in the 1830's and 1840's." . . .

---

*As the author and anti-immigration activist Peter Brimelow wrote in his 1995 book *Alien Nation,* "Americans have a legitimate interest in their country's racial balance . . . [and] a right to insist that their government stop shifting it." Himself an immigrant from England, Brimelow wants "more immigrants who look like me."

19   Does it not seem likely that today's immigrants—because of their numbers, the constant flow of even more newcomers, and their proximity to their countries of origin—will be unable or unwilling to assimilate as previous ethnic groups have done?

20   There is no question that some public policies in the U.S. have actively discouraged assimilation. Bilingual education, the dominant method of instruction of Hispanic immigrant children for some 30 years, is the most obvious culprit, with its emphasis on retaining Spanish. But bilingual education is on the wane, having been challenged by statewide initiatives in California (1998), Arizona (2000), and Massachusetts (2004), and by policy shifts in several major cities and at the federal level. States that have moved to English-immersion instruction have seen test scores for Hispanic youngsters rise, in some cases substantially.

21   Evidence from the culture at large is also encouraging. On most measures of social and economic integration, Hispanic immigrants and their descendants have made steady strides up the ladder. English is the preferred language of virtually all U.S.-born Hispanics; indeed, according to a 2002 national survey by the Pew Hispanic Center and the Kaiser Family Foundation, 78 percent of third-generation Mexican-Americans cannot speak Spanish at all. In education, 86 percent of U.S.-born Hispanics complete high school, compared with 92 percent of non-Hispanic whites, and the drop-out rate among immigrant children who enroll in high school after they come here is no higher than for the native-born. . . .

22   As for the effect of Hispanic immigrants on the country's social fabric, the NRC found that they are more likely than other Americans to live with their immediate relatives: 88.6 percent of Mexican immigrant households are made up of families, compared with 69.5 percent of non-Hispanic whites and 68.3 percent of blacks. These differences are partially attributable to the age structure of the Hispanic population, which is younger on average than the white or black population. But even after adjusting for age and immigrant generation, U.S. residents of Hispanic origin—and especially those from Mexico—are much more likely to live in family households. Despite increased out-of-wedlock births among Hispanics, about 67 percent of American children of Mexican origin live in two-parent families, as compared with 77 percent of white children but only 37 percent of black children.

23   Perhaps the strongest indicator of Hispanic integration into American life is the population's high rate of intermarriage. About a quarter of all Hispanics marry outside their ethnic group, almost exclusively to non-Hispanic white spouses, a rate that has remained virtually unchanged since 1980. And here a significant fact has been noted in a 2005 study by the Population Reference Bureau—namely, that "the majority of inter-Hispanic children are reported as Hispanic." Such intermarriages themselves, the study goes on, "may have been a factor in the phenomenal growth of the U.S. Hispanic population in recent years."

24   It has been widely predicted that, by mid-century, Hispanics will represent fully a quarter of the U.S. population. Such predictions fail to take into account that increasing numbers of these "Hispanics" will have only one grandparent or great-grandparent of Hispanic heritage. By that point, Hispanic ethnicity may well mean neither more nor less than German, Italian, or Irish ethnicity means today.

25   How, then, to proceed? Congress is under growing pressure to strengthen border control, but unless it also reaches some agreement on more comprehensive reforms, stauncher enforcement is unlikely to have much of an effect. With a growing economy and more jobs than our own population can readily absorb, the U.S. will continue to need immigrants. Illegal immigration already responds reasonably well to market forces. It has increased during boom times like the late 1990's and decreased again when jobs disappear, as in the latest recession. Trying to determine an ideal number makes no more sense than trying to predict how much steel or how many textiles we ought to import; government quotas can never match the efficiency of simple supply and demand. As President Bush has argued—and as the Senate has now agreed—a guest-worker program is the way to go.

26   Does this mean the U.S. should just open its borders to anyone who wants to come? Hardly. We still need an orderly process, one that includes background checks to insure that terrorists and criminals are not being admitted. It also makes sense to require that immigrants have at least a basic knowledge of English and to give preference to those who have advanced skills or needed talents.

27   Moreover, immigrants themselves have to take more responsibility for their status. Illegal aliens from Mexico now pay significant sums of money to "coyotes" who sneak them across the border. If they could come legally as guest workers, that same money might be put up as a surety bond to guarantee their return at the end of their employment contract, or perhaps to pay for health insurance. Nor is it good policy to allow immigrants to become welfare recipients or to benefit from affirmative action: restrictions on both sorts of programs have to be written into law and stringently applied.

28   A market-driven guest-worker program might be arranged in any number of ways. A proposal devised by the Vernon K. Krieble Foundation, a policy group based in Colorado, suggests that government-licensed, private-sector employment agencies be put in charge of administering the effort, setting up offices in other countries to process applicants and perform background checks. Workers would be issued tamper-proof identity cards only after signing agreements that would allow for deportation if they violated the terms of their contract or committed crimes in the U.S. Although the Krieble plan would offer no path to citizenship, workers who wanted to change their status could still apply for permanent residency and, ultimately, citizenship through the normal, lengthy process.

29   Do such schemes stand a chance politically? A poll commissioned by the Krieble Foundation found that most Americans (except those with less than a high-school education) consider an "efficient system for handling guest workers" to be more important than expanded law enforcement in strengthening the country's border. Similarly, a CNN tracking poll in May found that 81 percent of respondents favored legislation permitting illegal immigrants who have been in the U.S. more than five years to stay here and apply for citizenship, provided they had jobs and paid back taxes. True, other polls have contradicted these results, suggesting public ambivalence on the issue—and an openness to persuasion.

30   Regardless of what Congress does or does not do—the odds in favor of an agreement between the Senate and House on final legislation are still no better

than 50-50—immigration is likely to continue at high levels for the foreseeable future. Barring a recession or another terrorist attack, the U.S. economy is likely to need some 1.5 to 2 million immigrants a year for some time to come. It would be far better for all concerned if those who wanted to work in the U.S. and had jobs waiting for them here could do so legally, in the light of day and with the full approval of the American people.

FOR DISCUSSION

1. Chavez thinks that media attention and politics are responsible for the current spotlight on immigration—implying that the issue is hyped, overblown. Based on what you have read in this section and your own knowledge, would you agree? Why or why not?

2. Chavez makes a strong case for the economic necessity of immigrant workers. Summarize her position, including her effort to refute viewpoints such as FAIR's. Do you find her case convincing? Why or why not? If you agree, what implications does your assent have for immigration policy? If you disagree, what implications does your dissent have?

3. Compare Chavez's view of the assimilation of Mexican immigrants with Samuel Huntington's in his selection in this chapter. Who makes the stronger case? If you think Chavez does, what points does Huntington make that must be taken into account? If Huntington does, what does Chavez say that merits attention?

FOR RESEARCH AND CONVINCING

There is a great deal of resentment toward illegal immigration at the level of local government, both state and city. It is not hard to see why—local government bears much of the cost of services required for undocumented workers. Investigate this problem and then write a paper urging the federal government to take on more of the costs of illegal immigration.

The Border Patrol State

LESLIE MARMON SILKO

Whenever illegal immigration is discussed, someone asserts that we have lost control of our borders. The contention is typically accepted as a fact rather than thought about seriously. This classic article examines the notion seriously, while calling attention to violations of the civil rights of American citizens by Border Patrol agents.

Leslie Marmon Silko is a celebrated Native American writer. Her article appeared originally in *The Nation* (17 October 1994).

1   I used to travel the highways of New Mexico and Arizona with a wonderful sensation of absolute freedom as I cruised down the open road and across the vast desert plateaus. On the Laguna Pueblo reservation where I was raised, the people were patriotic despite the way the U.S. government had treated Native Americans. As proud citizens, we grew up believing the freedom to travel was our inalienable right, a right that some Native Americans had been denied in the early twentieth century. Our cousin, old Bill Pratt, used to ride his horse 300 miles overland from Laguna, New Mexico, to Prescott, Arizona, every summer to work as a fire lookout.

2   In school in the 1950s, we were taught that our right to travel from state to state without special papers or threat of detainment was a right that citizens under communist and totalitarian governments did not possess. That wide open highway told us we were U.S. citizens; we were free. . . .

3   Not so long ago, my companion Gus and I were driving south from Albuquerque, returning to Tucson after a book promotion for the paperback edition of my novel *Almanac of the Dead*. I had settled back and gone to sleep while Gus drove; but I was awakened when I felt the car slowing to a stop. It was nearly midnight on New Mexico State Road 26, a dark, lonely stretch of two-lane highway between Hatch and Deming. When I sat up, I saw the headlights and emergency flashers of six vehicles—Border Patrol cars and a van were blocking both lanes of the highway. Gus stopped the car and rolled down the window to ask what was wrong. But the closest Border Patrolman and his companion did not reply; instead, the first agent ordered us to "step out of the car." Gus asked why, but his question seemed to set them off. Two more Border Patrol agents immediately approached our car, and one of them snapped, "Are you looking for trouble?" as if he would relish it.

4   I will never forget that night beside the highway. There was an awful feeling of menace and violence straining to break loose. It was clear that the uniformed men would be only too happy to drag us out of the car if we did not speedily comply with their request (asking a question is tantamount to resistance, it seems). So we stepped out of the car and they motioned for us to stand on the shoulder of the road. The night was very dark, and no other traffic had come down the road since we had been stopped. All I could think about was a book I had read—*Nunca Mas*—the official report of a human rights commission that investigated and certified more than 12,000 "disappearances" during Argentina's "dirty war" in the late 1970s.

5   The weird anger of these Border Patrolmen made me think about descriptions in the report of Argentine police and military officers who became addicted to interrogation, torture and the murder that followed. When the military and police ran out of political suspects to torture and kill, they resorted to the random abduction of citizens off the streets. I thought how easy it would be for the Border Patrol to shoot us and leave our bodies and car beside the highway, like so many bodies found in these parts and ascribed to "drug runners."

6   Two other Border Patrolmen stood by the white van. The one who had asked if we were looking for trouble ordered his partner to "get the dog," and from the back of the van another patrolman brought a small female German shepherd on a leash. The dog apparently did not heel well enough to suit him, and the handler jerked the leash. They opened the doors of our car and pulled the dog's head into it, but I saw immediately from the expression in her eyes that the dog hated them, and that she would not serve them. When she showed no interest in the inside of the car, they brought her around back to the trunk, near where we were standing. They half-dragged her up into the trunk, but still she did not indicate any stowed-away human beings or illegal drugs.

7   The mood got uglier; the officers seemed outraged that the dog could not find any contraband, and they dragged her over to us and commanded her to sniff our legs and feet. To my relief, the strange violence the Border Patrol agents had focused on us now seemed shifted to the dog. I no longer felt so strongly that we would be murdered. We exchanged looks—the dog and I. She was afraid of what they might do, just as I was. The dog's handler jerked the leash sharply as she sniffed us, as if to make her perform better, but the dog refused to accuse us: She had an innate dignity that did not permit her to serve the murderous impulses of those men. I can't forget the expression in the dog's eyes; it was as if she were embarrassed to be associated with them. I had a small amount of medicinal marijuana in my purse that night, but she refused to expose me. I am not partial to dogs, but I will always remember the small German shepherd that night.

8   Unfortunately, what happened to me is an everyday occurrence here now. . . .

9   I was [also] detained once at Truth or Consequences, despite my and my companion's Arizona driver's licenses. Two men, both Chicanos, were detained at the same time, despite the fact that they too presented ID and spoke English without the thick Texas accents of the Border Patrol agents. While we were stopped, we watched as other vehicles—whose occupants were white—were waved through the checkpoint. White people traveling with brown people, however, can expect to be stopped on suspicion they work with the sanctuary movement, which shelters refugees. White people who appear to be clergy, those who wear ethnic clothing or jewelry and women with very long hair or very short hair (they could be nuns) are also frequently detained; white men with beards or men with long hair are likely to be detained, too, because Border Patrol agents have "profiles" of "those sorts" of white people who may help political refugees. (Most of the political refugees from Guatemala and El Salvador are Native American or mestizo because the indigenous people of the Americas have continued to resist efforts by invaders to displace them from their ancestral lands.) Alleged increases in illegal immigration

by people of Asian ancestry means that the Border Patrol now routinely detains anyone who appears to be Asian or part Asian, as well.

10   Once your car is diverted from the Interstate Highway into the checkpoint area, you are under the control of the Border Patrol, which in practical terms exercises a power that no highway patrol or city patrolman possesses: They are willing to detain anyone, for no apparent reason. Other law-enforcement officers need a shred of probable cause in order to detain someone. On the books, so does the Border Patrol; but on the road, it's another matter. They'll order you to stop your car and step out; then they'll ask you to open the trunk. If you ask why or request a search warrant, you'll be told that they'll have to have a dog sniff the car before they can request a search warrant, and the dog might not get there for two or three hours. The search warrant might require an hour or two past that. They make it clear that if you force them to obtain a search warrant for the car, they will make you submit to a strip search as well. . . .

11   This is the police state that has developed in the southwestern United States since the 1980s. No person, no citizen, is free to travel without the scrutiny of the Border Patrol. In the city of South Tucson, where 80 percent of the respondents were Chicano or Mexicano, a joint research project by the University of Wisconsin and the University of Arizona recently concluded that one out of every five people there had been detained, mistreated verbally or nonverbally, or questioned by I.N.S. [Immigration and Naturalization Service] agents in the past two years.

12   Manifest Destiny may lack its old grandeur of theft and blood—"lock the door" is what it means now, with racism a trump card to be played again and again, shamelessly, by both major political parties. "Immigration," like "street crime" and "welfare fraud," is a political euphemism that refers to people of color. Politicians and media people talk about "illegal aliens" to dehumanize and demonize undocumented immigrants, who are for the most part people of color. Even in the days of Spanish and Mexican rule, no attempts were made to interfere with the flow of people and goods from south to north and north to south. It is the U.S. government that has continually attempted to sever contact between the tribal people north of the border and those to the south.[1]

13   Now that the "Iron Curtain" is gone, it is ironic that the U.S. government and its Border Patrol are constructing a steel wall ten feet high to span sections of the border with Mexico. . . . Like the pathetic multimillion-dollar "antidrug" border surveillance balloons that were continually deflated by high winds and made only a couple of meager interceptions before they blew away, the fence along the border is a theatrical prop, a bit of pork for contractors. Border entrepreneurs have already used blowtorches to cut passageways through the fence to collect "tolls," and are doing a brisk business. . . .

[1]The Treaty of Guadalupe Hidalgo, signed in 1848, recognizes the right of the Tohano O'Odom (Papago) people to move freely across the U.S.–Mexico border without documents. A treaty with Canada guarantees similar rights to those of the Iroquois nation in traversing the U.S.–Canada border. [Author's note]

14   It is no use; borders haven't worked, and they won't work, not now, as the indigenous people of the Americas reassert their kinship and solidarity with one another. A mass migration is already under way; its roots are not simply economic. The Uto-Aztecan languages are spoken as far north as Taos Pueblo near the Colorado border, all the way south to Mexico City. Before the arrival of the Europeans, the indigenous communities throughout this region not only conducted commerce, the people shared cosmologies, and oral narratives about the Maize Mothers, the Twin Brothers and their Grandmother, Spider Woman, as well as Quetzalcoatl the benevolent snake. The great human migration within the Americas cannot be stopped; human beings are natural forces of the Earth, just as rivers and winds are natural forces. . . .

15   One evening at sundown, we were stopped in traffic at a railroad crossing in downtown Tucson while a freight train passed us, slowly gaining speed as it headed north to Phoenix. In the twilight I saw the most amazing sight: Dozens of human beings, mostly young men, were riding the train; everywhere, on flat cars, inside open boxcars, perched on top of boxcars, hanging off ladders on tank cars and between boxcars. I couldn't count fast enough, but I saw fifty or sixty people headed north. They were dark young men, Indian and mestizo; they were smiling and a few of them waved at us in our cars. I was reminded of the ancient story of Aztlán, told by the Aztecs but known in other Uto-Aztecan communities as well. Aztlán is the beautiful land to the north, the origin place of the Aztec people. I don't remember how or why the people left Aztlán to journey farther south, but the old story says that one day, they will return.

FOR DISCUSSION

1. Silko refers to the "weird anger" (paragraph 5) of the Border Patrol officers. Why does she call it "weird"? What might explain their anger?

2. "Immigration," like "street crime" and "welfare fraud," Silko claims, "is a political euphemism that refers to people of color." Is she right? What do these terms make you think of? How do such associations distort clear thinking about immigration, legal or illegal?

3. Originally "The Border Patrol State" appeared under the caption "America's Iron Curtain," an allusion to the Berlin Wall, one of the great symbols of tyranny for Americans of Silko's generation. Thus, the editors of *The Nation* compare our border walls to the Berlin Wall, torn down only a few years before Silko's article appeared. How apt is the analogy?

FOR RESEARCH, DISCUSSION, AND MEDIATION

Silko reminds us of how short-sighted views of immigration can be—they tend to focus on the current situation without much awareness of the history, for example, of peoples moving back and forth along the U.S. border with Mexico. Find out all you can about the movement of peoples along our southern border, being sure to go all the way back to when there was no border and the region was populated by Native Americans only. Answer these questions: What does the history tell us about cultural ties among the people who live on both sides of the current border? How much should what we know from history influence our thinking now about border control and immigration?

Write an essay proposing an approach to border control based on your new knowledge of history. Use your knowledge to propose a solution in between the current extremes: shutting off illegal immigration entirely and creating completely open borders.

FOR FURTHER READING

Huntington, Samuel P. *Who Are We? The Challenges to America's Identity.* New York: Simon and Schuster, 2004.

Jacoby, Tamar, ed., *Reinventing the Melting Pot: The New Immigrants and What It Means to Be American.* Basic Books, 2004.

Reason (August–September 2006). A series of provocative articles in a special section of the issue. See especially Carolyn Lockheed, "The Unexpected Consequences of Immigration Reform."

Wilson Quarterly (Summer 2006). Some interesting pieces on recent immigration trends, including legal immigration from Africa.

Zollberg, Aristide R. *A Nation by Design: Immigration Policy in the Fashioning of America.* Boston: Harvard UP, 2004.

The debate over health care reform drew heated language from protestors of the legislation at a demonstration in San Francisco in August of 2009.

Declining Civility:
Is Rudeness on the Rise?

Examples of rude behavior are not hard to find these days. On the roads, aggressive drivers seem more common than courteous ones. In the news, we see a tennis player verbally assault a line judge and a rap singer barge onstage to interrupt another singer's awards acceptance speech. At meals, people are texting while ignoring others sitting with them around the table. And in college classes, students and professors report that they regularly observe rude behavior such as text messaging, talking, sleeping, allowing cell phones to ring, and packing up books before the end of class.

On the political landscape, language has become more heated and divisive along party lines, with both major parties taking off the gloves and hurling insults and personal attacks. When Congressman Joe Wilson of South Carolina shouted "You lie!" during President Obama's speech on health care reform in September of 2009, even members of his own Republican Party criticized him as having gone too far. Politicians, news commentators, and radio talk show hosts have found that incivility gets them more attention than politeness.

Incivility, however, does not persuade. For Aristotle, good character—or ethos—was an essential element of persuasion. It is also an important element of democracy, which depends on cooperation. In this chapter, Michael Gerson of the *Washington Post* uses metaphors to describe this need: "Civility acts like grease in the democratic machine; disdain is sand thrown into the gears." His point is that even when people disagree they should show respect for each other's views and for each other as people. Civility makes all communication more effective. A course in college writing is therefore a good place to examine civility and its role in our personal and public lives.

The readings in this chapter begin with a definition of civility from a professor of literature, P. M. Forni, whose book *Choosing Civility* has become a best-seller since its publication in 2002. Civility "is imagination on a moral track." He advocates teaching civility in college to help students reach their full human potential. "To be fully human," he writes, "we must be able to imagine others' hurt and to relate it to the hurt we would experience if we were in their place." Other readings show examples of people's failure to act in civil ways, in private life such as texting at the dinner table and in the public world, when expressing political disagreement.

Assuming that incivility is actually on the rise, we should consider why that might be and what might be the consequences for our society. Janet Kinosian's article raises some possible causes of rudeness. Since the 1960s, children have been raised with an emphasis on the self, what Forni calls "the cult of the self." Individuals do whatever amuses or benefits them with no regard for whether their behavior might offend others. Other factors Kinosian sees as contributing to rudeness include the belligerence of cable news anchors and the crudeness of reality TV.

What are the consequences of incivility? If civility is, as Forni claims, moral behavior, then choosing incivility is choosing to be immoral. It is acting "in bad faith," as the blogger hilzoy says in "Fighting Words," with no concern for the truth or the pain that words can inflict. The uncivil person becomes increasingly full of hatred. However, communications professor Brian McGee argues that too much insistence on civility can hinder democratic progress. Protests against established positions are often "passionate and disorderly," while politeness, as he says, "can be boring." Incivility can bring about change.

That may be true, but do we really want a political climate where opponents do not at least listen respectfully to each other's positions? As Barack Obama asked in a "60 Minutes" interview, in an atmosphere where the "loudest, shrillest voices get the most attention . . . [h]ow can we make sure that civility is interesting?" The readings in this chapter should stimulate interest in the role of civility in the public realm and in our daily personal interactions.

What Is Civility?

P. M. FORNI

The first reading comes from a best-selling book, Choosing Civility: The Twenty-five Rules of Considerate Conduct. *The author is a professor of Italian literature and civility at Johns Hopkins University, where he directs the Johns Hopkins Civility Initiative. Before giving readers his "rules" for showing consideration towards others, Forni lays the groundwork with his careful definition of civility.*

Maybe I was coming down with change-of-season influenza. If so, I should really consider buying a little white half mask for my subway ride home.

—Sujata Massey

1   For many years literature was my life. I spent most of my time reading, teaching, and writing on Italian fiction and poetry. One day, while lecturing on the *Divine Comedy,* I looked at my students and realized that I wanted them to be kind human beings more than I wanted them to know about Dante. I told them that if they knew everything about Dante and then they went out and treated an elderly lady on the bus unkindly, I'd feel that I had failed as a teacher. I have given dozens of lectures and workshops on civility in the last few years, and I have derived much satisfaction from addressing audiences I could not have reached speaking on literature. I know, however, that reading literature can develop the kind of imagination without which civility is impossible. To be fully human we must be able to imagine others' hurt and to relate it to the hurt we would experience if we were in their place. Consideration is imagination on a moral track.

2   Sometimes the participants in my workshops write on a sheet of paper what civility means to them. In no particular order, here are a number of key civility-related notions I have collected over the years from those sheets:

Respect for others	Decency
Care	Self-control
Consideration	Concern
Courtesy	Justice
Golden rule	Tolerance
Respect of others' feelings	Selflessness
Niceness	Etiquette
Politeness	Community service
Respect of others' opinions	Tact
Maturity	Equality
Kindness	Sincerity
Manners	Morality
Being accommodating	Honesty
Fairness	Awareness

Trustworthiness	Going out of one's way
Friendship	Friendliness
Table manners	Lending a hand
Moderation	Propriety
Listening	Abiding by rules
Compassion	Good citizenship
Being agreeable	Peace

This list tells us that

- Civility is complex.
- Civility is good.
- Whatever civility might be, it has to do with courtesy, politeness, and good manners.
- Civility belongs in the realm of ethics.

3   These four points have guided me in writing this book. Like my workshop participants, I am inclusive rather than exclusive in defining civility. Courtesy, politeness, manners, and civility are all, in essence, forms of awareness. Being civil means being constantly aware of others and weaving restraint, respect, and consideration into the very fabric of this awareness. Civility is a form of goodness; it is gracious goodness. But it is not just an attitude of benevolent and thoughtful relating to other individuals; it also entails an active interest in the well-being of our communities and even a concern for the health of the planet on which we live.

4   Saying "please" and "thank you"; lowering our voice whenever it may threaten or interfere with others' tranquillity; raising funds for a neighborhood renovation program; acknowledging a newcomer to the conversation; welcoming a new neighbor; listening to understand and help; respecting those different from us; responding with restraint to a challenge; properly disposing of a piece of trash left by someone else; properly disposing of dangerous industrial pollutants; acknowledging our mistakes; refusing to participate in malicious gossip; making a new pot of coffee for the office machine after drinking the last cup; signaling our turns when driving; yielding our seat on a bus whenever it seems appropriate; alerting the person sitting behind us on a plane when we are about to lower the back of our seat; standing close to the right-side handrail on an escalator; stopping to give directions to someone who is lost; stopping at red lights; disagreeing with poise; yielding with grace when losing an argument, these diverse behaviors are all imbued with the spirit of civility.

5   *Civility, courtesy, politeness,* and *manners* are not perfect synonyms, as etymology clearly shows.

> In life courtesy and self-possession, and in the arts style, are the sensible impressions of the free mind, for both arise out of a deliberate shaping of all things, and from never being swept away, whatever the emotion, into confusion or dullness.
>
> —William Butler Yeats

Courtesy is connected to *court* and evoked in the past the superior qualities of character and bearing expected in those close to royalty. Etymologically, when we are courteous we are courtierlike. Although today we seldom make this connection, courtesy still suggests excellence and elegance in bestowing respect and attention. It can also suggest deference and formality.

> The very essence of politeness seems to be to take care that by our words and actions we make other people pleased with us as well as with themselves.
>
> —Jean de La Bruyere

6   To understand *politeness,* we must think of *polish.* The polite are those who have polished their behavior. They have put some effort into bettering themselves, but they are sometimes looked upon with suspicion. Expressions such as "polite reply," "polite lie," and "polite applause" connect politeness to hypocrisy. It is true that the polite are inclined to veil their own feelings to spare someone else's. Self-serving lying, however, is always beyond the pale of politeness. If politeness is a quality of character (alongside courtesy, good manners, and civility), it cannot become a flaw. A suave manipulator may appear to be polite but is not.

> There is always a best way of doing everything, if it be to boil an egg. Manners are the happy way of doing things; each once a stroke of genius or of love, now repeated and hardened into usage.
>
> —Ralph Waldo Emerson

7   When we think of good *manners* we often think of children being taught to say "please" and "thank you" and chew with their mouths closed. This may prevent us from looking at manners with the attention they deserve. *Manner* comes from *manus,* the Latin word for "hand." *Manner* and *manners* have to do with the use of our hands. A manner is the way something is done, a mode of handling. Thus *manners* came to refer to behavior in social interaction—the way we handle the encounter between Self and Other. We have good manners when we use our hands well—when we handle others with care. When we rediscover the connection of *manner* with *hand,* the hand that, depending on our will and sensitivity, can strike or lift, hurt or soothe, destroy or heal, we understand the importance—for children and adults alike—of having good manners.

> Being civil to one another is much more active and positive a good than mere politeness or courtesy, but like many other important goods, such as generosity, gratitude, or solidarity, it is not the sort of thing that can be "demanded" as a matter of duty, like a moral entitlement.
>
> —Robert B. Pippin

8   *Civility's* defining characteristic is its ties to *city* and *society.* The word derives from the Latin *civitas,* which means "city," especially in the sense of civic community. *Civitas* is the same word from which *civilization* comes. The age-old assumption behind civility is that life in the city has a civilizing effect. The city is where we enlighten our intellect and refine our social skills. And as we are shaped by the city,

we learn to give of ourselves for the sake of the city. Although we can describe the civil as courteous, polite, and well mannered, etymology reminds us that they are also supposed to be good citizens and good neighbors.

FOR DISCUSSION

1. Forni begins by arguing that learning to be kind to others is as important to a college education as learning literature—or presumably any other area of academic study. Do you think a university ought to play some role in developing students' character as well as their knowledge? If so, what are some of the ways this could happen?

2. Have you previously thought about reading literature as a way to develop empathy for other people? If so, what books, poems, and stories would you recommend?

3. In paragraph 3, Forni says awareness of others is the basis of civility. How do some of the examples in paragraph 4 show an awareness of others? What are some habits and conditions of daily life that hinder such awareness, causing our attentions to be self-directed?

4. Forni believes the etymology, or origins, of words can open up our understanding of meanings. How does the discussion of the origins of the words *courtesy*, *politeness*, and *manners* add to your understanding of what it takes to be a civil person?

FOR RESEARCH AND INQUIRY

Do research into the problem of incivility on college campuses (including observations on your own campus) and how schools are dealing with it. Many schools have instituted codes of conduct, which are often posted on the Internet. Then do research into opinions about the usefulness of such codes. How effective are they? What other solutions have been proposed? Conclude by endorsing a plan for dealing with the problem.

FOR RESEARCH AND CONVINCING OR MEDIATION

Many groups feel that hazing has a good purpose in forming bonds among members of an organization. It was common for first-year college students to be hazed, a tradition going back hundreds of years but now mostly eliminated by student codes of conduct. However, other campus institutions continue the practice to some degree. Look into arguments for and against hazing. Does it build character or teach incivility? Write an argument against the practice as uncivil, using some of the ideas of P. M. Forni about why colleges should teach civility. Or write an essay to mediate that arrives at a position that would satisfy people on both sides.

Play with Your Food, Just Don't Text

SARA RIMER

> This article, which originally appeared in the *New York Times* in 2009, offers a range of opinions about the common habit of texting at the table. Before reading, consider your own attitude toward texting while dining with others. Have you done it? How do you feel when others do it?

Danah Boyd and Gilad Lotan, a married couple, regularly bring their iPhones to the dinner table.

1 Anytime Anne Fishel and her family talk about behaviors that are out of bounds during family meals, they come back to the Yom Kippur Incident.

2 Two years ago, 14 people had gathered at her dining room table in Newton, Mass., to break the fast on the most solemn of Jewish holidays. As Dr. Fishel looked around, it seemed that everyone—her husband, their two college-age sons, Gabe and Joe, their friends—was enjoying her cooking and sharing the sense of an important family dinner.

3 Except, she noticed, for Gabe's friend from college. Wait a second, what was he doing? With a furtive downward glance, he was surreptitiously texting—and not just once or twice, but almost continuously, from the apple-squash soup to the roast turkey.

4 Dr. Fishel, who directs the family and couples therapy program at Massachusetts General Hospital, wasn't about to embarrass the young man. But another of Gabe's

friends, seated next to the stealth texter, spoke up. "You really shouldn't be doing that here," she admonished him, and not in a whisper.

5   "Why not?" the texter said. "It's not like this is a formal dinner or something."

6   Texting anarchy, Emily Post's great-granddaughter, Cindy Post Senning, calls it. "People are texting everywhere," she said.

7   Husbands, wives, children and dinner guests who would never be so rude as to talk on a phone at the family table seem to think it's perfectly fine to text (or e-mail, or Twitter) while eating.

8   Dr. Post Senning is here to tell you that it is not perfectly fine. Not at all. So new is the problem that her latest book, *Emily Post's Table Manners for Kids* (HarperCollins, 2009), written with Peggy Post, covered it only generally, in a blanket ruling: "Do NOT use your cell phone or any other electronic devices at the table."

9   She now finds it necessary to weigh in on the texting issue specifically: No texting at the dinner table, particularly at home. "The family meal is a social event," she said in a phone interview, "not a food ingestion event."

10   "Be aware that others can see your thumbs working even when they are in your lap," she wrote in a follow-up e-mail message, laying down the official rule of etiquette. "If you are in a situation where your attention should be focused on others, you should not be texting." And she means no e-mailing, either.

11   That means you, George d'Arbeloff. Or so his wife, P. A. d'Arbeloff, told him after she caught him peeking at the iPhone in his lap during Thanksgiving dinner at their home in the Jamaica Plain neighborhood of Boston. "I tried to catch his eye," said Ms. d'Arbeloff, director of the Cambridge Science Festival in Cambridge, Mass., "but he was looking down."

12   He may have been scrolling through work-related e-mail messages or, possibly, checking sports scores, conceded Mr. d'Arbeloff, who is the chairman of a Los Angeles–based dental laser company. Because the company is on the West Coast, e-mail messages tend to flood in just as he is sitting down to eat.

13   "I have never texted at the dinner table," he said in a telephone interview. "I will admit: I do read e-mails." He paused, listening to his wife, who was in the room with him. "P. A. says I send."

14   A few months ago, a family meeting was convened. The d'Arbeloffs' 7-year-old twin daughters made their feelings known. Their father agreed to cease using his iPhone during dinner. "I'm 95 percent reformed," he said.

15   "Maybe people think they can time-share: both texting and talking at once," said Harry Lewis, a Harvard computer science professor and one of the authors of *Blown to Bits: Your Life, Liberty and Happiness After the Digital Explosion* (Addison-Wesley, 2008). Beware, he says: You're not fooling anybody. "No one thinks someone on the cellphone can really be paying attention to another person."

16   Texting while eating has become a major issue among couples in counseling, says Evan Imber-Black, a prominent family therapist. And, yes, she says, it seems the men are the ones who can't sit down for dinner for a half-hour without tapping away at their phones. (The reverse is true among teenagers, where the girls are the nonstop texters.)

17   "I think it has to do with the erosion of a boundary between work and family, particularly for men in any kind of business where they're just afraid to stop working practically 24-7," said Dr. Imber-Black, one of the authors of the book *Rituals in Families and Family Therapy.*

18   Evvajean Mintz's husband, Richard, a partner in a Boston law firm, arrives at the table with his BlackBerry clipped to his belt. "If there's one second of spare time, and if you look away from him and lose eye contact, he immediately whips it out and starts looking at it," she said. "I suggested I'd throw it out the window."

19   Like a lot of couples, the Mintzes have conflicting views of the rate of tableside BlackBerry use. Mr. Mintz, who is working part time at 87, thought he was doing it only when his wife was preoccupied—when, for example, she ducks into another room to catch a few minutes of television.

20   "I try not to do it in a way that upsets her," Mr. Mintz said. "I guess I'm not doing it as well as I should."

21   Another family therapist, Peter Fraenkel, director of the Center for Work and Family at the Ackerman Institute for the Family in Manhattan, said he recently counseled a real estate broker and his wife, who works as a headhunter. The couple has two children, ages 6 and 4. She wanted two BlackBerry-free hours each night, including dinner.

22   Dr. Fraenkel said that he had the husband log his incoming e-mail messages, texts and calls for two weeks. Which ones had to be handled immediately, or else the deal would be lost?

23   After the husband concluded that none of the calls were urgent, Dr. Fraenkel said, he was able to create the two-hour BlackBerry-free family zone.

24   As for teenagers and texting, says Danah Boyd, a researcher at Microsoft who studies the ways young people use technology, they're just doing what they've always done: hanging out with their friends.

25   The cellphone makes it possible to bring your social circle to the dinner table. "You don't really have to disconnect," she said.

26   Brigid Wright, 17, from Needham, Mass., said that like many teenagers, she has honed the skill of eating with one hand and texting with the other. But, she said (and her family confirms), she does not text at the table at home.

27   "No teenager wants to look up from a glowing cellphone screen to see a disappointed parent frowning across the table," she wrote in an e-mail message.

28   Ms. Boyd is 31. Sometimes she looks up from her glowing iPhone screen to see her husband, Gilad Lotan, a Microsoft designer, frowning at her across the table.

29   "If I'm sitting there privately responding to messages, Gilad might say, 'Hey, I thought we were at dinner,'" she said. "I'll be, like, 'Hmm, sorry, just doing this quickly.'"

30   They both bring their iPhones to the table, she said, using them as conversational tools. If they're debating a question, for instance, they might use their phones to look up the answer.

31   They try to avoid texting, she said, "if it's a dinner where we're trying to be engaged." (As opposed to a dinner "where we both need food in our systems so we can both get back to work.")

32   There is no texting or e-mailing at the dinner table in Lydia Shire's home, in Weston, Mass. "My son would never dream of texting at the table," said Ms. Shire, a chef and restaurant owner in Boston. "And he wouldn't do it at anyone else's table, either."

33   True, said her 19-year-old son, Alex Pineda. To take out his BlackBerry Dream would be to distract from his mother's amazing cooking, and the conversation with her and his father.

34   But he did have to explain it to a friend who came to dinner not long ago. Just as they were sitting down at the table, Alex said, "he started texting."

35   Fortunately, his mother was still occupied with serving the food. "She didn't notice," Alex said. "I told him to put it away."

QUESTIONS FOR DISCUSSION

1. The "Yom Kipper Incident" seems like an egregious breach of manners. Why do you think the texting college student was not aware that others would find his actions very rude?

2. Cell phones and laptops have made it possible to combine work and personal life. What does this habit reveal about the values and priorities of those who do not establish a boundary between work and family life? Why might they be afraid to be unconnected to their work?

3. What is Danah Boyd's attitude toward teens texting at the table? Is there anything wrong with teens preferring to socialize with their friends rather than with their family at the table?

FOR PERSUASION

Do research into the benefits of the family dinner hour, where children and parents sit down to a technology-free social exchange rather than a "food ingestion event," to use the words of the etiquette writer Cindy Post Senning. Make a persuasive argument to parents about the value of reestablishing a technology-free family dinner hour.

Ours Is a Rude Age, but Have a Nice Day

JANET KINOSIAN

> Janet Kinosian is a journalist who writes for *Reader's Digest, People,* and the *Los Angeles Times,* where this column originally appeared in May of 2009. Are you convinced that we live in a "rude age" or just a more open and casual world than the one your grandparents lived in?

1   Manners have always had their thoughtful admirers, along with their merely numerous ones. After all, manners—good ones—help grease life's highways. Parents teaching their children manners was once considered tantamount to putting shoes on their feet.

2   But given 40-odd years worth of toxicological reduced decorum—what civility experts term the post-Woodstock decline—is it any wonder parents are feeling a little lonely, a little edgy?

3   What is a parent's plea for "thank you" and "sir" and "ma'am" and "please" amid Internet raunch and mayhem, guns at school and on freeways, tantrum-throwing and spitting sports figures, the drones of trashy misfits exploited on reality TV and cable news shows where politicos yell at one another in lieu of civilized discourse?

4   Worse yet, bad manners are now being culturally held up as big business—via the Howard Stern's and Rush Limbaugh's and Glenn Beck's of the world. Don't just have bad manners, goes the line, have atrocious manners and watch what happens. You'll get noticed, and maybe even rich and famous.

5   Take the recent Joe Wilson debacle. When the Republican congressman from South Carolina shouted out "You lie!" to the world's most powerful man during Obama's recent health care reform speech, half the world was appalled at the rudeness—and the other half [presumably the less-mannered half] fawn on him as a hero, to the tune of $1 million in campaign funds culled in just one week.

6   Since it pays to be rude and crude in today's hyped-up 24-hour worldwide opinion-fest, where do good manners fit in?

7   A *U.S. News & World Report* survey shows just how worried people are by all of this. Conducted in association with Bozell Worldwide, the survey showed that the vast majority of Americans feel we've reached a rude-mannered watershed.

8   Nine of 10 think incivility is a serious problem, and nearly half think it's extremely serious. Seventy-eight percent believe the level of rudeness in society probably has worsened dramatically in the last 10 years and more than 90% think it contributes directly to the increase in today's violence. Eighty-five percent think rudeness is puncturing the social fabric of the country.

9   Top on this list of punctures is the 1960s-born "cult of the self," says Pier Massimo Forni, a Johns Hopkins University professor who has studied the decline of civility in America and other countries for many years, and started The Civility Institute at Johns Hopkins in 2000. His book, *Choosing Civility* (2002), is a perennial bestseller.

10   In the past, Forni says, "children had never heard of the aggrandizement of the self over decorum. Children were never taught they were No. 1, and that their feelings, thoughts, desires were equal or more important than anything or anyone else."

11   That lesson is in direct contrast to the root of manners, he says: that you can transcend the self and be more aware of others. And thus the massive boombox blaring two inches from a stranger's head; you got a problem with that?

12   He says because many Americans fear we've become a "nation of strangers," manners have taken a plunge.

13   Explains Forni: "When people feel anonymous, their behavior tends to reflect less restraint. Why not be verbally abusive on the road? Who will ever know? Strangers have no reputations, and less guilt." He says the anonymity also shows up in American over-friendliness, such as the gushing "have a nice day," intimate chit-chat with waiters and business routinely conducted on a first-name basis. "Two sides to the same coin," he says.

14   A loosely formed civility and manners movement has been building. The U.S. government got into the act in the past decade, sponsoring new study commissions and offering podiums for groups like former Georgia Sen. Sam Nunn and former Education Secretary William Bennett's National Commission on Civic Renewal.

15   Patricia Schroeder headed a "New Century/New Solution" project sponsored by the Boston-based Institute for Civil Society, begun a decade ago from an anonymous grant of $35 million. Some of the institute's goals? To recenter the concept that civility, manners and well-bred social intercourse are safeguards for a democratic society.

16   "People are concerned about a culture that's getting more vulgar and out of control," says Pam Solo, director of the institute.

17   However, not everyone is comfortable with a manners crusade. Some see it as elitist or intolerant. Traditionally, manners have been used to distinguish the well-bred from the lower classes and, in a multicultural, pluralistic, democratic society, there's danger in labeling one behavior better than another, or so the argument goes.

18   "It's less about societal snobbishness than it is about what society will tolerate and what the parameters are for behavior," counters Arlene Isaacs, a New York–based consultant to corporations in manners awareness.

19   "The sooner kids know life isn't a free-for-all, and that the way you are perceived is the way you will be received, the better," Isaacs says. "The question I use is this: Do you want to be invited to the party—and more importantly, do you want to be invited back? Then you better watch your manners."

20   Her sentiments are echoed by writer James Morris in the *Wilson Quarterly,* who claims we are "in the Age of Whatever." He says that society needs to make some judgments about tolerable and even preferable behavior. He says even the trend toward casual and sloppy attire cries out to be rethought. "People appear in public in clothes that must scare the hangers in a dark closet," he writes.

21   "We've had a legacy of the '60s that manners are bad because they're artificial, and we should behave naturally," says Judith Martin, better known as Miss Manners for her syndicated newspaper column.

22   "We've seen where that's gotten us."

FOR DISCUSSION

1. In what ways does this reading show that it pays to be rude? How can you explain the apparent contradiction between the popularity of rudeness in politics and media and the survey results showing that people see rudeness as a serious problem?

2. This article includes some analysis of the problem by P. M. Forni, the author of this chapter's first reading, "What Is Civility?" What are two causes Forni sees for the rise in rudeness? What evidence do you have for agreeing with him about each of these causes? Can you suggest any other possible causes?

3. Paraphrase the argument in paragraph 17, which offers an opposing view. Do you think good manners are a sign of high social status? Is it snobbish to judge people based on their knowledge of etiquette?

4. Do you agree with James Morris that Americans are too casual in their clothing? Why might wearing jeans or shorts on certain occasions be a breach of good manners? Is it a breach of manners if everyone agrees that jeans and shorts are appropriate for a certain occasion, such as a church service?

FOR INQUIRY

Inquire into the arguments for dress codes in schools. Do these arguments address issues having to do with civility? Has there been evidence that a more formal style of dress correlates with higher grades and a better educational environment than when students are permitted to wear whatever they want to school? Arrive at a conclusion about the relationship of clothing and civility in a school environment.

FOR RESEARCH AND CONVINCING

Look into the gradual increase in informality in our culture, such as the use of first names even among strangers and the disappearance of coats and ties as regular business attire. If manners are simply what a culture agrees to tolerate, is there any argument to be made against agreeing to live in an informal atmosphere? Make an argument to convince readers that this informality is a positive move toward a more open and natural society or a negative move toward a decline in civility.

The Rhetoric of the Rant

MICHAEL GERSON

> The following column is by *Washington Post* opinion writer Michael Gerson. Gerson
> also is a senior research fellow at the Institute for Global Engagement and author of
> the book *Heroic Conservatism* (Harper, 2007). He is concerned here about the
> popularity of ranting, an intentionally mean and aggressive kind of discourse. The
> opening paragraphs refer to a performance by Wanda Sykes, a stand-up comedian, at
> a Washington press event in which she attacked the well-known conservative
> commentator Rush Limbaugh, known for his own ranting abilities.

1   The first response to the performer on a public stage wishing the death of a stranger
for political reasons was discomfort. Wanda Sykes had "crossed a line" at the White
House Correspondents' Association Dinner in accusing Rush Limbaugh of terrorism
and treason, mocking his past drug addiction* and wishing his kidneys would fail.
But a counter reaction soon developed: Humor often is transgressive, and if you
can't take it, don't dish it, and let's everyone lighten up a bit, and can't anyone
take a joke anymore?

2   The initial reaction was more human.

3   Sykes' defenders found her pungency unexceptional, and it is. It represents a
whole genre of political discourse: the rhetoric of the rant. This approach recently
introduced the "c" word into the national debate on gay marriage. It leads some
spotlight-chasing conservatives to attack opponents as "traitors" and to employ
racist epithets. It is the dominant form of public comment on the Internet, where
the pithy, personal, scatological attack has become a minor art form, rather like
sculpting in excrement.

4   What I'm describing is not the blunt earthiness of the farmer or the unguarded
political overstatement among friends. It is a practiced form of verbal aggression,
combining harshness and coarseness to shock and intimidate.

5   The practitioners of the rant have their own television shows, radio programs
and Web sites. And now it seems they will have their own elected representative,
the author of *Rush Limbaugh Is a Big Fat Idiot.* Al Franken has made a career of such
rants, supposedly asking "Isn't Cardinal O'Connor an [expletive]?" calling opponents
"human filth" and suggesting that his next book might bear the title: "I [expletive]
Hate Those Right-Wing Mother [expletives]!" Which many Minnesotans apparently
found refreshing.

6   The advocates of this approach often describe it (and themselves) as courageous.
Franken explains, "My dad did say, 'If you stand up to bullies they usually back
down." But those who make their living beating up others to take their lunch
money must eventually be categorized as bullies themselves. They take perhaps the
most common human vice—self-indulgent anger—and cloak it as a rare virtue. But
it is a strange moral inversion to talk of the "courage" of the raised middle finger.
Perhaps adolescent rudeness. Maybe boorishness. Not courage, which involves

*In 2003, Limbaugh publically addressed his addiction to prescription pain medications and began treat-
ment to overcome it.

standing up for a belief, not dehumanizing those who don't share it. America doesn't need another scolding lecture on the importance of civility. Well, apparently it does. So here goes.

7 The practice of civility is important to democracy. In his book, *Civility: Manners, Morals and the Etiquette of Democracy,* Stephen L. Carter defines civility as "the sum of the many sacrifices we are called to make for the sake of living together. . . . We should make sacrifices for others not simply because doing so makes social life easier (although it does), but as a signal of respect for our fellow citizens, marking them as full equals, both before the law and before God."

8 Respect makes cooperation for the common good possible. Civility acts like grease in the democratic machine; disdain is sand thrown into the gears. But civility is also a direct reflection of our belief in human equality. Even people we vehemently disagree with on the largest issues possess a democratic value equal to our own. Carter argues that this recognition does not preclude "passionate disagreement," but it does require "civil listening"—and I'd guess it forbids hoping for the death of political opponents.

9 So civility has an unavoidably moral component. The proper treatment of others conveys regard and demonstrates self-control. Rudeness sets out to dominate and humiliate. This is not only true in politics. "Precisely because rudeness is quite common," says philosophy professor Emrys Westacott, "it is not a trivial issue. Indeed, in our day-to-day lives it is possibly responsible for more pain than any other moral failing." Verbal violence can leave people smarting for days, or scarred for years, or pushed like a vulnerable middle-schooler toward suicide. Such hostility is broadly and correctly condemned. Why does politics seem to numb this rudimentary moral sense?

10 The answer, of course, is the infectious nature of incivility itself. Every excess provides the excuse for greater and opposite excess—a search for more vicious put-downs and more startling obscenities. Avoiding this escalation is one of the primary challenges of the schoolyard and one of the important attributes of a citizen. Everyone has grievances; fewer have the courage of manners. All of us need more of it.

QUESTIONS FOR DISCUSSION

1. Gerson describes two responses to Sykes's remarks about Limbaugh— "discomfort" at first, followed by laughter as the audience put the remarks into the context of humorous ranting. This editorial, however, argues against mean-spirited ranting, even as a joke. What are Gerson's reasons for opposing it?

2. In paragraph 9, Gerson extends his argument from the political use of ranting to the verbal violence people experience in day-to-day life, such as in school and in the workplace. Do you agree with him about the power of words to leave lasting scars? Does it make a difference, morally, if the words are intended as humor?

3. Rush Limbaugh himself is known for his "transgressive" humor, such as referring to Barack Obama as a "Halfrican American." Do you think Limbaugh's own aggressive style in any way justifies the language of Sykes and Franken?

FOR CONVINCING

Since ranting is like preaching to the choir, what is its purpose? Analyze some examples of speeches or transcripts of talk shows that illustrate the genre of the rant. What kind of language does ranting use? Scatological? Who are the politicians that employ this? What is the relationship between ranting and an educated class of people?

If one politician calls another a traitor, does that make it all right for someone to call the accuser a traitor as well? Or is this a race to the bottom of political discourse?

Edgy humor?

Can Political Rhetoric Be Too Civil?

BRIAN MCGEE

> This guest editorial in the Charleston, South Carolina newspaper, *The Post and Courier,* was written by Brian McGee, chairman of the Department of Communication at the College of Charleston. Consider whether ranting might qualify as an example of the impolite kinds of discourse he says are sometimes necessary.

1 Every few years, in response to one or more widely publicized episodes of rowdiness or rudeness, someone bemoans the decline of civility in U.S. politics.

2 Such complaints sometimes suggest the good old days were more polite than they are today, as when the *New York Times* noted in 1997 an "epidemic of incivility" in public meetings.

3 In other instances Americans are described as worrisomely inconsiderate. Turning once again to the *New York Times,* we find the editors opining in 1876 that the U.S. was the "rudest of nations," with a problem of "national incivility."

4 This time-honored anxiety about civility is with us today. Harry Pastides, president of the University of South Carolina, is worried about the "decline in the civil tenor of our national discourse." Pastides has committed the eight campuses of his university to teaching civility because "the people of this nation deserve better."

5 I do not doubt that Pastides's goals are admirable and the product of deeply held convictions. However, I don't think his efforts will be successful.

6 Initially, any commitment to teaching civility to university students implies they do not fully understand the merits of politeness or the political and societal advantages of civility.

7 I have no first-hand experience with Pastides's students, but my institution's students are the politest people I've ever met in a teaching career that covers 20 years and six states. Individually, some of my students are rude on some days, but they long ago learned they shouldn't be. They understand the basic rules of civility, even if they choose to ignore those rules.

8 Moreover, Pastides isn't talking about student-teacher interactions. He wants more civil discourse about politics, which I certainly appreciate. The problem is that 22-year-olds and graduate students are not the primary sources of shouting in contemporary political forums, as far as I can tell. Retirees and middle-aged workers have been responsible for more than their fair share of incivility in town hall meetings. A revised university code of conduct isn't going to influence the over-40 crowd.

9 So, my sense is that familiarity with politeness norms is most productively and most commonly cultivated in grade school and in family life. There is no student knowledge vacuum in the area of decorum and civil discourse that universities must rush to fill.

10 Our students have the basic idea. Politeness generally is good. Rudeness generally is not.

11 What can universities do about incivility? In part, they can study why ordinarily civil people choose to be uncivil. As one example, I want to suggest why incivility has a role to play in American politics and in any democratic society.

12   Those who hold political power always would prefer to have a polite debate, hold a vote in which their side will prevail, and consider the democratic niceties fulfilled.

13   Politeness, as the politically powerful know, is boring. Incivility attracts attention. Those in the minority are particularly likely to be uncivil because incivility encourages uncommitted voters and media organizations to pay attention, to consider and promote minority views and, possibly, to change hearts and minds.

14   The list of impolite people and groups in politics is long and distinguished. There is good reason to believe that incivility was important in the successes of the movements to end slavery; secure civil rights for African Americans, women, and gay men; and reduce property taxes in California and other states, among many other causes.

15   Like most people, I prefer friendly and civil conversations about all topics, including politics. Debate about important issues in most cases can and should be both spirited and cordial.

16   In saying so, however, I would not uncritically make civil discourse into another tool of congressional or legislative majorities, whether Democratic or Republican. If political ideas, whether conservative or liberal, cannot withstand the passionate and disorderly speech of the minority, those political ideas usually will not endure in the long run.

17   So, at all our universities, let's explain why talk should be preferred to violence, and why all points of view must be heard if we want democracy to work. But let's celebrate the merits of civility with some qualification. In particular, let's not maintain that incivility is OK for our side, but terrible when it comes from the other side.

18   Politics in a democratic society can be a messy, unpleasant business. We always will be happiest when politics and politeness coexist in a productive way. Sometimes, however, the people of this nation both want and need a little incivility.

QUESTIONS FOR DISCUSSION

1. Several of the readings in this chapter refer to concern over rising incivility. McGee was motivated to write this column in response to the decision of the University of South Carolina president, Harry Pastides, to teach civility on all campuses in the state system. Why does McGee oppose the idea? Do you agree that college students already have the needed knowledge about civility?

2. Would you agree that impolite discourse is often initiated by those who do not hold the power in any political situation? What examples can you give to show that minorities have had to be impolite or not civil in order to get the attention that will dislodge the status quo? Consider the examples of progress McGee mentions in paragraph 14: What are some examples of political discourse that helped lead to these examples of progress?

3. What is the difference between the kind of speech that greases the wheels of democracy and the kind that throws sand in the wheels? What is the difference between "messy and unpleasant" but necessary versus divisive and counterproductive to a democratic government?

FOR INQUIRY AND CONVINCING

Examine a famous speech that helped to bring about some progressive legislation such as the end of segregation in the South. (A powerful example is Susan B. Anthony's 1873 speech for woman's right to vote, just a little over five hundred words and readily available on the Internet.) Does your analysis of this particular speech—or another of your choice—support McGee's point that people wishing to challenge the status quo must use uncivil language?

Fighting Words

HILZOY

> This reading is a blog post by "hilzoy," who identifies herself as "a philosophy professor who specializes in ethics." Hilzoy wrote on the liberal political blog *Obsidian Wings* in response to a post by another blogger, Erick Erickson, on *RedState,* which describes itself as "the leading blog for right of center online activists."

1 I am trying to figure out what would possess Erick Erickson to write something like this:

> You only thought leftists got excited when American soldiers got killed. As I've written before, leftists celebrate each and every death of each and every American solider because they view the loss of life as a vindication of their belief that they are right.

2 "Some" leftists, perhaps: there are a lot of people on the left, as there are on the right, and thus I imagine you could find members of either group who do any number of loathsome things. But Erick Erickson didn't write "some leftists." He wrote that "leftists celebrate each and every death of each and every American solider" [sic]. All of us.

3 Even those of us who are serving in Iraq or Afghanistan, or who have family or friends there. Even those of us whose family or friends have died. We all *got excited. We celebrated. Each and every time* a soldier died.

4 Duels have been fought for less.

5 I'm not interested in 'explanations' like: he's on the right, so of course he says idiotic things. Treating his opponents as one big undifferentiated cartoonish mass is part of what makes what Erick wrote so objectionable, and I have no interest in following his example. Nor is hyperbole a good explanation: it's not true that everyone on the left is happy when soldiers die, but that we don't go so far as to *celebrate.*

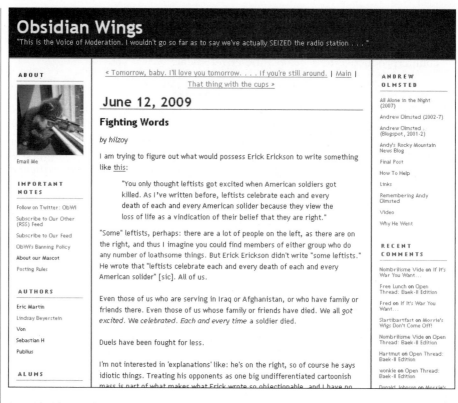

Obsidian Wings

"This is the Voice of Moderation. I wouldn't go so far as to say we've actually SEIZED the radio station . . . ."

ABOUT

Email Me

IMPORTANT NOTES

Follow on Twitter: ObWi

Subscribe to Our Other (RSS) Feed

Subscribe to Our Feed

ObWi's Banning Policy

About our Mascot

Posting Rules

AUTHORS

Eric Martin

Lindsay Beyerstein

Von

Sebastian H

Publius

ALUMS

« Tomorrow, baby. I'll love you tomorrow. . . . If you're still around. | Main | That thing with the cups »

June 12, 2009

Fighting Words

by hilzoy

I am trying to figure out what would possess Erick Erickson to write something like this:

> "You only thought leftists got excited when American soldiers got killed. As I've written before, leftists celebrate each and every death of each and every American soldier because they view the loss of life as a vindication of their belief that they are right."

"Some" leftists, perhaps: there are a lot of people on the left, as there are on the right, and thus I imagine you could find members of either group who do any number of loathsome things. But Erick Erickson didn't write "some leftists." He wrote that "leftists celebrate each and every death of each and every American solider" [sic]. All of us.

Even those of us who are serving in Iraq or Afghanistan, or who have family or friends there. Even those of us whose family or friends have died. We all *got excited*. We *celebrated*. Each and every time a soldier died.

Duels have been fought for less.

I'm not interested in 'explanations' like: he's on the right, so of course he says idiotic things. Treating his opponents as one big undifferentiated cartoonish mass is part of what makes what Erick wrote so objectionable, and I have no

ANDREW OLMSTED

All Alone in the Night (2007)

Andrew Olmsted (2002-7)

Andrew Olmsted (Blogspot, 2001-2)

Andy's Rocky Mountain News Blog

Final Post

How To Help

Links

Remembering Andy Olmsted

Video

Why He Went

RECENT COMMENTS

Nombrilisme Vide on If It's War You Want

Free Lunch on Open Thread: Baek-Il Edition

Fred on If It's War You Want. . .

Slartibartfast on Morrie's Wigs Don't Come Off!

Nombrilisme Vide on Open Thread: Baek-Il Edition

Hartmut on Open Thread: Baek-Il Edition

wonkie on Open Thread: Baek-Il Edition

Donald Johnson on Morrie's

June 12, 2009, Fighting Words blog posting

http://obsidianwings.blogs.com/obsidian_wings/2009/06/fighting-words.html

6   I think we can rule out the possibility that he believes this in good faith: that he asked himself, before writing this, "Is this really true?", thought about (for instance) the 44% of military voters who voted for Obama, liberals presently serving in combat, or the liberals on VetVoice, asked himself whether they actually celebrate when one of their own is killed in combat, and answered: "Yes."

7   He might be a pure hack, like those expert witnesses that the tobacco companies used to trot out to testify that nicotine is not addictive. But I suspect he's not.

8   The alternative is that he believes this in bad faith. Maybe, for him, writing blog posts has become a game: you score points when you can, and whether or not the things you write are actually true has ceased to be a concern. Or maybe hatred has got the better of him, like the person C. S. Lewis describes here:

> Suppose one reads a story of filthy atrocities in the paper. Then suppose that something turns up suggesting that the story might not be quite true, or not quite so bad as it was made out. Is one's first feeling, "Thank God, even they aren't quite so bad as that," or is it a feeling of disappointment, and even a determination to cling to the first story for the sheer pleasure of thinking your enemies are as bad as possible? If it

is the second then it is, I am afraid, the first step in a process which, if followed to the end, will make us into devils. You see, one is beginning to wish that black was a little blacker. If we give that wish its head, later on we shall wish to see grey as black, and then to see white itself as black. Finally we shall insist on seeing everything—God and our friends and ourselves included—as bad, and not be able to stop doing it: we shall be fixed forever in a universe of pure hatred. (*Mere Christianity*)

If you give in to "the sheer pleasure of thinking your enemies are as bad as possible," it's easy to see how you could end up thinking things about them that it is implausible to think about any group of human beings: for instance, that when a nineteen year old who enlisted because he wanted to serve his country gets blown up by an IED, your enemies think that that's cause for celebration. Your opponents become cartoons in your mind, and the normal duty to be charitable and generous, or even realistic, in your views about other people seems not to apply to them. You stop thinking of them as fellow human beings, and start thinking of them as enemies.

9   I suspect that this is the state of mind in which people laughed along with Rush Limbaugh when he said that Chelsea Clinton was "the family dog." No one who laughed at that could have been thinking of Chelsea Clinton as an *actual adolescent girl* whose looks were being ridiculed by the biggest talk radio host in the country. Had they done so, Limbaugh's sheer cruelty would have been obvious, and the only people who would have laughed are the kind of people who would laugh if they saw a dog being set on fire.

10   But Chelsea Clinton wasn't a human being; she was *an opponent*. And Limbaugh was scoring points. And the thought that an actual girl, and one who had never asked to be in politics, was being made fun of on national radio probably never crossed their minds, any more than the thought of actual human beings who are liberals and who are, or care about, soldiers, crossed Erick's.

11   No one—not liberals, not conservatives—should forget that their opponents are human beings. And no one can afford to start down the road Lewis describes, in which you allow yourself to be *disappointed* when your opponents aren't as bad as you first thought, or *want* them to be as bad as possible. And no one should get so wrapped up in political fights that in focusing on the mote in someone else's eye, they lose sight of the beam in their own.

QUESTIONS FOR DISCUSSION

1. Hilzoy opens with the quoted passage from Erick Erickson's blog and then asks how he could have written something so obviously not true. What possible explanations does she reject, and why? Why does she think he could not have been writing "in good faith"? What explanation does she think is most likely?

2. Hilzoy uses a passage from the Christian author C. S. Lewis, author of *The Chronicles of Narnia*, to argue against the temptation to exaggerate the evils of your opponents. How would you paraphrase Lewis's argument in the quoted passage? Why should people not do this?

3. Rush Limbaugh's remark about Chelsea Clinton was obviously intended as a joke that his conservative audience would find funny because of its rudeness. Limbaugh helped to establish the "shock jock" style of radio talk show—incivility as entertainment. Would you put this kind of joke in the same category as the blog post by Erickson?

4. Hilzoy's title for this post is "Fighting Words," meaning words that are intended to stir up a fight. Political blogs are notoriously shrill and combative, not intended to persuade those with opposing viewpoints but to rally the like-minded and "score points" in a war of words. Does it matter whether they use "fighting words" or not? What does hilzoy mean by the comment "duels have been fought for less"?

FOR INQUIRY

Hilzoy's blog post raises the issue of how the Internet has changed political commentary from the days when commentary appeared only in mainstream newspapers, written by professional journalists. Now, anyone can write opinion columns on a blog of their own or join one of the many partisan blogging groups on the Web. Do research into opinions on this change to a more popular and democratic kind of journalism. What are the advantages and disadvantages when anyone can say anything and gain a readership?

FOR FURTHER READING

Calandra, Lion. "Public Grooming: Duck! It's a Wayward Toenail Clipping." *New York Times.* Nytimes.com. 8 Nov. 2009. Web. 10 Jan. 2010.

Carter, Stephen L. *Civility: Manners, Morals, and the Etiquette of Democracy.* New York: Basic Books, 1998. Print.

Forni, P. M. *Choosing Civility: The Twenty-five Rules of Considerate Conduct.* New York: St. Martin's, 2002. Print.

——. *The Civility Solution: What to Do When People Are Rude.* New York: St. Martin's, 2009. Print.

Gilroy, Marilyn. "Colleges Grappling with Incivility." *Education Digest.* Dec. 2008 74:4, pp. 36–40. Ebscohost. Web. 13 Jan. 2010.

"Minding Manners: Civility Project Compiles Rules Using Washington's Models." *The University of Virginia Magazine.* Winter 2009. Web. 22 Jan. 2010.

Parker, Kathleen. "'New' Media Have Fueled Our Incivility." *Arizona Daily Star.* 17 Nov. 2009. Web. AzStarNet.com 9 Jan. 2010.

Siegel, Lee. *Against the Machine: Being Human in the Age of the Electronic Mob.* New York: Random House, 2008. Print.

Twenge, Jean. "Incivility—or Narcissism?" *The Narcissism Epidemic.* Psychologytoday.com. 18 Sept. 2009. Web. 20 Jan. 2010.

Enhancing Humans: How Far Is Too Far?

Human beings have always found ways to enhance their lives by improving on what nature provides. That is what technology is all about, from the first stone tools to today's computers and cell phones. Now technology has the potential to alter not only the tools we use but also our genetic makeup, the "software" that tells our bodily "hardware" what shapes to take and what to do. The question is: How far is too far? Where should our nearly compulsive efforts to enhance ourselves stop?

Genetic engineering receives much attention in the news, but at present manipulating genes is not a significant share of enhancement. Rather, as Carl Elliott points out in the first selection, using drugs intended to treat disease for their capacity to enhance our energy level, increase our capacity to focus, reduce anxiety, and in other ways make us more productive dominate the scene. We refer not to illegal drugs but prescription drugs such as Adderall, Ritalin, Provigil, and Aricept, developed to treat clinical problems like attention-deficit disorder (ADD) and Alzheimer's, but now used by healthy people as "brain enhancers." As the second and third selections in this chapter indicate, the use of such drugs is widespread on and off college campuses, and not just by students wanting a boost during final exams, but by professors, workaholic executives, and the like.

Outside of breaking the law by using prescription medications intended for somebody else in off-label ways, what is the problem? After all, we have "real" drug problems, such as crystal meth and heroin, against which someone getting a dose or two of Ritalin from an ADD patient for occasional use may seem trivial. But in fact the abuse of prescription drugs is a major concern, a bigger problem in some ways than the traffic in illegal drugs. They pose health risks and raise ethical questions such as how fair it is for a student to seek an advantage on a test that comes from anything else than studying hard. Will other students feel pressure to take drugs such as Ritalin to maintain their competitive edge? Are we headed toward a society not just addicted to Starbucks but where doping is as routine as coffee and energy drinks?

In general, our drive to enhance ourselves in all ways requires careful thought, each choice a balancing of such considerations as benefit, risk, effort expended, and cost. Where to draw the line is never easy: even dieting and exercise can go too far.

More specifically, we will face increasing temptations to use knowledge of genetics not just to prevent and treat disease—surely a legitimate use of the technology—but to increase the chances to have children that are smarter, more attractive, more talented, and so on than the roll of the dice in ordinary human mating permits. Gregory Stock and C. Ben Mitchell address these temptations with different attitudes and ways of thinking, but both alert us to how serious such choices are. Again, the question is, How far is too far? Should we stop with restoring normal function, using stem cells, for instance, to help a paralyzed person walk again? Or should we aim at fashioning better human beings, better in the sense of having higher IQs? Is it possible to be too smart? Or to have too much athletic or musical talent? These are hard questions that must be pondered as a powerful technology unfolds before our eyes.

The Tyranny of Happiness

CARL ELLIOTT

Carl Elliott teaches philosophy and bioethics at the University of Minnesota. The following selection comes from the last chapter of his book *Better Than Well: American Medicine Meets the American Dream.*

Elliott is concerned with the American passion for—some would say "compulsion toward"—enhancement of all kinds. He analyzes its motives and traces it to self-fulfillment as the goal of happiness. The problem is that such a notion of the good lacks social connection and eludes definition and assessment. How can we know what fulfills us? How can we know when we are fulfilled?

In America I have seen the freest and best educated of men in circumstances the happiest to be found in the world, yet it seemed to me that a cloud habitually hung on their brow, and they seemed serious and almost sad even in their pleasures.

—Alexis de Tocqueville

1 Thirty-five years ago, at the beginning of a twelve-year Senate inquiry into the drug industry, Senator Gaylord Nelson opened the session on psychotropic drugs by comparing them to the drugs in *Brave New World.* "When Aldous Huxley wrote his fantasy concept of the world of the future in the now classic *Brave New World,* he created an uncomfortable, emotionless culture of escapism dependent on tiny tablets of tranquility called soma."[1] Thirty-five years later, *Brave New World* is still invoked, time and again, as a warning against the dangers that await us if we embark on new enhancement technologies. News stories about psychotropic drugs, stem cells, reproductive technologies, or genetic engineering inevitably appear with headlines reading Brave New Medicine, Brave New Babies, Brave New Minds, or Brave New People. It is as if we have no other metaphors for these technologies, no competing visions of possible futures. Whatever the new technology of the moment happens to be, we hear the same cautionary tale: it will lead us to a totalitarian society where generic workers are slotted into castes and anesthetized into bliss. The people in these totalitarian societies are not so much unhappy as they are ignorant of what true happiness is, because they have been drugged and engineered to want nothing more than that which their station allows them.

2 We keep returning to this story, I suspect, partly because we like stories of individuals battling the forces of authority, and partly because it allows both teller and listener to collude in the shared sense that we, unlike our neighbors and coworkers and maybe even our family members, have figured out what is really bad about a technology that looks so good. This story says, "Our neighbors may have been sold a bill of goods, they may think that they have found happiness in a Prozac tablet and a Botox injection, but you and I know it's a crock. You and I are too smart to believe the cosmetic surgery Web sites, the drug companies peddling Sarafem and Paxil, and the psychiatrists who tell us we have adult ADHD." Yet as much as we like the *Brave New World* story, as many times as we read it and repeat it and write high school essays about it, somehow it never seems to apply to us. For men, the story of enhancement technologies is about the vanity of women; for women, it is about the sexual gaze of men; for Europeans and

Canadians, it is about shallowness of American values; for Americans, it is about "other" Americans—the ones who are either too crooked or deluded to acknowledge what is really going on. If we blame anyone for the ill effects of enhancement technologies, it is either someone in power (the FDA, the media, Big Pharma, "the culture") or the poor suckers who have allowed themselves to be duped (Miss America contestants, neurotic New Yorkers, Michael Jackson). We imagine second-rate TV stars lining up for liposuction and anxious middle managers asking their family doctors for Paxil, and we just shake our heads and laugh. "Why can't they learn to accept themselves as they are?" we ask. Then we are asked to sing a solo in the church choir and can't sleep for a week, or our daughter starts getting teased at school for her buck teeth, and the joke doesn't seem so funny anymore.

3   We all like to moralize about enhancement technologies, except for the ones we use ourselves. Those technologies never seem quite so bad, because our view of them comes not from television or magazines but from personal experience, or the shared confidences of our troubled friends. There is often striking contrast between private conversation about enhancement technologies and the broader public discussion. In public, for example, everyone seems to be officially anti-Prozac. Feminists ask me why doctors prescribe Prozac more often for women than for men. Undergraduates worry that Prozac might give their classmates a competitive edge. Philosophy professors argue that Prozac would make people shallow and uncreative. Germans object that Prozac is not a natural substance. Americans say that Prozac is a crutch. Most people seem to feel that Prozac is creating some version of what historian David Rothman called, in a *New Republic* cover story, "shiny, happy people."

4   In private, though, people have started to seek me out and tell me their Prozac stories. They have tried Prozac and hated it; they have tried Prozac and it changed their life; they have tried Prozac and can't see what the big deal is. It has begun to seem as if everyone I know is on Prozac, has been on Prozac, or is considering taking Prozac, and all of them want to get my opinion. Most of all, they want me to try Prozac myself. "How can you write about it if you've never even tried it?" I can see their point. Still, it strikes me as a strange way to talk about a prescription drug. These people are oddly insistent. It was as if we were back in high school, and they were trying to get me to smoke a joint.

5   People who look at America from abroad often marvel at the enthusiasm with which Americans use enhancement technologies. I can see why. It is a jolt to discover the rates at which Americans use Ritalin or Prozac or Botox. But "enthusiasm" is probably the wrong word to describe the way Americans feel about enhancement technologies. If this is enthusiasm, it is the enthusiasm of a diver on the high platform, who has to talk himself into taking the plunge. . . . I don't think Americans expect happiness in a handful of tablets. We take the tablets, but we brood about it. We try to hide the tablets from our friends. We worry that taking them is a sign of weakness. We try to convince our friends to take them too. We fret that if we don't take them, others will outshine us. We take the tablets, but they leave a bitter taste in our mouths.

6   Why? Perhaps because in those tablets is a mix of all the American wishes, lusts, and fears: the drive to self-improvement, the search for fulfillment, the desire

to show that there are second acts in American lives; yet a mix diluted by nagging anxieties about social conformity, about getting too much too easily, about phoniness and self-deception and shallow pleasure. This is not a story from *Brave New World.* It is not even a story of enhancement. . . . It is less a story about trying to get ahead than about the terror of being left behind, and the humiliation of crossing the finish line dead last, while the crowd points at you and laughs. You can still refuse to use enhancement technologies, of course—you might be the last woman in America who does not dye her gray hair, the last man who refuses to work out at the gym—but even that publicly announces something to other Americans about who you are and what you value. This is all part of the logic of consumer culture. You cannot simply opt out of the system and expect nobody to notice how much you weigh.

7   Why here, why now? On one level, the answer seems obvious: because the technology has arrived. If you are anxious and lonely and a drug can fix it, why stay anxious and lonely? If you are unhappy with your body and surgery can fix it, why stay unhappy? The market moves to fill a demand for happiness as efficiently as it moves to fill a demand for spark plugs or home computers. It is on a deeper level that the question of enhancement technologies becomes more puzzling. What has made the ground for these technologies so fertile? The sheer variety of technologies on display is remarkable. . . . Black folks rub themselves with cream to make their skin lighter, while white folks broil in tanning parlors to make their skin darker. Bashful men get ETS surgery to reduce blood flow above the neck, while elderly men take Viagra to increase blood flow below the belt. Each technology has its own rationale, its own cultural niche, a distinct population of users, and an appeal that often waxes or wanes with changes in fashion or the state of scientific knowledge. But do they have anything in common? Is there anything about the way we live now that helps explain their popularity?

8   The "self that struggles to realize itself," as philosopher Michael Walzer puts it, has become a familiar notion to most people living in the West today.[2] We tend to see ourselves as the managers of life projects that we map out, organize, make choices about, perhaps compare with other possible projects, and ultimately live out to completion. From late adolescence onward, we are expected to make important decisions about what to do for a living, where to live, whether to marry and have children, all with the sense that these decisions will contribute to the success or failure of our projects. Yet as Walzer points out, there is nothing natural or inevitable about this way of conceptualizing a life. Not everyone in the West today will think of their lives as planned projects, and most people at most times in history have probably thought of their lives differently. Marriages are arranged; educational choices are fixed; gods are tyrannical or absent. A life might be spontaneous, rather than planned; its shape might be given to us, rather than created. The shapes of lives can be determined not by the demands of personal values or self-fulfillment, but by those of God, family, social station, caste, or one's ancestors.

9   This notion of life as a project suggests both individual responsibility and moral uncertainty. If I am the planner and manager of my life, then I am at least partly

responsible for its success or failure. Thus the lure of enhancement technologies: as tools to produce a better, more successful project. Yet if my life is a project, what exactly is the purpose of the project? How do I tell a successful project from a failure? Aristotle (for example) could write confidently about the good life for human beings because he was confident about what the purpose of being a human being was. Just as a knife has a purpose, so human beings have a purpose; just as the qualities that make for a good knife are those that help the knife slice, whittle, and chop, the qualities that make a human being better are those that help us better fulfill our purpose as human beings.

10   Our problem, of course, is that most of us don't have Aristotle's confidence about the purpose of human life. Good knives cut, that much we can see, but what does a good human being do, and how will we know when we are doing it? Is there even such a thing as a single, universal human purpose? Not if we believe what we are told by the culture that surrounds us. From philosophy courses and therapy sessions to magazines and movies, we are told that questions of purpose vary from one person to the next; that, in fact, a large part of our life project is to discover our own individual purpose and develop it to its fullest. This leaves us with unanswered questions not just about what kinds of lives are better or worse, but also about the criteria by which such judgments are made. Is it better to be a successful bail bondsman or a second-rate novelist? On what yardstick do we compare the lives of Reform Jews, high-church Episcopalians, and California Wiccans? Where exactly should the choices we make about our lives be anchored?

11   Many people today believe that the success or failure of a life has something to do with the idea of self-fulfillment. We may not know exactly what a successful life is, but we have a pretty good suspicion that it has something to do with being fulfilled—or at the very least, that an unfulfilled life runs the risk of failure. In the name of fulfillment people quit their jobs in human resources and real estate to become poets and potters, leave their dermatology practices to do medical mission work in Bangladesh, even divorce their husbands or wives (the marriage was adequate, but it was not fulfilling). Women leave their children in day care because they believe that they will be more fulfilled with a career; they leave their jobs because they believe that it will be more fulfilling to stay home with the kids. Fulfillment has a strong moral strand to it—many people feel that they *ought* to pursue a career, that they *ought* to leave a loveless marriage—but its parameters are vague and indeterminate. How exactly do I know if I am fulfilled? Fulfillment looks a little like being in love, a little like a successful spiritual quest; it is a state centered largely on individual psychic well-being. If I am alienated, depressed, or anxious, I can't be completely fulfilled.

12   If I am not fulfilled, I am missing out on what life can offer. Life is a short, sweet ride, and I am spending it all in the station. The problem is that there is no great, overarching metric for self-fulfillment, no master schedule that we can look up at and say, "Yes, I've missed the train." So we look desperately to experts for instructions—counselors, psychiatrists, advice columnists, self-help writers, life coaches, even professional ethicists. We read the ads on the wall for cosmetic

dentistry, and we look nervously at the people standing next to us in line. Does she know something that I don't? Is she more fulfilled? How does my psychic well-being compare to hers? . . .

13   In other times and places, success or failure in a life might have been determined by fixed and agreed-upon standards. You displeased the ancestors; you shamed your family; you did not accept Jesus Christ as your personal savior. You arrived late to the station, and the train left without you. But our situation today is different—not for everyone, of course, but for many of us. We have gotten on the train, but we don't know who is driving it, or where, some point off in the far distance, the tracks are leading. The other passengers are smiling, they look happy, yet underneath this facade of good cheer and philosophical certainty, a demon keeps whispering in our ears: "What if I have gotten it all wrong? What if I have boarded the wrong train?"

14   Tocqueville hinted at this worry over 150 years ago when he wrote about American "restlessness in the midst of abundance." Behind all the admirable energy of American life, Tocqueville saw a kind of grim relentlessness. We build houses to pass our old age, Tocqueville wrote, then sell them before the roof is on; we clear fields, then leave it to others to gather the harvest; we take up a profession, then leave it to take up another one or go into politics. Americans frantically pursue prosperity, and when we finally get it, we are tormented by the worry that we might have gotten it quicker. An American on vacation, Tocqueville marveled, "will travel five hundred miles in a few days as a distraction from his happiness."[3]

15   Tocqueville may well have been right about American restlessness, but it took another Frenchman, surrealist painter Phillipe Soupault, to put his finger on the form that it has taken today. According to Soupault, Americans see the pursuit of happiness not just as a right, as the Declaration of Independence states, but as a strange sort of duty. In the United States, he wrote, "one is always in danger of entrapment by what appears on the surface to be a happy civilization. There is a sort of obligation to be happy." Humans are born to be happy, and if they are not, something has gone wrong. As Soupault puts it, "Whoever is unhappy is suspect."[4] Substitute self-fulfillment for happiness and you get something of the ethic that motivates the desire for enhancement technologies. Once self-fulfillment is hitched to the success of a human life, it comes perilously close to an obligation—not an obligation to God, country, or family, but an obligation to the self. We are compelled to pursue fulfillment through enhancement technologies not in order to get ahead of others, but to make sure that we have lived our lives to the fullest. The train has left the station and we don't know where it is going. The least we can do is be sure it is making good time.

NOTES

1. Mickey Smith, *A Social History of the Minor Tranquilizers: The Quest for Small Comfort in an Age of Anxiety* (New York: Praeger, 1989) 178.
2. Michael Walzer, *Thick and Thin: Moral Argument at Home and Abroad* (South Bend: Notre Dame UP, 1994) 23–24.

3. Alexis de Tocqueville, *Democracy in America,* trans. George Lawrence, ed. J. P. Mayer (New York: Harper and Row, 1988) 536.

4. Philippe Soupault, "Introduction to Mademoiselle Coeur Brise (Miss Lonely-hearts)," *Nathanael West: A Collection of Critical Essays,* ed. Jay Martin (Englewood Cliffs: Prentice-Hall, 1971) 112–13.

FOR DISCUSSION

1. According to Elliott, why do people appeal so often to Huxley's novel, *Brave New World,* when enhancement technologies, especially new ones, are discussed? Why does he consider the connection essentially misleading?

2. Elliott claims that American culture and values emphasize "life as a project"—hence, "the lure of enhancement technologies: as tools to produce a better, more successful project." Do you see this as the drive behind such popular TV shows as *What Not to Wear* and *Extreme Makeover?*

3. "If I am alienated, depressed, or anxious, I can't be completely fulfilled," Elliott says, and the solution becomes a pill, plastic surgery, occupational change, divorce—something that will "fix" the problem. But are there circumstances when people ought to feel alienated, depressed, or anxious? Can such feelings be positive and productive rather than negative and counterproductive?

4. Elliott cites the French surrealist painter Phillipe Soupault, who claims that in the United States "there is a sort of obligation to be happy. . . . Whoever is unhappy is suspect." Thus, according to Elliott, the pursuit of happiness is not a right but rather "a strange sort of duty . . . an obligation to the self." Do you find this diagnosis persuasive? What, according to Elliott, makes such an understanding of the pursuit of happiness unsatisfying and ultimately self-defeating?

FOR PERSUASION

"Our problem," Elliott claims, "is that most of us don't have Aristotle's confidence about the purpose of human life. . . . [W]hat does a good human being do, and how will we know when we are doing it?"

Are we Americans so much in doubt about what we ought to be doing as Elliott claims? Write an essay arguing against his assertion of complete relativity where our notion of the good is concerned. Support it by referring to popular culture—to movies and TV dramas, for instance—which often reflect our values and sometimes expose them for reflection.

Brain Enhancement Is Wrong, Right?

BENEDICT CAREY

Benedict Carey is a writer on science and medical topics for the *New York Times.* The following article appeared on March 9, 2008.

© 2008 The New York Times. Reprinted by permission.

1   So far no one is demanding that asterisks be attached to Nobels, Pulitzers or Lasker awards. Government agents have not been raiding anthropology departments, riffling book bags, testing professors' urine. And if there are illicit trainers on campuses, shady tutors with wraparound sunglasses and ties to basement labs in Italy, no one has exposed them.

2   Yet an era of doping may be looming in academia, and it has ignited a debate about policy and ethics that in some ways echoes the national controversy over performance enhancement accusations against elite athletes like Barry Bonds and Roger Clemens.

3   In a recent commentary in the journal *Nature,* two Cambridge University researchers reported that about a dozen of their colleagues had admitted to regular use of prescription drugs like Adderall, a stimulant, and Provigil, which promotes wakefulness, to improve their academic performance. The former is approved to treat attention deficit disorder, the latter narcolepsy, and both are considered more effective, and more widely available, than the drugs circulating in dorms a generation ago.

4   Letters flooded the journal, and an online debate immediately bubbled up. The journal has been conducting its own, more rigorous survey, and so far at least 20 respondents have said that they used the drugs for nonmedical purposes, according to Philip Campbell, the journal's editor in chief. The debate has also caught fire on the Web site of the *Chronicle of Higher Education,* where academics and students are sniping at one another.

5   But is prescription tweaking to perform on exams, or prepare presentations and grants, really the same as injecting hormones to chase down a home run record, or win the Tour de France?

6   Some argue that such use could be worse, given the potentially deep impact on society. And the behavior of academics in particular, as intellectual leaders, could serve as an example to others.

7   In his book *Our Posthuman Future: Consequences of the Biotechnology Revolution,* Francis Fukuyama raises the broader issue of performance enhancement: "The original purpose of medicine is to heal the sick, not turn healthy people into gods." He and others point out that increased use of such drugs could raise the standard of what is considered "normal" performance and widen the gap between those who have access to the medications and those who don't—and even erode the relationship between struggle and the building of character.

8   "Even though stimulants and other cognitive enhancers are intended for legitimate clinical use, history predicts that greater availability will lead to an increase in diversion, misuse and abuse," wrote Dr. Nora Volkow, director of the National Institute on Drug Abuse, and James Swanson of the University of California at Irvine, in a letter to *Nature.* "Among high school students, abuse of prescription medications is second only to cannabis use."

9   But others insist that the ethics are not so clear, and that academic performance is different in important ways from baseball, or cycling.

10   "I think the analogy with sports doping is really misleading, because in sports it's all about competition, only about who's the best runner or home run hitter," said Martha Farah, director of the Center for Cognitive Neuroscience at the University of Pennsylvania. "In academics, whether you're a student or a researcher, there is an element of competition, but it's secondary. The main purpose is to try to learn things, to get experience, to write papers, to do experiments. So in that case if you can do it better because you've got some drug on board, that would on the face of things seem like a plus."

11   She and other midcareer scientists interviewed said that, as far as they knew, very few of their colleagues used brain-boosting drugs regularly. Many have used Provigil for jet lag, or even to stay vertical for late events. But most agreed that the next generation of scientists, now in graduate school and college, were more likely to use the drugs as study aids and bring along those habits as they moved up the ladder.

12   Surveys of college students have found that from 4 percent to 16 percent say they have used stimulants or other prescription drugs to improve their academic performance—usually getting the pills from other students.

13   "Suppose you're preparing for the SAT, or going for a job interview—in those situations where you have to perform on that day, these drugs will be very attractive," said Dr. Barbara Sahakian of Cambridge, a co-author with Sharon Morein-Zamir of the recent essay in *Nature.* "The desire for cognitive enhancement is very strong, maybe stronger than for beauty, or athletic ability."

14   Jeffrey White, a graduate student in cell biology who has attended several institutions, said that those numbers sounded about right. "You can usually tell

who's using them because they can be angry, testy, hyperfocused, they don't want to be bothered," he said.

15   Mr. White said he did not use the drugs himself, considering them an artificial shortcut that could set people up for problems later on. "What happens if you're in a fast-paced surgical situation and they're not available?" he asked. "Will you be able to function at the same level?"

16   Yet such objections—and philosophical concerns—can vaporize when students and junior faculty members face other questions: What happens if I don't make the cut? What if I'm derailed by a bad test score, or a mangled chemistry course?

17   One person who posted anonymously on the *Chronicle of Higher Education* Web site said that a daily regimen of three 20-milligram doses of Adderall transformed his career: "I'm not talking about being able to work longer hours without sleep (although that helps)," the posting said. "I'm talking about being able to take on twice the responsibility, work twice as fast, write more effectively, manage better, be more attentive, devise better and more creative strategies."

18   Dr. Anjan Chatterjee, an associate professor of neurology at the University of Pennsylvania who foresaw this debate in a 2004 paper, argues that the history of cosmetic surgery—scorned initially as vain and unnatural but now mainstream as a form of self-improvement—is a guide to predicting the trajectory of cosmetic neurology, as he calls it.

19   "We worship at the altar of progress, and to the demigod of choice," Dr. Chatterjee said. "Both are very strong undercurrents in the culture and the way this is likely to be framed is: 'Look, we want smart people to be as productive as possible to make everybody's lives better. We want people performing at the max, and if that means using these medicines, then great, then we should be free to choose what we want as long as we're not harming someone.' I'm not taking that position, but we have this winner-take-all culture and that is the way it is likely to go."

20   People already use legal performance enhancers, he said, from high-octane cafe Americanos to the beta-blockers taken by musicians to ease stage fright, to antidepressants to improve mood. "So the question with all of these things is, Is this enhancement, or a matter of removing the cloud over our better selves?" he said.

21   The public backlash against brain-enhancement, if it comes, may hit home only after the practice becomes mainstream, Dr. Chatterjee suggested. "You can imagine a scenario in the future, when you're applying for a job, and the employer says, 'Sure, you've got the talent for this, but we require you to take Adderall.' Now, maybe you do start to care about the ethical implications."

FOR DISCUSSION

1. "The desire for cognitive enhancement is very strong, maybe stronger than for beauty, or athletic ability," Carey cites Barbara Sahakian as saying. Does this statement seem true to you? If so, what are its implications?

2. Reread paragraph 17 carefully, noting the claims of the person who posted to the *Chronicle of Higher Education's* Web site. He believes that Adderall has "transformed his career," which makes the scenario discussed in the last paragraph not as unrealistic as it may seem. What are the ethical implications of being *required* to take performance-enhancing drugs, say, to be an air traffic controller?

FOR DISCUSSION AND MEDIATION

The strength of Carey's article is that he reports the opposing positions on performance-enhancing drugs so well. Reread the article, paying special attention to the views of Francis Fukuyama, Nora Volkow, Martha Farah, and Anjan Chatterjee. Then consider the proposition that, good or bad, greater use of such drugs will almost certainly happen.

Given that people will use them, what would be the best position for us to take regarding *responsible and ethical use?* That is, take and defend a position designed to draw the assent of the widest possible audience, one that will take into account both the viewpoints of those who oppose the use of performance-enhancers and those who see no objection to them.

Professor's Little Helper?

BARBARA SAHAKIAN AND NORA VOLKOW

Perhaps no one knows more about cognitive-enhancing drugs than Barbara Sahakian, a neourologist at Cambridge University, and Nora Volkow, head of the National Institute of Drug Abuse in the United States. They were interviewed by Lynn Neary on "Talk of the Nation," a National Public Radio program, on March 17, 2008. We offer an abridged version of the transcript here.

1   I'm Lynn Neary in Washington.

2   If you could take a drug that might help you think better or perform more effectively and efficiently in school or at work, would you do it? And if so, do you think that's the same as taking a drug that helps you hit more home runs? That's one of the questions being raised in the debate over brain-enhancement drugs. Once prescribed mainly for people with disabilities, brain-enhancement drugs are now being used more frequently by students who are about to take a tough test or by academics and other professionals who may be getting ready for a big presentation. Is it cheating or not?

3   Joining us now from the BBC studios in Cambridge, England, is Barbara Sahakian. She is professor of clinical neuropsychology at Cambridge University. Her commentary on brain-enhancement drugs, titled "Professor's Little Helper," appeared in the journal *Nature*.

4   **Neary:** What drugs are we talking about?

5   **Prof. Sahakian:** [Among others, she mentions Ritalin, for treating attention deficit hyperactivity disorder (ADHD) and Aricept, for treating Alzheimer's.]

6   **Neary:** So if you do not have any kind of disability or condition that requires the use of these drugs, how does it affect you?

7   **Prof. Sahakian:** We've done studies with Ritalin using Cambridge undergraduates who are already functioning very well. But even Cambridge undergraduates show improvements when they take Ritalin on the different tests that we've used, such as test of what we call working memory [recall of information for a short time]. We showed very good enhancement.

8   Another drug we used was modafinil, known as Provigil, for the treatment of excessive daytime sleepiness or narcolepsy. We've shown that normal, healthy volunteers do very well on that and increased their memory, planning ability and so forth.

9   **Neary:** So people now are using these drugs for what purpose? Give me an example of why somebody might take one of these drugs?

10   **Prof. Sahakian:** We gave a questionnaire to some colleagues I knew who were taking these drugs. They say they take them for jetlag. If they have to give a big lecture and feel that they've got jetlag, they take the drug. And they say it improves their ability to attend, their working memory, and word finding, which you can imagine for a lecturer is very important.

11   I have colleagues also who they say they took it because they want to just increase their mental energy and improve their thinking when they're trying to have a particularly productive day.

12   **Neary:** When we talk about performance-enhancing drugs in sports or in physical activity, we say that it makes you stronger. Can you say that these drugs make you smarter?

13   **Prof. Sahakian:** It depends what you mean by smarter. We're not talking I.Q., but it helps to keep your attention focused and to remember what you're trying to do in order to complete the task.

14   **Neary:** So this is where some of the ethical questions might come up. In this country, for instance, there's the SAT, the college entrance exams. If some students are starting to take these drugs to help them perform better and others are not, then those who are taking them might have an unfair advantage.

15   **Prof. Sahakian:** Well, exactly, that's one of the ethical questions because it could result in coercing other people to take the drug because they fear they will be at a disadvantage if they don't. . . .

16   I don't know if you're aware but at some college campuses where they've done surveys about 16 to 20 percent of college students have used Ritalin for studying purposes and to enhance cognition for exams. So it's fairly widespread in the USA on college campuses.

17   **Neary:** We are talking about brain-enhancement drugs and debate over some of the ethical issues involved. If you'd like join our discussion, our number is 800-989-8255. We're going to take a call now from Conway, Arkansas.

18   **Caller:** I'm a student here in Conway, a senior, graduating this year. And I've taken these brain-enhancing drugs and it's difficult because it seems students that are really excelling are taking them and it's hard to compete in a busy academic environment without the drugs. There's so many people overloading themselves and using them to improve their performance.

19   **Neary:** So you started doing it because you felt other kids were doing it to keep up?

20   **Caller:** I did it the first time because I was behind and I had too much work to do and it was an easy way out. You just see how many people do it, especially during finals and keeping them awake to write papers.

21   **Neary:** Can you explain what the effect is, exactly?

22   **Caller:** It makes it easier to stay up for long amounts of time and focus on a single task without getting distracted, which is really easy to do when you're surrounded by thousands of people.

23   **Neary:** I'm assuming that there's an underground, a way of buying them on campus?

24   **Caller:** It's not really underground; it's pretty open. There's a lot of people that are prescribed Ritalin and Adderall, and it's not hard to find some of it.

25   **Neary:** Do you have any concerns about what you are able to accomplish with these drugs as compared to a friend who does not take them?

26 **Caller:** I don't necessarily feel that it gives me an advantage, just that I am able to do more work when I am stressed out. . . . I've stopped using the drugs. They give me the jitters, make me feel bad afterwards.

27 **Neary:** Thank you so much for calling in. Barbara Sahakian, can you comment?

28 **Prof. Sahakian:** I think what he said is very typical, so it was helpful that he was forthright about it. We had letters responding to my "Professor's Little Helper" commentary, and one of the letters came from Nora Volkow, head of the National Institute of Drug Abuse in America. Her point was that there is a large amount of these prescriptions that are being passed on or sold, a concern for the NIDA.

29 **Neary:** We have to take a break here and when we come back, Dr. Volkow is going to join us. . . .

30 It's so good to have you with us. Welcome to the program. Dr. Volkow, can you tell us how addictive these drugs are?

31 **Dr. Nora Volkow:** Stimulant medications have an effect that is similar to that of drugs of abuse. So yes, indeed, both amphetamine as well as Ritalin has the potential for producing dependency.

32 **Neary:** We heard from a caller already who was describing the effect. He said, sometimes you get jittery from these drugs. I wonder if you can expand on this.

33 **Dr. Volkow:** Well, responses to stimulant medication vary enormously and the effects of Ritalin are somewhat different from those of amphetamine. Amphetamine is more potent and its effects longer lasting. And because it's stimulating dopamine [a brain chemical] at much higher levels than normal, these can be perceived by individuals as making them restless or jittery, and these can be very, very uncomfortable.

34 Also, he mentioned that he didn't like how he felt after the drug's effects are over. It is described by some individuals as feeling like a crash. They lack energy and cannot concentrate.

35 When you use these medications outside the prescribed purposes, you produce adaptation changes in your brain that can be deleterious to performance.

36 Furthermore, not everybody improves when they take a stimulant medication. There are numerous stories that for some individuals and certain tasks, performance can actually deteriorate.

37 **Neary:** How would they deteriorate?

38 **Dr. Volkow:** For example, you can concentrate much better but that concentration can go to the extreme, make you perseverate on that particular task when you need to shift to another. . . .

39 **Neary:** Oh, I see, so you're focusing so intensely on one thing that you're not able to go back and forth and . . .

40 **Dr. Volkow:** Exactly.

41   **Neary:** You don't have the breadth that you need for true knowledge, really?

42   **Dr. Volkow:** Exactly.

43   **Neary:** Okay. Let's take a call. We're going to go to Joe. He is calling from Salt Lake City, Utah.

44   Joe, go ahead.

45   **Joe:** Thank you for letting me participate. I'm a physician and I've prescribed stimulants as well as Provagil. And I was with a group of other physicians discussing the ethical aspects of it, and two things came to us. One was whether or not the drugs were addictive; the other was whether or not there was competition, in the same way sports players take steroids to enhance their performance.

46   We thought it was ethically dubious for a student who otherwise doesn't have a diagnosis to be taking a stimulant to improve test scores. It made it unfair for them to be in the same arena as students who aren't taking stimulants. However, we thought it may not be as ethically dubious for individuals who are not directly competing, such as, say, the physician who is a resident, who has been on call late nights and he takes modafinil to be more alert the next day—or the long-haul truck driver who may be taking it to be more alert.

47   **Neary:** So you're saying that, as a doctor, you would prescribe this drug to someone who doesn't have a physical or mental condition where they need it but for their job?

48   **Joe:** Yes—well, yes and no. Modafinil is indicated for shift workers, and residents and truck drivers do shift work. I wouldn't necessarily prescribe it to someone who's livelihood or safety doesn't depend on it, but I actually haven't had anyone ask me to prescribe it to them.

49   **Neary:** Oh, I see. Okay. . . .

50   Barbara Sahakian, let me ask you to reply, to respond first.

51   **Prof. Sahakian:** I thought Joe's point was very interesting because it has been suggested that there may be conditions in which we want to encourage people to take cognitive-enhancing drugs—for instance, air-traffic controllers.

52   And he also pointed out that, thus far anyway, modafinil doesn't seem to have the same abuse potential, true also of some other drugs.

53   **Neary:** Dr. Volkow was turning thumbs down on a certain point when you were talking, so I just want to hear what she was responding to.

54   **Dr. Volkow:** I think that giving stimulant medication for people on night shifts is accepted medical practice. At the same time, there has been concern that some judgments have been inadequate when people have been sleep deprived—many misjudgments have been directly linked with the effects of amphetamine. Amphetamine can not only increase paranoid thinking but also cause sleep deprivation. So, again, not everybody responds well to stimulant medications.

55   I was smiling at modafinil because new studies done on humans show that, just like stimulants, it increases dopamine in the brain.

56   **Neary:** I was going to ask you, what's the difference between this and, say, what used to be called speed, which kids used to use before exams.

57   **Dr. Volkow:** Well, Dexedrine or speed is an amphetamine-like compound and with Adderall, you have Dexedrine plus amphetamine. That's a very effective medication for attention deficit disorder.

58   **Neary:** All right. We're going to take a call now. Carolyn. She's calling from San Jose, California.

59   **Carolyn:** Hi. Thank you for taking my call. Good program. I just am concerned at the widespread use of drugs for everything and nothing in our culture. And you know, Dr. Joe a little while ago was talking about prescribing these drugs for the resident who didn't get a good night's sleep. Frankly, I'd rather be treated by a resident who did have a good night's sleep and not by one who's on drugs. And what's next? Are we going to drug test students?

60   **Neary:** All right, thanks so much for calling, Carolyn.
61   Barbara Sahakian or Dr. Volkow?

62   **Prof. Sahakian:** Well, I'd like to respond. First, to the very important point she made: our drug use is a reflection of our society and we should really be looking at the broader context of why healthy people would choose to use a drug in the first place. There are other options for coping with everyday stresses. We could improve the work–life balance or learn relaxation techniques. And the best way to enhance cognition is through education and other means. So we have other ways of tackling these problems.

63   Yes, we may have to drug-test, I suppose, if people are against using the drugs in competitive situations.

64   **Neary:** Dr. Volkow.

65   **Dr. Volkow:** There's another aspect that is important to consider which we haven't discussed. It has been shown that ADHD kids on stimulant medications perform better, but when tested off the stimulant, they actually perform worse than they did before initiation of the stimulant. They recover, but there's a period where the performance is actually worse than it was before. And this is likely to happen when people are taking stimulants outside the context of ADHD.

66   Furthermore, if a stimulant medication helps you pass an exam, what will be the outcome two or three months later? Will you be able to remember as well the information as you might have done with proper sleep and putting in the hours that it takes to learn without sleep deprivation? If you're doing it just to pass an exam—well, that's one issue—but if you're doing it to build up a knowledge base that will allow you to succeed—well, we do not have any information about these medications on that score.

FOR DISCUSSION

1. Is there any difference between taking a cognitive-enhancing drug to do better on the SAT and taking steroids to hit more home runs? Do both amount to cheating?

2. The college student identified as Caller, who called in from Conway, Arkansas, mentions that his peers are "overloading themselves." Would you say that you or some of your friends are doing too much, either as a matter of choice or necessity? Is that the underlying reason why drugs like Ritalin and Provigil appeal so much?

3. Nora Volkow supplies a number of reasons not to use the drugs. What are they? Which do you find most persuasive?

FOR DISCUSSION AND INQUIRY

"Our drug use is a reflection of our society," Barbara Sahakian correctly says, "and we should be looking at the broader context of why healthy people would choose to use a drug in the first place." Explore this statement in class, drawing on all the selections in this chapter so far.

Then write an exploratory essay offering your own tentative explanation for why healthy people resort so often to over-the-counter and prescription drugs. What needs to change for this kind of drug abuse to diminish? Draw on your own experience or that of people you know.

Choosing Our Genes

GREGORY STOCK

> Gregory Stock is director of the Program on Medicine, Technology, and Society at UCLA and author of the best-seller *Redesigning Humans.* In his book and the following article from *The Futurist,* he offers a detailed discussion of what is likely to happen soon in applying genetics to enhance human beings.

1   Technologies giving us control over our genetic destiny will be developed, whether they are banned or not. But clumsy regulatory efforts could greatly impede our progress toward improving the future health and well-being of our descendants.

2   What is causing all the fuss are technologies that will give parents the ability to make conscious choices about the genetics and traits of their children. For the foreseeable future, genetically altering adults is not in the cards, other than for treating a handful of specific diseases like cystic fibrosis. Changing the genes of an adult is far too daunting, and there are simpler, safer, and more effective ways of intervening to restore or enhance adult function.

3   Germinal choice technology refers to a whole realm of technologies by which parents influence the genetic constitutions of their children at the time of their conception. The simplest such intervention would be to correct genes. It is not a particularly radical departure, since it would have exactly the same effect as could be accomplished by screening multiple embryos and picking one with the desired genes. In fact, such embryo screening is being done now in preimplantation genetic diagnosis. Such technology has been in use for more than a decade, but what can be tested for is going to become increasingly sophisticated in the next 5 to 10 years. And as these technologies mature, the kinds of decisions that parents can make will become much more complex.

4   Farther into the future will be germline interventions—alterations to the egg, sperm, or more likely the first cell of an embryo. These procedures are being done already in animal systems, but using approaches that don't have the safety or reliability that would be required in human beings. . . .

GOALS OF GERMINAL CHOICE

5   The prevention of disease will likely be the initial goal of germinal choice. And the possibilities may soon move well beyond the correction of aberrant genes. Recent studies suggest, for example, that children who have Down syndrome have close to a 90% reduction in the incidence of many cancers. It is possible that trisomy 21—i.e., having a third copy of chromosome 21, with increased gene expression levels that lead to the retardation and other symptoms of Down syndrome—may be protective against cancer. What if we could identify which of the genes on that chromosome are responsible for this protection from cancer? Geneticists might take a set of those genes and place them on an artificial chromosome, then add it to an embryo to reduce the incidence of cancer to the levels seen with Down syndrome, but without all the problems brought by the duplication of the other genes on chromosome 21. Many other similar possibilities will no doubt emerge, and some will almost certainly prove beneficial.

6   The use of artificial chromosomes might work quite well, particularly because the chromosomes themselves could be tested within the laboratory environment before any human use. They could be tested on animals, validated, and used in humans in essentially the same state they were tested in. Today, each gene therapy is done anew, so it is impossible to gain that kind of reliability. . . .

7   All sorts of ideas will occur to future gene therapists, who will then test them out to see if they are possible. If they are, then we will not forgo them. Reducing the incidence of cancer and heart disease, for example, or retarding aging are health enhancements that will be seen as very, very desirable.

GENETICALLY EXTENDING LIFESPANS

8   Antiaging will be an especially significant area of research because such interventions seem so plausible and are so strongly desired by large numbers of people. If it turns out that there are interventions that could—through our unraveling of the underlying process of aging—allow us to develop pharmaceutical and other interventions that are effective in adults, then that is what everybody would want. . . .

9   But embryo engineering will likely be easier and more effective than gene therapy in an adult. This is because genes placed in an embryo are copied into every single cell in the body and could be given tissue-specific control elements. So there may well be interventions to an embryo that are infeasible in an adult. And in this case, parents will likely look at conception as their one chance to give their child significant health advantages—a chance that will never again be available.

10   A "cure for aging" might be greatly accelerated by an infusion of funds into research on the biology of aging. Right now, the area is rather underfunded. Much more money is being spent to find treatments for diseases of aging than to understand the underlying process that may be responsible for a wide variety of age-related diseases, such as cancer, heart disease, Alzheimer's, arthritis, and diabetes. . . .

11   Antiaging—offering one's children longer lifespans—will probably be a key goal of germline interventions, but not the only one. To do what is best for our children is a very human response. In fact, international polls have shown that in every country polled there is at least a significant minority who are interested in enhancing the physical or mental well-being of their children. They are thinking not of simple therapy to avoid particular diseases, but interventions aimed at actually improving (at least in their eyes) a child's beauty, intelligence, strength, altruism, and other qualities.

AN UNWELCOME CHOICE?

12   Society may not welcome some parents' choices. Sex selection is legal in the United States, but illegal in Britain and a number of other countries. And quite a few people think the procedure should be illegal in the United States as well, despite the fact that in the West, where no serious gender imbalances arise, it is hard to see who is injured by such choices. Another immediate decision will be whether parents screen for broad numbers of genetic diseases, some of which may not be terribly serious. And soon, parents will likely be able to make choices about the

height or IQ of their children, or other aspects of temperament and personality—predispositions and vulnerabilities that may soon be rather obvious in each of our genetic readouts.

13   The first wave of possibilities from germinal choice technology will be in genetic testing and screening, choosing one embryo instead of another. Initially, it will be very difficult for a lot of people to accept this, but it will be almost impossible to regulate, since any such embryo could have arrived completely naturally. These choices may prove agonizing, but they won't be dangerous, and I suspect they will bring us more benefits than problems.

14   Some people worry about a loss of diversity, but I think a more wrenching issue may be parents who decide to specifically select an embryo that would result in a child with a serious health condition. Should parents be allowed to make such choices?

15   In the deaf community, for instance, there is a whole movement that is very opposed to the use of cochlear implants, because it hurts deaf culture and treats deafness like a disability. This is exactly the way most hearing people view it. And there are deaf parents who say that they would use germinal choice technology to ensure that their children were deaf. That is not to say they would take an embryo and damage it, but they would select an embryo that would develop into a deaf child.

16   That becomes a real issue for society when, for example, such health problems have medical costs that society must bear. If we feel that parents do have the right to make such choices and that there is no reason to value the birth of a healthy individual any more than someone with serious health challenges, then we won't regulate such choices. But if we decide there is a problem, and really want to come to grips with it, we may find it very challenging.

FRIGHTENING OURSELVES TO DEATH

17   Shortly after reports were heard of the first pregnancy resulting from a human cloning program (reports that most scientists believe are a total fabrication), U.S. President George W. Bush voiced his support for a Senate bill that would outlaw all forms of human cloning, including biomedical research aimed at creating embryonic stem cells that would not be rejected when transplanted, so-called therapeutic cloning.

18   I believe such a ban is premature, futile, extremely misguided, and just plain wrong. It would not significantly delay the arrival of reproductive cloning, which in my view is almost certain to occur within this decade somewhere in the world. It would inject politics, religion, and philosophy into the workings of basic research and inquiry, which would be a dangerous precedent. It would legislate greater concern for a microscopic dot of cells than for real people with real diseases and real suffering. And it would threaten embryo researchers with criminal penalties so extreme (10 years in prison) that they are almost unbelievable in the United States, a country where women during their first trimester have the right to an abortion for any reason whatsoever.

19   U.S. restraints on embryo research have already had an impact on the development of biomedical technologies directed toward regenerative medicine. Those

restraints have slowed progress in this realm in the United States, which has the most powerful biomedical research effort in the world. Such research has now moved to Britain and other countries, such as Singapore, which is funding a huge program to explore embryonic stem cells. But such delays are very unfortunate because of the might-have-beens that still are not. For most people, a delay of a decade or two is not a big problem, but this is not so for people like actor Michael J. Fox and others who are undergoing progressive decline from serious diseases like Parkinson's or Alzheimer's. . . .

20   No matter how much it disturbs us, human germinal choice is inevitable. Embryo selection is already here, cloning is on the way, and even direct germline engineering in humans will arrive. Such technology is inevitable because many people see it as beneficial, because it will be feasible in thousands of labs all over the world, and, most importantly, because it will be a mere spin-off of mainstream biomedical research to decipher our biology. . . .

A DEMOCRATIZING TECHNOLOGY?

21   The effort to block these new reproductive technologies renders them extremely divisive socially, because it will guarantee that they are only available to the wealthy who are able to circumvent any kinds of restrictions rather easily, either by traveling to other locations or by simply paying money to get black-market services.

22   At their core, germinal choice technologies—if handled properly—could be very democratizing, because the kinds of interventions that will be available initially are going to compensate for deficits. It will be much easier to lift someone with an IQ of 70 up to 100 (the population average) than to raise someone's IQ from 150 (the top fraction of a percent of the population) up to 160. And the same will be true in selecting the predispositions of future children. . . .

23   The genetic lottery can be very, very cruel. Ask anybody who is very slow or has a genetic disease of one sort or another. They don't believe in some abstract principle of how wonderful the genetic lottery is. They would like to be healthier or have more talent in one way or another. The broad availability of these technologies would thus level the playing field in many ways, because it would give opportunities to those who otherwise would be genetically disadvantaged.

24   Another point is that these technologies, as do any technologies, evolve rather rapidly. The differences will not so much be between the wealthy and the poor in one generation (although obviously there will be more things available to those who have more resources), but between one generation and the next. Today, even a Bill Gates could not obtain the genetic enhancements or services for his child that will seem primitive compared with what any middle-class person is going to have access to in 25 years. . . .

LOSING OUR HUMANITY—OR CONTROLLING IT?

25   Another misplaced fear is that, by tampering with our biology, we risk losing our humanity. But does "humanity" have to do with very narrow aspects of our biology, or does it have to do with the whole process of engaging the world and with our interactions with one another? For instance, if our lifespan were to double, would

that make us "not human" in some sense? It would certainly change the trajectory of our lives, the way we interact with one another, our institutions, our sense of family, and our attitudes about education. But we would still be human, and I daresay we would soon adjust to these changes and wonder how we could ever have lived without them. . . .

26   Humans now are just in the very early stages of their evolution—early adolescence at most. A thousand years from now, when future humans look back at this era, they're going to see it as a primitive, difficult, and challenging time. They will also see it as an extraordinary, rather glorious moment when we laid down the foundations of their lives. It is hard to imagine what human life will be like even a hundred years from now, but I suspect that the reworking of our own biology will figure heavily in our future.

FOR DISCUSSION

1. According to Stock, why is genetic alteration of adults "not in the cards" for the most part?

2. "Correcting genes" in embryos would not be, Stock claims, "a particularly radical departure" from current practices used in in vitro fertilization. Why does he say this? How does it differ from what he calls "preimplantation genetic diagnosis"?

3. Stock points to an interesting "side effect" of Down syndrome—that children afflicted by it also "have close to a 90% reduction in the incidence of many cancers" (paragraph 5). How does he propose that such knowledge could be used to reduce cancer in the general population?

4. "Society may not welcome some parents' choices," Stock admits. He points out that some deaf parents will want deaf children as an example. What other choices might society find troubling?

5. Stock argues that genetic manipulation of human embryos could be a democratizing technology. What does he offer to support his view?

6. How does Stock view the question of what makes human beings human? Do you agree that gene manipulation will not fundamentally change what it means to be human?

FOR RESEARCH AND DISCUSSION

"The genetic lottery can be very, very cruel," Stock observes, and to verify that all you need to do is visit the cancer ward at a children's hospital or encounter an example or two of other congenital diseases. It is difficult to extol natural processes when about 2% of all live births result in genetically impaired children.

Compile a list of diseases linked to genetic defects. Individually or in groups, select a disease, then find out about symptoms and current, nongenetic treatment, including what it costs. Give a short, informative presentation about each disease.

Then discuss this question in class: Can there be any reasonable objection to genetic research designed to prevent such diseases either through screening embryos or through altering germ cells that produce or can produce genetic illnesses?

FOR CONVINCING

Stock points to the area of greatest controversy where applications of genetic knowledge are concerned—enhancing human traits a culture considers desirable. It is one thing to cure disease, the common argument goes, quite another to extend lifetimes or raise IQs or design children to be more attractive or less susceptible to depression.

Suppose that we have the knowledge and the means to select the traits our children will have. Suppose also that it is affordable and that conception would be the result of sexual intercourse only—no petri dishes and artificial means of insemination. In a short essay, make a case for using or not using that technology.

Cartoon: Gene-Splicing as Big Business

LARRY GONICK AND MARK WHEELIS

If you want to learn about genetics and have fun at the same time, read *The Cartoon Guide to Genetics* (HarperCollins, 1991), from which the following satire comes.

From *The Cartoon Guide to Genetics* by Larry Gonick and Mark Wheelis. © Larry Gonick and Mark Wheelis. All rights reserved. Reprinted with permission.

FOR DISCUSSION

There has been a great deal of concern about the alliance between business and American colleges in recent years. So the questions raised by the appalled academics in the cartoon are serious questions, even if the economic incentives for turning discoveries into profits are so great that they tend to overwhelm them. What do you think about the issues raised, especially as they bear on business applications of genetic engineering?

On Human Bioenhancements

C. BEN MITCHELL

> C. Ben Mitchell is Graves Professor of Moral Philosophy at Union University and editor
> of *Ethics and Medicine,* the journal in which the following editorial appeared in Fall 2009.

1   Human beings are obsessive innovators. *Homo sapiens* (knower) is by nature *Homo faber* (fabricator). Life without what philosopher Michael Novak has called "the fire of invention" doubtless would be nasty, bloody, and brutish. Since biomedicine and biotechnology are two spheres where innovation is especially rewarded, it is no surprise that we stand on the threshold of the development of human biological enhancements.

2   We have attempted enhancement in many different ways, especially for our children: diet, exercise, music lessons, tutoring, athletics, and even cosmetic surgery. But for many people, there is something deeply troubling about bioenhancement technologies, whether they are reproductive, genetic, neurological, or prosthetic technologies. By 'bioenhancement' I mean that these technologies magnify human biological function *beyond species typical norms.*

THERAPY VERSUS ENHANCEMENT

3   Ethical reflection about these technologies requires that we make some distinction between therapy and enhancement. Therapies would include medical interventions that restore human functioning to species typical norms. So, kidney dialysis, lasik surgery, and angioplasty are therapies; but adding twenty IQ points to someone who already has a normal IQ would be an enhancement.

4   Both proponents and critics of bioenhancements have argued, however, that the line between therapy and enhancement is vanishingly thin. But it may not be as faint as some imagine. I was once in a conversation with a prominent fertility specialist who used preimplantation genetic diagnosis (PGD) to help couples have children without genetically-linked diseases. He told of a couple who came to him requesting that he assist them to have a child who would have perfect musical pitch. Since they were both orchestral musicians and because there may be a gene associated with aural acuity, they wanted a child to follow in their footsteps. He steadfastly refused. He said he could not say exactly why, but his intuition was that it was unethical. Just because we cannot always make finely tuned distinctions does not mean distinctions are impossible. Just because a bright line may not be drawn does not mean no line can be drawn.

5   We should resist human bioenhancement technologies at least for a number of reasons, including their inconsistency with the goals of medicine, their violation of the principle of justice, and their complicity with cultural stereotypes.

THE GOALS OF MEDICINE

6   Human bioenhancements should be resisted, first, because they are inconsistent with the goals of medicine. The first goal of medicine is healing for the "patient's

good." The principle of medical beneficence assumes either that a patient is enjoying homeostasis, and the role of the physician is to assist him or her to maintain or optimize normal functioning, or that a patient is suffering diminished capacity due to illness or disease, and medicine's role is to help restore as much normal function as possible. This aim of medicine is as old as the Hippocratic Oath. Whether we call it healing, wellness, or shalom, the goals of medicine are restorative and preventive.

7   Only recently have we begun to imagine medicine as a way to move beyond therapy. Medicine is seen less today as a profession and more as a commercial service. Physicians are not seen as professionals, they are merely body plumbers (no offense to plumbers). Consumerism thrives on giving the customer what he or she desires. While human bioenhancements are not consistent with the traditional aims of medicine, they are very consistent with desire-satisfaction where, as ethicist Carl Elliott so elegantly puts it, "American medicine meets the American dream." So now consumers employ doctors to make them "better than well."

THE PRINCIPLE OF JUSTICE

8   Another reason to reject bioenhancements is the principle of justice. Having recently witnessed the Olympic games in Beijing, and heard the hoopla over doping in the Tour de France, we should be sensitive to the ways even the hint of enhancements threaten the fairness of competition. By analogy, technologically enhanced IQ, speed, dexterity, hearing, musical ability, etc., would create injustices, at least in cultures where those qualities are valued. The enhanced individual potentially would have unfair advantage over others in employment or life, just as blood-doping and steroids created advantages over other athletes. Furthermore, enhancing already wealthy Westerners while so many individuals lack access to basic therapeutic medicine, seems patently unjust. In fact, most of the world's people do not want enhancements, they want basic healthcare.

THE PROBLEM OF CULTURAL COMPLICITY

9   Georgetown philosopher Margaret Little has argued that enhancements contribute to cultural differences that lead to personal dissatisfaction and even stigmatization. For instance, Western culture's valorization of the Barbie-doll figure leads to body dysmorphic disorder among American teenage girls. Some Asian girls are having cosmetic surgery to make their eyes rounder and less almond-shaped in order to fit the Western ideal. For a culture to legitimize enhancement is to be complicit in these pathologies. And this would seem especially heinous after spending untold social capital, tax-dollars, and educational resources trying to convince our culture that persons with disabilities should be respected equally as those without them.

10   Human bioenhancements seem to be a very dubious investment of time and other scarce resources. Only those already well-off can afford the luxury of enhancements. The sick need a physician.

FOR DISCUSSION

1. In paragraph 4, Mitchell describes a case where a doctor refused to help a couple engineer a child with perfect pitch, obviously an asset for musicians. The doctor said "his intuition was that it [the request] was unethical." Do you agree? If so, can you give reasons for turning the couple down?

2. One of Mitchell's reasons for resisting bioenhancements is that money and resources are expended "to magnify human biological function" when so many people in the world lack even basic medical care, including millions in the United States. Should individual choice be limited by such considerations? How do you feel about wealthy people having access to biological enhancements when the vast majority of people in the United States and other countries do not?

FOR RESEARCH AND CONVINCING

"Medicine is seen less today," Mitchell claims, "as a profession and more as a commercial service." Do research on how medicine is practiced today to discover how much truth there is in Mitchell's assertion. If you see the commercialization of medicine as a problem, propose a solution that would move the practice of medicine more toward professional responsibility. If you see the commercialization of medicine as free enterprise at work, defend current practice against Mitchell's criticism.

FOR FURTHER READING

Chapman, Audrey R., and Mark S. Frankel, eds., *Designing Our Descendants: The Promises and Perils of Genetic Engineering.* New York: Farrar, 2002.

Elliott, Carl. *Better Than Well: American Medicine Meets the American Dream.* New York: Norton, 2003.

Fukuyama, Francis. *Our Posthuman Future: Consequences of the Biotechnology Revolution.* New York: Farrar, 2002.

Gonick, Larry, and Mark Wheelis, *The Cartoon Guide to Genetics.* New York: Harper, 2005.

Gregory Stock, *Redesigning Humans: Our Inevitable Genetic Future.* Boston: Houghton, 2002.

A Brief Guide to Editing and Proofreading

Editing and proofreading are the final steps in creating a finished piece of writing. Too often, however, these steps are rushed as writers race to meet a deadline. Ideally, you should distinguish between the acts of revising, editing, and proofreading. Because each step requires that you pay attention to something different, you cannot reasonably expect to do them well if you try to do them all at once.

Our suggestions for revising appear in each of Chapters 8–11 on the aims of argument. *Revising* means shaping and developing the whole argument with an eye to audience and purpose; when you revise, you are ensuring that you have accomplished your aim. *Editing,* on the other hand, means making smaller changes within paragraphs and sentences. When you edit, you are thinking about whether your prose will be a pleasure to read. Editing improves the sound and rhythm of your voice. It makes complicated ideas more accessible to readers and usually makes your writing more concise. Finally, *proofreading* means eliminating errors. When you proofread, you correct everything you find that will annoy readers, such as misspellings, punctuation mistakes, and faulty grammar.

In this appendix, we offer some basic advice on what to look for when editing and proofreading. For more detailed help, consult a handbook on grammar and punctuation and a good book on style, such as Joseph Williams's *Ten Lessons in Clarity and Grace* or Richard Lanham's *Revising Prose.* Both of these texts guided our thinking in the advice that follows.

EDITING

Most ideas can be phrased in a number of ways, each of which gives the idea a slightly distinctive twist. Consider the following examples:

In New York City, about 74,000 people die each year.

In New York City, death comes to one in a hundred people each year.

Death comes to one in a hundred New Yorkers each year.

www.mhhe.com/**crusius**

For a wealth of online editing resources, check out the tools grouped under:

Editing

www.mhhe.com/**crusius**

To take a diagnostic test covering editing skills, go to:

Editing > Diagnostic Test

To begin an article on what becomes of the unknown and unclaimed dead in New York, Edward Conlon wrote the final of these three sentences. We can only speculate about the possible variations he considered, but because openings are so crucial, he almost certainly cast these words quite deliberately.

For most writers, such deliberation over matters of style occurs during editing. In this late stage of the writing process, writers examine choices made earlier, perhaps unconsciously, while drafting and revising. They listen to how sentences sound, to patterns of rhythm both within and among sentences. Editing is like an art or craft; it can provide you the satisfaction of knowing you've said something gracefully and effectively. To focus on language this closely, you will need to set aside enough time following the revision step.

In this section, we discuss some things to look for when editing your own writing. Don't forget, though, that editing does not always mean looking for weaknesses. You should also recognize passages that work well just as you wrote them, that you can leave alone or play up more by editing passages that surround them.

Editing for Clarity and Conciseness

Even drafts revised several times may have wordy and awkward passages; these are often places where a writer struggled with uncertainty or felt less than confident about the point being made. Introductions often contain such passages. In editing, you have one more opportunity to clarify and sharpen your ideas.

Express Main Ideas Forcefully

Emphasize the main idea of a sentence by stating it as directly as possible, using the two key sentence parts (*subject* and *verb*) to convey the two key parts of the idea (*agent* and *act*).

As you edit, first look for sentences that state ideas indirectly rather than directly; such sentences may include (1) overuse of the verb *to be* in its various forms (*is, was, will have been,* and so forth), (2) the opening words "There is . . ." or "It is . . . ," (3) strings of prepositional phrases, or (4) many vague nouns. Then ask, "What is my true subject here, and what is that subject's action?" Here is an example of a weak, indirect sentence:

> It is a fact that the effects of pollution are more evident in lower-class neighborhoods than in middle-class ones.

The writer's subject is pollution. What is the pollution's action? Limply, the sentence tells us its "effects" are "evident." The following edited version makes pollution the agent that performs the action of a livelier verb, "fouls." The edited sentence is more specific—without being longer.

> *Pollution* more frequently *fouls* the air, soil, and water of lower-class neighborhoods than of middle-class ones.

Editing Practice The following passage about a plan for creating low-income housing contains two weak sentences. In this case, the weakness results from wordiness. (Note the overuse of vague nouns and prepositional phrases.) Decide what the true subject is for each sentence, and make that word the subject of the verb. Your edited version should be much shorter.

> As in every program, there will be the presence of a few who abuse the system. However, as in other social programs, the numbers would not be sufficient to justify the rejection of the program on the basis that one person in a thousand will try to cheat.

Choose Carefully between Active and Passive Voice

Active voice and passive voice indicate different relationships between subjects and verbs. As we have noted, ideas are usually clearest when the writer's true subject is also the subject of the verb in the sentence—that is, when it is the agent of the action. In the passive voice, however, the agent of the action appears in the predicate or not at all. Rather than acting as agent, the subject of the sentence *receives* the action of the verb.

The following sentence is in the passive voice:

> The air of poor neighborhoods is often fouled by pollution.

www.mhhe.com/crusius

For more coverage of voice, go to:

Editing > Verb and Voice Shifts

There is nothing incorrect about the use of the passive voice in this sentence, and in the context of a whole paragraph, passive voice can be the most emphatic way to make a point. (Here, for example, it allows the word *pollution* to fall at the end of the sentence, a strong position.) But, often, use of the passive voice is not a deliberate choice at all; rather, it's a vague and unspecific way of stating a point.

Consider the following sentences, in which the main verbs have no agents:

> It *is believed* that dumping garbage at sea is not as harmful to the environment as *was* once *thought*.

> Ronald Reagan *was considered* the "Great Communicator."

Who thinks such dumping is not so harmful? environmental scientists? industrial producers? Who considered former president Reagan a great communicator? speech professors? news commentators? Such sentences are clearer when they are written in the active voice:

> Some environmentalists believe that dumping garbage at sea is not as harmful to the environment as they used to think.

> Media commentators considered Ronald Reagan the "Great Communicator."

In editing for the passive voice, look over your verbs. Passive voice is easily recognized because it always contains (1) some form of *to be* as a helping verb and (2) the main verb in its past participle form (which ends in *-ed, -d, -t, -en,* or *-n,* or in some cases may be irregular: *drunk, sung, lain,* and so on).

When you find a sentence phrased in the passive voice, decide who or what is performing the action; the agent may appear after the verb or not at all. Then decide if changing the sentence to the active voice will improve the sentence as well as the surrounding passage.

Editing Practice

1. The following paragraph from a student's argument needs to be edited for emphasis. It is choking with excess nouns and forms of the verb *to be,* some as part of passive constructions. You need not eliminate all passive voice, but do look for wording that is vague and ineffective. Your edited version should be not only stronger but shorter as well.

    Although emergency shelters are needed in some cases (for example, a mother fleeing domestic violence), they are an inefficient means of dealing with the massive numbers of people they are bombarded with each day. The members of a homeless family are in need of a home, not a temporary shelter into which they and others like them are herded, only to be shuffled out when their thirty-day stay is over to make room for the next incoming herd. Emergency shelters would be sufficient if we did not have a low-income housing shortage, but what is needed most at present is an increase in availability of affordable housing for the poor.

2. Select a paragraph of your own writing to edit; focus on using strong verbs and subjects to carry the main idea of your sentences.

Editing for Emphasis

When you edit for emphasis, you make sure that your main ideas stand out so that your reader will take notice. Following are some suggestions to help.

Emphasize Main Ideas by Subordinating Less Important Ones

Subordination refers to distinctions in rank or order of importance. Think of the chain of command at an office: the boss is at the top of the ladder, the middle management is on a lower (subordinate) rung, the support staff is at an even lower rung, and so on.

In writing, subordination means placing less important ideas in less important positions in sentences in order to emphasize the main ideas that should stand out. Writing that lacks subordination treats all ideas equally; each idea may consist of a sentence of its own or may be joined to another idea by a coordinator (*and, but,* and *or*). Such a passage follows with its sentences numbered for reference purposes.

(1) It has been over a century since slavery was abolished and a few decades since lawful, systematic segregation came to an unwilling halt. (2) Truly, blacks have come a long way from the darker days that lasted for more than three centuries. (3) Many blacks have

entered the mainstream, and there is a proportionately large contingent of middle-class blacks. (4) Yet an even greater percentage of blacks are immersed in truly pathetic conditions. (5) The inner-city black poor are enmeshed in devastating socioeconomic problems. (6) Unemployment among inner-city black youths has become much worse than it was even five years ago.

Three main ideas are important here—that blacks have been free for some time, that some have made economic progress, and that others are trapped in poverty—and of these three, the last is probably intended to be the most important. Yet, as we read the passage, these key ideas do not stand out. In fact, each point receives equal emphasis and sounds about the same, with the repeated subject-verb-object syntax. The result seems monotonous, even apathetic, though the writer is probably truly disturbed about the subject. The following edited version, which subordinates some of the points, is more emphatic. We have italicized the main points.

> *Blacks have come a long way* in the century since slavery was abolished and in the decades since lawful, systematic segregation came to an unwilling halt. Yet, although many blacks have entered the mainstream and the middle class, *an even greater percentage is immersed in truly pathetic conditions.* To give just one example of these devastating socioeconomic problems, *unemployment among inner-city black youths is much worse now than it was even five years ago.*

Although different editing choices are possible, this version plays down sentences 1, 3, and 5 in the original so that sentences 2, 4, and 6 stand out.

As you edit, look for passages that sound wordy and flat because all the ideas are expressed with equal weight in the same subject-verb-object pattern. Then single out your most important points, and try out some options for subordinating the less important ones. The key is to put main ideas in main clauses and modifying ideas in modifying clauses or phrases.

Modifying Clauses Like simple sentences, modifying clauses contain a subject and verb. They are formed in two ways: (1) with relative pronouns and (2) with subordinating conjunctions.

Relative pronouns introduce clauses that modify nouns, with the relative pronoun relating the clause to the noun it modifies. There are five relative pronouns: *that, which, who, whose,* and *whom.* The following sentence contains a relative clause:

> Alcohol advertisers are trying to sell a product *that is by its very nature harmful to users.*

> —Jason Rath (student)

Relative pronouns may also be implied:

> I have returned the library book [that] *you loaned me.*

Relative pronouns may also be preceded by prepositions, such as *on, in, to,* or *during:*

> Drug hysteria has created an atmosphere *in which civil rights are disregarded.*

Subordinating conjunctions show relationships among ideas. It is impossible to provide a complete list of subordinating conjunctions in this short space, but here are the most common and the kinds of modifying roles they perform:

> To show time: *after, as, before, since, until, when, while*
>
> To show place: *where, wherever*
>
> To show contrast: *although, though, whereas, while*
>
> To show cause and effect: *because, since, so that*
>
> To show condition: *if, unless, whether, provided that*
>
> To show manner: *how, as though*

By introducing it with a subordinating conjunction, you can convert one sentence into a dependent clause that can modify another sentence. Consider the following two versions of the same idea:

> Pain is a state of consciousness, a "mental event." It can never be directly observed.
>
> *Since pain is a state of consciousness, a "mental event,"* it can never be directly observed.
>
> —Peter Singer, *"Animal Liberation"*

Modifying Phrases   Unlike clauses, phrases do not have a subject and a verb. Prepositional phrases and infinitive phrases are most likely already in your repertoire of modifiers. (Consult a handbook if you need to review these.) Here, we remind you of two other useful types of phrases: (1) participial phrases and (2) appositives.

Participial phrases modify nouns. Participles are created from verbs, so it is not surprising that the two varieties represent two verb tenses. The first is present participles ending in *-ing:*

> *Hoping to eliminate harassment on campus,* many universities have tried to institute codes for speech and behavior.
>
> The desperate Haitians fled here in boats, *risking all.*
>
> —Carmen Hazan-Cohen (student)

The second is past participles ending in *-ed, -en, -d, -t,* or *-n:*

> Women themselves became a resource, *acquired by men much as the land was acquired by men.*
>
> —Gerda Lerner

Linked more to the Third World and Asia than to the Europe of America's racial and cultural roots, Los Angeles and Southern California will enter the 21st century as a multi-racial and multicultural society.

—Ryszard Kapuscinski

Notice that modifying phrases should immediately precede the nouns they modify.

An *appositive* is a noun or noun phrase that restates another noun, usually in a more specific way. Appositives can be highly emphatic, but more often they are tucked into the middle of a sentence or added to the end, allowing a subordinate idea to be slipped in. When used like this, appositives are usually set off with commas:

Rick Halperin, *a professor at Southern Methodist University,* noted that Ted Bundy's execution cost Florida taxpayers over six million dollars.

—Diane Miller (student)

Editing Practice

1. Edit the following passage as needed for emphasis, clarity, and conciseness, using subordinate clauses, relative clauses, participial phrases, appositives, and any other options that occur to you. If some parts are effective as they are, leave them alone.

    The monetary implications of drug legalization are not the only reason it is worth consideration. There is reason to believe that the United States would be a safer place to live if drugs were legalized. A large amount of what the media has named "drug-related" violence is really prohibition-related violence. Included in this are random shootings and murders associated with black-market transactions. Estimates indicate that at least 40 percent of all property crime in the United States is committed by drug users so they can maintain their habits. That amounts to a total of 4 million crimes per year and $7.5 billion in stolen property. Legalizing drugs would be a step toward reducing this wave of crime.

2. Edit a paragraph of your own writing with an eye to subordinating less important ideas through the use of modifying phrases and clauses.

Vary Sentence Length and Pattern

Even when read silently, your writing has a sound. If your sentences are all about the same length (typically fifteen to twenty words) and all structured according to a subject-verb-object pattern, they will roll along with the monotonous rhythm of an assembly line. Obviously, one solution to this problem is to open some of your sentences with modifying phrases and clauses, as we discuss in the previous section. Here we offer some other strategies, all of which add emphasis by introducing something unexpected.

1. Use a short sentence after several long ones.

   [A] population's general mortality is affected by a great many factors over which doctors and hospitals have little influence. For those diseases and injuries for which modern medicine can affect the outcome, however, which country the patient lives in really matters. Life expectancy is not the same among developed countries for premature babies, for children born with spina bifida, or for people who have cancer, a brain tumor, heart disease, or chronic renal failure. *Their chances of survival are best in the United States.*

   —John Goodman

2. Interrupt a sentence.

   The position of women in that hippie counterculture was, *as a young black male leader preached succinctly,* "prone."

   —Betty Friedan

   Symbols and myths—*when emerging uncorrupted from human experience*—are precious. Then it is the poetic voice and vision that informs and infuses—*the poet-warrior's, the prophet-seer's, the dreamer's*—reassuring us that truth is as real as falsehood. And ultimately stronger.

   —Ossie Davis

3. Use an intentional sentence fragment. The concluding fragment in the previous passage by Ossie Davis is a good example.

4. Invert the order of subject-verb-object.

   Further complicating negotiations is the difficulty of obtaining relevant financial statements.

   —Regina Herzlinger

   This creature, with scarcely two thirds of man's cranial capacity, was a fire user. Of what it meant to him beyond warmth and shelter, we know nothing; with what rites, ghastly or benighted, it was struck or maintained, no word remains.

   —Loren Eiseley

Use Special Effects for Emphasis

Especially in persuasive argumentation, you will want to make some of your points in deliberately dramatic ways. Remember that just as the crescendos stand out in music because the surrounding passages are less intense, so the special effects work best in rhetoric when you use them sparingly.

Repetition Deliberately repeating words, phrases, or sentence patterns has the effect of building up to a climactic point. Here is an example from the conclusion of an argument linking women's rights with environmental reforms:

> Environmental justice goes much further than environmental protection, a passive and paternalistic phrase. *Justice requires that* industrial nations pay back the environmental debt incurred in building their wealth by using less of nature's resources. *Justice prescribes that* governments stop siting hazardous waste facilities in cash-poor rural and urban neighborhoods and now in the developing world. *Justice insists that* the subordination of women and nature by men is not only a hazard; it is a crime. *Justice reminds us that* the Earth does not belong to us; even when we "own" a piece of it, we belong to the Earth.

> —H. Patricia Hynes

Paired Coordinators Coordinators are conjunctions that pair words, word groups, and sentences in a way that gives them equal emphasis and that also shows a relationship between them, such as contrast, consequence, or addition. In grade school, you may have learned the coordinators through the mnemonic *FANBOYS*, standing for *for, and, nor, but, or, yet, so.*

Paired coordinators emphasize the relationship between coordinated elements; the first coordinator signals that a corresponding coordinator will follow. Some paired coordinators are:

both _____ and _____
not _____ but _____
not only _____ but also _____
either _____ or _____
neither _____ nor _____

The key to effective paired coordination is to keep the words that follow the marker words as grammatically similar as possible. Pair nouns with nouns, verbs with verbs, prepositional phrases with prepositional phrases, and whole sentences with whole sentences. (Think of paired coordination as a variation on repetition.) Here are some examples:

> Feminist anger, or any form of social outrage, is dismissed breezily—*not* because it lacks substance *but* because it lacks "style."

> —Susan Faludi

> Alcohol ads that emphasize "success" in the business and social worlds are useful examples *not only* of how advertisers appeal to people's envy *but also* of how ads perpetuate gender stereotypes.

> —Jason Rath (student)

Emphatic Appositives While an appositive (a noun or noun phrase that restates another noun) can subordinate an idea, it can also emphasize an idea if it is placed at the beginning or the end of a sentence, where it will command attention. Here are some examples:

> *The poorest nation in the Western hemisphere,* Haiti is populated by six million people, many of whom cannot obtain adequate food, water, or shelter.
>
> —Sneed B. Collard III

> [Feminists] made a simple, though serious, ideological error when they applied the same political rhetoric to their own situation as women versus men: *too literal an analogy with class warfare, racial oppression.*
>
> —Betty Friedan

Note that at the end of a sentence, an appositive may be set off with a colon or a dash.

Emphatic Word Order   The opening and closing positions of a sentence are high-profile spots, not to be wasted on weak words. The following sentence, for example, begins weakly with the filler phrase "there are":

> *There are* several distinctions, all of them false, that are commonly made between rape and date rape.

A better version would read:

> My opponents make several distinctions between rape and date rape; all of these are false.

Even more important are the final words of every paragraph and the opening and closing of the entire argument.

Editing Practice

1.   Select one or two paragraphs from a piece of published writing you have recently read and admired. Be ready to share it with the class, explaining how the writer has crafted the passage to make it work.

2.   Take a paragraph or two from one of your previous essays, perhaps even an essay from another course, and edit it to improve clarity, conciseness, and emphasis.

Editing for Coherence

Coherence refers to what some people call the "flow" of writing; writing flows when the ideas connect smoothly, one to the next. In contrast, when writing is incoherent, the reader must work to see how ideas connect and must infer points that the writer, for whatever reason, has left unstated.

Incoherence is a particular problem with writing that contains an abundance of direct or indirect quotations. In using sources, be careful always to lead into the quotation with some words of your own, showing clearly how this new idea connects with what has come before.

Because finding incoherent passages in your own writing can be difficult, ask a friend to read your draft to look for gaps in the presentation of ideas. Here are some additional suggestions for improving coherence.

Move from Old Information to New Information

Coherent writing is easy to follow because the connections between old information and new information are clear. Sentences refer to previously introduced information and set up reader expectations for new information to come. Notice how every sentence fulfills your expectations in the following excerpts from an argument on animal rights by Steven Zak.

> The credibility of the animal-rights viewpoint . . . need not stand or fall with the "marginal human beings" argument.

Next, you would expect to hear why animals do not have to be classed as "marginal human beings"—and you do:

> Lives don't have to be qualitatively the same to be worthy of equal respect.

At this point you might ask upon what else we should base our respect. Zak answers this question in the next sentence:

> One's perception that another life has value comes as much from an appreciation of its uniqueness as from the recognition that it has characteristics that are shared by one's own life.

Not only do these sentences fulfill reader expectations, but each also makes a clear connection by referring specifically to the key idea in the sentence before it, forming an unbroken chain of thought. We have italicized the words that accomplish this linkage and connected them with arrows.

> The credibility of the animal-rights viewpoint . . . need not stand or fall with the *"marginal human beings"* argument.
>
> Lives don't have to be *qualitatively the same* to be worthy of *equal respect*.
>
> One's perception that *another life has value* comes as much from an *appreciation of its uniqueness* as from the recognition that it has characteristics that are shared by one's own life.
>
> One can imagine that the lives of various kinds of animals *differ radically*. . . .

In the following paragraph, reader expectations are not so well fulfilled:

> We are presently witness to the greatest number of homeless families since the Great Depression of the 1930s. The cause of this phenomenon is a shortage of low-income housing. Mothers with children as young as two weeks are forced to live on the street because there is no room for them in homeless shelters.

Although these sentences are all on the subject of homelessness, the second leads us to expect that the third will take up the topic of shortages of low-income housing. Instead, it takes us back to the subject of the first sentence and offers a different cause—no room in the shelters.

Looking for ways to link old information with new information will help you find problems of coherence in your own writing.

Editing Practice

1. In the following paragraph, underline the words or phrases that make the connections back to the previous sentence and forward to the next, as we did earlier with the passage from Zak.

   The affluent, educated, liberated women of the First World, who can enjoy freedoms unavailable to any women ever before, do not feel as free as they want to. And they can no longer restrict to the subconscious their sense that this lack of freedom has something to do with—with apparently frivolous issues, things that really should not matter. Many are ashamed to admit that such trivial concerns—to do with physical appearance, bodies, faces, hair, clothes—matter so much. But in spite of shame, guilt, and denial, more and more women are wondering if it isn't that they are entirely neurotic alone but rather that something important is indeed at stake that has to do with the relationship between female liberation and female beauty.

   —Naomi Wolf

2. The following student paragraph lacks coherence. Read through it, and put a slash (/) between sentences expressing unconnected ideas. You may try to rewrite the paragraph, rearranging sentences and adding ideas to make the connections tighter.

   Students may know what AIDS is and how it is transmitted, but most are not concerned about AIDS and do not perceive themselves to be at risk. But college-age heterosexuals are the number-one high-risk group for this disease (Gray and Sacarino 258). "Students already know about AIDS. Condom distribution, public or not, is not going to help. It just butts into my personal life," said one student surveyed. College is a time for exploration and that includes the discovery of sexual freedom. Students, away from home and free to make their own decisions for maybe the first time in their lives, have a "bigger than life" attitude. The thought of dying is the farthest from their minds. Yet at this point in their lives, they are most in need of this information.

Use Transitions to Show Relationships between Ideas

Coherence has to be built into a piece of writing; as we discussed earlier, the ideas between sentences must first cohere. However, sometimes readers need help in making the transition from one idea to the next, so you must provide signposts to help them see the connections more readily. For example, a transitional word like *however* can prepare readers for an idea in contrast to the one before it, as in the second sentence in this paragraph. Transitional words can also highlight the structure of an argument ("These data will show three things: first . . . , second . . . , and third . . ."), almost forming a verbal path for the reader to follow. Following are examples of transitional words and phrases and their purposes:

To show order: *first, second, next, then, last, finally*

To show contrast: *however, yet, but, nevertheless*

To show cause and effect: *therefore, consequently, as a result, then*

To show importance: *moreover, significantly*

To show an added point: *as well, also, too*

To show an example: *for example, for instance*

To show concession: *admittedly*

To show conclusion: *in sum, in conclusion*

The key to using transitional words is similar to the key to using special effects for emphasis: Don't overdo it. To avoid choking your writing with these words, anticipate where your reader will genuinely need them, and limit their use to these instances.

Editing Practice   Underline the transitional words and phrases in the following passage of published writing:

> When people believe that their problems can be solved, they tend to get busy solving them.
>
> On the other hand, when people believe that their problems are beyond solution, they tend to position themselves so as to avoid blame. Take the woeful inadequacy of education in the predominantly black central cities. Does the black leadership see the ascendancy of black teachers, school administrators, and politicians as an asset to be used in improving those dreadful schools? Rarely. You are more likely to hear charges of white abandonment, white resistance to integration, conspiracies to isolate black children, even when the schools are officially desegregated. In short, white people are accused of being responsible for the problem. But if the youngsters manage to survive those awful school systems and achieve success, leaders want to claim credit. They don't hesitate to attribute that success to the glorious Civil Rights movement.
>
> —William Raspberry

PROOFREADING

Proofreading is truly the final step in writing a paper. After proofreading, you ought to be able to print your paper out one more time; but if you do not have time, most instructors will be perfectly happy to see the necessary corrections done neatly in ink on the final draft.

Following are some suggestions for proofreading.

www.mhhe.com/**crusius**

For some advice and practice related to spelling, go to:

Editing > Spelling

Spelling Errors

If you have used a word processor, you may have a program that will check your spelling. If not, you will have to check your spelling by reading through again carefully with a dictionary at hand. Consult the dictionary whenever you feel uncertain. Note also that spell checkers can be unreliable; a word that is spelled correctly but is the wrong word won't be caught. You might consider devoting a special part of your writer's notebook to your habitual spelling errors: some students always misspell *athlete*, for example, whereas others leave the second *n* out of *environment*.

Omissions and Jumbled Passages

Read your paper out loud. Physically shaping your lips around the words can help locate missing words, typos (*saw* instead of *was*), or the remnants of some earlier version of a sentence that did not get fully deleted. Place a caret (^) in the sentence and write the correction or addition above the line, or draw a line through unnecessary text.

Punctuation Problems

Apostrophes and commas give writers the most trouble. If you have habitual problems with these, you should record your errors in your writer's notebook.

Apostrophes

Apostrophe problems usually occur in forming possessives, not contractions, so here we discuss only the former. If you have problems with possessives, you may also want to consult a good handbook or seek a private tutorial with your instructor or your school's writing center.

Here are the basic principles to remember.

1. Possessive pronouns—*his, hers, yours, theirs, its*—never take an apostrophe.
2. Singular nouns become possessive by adding -*'s*.

    A single parent's life is hard.

    A society's values change.

    Do you like Mr. Voss's new car?
3. Plural nouns ending in -*s* become possessive by simply adding an apostrophe.

    Her parents' marriage is faltering.

    Many cities' air is badly polluted.

    The Joneses' house is up for sale.
4. Plural nouns that do not end in -*s* become possessive by adding -*'s*.

    Show me the women's (men's) room.

    The people's voice was heard.

If you err by using apostrophes where they do not belong in nonpossessive words ending in -*s,* remember that a possessive will always have a noun after it, not some other part of speech such as a verb or a preposition. You may even need to read each line of print with a ruler under it to help you focus more intently on each word.

Commas

Because commas indicate a pause, reading your paper aloud is a good way to decide where to add or delete them. A good handbook will elaborate on the following basic principles. The example sentences have been adapted from an argument by Mary Meehan, who opposes abortion.

1. Use a comma when you join two or more main clauses with a coordinating conjunction.

   Main clause, conjunction (and, but, or, nor, so, yet) *main clause.*

   Feminists want to have men participate more in the care of children, but abortion allows a man to shift total responsibility to the woman.

2. Use a comma after an introductory phrase or dependent clause.

   Introductory phrase or clause, main clause.

   To save the smallest children, the Left should speak out against abortion.

3. Use commas around modifiers such as relative clauses and appositives unless they are essential to the noun's meaning. Be sure to put the comma at both ends of the modifier.

   _____, *appositive,* _____
   _____, *relative clause,* _____

   One member of the 1972 Presidential commission on population growth was Graciela Olivarez, a Chicana who was active in civil rights and antipoverty work. Olivarez, who later was named to head the Federal Government's Community Services Administration, had known poverty in her youth in the Southwest.

4. Use commas with a series.

   ___x___, ___y___, and ___z___

   The traditional mark of the Left has been its protection of the underdog, the weak, and the poor.

Semicolons

Think of a semicolon as a strong comma. It has two main uses.

1. Use a semicolon to join two main clauses when you choose not to use a conjunction. This works well when the two main clauses are closely related or parallel in structure.

   Main clause; main clause.

www.mhhe.com/**crusius**

For some additional coverage of comma use, go to:

Editing > Commas

www.mhhe.com/**crusius**

For more coverage of semicolons, go to:

Editing > Semicolons

Pro-life activists did not want abortion to be a class issue; they wanted to end abortion everywhere, for all classes.

As a variation, you may wish to add a transitional adverb to the second main clause. The adverb indicates the relationship between the main clauses, but it is not a conjunction, so a comma preceding it would not be correct.

Main clause; transitional adverb (however, therefore, thus, moreover, consequently), *main clause.*

When speaking with counselors at the abortion clinic, many women change their minds and decide against abortion; however, a woman who is accompanied by a husband or boyfriend often does not feel free to talk with the counselor.

2. Use semicolons between items in a series if any of the items themselves contain commas.

___,___ ; ___,___ ; ___,___

A few liberals who have spoken out against abortion are Jesse Jackson, a civil rights leader; Richard Neuhaus, a theologian; the comedian Dick Gregory; and politicians Mark Hatfield and Mary Rose Oakar.

Colons

www.mhhe.com/**crusius**

For some additional help using colons, go to:

Editing > Colons

The colon has two common uses.

1. Use a colon to introduce a quotation when both your own lead-in and the words quoted are complete sentences that can stand alone. (See the section in Chapter 6 entitled "Incorporating and Documenting Source Material" for more on introducing quotations.)

Main clause in your words: "Quoted sentence(s)."

Mary Meehan criticizes liberals who have been silent on abortion: "If much of the leadership of the pro-life movement is right-wing, that is due largely to the default of the Left."

2. Use a colon before an appositive that comes dramatically at the end of a sentence, especially if the appositive contains more than one item.

Main clause: appositive, appositive, and appositive.

Meehan argues that many pro-choice advocates see abortion as a way to hold down the population of certain minorities: blacks, Puerto Ricans, and other Latins.

Grammatical Errors

Grammatical mistakes can be hard to find, but once again we suggest reading aloud as one method of proofing for them; grammatical errors tend not to "sound right" even if they look like good prose. Another suggestion is to recognize your habitual errors and then look for particular grammatical structures that lead you into error.

Introductory Participial Phrases

Constructions such as these often lead writers to create dangling modifiers. To avoid this pitfall, see the discussion of participial phrases earlier in this appendix. Remember that an introductory phrase dangles if it is not immediately followed by the noun it modifies.

> *Incorrect:* Using her conscience as a guide, our society has granted each woman the right to decide if a fetus is truly a "person" with rights equal to her own.

(Notice that the implied subject of the participial phrase is "each woman," when in fact the subject of the main clause is "our society"; thus, the participial phrase does not modify the subject.)

> *Corrected:* Using her conscience as a guide, each woman in our society has the right to decide if a fetus is truly a "person" with rights equal to her own.

Paired Coordinators

If the words that follow each of the coordinators are not of the same grammatical structure, then an error known as nonparallelism has occurred. To correct this error, line up the paired items one over the other. You will see that the correction often involves simply adding a word or two to, or deleting some words from, one side of the paired coordinators.

> not only _____ but also _____
>
> *Incorrect:* Legal abortion not only protects women's lives, but also their health.
>
> *Corrected:* Legal abortion protects not only women's lives but also their health.

Split Subjects and Verbs

If the subject of a sentence contains long modifying phrases or clauses, by the time you get to the verb you may make an error in agreement (using a plural verb, for example, when the subject is singular) or even in logic (for example, having a subject that is not capable of being the agent that performs the action of the verb). Following are some typical errors:

> The *goal* of the courses grouped under the rubric of "Encountering Non-Western Cultures" *are* . . .

Here the writer forgot that *goal,* the subject, is singular.

> During 1992, *the Refugee Act of 1980,* with the help of President Bush and Congress, *accepted* 114,000 immigrants into our nation.

www.mhhe.com/**crusius**

For additional coverage of agreement, go to:

Editing > Subject/Verb Agreement

The writer here should have realized that the agent doing the accepting would have to be the Bush administration, not the Refugee Act. A better version would read:

> During 1992, the Bush administration accepted 114,000 immigrants into our nation under the terms of the Refugee Act of 1980.

Proofreading Practice Proofread the following passage for errors of grammar and punctuation.

> The citizens of Zurich, Switzerland tired of problems associated with drug abuse, experimented with legalization. The plan was to open a central park, Platzspitz, where drugs and drug use would be permitted. Many European experts felt, that it was the illegal drug business rather than the actual use of drugs that had caused many of the cities problems. While the citizens had hoped to isolate the drug problem, foster rehabilitation, and curb the AIDS epidemic, the actual outcome of the Platzspitz experiment did not create the desired results. Instead, violence increased. Drug-related deaths doubled. And drug users were drawn from not only all over Switzerland, but from all over Europe as well. With thousands of discarded syringe packets lying around, one can only speculate as to whether the spread of AIDS was curbed. The park itself was ruined and finally on February 10, 1992, it was barred up and closed. After studying the Swiss peoples' experience with Platzspitz, it is hard to believe that some advocates of drug legalization in the United States are urging us to participate in the same kind of experiment.

Fallacies—and Critical Thinking

Arguments, like [people], are often pretenders.

—Plato

Throughout this book we have stressed how to argue well, accentuating the positive rather than dwelling on the negative, poor reasoning and bad arguments. We would rather say "do this" than "do not do that." We would rather offer good arguments to emulate than bad arguments to avoid. In stressing the positive, however, we have not paid enough attention to an undeniable fact. Too often unsound arguments convince too many people who should reject them. This appendix addresses a daily problem—arguments that succeed when they ought to fail.

Traditionally, logicians and philosophers have tried to solve this problem by exposing "fallacies," errors in reasoning. About 2,400 years ago, the great ancient Greek philosopher Aristotle was the first to do so in *Sophistical Refutations*. "Sophistry" means reasoning that *appears* to be sound. Aristotle showed that such reasoning only seems sound and therefore should not pass critical scrutiny. He identified thirteen common errors in reasoning. Others have since isolated dozens more, over a hundred in some recent treatments.

We respect this ancient tradition and urge you to learn more about it. Irving M. Copi's classic textbook, *Introduction to Logic*, offers an excellent discussion. It is often used in beginning college philosophy courses. However, our concern is not philosophy but arguments about public issues, where a different notion of fallacy is more useful. Let's start, then, with how we define it.

WHAT IS A FALLACY?

Our concern is arguing well, both skillfully and ethically, and arguments have force through *appeals to an audience*. Therefore, we define *fallacy* as "the misuse of an otherwise common and legitimate form of appeal."

609

A good example is the appeal to authority, common in advancing evidence to defend reasons in an argument. If I am writing about flu epidemics, for instance, I may cite a scientist studying them at the national Centers for Disease Control to support something I have said. As long as I report what he or she said accurately, fully, and without distortion, I have used the appeal to authority correctly. After all, I am not a flu expert and this person is—it only makes sense to appeal to his or her authority.

But suppose that my authority's view does not represent what most experts believe—in fact most leading authorities reject it. Perhaps I just do not know enough to realize that my authority is not in the mainstream. Or perhaps I do know, but for reasons of my own I want my audience to think a minority view is the majority view. It does not matter whether I intend to deceive or not—if I present my authority in a misleading way, I have misused the appeal to authority. I have committed a fallacy in the meaning we are giving it here.

Here is the point of our definition of fallacy: There is nothing wrong with the appeal to authority itself. Everything depends on how it is used in a particular case. That is why fallacies must be linked with critical thinking. Studying fallacies can lead to mindless "fallacy hunts" and to labeling all instances of a kind of appeal as fallacious. Fallacies are common, but finding them requires *thinking through any appeal that strikes us as suspect for some reason*. We have to decide in each case whether to accept or reject the appeal—or more often, how much we should let it influence our thinking.

WHY ARE FALLACIES SO COMMON?

Fallacies are common because they are deeply rooted in human nature. We must not imagine that we can eliminate them. But we can understand some of their causes and motivations and, with that understanding, increase our critical alertness.

We have distinguished unintended fallacies from intentional ones. We think most fallacies are not meant to deceive, so let's deal with this bigger category first. Unintentional fallacies can result from not knowing enough about the subject, which we may not realize for a number of reasons:

- *Inaccurate reporting or insufficient knowledge.* Arguments always appeal to the facts connected with a controversial question. Again, as with the appeal to authority, there is nothing wrong with appealing to what is known about something. It is hard to imagine how we would argue without doing so. But we have to get the facts right and present them in a context of other relevant information.

  So, for example, experts think that about 300,000 undocumented, foreign-born people immigrate to the United States each year. Not 3,000 or 30,000, but 300,000, and not per month or decade, but annually. The first way we can misuse the appeal to facts is not to report the information accurately. Mistakes of this kind occur often. Magazines and newspapers frequently acknowledge errors in their stories from previous issues.

If we cite the correct figure, 300,000 per year, to support a contention that the Border Patrol is not doing its job, we would be guilty of a fallacy if we did not know that about half of these immigrants come legally, on visas, and simply stay. They are not the Border Patrol's problem. So, even if we cite information accurately, we can still misrepresent what it means or misinterpret it. Accuracy is important but not enough by itself to avoid fallacies. We have to double-check our facts and understand what the facts mean.

- *Holding beliefs that are not true.* If what we do not know can hurt us, what we think we know that is false does more damage. We pick up such beliefs from misinformation that gets repeated over and over in conversation and the media. For example, many Americans equate Islam with Arabs. But most Muslims are not Arabs, and many Arabs are not Muslims. The linkage is no more than a popular association. Furthermore, many terrorists are neither Arabs nor Muslims—we just do not hear about them much. Unfortunately, even when informed people point out the facts just mentioned, they tend not to register or be forgotten quickly. Such is the hold of incorrect beliefs on the minds of many people.

- *Stubbornly adhering to a belief despite massive counterevidence.* At one time most climate scientists resisted the notion that human activities could influence the weather, much less cause global warming. But as more and more evidence accumulated, the overwhelming majority eventually came to agree that carbon dioxide emissions, especially from vehicles and power-generating plants, are the major cause of global warming. But dissenters still exist, and not all of them are being paid by oil companies. Some may sincerely feel that natural variation in the Earth's climate is the real cause of global warming. Some may enjoy the role of outsider or maverick. Some may say that often the majority opinion turns out to be wrong, which is true enough, and somebody needs to play the skeptic. Whatever the motivation may be, the dissenters are brushing aside an enormous amount of evidence. Their fallacious arguments have helped to convince too many Americans that we do not have a problem when we do. We cite this example to show that fallacies are not restricted to popular arguments. Scientists can be as stubborn as anyone. It is human nature, against which no degree of expertise can protect us.

- *Dodging issues we do not understand or that disturb or embarrass us.* The issues that immigration, both legal and illegal, raise, for example, are more often avoided or obscured than confronted. People talk about immigrants becoming "good Americans" and worry about whether the latest wave can or will "assimilate." But what is a "good American"?

The question is rarely posed. Exactly what does "assimilate" involve? Again, few ask the question. Thus, arguments about this subject often dodge the important questions connected with it. In many cases those making these arguments do so while thinking they are confronting it.

If you recognize yourself and people you know in some or all of these causes and motivations that drive fallacious arguments, welcome to the club. We are all guilty. Without meaning to, we all get the facts wrong; we all pick up notions we take to be true that are not; and we all are at times stubborn and evasive.

Fortunately, unintended fallacies usually have telltale signs we can learn to detect, such as these:

- the reported fact that seems unlikely or implausible
- the interpretation that reduces a complex problem to something too simple to trust
- the belief that does not fit what we know of the world and our own experience
- the argument that strains too hard to downplay or explain away data that would call it into question
- the argument that dances around issues rather than confronting them

The good news is that unintended fallacies are seldom skillful enough to fool us often or for long. They tend to give themselves away once we know what to look for and care enough to exercise our natural critical capacity.

The bad news is that arguments coldly calculated to deceive, although less common than arguments that mislead unintentionally, are often much harder to detect. What makes the problem especially tough is that deceit comes too often from people we want and even need to trust. Why? Why do people sometimes set out to deceive others? We think the philosopher and brilliant fallacy hunter Jeremy Bentham had the best answer. He called the motivation "interest-begotten prejudice." What did he mean?

He meant that all human beings have interests they consider vital—status, money, and power they either have and seek to protect or strive to acquire. As a direct result of these interests, their outlook, thinking, and of course their arguments are shot through with prejudices, unexamined judgments about what is good, desirable, worthwhile, and so on. For example, through much of American history, Native Americans had something the American government wanted—land. When it did not take it by force, it took it by treaty, by persuading Native Americans to make bad bargains that often the government never intended to keep anyway. The whole process rode on prejudices: Native Americans were savages or children in need of protection by the Great Father in Washington; besides that, they did not "do anything" with the land they had. Because the deceit paid off handsomely for its perpetrators, it went on until there was little land remaining to take.

We would like to tell you that deliberate deceit in argument does not work—that deceivers are exposed and discredited at least, if not punished for what they do. We would like to endorse Abraham Lincoln's famous statement: "You can fool all of the people some of the time, and some of the people all the time, but you can't fool all of the people all of the time." Maybe so—many Native Americans and some independent-thinking white people were not fooled by the false promises of the treaties. But the humorist James Thurber's less famous observation is probably closer to the truth: "You can fool too many of the people too much of the time." This is so because the interest-begotten prejudices of the powerful coincide with or cooperate with the prejudices of a large segment of the audience addressed. That is why Hitler and his propaganda machine was able to create the disastrous Third Reich and why Joseph Stalin, who murdered more Russians than Hitler did, remains a national hero for many Russians even now, after his brutal regime's actions have long been exposed.

So, what can be done about the fallacious arguments of deliberate deceivers, backed as they often are by the power of the state or other potent interests? The most important thing is to examine our own interest-begotten prejudices, because that is what the deceivers use to manipulate us. They will not be able to push our buttons so easily if we know what they are and realize we are being manipulated. Beyond that, we need to recognize the interests of others, who may be in the minority and largely powerless to resist when too many people are fooled too much of the time. We can call attention to the fallacies of deliberate deceivers, exposing their game for others to see. We can make counterarguments, defending enlightened stances with all our skill. There is no guarantee that what should prevail will, but at least we need not lend support to exploiters nor fall into silence when we ought to resist.

SOME COMMON FALLACIES

For reasons that should be clearer now, people often misuse legitimate forms of appeal. We have mentioned two examples already—the misuse of the appeal to authority and the misuse of the appeal to facts. All legitimate appeals can be misused, and because there are too many to discuss them all, we will confine our attention to those most commonly turned into fallacies.

In Chapter 10, "Motivating Action: Arguing to Persuade," we described and illustrated all the forms of appeal (pages 243–244). In sum, we are persuaded by

- *ethos:* the character of the writer as we perceive him or her
- *pathos:* our emotions and attitudes as the argument arouses them
- *style:* how well something is said
- *logos:* our capacity for logic, by the force of reasons and evidence advanced for a thesis

You will encounter people, including many professors, who hold that only logos, rational appeal, *should* persuade. Anything else from their point of view is irrelevant and probably fallacious. We say in response that, regardless of what should be the case, people *are* persuaded by all four kinds of appeal—that we always have been and always will be. It therefore does not help to call appeals to ethos, pathos, and style fallacious. It *can* help to understand how these legitimate forms of appeal can be misused or abused.

The Appeal to Ethos

We do not know many people well whose arguments we encounter in print or in cyberspace. Typically, we do not know them at all. Consequently, we ordinarily rely on their qualifications and reputation as well as our impression of their character from reading what they have written. If ethos is not important or should not matter, we would not find statements about an author's identity and background attached to articles and books they have written. Speakers would not be introduced by someone providing similar information. But ethos does matter; as Aristotle said long ago, it is probably the most potent form of appeal. If we do not trust the person we are hearing or reading, it is highly unlikely we will be persuaded by anything said or written. If we do, we are inclined to assent to all of it. Consequently, appeals to ethos are often misused. Here are some of the common ways.

Personal Attack

There are people we ought never to trust—confidence men who bilk people out of their life savings, pathological liars, and so on. There is nothing wrong with exposing such people, destroying the ethos they often pretend very persuasively to have, thereby rendering their arguments unpersuasive.

But too often good arguments by good people are undermined with unjustified personal attacks. The most common is name-calling. Someone offers an argument opponents cannot see how to refute, so instead of addressing the argument, they call him or her "a liberal," a "neocon," or some other name the audience equates with "bad."

This fallacy is so common in politics that we now refer to it as "negative ads" or "negative campaigning." We ought not to dismiss it because experience and studies show that it often works. It works because once a label is attached to someone it is hard to shake.

Common Opinion

It is hard to find any argument that does not appeal to commonly accepted beliefs, many of which are accurate and reliable. Even scientific argument, which extols the value of skepticism, assumes that some knowledge is established beyond question and that some ways of doing things, like experimental design, are the right ways. When we indicate that we share the common opinions of our readers, thinking and behaving as they do, we establish or increase our ethos.

Used fallaciously, a writer passes off as commonly accepted either a belief that is not held by many informed people or one that is held commonly but is false or highly doubtful. "Of course," the writer says, and then affirms something questionable as if it was beyond question. For example, "Everybody knows that AIDS is spread by promiscuous sexual behavior." Sometimes it is, but one sexual act with one person can transmit the virus, and infection need not be transmitted sexually at all—babies are born with it because their mothers have AIDS, and addicts sharing needles is another common way AIDS is spread. Furthermore, health care workers are at higher risk because they often are exposed to bodily fluids from infected people. The common opinion in this and many other instances is no more than a half-truth at best.

Tradition

Few can see the opening of the musical *Fiddler on the Roof* and not be at least temporarily warmed by the thought of tradition. Tradition preserves our sense of continuity, helps us maintain stability and identity amid the often overwhelming demands of rapid change. No wonder, then, that writers appeal to it frequently to enhance their ethos and often in ways that are not fallacious at all. It was hardly a fallacy after 9/11, for instance, to remind Americans that part of the price we pay for liberty, our supreme traditional value, is greater relative vulnerability to terrorism. A closed, totalitarian society like North Korea can deal with terrorism much more "efficiently" than we can, but at the price of having no liberty.

Many of the abuses of tradition as a source of ethical appeal are so obvious as to need no discussion: politicians wrapping themselves in the flag (or at least red, white, and blue balloons), television preachers oozing piety to get donations. You can easily provide your own examples. Much more difficult to discern is invoking tradition not to dupe the naïve but to justify resisting constructive change. Tradition helped to delay women's right to vote in the United States, for example, and plays a major role in the high illiteracy rate for women in India and many other countries now.

Like all fallacious uses of legitimate appeals, ethical fallacies can be revealed by asking the right questions:

For *personal attack,* ask, "Are we dealing with a person whose views we should reject out of hand?" "Is the personal attack simply a means to dismiss an argument we ought to listen to?"

For *common opinion,* ask, "Is this belief really held by well-informed people?" If it is, ask, "Does the common belief hold only in some instances or in every case?"

For *tradition,* ask, "Have we always really done it that way?" If so, ask, "Have conditions changed enough so that the old way may need to be modified or replaced?"

The Appeal to Pathos

After people understand the indispensable role ethos plays in persuasion, few continue to view it only negatively, as merely a source of fallacies. Pathos is another matter. In Western culture, the heart is opposed to the head, feeling and emotion contrasted with logic and clear thinking. Furthermore, our typical attitudes toward pathos affect ethos as well: Emotional people cannot be trusted. Their arguments betray a disorganized and unbalanced mind.

With cause, we are wary of the power of emotional appeal, especially when passionate orators unleash it in crowds. The result often enough has been public hysteria and sometimes riots, lynchings, and verbal or physical abuse of innocent people. We know its power. Should it, then, be avoided? Are emotional appeals always suspect?

Let's take a brief look at a few of them.

Fear

"The only thing we have to fear is fear itself," Franklin Roosevelt declared, at a time when matters looked fearful indeed. The Great Depression was at its height; fascism was gaining ground in Europe. The new president sought to reduce the fear and despair that gripped the United States and much of the world at the time.

About a year later, in 1933, Hitler came to power, but the authorities in Britain, France, and other countries failed to realize the threat he represented soon enough, despite warnings from Winston Churchill and many others. As a result, the Allied powers in Europe fell to the Nazis, and Britain came to the brink of defeat. Fear can paralyze, as Roosevelt knew, but lack of it can result in complacency when genuine threats loom.

How can we tell the difference? With appeals to fear, as with all appeals to any emotion, this hard-to-answer question is the key: *Does reality justify the emotion a speaker or writer seeks to arouse or allay?* Recently, for instance, it has been easy to play on our fear of terrorists. But the odds of you or me dying in a terrorist plot are very low. The risk of death is greater just driving a car. Far more Americans will die prematurely from sedentary ways than Osama bin Laden and his associates are ever likely to kill. 9/11 has taught us yet again that "eternal vigilance is the price of liberty," but the sometimes nearly hysterical fear of terrorism is not justified.

Pity

Fear has its roots in the body, in the fight-or-flight rush of adrenaline that helps us to survive. Pity, the ability to feel sorry for people suffering unjustly, has social roots. Both are fundamental emotions, part of being human.

Like the appeal to fear, the appeal to pity can be used fallaciously, to mislead us into, for example, contributing to a seemingly worthy cause which is really just a front for con artists. But if pity can be used to manipulate us, we can also fail to respond when pity is warranted. Or we can substitute the emotion for action. The suffering in Darfur in recent years has been acute, but the response of the rest of the world has usually been too little, too late. Like fear, then, we can fail to respond to appeals for pity when they are warranted.

Which is worse? To be conned sometimes or to be indifferent in the face of unjust suffering? Surely the latter. Because fear can lead to hysteria and violence, we should meet appeals to it skeptically. Because unjust suffering is so common, we should meet appeals to pity in a more receptive frame of mind. But with both emotions we require critical thinking. "I just feel what I feel" is not good enough. We have to get past that to distinguish legitimate emotional appeals from fallacious ones.

Ridicule

We mention ridicule because student writers are often advised to avoid it. "Do not ridicule your opponents in an argument" is the standard advice, advice you will find elsewhere in this book. So, is ridicule always fallacious, always a cheap shot, always a way to win points without earning them?

Well, not always. With most positions on most issues, we are dealing with points of view we may not agree with but must respect. But what if a position makes no sense, has little or no evidence to support its contentions, and yet people persist in holding it? What then? Is ridicule justified, at least sometimes?

If it is not, then satire is not justified, for satire holds up for scorn human behavior the satirist considers irrational and destructive. We all enjoy political cartoons, which thrive on ridicule of the absurd and the foolish. How many stand-up comedians would have far less material if ridicule was never justified?

Like pity, ridicule is a social emotion. It tries to bring individuals who have drifted too far away from social norms back into the fold. It allows us to discharge our frustration with stupid or dishonest positions through largely harmless laughter—far better than "let's beat some sense into old So-and-So." Ridicule, then, has its place and its functions.

But it also has its fallacies. Most commonly an intelligent, well-reasoned, and strongly supported position suffers ridicule simply because it is unpopular, because most people have difficulty getting their minds around it. Clearly, the fact that an argument has been dismissed as ridiculous or absurd does not mean that it is, and we must be especially careful when we unthinkingly join in the ridicule.

Like the fallacies related to ethos, pathetic fallacies can be revealed with the right questions:

1. Is the emotion appropriate to the situation, in proportion to what we know about what is going on in the world?

2. What are the consequences of buying into a particular emotional appeal? Where will it take us?

3. Does the emotional appeal *substitute* for reason, for a good argument, or does it reinforce it in justified ways?

4. What is the relation of the appeal to unexamined and possibly unjustified prejudice or bias? Are we being manipulated or led for good reasons to feel something?

The Appeal to Style

Most experienced and educated people are aware of the seductions of ethos and pathos. They know how easy it is to be misled by people they trust or manipulated by emotion into doing something they ordinarily would not and should not do. They have been fooled enough to be wary and therefore critical. However, even experienced and educated people often are not alert to the power of style, to the great impact that something can have *just because it is stated well.* One of the great students of persuasion, the American critic Kenneth Burke, explained the impact of style. He said that when we like the *form* of something said or written, it is a small step to accepting the *content* of it as well. We move very easily from "Well said" to "I agree," or even "It must be true." It is almost as if we cannot distrust at a deep level language that appeals to our sense of rhythm and sound.

Yet fallacies of style are a major industry. It is called advertising. People are paid handsomely to create slogans the public will remember and repeat. From some time ago, for instance, comes this one: "When guns are outlawed, only outlaws will have guns." Has a nice swing to it, doesn't it? The play on words is pleasing, hard to forget, and captures in a powerful formula the fears of the pro-gun lobby. Of course, in reality there has never been a serious movement to outlaw guns in the United States. No one is going to take away your guns, so the slogan is nothing more than scaremongering at best.

Now compare this slogan with another memorable phrase: "Justice too long delayed is justice denied." Martin Luther King used it to characterize the situation of black Americans in 1963 in his classic "Letter from Birmingham Jail." He got the phrase from a Supreme Court justice, but its appeal has less to do with the source of the statement than with its formula-like feeling of truth. It stuck in King's mind so he used it in his situation, and once you read it, you will not forget it either. In other words, it works in much the same way that the fallacious slogan works. But King's use of it is not at all fallacious. As a matter of undisputed fact, black Americans were denied their civil rights legally and illegally for more than a century after the Emancipation Proclamation.

The point, of course, is that the form of a statement says nothing about its truth value or whether it is being used to deceive. If form pushes us toward unthinking assent, then we must exert enough resistance to permit critical thought. Even "justice too long delayed is justice denied" may require some careful thought if it is applied to some other situation. Many people who favor the death penalty, for example, are outraged by the many years it usually takes to move a murderer from conviction to execution. They could well apply the phrase to this state of affairs. How much truth should it contain for someone who has no legal, moral, or religious objections to capital punishment? It is true that often the relatives of a victim must wait a decade or more for justice. It is true that sometimes, for one reason or another, the execution never happens. Is that justice denied? But it is also true that convicted felons on death row have been found innocent and released. Some innocent ones have been executed. Has justice been too long delayed or not? Would it be wise to shorten the process? These are serious questions critical thought must address.

The appeal of style goes well beyond slogans and formulas. We have not offered a list of common stylistic devices and how they may be misused because there are far too many of them. All can be used to express the truth; all can be used to package falsehood in appealing rhythm and sound. Separating ourselves from appeals of language long enough to think about what is being said is the only solution.

The Appeal to Logos

Before we present a short list of common errors in reasoning, the traditional focus of fallacy research, let's review a fundamental point about logic: An argument can be free of errors in reasoning, be logically compelling, and yet be false. Logic can tell us whether an argument makes sense but not whether it is true. For example, consider the following statements:

> Australia began as a penal colony, a place where criminals in England were sent.

> Modern Australians, therefore, are descendents of criminals.

There is nothing wrong with the logical relation of these two statements. But its truth value depends on the *historical accuracy* of the first statement. It depends also on the *actual origins* of all modern Australians. As a matter of fact, Australia was used by the English as a convenient place to send certain people the authorities considered undesirable, but they were not all criminals. Furthermore, native Australians populated the country long before any European knew it existed. And most modern Australians immigrated long after the days of the penal colony. So the truth value of these perfectly logical statements is low. It is true enough for Australians to joke about sometimes, but it is not really true.

Here is a good rule of thumb: *The reality of things reasoned about is far more varied and complex than the best reasoning typically captures.* Sometimes errors in reasoning lead us to false conclusions. But false conclusions result much more often from statements not being adequate to what is known about reality.

With that in mind, let's look at a few fallacies of logical appeal.

False Cause

We have defined *fallacy* as the misuse of a legitimate form of appeal. There is nothing more common or reasonable than identifying the cause of something. We are not likely to repair a car without knowing what is causing that wobble in the steering, or treat a disease effectively, or come up with the right solution to almost any problem without knowing the cause.

The difficulty is that just because "a" follows "b," "b" did not necessarily cause "a." Yet we tend to think so, especially if "a" always follows "b." Hence, the possibility of "false cause," reasoning that misleads by confusing sequence with cause. If we flip a light switch and the light does not go on, we immediately think, "The bulb is burned out." But if we replace the bulb, and it still does not work, we think the problem must be the switch. We may tinker with that for a while before we realize that none of the lights are working: "Oh, the breaker is cut off." By a process of trial and error, we eliminate the false causes to find the real one.

But if we are reasoning about more complex problems, trial and error usually is not an option. For example, a recent newspaper article attributed the decline in the wages of Americans despite increased productivity to the influx of illegal aliens, especially from Mexico. Because they are paid less than most American citizens are, attributing the cause of lower wages to them may seem plausible. But actually some groups of Americans have endured a steady decline for some time, as high-paying industrial jobs were lost and lower-paying service work took their place. Globalization has allowed companies to force wages down and reduce the power of labor unions by taking advantage of people in other countries who will work for much less. It is highly unlikely that depressed wages are caused by illegal aliens alone. But if we do not like them, it is especially tempting to blame them for a more complex problem with which they are only associated. That is called *scapegoating*, and false cause is how the reasoning works that justifies it.

As a rule of thumb, let's assume that complex problems have multiple causes, and let's be especially suspicious when common prejudices may motivate single-cause thinking.

Straw Man

Nothing is more common in argument than stating an opponent's position and then showing what is wrong with it. As long as we state our opponent's position fully and accurately and attack it intelligently, with good reasons and evidence, there is nothing fallacious about such an attack.

The temptation, however, is to seek advantage by attributing to our opponents a weak or indefensible position they do not hold but which resembles their position in some respects. We can then knock it down easily and make our opponents look dumb or silly in the process. That is called "creating a straw man," and it is a common ploy in politics especially. It works because most people are not familiar enough with the position being distorted to realize that it has been misrepresented, and so they accept the straw man as if it was the real argument. Often people whose views have been caricatured fight an uphill battle, first to reestablish their genuine position and then to get it listened to after an audience has accepted the distorted one as genuine. Thus, many fallacies succeed because of ignorance and ill will on the part of both the fallacious reasoner and the audience.

Slippery Slope

Human experience offers many examples of "one thing leading to another." We decide to have a baby, for instance, and one thing follows another from the first diaper change all the way to college graduation, with so much in between and beyond that a parent's life is altered forever and fundamentally. Furthermore, it is always prudent to ask about any decision we face, "If I do *x*, what consequent *y* am I likely to face? And if *y* happens, where will that lead me?"

The slippery-slope fallacy takes advantage of our commonsense notion that actions have consequences, that one thing leads to another. The difference between the truth and the fallacy is that the drastic consequences the arguer envisions could not or are not likely to happen. Those who opposed making the so-called morning-after pill available without a prescription sometimes warned of a wholesale decline in sexual morality, especially among young adults. That has not happened, and in any case, technology is one thing, morality another. What makes sex right or wrong has little to do with the method of contraception.

The slippery-slope fallacy plays on fear, indicating one of the many ways that one kind of appeal—in this case, to logic, or reasoning about consequences—connects with other kinds of appeal—in this case, to emotion. Working in tandem, such appeals can be powerfully persuasive. All the more reason, then, to stand back and analyze any slope an argument depicts critically. Is the predicted slide inevitable or even probable? In many cases, the answer will be no, and we can see through the appeal to what it often is: a scare tactic to head off doing something that makes good sense.

Hasty Generalization

We cannot think and therefore cannot argue without generalizing. Almost any generalization is vulnerable to the charge of being hasty. All that is required for what some logicians label as "hasty generalization" is to find a single exception to an otherwise true assertion. So "SUVs waste gas." But the new hybrid SUVs are relatively gas efficient. "Since 9/11 American Muslims have felt that their loyalty to the United States has been in doubt." Surely we can find individual Muslims who have not felt insecure at all.

The problem with hasty generalization is not exceptions to statements that are by and large true. The problem, rather, is generalization based on what is called a biased (and hence unrepresentative) sample, which results in a generalization that is false. If you visit an institution for the criminally insane, you will probably encounter some schizophrenics. You may conclude, as many people have, that schizophrenics are dangerous. Most of them, however, are not, and the relatively few who are do not pose a threat when they stay on their meds. The common fear of "schizo street people" results from a hasty generalization that can do real harm.

Begging the Question

We end with this because it is especially tricky. Every argument makes assumptions that have not been and in some cases cannot be proven. We simply could not argue at all if we had to prove everything our position assumes. Hence, virtually all arguments can be said to "beg the question," to assume as true that which has not been shown definitively as true. Furthermore, we can never tell when an assumption that almost no one doubts can turn out to be very doubtful as new information emerges. Assumptions we used to make routinely can become hot issues of controversy.

Consequently, we should confine "begging the question" to *taking as settled the very question that is currently at issue.* Someone is charged with a crime, and the press gives it much ink and air time. Inevitably, some people jump to the conclusion that the accused is guilty. This can be such a big problem that it is hard to impanel a jury that has not been hopelessly biased by all the coverage.

We beg the question whenever we assume something that can not be assumed because it is the very thing we must prove. Fallacies of this kind are usually no harder to spot than the juror who thinks the defendant is guilty simply because he or she has been charged with a crime. Pro-lifers, for example, argue in ways that depend on the fetus having the legal status of a person. Of course, if the fetus is a person, there is no controversy. Abortion would be what pro-lifers say it is, murder, and thus prohibited by law. The personhood of the fetus is *the* issue; assuming the fetus is a person is begging the question.

The following exercise does not include what many such exercises offer—fallacies so obvious they would fool no one over the age of ten. You will have to think them through, discuss them at length. In some cases, rather than flatly rejecting or accepting the arguments, you may want to give them "partial credit," a degree of acceptance. That is fine, part of learning to live with shades of gray.

EXERCISE

The following examples come from instances of persuasion that appeared in earlier editions of this book. Some may not be fallacious in any way. Assess them carefully and be prepared to defend the judgment you make.

1. From an ad depicting the VW Beetle: "Hug it? Drive it? Hug it? Drive it?"

2. From a cartoon depicting a man holding a pro-life sign, above which appear two specimen jars, one containing "a dead abortion doctor,"

the other "a dead fetus." The man is pointing at the jar with the dead fetus. The caption reads "We object to this one."

3. From an essay called "The End of Life," James Rachels offers the following interpretation of the Biblical prohibition against taking human life: "The sixth commandment does not say, literally, 'Thou shalt not *kill*'—that is a bad translation. A better translation is, Thou shalt not commit *murder,* which is different, and which does not obviously prohibit mercy killing. Murder is by definition *wrongful killing;* so, if you do not think that a given kind of killing is wrong, you will not call it murder" [author's emphasis].

4. From a panel discussion in *Newsweek* about violence in the media: The moderator asks a representative of the movie industry why the rating NC-17 is not applied to "gratuitously violent movies." The response is "because the definition of 'gratuitous' is shrouded in subjectivity. . . . Creative people can shoot a violent scene a hundred different ways. Sex and language are different, because there are only a few ways [you can depict them on screen]. . . . Violence is far more difficult to pin down."

5. From an essay critical of multiculturalism comes the following quotation from the political scientist Samuel B. Huntington, whose view the essay's author endorses: "Does it take an Osama bin Laden . . . to make us realize that we are Americans? If we do not experience recurrent destructive attacks, will we return to the fragmentation and eroded Americanism before September 11?"

6. From an essay advocating multiculturalism: "The attack on affirmative action isn't really about affirmative action. Essentially it is another tactic in today's war on the gains of the 1960's, a tactic rooted in Anglo resentment and fear. A major source of that fear: the fact that California will almost surely have a majority of people of color in 20 to 30 years at most, with the nation as a whole not far behind."

7. From an essay urging us to move beyond the multiculturalism debate, written by a naturalized American citizen who was born in India: "I take my American citizenship very seriously. I am a voluntary immigrant, and not a seeker of political asylum. I am an American by choice, and not by the simple accident of birth. I have made emotional, social, and political commitments to this country. I have earned the right to think of myself as an American."

8. From an article arguing that militant Islam and Islamic terrorism is like Nazism: "Once again, the world is faced with a transcendent conflict between those who love life and those who love death both for themselves and their enemies. Which is why we tremble."

9. From an article arguing that American foreign policy provokes terrorism and that the root of it all is "our rampant militarism": "Two

of the most influential federal institutions are not in Washington but on the south side of the Potomac River: the Defense Department and the Central Intelligence Agency. Given their influence today, one must conclude that what the government outlined in the Constitution of 1787 no longer bears much relationship to the government that actually rules from Washington. Until that is corrected, we should probably stop talking about 'democracy' and 'human rights.'"

10. From an article that attempts to explain human mating in evolutionary terms: "Feelings and acts of love are not recent products of particular Western views. Love is universal. Thoughts, emotions, and actions of love are experienced by people in all cultures worldwide—from the Zulu in the southern tip of Africa to the Eskimos in the north of Alaska."

For additional examples of fallacies for analysis, see "Stalking the Wild Fallacy" <http://www.fallacyfiles.org/examples.html>.

active voice A statement that has the doer of the action as the subject of the sentence, followed by the verb and the person or thing that receives the action. "The President (subject) criticized (verb) the Congress (receiver of the action) for delaying passage of the legislation. See also **passive voice.** Favor active voice sentences because they are easier to understand and make a stronger impression on readers.

allusion A reference to a person, event, or text the author thinks readers will recognize without explanation. Usually a quick Google search will clarify allusions you do not recognize.

American Psychological Association (APA) style sheet or handbook The guide to research papers used in most natural and social science courses. Most of the information is accessible online. See also **Modern Language Association (MLA) style sheet or handbook.**

annotation Typically a handwritten note in the margins of something we are reading that, for instance, helps us to relocate a major point in a text or raises a question about something the author has said. Form the habit of writing in the margins of print texts and typing in comments for electronic ones, necessary for both critical reading and research.

argument An opinion backed by a reason—for instance, "We should cap tuition (opinion) because too many college students cannot afford the increasing costs" (reason). Arguments are developed into cases by adding more reasons and evidence that supports each reason.

assumptions Principles or values an argument takes for granted and so does not state or defend. "We should cap tuition because too many college students cannot afford the increasing costs" assumes what most Americans take for granted: that extending higher education to as many people as possible is a good thing. When we make

arguments, we should examine our assumptions to make sure that they do not need defending. When we assess the arguments of other people, we should expose the assumptions to make sure they should go unchallenged.

audience Also called "readership," designates the particular group of people we hope to reach with an argument. There is no point in trying to convince an audience that already agrees with us, nor an audience unalterably opposed to our opinion. Choose an audience weakly inclined your way, inclined against you but open to reason, or with no position at all. In this middle range of groups, pick the audience you know best and then consciously develop your argument to appeal to their values and interests.

bibliography A list of sources on a particular topic, arranged in alphabetical order according to the last name of the author or, in the case of sources with no author, the first major word in the title. Called "Works Cited" in the Modern Language Association (MLA) handbook used in most English courses.

blog Short for "web log," designates online sites maintained by people who wish to register their opinions on many issues. A vast, democratic expansion of access for popular opinion as compared to print. Increasingly important for the discussion of controversial subjects worldwide.

brief Also called "case structure," an outline of a case, including the claim or thesis you are defending, the reasons that justify or explain your thesis, and the evidence you will offer to develop and support each reason. Useful as a plan for writing a paper. Typically does not include your ideas for beginning and ending the paper and perhaps other details, such as showing why a possible objection to your case does not hold. See also **case strategy** and **refutation.**

case strategy The moves a writer makes to have maximum impact on an audience, including selecting, wording, and ordering reasons and evidence. Audience awareness is the key to case strategy. For instance, if you are arguing for a ban on cell phone use by drivers, you need to propose ways to minimize the loss of freedom and the inconvenience such a ban would cause.

case structure See **brief.**

claim Also called "thesis," the central statement an argument defends, the belief or action you want your audience to accept. A claim is a carefully stated and more specific version of your opinion about something. For example, you may be opposed to the war in Afghanistan (opinion) but your claim might be, "We should withdraw all American troops from Afghanistan within the next year."

climate of opinion The range of existing common viewpoints on any controversial question. As an arguer you need to be acquainted with what people are thinking and what motivates the varying points of view, which usually amounts to the perceived interests of the contending parties.

common knowledge A convention that governs the need for citation of sources. If the information is widely known—say, the kind of information available in a general use encyclopedia or what people who keep up with the news would know—there is no need to provide parenthetical notation or an entry in your Works Cited page. Our advice is to cite anyway if you are in doubt about whether an item qualifies as common knowledge.

connotation What a word or statement implies. For instance, both "famous" and "notorious" mean that someone is well known, but "notorious" implies well known for bad reasons. Because the connotations of words register unconsciously most of time, and therefore are not usually criticized, choosing words carefully for their connotations has a powerful impact on readers. See also **denotation.**

context A word with many meanings, used most commonly in two ways: context of text, which means the place from which a quotation is taken, and context of situation, which means the circumstances in which a writer writes or an interpreter of a text interprets. So, Abraham Lincoln's famous words, "With malice toward none, with charity for all," come near the end of his Second Inaugural, where he is discussing the attitude he would take in victory when the Civil War is over (context of text), a position he argued against those that would punish the South for starting the war (context of situation). See also **rhetorical context.**

conviction An earned opinion achieved through thought, research, and discussion. We often have casual opinions that need to be examined thoroughly to see what they are worth. Many Americans believe, for instance, that Japanese- and German-made vehicles are always better than domestics—are they? What does the best current data show? We should argue (make claims about) only opinions that we have earned.

convincing One of the four aims of argument; to seek assent to a claim not directly tied to taking action. Convincing, or case-making, is especially valued in the academic world, where we are often debating issues or topics about which no action can be taken. "What caused the Great Depression?" for example, is an important question in an American history course, crucial to understanding the past.

critical reading Also called "close reading," a thoughtful examination of a text with the intent of analyzing and evaluating it. Instead of reading a text just to know what it says, we slow down enough to think through what it says and whether or not we should accept what it says as accurate and true.

denotation The dictionary meaning of a word, apart from what it implies. The term "white," for example, in the United States designates anyone whose skin color and facial features allows him or her to pass as white whatever the racial mix in ancestry might be. See also **connotation.**

dialogue Also known as "dialectic," a serious conversation where opinions are both offered and examined critically, often through a process of questioning. If someone says, "We must secure our borders," a legitimate question for exploring the assertion would be, "What do you mean by 'secure'?" What sort of people do you want to prevent entering or leaving our country without documents?

editing As contrasted with revision, or significant rewriting of a paper to improve content, designates attention to such matters as awkward sentences, paragraph coherence, and errors; as such, editing comes after revision and before proofreading. Editing is indispensable to writing well. See also **revision** and **proofreading.**

ethos A word that means "character" in Greek, used to designate how a writer appeals through self-presentation, conforming to what readers admire: being intelligent, well informed, fair, aware of reader fears and desires, and so on. Perhaps the most potent form of appeal because people we do not trust cannot convince or persuade us.

evidence Reasoning, data, and expert opinion advanced to justify or confirm a reason. The amount of evidence needed to support a reason depends on the degree of resistance you estimate your audience will have.

fallacies The misuse of a legitimate form of appeal, sometimes with the intent to deceive. For example, on matters requiring specialized knowledge, we cite expert opinion, as in the case of the law with regard to a particular practice. There is nothing wrong with citing expert opinion, but we must cite a genuine expert and represent his or her opinion accurately to avoid committing a fallacy.

field research Generating your own information through observation, experiment, surveys, and the like rather than using sources. A valuable way to test your opinions and to provide evidence about issues that existing data do not address. If you want to know what students at your college think about living together before marriage, for instance, conducting a survey may be the only way to secure such information.

graphics Visual supplements to a text, including tables, charts, pie graphs, drawings, and the like. Widely used in publications but not exploited nearly enough in academic writing by students.

identification Linking the reader's interest and values with what a writer has said, achieved most commonly and powerfully through shared experiences, such as participation in the same war, the same activity or place, and so on. The writer who advocates preservation of nature by describing a trip as a child to a national park is seeking the identification of readers with the cause.

implied questions All statements we write or read answer (mostly unstated) questions, so that the statement, "The first one hundred days of a new President are not as important as many people think," answers the question, "How well does the first one hundred days predict the success of an administration?" Learning to ask what questions a statement implies can help you with argument in two ways: With your own arguments, you can see better the sequence of questions your sentences are answering, and possibly detect other questions you need to answer and a better sequence for the ones you have answered. With the arguments of others, you can more easily detect different possible answers to the questions the writer's sentences imply.

inquiry One of the four aims of argument, inquiry uses reasoning to analyze and critique existing arguments, as part of the process of arriving at the truth as you see it. Asking and pursuing questions is the key to effective inquiry. See also **conviction.**

issue A controversial question connected to a subject matter or topic. If we are discussing health care, for example, an issue would be, "Should access to health care be considered a right for all U.S. citizens?" See also **stasis.**

logos A Greek word that means "reasoning," used to designate the logical appeal of an argument. Readers respond to well-reasoned cases by saying "This makes sense to me" or "Your logic is compelling," the kind of response logical appeal seeks.

mature reasoning As contrasted with much undisciplined popular reasoning, a mature reasoner is well informed, self-critical, and open to constructive criticism from others; argues with reader needs and concerns in mind; and has a sense of context, the circumstances to which an argument must respond. Mature reasoning is the goal of this book.

mediation One of the four aims of argument, used to find common ground and agreement on a course of action when parties to a dispute are in sharp and seemingly irreconcilable conflict. You will encounter mediating positions on all controversial topics, from which you can learn the valuable skill of bringing people together who, in many cases, have stopped talking to one another.

middle style The kind of style typical of argument, not as passionate and formal as oratory, nor as chatty and familiar as, say, texting a friend. We use middle style when we talk or write to people we do not know well whose opinion of us matters.

Modern Language Association (MLA) style sheet or handbook The guide to research papers used in most liberal arts courses. Most of the information is accessible online. See also **American Psychological Association (APA) style sheet or handbook.**

opinion Most arguments begin with opinions, with something as simple as "I didn't like that movie." When we take an opinion like this and think it through, developing it into a thesis or claim we could defend in a movie review, including good reasons and evidence, we have moved to what we need for arguing well. The same as **position**; contrast with **conviction.**

paraphrase To state what someone else has said or written in your own words, the alternative to quoting someone. You should paraphrase your sources more often than you quote them, reserving quotation for statements from sources where the exact wording matters—for instance, when you want to comment on the wording.

passive voice A sentence where the doer or subject of the verb's action is either left out or moved to a position after the verb. "Congress was criticized by the President for delaying passage of the legislation." Passive voice is harder for readers to understand, and so active voice is preferred. However, passive voice is useful when you do not know who did something or when you do not want to emphasize responsibility for an action. Prefer active voice, but use passive voice when you have a good reason to do so. See also **active voice.**

pathos A Greek word that means "feeling" or "emotion," used to refer to moving readers to act by, for example, showing photographs of people suffering from a natural disaster that has left then destitute. When appropriate emotional appeals are used to supplement sound reasoning, pathos is a legitimate way to persuade others.

persuasion One of the four aims of argument, persuasion moves people to act by combining logical argument with emotional appeals. Advertising is the most common form of persuasion in our culture, but you will find it whenever action is at stake, such as an election, a vaccination campaign, contributions for disaster relief, and so on.

plagiarism The act of presenting someone else's words or ideas as your own, without acknowledging the source. The most common forms of plagiarism result from not supplying parenthetical documentation for information you have paraphrased or paraphrasing in language too close to your source even with documentation. Be careful to supply all documentation and put your source aside when you paraphrase to avoid using the language of your source. See also **paraphrase.**

position An overall, summarizing attitude or judgment about some topic or issue. "I don't like same-sex marriage" is a position that could become an earned opinion and then a thesis or claim in an argument. Positions need to be thought through, researched, discussed, and stated carefully to function well in argumentation. See also **conviction** and **claim.**

prewriting The same as preparing to write, designates everything done prior to the first draft. Good writing results from effort in prewriting and revision, or rewriting. You cannot put too much effort into preparing to write and into revision of first drafts.

proofreading The last phase of writing, coming after revision and editing, the purpose of which is to detect small remaining errors, such as typos and misspellings. A good technique is to read your paper slowly, sentence-by-sentence, beginning with the last paragraph and working back toward the first. This will help you detect errors by breaking up the flow of the prose. See also **revision** and **editing.**

qualifier Acknowledging the strength of one's claim: "Counterinsurgency usually fails when the government of a country lacks popular support." The word "usually" is a qualifier, allowing for exceptions to the claim.

refutation Anticipating objections to your argument a reader is likely to have and showing why they do not hold. Normally appears after you make your case, but if the objections to your case are strongly adhered to by your audience, sometimes the refutation should come first.

revision Literally, "to see again," refers to big changes to improve the quality of a first draft, such as adding content, rearranging the order of presentation, and rewriting to make points clearer and more forceful. See also **editing** and **proofreading.**

rhetoric The art of argument, techniques that convince or persuade. See also **mature reasoning.**

rhetorical context The knowledge of circumstances required to understand a text and therefore to respond to it well: information about the time and place in which it was written, about the author, who published it, and the ongoing debate to which it contributed. Online searches can turn up helpful information quickly and with little effort.

rhetorical prospectus A plan for writing that includes a statement of the thesis, aim of argument or purpose, audience, and organizational plan. See also **brief** and **case strategy.**

sampling A fast and not necessarily sequential reading of a text, such as reading the first sentence in each paragraph, to get a feeling for the territory it covers and as preparation for a more careful reading.

stasis Means "stop" or "stay," and refers to ordering the issues connected with a controversial topic to discover what you should argue. For instance, the proposed sending of astronauts to Mars begins with the question, "Is such a mission worthwhile?" If you say "no," then you stop with this issue and make your case. If you say "yes," then the next issue is technical feasibility. "Can we actually send a human mission to Mars?" If you say "yes," you make your case that it should and can be done. And so on, through other issues connected with the Mars mission. Stasis is a valuable approach to understanding how issues connected with a topic relate to one another. See also **issue.**

thesis See **claim.**

topic A subject matter, such as "American policy in the Middle East." Typically arguments are restricted to some part of a topic, and often to a single issue related to it. Narrowing topics to something that can be handled within the length allowed for an assignment is an important part of prewriting or preparing to write. See also **issue.**

visual rhetoric The use of images, sometimes with sound or other appeals to the senses, to persuade one's audience to act as the image-maker would have them act. Advertising and political cartoons are examples of visual rhetoric.

voice Your voice in writing should be a slightly more formal version of how you speak when you are talking to people you do not know well and whose opinion of you matters. The result is "conversational prose," in general the norm of good writing now. Voice also needs to be adapted to your subject matter, audience, and purpose, so that, for instance, writing about the quality of medical care available to wounded veterans has a high seriousness that, say, a parking problem does not.

CREDITS

Text and Illustration Credits

Noelle Alberto, "Multitasking: A Poor Study Habit." Reprinted by permission.

The American Heritage Dictionary of the English Language, excerpts from definitions of "mature" and "critical." Copyright © 2006 by Houghton Mifflin Company. Reproduced by permission from *The American Heritage Dictionary of the English Language, Fourth Edition.*

Tim Appenzeller, "The Coal Paradox," *National Geographic,* March 2006. Reprinted by permission of National Geographic Society.

Tom Beaudoin, "Consuming Faith: Integrating Who We are With What We Buy," Jul/Aug 2004. © 2004 Tom Beaudoin. Reprinted from Tikkun: A Bimonthly Interfaith Critique of Politics, Culture, & Society.

Sissela Bok, "Media Literacy" from *Mayhem: Violence as Public Entertainment* by Sissela Bok. Copyright © 1998 by Sissela Bok. Reprinted by permission of Da Capo Press, a member of Perseus Books Group.

Benedict Carey, "Brain Enhancement is Wrong, Right?" From *New York Times,* © March 9, 2008 The New York Times. All Rights Reserved. Used by permission and protected by the Copyright Laws of the United States.

Linda Chavez, "The Realities of Immigration," *Commentary,* July–August 2006, pp. 34–39. Reprinted by permission of *Commentary* Magazine.

The Chronicle of Higher Education, "This Year's Freshmen at 4-year Colleges: A Statistical Profile" © 2009, The Chronicle of Higher Education. Reprinted with permission.

Ross Douthat and Jenny Woodson, "The Border," *The Atlantic Monthly,* January/February 2006, pp. 54–55. Copyright 2006 The Atlantic Monthly Group, as first published in *The Atlantic Monthly.* Distributed by Tribune Media Services. Chart: Data courtesy of U.S. Customs and Border Protection, Border Patrol, FY 2004.

Tamara Draut, from *Strapped: Why America's 20- and 30-Somethings Can't Get Ahead* by Tamara Draut, copyright © 2005 by Tamara Draut. Used by permission of Doubleday, a division of Random House, Inc.

Gregg Easterbrook, "Some Convenient Truths," *The Atlantic Monthly,* September 2006, pp. 29–30. Copyright © 2006 by Gregg Easterbrook. Reprinted by permission of InkWell Management, LLC.

Carl Elliott, "The Tyranny of Happiness," from *Better Than Well: American Medicine Meets the American Dream* by Carl Elliott. Copyright © 2003 by Carl Elliott. Used by permission of W. W. Norton & Company, Inc.

Ian Fagerstrom, "Comparison of Perspectives on Narcissism" © Ian Fagerstrom. Reprinted by permission.

Helen Fisher, adapted from "'That First Fine Careless Rapture': *Who We Choose*" and "Notes" from *Why We Love: The Nature and Chemistry of Romantic Love* by Helen Fisher. Copyright 2004 by Helen Fisher. Reprinted by permission of Henry Holt and Company.

James Forman, Jr., "Arrested Development: The Conservative Case against Racial Profiling." From *The New Republic,* September 10, 2001. Reprinted by permission of The New Republic. Copyright © 2001 The New Republic, L.L.C.

P. M. Forni, Choosing Civility: The Twenty-five Rules of Considerate Conduct. © 2002 by the author and reprinted by permission of St. Martin's Press, LLC.

Helen Fremont, "First Person Plural" from *Why I'm Still Married: Women Write Their Hearts Out on Love, Loss, Sex, and Who Does the Dishes,* edited by Karen Propp and Jean Trounstine. Hudson Street Press, published by Penguin Group, 2006. Copyright © 2005 by Helen Fremont. All rights reserved. Reprinted by permission of the author.

David Fryman, "Open Your Ears to Biased Professors," The Justice (Brandeis U.), Sept. 1, 2004, 10. © 2004. David Fryman and The Justice at Brandeis University.

Michael Gerson, "The Rhetoric of the Rant." © May 15, 2009. *The Washington Post.* Reprinted with permission from The Washington Post.

Gerald Graff, "An Argument Worth Having." From The New York Times. © September 5, 2009. The New York Times. All Rights Reserved. Used by permission and protected by the Copyright Laws of the United States.

Duncan Greenberg, "Generation Y and the New Myth of Narcissus." From the Yale Herald. ©

Angi Grellhesl, "Mediating the Speech code Controversy." Reprinted by permission Angi Grellhesl.

Jack Grimes, "Hook-Up Culture." Jack Grimes, *Tufts University Daily,* March 30, 2004. Reprinted with permission.

David J. Hanson, "Responses to Arguments Against the Minimum Drinking Age," Reprinted with permission of David J. Hanson, Prof. Emeritus.

Natsumi Hazama, "Is Too Much Pressure Healthy?" Reprinted with permission from Natsumi Hazama.

Caroline Heldman, "Out-of-Body Image," Reprinted by permission of *Ms.* Magazine, © 2008

Tamar Jacoby, from *Reinventing the Melting Pot: The New Immigrants and What It Means to Be American,* edited by Tamar Jacoby. Copyright © 2004 by Tamar Jacoby. Reprinted by permission of Basic Books, a member of Perseus Books Group.

Pat Joseph, "Start by Arming Yourself with Knowledge: Al Gore Breaks Through with His Global-Warming Message," *Sierra,* September/ October 2006. Reprinted with permission from *Sierra,* the magazine of The Sierra Club.

Olivia Judson, "Optimism in Revolution," From The New York Times, © August 13, 2008, The New York Times. Reprinted by permission.

Anya Kamenetz, "Waking Up and Taking Charge," from *Generation Debt* by Anya Kamenetz, copyright © 2006 by Anya Kamenetz. Used by permission of Riverhead Books, an imprint of Penguin Group (USA) Inc.

Daniel M. Kammen, "The Rise of Renewable Energy," *Scientific American*, September 2006. Text: Reprinted with permission. Copyright © 2006 by Scientific American, Inc. All rights reserved. Illustrations: Illustration of wind turbines by Kenn Brown/Mondolithic Studios. Reprinted with permission. "Growing Fast, but Still a Sliver" by Jen Christiansen (Sources: *PV News*, BTM Consult, AWEA, EWEA, F. O. Licht and *BP Statistical Review of World Energy 2006*), originally printed in *Scientifi c American*; "Wind Power" (map) by Jen Christiansen (Source: National Renewable Energy Laboratory), originally printed in *Scientific American*; "R&D Is Key" by Jen Christiansen (Source: Reversing the Incredible Shrinking Energy R&D Budget, D. M. Kammen and G. Nemet, in *Issues in Science and Technology*, Fall 2005), originally printed in *Scientific American*. Reprinted by permission of Jen Christiansen.

Roger Kimball, "Institutionalizing Our Demise: America vs. Multiculturalism" from *Lengthened Shadows: America and Its Institutions in the Twenty-First Century*, edited by Roger Kimball and Hilton Kramer. San Francisco: Encounter Books, 2004. First published by Encounter Books. Reprinted by permission of the author.

Martin Luther King, Jr., "Letter from Birmingham Jail." Reprinted by arrangement with The Heirs to the Estate of Martin Luther King Jr., c/o Writers House as agent for the proprietor, New York, NY. Copyright 1963 Dr. Martin Luther King Jr.; Copyright renewed 1991 Coretta Scott King.

Janet Kinosian. "Ours Is a Rude Age, but Have a Nice Day." © The Los Angeles Times, May 4, 2009. Reprinted by permission of The Los Angeles Times.

Alex Kotlowitz, "False Connections." From *Consuming Desires: Consumption, Culture, and the Pursuit of Happiness*, edited by Roger Rosenblatt. Copyright © 1999 by Island Press. Reproduced by permission of Island Press, Washington, DC.

Eve LaPlante, "18,260 Breakfasts." Reprinted by permission of International Creative Management, Inc. Copyright © 2005 by Eve LaPlante. From *Why I'm Still Married: Women Write Their Hearts Out on Love, Loss, Sex, and Who Does the Dishes*, edited by Karen Propp and Jean Trounstine. Hudson Street Press, 2006.

Russ Linden, "The Promise of the Millennial Generation," This column originally appeared on Governing.com, February 18, 2009. Copyright © 2009 The President and Fellows of Harvard College.

Amory Lovins, "How America Can Free Itself of Oil— Profitably," *Fortune*, October 4, 2004. © 2004 Time Inc. All rights reserved.

Elizabeth Martínez, "Reinventing 'America': Call for a New National Identity" from *De Colores Means All of Us: Latina Views for a Multi-Colored Century* by Elizabeth Martínez. Copyright © 1998 by Elizabeth Martínez. Reprinted by permission of South End Press.

William F. May, "Rising to the Occasion of Our Death." Copyright © 1990 by the *Christian Century*. Reprinted by permission from the July 11–18, 1990, issue of the *Christian Century*.

Brian McGee "Too much civility can serve agenda of the powers that be." © November 21, 2009. Reprinted with permission of Brian McGee and Post & Courier.

C. Ben Mitchell, "On Human Bioenhancements," Ethics and Medicine © Fall 2009. Reprinted with permission of Bioethics Press.

Richard Moe, "Battling Teardowns, Saving Neighborhoods." Speech given to the Commonwealth Club, San Francisco, California, June 28, 2006. © 2006 National Trust for Historic Preservation. Reprinted with permission.

Bharati Mukherjee, "Beyond Multiculturalism: A Two-Way Transformation," in *Multi-America: Essays on Cultural Wars and Cultural Peace*, ed. Ishmael Reed. Viking, 1997. Copyright © 1997 by Bharati Mukherjee. Reprinted with permission of author.

Michelle Nijhuis, from "Selling the Wind" by Michelle Nijhuis. First published in *Audubon* magazine, September–October 2006. © 2006 by the National Audubon Society. Reprinted by permission of *Audubon* magazine.

The Oxford English Dictionary, excerpt from definition of "narcissism." Editing by Simpson & Weiner; reproduced by permission from Oxford Publishing Limited.

Don Peck and Ross Douthat, "Does Money Buy Happiness?" *The Atlantic Monthly*, January/February 2003, pp. 42–43. Copyright 2003 The Atlantic Monthly Group, as first published in *The Atlantic Monthly*. Distributed by Tribune Media Services.

T. Boone Pickens, "The Pickens Plan to Free the United States from Dependency on Oil" on http://www.pickensplan.com. Reprinted with permission.

Leonard Pitts, "The Other F Word," *Miami Herald*, February 14, 2008, p. 19A. Copyright 2008 by McClatchy Interactive West. Reproduced with permission of McClatchy Interactive West in the format Textbook via Copyright Clearance Center.

Virginia Postrel, pages 4–9 from "The Aesthetic Imperative" from *The Substance of Style* by Virginia Postrel. Copyright © 2003 by Virginia Postrel. Reprinted by permission of HarperCollins Publishers.

Alissa Quart, "X-Large and X-Small" from *Branded: The Buying and Selling of Teenagers* by Alissa Quart. Copyright © 2003 by Alissa Quart. Reprinted by permission of Basic Books, a member of Perseus Books Group.

Richard Rhodes, "Hollow Claims about Fantasy Violence." From *New York Times*, September 17, 2000. Copyright © 2000 The New York Times. Reprinted by permission.

Wilbert Rideau, "Why Prisons Don't Work" from Time (March 21, 1994). Copyright © 1994 by Wilbert Rideau. Reprinted with the permission of the author, c/o The Permissions Company, www.permissionscompany.com.

Sarah Rimer, "Play With Your Food, Just Don't Text." From The New York Times © 27 May 2009. All rights reserved. Used by permission and protected by the Copyright Laws of the United States.

Andy Rudd, "Which 'Character' Should Sport Develop," from Physical Educator 62.4 ©2005 pp. 205–212. By permission of Phi Epsilon Kappa Fraternity.

William F. Ruddiman, "Consuming Earth's Gifts" from Plows, Plagues, and Petroleum: How Humans Took Control of Climate by William

Barbara Sahakian and Nora Volkow, "Professor's Little Helper," National Public Radio Broadcast, March 17, 2008, Talk of the Nation, 3:00 pm EST. By permission of National Public Radio.

Photo Credits